Prisons and Prisoners

Prisons and Prisoners

*Edited by Michael Tonry
and Sandra Bucerius*

VOLUME 51

The University of Chicago Press, Chicago and London

The University of Chicago Press, Chicago 60637
The University of Chicago Press, Ltd., London

© 2022 by The University of Chicago
All rights reserved.
Printed in the United States of America

ISSN: 0192-3234
E-ISSN: 2153-0416

ISBN-13: 978-0-226-82505-2 (cloth)
ISBN-13: 978-0-226-82507-6 (paper)
eISBN-13: 978-0-226-82506-9 (e-book)

LCCN: 2022951056

The paper used in this publication meets the minimum requirements of American National Standard for Information Sciences—Permanence of Paper for Printed Library Materials, ANSI Z39.48-1984. ⊚

Contents

Preface

Crime and Justice from its inception has been a peer-reviewed scholarly journal that commissions, vets, and publishes state-of-the-art syntheses of knowledge: What do we know and with what degree of confidence? When and how did we learn it? What more do we need to learn?

In the early years the series conceived of itself as and was called an annual review of criminology; each volume covered a wide, interdisciplinary range of subjects. That became confining. Some subjects in some times are so large or topical or important that no single essay—or several—can do them justice. Early days examples from the 1980s and 1990s included family violence, white collar crime, drugs and crime, police reform, youth violence, and prisons. The solution was sometimes to publish thematic volumes dealing with many facets of a single, broad subject. In recent decades the series has roughly alternated between traditional, multiple-topic volumes (e.g., vols. 47 and 50) and thematic ones (e.g., *American Sentencing* [vol. 48] and *Organizing Crime* [vol. 49]).

This volume is the first that will reprise a predecessor, *Prisons* (1999), which the late Joan Petersilia and I organized. We were proud of it and believed it proved more useful and accessible to researchers, practitioners, and policy makers than scholarly writings usually do. Sandra Bucerius and I, for several reasons, decided the subject warrants a revisit. First, "mass incarceration" has been the overriding, brooding metaphor for American criminal justice for two decades and has only slightly diminished since imprisonment rates peaked in 2007. Second, not surprisingly, various of its features and effects have catalyzed large new literatures, which is the primary reason *Prisons* is out of date. What people want to know, and do know, is substantially different from what it was 20 years ago. Third, prisons research has become international. Twenty years ago, most was done by American and to a lesser extent British researchers, dealt with American and British prisons, and was published in English. The contemporary research community is international, important work is being done in many countries and comparatively, and, although the literature continues predominantly to be published in English, many important works appear in other languages.

For this volume, Sandra and I mostly followed the standard *Crime and Justice* developmental process for a thematic volume. Essays were commissioned from well-known, highly respected scholars. Drafts were distributed to paid referees for critical reactions and suggestions for improvement. The referees were Eric Baumer, Katherine Beckett, Martin Bouchard, Todd Clear, Megan Comfort, Anthony Doob, John Hagedorn, Craig Haney, Krzystof Krajewski, Candace Kruttschnitt, Shadd Maruna, Joseph Murray, Tapio Lappi-Seppälä, Christopher Lyons, Tim Newburn, Harold Pollack, Eric Sevigny, Cassia Spohn, and Dirk van Zyl Smit. Sandra and I provided our own questions, comments, and suggestions. Each essay was then rewritten, sometimes more than once. The "mostly" in the opening sentence to this paragraph refers—thanks to the coronavirus—to our inability to convene a first-draft conference at which the writers, the editors, and other specialists from the United States and Europe could dissect and illuminate initial drafts. We made a first attempt for October 2021 and a second for January 2022, but air travel constraints made us decide to cancel both. Reviewing processes were unusually intense, however, and we doubt that many if any of the writers will complain that their essays received insufficient critical attention.

Many people have served as coeditors of *Crime and Justice* thematic volumes. Some extensively participated in developing the volumes their names adorn; some did not. Sandra is among the heavy lifters. She and I have been active collaborators throughout. We lengthily discussed topics and writers and referees and drafts. She read and commented on all the initial and revised drafts, cowrote the introduction, and advised on the dust jacket and this preface. I am in her debt.

The writers endured a long, arduous process with remarkable patience and goodwill. Referees prepared reports substantially more detailed and reflective than is common; writers took the reports seriously. We are grateful to them all. Readers will decide for themselves whether those efforts were worthwhile.

Michael Tonry

Bagnaia, Isola d'Elba, September 2022

Sandra Bucerius and Michael Tonry

Has the Prison a Future?

The prison may or may not be always with us. Only time will tell. Half a century ago, it appeared to be in terminal decline. Imprisonment rates were falling in most developed countries, including the United States. Prison abolition movements were emerging, particularly in Scandinavia and the Netherlands, and a call for a "national moratorium on prison construction" was being heard in the United States.[1] Foundations were being laid for what later became known as the restorative justice movement. New community programs for diversion of cases from the criminal justice system were everywhere proliferating. Most of what we now think of as community-based penalties—community service, victim-offender mediation, home confinement, day reporting centers, intensive probation supervision, electronic monitoring, financial penalties including day fines, prosecutorial diversion—were being invented or greatly expanded.

From the 1940s through the mid-1970s, leading practitioners and scholars believed the prison's days were numbered, except possibly residually for the very most serious crimes and most troubled offenders. In 1942, Hermann Mannheim of the London School of Economics, then and in following decades Britain's most influential criminologist, observed, "The days of imprisonment as a method of mass treatment of lawbreakers are largely over. What remains of it will have to employ much more scientific methods of selection and treatment in order to survive" (1942, p. 222).

---

[1] The proposed moratorium, sponsored by the National Council on Crime and Delinquency, was not a law reformer's fantasy. In 1973, the National Advisory Commission on Criminal Justice Standards and Goals, appointed by Republican President Richard Nixon and chaired by Russell Peterson, the Republican governor of Delaware, proposed a 10-year moratorium on prison construction, a permanent ban on building of juvenile prisons and closure of existing ones, repeal of all mandatory sentence laws, and abolition of plea bargaining (NACCJSG 1973).

Electronically published October 3, 2022

Crime and Justice, volume 51, 2022.
https://doi.org/10.1086/722453

Norval Morris, author of *The Future of Imprisonment* (1974), coeditor of *The Oxford History of the Prison* (Morris and Rothman 1995), and America's most prominent prison scholar from the 1970s through the 1990s, in 1965 wrote that "it is confidently predicted that, before the end of this century, prison in [its current] form will become extinct, though the word may live on. . . . [The prison's] origins were makeshift, its operation is unsatisfactory, and its future lacks promise" (1965, p. 268).

Mannheim and Morris were not armchair criminologists. They spent time in prisons and jails and probation offices and courts. Many smart sophisticated people, practitioners, policy makers, and professors alike, thought what they thought. In the early nineteenth century, the prison was a humanitarian reform, a replacement for capital and corporal punishment and banishment. By the mid-twentieth century those aims seemed close to achievement: corporal punishment and banishment were relics of a benighted past; use of capital punishment had been ended in most developed countries and was rapidly declining elsewhere. The prison era seemed to be passing, even in the United States.

By the middle of the twentieth century, it was clear that prisons were mostly horrible places that damaged many who were sent there and accomplished little that was good or useful. Not surprisingly in that intellectual environment, the US prison population fell throughout the 1960s and early 1970s, as did those of other developed countries.

It is easy to see why, especially for people who came of age in the 1970s or later, the prison's end or near end appears to be an impossible dream. In many Western countries, the combination of sharply rising crime rates in the 1970s and 1980s and the politicization of crime as a public policy subject led to modest-to-enormous increases in the number of people locked up. The Netherlands, where the imprisonment rate increased from 23 per 100,000 in the early 1970s to 140 in 2005, and the United States, where it increased from 160 in 1973 to 763 in 2007, were the extreme cases. A few countries, notably the Scandinavians, Germany, France, and Canada, in various ways modulated the increases. Imprisonment rates in most Western countries have since fallen from their peaks, sometimes as in the Netherlands drastically, but remain at or near record levels in the English-speaking countries (except Canada).

We decided that this is a good time to take stock of what is now known about the use and effects of imprisonment. Michael and the late, great Joan Petersilia long ago edited an earlier *Crime and Justice* thematic volume, *Prisons* (Tonry and Petersilia 1999), but its contents are dated and its interest is principally historical. In the intervening two-plus decades, research on prisons and prisoners has expanded enormously.

In 1999, most scholarly research—as opposed to operational, management research—concerned developments in Britain and the United States and was published in English. Much of that was sociological, focused on inmate subcultures, or psychological, focused on how prisoners coped with and adapted to prison life. Some, principally by economists and statisticians, sought to measure the crime-preventive effects of imprisonment generally and the deterrent effects of punishments of greater and lesser severity.

In 2022, serious scholarly research on prisoners, prisons, and the effects of imprisonment has been published and is underway in many countries. That greater cosmopolitanism is reflected in the pages of this volume. Several essays concern developments in places other than Britain and the United States. Several are primarily comparative and cover developments in many countries. Those primarily concerned with American research draw on work done elsewhere.

The subjects of prison research have also changed. Work on inmate subcultures and coping and adaptation has largely fallen by the wayside. Little is being done on imprisonment's crime-preventive effects, largely because, as the National Academy of Sciences Committee on the Causes and Consequences of High Rates of Incarceration concluded, they are at best modest and often perverse (Travis, Western, and Redburn 2014). A recent *Crime and Justice* essay, examining the 116 studies then published on the effects of imprisonment on subsequent offending, concluded that serving a prison term makes ex-prisoners on average more, not less, likely to reoffend (Petrich et al. 2021).

In 1999, little research had been done on the effects of imprisonment on prisoners' families, children, or communities, or even—except for recidivism—on ex-prisoners' later lives: family life, employment, housing, physical and mental health, or achievement of a conventional, law-abiding life. The first comprehensive survey of what was then known was published in the earlier *Crime and Justice* prisons volume (Hagan and Dinovitzer 1999). An enormous literature has since emerged, as essays in this volume demonstrate. Comparatively little work had been done by 1999 on the distinctive prison experiences of women and members of non-White minority groups. That too has changed, as several of the essays make clear.

What is not clear is the future of imprisonment. Prison abolition or, as Mannheim and Morris predicted and the 1973 National Advisory

Commission proposed, its near abolition seems nowhere to be in the cards in any foreseeable future. Their critiques are as valid now as when they were offered: imprisonment accomplishes little that is good and much that is harmful. In some developed countries imprisonment is increasingly seen as a last resort, to be used sparingly, only if nothing else has worked or will do; use of alternative community sanctions is increasing, and imprisonment rates are declining. Less starkly but encouragingly, imprisonment use and rates in Eastern Europe have mostly sharply declined in recent decades. In the United States, Britain, Australia, and New Zealand, it is business as usual.

Were one of us czar or czarina, we would end the imprisonment era, not abruptly, not without developing much stronger social welfare policies whose absence blights lives and leads young people to lives of crime, not without devising better ways to meet ex-prisoners' needs and help them lead satisfying law-abiding lives, and not without addressing the challenges posed by the tiny numbers of people who are pathologically violent or fundamentally committed to lives of crime. Should those changes eventually occur, Mannheim and Morris's prediction will come to be seen as prescient, albeit possibly a bit premature.

REFERENCES

Hagan, John, and Ronit Dinovitzer. 1999. "Collateral Consequences of Imprisonment for Children, Communities, and Prisoners." In *Prisons*, edited by Michael Tonry and Joan Petersilia. Vol. 26 of *Crime and Justice: A Review of Research*, edited by Michael Tonry. Chicago: University of Chicago Press.

Mannheim, Hermann. 1942. "American Criminology and Penology in War Time." *Sociological Review* 34:222–34.

Morris, Norval. 1965. "Prison in Evolution." In *Criminology in Transition: Essays in Honour of Hermann Mannheim*, edited by Tadeusz Grygier, Howard Jones, and John C. Spencer. London: Tavistock.

Morris, Norval. 1974. *The Future of Imprisonment*. Chicago: University of Chicago Press.

Morris, Norval, and David J. Rothman, eds. 1995. *The Oxford History of the Prison*. New York: Oxford University Press.

NACCJSG (National Advisory Commission on Criminal Justice Standards and Goals). 1973. *A National Strategy to Reduce Crime*. Washington, DC: US Government Printing Office.

Petrich, Damon M., Travis C. Pratt, Cheryl Lero Jonson, and Francis T. Cullen. 2021. "Custodial Sanctions and Reoffending: A Meta-analytic Review." In

Crime and Justice: A Review of Research, vol. 50, edited by Michael Tonry. Chicago: University of Chicago Press.

Tonry, Michael, and Joan Petersilia, eds. 1999. *Prisons*. Vol. 26 of *Crime and Justice: A Review of Research*, edited by Michael Tonry. Chicago: University of Chicago Press.

Travis, Jeremy, Bruce Western, and Steve Redburn, eds. 2014. *The Growth of Incarceration in the United States: Exploring Causes and Consequences*. Report of the National Academy of Sciences Committee on the Causes and Consequences of High Rates of Incarceration. Washington, DC: National Academies Press.

Michael Tonry

Punishments, Politics, and Prisons in Western Countries

ABSTRACT

Imprisonment rates and patterns and the professionalism and decency of prison operations vary widely between countries and, within the United States, between states. The explanations for differences are deeply embedded in national or local histories and political cultures; substantial changes are hard to achieve. Day-to-day life even in the "best" prisons is usually drab, monotonous, and unpleasant; in the worst it is squalid, unhealthy, and sometimes terrifying. Conditions for guards and other staff are often little better. The big difference is that they can go home at shift's end. They are often poorly paid and little respected; work in claustrophobic, stultifying environments; and deal daily with angry, depressed, mentally ill, and otherwise troubled people. The best run, most humane prisons address those challenges as best they can—in some countries, sometimes, reasonably well. Many prisons—in some countries, most—are terrible places. Sometimes that is because policy makers cannot or will not spend the money needed to run them decently, sometimes because they do not much care what goes on inside, and sometimes because they affirmatively want prisoners to suffer. Staff miseries are collateral damage.

Countries' prisons serve as the moral equivalent of canaries in coal mines. Dead canaries attest to the presence of poisonous gases; overcrowded, squalid prisons, to an absence of respect for human dignity. "The degree

Michael Tonry was formerly professor of law and public policy and director of the Institute of Criminology at Cambridge University. I am grateful to Sandra Bucerius, Klára Kereszi, Krzysztof Krajewski, Miklós Lévay, Rossella Selmini, Tapio Lappi-Seppälä, and Tim Newburn for critical readings of an earlier draft.

Electronically published September 27, 2022

Crime and Justice, volume 51, 2022.

of civilization in a society," Fyodor Dostoyevsky wrote, in *House of the Dead* (1861), "can be judged by entering its prisons." Winston Churchill in a House of Commons speech in 1910, when he was Home Secretary of England and Wales,[1] observed more fulsomely:

> The mood and temper of the public in regard to the treatment of crime and criminals is one of the most unfailing tests of any country. A calm, dispassionate recognition of the rights of the accused and even of the convicted criminal, . . . tireless efforts towards the discovery of curative and re-generative processes; unfailing faith that there is a treasure, if you can only find it, in the heart of every man. These are the symbols which, in the treatment of crime and the criminal, mark and measure the stored-up strength of a nation, and are the sign and proof of the living virtue within it.

How prisoners are treated says much about political cultures and fundamental values. Enlightenment ideas about rationality, fairness, justice, and equality were in the air when the precursors to modern prisons took shape early in the nineteenth century, as the American Declaration of Independence in 1776, the French Declaration of the Rights of Man and of the Citizen in 1789, and democratic political uprisings throughout Europe in 1832 and 1848 demonstrate.

Those ideas continue to reverberate. Human rights activists, prison reformers, and many correctional officials draw on them to evaluate prisons and their treatment of prisoners. By those measures, countries vary enormously. Regimes in many places—Russia, China, much of Central and South America—pay little attention to Enlightenment values, have always treated prisoners terribly, and still do. Northern European countries—the Netherlands, the German-speaking countries, Switzerland, the Nordic countries—are at the opposite pole. Imprisonment rates are low, prison terms are usually short and proportionate to the seriousness of the crimes for which they are imposed, prisons are usually small (typically low hundreds of inmates or fewer), and prisoners are treated respectfully and compassionately.[2] The aspirations are clear, and widely supported, even

---

[1] Hereafter, with apologies to the Welsh, I refer to the country as England. Devolution has brought Wales some degree of autonomy within the United Kingdom, but, unlike Scotland and Northern Ireland, it does not have a separate legal system.

[2] That does not mean that prisoners anywhere generally regard imprisonment as a pleasant experience, although, as Bucerius, Haggerty, and Dunford (2020), Bucerius and Sandberg (2022), and Tetrault (2022) observe, sometimes some prisoners value security

if like all human aspirations they are not always realized. Prisoners are citizens behind bars, entitled to the rights and benefits of other citizens except unfettered mobility including—an important symbolic indicator— the right to vote.

Prisons in the United States, and to lesser extents other English-speaking countries that were once British colonies, are a middle case. They pay lip service to Enlightenment values and in some ways—generally not wholeheartedly—honor them. Imprisonment rates are higher than in Western Europe, sentences are often long and disproportionately severe, many prisons are enormous (sometimes thousands of inmates), conditions are often squalid, and services and programs are usually sparse. To advert to a symbol: prisoners are seldom entitled to vote—in the United States, only in Maine and Vermont.[3] British Prime Minister David Cameron no doubt spoke for many English speakers when he denounced the European Court of Human Rights decision in *Hirst v. United Kingdom* (No. 2) (2005) ECHR 681, which affirmed British prisoners' right to vote. The decision, Cameron declared, "made me physically ill even to contemplate" (*Times* 2010).

In this essay I explore why prison use, prison conditions, and prisoners' experiences vary enormously from place to place and some of the implications of those reasons. The short explanation is that democratic countries have prisons that electoral majorities want or will tolerate, but that raises the question of why wants and tolerances vary so widely. Reasonably convincing accounts involve distinctive features of national histories and political cultures that shape attitudes toward crime, criminals, and punishment and respect for human dignity generally. Norval Morris and David Rothman (1995, p. viii) observed in *The Oxford History of the Prison* that "the history of the prison serves to illuminate the history of all social institutions." In the United States, most prisons and jails are barren and

---

or services some prisons provide. David Downes (1988) long ago showed that English prisoners in the Netherlands were pleasantly surprised by Dutch prison conditions; Dutch prisoners were mortified by the awfulness of English prisons. That does not imply that Dutch prisoners liked Netherlands prisons. Contemporary Scandinavian prisoners presumably generally dislike their confinement; were they magically transported to prisons in California or—perish the thought!—Alabama or Louisiana, they would likely be horrified.

[3] Canada is an exception but not because provincial and national legislators were especially solicitous of prisoners' interest in voting; lower courts upheld some disenfranchisement laws and struck down others until the Canadian Supreme Court settled the matter by declaring denial of voting rights to prisoners to be unconstitutional (*Sauvé v. Canada [Chief Electoral Officer]*, 2002 SCC 68, [2002] 3 SCR 519).

dehumanizing; neither sympathy nor empathy for prisoners is much evident. This, I have shown elsewhere, is because criminal justice policies, practices, and institutions resonate to distinctive American histories of race relations, politicization of the criminal law, and moral judgmentalism associated with fundamentalist Protestantism (Tonry 2021).[4] Racial bias, indifference to racial disparities, political interference in processing of individual criminal cases, and vindictive moralism permeate American criminal justice systems. Equally distinctive but different considerations explain the nature and uses of prisons in other countries including, for example, why Finland reduced its imprisonment rate by two-thirds in the late twentieth century; operates small, service-rich institutions; and by American standards punishes convicted people modestly (Lappi-Seppälä 2016). Different historical and cultural contexts explain why imprisonment rates in the Netherlands have often since the 1950s been among the lowest in Western countries (Tonry and Bijleveld 2007; Boone, Pakes, and van Wingerden 2020), why many European countries in the 1970s and 1980s responded to rising crime rates by establishing new community punishments rather than by sending many more people to prison, and why mass amnesties and pardons were commonplace and uncontroversial in France and Italy for nearly two centuries (Lévy 2007).

I cannot in one essay discuss the historical and cultural underpinnings of many countries' criminal justice systems. Instead I discuss things that shape imprisonment—punishment philosophies, politics, and policies—in Sections II and III, after surveying patterns of imprisonment in European and English-speaking countries in Section I and before summing

---

[4] In this essay, I mostly discuss facets of imprisonment policies and use in Western countries rather than "determinants of penal policies" (Tonry 2007; Lacey, Soskice, and Hope 2018). A sizable literature on determinants that began to develop in the mid-1990s focused successively on populist punitiveness (Bottoms 1995), conditions of late modernity (Garland 2001), penal populism (Pratt 2007), neoliberalism (Cavadino and Dignan 2005), and political economy (Lacey 2008). Tapio Lappi-Seppälä (2008) showed that moderate penal policies and low imprisonment rates are at a global level correlated with citizens' trust in one another, government legitimacy in citizens' eyes, low levels of income inequality, and high levels of social welfare spending. I showed that moderate policies and low imprisonment rates are associated with consensus rather than conflict political systems (Lijphart [1984, 1999] explains the difference), policy reliance on professional expertise rather than public opinion, and use of career civil service lawyers and judges rather than elected or politically appointed ones (Tonry 2007). Lappi-Seppälä's and my findings necessarily raise the question of why countries do and do not have particular attributes. The answers, the most exhaustive and authoritative surveys of the determinants literature agree, are to be found in countries' distinctive histories and political cultures (Garland 2018, 2020; Lacey, Soskice, and Hope 2018).

up in Section IV. Imprisonment in many countries could be more just, humane, respectful, and effective than it now is—other countries' experiences show it is possible—but that will seldom happen easily or quickly.

I. Patterns of Imprisonment Use

Prisons, it is commonly said, first came into widespread use as mechanisms of punishment in the nineteenth century in the United States. That is not entirely true. Earlier institutions recognizably akin to prisons existed in Europe, on a smaller scale, as did pretrial detention and post-conviction confinement of people sentenced to death or in Great Britain to transportation. So too on a larger scale did asylums for "the insane" and debtors' prisons, both performing latent functions of modern prisons. In other respects, though, the claim is true. Early Quaker-influenced institutions, especially Philadelphia's Walnut Street Jail and Eastern State Penitentiary, predicated on ideas about penitence as a basis for moral reformation (thence "penitentiaries"), captured the imaginations of reformers elsewhere. Among many others, Alexis de Tocqueville, Charles Dickens, Frances Trollope, and Hans Christian Anderson famously traveled to America in the first half of the nineteenth century to visit prisons. Their reports were not uniformly positive, but that does not seem to have mattered. Prisons based on American models were built throughout Europe, especially in Great Britain, and elsewhere. We live with the results. Some prisons continue to be called penitentiaries or reformatories, although the Quaker ideas soon lost favor. The solitary confinement regimes they specified proved to be destructive and inhumane (Morris and Rothman 1995; Smith 2006).

The use of imprisonment varies widely. To some critics, comparatively few, having any prisons at all is a problem: abolition is the solution. Most people outside abolitionist circles, however, accept that imprisonment has or may serve useful public functions—or is in any case unlikely to disappear any time soon. Almost all critics believe prisons could be operated more constructively and humanely.

The punitiveness of national criminal justice systems is usually measured by the number of people locked up per 100,000 population. That rate provides some information but obscures important differences. Some countries send many people convicted of crimes to prison; others comparatively few. Terms longer than a year are rare in some countries and common in others. Pretrial confinement is common in some places, comparatively rare in others. As a result, two countries with similar imprisonment rates may punish their residents in very different ways, one imprisoning many people for short periods (e.g., the Netherlands), another imprisoning comparatively few but usually for longer (e.g., Germany; Aebi et al. 2021).

Reasonably reliable data on prison admissions and populations are available globally (Fair and Walmsley 2021), in Europe (Aebi and Tiago 2021; Aebi et al. 2021), and in the United States (e.g., Carson 2021).[5] Imprisonment use varies greatly in absolute scale but also in other ways I describe below. Table 1 shows total rates—in American terms, for jails and prisons combined—for five English-speaking, seven Western European, and five Eastern and Central European countries at roughly half-decade intervals since 1998–99.[6] The final column lists countries by increasing imprisonment rates in 2019–21. The variation is enormous: the American rate of 629 per 100,000 population was more than 12 times Finland's 50 and six to 10 times those of most other Western European countries. Patterns leap out. Fluctuations over two decades were modest in the eight countries— all in Western Europe except Canada—with the lowest rates. Rates have fallen in most countries in recent years. They are lowest in Western Europe, substantially higher in the English-speaking countries (except Canada),

[5] These sources vary in nature, completeness, and comparability. Most—including others compiled by the United Nations and Eurostat—are compilations of data provided by national or state/regional/provincial agencies that vary substantially in completeness and comparability (are juveniles, people held in police custody, and immigration detainees [any, all, only those in criminal as opposed to administrative detention?] included or excluded?). The most comparable international data are provided by the Council of Europe's SPACE I statistics (Aebi and Tiago 2021), which are based on templates that have evolved over several decades and incorporate standardizing adjustments to make national data comparable (e.g., to remove juvenile system and immigrant administrative detention data). SPACE I data are thus for many countries closely comparable in a given year and over time. Noncomparability issues in other data systems make rates less equivalent but are unlikely significantly to affect orders of magnitude: Finnish and Dutch rates, for example, would remain low, French and Canadian rates middling, Hungarian and New Zealand rates high, Russian rates very high, and American rates enormous if perfectly consistent classification systems were used.

[6] In most developed countries, pretrial detention is called remand. The American distinction between local jails for most pretrial detention and short terms of confinement and state or federal prisons for longer terms does not exist in most other countries (Canada comes closest: people awaiting trial or serving terms of 2 years or less are held in provincial prisons; federal prisons hold people serving longer terms). Because most readers of this essay are likely to be Americans, I often use the American terminology. To belabor the point: imprisonment and admission data in tables 1–6, and expository text, refer to "jail" and "prison" numbers combined.

TABLE 1

Imprisonment Rates per 100,000 Population, 17 Countries, Various Years

Country	1998–99	2007–8	2011–13	2019–21
Finland	45 (12/31/99)	64 (1/1/08)	57.6 (9/1/13)	49.9 (1/31/20)
Netherlands	90 (12/31/99)	100 (8/31/08)	62.9 (9/1/13)	58.5 (1/31/20)
Norway	60 (9/30/99)	69 (8/1/08)	72.2 (9/1/13)	58.8 (1/31/20)
Sweden	60 (9/20/99)	74 (10/1/07)	61.4 (9/1/13)	65.0 (1/31/20)
Germany	95 (1/31/99)	89 (8/31/08)	84.1 (9/1/13)	76.2 (1/31/20)
Switzerland	85 (9/1/99)	76 (9/5/07)	88.0 (9/1/13)	80.2 (1/31/20)
Canada	110 (1998–99 mean)	116 (2007–8 mean)	118 (9/30/11)	104 (3/31/19)
France	90 (9/1/99)	96 (7/1/08)	119.5 (9/1/13)	105.3 (1/31/20)
England and Wales	125 (11/31/99)	153 (11/28/08)	147.2 (9/1/13)	138 (1/31/20)
Ukraine	430 (12/99)	323 (1/1/08)	305 (9/1/13)	139 (10/1/21)
New Zealand	150 (1999 mean)	185 (6/30/08)	192 (6/30/13)	164 (6/30/21)
Australia	110 (1999 mean)	129 (6/30/08)	130 (6/30/12)	167 (3/1/21)
Hungary	150 (12/31/99)	149 (9/2/08)	180.6 (9/1/13)	171.8 (1/31/20)
Poland	145 (12/31/99)	221 (10/31/08)	205.2 (9/1/13)	195.3 (1/31/20)
Lithuania	385 (10/3/99)	234 (1/1/08)	314.6 (9/1/13)	219.7 (1/31/20)
Russia	730 (12/31/99)	629 (11/1/08)	475 (9/1/13)	356.1 (1/31/20)
United States	680 (6/30/99)	763 (12/31/07)	709 (12/31/13)	629 (6/30/19)

Sources.—For 1998–98 rates (Walmsley 2000); 2007–8 rates (Walmsley 2009); 2011–13 rates: for continental Europe except Ukraine (Aebi and Delgrande 2014, table 1); for Australia, Canada, New Zealand, and Ukraine (Walmsley 2014, tables 2, 4, and 5); for the United States (Carson 2014; Minton and Golinelli 2014); 2019–21 rates: for continental Europe except Ukraine (Aebi and Tiago 2021); for all others, World Prison Brief, Institute for Criminal Policy Research, Birkbeck College, University of London, https://www.prisonstudies.org/world-prison-brief-data (accessed November 30, 2021).

higher still in Eastern and Central Europe, and highest by far in the United States. Among traditionally high-rate countries, rates have declined much more in Lithuania, Ukraine, and Russia than in the United States.

Little about these differences will surprise informed people in particular countries. They mostly reflect deliberate policy choices. During two decades of rising crime rates in all Western countries that began in the late 1960s (Tonry 2014), for example, American politicians and practitioners chose to increase imprisonment rates substantially, Finnish politicians and practitioners to reduce theirs by two-thirds, and German politicians and practitioners to hold theirs level (Tonry 2004, figs. 2.1–2.3). Imprisonment rates dropped precipitately in most former Warsaw Pact countries after 1989 as a result of deliberate policy choices in the aftermath of collapse of authoritarian regimes. Rates fell more slowly and later in the former Soviet Socialist Republics (SSRs); previous political regimes remained in power after the Soviet Union collapsed and were presumably less inclined to emulate Western European norms and patterns.

Comparisons of imprisonment rates per 100,000 population can, however, be misleading. They obscure big variations in use of pretrial detention, in the likelihood that convicted people are sentenced to imprisonment, and in the lengths of sentences, as tables 2 and 3 show.

Table 2 is taken from the first major comparative effort to look closely at national differences in use of imprisonment (Young and Brown 1993). Only a few such detailed comparative analyses have been published, with comparable results (e.g., Kommer 1994, 2004). The differences this classic albeit elderly analysis demonstrates would be similar except in details were similar analyses done using recent data (e.g., from Aebi and Tiago 2021).

Table 2 shows imprisonment rates in 1990 and rates for total, pretrial, and postconviction prison admissions in 1987 in three English-speaking and four Western European countries. The "rankings" vary widely. Sweden, for example, had the second-lowest imprisonment rate overall but by far the highest rates of total and pretrial admissions and the second highest rate of postconviction admissions. Sweden locked up lots of people before trial and goodly numbers afterward (given its low imprisonment rate, for relatively short times). Sweden's imprisonment rate was significantly lower than those of Germany and France, but total admissions were three and a half times higher and pretrial admissions were four to five times higher.

TABLE 2

Imprisonment Rates: Sentenced, Remand, and Total Admission Rates per 100,000, Seven Countries

Country Rank	Imprisonment (1990)	Sentenced Admissions (1987)	Remand Admissions (1987)	Total Admissions (1987)
1	New Zealand (106)	New Zealand (190)	Sweden (405)	Sweden (583)
2	England and Wales (93)	Sweden (178)	Scotland (335)	Scotland (434)
3	Scotland (95)	Netherlands (137)	New Zealand (203)	New Zealand (393)
4	France (82)	England and Wales (137)	England and Wales (169)	England and Wales (306)
5	West Germany (78)	Scotland (99)	France (104)	France (168)
6	Sweden (58)	West Germany (84)	West Germany (78)	West Germany (162)
7	Netherlands (44)	France (64)	Netherlands (NA)	Netherlands (NA)

Source.—Young and Brown (1993).

Table 3 shows prison admission and sentence length data for 10 European countries in 2015, the most recent year for which such data are available (Aebi et al. 2021). An American frame of reference may be useful. In 2009, the latest year for which national data are available, 73 percent of convicted people charged with felonies in American state courts were sentenced to imprisonment (Reaves 2013, tables 24–26). By stark contrast, 3 percent (in Finland) to 28 percent (in the Netherlands) of people convicted of crimes in 2015 in the 10 European countries were sentenced to imprisonment.[7]

The European/American contrast concerning lengths of prison sentences is equally stunning. In 2009, maximum state prison sentences for people convicted of any offense following a felony charge in American state courts averaged 91 months for violent offenses, 40 months for

---

[7] The American 73 percent and data in the following paragraph on average sentence lengths provide a chastening contrast, I believe. The American data refer to cases initially prosecuted as felonies (although some resulted in misdemeanor convictions, usually as a product of plea bargaining). The European data refer to all convicted cases except traffic and administrative offenses. Unfortunately no credible national US data on sentencing exist except for felony cases, and no data are available on sentence lengths overall. Reliable European data on mean sentences following convictions for specific offenses likewise do not exist. Even with those differences, it is impossible not to conclude that American sentencing is vastly harsher.

TABLE 3
Imposition and Length of Unsuspended Prison Sentences in Months: Selected European Countries and United States, 2015

Country	Imprisonment Rate per 100,000 (1/31/20)	% Prison Sentences, Unsuspended						
		Total	Of Which, <6 Months	Of Which, 6 to <12 Months	Of Which, 12 to <24 Months	Of Which, 24 to <60 Months	Of Which, 60 to <120 Months	Of Which, ≥120 Months
Finland	49.1	2.8	60.2	10.2	13.7	12.2	2.7	.2
France	105.3	22.1	54.6	24.0	16.5	3.0	1.7	.1
Germany	76.2	4.8	22.7	29.4	19.1	24.3	4.0	.7
Hungary	171.8	10.7	2.1	16.3	35.8	32.3	10.8	2.3
Netherlands	58.5	28.5	84.4	7.3	5.4	3.4	.8	.3
Norway	58.8	3.7	74.8	12.0	9.7	1.9	1.4	.3
Poland	195.3	13.1	20.4	32.4	33.9	10.7	1.8	.7
Sweden	65.0	10.2	64.2	14.2	13.2	5.3	2.2	.3
Switzerland	80.2	9.6	77.3	8.6	6.1	6.4	1.3	.7
England	138.0	7.2	14.7	16.1	35.5	34.1	10.1	2.9
United States	629 (2019)	73 (2009)*						

SOURCES.—European imprisonment rates on January 31, 2020 (Aebi and Tiago 2021, table 3); European prison sentences, 2015 (Aebi et al. 2021, tables 3.2.3.1 and 3.2.5.1); US imprisonment rate (see table 1); US prison admission rate (Reaves 2013).

* Data are for sentenced cases initially charged as felonies in the 75 most populous counties that resulted in felony or misdemeanor convictions.

property offenses, and 52 months for any offense. For intentional homicide, rape, and robbery the means were 373, 142, and 90 months (Reaves 2013, tables 24–26).[8]

By contrast, as table 3 shows, prison terms longer than 1 year were rare in Europe, constituting only 1 or 2 percent of all sentences in most countries. Most prison sentences were for a year or less. In six of the 10 countries, half to two-thirds of prison sentences were for 6 months or less. At the other extreme, more than 80 percent of prison sentences in Hungary and England and Wales, and nearly 50 percent in Poland, were for a year or longer. Those countries were simply substantially more punitive than most of the others.

Germany is a special case. Prison admissions were third lowest in 2015 at 4.8 percent of convicted people, but sentence lengths were comparatively long. Nearly a third were for 2 years or more. This is because German law has long strongly discouraged use of short prison sentences, authorized penal orders that require a guilty plea but do not allow a prison sentence, and encouraged use of conditional dismissals in lieu of prosecutions (Weigend 1997, 2016).

Except in Germany, Hungary, and England, only 1–3 percent of people sentenced to imprisonment received sentences of 5 years or longer. Even those numbers look misleadingly large because few convicted people receive prison sentences at all. In Germany, 4.7 percent of sentences were for 5 years. That is 4.7 percent, however, of the 4.8 percent of convicted people overall who received any prison sentence. In other words, less than three-tenths of 1 percent of all convicted persons received sentences of 5 years or longer.[9]

Several observations emerge. First, countries vary enormously in their use of imprisonment: there are order-of-magnitude differences in locking people up, illustrated by the more than twelvefold difference between

---

[8] This is serious time. Release before serving a substantial part of the sentence is uncommon. Good time/remission can reduce maximum sentences by 15–33 percent, varying by state. Parole release is possible in two-thirds of the states, although comparatively rare for people serving long sentences. An overlapping half of the states have enacted truth-in-sentencing laws applicable to most serious crimes; they require service of 85 percent of the maximum sentence before eligibility for release (Tonry 2016).

[9] Even the few longer sentences provide a misleading impression of absolute severity (Weigend 2016). In many European countries, prisoners receive an automatic or nearly automatic one-third reduction in their sentences, usually called "remission," basically the same as American "time off for good behavior." Discretionary release is also possible in many countries, often after serving half of the nominal sentence.

American (629) and Finnish (50) imprisonment rates. Second, some countries much more often than others confine defendants before trial. Third, much larger fractions of people convicted of crimes receive prison sentences in some countries than in others. Fourth, average lengths of prison sentences vary widely. Fifth, those differences usually result from conscious decisions by policy makers and practitioners, for reasons they can explain. I discuss some of those reasons and their implications in Section III.

Before that, because deprivation of liberty in a free society should be justifiable in principle, and policy makers sometimes claim to act on principled grounds, I discuss the nature and pertinence of prevailing ideas about punishment.

II. Principles and Purposes

People are sentenced to imprisonment as punishment. That is a big deal, something that should be explainable in terms of justice, public benefit, or both. Those explanations are often embedded in, or justifiable under, theories or philosophies of punishment but often—probably usually—involve other considerations.

The philosophies, conventionally described as retributive, consequentialist, or mixed, offer analytical frameworks. However, policy decisions and punishments imposed on individuals are in practice also influenced by other expressive, symbolic, and self-interested considerations. The philosophies are normative; the other considerations are expediencies aimed at achievement of objectives other than just punishments or crime prevention.

A. Norms

Retributive ways of thinking are conventionally associated with the German philosophers Immanuel Kant ([1797] 2017) and Georg Wilhelm Friedrich Hegel ([1821] 1991), consequentialism with the English polymath Jeremy Bentham ([1789] 1970), and mixed theories with the twentieth century's H. L. A. Hart (1968) and Norval Morris (1974). Huge literatures explore, challenge, and build on their ideas, but for my purposes their main themes and the differences among them are what is important.

Retributivism centers on respect for moral autonomy, human dignity, and inalienable human rights; consequentialism on collective interests, benefits, and costs; and mixed theories on reconciling the two. All three acknowledge and wrestle with tensions between individual and collective interests, between treating individuals justly and preventing crime.

1. *Retributivism.* There are many well-elaborated retributive theories.[10] In all of them the moral gravity of an individual's wrongdoing should be the, or a, primary consideration in deciding whether and how much he or she may justly be punished. Critics of retributivism say it is bloodthirsty, causing and rationalizing suffering, often for no good practical reason. Retributivists disagree, saying that their approach, by attaching proportionate consequences to blameworthy acts, respects human dignity and celebrates moral autonomy. Hegel, for example, observed that with retributive punishment, "The criminal is *honoured* as a rational being. He is denied this honour if the concept and criterion of his punishment are not derived from his own act; and he is also denied it if he is regarded simply as a harmful animal which must be rendered harmless, or punished with a view to deterring him or reforming him" ([1821] 1991, p. 127).

2. *Consequentialism.* There are fewer well-elaborated consequentialist theories. Often they identify a wide range of considerations (e.g., deterrence, incapacitation, rehabilitation, retribution, moral education, acknowledgment of public concerns, appeasement of public anger, maintenance of state legitimacy) and direct decision makers to take them into account as appears appropriate in individual cases (e.g., Hart 1958). Most share with Bentham's utilitarianism a premise that preventing or minimizing crime should be the, or a, primary consideration in deciding whether, how, and how much a wrongdoer should be punished.[11] Critics claim that Bentham's utilitarianism would justify punishing innocent people if the crime prevention effects were substantial. Most utilitarians deny this, saying either that such punishments would inevitably become known and the criminal law would lose legitimacy, credibility, and effectiveness as a result or that state punishment may by definition be imposed only on people convicted of crimes. Many consequentialists believe some convicted people may appropriately be punished disproportionately severely because they are believed to be dangerous and should be incapacitated, because

---

[10] Classic overviews of "varieties of retributivism" include Hart (1968, appendix), Cottingham (1979), and Walker (1991).

[11] Two principal exceptions are Braithwaite and Pettit's (1990, 2001) "republican theory of justice," usually associated with restorative justice, which would seek to maximize dominion (individuals' control over their own lives) and economists' theories that seek to maximize profits (crime prevention) and minimize costs (suffering by punished people; e.g., Posner 2007). Both differ from retributive and mixed theories in taking no account of retributive considerations of deserved or proportionate punishment.

they are incorrigible and cannot be rehabilitated, or because deterrent considerations justify harsh, exemplary punishments.

3. *Mixed Theories.* Hart (1968) and Morris (1974) were not retributivists but worried that starkly disproportionate punishments undermine the law's legitimacy in citizens' eyes and with that its moral authority. Both urged that retributive and consequentialist considerations be balanced. Morris promoted "limiting retributivism": the seriousness of the crime sets upper and lower limits of deserved punishment, within which preventive considerations may sometimes be taken into account. Hart (1968, p. 233) was vaguer, allowing "some place, though a subordinate one, to ideas of equality and proportion in the gradation of the severity of punishment."

Policy makers and practitioners no doubt sometimes think about imposition of deserved punishments, efforts to prevent crimes, and trade-offs between them but often also have other objectives in mind. As table 2 showed, for example, there are enormous differences between countries in use of pretrial confinement. Because defendants are presumed to be innocent, pretrial confinement is used sparingly in many countries. Defendants in Sweden, by contrast, were for long routinely held in isolation before trial in order to facilitate investigations and prosecutions; this was in theory meant to prevent tampering with evidence or suborning witnesses (Smith 2006). As table 3 showed, use of prison sentences and sentence lengths vary widely between countries. Policy makers in English-speaking countries in recent decades often enacted laws permitting or requiring unjustly long prison sentences. American three-strikes laws and English sentences to "imprisonment for public protection" are paradigm instances.

B. Expediency

Decisions about punishment and imprisonment are often influenced by considerations other than justice and crime prevention. Policies are sometimes adopted and individuals punished for expressive, symbolic, or expedient reasons that have little or nothing to do with normative ideas about justice or good faith efforts to prevent crime (Tonry 2006).

1. *Expressive Punishments.* State actions and decisions by state agents are often intended or interpreted expressively, as endorsements of propositions about the world or about values, or as acknowledgment of the validity of beliefs or opinions. In recent decades, many governments enacted harsher laws concerning violence generally, child abuse, sexual predation, and hate crimes at least in part to acknowledge putative

concerns or preferences of citizens. In his landmark book, *The Culture of Control*, David Garland (2001) argued that British and American governments adopted expressive crime policies in the 1990s without necessarily believing harsher laws would have preventative effects. A primary goal was reinforcement or enhancement of governmental legitimacy in citizens' eyes. Likewise, individuals are often prosecuted, especially in Common Law countries, to send expressive messages. Think about the MeToo movement and recent sexual assault prosecutions of comedian Bill Cosby, producer Harvey Weinstein, and other prominent men. Their behaviors were morally and ethically terrible. Prosecutions were warranted, but they were often meant at least as much to express sympathy for or solidarity with victims and the MeToo movement as dispassionately to prove wrongdoing and determine just punishments. British politicians often say that harsh crime policies are meant to maintain or restore "public confidence" in the legal system. Prominent examples include abolition of the centuries-old Common Law double jeopardy rule and of a long-standing prohibition of state appeals of sentences in individual cases (Windlesham 1993; Tonry 2012*b*).[12]

2. *Symbolic Punishments.* Symbolic punishments and policies are slightly different. Sometimes they overlap with expressive actions, which usually at least purport to have or pursue real world effects. Other times, their proponents do not pretend to expect practical consequences. The aim is to go on record.

The symbolic statements sometimes are purposely cruel, as when politicians decry "country club prisons" and threaten or require elimination of programs and amenities for explicitly punitive purposes. Some American judges in the 1960s and 1970s imposed prison sentences expressed in centuries on people they knew would likely be released on parole after at most a few years. "Texan Given 1,500 Years," a *New York Times* (1970) headline

---

[12] Consider the following quotations on the need for a law authorizing prosecutorial sentence appeals from *House of Lords Debates*, 26 October 1987, vol. 489, cols. 314–401; *House of Commons Debates*, 28 January 1988, vol. 125, cols. 681–767: "Lenient sentences are one 'problem too important to ignore' because of the 'harm to public confidence which the occasional over-lenient sentence can cause'" (Noble Earl); in "serious cases where public emotions can be understandably engaged," unduly lenient sentences arouse "widespread concern ... [and] govern the confidence of the citizen in the machinery for his protection" (Lord Elwyn-Jones); "When a manifestly over-lenient sentence is passed, the damage to public confidence in the system is out of all proportion to the significance of the case. ... That is why the problem, though small in scale, is of great importance" (Douglas Hurd [Home Secretary]). Lord Windlesham (1993) discusses the debates and arguments in detail.

announced regarding a man "convicted of possession and sale of heroin. It was the longest sentence in Texas history. Sentences of 1000 years and more have been given recently in cases of rape, robbery, and assault." One might wonder what the judges involved would have thought appropriate for gangland killings, political assassinations, or killings following extended torture? More recently, 71-year-old securities law violator Bernard Madoff was sentenced to 150 years imprisonment in 2009 despite ill health that made anything more than a few years window dressing; even when terminally ill he was denied compassionate release. Republican New York Senator Alfonso D'Amato, after proposing harsh amendments to a federal mandatory sentencing law, "conceded that his two successful amendments, which Justice Department officials say would have little practical effect on prosecution of crimes, might not solve the problem. 'But,' he said, 'it does bring about a sense that we are serious'" (Ifill 1991). Some American three-strikes laws were for that reason drafted so complexly that—legislators realized and intended—they would seldom or never be applied (Dickey and Hollenhurst 1998). Other such laws (e.g., California's original three-strikes law and many life-without-parole laws) were expected to be applied, but legislators' votes in support were often simply symbolic statements about their toughness.

3. *Political Expediency.* Louis Renault, the French police officer in *Casablanca*, when ordered by a German officer to close Rick's Bar (and casino), declared, "I'm shocked, shocked, to find that gambling is going on in here." Captain Renault was not shocked. Few people are likewise likely to be surprised that expediency influences punishment policies and practices, albeit much more in some countries than in others. Rod Morgan (2006, p. 111), formerly head of the English Youth Justice Board and later Her Majesty's Chief Inspector of Probation, attributed the crime policies of Tony Blair's Labour Government to pursuit of "short-term electoral gain rather than effectiveness in changing behaviour or creating a safer world." Jonathan Simon in *Governing through Crime* (2007) observed that campaigning American politicians often try to win votes by provoking voters' anxieties and anger about crime and then promising to respond by supporting harsh policies. They are seldom especially interested in crime, he wrote; they need to be elected to do other things they care more about.

Republicans successfully used tough-on-crime appeals policies to win American elections for decades (Edsall and Edsall 1991). Bill Clinton stalemated them by adopting a strategy of always being equally tough or tougher. That is a principal cause of unprecedentedly harsh American sentencing policies and enormous imprisonment rates. Clinton (e.g., 1996) and then senator Joe Biden celebrated their roles in passing the now infamous Violent Crime Control and Law Enforcement Act of 1994 that enacted the federal three-strikes law, lengthened mandatory minimum sentences, authorized the death penalty for 60 additional federal offenses, and authorized billions for prison construction to states that effectively abolished parole for people convicted of many offenses (Windlesham 1998; Gest 2001).

Similar stories can be told about post-1989 developments in Eastern and Central Europe (e.g., Krajewski 2010; Haney 2011, 2016; Lévay 2012a, 2012b). Fidesz-dominated governments of Viktor Orbán in Hungary, for example, have regularly focused campaigns and governance on toughness and regularly enacted severe punishment laws (including in 1999, 2009, and 2010).

But champions include not only legislators and chief executives. When elections loom, many American prosecutors become more aggressive (e.g., Dyke 2007; McCannon 2013; Bandyopadhyay and McCannon 2014), and many judges become more punitive (e.g., Huber and Gordon 2004; Berdejó and Yuchtman 2013; Berry 2015; Munir 2020). These are especially acute American problems because most state judges and chief prosecutors are elected. Practitioners everywhere, however, are no doubt sometimes tempted to take their own wishes for approval, promotion, or publicity into account when dealing with individual cases (Tonry 2006, 2012a).

C. Juxtaposing Punishment Philosophies and Expediency

Punishment philosophies and expediency considerations intermingle. A particular policy or punishment decision might be thought just in principle, an appropriate expression of condemnation, a symbol of a decision maker's determination, and professionally or personally advantageous to him or her. So the prosecutors in the Bill Cosby, Harvey Weinstein, and Bernard Madoff cases may have thought. Often, however, punishment philosophies and expediency point in different directions.

Consider two examples, one concerning a policy, one an individual case. The US Congress in 1986 enacted a "100-to-1" law that mandated the same 5-, 10-, and 20-year minimum prison sentences for sales of designated quantities of crack cocaine and sales of powder cocaine 100 times larger. Because street-level crack sellers were mostly young minority males, massive racial disparities in imprisonment were predicted and resulted (McDonald and Carlson 1993; Tonry 1995). No informed person believed the severe punishments would significantly affect drug sales or use. Conservative New York Senator Daniel Patrick Moynihan (1993, p. 362), for example, observed that "'drug busts' are probably necessary symbolic acts but nothing more." James Q. Wilson (1990, p. 534), for several decades America's most politically influential criminologist, similarly wrote that the effects of street-level arrests were "likely to be small. . . . I know of no serious law-enforcement official who disagrees with this conclusion. Typically, police officials tell interviewers that they are fighting a losing war or, at best, a holding action."

Here is the second example. Arkansas Governor Bill Clinton flew home to Little Rock during his 1992 campaign for the Democratic presidential nomination to preside over the execution of Ricky Ray Rector, a brain-damaged man who shot himself in the forehead when he realized he had unintentionally killed someone during a robbery. Scheduled for execution at midnight, Rector pushed aside the pecan pie he had ordered for his last supper, saving it for breakfast. Clinton denied the petition for commutation (Frady 1993).

Reasonable people differ in their beliefs about why, when, and how people may justly be punished. Reasonable people no doubt differ about the appropriateness or value of particular expressive policies and symbolic actions. It is difficult, however, to imagine anyone openly declaring, "I am voting for this bill even though I know it requires unjustly severe punishments and unnecessarily exacerbates racial disparities" or "I wouldn't insist on such a harsh punishment in your case, [or allow you to be executed], but I need to; it'll help me get elected." Such things happen in the United States sadly often.

III. Principles, Politics, and Policies

Differences in punishment policies and practices are not simply by-products of national differences in crime levels or patterns, changes in population composition, or economic ups and downs.[13] They result mostly

[13] This essay is long enough without detailed discussion of every assertion. As this one is fundamental, I offer some brief explanation. The first point (crime rates) is demonstrated in Sec. I: crime rates rose steeply in all developed Western countries in the 1970s and 1980s (Tonry 2014); imprisonment rates in different countries rose sharply, rose a little, remained broadly stable, or declined during those years. The second (population composition)

from conscious decisions by policy makers and practitioners who are influenced by norms, traditions, and expediency interests. This means that differences can largely be explained and in an analytical sense understood. It also means that major or rapid changes are difficult to accomplish unless they are willed by dominant political elites. In this section, I discuss four kinds of changes that have succeeded and failed in different places: shifts in punishment norms, imprisonment rates, prison diversion programs, and prison conditions.

A. Changes in Philosophies and Purposes

Punishment philosophies and purposes shape imprisonment levels, policies, and practices. They undergird the laws that determine who goes to prison and for how long. They influence the legislative, financial, and management decisions that shape prison conditions and programming.

Tensions between retributivism and consequentialism, between thinking about justice and thinking about crime prevention, exist in all times and places, probably also in most people's heads. Prevailing beliefs and emphases change within countries and vary between them. From the late 1800s through the 1960s, consequentialist ideas, principally focused on rehabilitation, secondarily on incapacitation, were influential in all Western countries. Their manifestations, however, varied widely.

The United States was the polar case. The key institutions and practices—the rehabilitative prison, the reformatory, probation, parole, the juvenile court; individualization as a method and an aspiration—took shape in the second half of the nineteenth century (Rothman 1971, 1980). Most developed Western countries emulated them. Between the early 1930s and 1975, every American state and the federal government operated an indeterminate sentencing system. Punishments were to be individualized to take account of offenders' circumstances and characteristics. Parole boards determined the lengths of prison sentences. Herbert Wechsler (1961, p. 468), twentieth-century America's most influential criminal

---

should be self-evident, demonstrated by stable and declining imprisonment rates throughout most of Western Europe and Canada during recent decades of large-scale population movement and increased diversity. The third (economic developments) can be seen by noting the stability of most countries' imprisonment rates despite recurring ups and downs. The US prison population grew continuously for more than three decades (1973–2007) amid alternating recessions and booms and has been gradually declining since 2007 despite substantial economic fluctuations.

law scholar and primary draftsman of the Model Penal Code, made the governing premise clear: "The rehabilitation of an individual who has incurred the moral condemnation of the law is in itself a social value of importance, a value, it is well to note, that is and ought to be the prime goal." In the most thorough-going indeterminate systems, in California and Washington State, judges sentenced people to prison but had no voice in how long they stayed. Every prison sentence was fully indeterminate (from 1 year to the statutory maximum). Parole boards set release dates. More commonly, judges set minimum terms, maximums, or both. Parole boards operated within those constraints.[14]

No other country went so far—England, for example, established a parole board only in 1968[15]—but ideas about individualization and rehabilitation were influential in every Western country (Bottomley 1990). Germany's Franz von Liszt (e.g., 1897, 1905) and Italy's Enrico Ferri (e.g., 1881, 1917), the most influential early European proponents of indeterminate sentencing, and their followers, were enormously influential (Pifferi 2022; Wetzell 2022). After decades of debate, most European policy makers and scholars acknowledged the importance and relevance of rehabilitation but by 1930 concluded that, except for young offenders, retributive considerations are at least equally important (Pifferi 2012). Indeterminate sentencing was rejected in principle, except for small numbers of offenders deemed extraordinarily dangerous or incorrigible.[16] Not so in the United States. Herbert Wechsler and his mentor Jerome Michael acknowledged that retribution may represent "the unstudied belief of most men" but insisted that "no legal provision can be justified merely

---

[14] Minimums and maximums seldom offered much constraint. Some states allowed judges to specify minimums, which usually had to be no more than a third of the maximum. Others authorized judges to set only maximums; parole boards could release any prisoner who had served a year or more.

[15] In a half-baked way that demonstrates the limited influence of retributive ideas in 1960s England. The parole board consisted of more than 100 members who met infrequently and in small groups. Decisions inevitably reflected the hearing panel's makeup. Achieving overall consistency and correcting or avoiding disparities were neither goals nor possible. Unlike American boards that autonomously decided release dates, the English Parole Board made and makes recommendations to government ministers who sometimes reject them, almost always for reasons of political expediency and usually mentioning public opinion.

[16] This was the origin of the common European distinction between "sanctions" (punishments, for which retributive proportionality is important) and "measures" (controls, which need not be proportionate, to address extraordinary public safety threats; de Keijser 2011; Pifferi 2012).

because it calls for the punishment of the morally guilty by penalties proportioned to their guilt, or criticized merely because it fails to do so" (Michael and Wechsler 1940, pp. 7, 11).

In the 1970s, rehabilitation fell from favor, initially in the United States and subsequently in most Western countries (e.g., Home Office 1990 [England and Wales]; Albrecht 2004 [Germany]; Junger-Tas 2004 [Netherlands]; Lappi-Seppälä 2016 [Scandinavia]). In the United States, sentencing disparities, risks and realities of racial bias, and beliefs that punishments should be consistent and proportionate were influential. So, however, were the "Nothing Works" implications of surveys of social science research on the effectiveness of rehabilitative programs (e.g., Martinson 1974; Lipton, Martinson, and Wilks 1975). In other Western countries, retributive ideas about deserved punishment and concerns that nothing works drove major changes. Rehabilitative aspirations and programs did not disappear but became less central.

The shifts resulted not from top-down decisions of policy makers but from changes in prevailing ways of thought. In earlier times, rehabilitation and crime prevention seemed to many people to be self-evidently more important than "doing justice" by means of proportionate punishments. Criminal behavior was widely believed (including by, e.g., Ferri, von Liszt, and Wechsler) to be largely or entirely determined by environmental conditions and innate psychological characteristics for which individuals are not morally responsible.[17] People do not choose their parents, their natal social class, or their disabilities. By the 1970s, that reasoning persuaded many fewer people; crimes were more often seen as blameworthy actions by morally culpable people. Influential proposals for emphasis on deserved punishments and development of sentencing guidelines were made in the United States (e.g., Morris 1974; von Hirsch 1976), Australia (Australian Law Reform Commission 1980), Canada (Canadian Sentencing Commission 1987), and England and Wales (Home Office 1990). Expert bodies in Finland and Sweden proposed and parliaments enacted statutory overhauls to decrease sentencing disparities and apportion punishments to offenses' "penal value" (Lappi-Seppälä 2016). Comprehensive changes

---

[17] Here is a classic German statement, similar to contemporaneous others by writers in many countries (Pifferi 2016): "Man is the product," Hugo Appelius (1892) wrote in the *Zeitschrift für die gesamte Strafrechtswissenschaft*, "of his descent, his upbringing, and the changing environments of his life to such a degree that these influences determine his actions with compelling force, without his being able to resist this force through any free or independent decision" (trans. Richard F. Wetzell 2022, p. 44).

in sentencing laws did not occur in most continental European countries or Canada, but emphases on rehabilitation as a rationale for imprisonment declined.

The changed emphases played out very differently. In the United States, the shift was hugely influential. In the 1970s and early 1980s every state and the federal government developed sentencing guidelines systems of one sort or another or enacted entirely new sentencing laws, many jurisdictions abolished parole release, and some did all three (Blumstein et al. 1983). Since the 1980s, retributive ideas have remained influential among scholars but not among policy makers.[18] They were replaced by political expediency and lip service to consequentialist concerns about deterrence, incapacitation, and public safety.[19] Results include mandatory minimum sentencing laws in every US state, three-strikes laws in 26 states, truth-in-sentencing laws in an overlapping 26 states, life-without-parole laws in 49 states, and all of them in the federal system. Together those laws have been the primary drivers of American imprisonment rates and patterns (Tonry 2016).

England and Wales especially but also Australia, New Zealand, and Canada (under the conservative Stephen Harper government, 2006–15) followed the American lead and adopted expedient and consequentialist policies that led (except in Canada) to steeply higher imprisonment rates (Doob and Webster 2016 [Canada]; Freiberg 2016 [Australia]; Roberts and Ashworth 2016 [England]; Pratt 2017 [New Zealand]).[20] In at least

[18] The story is much the same in England and Wales (Newburn 2007; Downes and Newburn 2022). A Home Office white paper written by David Faulkner (Home Office 1990), the senior civil servant handling criminal justice policy, proposed "just desserts" as a guiding rationale for punishment and proposed major statutory changes that were enacted in the Criminal Justice Act 1991; appellate courts quickly nullified major changes and Parliament repealed others (Ashworth 2001). Mandatory minimum sentencing laws and the Labour Party's "tough on crime" platform soon followed. A decade later, another senior civil servant, John Halliday, led a study commission that endorsed Norval Morris's "limiting retributivism" and proposed statutory changes (Home Office 2001). In its wake were the Criminal Justice Act 2004, abolition of the centuries-old double jeopardy rule, and indeterminate sentences of "imprisonment for public protection" (Roberts and Ashworth 2016).

[19] Then, as now, the state of the art of scientific knowledge cautioned against beliefs that deterrent and incapacitative effects of punishment or imprisonment are significant. The findings of National of Sciences Panels in 1978 (Blumstein, Cohen, and Nagin 1978) and 2014 (Travis, Western, and Redburn 2014) are closely similar; the latter is more emphatic.

[20] Probably demonstrating greater judicial commitment to human rights values in Canada than in other Common Law countries, Canadian courts declared many of the "tough" laws enacted under the Harper regime to be unconstitutional or significantly limited their scope (Doob and Webster 2016). The key cases are discussed in n. 29.

the United States and England, de-emphasis of rehabilitation resulted in spending and personnel cuts, withdrawal of programs and services, and diminution in the quality of life experienced by prisoners.

Changes in continental Europe were less stark. Skepticism about the effectiveness of rehabilitative programs and concern that rehabilitation cannot by itself justify imprisonment or harsher punishments have been influential, but pre-1970 ways of doing business were not abandoned, radically severe sentencing laws were not enacted, and imprisonment rates (except in Eastern and Central Europe; discussed below) have for long remained broadly stable in most countries (as table 1 shows). Traditional court and prosecutorial processes changed comparatively little except for development and expansion of diversion programs for people charged with low-level offenses. Examples, widely emulated elsewhere, include "transactions" (suspension and later dismissal of charges if suspects pay financial penalties scaled to offense seriousness) in the Netherlands and Belgium, "conditional dismissals" (much like transactions) in Germany, and "penal orders" (a conviction but no trial if suspects agree to financial or other nonconfinement penalties) in Sweden and other countries (Asp 2012; van de Bunt and van Gelder 2012; Weigend 2016).

Developments in the Nordic countries are probably representative of those elsewhere in Europe. Major overhauls of sentencing laws in Finland in the 1970s and Sweden in the 1980s repudiated rehabilitation as a governing purpose and sought to assure modest, consistent, and proportionate use of prison sentences. Sentences for some violent and sexual offenses have over time since increased—modestly by US standards—but were offset by increased use of diversionary programs and prison alternatives including mediation, penal orders, community service, and electronic monitoring (Lappi-Seppälä 2016). Imprisonment rates remained broadly stable, rising a bit in the 1990s and early 2000s and more recently significantly declining.

The takeaway: changes in prevailing punishment norms have consequences that vary widely between countries. Punishment severity in most major English-speaking countries rose substantially after enthusiasm for rehabilitation declined. Most Western European countries and Canada, by contrast, accommodated the shifts in thinking without fundamentally destabilizing institutions and practices. Investments in rehabilitation and social services for convicted people continued and grew but as elements of community punishments and within prisons. Rehabilitation ceased being a purpose of imprisonment but remained a primary goal.

B. *The Scale of Imprisonment*

Imprisonment rates are imperfect but reasonably discriminating measures of the severity of countries' criminal justice systems (Lappi-Seppälä 2008). They are mostly products of policy choices, sometimes explicit, as with Finland's multiple decade decline "to the Scandinavian level," and other times are foreseeable effects of policy changes, as with the fivefold US increase in imprisonment rates after 1973 and substantial but smaller increases in Australia (Freiberg 2016), England (Roberts and Ashworth 2016), and New Zealand (Pratt 2017) beginning in the 1990s. A small case-study literature documents successes and failures of efforts to reduce use of imprisonment.

Liberal law reformers and human rights activists in the United States and England and Wales have long, largely unsuccessfully, sought to reduce use of imprisonment. Prison abolition movements have existed in many countries, without notable influence or success. Some countries and a few American states have managed to reduce rates deliberately for long periods or for a time. In other places such as Germany and Scandinavia policy changes have stabilized use of imprisonment or prevented significant increases.

The only generalization that emerges is that sizable decreases or stabilization in rates can be achieved over extended periods as the Finnish experience, initiatives in Alberta and North Carolina in the 1990s, and recent decades of experience in many Eastern and Central European countries demonstrate. Some American states, most conspicuously Minnesota, Washington, and Oregon, managed to limit prison population growth in the 1980s in a context of rapidly rising rates nationally (in the 1990s the necessary political will dissolved and imprisonment rates shot up in all three states).

Significant changes occur when dominant policy elites wish it so. Their aims, beliefs, and interests are determinative and only sometimes coincide with popular beliefs. Public opinion research, for example, has long shown that opinions and beliefs about punishment are more ambivalent and less punitive in English-speaking countries than many politicians appear to believe (Roberts et al. 2003).[21] In countries in which crime is a

---

[21] Research has for at least 30 years shown stark differences in people's expressed opinions and beliefs depending on the methodologies used to investigate them. Immediate-response phone surveys elicit much harsher patterns of answers to questions such as "Do you favor capital punishment?" "Do you favor mandatory minimum 10-year prison sentences for robbers?" and "Should people convicted of violent offenses be ineligible for

contentious political issue, however, many politicians act as if they believe public attitudes are always highly punitive, probably on the reasoning—paralleling Pascal's argument for belief in God—that if they are wrong, they will suffer no harm. Elections are seldom lost because politicians are too tough on crime.

1. *Long-Term Success.* Finland's remarkable two-thirds reduction in imprisonment rates over several decades is the best known success story (e.g., Törnudd 1993; Lappi-Seppälä 2001). There are others. The US state of North Carolina stabilized imprisonment rates in the early 1990s and avoided subsequent increases, although the national rate continued to climb until 2007. It peaked at 763 per 100,000 and was about 629 at the end of 2019,[22] necessarily meaning that rates declined in some—about half—of the states. California's is the only substantial recent drop resulting largely from ambitious policy choices of political leaders. Declines elsewhere have resulted from congeries of causes including lower crime rates; piecemeal changes in prosecutorial, parole, and probation practices; modest changes in sentencing laws; and a general softening in political posturing. Former Warsaw Pact countries and SSRs, including Russia, substantially reduced imprisonment rates after 1989, although the timing of declines varied widely. Western European countries—for example, Germany, Switzerland, and the Scandinavians—avoided significant increases during the two-decade rise in crime rates that ended in the 1990s, by creating new diversionary programs and community penalties. The Finnish story has often been told, so I do not repeat it. I briefly summarize developments in North America and East and Central Europe.

North Carolina has more successfully managed the size of its prison population over an extended period than any other state. During the 1970s and 1980s, when the national rate tripled, officials sought to restrain growth by enacting a determinate sentencing law, increasing use of parole release, and establishing an overcrowding-triggered emergency release program.

---

community penalties?" than are elicited by deliberative polling, focus groups, or scenario studies. When the latter methods are used, all of which involve looking closely at particular (or particular types of) offenses and offenders, respondents are less likely to prefer harsh punishments, more likely to favor use of community penalties and rehabilitative programs, and more likely to want offenders' characteristics and offense circumstances taken into account in making decisions about them (Pickett 2019).

[22] This is somewhat misleading. Much of the decrease results from increases in the size of the US resident population. Put differently, the denominator of the imprisonment rate grew significantly faster than the numerator declined. Rates would have declined even if the number of people in prison did not change or increased modestly.

When those efforts failed, observing that Minnesota and Washington successfully used sentencing guidelines to restrain population growth, North Carolina established a sentencing commission. Like Minnesota's, Washington's, and Oregon's commissions, it adopted a "capacity constraint" policy that tailored projected needs for prison beds to available capacity. The guidelines, based on statistical projections that proved to be remarkably accurate, took effect in 1994. They worked (Wright 2002). The imprisonment rate fell from first among the 50 states in 1980 to thirty-first by 1999 and has remained at that level (thirtieth in 2020; Carson 2021). North Carolina's rate is by far the lowest among southern states.

California's recent experience, based on several decades of prisoners' rights lawsuits culminating in the US Supreme Court decision in *Brown v. Plata*, 563 U.S. 493 (2011), provides a second success story. *Plata*, predicated on persistent and egregious failures to provide constitutionally adequate medical care, declared prison conditions generally to be constitutionally inadequate. Following up, a lower federal court ordered a sizable reduction in the number of state prisoners. Governor Jerry Brown persuaded the legislature to enact the 2011 "realignment law," a state-to-county reallocation of responsibility. It did not require release of existing prisoners but mandated that many people subsequently convicted of less serious offenses be held in county jails rather than in state prisons. Supervision of many released prisoners was shifted from state parole authorities to county probation officers. The law specified local, not state, confinement for violations of conditions and for shorter terms (Weisberg 2019).

Federal court orders provided the immediate impetus. A series of successful citizen initiatives, organized by prison reform activists and supported by Governor Brown, was also important. Proposition 36 (2012) mitigated the harshness of the three-strikes law; Proposition 47 (2014) reduced large numbers of low level felonies to misdemeanors, thereby precluding state imprisonment; and Proposition 57 (2016) authorized parole eligibility for large numbers of long-term prisoners. All passed by wide margins. The changes worked. California's prison population declined from 149,169 in 2011 to 97,319 in 2020, the most recent year for which data are available, and the state imprisonment rate fell by nearly 40 percent, from 393 per 100,000 in 2011 to 247 in 2020 (Carson and Golinella 2013; Carson 2021).[23]

---

[23] These California rates are not comparable to other countries' because they do not include pretrial detainees and people serving short terms of confinement in county jails. Total rates including jail and prison inmates are usually 50 percent higher than state

Policy initiatives in several American states controlled or reduced populations for a time. Sentencing commissions in Minnesota, Washington, and Oregon adopted capacity constraint policies in the 1980s on which the subsequent North Carolina policy was based (Tonry 1996). Compared with rapidly rising rates in most states and nationally, all successfully constrained population growth through the early 1990s; after that, state governments in various ways undermined and overrode the guidelines. Minnesota's commission in the 1990s doubled the lengths of presumptive sentences for many offenses in response to legislative pressure. A citizen-initiated referendum in Oregon in 1994 established lengthy mandatory minimum prison sentences for many offenses. Legislatures literally (Oregon) or effectively (Washington) eliminated their states' sentencing commissions (Frase 2013).

2. *Short-Term Success.* There are two reasonably well-documented instances of successful reductions of prison use based primarily on economic rather than human rights considerations. California in the 1960s under Governor Ronald Reagan, and the Canadian province of Alberta in the 1990s under Premier Ralph Klein, attempted and managed significantly to reduce prison populations.

The California success was short-lived. The imprisonment rate in 1968, Reagan's second year in office, was 146 per 100,000 residents. In 1972, it was 96, 34 percent lower and the lowest since 1950. The reduction resulted from a number of changes: fewer people were sentenced to imprisonment because many were diverted to state-subsidized county probation programs, parole release rates increased, and parole revocations fell. Reagan took credit for the decrease, but there is no evidence that he was motivated to reduce prison use. The evidence is ambiguous: "Reducing the size and the cost of government, a key element in Reagan's political ideology, could have been the most important factor. Reagan in any event acquiesced in and did not interfere with the population-reducing initiatives" (Gartner, Doob, and Zimring 2011, p. 312). The "success" was short-lived. After the 4-year decline, imprisonment rates rose continuously for nearly 40 years (Weisberg 2019).

The story in Alberta, often described as Canada's most conservative province, partly parallels California's. A conservative chief executive,

---

imprisonment rates alone. California's total rate in 2020 thus was approximately 375, vastly higher than any in Western Europe and—except for Russia—substantially higher than those of any of the Eastern and Central European countries shown in tables 1 and 5.

motivated by fiscal concerns, empowered officials to change policies and practices. Webster and Doob (2014, pp. 5, 22) observe that "the impetus for this change had nothing directly to do with imprisonment, crime or criminal justice. . . . Decarceration constituted—from a political perspective—simply a means to an end but never an end in itself." It began when Premier Klein promised to balance the provincial budget by cutting spending but not—he was emphatic—by increasing revenue. His May 1993 budget required an across-the-board spending cut of approximately 20 percent. In response, corrections officials closed two prisons and established new community punishment programs; prosecutors altered their practices to reduce prison admissions. Imprisonment rates declined by a third—from 102 per 100,000 in 1993 to 69 in 1997, a level around which it hovered for nearly a decade (Webster and Doob 2014). The rate has since stabilized at 80–90 per 100,000.[24]

Reductions in California and Alberta resulted from administrative actions rather than from changes in laws. Changes in punishment practices may be easier to accomplish under conservative leaders motivated by fiscal rather than human rights concerns.

3. *Eastern and Central Europe.* Eastern and Central Europe is a large, diverse region consisting of many countries, but imprisonment rate developments have been strikingly similar. Rates have declined sharply since 1989 in almost all countries, usually later in the former SSRs and often with major fluctuations, but the overall direction is clear. Rates have, however, been much more volatile than in Western Europe or Canada. Human rights aspirations to reduce prison use have recurrently contended with populist tough-on-crime initiatives.

Roy King (1997, p. 7), for several decades Britain's preeminent prison scholar, described two early phases shown in table 4:

In the first, the euphoria following independence and the winning of new freedoms focused attention on prisons largely because they symbolised past oppression. . . . There was also a need to expunge at least the worst excesses of the past. . . . New prison directors were

---

[24] This may or may not be a long-term "success" story. Canadian national rates have fluctuated around 100 per 100,000 since 1950, which means that stability is the national pattern and norm. However, Alberta's post-1993 rates have been consistently lower than rates in the 1980s. Alberta imprisonment rate data were downloaded on February 1, 2022, from Statistics Canada: https://www.statcan.gc.ca/.

TABLE 4

Imprisonment in Central and Eastern Europe: Selected Countries, 1985–94

Country	1985–87 Total	Peak Rate	1989–91 Total	Trough Rate	1994 Total	1994 Rate
Russia			698,000	470	885,000	590
Ukraine			120,000	230	180,000	345
Belarus	31,204	310	14,235	140	35,720	345
Lithuania	14,888	415	8,586	230	12,782	340
Poland	110,182	295	40,321	105	62,719	165
Romania	60,269	265	16,429	70	43,990	195

SOURCE.—King (1997).

appointed, existing staff ... were dismissed or chose to leave, and ... new legislation and penal executive codes were introduced or planned. Prison populations fell, in some cases dramatically. In the second phase ... prison populations have grown almost as dramatically as they fell, sometimes more so. . . . There has been a remarkably similar pattern: from recent high levels in the use of custody during the period 1985–7 ... to unprecedentedly low points in the period 1989–91, . . . only for prison populations to rise again to new highs in 1994. The pattern is probably typical of most jurisdictions, even if it does not hold for all.

Three longer-term patterns stand out in Eastern and Central Europe.[25] The first is that rates in most countries initially fell substantially after 1989, sometimes in part because of broad-based amnesties. In former Warsaw Pact countries such as Hungary and Poland, as table 5 shows, rates initially fell rapidly. New governments wanted, as Krzysztof Krajewski put it (2004, pp. 377–78), "to get rid of the Soviet inheritance

---

[25] Support for the three generalizations is provided by data shown in tables 4–6. The English-language literature on imprisonment and penal policy in Eastern and Central Europe is sparse: many offhand comments but few focused writings (there are no doubt sizable literatures in national languages and on narrower topics). There is a small literature on developments in particular countries (e.g., Krajewski 2004, 2012, 2013, 2014, 2016 [Poland]; Válková and Hulmáková 2007 [Czech Republic]; Lévay 2012a, 2012b, 2014 [Hungary]; Drápal 2021 [Czech Republic]). There are a few comparative works: Haney (2011, 2016; Czech Republic, Hungary, Poland, Slovakia) and Lévay (2012b; Czech Republic, Hungary, Poland, and Slovenia). There are a few brief but more comprehensive surveys (Lévay 2005; Krajewski 2010, 2014).

TABLE 5

Imprisonment Rates per 100,000: Hungary and Poland, Selected Years, 1980s–2020

Country	1980s	1990	1992	1994	1996	1998	2000	2002	2005	2010	2015	2020
Hungary	193 (1988)	122	159	126	1,277	143	155	178	156	163	187	172
Poland	295 (1986)	120	160	163	144	141	181	208	217	210	191	190

SOURCES.—Krajewski (2004), Lévay (2005; Hungarian National Prison Administration), Walmsley (2015), and Fair and Walmsley (2021).

and to join or (as some prefer to say) rejoin western Europe in every possible respect, including membership of the European Union. This applies to crime, criminal justice and crime control as to every other field." Miklós Lévay (2006, p. 235) observed that between 1988 and 1998 Hungary's "prison population decreased by half. During this time, the rate of immediate imprisonment sentences also declined." The changes were motivated by efforts to emulate "the sentencing practices of Western European states, and the requirements of membership in the Council of Europe." Something similar happened, mostly later, in former SSRs.

Second, as table 5 also shows, the liberal reform impulses in Hungary and Poland lost momentum by the late 1990s. Imprisonment rates initially plummeted and remained modest through mid-decade but then increased to significantly higher levels where they remain.[26] Rapidly rising crime rates in the 1990s and election of populist, neoconservative governments led to politicization of crime and punishment and to harsher policies and practices. Miklós Lévay (2006, p. 235), later a judge of the Hungarian Constitutional Court, described liberalizing changes in Hungary in the mid-1990s but then observed, "This process came to a halt at the highly politicized and 'law and order' perspective-guided amendment of the Penal Code in 1998."

Third, though, compared with pre-1989 levels, imprisonment rates have fallen substantially in all former Warsaw Pact countries and SSRs

---

[26] Krajewski (2016), while acknowledging that the politics of law and order partly explains high Polish imprisonment levels, argues that another part of the explanation is more benign: judges have taken to heart the desirability of diverting many convicted people to the community. The difficulty is that many programs are inadequately funded and managed; large numbers of people assigned to them have their participation revoked and are returned to court for resentencing.

in Europe. As table 1 shows, for example, Ukraine's imprisonment rate fell by two-thirds between 1998–99 and 2020 (430 per 100,000 population to 139), Lithuania's by half (385 to 220), and Russia's by half (730 to 356).

Table 6 provides data for a wider range of Eastern and Central European countries. Despite major differences in recent and long-term histories, steep overall decreases are evident. Some of these countries were once part of the Austro-Hungarian Empire, others were dominated by Russia or the Soviet Union, and still others were under Prussian or German suzerainty. The trend lines not surprisingly vary. Steep declines occurred earlier in the former Warsaw Pact countries, later in the former SSRs. Some experienced steady long-term declines, some more recent ones.

Nonetheless, the ambition to "reach the European level" appears to have been widely shared. Krzysztof Krajewski (2014, p. 95) observed that it is "striking that countries of Central and Eastern Europe are commonly known for their rather harsh criminal justice systems and sentencing patterns as compared with Western Europe. These countries were known for extremely high levels of punitiveness before 1989, which was understandable considering their authoritarian political systems imposed by Soviet dominance."

Current rates remain relatively high compared with Western Europe, where per capita rates of 60 per 100,000 were common in 2020–21 but

TABLE 6
Imprisonment Rates per 100,000: Eastern European Countries, Selected Years, 1983–2020

Country	1983	Late 1980s	1995	2000	2008	2014*	2021†
Bulgaria	149		109	121	148	151	93
Czech Republic	250		189	210	201	154	177
Estonia			297	341	282	236	168
Hungary	132	193 (1988)	121	148	152	186	172
Latvia			313		291	304	165
Lithuania			362	280	217	329	184
Poland	226	295 (1986)	171	169	216	217	190
Romania			205	221	123	155	120
Russia				730	629	475	326
Ukraine				439 (1999)	323	305	140

SOURCES.—Walmsley (2000, 2009, 2014), Lévay (2005), Krajewski (2010, 2014), and Fair and Walmsley (2021).

* Counting dates vary between 2011 and 2013; most are 2012.

† Counting dates vary between 2019 and 2021; most are 2021.

not always. Bulgaria's 93 per 100,000 would be mainstream in Western Europe, Romania's 120 and Ukraine's 140 are comparable to England and Wales's 138 (table 1). With the exception of Russia, the other countries have imprisonment rates (168–90) comparable to those in Australia (167; table 1) and New Zealand (164; table 1) and of course much lower than America's 629 (table 1). Eastern and Central Europe have reached the Anglo-Saxon level.

All that is required is political will. Sometimes shifts in the zeitgeist result in major changes in use of imprisonment. The Eastern and Central European declines since 1989 offer downward examples. California's experience since 2011 may be another. The doubling of American imprisonment rates in the 1970s, before major new tough-on-crime legislation was enacted in the 1980s, is an upward example (Blumstein 1988; Blumstein and Beck 1999).

C. Diversionary Programs

Particularly during periods of rising crime rates, the simplest way to avoid prison population increases is to send fewer people to prison. Many countries have in recent decades created and expanded community penalties to serve as prison alternatives. That worked conspicuously well in Europe and failed miserably in the United States and England. I have written about this elsewhere (Morris and Tonry 1990; Tonry 1999), so I offer only a summary here. In Germany, use of day fines, conditional dismissals, penal orders, and limits on imposition of short prison sentences prevented rapid increases in imprisonment during an extended period of rising crime rates in the 1970s, 1980s, and early 1990s. Legislation in 1968 that discouraged imposition of short prison sentences proved to be the most effective documented prison diversion initiative in any country: the number of sentences of 6 months or less fell from 184,000 in 1968 to 56,000 (two-thirds of which were suspended) in 1970 and has remained at the lower level. The proportion of convicted suspects receiving unsuspended prison sentences fell by two-thirds from 24 to 7 percent (Weigend 2001). Scandinavian countries adopted numerous diversionary and early release programs including community service, electronic monitoring, and mediation that greatly reduced use of prison sentences (Lappi-Seppälä 2016). Building on successful pilot projects and implementation in England, community service soon spread to Scotland and the Netherlands in the 1980s and subsequently throughout Europe (Albrecht 2001). Similar stories can no doubt be told for most Western European and some Eastern and Central European countries (e.g., Romania: Durnescu and Haines 2012; Poland: Krajewski 2016).

The United States and England, although they initiated use of many diversionary community punishments, have done less well. The United States pioneered use of community service and victim-offender mediation as diversions from imprisonment in the 1960s and 1970s and electronic monitoring and home detention in the 1980s but largely abandoned them as alternatives to imprisonment by the beginning of the 1990s. All remained in use but as conditions of probation or parole rather than as independent front-end diversions (Morris and Tonry 1990). England adopted and widely used community service as a prison alternative in the 1970s and 1980s, but thereafter its use waned sharply. England adopted and widely used electronic monitoring beginning in the 1990s but mostly confined its use to people released from imprisonment. Both countries experimented with day fines in the 1980s. The American experiments failed when judges and prosecutors refused to cooperate with randomized evaluations of pilot projects (Morris and Tonry 1990). The English pilots were adjudged a success, but legislation in 1991 that authorized their use was repealed in 1993 (Ashworth 2001). The mentality in both countries was, and is, that imprisonment is the only credible punishment for nontrivial crimes.

These stories lead to one conclusion. Countries and states or provinces in which dominant political elites want to increase, decrease, or stabilize use of imprisonment can do so. It can be done directly as in North Carolina, California, Germany, Finland, or Scandinavia generally, indirectly by creating credible alternative dispositions, or both. Tapio Lappi-Seppälä (2016) has provided detailed accounts of policy changes over several decades that increased or decreased the use of imprisonment in Denmark, Finland, Norway, and Sweden.

D. Prison Conditions and Programs

What matters most to people sentenced to imprisonment—other than the wish to be elsewhere—are the character of their day-to-day lives inside and the scope and quality of services and programs available to them. I discuss this only briefly, partly because I have little firsthand knowledge of life inside prisons in different countries but mostly because there is but a scant comparative scholarly literature. Gaining access to prisons to conduct systematic studies of life inside is difficult in most countries (nearly impossible in many), which makes comparative studies of life inside prisons in two or more countries exceedingly difficult.[27] There are, of course, single country (usually single prison) studies, books and articles that tell prisoners' and administrators' stories, journalistic accounts, judicial opinions in cases challenging prison conditions, reports by organizations such as Human Rights Watch, and for Europe reports of the Committee for the Prevention of Torture and Inhuman or Degrading Treatment or Punishment (CPT). Few of these sources are comparative.

If, invoking Churchill, "the treatment of crime and the criminal . . . are the sign and proof of the living virtue within [a country]," any examination of relevant sources of information will demonstrate that national differences in living virtue are enormous (likewise within countries as, e.g., US comparisons between Minnesota and Alabama graphically would demonstrate). David Downes (1988), for example, interviewing English prisoners in the Netherlands and Dutch prisoners in England, found that Dutch prisoners were shocked by English prison conditions and English prisoners were pleasantly surprised in the Netherlands. Candace Kruttschnitt and Anja Dirkzwager (2011) replicated Downes's study two decades later and found the same thing. Historian James Q. Whitman (2003) was struck by stark differences in conditions in American and English compared with German and French prisons and tried to explain them. English and European elites responded to post-Enlightenment celebration of equality and human rights, he concluded, in fundamentally different ways. Previously members of elites in most countries were often treated decently—comfortable quarters, adequate food, servants, visitors—and lesser folk almost always miserably. Europeans, Whitman observed, leveled up and aspired to treat all offenders comparably and decently; the English leveled down. Both patterns, he suggests, have long endured.

Efforts to improve prison conditions are as much a product of national histories and cultures as are efforts to reduce or stabilize use of imprisonment. European governments and politicians often resent decisions of the

---

[27] Jon Vagg's (1994) comparative study of accountability systems in England, France, Germany, and he Netherlands is a rare exception, but it was not based on research conducted inside prisons. A small comparative literature is beginning to emerge (e.g., Bergman and Fondevila 2021 [Latin America]; Morelle, Le Marcis, and Hornberger 2021 [Africa]; Bucerius and Sandberg 2022 [Canada, Mexico, Norway]; Crewe et al. 2022 [England and Norway]).

European Court of Human Rights (ECHR) concerning prisons and prisoners and findings and recommendations of the CPT, but they usually accept and comply (not always completely or promptly, of course, and varying significantly between countries; Snacken 2021).

The American experience has been very different. The prisoners' rights movement won countless lawsuits in federal courts from the late 1960s to the early 1990s, and conditions improved markedly (Jacobs 1980; Schlanger 2003; Schoenfeld 2010; Harris 2020). In 1995, however, the US Congress enacted the ironically titled Prison Litigation Reform Act, which effectively deprived federal courts of jurisdiction over prison litigation; the "reform" targeted not inadequate prison conditions but litigation challenging them. Lawsuits in federal courts have largely disappeared; courts' capacity to maintain continuing oversight of remedial measures was eliminated for some kinds of cases and weakened for others. Conditions vary widely between states—in some states, especially in the South, they are horrifying—as they did before the prisoners' rights movement began (Dolovich 2022).

The English story is little cheerier. English governments have always resented and resisted ECHR and CPT findings, as Prime Minister Cameron's hostile reaction to an ECHR decision on prisoners' voting rights, quoted above, illustrates. Reports by Her Majesty's (independent) Inspectors of Prisons have over the years sometimes been influential but generally not. They regularly document terrible conditions and offer incisive critiques and recommendations, but any reader of English newspapers knows that conditions have worsened in recent years, especially as a result of drastic staffing and spending cuts by recent Conservative governments. Here are excerpts from the 2021 Annual Report of HM Chief Inspector of Prisoners (2021, pp. 7–8, emphasis added):

> As my predecessor observed in his annual report introduction last year, *the entrenched problems the Inspectorate had identified over recent years did not disappear* because of the pandemic. Violence, for instance, may have been suppressed by locking people up for almost all of the day, but its underlying causes have not gone away. . . . It was understandably difficult for prisons to deliver full programmes of education, training, and rehabilitation during COVID-19, but *we have found poor outcomes in purposeful activity and failures in rehabilitation and release planning for many years.* . . .
>
> [Most prisoners] have spent the pandemic locked in their cells for 22.5 hours a day. For many this has meant living their lives in a

small cell that has limited ventilation, a toilet that may or may not have a curtain in front of it, a television and a cell mate. . . .

[These observations] are particularly concerning in light of our other inspection findings. We found that most mental health services had ceased routine assessments or interventions. . . . Over half of prisoners told us they had mental health problems (52%) but less than a quarter said it was easy to see mental health workers (22%). There was also widespread curtailment of other health care services that left a long backlog of cases. At one prison we found prisoners waiting more than a year to see the GP. There is no doubt that rehabilitation should be one of the main purposes of prisons, yet too *many prisoners were locked up with too little to do before the pandemic and the situation became much worse this year.*

The coronavirus presented challenges to prison managers everywhere, of course. That is why I italicized passages referring to chronic problems.

Compassion for prisoners and empathy for the circumstances in which they live are conspicuously absent in England, many American jurisdictions, and no doubt elsewhere (but not everywhere). Compassion and empathy in correctional institutions no doubt vary between countries, but in recent decades the ECHR and CPT have effectively provided external pressures for decency in Europe. Nothing comparable exists in the United States and England.

IV. Imprisonment Prognoses

There are enormous differences between countries in levels of imprisonment, in how it is used, in confinement conditions, and in the availability, character, and use of diversion programs and community penalties. Levels of imprisonment are relatively stable in some countries and volatile in others. Patterns and levels of imprisonment can be changed when dominant political leaders want that to happen but are largely impervious to law reform efforts initiated by others. Change can happen, even sometimes changes about which domestic political elites are unhappy, under pressure from powerful outside institutions such as the ECHR and the CPT or for several decades federal court orders in the United States. In principle, prison inspectorates such as in England provide credible, independent, expert assessments of conditions and propose improvements and policy changes; in practice, elected politicians can and often do ignore inspectors' reports and recommendations. Without credible pressures from outside, and in the absence of political will, major changes and improvements range from slow and piecemeal to nonexistent.

Prisons everywhere should look like those in Scandinavia, Germany, Switzerland, and the Netherlands. Prisoners would be viewed and treated as citizens behind bars, entitled to the respect and support due all citizens and to the special services needed to help them achieve satisfying, law-abiding lives later on. That does not happen in many countries.

Below, I offer five generalizations that emerge from the previous sections. First, though, I briefly return to the discussion in Section II of principles and expedience. If, as is inevitable, ideas about governing principles and purposes of punishment vary between individuals and countries and over time, it should be no surprise that punishment policies and practices vary. Sometimes even countries with comparable imprisonment rates differ greatly in how prisons is used. In Germany, both rehabilitation and dehabilitation count; that is why short prison sentences are disfavored, relatively few people are sentenced to prison terms, and those few receive—by Western European standards—comparatively long sentences. In the Netherlands, relatively many convicted people are sentenced to imprisonment but mostly—by almost any standard—for comparatively short terms. Punishment jurisprudence in both countries values consistency, proportionality, and equal treatment, but those values are expressed in substantially different ways. No doubt someone with deep, rich knowledge of both countries could offer plausible explanations. In both countries, retributive beliefs are important, consequentialist beliefs are less important, and decision-making based on political or personal expediency is widely condemned (although, of course, not nonexistent).

In England and Wales, Australia, New Zealand, and the United States, by contrast, retributive beliefs are relatively unimportant, consequentialist beliefs (especially concerning deterrence and incapacitation) are at least often asserted, and expediency is a commonplace consideration in policy making. Two elaborations. First, many American politicians and practitioners, especially prosecutors, would say they are retributivists. By "retributive punishments," however, many simply mean "punitive" or "very severe," rather than what a philosopher or a Scandinavian judge would: "proportionate to the seriousness of the crime and to punishments received by others for the same and different crimes." The American policy maker's "retributivism" is often a decontextualized primal scream. Otherwise the federal 100-to-1 law would not have mandated longer sentences for street-level sales of 5 grams of crack than those prescribed under federal sentencing guidelines for sales of 500 grams of powder cocaine, sexual abuse of children, million-dollar securities frauds, and many robberies.[28] Similarly, it is difficult to discern any retributive proportionality in a 150-year, nonparolable prison sentence for a seriously ill 71-year-old white collar offender (Bernard Madoff). Punishments like Madoff's are not common even in the United States, but nonparolable life sentences and decades-long prison terms are.

Second, political expediency has often motivated enactment of harsh sentencing laws, for "expressive" or "symbolic" reasons or to try to improve reelection prospects, in English-speaking countries, Eastern and Central Europe, and less often elsewhere. I provided examples in Section II. In the United States expediency interests sometimes motivate prosecutors in their charging and plea bargaining and judges in sentencing (much less often than prosecutors, I hope and believe). My impression is that unprincipled practitioner expediency is—compared with other English-speaking and most European countries—a distinctively American disease.[29]

Now to the five generalizations. *First, punishment principles matter*. Indeterminate sentencing premised on consequentialist (mostly rehabilitative) aspirations in the United States was never implemented perfectly, or in retrograde states minimally adequately, but for many decades was widely accepted. From the 1930s through the early 1970s, imprisonment rates remained stable despite rises and falls in crime rates, and crime control was not an important political issue (Blumstein and Cohen 1973). In Western Europe, commitment to retributive and human rights ideas has long shaped punishment practices and policies. The Finnish and Swedish sentencing law reforms, Germany's disapproval of short prison stays, and Eastern and Central European efforts to model their systems on Western European norms are but some of many examples.

Second, differences in national history and culture matter. Recent decades' developments in Eastern and Central Europe demonstrate the long tail

---

[28] I provide details in Tonry (2016, table 6.1). The 100-to-1 law is but one of many examples I could have given. Something similar could be said about most mandatory minimum, three-strikes, and life-without-parole laws. In California, for example, many property misdemeanors (e.g., notoriously, thefts of three pizza slices, three golf clubs, several blank CDs) could count as a third strike and trigger a mandatory 25-year or life sentence.

[29] Although it is not uniquely American: Krzysztof Krajewski (2012) tells hair-raising tales of political prosecutions in Poland. Selmini (2020) and Bernat and Whyte (2022) discuss recent political prosecutions and imprisonments of Catalonian politicians in Spain. Turkish prisons hold thousands of political prisoners.

of Russian and Soviet domination, aspirations to emulate Western norms and practices, and the consequences of election of neoliberal and populist governments. Scandinavian, German, and Dutch practices, policies, and prison use patterns generally remained moderate and humane both during decades in which rehabilitative thinking was highly influential and since. In the English-speaking countries, except Canada, political expediency has in recent decades dominated crime control policies and influenced prosecutorial and sentencing practices. For a short period in the 1970s and early 1980s, the shift from consequentialism to retributivism in the United States produced widespread policy changes aiming at greater consistency, fairness, and equal treatment. After that, political expediency took over. Were retributive ideas about proportionate sentencing influential in American political culture, and support for human rights and respect for human dignity stronger, imprisonment policies and practices would be substantially different. So would those in Australia, England, and New Zealand.

Third, countries can fundamentally change punishment policies and practices if political will to do so exists. Substantial changes in Western Europe in diversion programs and prison alternatives in recent decades provide unglamorous and generally uncontroversial examples of successful policy innovation. The Finnish, North Carolinan, post-2011 Californian, post-1989 Eastern and Central European, and possibly the Albertan stories show that imprisonment rates can be substantially reduced when dominant policy elites want that to happen. The 1960s California story shows that imprisonment use can quickly be reduced but that the changes are likely to be fragile and short-lived when they are not based on long-term resolve.

Fourth, political expediency and self-interest often influence punishment policies and practices and are difficult to restrain. The rise and fall of the American prisoners' rights movement and the limited influence of Her Majesty's Inspectors of Prisons in England are illustrative. So are the increased imprisonment rates in some Eastern and Central European countries that followed election of populist and neoconservative governments. By contrast, despite their limitations, the ECHR and the CPT in Europe have shown that establishment of credible external standards and enforcement mechanisms can substantially restrain politicians from adoption of unjust and inhumane policies and continuation of inhumane practices (e.g., Snacken 2021). The Canadian Supreme Court, interpreting and applying the Canadian constitution, does that; its near nullification of mandatory minimum sentencing laws enacted by the Harper government is illustrative (Kerr and Berger 2020) as is its recent declaration that sentences of life without possibility of parole violate the Canadian constitution.[30]

Fifth, values matter. Assume for a moment that the phenomena I have discussed are reasonably accurately depicted and the inferences I draw are plausible. The picture that emerges is not an appealing one. Decent prisons, moderate and proportionate sentencing policies, and humane punishment practices are achievable in places where human rights ideals are widely shared and supported, but less so or not at all—or only strategically for limited periods—in places where they are not. A number of things follow.

One is that seemingly successful efforts to increase justice, fairness, and equal treatment in places in which those ideals are not widely shared will be fragile and over time likely to fail. Another is that commitment to human rights ideals and creation and maintenance of decent sentencing and prison systems are consequences of distinctive national histories and cultures. Tapio Lappi-Seppälä (e.g., 2008) has repeatedly shown that high levels of governmental legitimacy in citizens' eyes, trust in fellow citizens, low levels of income inequality, strong social welfare policies, and high fractions of gross domestic product devoted to public spending are principal correlates of moderate criminal justice policies and low imprisonment

---

[30] Three recent decisions have established strong proportionality limits. Two, *R. v. Nur*, [2015] S.C.J. No. 15, 2015 SCC 15, and *R. v. Lloyd*, [2016] S.C.J. No. 13, 2016 SCC 13, concern mandatory minimum sentences. *Lloyd* at para. 23 observed: "The question, put simply, is this: In view of the fit and proportionate sentence, is the mandatory minimum sentence grossly disproportionate to the offence and its circumstances? If so, the provision violates s. 12." Remarkably, by American constitutional standards, a law must be struck down if the mandated sentence fails that test for a hypothetical offender who might be affected by it even if in the appealed case the sentence is not disproportionately severe: the sentence might stand, but the law must fall. In the third decision, the court forbade imposition of sentences of life without possibility of parole or of consecutive "life" sentences for multiple murders that would deny any opportunity to appeal for parole (life sentences are parolable after 25 years). The court unanimously observed: "Section 745.51 of the *Criminal Code* is contrary to s. 12 of the *Charter* and ... must be declared to be of no force or effect immediately under s. 52(1) of the *Constitution Act, 1982*, and the declaration must strike down the impugned provision retroactively to the date it was enacted. In the case of multiple first degree murders, s. 745.51 authorizes the imposition of sentences of imprisonment that effectively deprive all offenders who receive such sentences of a realistic possibility of being granted parole before they die. Such sentences are degrading in nature and thus incompatible with human dignity, because they deny offenders any possibility of reintegration into society, which presupposes, definitively and irreversibly, that they lack the capacity to reform and re-enter society. B's total parole ineligibility period must therefore be 25 years, in accordance with the law as it existed prior to the enactment of s. 745.51" (*R. v. Bissonnette*, [2022] SCC 23, File No.: 39544).

levels (and almost certainly humane prison conditions, although that was not his focus). Countries and their political cultures have those characteristics for reasons.

The overriding implication is that advocates of humanizing criminal justice system changes should concentrate as much or more on normative changes and arguments as on empirical claims about cost savings and recidivism decreases. Motivated practitioners and politicians should of course work to improve and humanize practices and policies they can influence, but piecemeal technocratic improvements are unlikely to achieve fundamental system changes. What is wrong with mass incarceration, high imprisonment rates, and squalid prison conditions is not that their deterrent and incapacitative effects are modest or nonexistent, or that costs are too high, but that they are profoundly unjust.

REFERENCES

Aebi, Marcelo F., Stefano Caneppele, Stefan Harrendorf, Yuji Z. Hashimoto, Joerg-Martin Jehle, Tara S. Khan, Olivia Kühn, Chris Lewis, Lorena Molnar, Rannveig Þórisdóttir, and Paul Smit, eds. 2021. *European Sourcebook of Crime and Criminal Justice Statistics*, 6th ed. Strasbourg: Council of Europe.

Aebi, Marcelo F., and Natalia Delgrande, eds. 2014. *Council of Europe Annual Penal Statistics: SPACE I, Prison Populations, 2013 Survey*. Strasbourg: Council of Europe.

Aebi, Marcelo F., and Mélanie M. Tiago. 2021. *SPACE I—2020—Council of Europe Annual Penal Statistics: Prison Populations*. Strasbourg: Council of Europe.

Albrecht, Hans-Jörg. 2001. "Post-adjudication Dispositions in Comparative Perspective." In *Sentencing and Sanctions in Western Countries*, edited by Michael Tonry and Richard S. Frase. New York: Oxford University Press.

Albrecht, Hans-Jörg. 2004. "Youth Justice in Germany." In *Youth Crime and Youth Justice: Comparative and Cross-National Perspectives*, edited by Michael Tonry and Anthony N. Doob. Vol. 31 of *Crime and Justice: A Review of Research*, edited by Michael Tonry. Chicago: University of Chicago Press.

Appelius, Hugo. 1892. "Die Reformbestrebungen auf dem Gebiet der Strafrechtspflege und das heutige Strafrecht." *Zeitschrift für die gesamte Strafrechtswissenschaft* 12:1–33.

Ashworth, Andrew. 2001. "The Decline of English Sentencing and Other Stories." In *Sentencing and Sanctions in Western Countries*, edited by Michael Tonry and Richard S. Frase. New York: Oxford University Press.

Asp, Petter. 2012. "The Prosecutor in Swedish Law." In *Prosecutors and Politics: A Comparative Perspective*, edited by Michael Tonry. Vol. 41 of *Crime and Justice: A Review of Research*, edited by Michael Tonry. Chicago: University of Chicago Press.

Australian Law Reform Commission. 1980. *Sentencing of Federal Offenders*. Canberra: Australian Government Publishing Service.

Bandyopadhyay, Siddhartha, and Bryan C. McCannon. 2014. "The Effect of the Election of Prosecutors on Criminal Trials." *Public Choice* 161(1–2):141–56.

Bentham, Jeremy. (1789) 1970. *An Introduction to the Principles of Morals and Legislation*, edited by J. H. Burns and H. L. A. Hart. Oxford: Clarendon.

Berdejó, C., and N. Yuchtman. 2013. "Crime, Punishment, and Politics: An Analysis of Political Cycles in Criminal Sentencing." *Review of Economic Statistics* 95:741–56.

Bergman, Marcelo, and Custavo Fondevila. 2021. *Confinement, Punishment and Prisons in Africa*. Abingdon: Routledge.

Bernat, Ignasi, and David Whyte. 2022. "Criminalization as a Strategy of Power: The Case of Catalunya, 2017–2020." In *Criminalization of Activism: Historical, Present and Future Perspectives*, edited by Valeria Vegh Weis. Abingdon: Routledge.

Berry, Kate. 2015. *How Judicial Elections Impact Criminal Cases*. New York: New York University, Brennan Center for Justice.

Blumstein, Alfred. 1988. "Prison Populations: A System Out of Control?" In *Crime and Justice: A Review of Research*, vol. 10, edited by Michael Tonry. Chicago: University of Chicago Press.

Blumstein, Alfred, and Allen J. Beck. 1999. "Population Growth in U. S. Prisons, 1980–1996." In *Prisons*, edited by Michael Tonry and Joan Petersilia. Vol. 26 of *Crime and Justice: A Review of Research*, edited by Michael Tonry. Chicago: University of Chicago Press.

Blumstein, Alfred, and Jacqueline Cohen. 1973. "A Theory of the Stability of Punishment." *Journal of Criminal Law and Criminology* 64(2):198–206.

Blumstein, Alfred, Jacqueline Cohen, Susan E. Martin, and Michael Tonry, eds. 1983. *Research on Sentencing: The Search for Reform*. 2 vols. Washington, DC: National Academy.

Blumstein, Alfred, Jacqueline Cohen, and Daniel Nagin, eds. 1978. *Deterrence and Incapacitation: Estimating the Effects of Criminal Sanctions on Crime Rates*. Washington, DC: National Academy of Sciences.

Boone, Miranda, Francis Pakes, Sigrid van Wingerden. 2020. "Explaining the Collapse of the Prison Population in the Netherlands: Testing the Theories." *European Journal of Criminology* 17(1):1–18.

Bottomley, A. Keith. 1990. "Parole in Transition: A Comparative Study of Origins, Developments, and Prospects for the 1990s." In *Crime and Justice: A Review of Research*, vol. 12, edited by Michael Tonry. Chicago: University of Chicago Press.

Bottoms, Anthony E. 1995. "The Philosophy and Politics of Punishment and Sentencing." In *The Politics of Sentencing Reform*, edited by Chris Clarkson and Rod Morgan. Oxford: Oxford University Press.

Braithwaite, John, and Philip Pettit. 1990. *Not Just Deserts: A Republican Theory of Criminal Justice*. New York: Oxford University Press.

Braithwaite, John, and Philip Pettit. 2001. "Republicanism and Restorative Justice: An Explanatory and Normative Connection." In *Restorative Justice: Philosophy to Practice*, edited by John Braithwaite and Heather Strang. Burlington, VT: Ashgate.

Bucerius, Sandra, and Sveinung Sandberg. 2022. "Women in Prisons." In *Prisons and Prisoners*, edited by Michael Tonry and Sandra Bucerius. Vol. 51 of *Crime and Justice: A Review of Research*, edited by Michael Tonry. Chicago: University of Chicago Press.

Bucerius, Sandra M., Kevin D. Haggerty, and David T. Dunford. 2020. "Prison as Temporary Refuge: Amplifying the Voices of Women Detained in Prison." *British Journal of Criminology* 61(2):519–37.

Canadian Sentencing Commission. 1987. *Sentencing Reform: A Canadian Approach*. Ottawa: Canadian Government Publishing Centre.

Carson, E. Ann. 2014. *Prisoners in 2013*. Washington, DC: US Department of Justice, Bureau of Justice Statistics.

Carson, E. Ann. 2021. *Prisoners in 2020*. Washington, DC: US Department of Justice, Bureau of Justice Statistics.

Carson, E. Ann, and Daniela Golinella. 2013. *Prisoners in 2012: Advanced Counts*. Washington, DC: US Department of Justice, Bureau of Justice Statistics.

Cavadino, Michael, and James Dignan. 2005. *Penal Systems: A Comparative Approach*. London: Sage.

Clinton, Bill. 1996. *Between Hope and History: Meeting America's Challenges for the 21st Century*. New York: Crown.

Cottingham, John G. 1979. "Varieties of Retributivism." *Philosophical Quarterly* 29:239–46.

Crewe, Ben, Alice Levins, Simon Larmour, Julie Laursen, Kristian Mjåland, and Anna Schliehe. 2022. "Nordic Penal Exceptionalism: A Comparative, Empirical Analysis." *British Journal of Criminology*. https://doi.org/10.1093/bjc/azac013.

de Keijser, Jan. 2011. "Never Mind the Pain; It's a Measure! Justifying Measures as Part of the Dutch Bifurcated System of Sanctions." In *Retributivism Has a Past: Has It a Future?*, edited by Michael Tonry. New York: Oxford University Press.

Dickey, Walter J., and Pam Hollenhurst. 1998. *"Three Strikes": Five Years Later*. Washington, DC: Campaign for an Effective Crime Policy.

Dolovich, Sharon. 2022. "The Failed Regulation and Oversight of American Prisons." *Annual Review of Criminology* 5:153–77.

Doob, Anthony N., and Cheryl Marie Webster. 2016. "Weathering the Storm? Testing Long-Standing Canadian Sentencing Policy in the Twenty-First Century." In *Sentencing Policies and Practices in Western Countries: Comparative and Cross-National Perspectives*, edited by Michael Tonry. Vol. 45 of *Crime and Justice: A Review of Research*, edited by Michael Tonry. Chicago: University of Chicago Press.

Downes, David. 1988. *Contrasts in Tolerance: Post-war Penal Policy in the Netherlands and England and Wales*. Oxford: Clarendon.

Downes, David, and Tim Newburn. 2022. *The Politics of Law and Order*. Vol. 4 of *The Official History of Criminal Justice in England and Wales*. Abingdon: Routledge.

Drápal, Jakub. 2021. "Punitive by Negligence? The Myths and Reality of Penal Nationalism in the Czech Republic." *European Journal of Criminology*. https://doi.org/10.1177/14773708211063753.

Durnescu, Ioan, and Kevin Haines. 2012. "Probation in Romania: Archaeology of a Partnership." *British Journal of Criminology* 52(5):889–907.

Dyke, Andrew. 2007. "Electoral Cycles in the Administration of Criminal Justice." *Public Choice* 133:417–37.

Edsall, Thomas, and Mary Edsall. 1991. *Chain Reaction: The Impact of Race, Rights, and Taxes on American Politics*. New York: Norton.

Fair, Helen, and Roy Walmsley. 2021. *World Prison Brief*, 13th ed. London: Institute for Criminal Policy Studies, Birkbeck College, University of London.

Ferri, Enrico. 1881. *I Nuovi Orizzonti del Diritto e della Procedura Penale*. Bologna: Zanichelli.

Ferri, Enrico. 1917. *Criminal Sociology*. Boston: Little, Brown. (First Italian edition 1881.)

Frady, Marshall. 1993. "Death in Arkansas." *New Yorker*, February 22, 105–33.

Frase, Richard. 2013. *Just Sentencing: Principles and Procedures for a Workable System*. New York: Oxford University Press.

Freiberg, Arie. 2016. "The Road Well Travelled in Australia: Ignoring the Past, Condemning the Future." In *Sentencing Policies and Practices in Western Countries: Comparative and Cross-National Perspectives*, edited by Michael Tonry. Vol. 45 of *Crime and Justice: A Review of Research*, edited by Michael Tonry. Chicago: University of Chicago Press.

Garland, David. 2001. *The Culture of Control: Crime and Social Order in Contemporary Society*. Chicago: University of Chicago Press.

Garland, David. 2018. "Theoretical Advance and Problems in the Sociology of Punishment." *Punishment and Society* 20(1):8–33.

Garland, David. 2020. "Penal Controls and Social Controls: Toward a Theory of American Penal Exceptionalism." *Punishment and Society* 22(3):321–52.

Gartner, Rosemary, Anthony Doob, and Franklin E. Zimring. 2011. "The Past as Prologue: Decarceration in California Then and Now." *Criminology and Public Policy* 10(2):291–325.

Gest, Ted. 2001. *Crime and Politics: Big Government's Erratic Campaign for Law and Order*. New York: Oxford University Press.

Haney, Lynne. 2011. "The Politics of Punishment in Post-socialist Eastern Europe." Working Paper no. 06/11. New York: New York University Law School, Straus Institute.

Haney, Lynne. 2016. "Prisons of the Past: Penal Nationalism and the Politics of Punishment in Central Europe." *Punishment and Society* 18(3):346–68.

Harris, Jamie. 2020. "Social Movement Lessons from the US Prisoners' Rights Movement." New York: Sentience Institute.

Hart, H. L. A. 1968. *Punishment and Responsibility: Essays in the Philosophy of Law*. Oxford: Oxford University Press.

Hart, Henry M. 1958. "The Aims of the Criminal Law." *Law and Contemporary Problems* 23:401–42.

Hegel, Georg Wilhelm Friedrich. (1821) 1991. *Elements of the Philosophy of Right*, edited by Allen W. Wood. Translation by H. B. Nisbet. Cambridge: Cambridge University Press.

HM Chief Inspector of Prisoners. 2021. "Annual Report." London: HM Chief Inspector of Prisoners.

Home Office. 1990. *Crime, Justice, and Protecting the Public*. Cm 965. London: HM Stationery Office.

Home Office. 2001. *Making Punishments Work: Report of a Review of the Sentencing Framework for England and Wales*. London: Home Office Communication Directorate.

Huber, Gregory A., and Sanford C. Gordon. 2004. "Accountability and Coercion: Is Justice Blind When It Runs for Office?" *American Journal of Political Science* 48:247–63.

Ifill, Gwen. 1991. "Senate's Rule for Its Anti-crime Bill: The Tougher the Provision, the Better." *New York Times*, July 8, national ed., A6.

Jacobs, James B. 1980. "The Prisoner's Rights Movement and Its Impacts, 1960–80." In *Crime and Justice: A Review of Research*, vol. 2, edited by Norval Morris and Michael Tonry. Chicago: University of Chicago Press.

Junger-Tas, Josine. 2004. "Youth Justice in the Netherlands." In *Youth Crime and Youth Justice: Comparative and Cross-National Perspectives*, edited by Michael Tonry and Anthony N. Doob. Vol. 31 of *Crime and Justice: A Review of Research*, edited by Michael Tonry. Chicago: University of Chicago Press.

Kant, Immanuel. (1797) 2017. *The Metaphysics of Morals*, rev. ed., edited by Lara Denis. Translation by Mary J. Gregor. Cambridge: Cambridge University Press.

Kerr, Lisa, and Benjamin L. Berger. 2020. "Methods and Severity: The Two Tracks of Section 12." *Supreme Court Law Review* 94:235–55.

King, Roy. 1997. "Prisons in Eastern Europe." *Criminal Justice Matters* 27(1):7–8.

Kommer, Max. 1994. "Punitiveness in Europe: A Comparison." *European Journal of Criminal Policy and Research* 2(1):29–43.

Kommer, Max. 2004. "Punitiveness in Europe Revisited." *Criminology in Europe* 3(1):1, 8–12.

Krajewski, Krzysztof. 2004. "Crime and Criminal Justice in Poland." *European Journal of Criminology* 1(3):377–407.

Krajewski, Krzysztof. 2010. "Why Central and Eastern European Countries Have High Imprisonment Rates." *Criminology in Europe* 9(3):3, 7–10.

Krajewski, Krzysztof. 2012. "Prosecution and Prosecutors in Poland: In Quest of Independence." In *Prosecutors and Politics: A Comparative Perspective*, edited by Michael Tonry. Vol. 41 of *Crime and Justice: A Review of Research*, edited by Michael Tonry. Chicago: University of Chicago Press.

Krajewski, Krzysztof. 2013. "Penal Developments in Poland: New or Old Punitiveness?" In *European Penology*, edited by Tom Daems, Dirk van Zyl Smit, and Sonja Snacken. Oxford: Hart.

Krajewski, Krzysztof. 2014. "Different Penal Climates in Europe." *Kriminologijos Studijos* 2014(1):86–111.

Krajewski, Krzysztof. 2016. "Sentencing in Poland: Failed Attempts to Reduce Punitiveness." In *Sentencing and Punishment in Western Countries since 2000*, edited by Michael Tonry. Vol. 45 of *Crime and Justice: A Review of Research*, edited by Michael Tonry. Chicago: University of Chicago Press.

Kruttschnitt, Candace, and Anja Dirkzwager. 2011. "Are There Still Contrasts in Tolerance? Imprisonment in the Netherlands and England 20 Years Later." *Punishment and Society* 13(3):283–306.

Lacey, Nicola. 2008. *The Prisoner's Dilemma: Political Economy and Punishment in Contemporary Democracies*. Cambridge: Cambridge University Press.

Lacey, Nicola, David Soskice, and David Hope. 2018. "Understanding the Determinants of Penal Policy: Crime, Culture, and Comparative Political Economy." *Annual Review of Criminology* 1:195–217.

Lappi-Seppälä, Tapio. 2001. "Sentencing and Punishment in Finland: The Decline of the Repressive Ideal." In *Sentencing and Sanctions in Western Countries*, edited by Michael Tonry and Richard S. Frase. New York: Oxford University Press.

Lappi-Seppälä, Tapio. 2008. "Trust, Welfare, and Political Culture: Explaining Differences in National Penal Policies." In *Crime and Justice: A Review of Research*, vol. 37, edited by Michael Tonry. Chicago: University of Chicago Press.

Lappi-Seppälä, Tapio. 2016. "Nordic Sentencing." In *Sentencing Policies and Practices in Western Countries: Comparative and Cross-National Perspectives*, edited by Michael Tonry. Vol. 45 of *Crime and Justice: A Review of Research*, edited by Michael Tonry. Chicago: University of Chicago Press.

Lévay, Miklós. 2005. "Imprisonment Patterns in Central and Eastern Europe." *Criminology in Europe* 4(3):3, 13–15.

Lévay, Miklós. 2006. "European Integration and the Challenges in Criminal Sanctions: The Case of Hungary." In *Közjogi tanulmányok Lőrincz Lajos 70. születésnapja tiszteletére*, edited by Imre Miklós, Lamm Vanda, and Máthé Gábor. Budapest: Corvinus Egyetem.

Lévay, Miklós. 2012*a*. "Human Rights and Penalization in Central and Eastern Europe: The Case of Hungary." In *Resisting Punitiveness in Europe? Welfare, Human Rights, and Democracy*, edited by Sonja Snacken and Els Dumortier. London: Routledge.

Lévay, Miklós. 2012*b*. "Penal Policy, Crime, and Political Change." *Crime and Transition in Central and Eastern Europe*, edited by Alenka Šelih and Aleš Završnik. London: Springer.

Lévay, Miklós. 2014. "Of Hungarian Criminology and Development of Criminal Policy in Hungary since Changing the Regime in 1989–90." In *Beyond Punitiveness: Crime and Crime Control in a Comparative Perspective*, edited by Valeria Kiss. Budapest: Hungarian Society of Criminology.

Lévy, René. 2007. "Pardons and Amnesties as Policy Instruments in Contemporary France." In *Crime, Punishment, and Politics in a Comparative Perspective*, edited by Michael Tonry. Vol. 36 of *Crime and Justice: A Review of Research*, edited by Michael Tonry. Chicago: University of Chicago Press.

Lijphart, Arend. 1984. *Democracies: Patterns of Majoritarian and Consensus Government in Twenty-One Countries*. New Haven, CT: Yale University Press.

Lijphart, Arend. 1999. *Patterns of Democracy: Government Forms and Performance in Thirty-Six Countries*. New Haven, CT: Yale University Press.

Lipton, Douglas, Robert Martinson, and Judith Wilks. 1975. *Effectiveness of Correctional Treatment: A Survey of Treatment and Evaluation Studies*. New York: Praeger.

Martinson, Robert. 1974. "What Works? Questions and Answers about Prison Reform." *Public Interest* 35(2):22–54.

McCannon, Bryan C. 2013. "Prosecutor Elections, Mistakes, and Appeals." *Journal of Empirical Legal Studies* 10(4):696–714.

McDonald, Douglas C., and Kenneth C. Carlson. 1993. *Sentencing in the Federal Courts: Does Race Matter?* Washington, DC: Bureau of Justice Statistics, US Department of Justice.

Michael, Jerome, and Herbert Wechsler. 1940. *Criminal Law and Its Administration*. Chicago: Foundation.

Minton, Todd D., and Daniela Golinelli. 2014. *Jail Inmates at Midyear 2013: Statistical Tables*. Washington, DC: US Department of Justice, Bureau of Justice Statistics.

Morelle, Marie, Frédéric Le Marcis, and Julia Hornberger, eds. 2021. *Confinement, Punishment and Prisons in Africa*. Abingdon: Routledge.

Morgan Rod. 2006. "With Respect to Order, the Rules of the Game Have Changed: New Labour's Dominance of the 'Law and Order' Agenda." In *The Politics of Crime Control: Essays in Honour of David Downes*, edited by Tim Newburn and Paul Rock. Oxford: Oxford University Press.

Morris, Norval. 1974. *The Future of Imprisonment*. Chicago: University of Chicago Press.

Morris, Norval, and David J. Rothman, eds. 1995. *The Oxford History of the Prison*. New York: Oxford University Press.

Morris, Norval, and Michael Tonry. 1990. *Between Prison and Probation: Intermediate Punishments in a Rational Sentencing System*. New York: Oxford University Press.

Moynihan, Daniel Patrick. 1993. "Iatrogenic Government-Social Policy and Drug Research." *American Scholar* 62(3):351–62.

Munir, Haley. 2020. "Legal Actors and Electoral Competition: How Electoral Incentives Impact Fairness in the Judicial Process." PhD dissertation, Department of Political Science, Binghamton University.

New York Times. 1970. "Texan Given 1,500 Years." *New York Times*, June 20.

Newburn, Tim. 2007. "'Tough on Crime': Penal Policy in England and Wales." In *Crime, Punishment, and Politics in Comparative Perspective*, edited by Michael Tonry. Vol. 36 of *Crime and Justice: A Review of Research*, edited by Michael Tonry. Chicago: University of Chicago Press.

Pickett, Justin T. 2019. "Public Opinion and Criminal Justice Policy: Theory and Research." *Annual Review of Criminology* 2:405–28.

Pifferi, Michele. 2012. "Individualization of Punishment and the Rule of Law: Reshaping Legality in the United States and Europe between the 19th and the 20th Century." *American Journal of Legal History* 52:325–76.

Pifferi, Michele. 2016. *Reinventing Punishment: A Comparative History of Criminology and Penology in the 19th and 20th Century*. Oxford: Oxford University Press.

Pifferi, Michele, ed. 2022. *The Limits of Criminological Positivism: The Movement for Criminal Law Reform in the West, 1870–1940*. Abingdon: Routledge.

Posner, Richard A. 2007. *Economic Analysis of Law*, 7th ed. New York: Aspen.

Pratt, John. 2007. *Penal Populism*. Abingdon: Routledge.

Pratt, John. 2017. "New Zealand Penal Policy in the Twenty-First Century." In *The Palgrave Handbook of Australian and New Zealand Criminology, Crime and Justice*, edited by Antje Deckert and Rick Sarre. London: Palgrave Macmillan.

Reaves, Brian A. 2013. *Felony Defendants in Large Urban Counties, 2009: Statistical Tables*. Washington, DC: US Department of Justice, Bureau of Justice Statistics.

Roberts, Julian V., and Andrew Ashworth. 2016. "The Evolution of Sentencing Policy and Practice in England and Wales, 2003–2015." In *Sentencing Policies and Practices in Western Countries: Comparative and Cross-National Perspectives*, edited by Michael Tonry. Vol. 45 of *Crime and Justice: A Review of Research*, edited by Michael Tonry. Chicago: University of Chicago Press.

Roberts, Julian V., Loretta J. Stalans, David Indermaur, and Mike Hough. 2003. *Penal Populism and Public Opinion: Lessons from Five Countries*. Oxford: Oxford University Press.

Rothman, David. 1971. *The Discovery of the Asylum: Social Order and Disorder in the New Republic*. Boston: Little, Brown.

Rothman, David. 1980. *Conscience and Convenience: The Asylum and Its Alternatives in Progressive America*. Boston: Little, Brown.

Schlanger, Margo. 2003. "Inmate Litigation." *Harvard Law Review* 116(6):1555–706.

Schoenfeld, Heather. 2010. "Mass Incarceration and the Paradox of Prison Conditions Litigation." *Law and Society Review* 44(3–4):731–68.

Selmini, Rossella. 2020. "Criminalizzazione e Repressione del Dissenso Politico: Il Caso della Mobilitazione Indipendentista Catalana." *Criminalia* 2020:431–59.

Simon, Jonathan. 2007. *Governing through Crime: How the War on Crime Transformed American Democracy and Created a Culture of Fear*. New York: Oxford University Press.

Smith, Peter Scharf. 2006. "The Effects of Solitary Confinement on Prison Inmates: A Brief History and Review of the Literature." In *Crime and Justice: A Review of Research*, vol. 24, edited by Michael Tonry. Chicago: University of Chicago Press.

Snacken, Sonja. 2021. "Human Dignity and Prisoners' Rights in Europe." In *Crime and Justice: A Review of Research*, vol. 50, edited by Michael Tonry. Chicago: University of Chicago Press.

Tetrault, Justin E. C. 2022. "Indigenizing Prisons: A Canadian Case Study." In *Prisons and Prisoners*, edited by Michael Tonry and Sandra Bucerius. Vol. 51 of *Crime and Justice: A Review of Research*, edited by Michael Tonry. Chicago: University of Chicago Press.

Times. 2010. "Cameron Sickened by Prisoner Vote." *Times* (London), November 3. https://www.thetimes.co.uk/article/cameron-sickened-by-prisoner-vote-j3zf67bbm2t.

Tonry, Michael. 1995. *Malign Neglect: Race, Crime, and Punishment in America*. New York: Oxford University Press.

Tonry, Michael. 1996. *Sentencing Matters*. New York: Oxford University Press.

Tonry, Michael. 1999. "Parochialism in American Sentencing Policy." *Crime and Delinquency* 45:48–65.

Tonry, Michael. 2004. *Thinking about Crime: Sense and Sensibility in American Penal Culture*. New York: Oxford University Press.

Tonry, Michael. 2006. "Purposes and Functions of Sentencing." In *Crime and Justice: A Review of Research*, vol. 34, edited by Michael Tonry. Chicago: University of Chicago Press.

Tonry, Michael. 2007. "Determinants of Penal Policies." In *Crime, Punishment, and Politics in Comparative Perspective*, edited by Michael Tonry. Vol. 36 of *Crime and Justice: A Review of Research*, edited by Michael Tonry. Chicago: University of Chicago Press.

Tonry, Michael. 2012a. "Prosecutors and Politics in Comparative Perspective." In *Prosecutors and Politics: A Comparative Perspective*, edited by Michael Tonry. Chicago: University of Chicago Press.

Tonry, Michael. 2012b. "'Wrongful' Acquittals and 'Unduly Lenient' Sentences: Misconceived Problems That Provoke Unjust Solutions." In *Principled Approaches to Criminal Law and Criminal Justice: Essays in Honour of Professor Andrew Ashworth*, edited by Julian V. Roberts and Lucia Zedner. Oxford: Oxford University Press.

Tonry, Michael. 2014. "Why Crime Rates Are Falling throughout the Western World." In *Why Crime Rates Fall and Why They Don't*, edited by Michael Tonry. Vol. 43 of *Crime and Justice: A Review of Research*, edited by Michael Tonry. Chicago: University of Chicago Press.

Tonry, Michael. 2016. *Sentencing Fragments: Penal Reform in America, 1975–2025*. New York: Oxford University Press.

Tonry, Michael. 2021. "Fatalism and Indifference: The Influence of the Frontier on American Criminal Justice." In *Crime and Justice: A Review of Research*, vol. 50, edited by Michael Tonry. Chicago: University of Chicago Press.

Tonry, Michael, and Catrien Bijleveld. 2007. "Crime, Criminal Justice, and Criminology in the Netherlands." In *Crime and Justice in the Netherlands*, edited by Michael Tonry and Catrien Bijleveld. Chicago: University of Chicago Press.

Törnudd, Patrik. 1993. *Fifteen Years of Declining Prisoner Rates*. Research Communication no. 8. Helsinki: National Research Institute of Legal Policy, Finnish Ministry of Justice.

Travis, Jeremy, Bruce Western, and Steve Redburn, eds. 2014. *The Growth of Incarceration in the United States: Exploring Causes and Consequences*. Report of the National Academy of Sciences Committee on the Causes and Consequences of High Rates of Incarceration. Washington, DC: National Academies.

Vagg, Jon. 1994. *Prison Systems: A Comparative Study of Accountability in England, France, Germany, and the Netherlands*. Oxford: Clarendon.

Válková, Helena, and Jana Hulmáková. 2007. "Crime and Criminal Justice Reforms in the 'New Central European Countries,' and the Example of the Czech Republic." In *Penal Policy, Justice Reform, and Social Exclusion*, edited by Kauko Aromaa. Helsinki: Helsinki European Institute for Crime Prevention and Control.

van de Bunt, Henk, and Jean-Louis van Gelder. 2012. "The Dutch Prosecution Service." In *Prosecutors and Politics: A Comparative Perspective*, edited by Michael Tonry. Vol. 41 of *Crime and Justice: A Review of Research*, edited by Michael Tonry. Chicago: University of Chicago Press.

von Hirsch, Andreas [Andrew]. 1976. *Doing Justice: The Choice of Punishments*. New York: Hill & Wang.

von Liszt, Franz. 1897. "Die strafrechtliche Zurechnungsfähigkeit: Vortrag gehalten am 4. August 1896 auf dem III. Internationalen Psychologenkongress." *Zeitschrift für die gesamte Strafrechtswissenschaft* 17:70–84. (Repr. in *Strafrechtliche Aufsätze und Vortrige*, vol. 2, edited by Franz von Liszt. Berlin: Guttentag, 1905.)

von Liszt, Franz. 1905. "Die Kriminalitat der Jugendlichen." In *Strafrechtliche Aufsätze und Vortrige*, vol. 2, edited by Franz von Liszt. Berlin: Guttentag.

Walker, Nigel. 1991. *Why Punish?* Oxford: Oxford University Press.

Walmsley, Roy. 2000. *World Prison Population List*, 2nd ed. London: Home Office Research, Development, and Statistics Directorate.

Walmsley, Roy. 2009. *World Prison Brief*, 8th ed. London: King's College, International Centre for Prison Studies.

Walmsley, Roy. 2014. *World Prison Brief*, 10th ed. Colchester: International Centre for Prison Studies, University of Essex.

Walmsley, Roy. 2015. *World Prison Population Brief*, 11th ed. London: Institute for Criminal Policy Research, Birkbeck College, University of London.

Webster, Cheryl Marie, and Anthony N. Doob. 2014. "Penal Reform 'Canadian Style': Fiscal Responsibility and Decarceration in Alberta, Canada." *Punishment and Society* 16(1):3–31.

Wechsler, Herbert. 1961. "Sentencing, Correction, and the Model Penal Code." *University of Pennsylvania Law Review* 109(4):465–93.

Weigend, Thomas. 1997. "Germany Reduces Use of Prison Sentences." In *Sentencing Reform in Overcrowded Times*, edited by Michael Tonry and Kathleen Hatlestad. New York: Oxford University Press.

Weigend, Thomas. 2001. "Sentencing and Punishment in Germany." In *Sentencing and Sanctions in Western Countries*, edited by Michael Tonry and Richard S. Frase. New York: Oxford University Press.

Weigend, Thomas. 2016. "No News Is Good News: Sentencing in Germany since 2000." In *Sentencing and Punishment in Western Countries since 2000*, edited by Michael Tonry. Vol. 45 of *Crime and Justice: A Review of Research*, edited by Michael Tonry. Chicago: University of Chicago Press.

Weisberg, Robert. 2019. "The Wild West of Sentencing Reform: Lessons from California." In *American Sentencing*, edited by Michael Tonry. Vol. 48 of *Crime and Justice: A Review of Research*, edited by Michael Tonry. Chicago: University of Chicago Press.

Wetzell, Richard F. 2022. "Penal Reform in Imperial Germany: Conflict and Compromise." In *The Limits of Criminological Positivism: The Movement for Criminal Law Reform in the West, 1870–1940*, edited by Michele Pifferi. London: Routledge.

Whitman, James Q. 2003. *Harsh Justice: Criminal Punishment and the Widening Divide between America and Europe*. New York: Oxford University Press.

Wilson, James Q. 1990. "Drugs and Crime." In *Drugs and Crime*, edited by Michael Tonry and James Q. Wilson. Vol. 13 of *Crime and Justice: A Review of Research*, edited by Michael Tonry and Norval Morris. Chicago: University of Chicago Press.

Windlesham, David. 1993. *Responses to Crime: Penal Policy in the Making*. Oxford: Oxford University Press.

Windlesham, David. 1998. *Politics, Punishment, and Populism*. New York: Oxford University Press.

Wright, Ronald. 2002. "Counting the Cost of Sentencing in North Carolina, 1980–2000." *Crime and Justice: A Review of Research*, vol. 29, edited by Michael Tonry. Chicago: University of Chicago Press.

Young, Warren, and Mark Brown. 1993. "Cross National Comparisons of Imprisonment." In *Crime and Justice: A Review of Research*, vol. 17, edited by Michael Tonry. Chicago: University of Chicago Press.

Shadd Maruna, Gillian McNaull, and Nina O'Neill

The COVID-19 Pandemic and the Future of the Prison

ABSTRACT

Since the discovery of the "jail disease," probably typhus, in the eighteenth century, health experts have recognized that the prison is a near perfect in-cubator of contagious disease. Early in the COVID-19 pandemic, therefore, public health authorities and human rights groups advocated immediate and sustained decarceration of overcrowded prisons to save lives and stop the spread of the virus. Yet, decarceration efforts globally were uneven and largely failed to live up to expectations. Instead, prison systems typically sought to control the spread of COVID-19 by imposing strict "lockdowns" on prisoner movement that bordered on long-term solitary confinement in many jurisdictions. The consequences of these severe conditions on prisoners' mental and physical health are only just emerging. The ramifications for future prison reform efforts may be more profound. If a deadly pandemic is not enough to instigate a reimagining of the role of prison in society, it is unclear what could.

Disease has played a central role in shaping episodes of public controversy about the humanity of punishment. "Disease has a distinctive power to strip away the general invisibility of life that takes place behind the walls of prison, and narrow the gulf that normally separates the fate of prisoners from the imagination of the free. These moments have been particularly conse-quential because of their potential to motivate legal elites ... to 'see' the existing penal regime anew and actively to reimagine the American prison" (Simon 2013, p. 223). In his sweeping history of the "medical model" in

Shadd Maruna is professor of criminology and Gillian McNaull and Nina O'Neill are postdoctoral fellows at Queen's University Belfast.

Electronically published October 20, 2022

Crime and Justice, volume 51, 2022.
https://doi.org/10.1086/722434

prison, Jonathan Simon argues that disease has been the primary catalyst of change in prison policy and practice since the origins of the institution. Beginning with what the English reformer John Howard described as the "jail disease" (presumably typhus) that spread through prisons in the late 1700s, Simon argues that the correctional enterprise has been "repeatedly reshaped by moments of heightened concern about disease, prisons, and the general health of the public" (p. 218). New diseases and new discoveries in medicine and public health, he argues, led to "periodic transformations [in] ... correctional philosophy and ultimately constitutional understandings of the prison" (p. 218).

Labeled the worst public health crisis for a generation (Maycock and Dickson 2021; Maycock 2022), the COVID-19 pandemic appears to be a perfect example of history repeating itself. From its onset, the pandemic has highlighted the extreme vulnerability of incarcerated populations. By February 29, 2020, half of reported Wuhan COVID-19 cases were within the city's penal institutions, and an outbreak at a prison 450 miles away was traced to Wuhan officials who had visited and possibly infected seven prison guards and 200 prisoners (Barnert, Ahalt, and Williams 2020). The first COVID-19 diagnosis in a US prison was announced in March 2020 (Pitts and Inkpen 2020), and the first death was only weeks later, on March 26, 2020. Within 8 months, the number of prisoner deaths from COVID-related illnesses exceeded the number of prisoners executed in the United States during the preceding 30 years, creating a "new death penalty" (Mortaji et al. 2021, p. 801).

In 2021, the UN Office on Drugs and Crime estimated that approximately 550,000 prisoners around the world had contracted the virus at that point, resulting in an estimated 4,000 fatalities (UNODC 2021). By July 15, 2022, the US prison death toll alone reached nearly 2,900, with over 600,000 reported cases tracked according to the COVID Prison Project (https://covidprisonproject.com/). COVID-related mortality rates have been estimated to be at least 2.5 times higher in prison than in the general population in different jurisdictions (Braithwaite et al. 2021; Toblin and Hagan 2021), and infection rates are estimated to be up to 5.5 times higher (Edge et al. 2021; Marquez et al. 2021; Byrne et al. 2022). These figures are almost certainly underestimates, as many prison systems are suspected of not disclosing complete or accurate information (Lemasters et al. 2020; Natoli et al. 2021). Human Rights Watch (HRW 2022, para. 1) observes: "Many countries around the world are not monitoring and reporting on Covid-19 infection, death, and mitigation efforts in detention settings." Furthermore, these figures do not include deaths of infected prisoners after release, nor do they include populations in jails where controlling COVID can have a dramatic impact (Byrne et al. 2022). For instance, at the end of 2021, Rikers Island in New York City reported that over 17 percent of its jail population tested positive (Morales 2021). Similar patterns can be found in penal institutions around the world (Franco-Paredes et al. 2020; Dünkel, Harrendorf, and van Zyl Smit 2022).

As Simon suggests, this pandemic will almost certainly reshape how prisons are understood and incarceration is practiced. What that impact will look like, however, is not obvious. At the outset of the pandemic, penal systems internationally had to choose between at least two potential responses if they were to save lives and prevent the spread of the disease inside and outside the justice system. The most obvious option—advocated by the United Nations and numerous human rights organizations—was large-scale decarceration, defined by the National Academies of Science, Engineering, and Medicine (NASEM 2020, p. 15) as "the process of reducing the number of people in correctional facilities by releasing those currently incarcerated and by diverting those who might otherwise be incarcerated."

The pandemic led to the previously unthinkable shutting of schools, universities, workplaces, funeral homes, sporting events, and nearly every other aspect of social life in order to save lives and stop the spread of disease. Penal institutions are almost unparalleled in their ability to spread COVID-19 internally and to the wider community (Presidential COVID-19 Health Equity Task Force 2021). Overcrowded prison systems and jails could have enacted decarceration and excarceration measures (defined by Drucker [2018], respectively, as getting people out of prison and stopping putting more people in) to prevent deaths and protect the public. Of course, this is exactly what several countries around the globe did (HRW 2020a).

By far the more common response, however, was to enact penal "lockdowns" involving heightened levels of isolation and containment (Dünkel, Harrendorf, and van Zyl Smit 2022). Rather than decarceration, prison systems around the world implemented an experiment in solitary confinement at a massive scale. In other words, in order to save lives, prison systems did more of what prisons do best: isolating residents from human contact.

This stark choice between decarceration and heightened lockdown could shape the future of the prison for decades (Simon 2013). In the following sections, we examine both options in depth. In Section I, we begin with an analysis of the spread of disease both within penal institutions and from prisons to the wider public. Prison populations are uniquely vulnerable to viruses like COVID-19, both because of the backgrounds of people in prison and because of the nature of penal institutions. We begin Section II by reviewing the case for substantial decarceration in light of these vulnerabilities. The reality of decarceration fell badly short of the ambitions of reformers who called for swift action to reduce overcrowding and save lives. In this section we review both the successes and the multiple failings of decarceration in practice and address the question of "what went wrong" with prison releases worldwide.

In Section III, we review what happened to the people who remained inside prison during the pandemic. Instead of or in addition to decarcerating, most prison systems engaged in forms of "lockdown" resembling widespread solitary confinement. We assess emerging research regarding the effects of this vast lockdown on prisoners' mental health and well-being. In doing so, we draw on an array of global examples; however, most of our focus is on the United States, which has the world's highest incarceration rate (Fair and Walmsley 2021). In Section IV, we also draw on original data collected as part of our own 18-month study, coproduced with the User Voice organization, involving 10 prisons in England and Wales. British prisons experienced a dramatic, system-wide lockdown that has had a measurable impact on the mental health and well-being of the incarcerated.

Finally, Section V concludes that, with some notable exceptions, state responses to the pandemic in prisons around the globe have been an immense failure, on almost every level but most especially a failure of imagination or what Davis (2003, p. 20) calls the "stultifying idea that nothing lies beyond the prison." Decarceration responses were far too cautious, in most jurisdictions releasing only small numbers of prisoners at the lowest risk levels. Yet, the pandemic exposed the prison's enormous vulnerabilities for public health. As almost perfect incubators for the spread of infectious diseases such as COVID, prisons presented serious health risks to both those living and working inside them and the wider communities outside. In short, prisons put communities at heightened risk. Stripped of any pretense toward rehabilitation or any countervailing policy justification, the prison's survival is deeply puzzling, especially when so many other institutions (from schools to offices to places of worship) were closed and reinvented through use of technology in order to prevent the spread of disease.

Prisons have not survived the pandemic unchanged, however. They were radically transformed. Yet, in many jurisdictions, this took the form of a regression to their most basic state of pure punishment and social isolation. Emerging research suggests that this massive social experiment in prolonged solitary confinement—explicitly prescribed by the United Nations revised Standard Minimum Rules for the Treatment of Prisoners, known as the "Mandela Rules"—may be having enormous adverse effects on the mental health and well-being of those confined in these extraordinary conditions. The long-term effects will be shouldered by communities over the next decade.

The implications for the future of the prison are particularly bleak, suggesting the near impenetrability of carceral logic in many countries with the largest prison systems. That is, if states cannot decarcerate during a pandemic, it is difficult to imagine a context in which substantial decarceration could be contemplated. At the same time, the efforts of a minority of prison systems globally give hope that the structural mechanisms exist for rapid decarceration if states have the political will to make it happen. The experiences of the pandemic in prisons over the last 3 years have raised awareness within the medical community of the considerable public health threats posed by mass incarceration. This may ultimately expand the base of support for decarceration and penal abolition.

I. Confinement and Contagion

Since their origins, prisons have been places of illness and disease (Braun et al. 1989; Valway et al. 1994; Young et al. 2005; Franco-Paredes et al. 2020). For instance, well before the 2020 COVID outbreak, San Quentin Prison in California was the site of two previous influenza epidemics (Chaddock 2018) and an eruption of swine flu in 2009 (Reutter 2010). The first influenza outbreak was documented by Dr. Leo Stanley; between 500 and 1,000 of San Quentin's 1,900 prisoners contracted the "Spanish Flu" in 1918 (Arnold 2018; Hawks, Woolhandler, and McCormick 2020). Stanley (1919), who had worked in the prison since 1913, traced the first wave to one prisoner who was transferred from Los Angeles County Jail on April 13, 1918. By May 26 of that year, Stanley reported 101 admissions to the prison hospital, seven cases of bronchial pneumonia, and three deaths. Since then, there have been multiple waves of influenza outbreaks among prison populations internationally, especially in 1957–58 and 2003 (Franco-Paredes et al. 2020).

In a systematic review of existing studies, Baussano and colleagues (2010) found that the rate of tuberculosis in prisons was as much as 23 times higher than in the general population and that the rate of latent tuberculosis infections was as much as 26.4 times higher. Hepatitis rates are nine times higher among prison populations than in the general population (Gough et al. 2010; Dolan et al. 2016; Getaz 2019; Kinner et al. 2020; Wegel, Wardak, and Meyer 2022), with around 15 percent of prisoners internationally testing positive for hepatitis C (HRI 2020). Finally, approximately 3.8 percent of prisoners globally are thought to be living with HIV. Research suggests that these individuals can face fear, hostility, prejudice, and indifference from prison staff (Belenko et al. 2016).

Prisons are vulnerable to outbreaks of infection and disease for many reasons. They include preexisting health conditions of the incarcerated population, widespread overcrowding, high mobility of staff and short-term inmates, poor living conditions, and limited access to health care (Maruschak, Berzofsky, and Unangst 2015; Novisky 2018; Akiyama, Spaulding, and Rich 2020).

Prison populations may be disproportionately ill equipped to fight (and survive) infectious diseases because of preexisting health vulnerabilities. First, the prison population now contains a far greater number of medically vulnerable, elderly prisoners as a result of the extraordinary lengthening of US prison sentences over the past four decades (Tonry 2016)—including a quadrupling of the number of people serving life sentences between 1984 and 2017 (Nellis 2017). Indeed, between 1993 and 2018, US prisons experienced a 400 percent increase in the number of adult inmates age 55 or older (Carson and Sabol 2016; Bronson and Carson 2019). Second, prison populations have disproportionately high rates of chronic medical conditions such as obesity, diabetes, cardiovascular disease, and hypertension (Williams et al. 2012). Of course, incarcerated people are also far more likely to suffer from mental health problems, especially addiction and substance abuse disorders (Haugebrook et al. 2010). These issues are compounded by health inequities relating to socioeconomic status, race, and incarceration (Link and Phelan 1995; Phelan and Link 2015; Franco-Paredes et al. 2020; Lemasters et al. 2020). All these factors make the prison population much more vulnerable to hospitalization or death as a result of contracting the coronavirus (see esp. Prost et al. 2021).

The experience of imprisonment is in itself a serious risk factor for numerous diseases. Drawing on Link and Phelan's (1995) "social cause" framework, Novisky and colleagues (2021, p. 1630) argue that "incarceration is a potent structural driver of health inequalities that must be considered as a fundamental social cause of disease." This framework explains correlations between socioeconomic status and health "across time and place," indicating that social factors are integral to understanding health inequity due to unequal access to resources that create health protection in some groups and increase risk for others. Novisky and colleagues extend this conception by proposing that incarceration is a fundamental cause of health disparity, due to its relation to the four fundamental social cause criteria: multiple disease outcomes, multiple risk factors for disease and death, access to resources, and the reproduction of this association between prison and health across time and place. These risks are compounded by "intramural factors," policies within facilities that increase vulnerability to viruses, and "extramural factors" including the levels of prison staff rotating in and out of facilities daily, population "churn," and the absence of mass testing of residents and staff (Novisky 2021, pp. 1637–38).

Overcrowding, chief among these intramural factors, has been the subject of the most research on the public health risks of incarceration. Research on the differential manifestation of COVID-19 in prison suggests that every 10 percent increase in prison population results in a 14 percent risk increase in contracting COVID-19. Prisons running at 70–100 percent capacity increase their risk threefold, and those at 100 percent capacity increase risk fivefold (Leibowitz et al. 2021). With prisons in at least 125 countries chronically overcrowded (HRW 2020b), this is a considerable issue. Research further suggests that contagion risk is heightened by poor ventilation, lack of sanitation and hygiene, poor nutrition, lack of autonomy regarding preventative measures, and inequitable medical care—all of which are endemic in penal environments globally (Lemasters et al. 2020; Altibi et al. 2021; Chin et al. 2021; Toblin and Hagan 2021; Kim et al. 2022; Klein et al. 2022).

Movement of incarcerated people from one facility to another for administrative reasons also increases risks of contamination (Parsons and Worden 2021). Using analyses of time series data from one midsize prison in the United States, Brinkley-Rubenstein and colleagues (2021) found significant associations between the rate of weekly transfers and positive COVID-19 cases. For example, in May 2020, 122 men were transferred from California Institute for Men to San Quentin, and within days, almost a third of the San Quentin population tested positive for COVID-19, with 28 individuals dying.

Those in prison are also more likely to suffer serious health consequences after contracting COVID-19. Altibi et al. (2021) found that of all patients hospitalized in two settings in Michigan, incarcerated people during a 2-month period were more likely to present with fever, tachypnea, hypoxemia, and markedly elevated inflammatory markers than were their community-based counterparts. Furthermore, the study found that people in prison were more commonly admitted to intensive care and had higher rates of mortality within 30 days of admission (Altibi et al. 2021). Brelje and Pinals (2021, p. 197) observe: "Impaired provision of health care is particularly problematic because, at baseline, the imprisoned population has an increased rate of chronic medical conditions compared to the general population. . . . These chronic conditions increase prisoners' risk of morbidity and mortality if infected by SARS-CoV-2."

The ramifications of these intramural and extramural factors, moreover, follow prisoners after release, creating "significant implications" for "spread of and susceptibility to Covid-19" (Novisky et al. 2021, p. 1638). These factors include insecure housing, barriers to health care access, and return to neighborhoods with disproportionate levels of COVID-19 due to "structural marginalization" regarding health care access, unemployment, housing density and stability, and structural discrimination.

This is just one way in which the pandemic risks of penal institutions extend into the communities in which they are sited (Drucker 2013). For instance, failure to contain the spread of COVID in custodial settings carried severe potential consequences for diverse communities outside the prison gates, from "the homeless encampments in Los Angeles, California, to the rural households surrounding Maine State Prison" (Barnert, Ahalt, and Williams 2020, p. 966): "Outbreaks that occur within these facilities are likely to spread to the community, and outbreaks in communities are likely to spread to prisons. Preventing significant outbreaks within these facilities will, therefore, benefit not only the prisoners who are uniquely situated but also the general public" (Brelje and Pinals 2021, p. 195).

Big city jails in particular, with their daily influx of detainees, often briefly released for court and health appointments, become hot spots of contamination, both inside institutions and in their wider communities (Barnert, Ahalt, and Williams 2020, p. 964; see also Collica-Cox and Molina 2020). With their transient, short-term populations rotating in and out, porous city jails, especially, can act as vectors for infection to the communities around them. Reinhart (2021, sec. 2, para. 2) notes:

"Neglect of the welfare of incarcerated populations boomerangs back upon the rest of the United States, multiplying harm in many forms: biological, psychiatric, economic, and social. Even just short pre-trial detention in a jail followed by acquittal inflicts long-term disadvantages on individuals and their communities." In addition to the churn of entering and exiting prisoners, the long list of commuters into and out of penal facilities includes prison staff, medical staff, legal professionals, maintenance workers, outside rehabilitation and education providers, and, in normal times, visitors, inspectors, and researchers.

Although proving a causal link between these institutions and community outbreaks is difficult (Murphy 2021), several studies have highlighted broad public health implications, including increased COVID-19 infection rates in areas surrounding jails and prisons (Hooks and Sawyer 2020; Lofgren et al. 2020; Sims, Foltz, and Skidmore 2021). Reinhart and Chen (2020) explored this at Cook County Jail in Chicago, which reported in January 2022 that over 450 staff members and over 430 detainees had tested positive. They found that jail-community cycling accounted for 55 percent of case rate variance across Chicago ZIP codes and 37 percent of variance across Illinois. By April 19, 2020, jail-community cycling through Cook County was associated with 15.7 percent of documented Illinois cases. In Reinhart and Chen's view, current arrest and jailing practices "in highly policed neighborhoods" were turning arrested people into "potential disease vectors" in their communities. They argue that this may "bear partial responsibility" for the "striking racial disparities" of COVID-19 with the African American population (p. 1417).

II. The COVID Decarceration: What Went Wrong?

From the beginning of the pandemic, the potentially catastrophic effects of COVID-19 on people living in or near penal institutions were widely recognized by experts in fields ranging from epidemiology to criminology to medicine and law (Jiménez et al. 2020; Hwang, Kim, and Havins 2021; Leibowitz et al. 2021; Murphy 2021). Early modeling in these fields suggested that decreasing overcrowding through prison depopulation should be a central strategy in saving lives and reducing COVID-19 transmissions (NASEM 2020; Malloy et al. 2021). As a result, almost immediately, numerous calls for large-scale decarceration measures emerged (Strassle and Berkman 2020). The primary justifications can be broken down into cases based on human rights (Commissioner for Human Rights 2020;

IACHR 2020*a*; Bagaric, Isham, and Svilar 2021), public health and epidemiology (Barnert, Ahalt, and Williams 2020; Sivashanker et al. 2020; Murphy 2021), and ethics and social justice (Reinhart and Chen 2020; Denney and Valdez 2021). Despite these overlapping arguments, the numbers released during the first 2 years of the pandemic fell far short of expectations (Clear 2021; Lockwood 2021), begging the question of what went wrong.

A. The Case for Decarceration

When cases began spreading in prisons and jails in early 2020, the UN High Commissioner for Human Rights, Michelle Bachelet, highlighted the urgent need for governments to take action to protect incarcerated people, including pressing states to reduce prisoner numbers (OHCHR 2020*b*). In particular, she highlighted the need to release "those particularly vulnerable to Covid-19 … older detainees and those who are sick, as well as low-risk offenders," while providing for "the specific health-care requirements of women prisoners, including those who are pregnant, as well as those of inmates with disabilities and of juvenile detainees" (para. 7). This was reinforced by the UN Inter-agency Standing Committee (IASC), which called for prioritizing the release of "children, persons with underlying health conditions, persons with low risk profiles and who have committed minor and petty offenses, persons with imminent release dates and those detained for offenses not recognized under international law" (IASC 2020, p. 3).

Releasing incarcerated people during a contagion crisis was framed as an issue of international human rights law, with the UN Standard Minimum Rules for the Treatment of Prisoners (UNODC 2015) setting out the obligation of states to safeguard the mental health and well-being of prisoners (OHCHR 2020*b*). The Council of Europe Commissioner for Human Rights (2020) reminded member states that efforts should be made to find alternatives to the deprivation of liberty in order to safeguard human rights standards, as outlined by the European Committee for the Prevention of Torture and Inhuman or Degrading Treatment or Punishment in its COVID-19 "Statement of Principles" (CPT 2020). This aim was reiterated by the Inter-American Commission on Human Rights (IACHR 2020*a*) in Resolution 1/2020, "Pandemic and Human Rights in the Americas," calling for identification of those whose status could be converted to an alternative to imprisonment (IACHR 2020*b*). In addition, the IASC stressed that the pandemic provided "an opening for engagement with police ... [and other] law enforcement institutions as well as the judiciary about risks and opportunities related to pre-trial detention" (IASC 2020, p. 3).

Medical experts focused on the public health threat posed by imprisonment. In an editorial, the *American Journal of Public Health* emphasized that the most urgent frontline strategy for correctional facilities must be population reduction "to limit spread and improve containment" (Barnert, Ahalt, and Williams 2020, p. 964). Likewise, the *British Medical Journal* urged that "healthcare needs to lead the charge ... (and) urgently organize to advocate for safe decarceration." The pandemic was seen to highlight "the deep interconnections between public health and social justice," further widening inequalities in communities at the intersection of race and disability who disproportionately bore "the human and economic cost" of incarceration (Sivashanker et al. 2020, p. 1). States were urged to develop comprehensive plans to address custodial setting risk, in an effort to prevent incarceration enacting "cruel and unusual punishment" (Barnert, Ahalt, and Williams 2020, p. 965). Early in the pandemic, with support from Arnold Ventures and the Robert Wood Johnson Foundation, the National Academies of Science, Engineering, and Medicine (NASEM 2020) formed an ad hoc committee with expertise in law, medicine, public health, and social sciences to provide a blueprint for decarceration during the COVID pandemic. Their report recommended that large-scale release and decarceration efforts were "an appropriate and necessary mitigation strategy" for containing COVID-19 (p. 88).

From a social justice perspective, the emerging picture of prison and jail contagion risk levels led to grassroots mobilization, with activists inside and outside prisons rallying around decarceration demands. A significant element of this mobilization in the United States focused on the effects of COVID-19 on specific racial and ethnic groups in and out of prison (Reinhart and Chen 2020; APM Research Lab 2021; Farr 2021; Novisky et al. 2021). The Color of Coronavirus Project reports that the national COVID-19 mortality rate for Pacific Islander, Latino, Indigenous, and Black Americans between March 2020 and February 2021 was twice that of the White and Asian population, a difference that triples when adjusted for age (APM Research Lab 2021). Farr (2021, p. 194) observes, "Neither public health nor political strategies for COVID-19 prevention and containment have provided Black, Latinx, and Indigenous people the necessary means to protect themselves," with mass incarceration and the "deeper history of racialized custody" key factors these communities face. Denney and Valdez (2021, p. 863) argue that preexisting "racial vulnerability" fed into the spread of COVID-19 in prison, "mainly among race-class subjugated (RCS) communities."

The impact of the pandemic on these groups was heightened by three enmeshed factors that "compound[ed] racial vulnerability": health care inequity on the basis of class and race, "external shocks" disproportionately affecting RCS communities, and government responses that entrenched the inequitable effects (Denney and Valdez 2021, p. 863). Predictors of higher community COVID-19 rates including mean household size, proportion of food service workers, number of foreign-born noncitizens, and preexisting health issues are all prevalent features of RCS populations. These factors were compounded by government responses that "disregarded or harmed RCS communities," including rushed reopening of the economy and slackening of public health measures, despite rising death rates within these communities (p. 865).

Finally, an additional element of the grassroots mobilization was the "ableist" implications of COVID-19 responses. The American Civil Liberties Union (ACLU 2020) and disability rights groups campaigned for release of disabled persons imprisoned for nonviolent offenses. As Schotland (2021, para. 1) observed, disabled prisoners face "multiple and overlapping injustices and oppressions" including "race and ethnic discrimination, poverty, trauma, multiple physical impairments, mental illness, and/or cognitive limitations." In the US prison system, disability levels are three times higher than in the general population, and in US jails, four times higher (Schotland 2021). Disability added an intersecting and additional risk to justifications for court sentences when "conditions of confinement are so dangerous they violate human rights" (para. 3).

In short, the public health risks of COVID-19 intersected with human rights and ethical concerns creating a broad coalition of support for decarceration. Beyond the risk of prisons acting as an amplifying contagion vortex during the pandemic, the risks inside were seen potentially to breach both the Eighth Amendment of the US Constitution's prohibition of "cruel and unusual punishment" and, more broadly, obligations of governments set out in the European Convention on Human Rights (1950) and the United Nation's Mandela Rules (UNODC 2015). For legal observers, the elevated "risk" of incarceration caused by the pandemic raised additional issues regarding the legal principle of "proportionality" that requires that severity of punishments be proportionate to the seriousness of breaches of law for which they are imposed. With imprisonment during the pandemic "more burdensome than was previously understood," decarceration was a policy more "consistent with the proportionality principle" (Bagaric, Isham, and Svilar 2021, p. 127).

B. Decarceration in Practice

Despite these arguments from disparate quarters, the numbers of released prisoners in the first 2 years of the pandemic were far lower than anticipated in most countries (Lockwood 2021). Across the globe, reviews by Harm Reduction International and Human Rights Watch suggested that at least 109 countries enacted decarceration measures between March and June 2020, with the potential to release around 5–6 percent of the 11 million people in prison worldwide (HRI 2020; HRW 2020b). However, not all announced release schemes were actually implemented (Grierson 2020a; HRW 2020a, 2020b), and many of those that were fell "significantly short of expectations and the significant political commitments made in the name of public health" (HRI 2020, para. 6). Moreover, many releases were temporary, with released prisoners reimprisoned at later stages of the pandemic. By the end of 2021, the global prison population was estimated to be 10,771,204, a rate of 140 per 100,000. This represented an increase from 10,743,619 prisoners in 2018 but a decrease in real terms from 45 per 100,000, with all continents but the Americas experiencing population drops (Fair and Walmsley 2021). Penal Reform International's "Global Prison Trends" (2022) describes current prison expansion globally to be "at an all-time high," with a population around 11.5 million.

Some countries did, however, achieve more substantial and sustained decarceration. This was especially the case in countries with long-standing issues with prison overcrowding. Before the pandemic, the Philippines had one of the world's most overcrowded prison systems, operating at 537 percent of capacity in its 400 prisons and jails (Arambulo et al. 2021). By October 2020, nearly 82,000 prisoners and detainees were released in one of the largest such initiatives globally (Arambulo et al. 2021). In Kenya, reduction initiatives included scaling down services and activities in the justice system for 30 days, a directive to dispense with police bonds for low-level offenses, and suspension of new admissions to custodial institutions. Additionally, after reviewing 19,000 case files, the High Court in Kenya decided that 15,379 prisoners should be released, have their sentences reduced, or be placed on a community service order (Deche and Bosire

2020). Other decarceration efforts highlighted by the Harm Reduction International analysis in 2020 include India releasing over 66,000 people (14 percent of the population), Iran issuing 10,000 pardons and releasing 75,000 of its 240,000 prisoners (over 30 percent), Iraq reducing its 45,000 population by just under 40 percent, and Myanmar pardoning 27 percent of its 92,000 prisoners (HRI 2020).

The Council of Europe (2022) reports that the COVID-19 pandemic resulted in prison population reductions in 49 prison administrations of 52 member states, due largely to reduced crime rates and court backlogs in conjunction with various release schemes. The Portuguese government in 2020 planned to release around 10 percent of the prison population, approximately 2,000 prisoners, including those serving sentences under 2 years and those nearing the end of a sentence for nonviolent crimes, corruption, drug trafficking, or state actors. Portugal also enacted an "exceptional presidential pardon" for the release of many individuals over age 65 with preexisting health issues (Fróis 2020, p. 25). Likewise, France decreased its prison population by an estimated 20 percent in the pandemic's first year (HRI 2020).

These were exceptions to the general rule, however. Decarceration was far less successful in most countries. Zeveleva and Nazif-Munoz (2022) found that only 16 of 47 jurisdictions in the Council of Europe effectively implemented decarceration measures in the first year of the pandemic. Overall, imprisonment rates decreased by only around 2.3 percent across the continent primarily due to decreases in crime and backlogs in the courts (Council of Europe 2022). The Prison Service of England and Wales had a particularly troubled experience. In April 2020, the Ministry of Justice announced that it would release up to 4,000 prisoners, about 5 percent of the population (Grierson 2020c). Over 2,000 electronic monitoring tags were purchased to facilitate the releases. The chair of the Independent Advisory Panel on Deaths in Custody warned that the scheme was "hard to understand, difficult to explain and close to impossible to deliver" with processes and eligibility criteria "mired in complexity and risk aversion" (Grierson 2020b, paras. 2–6). By the end of June 2020, only 57 individuals had been released, six mistakenly. The Conservative Government lost its political nerve. By October 2020, the scheme was "closed." In total, 275 individuals were released, a fraction of 1 percent of the overall prison population (Grierson 2020a).

Of course, the success of decarceration around the world largely depended on the United States, which holds a quarter of the world's prisoners (Fair and Walmsley 2021). The scale and complexity of criminal justice systems in the United States means that a wide variety of disparate strategies were required rather than the centralized, top-down approach taken in smaller countries with a single prison system. For example, California expanded use of "good time" credits to promote prisoner release while also establishing a statewide emergency bail schedule to reduce use of cash bail and lower jail populations (Prison Policy Initiative 2022). Inevitably, these multiple, overlapping, and enmeshed local, state, and national initiatives were neither universally nor consistently implemented, resulting in wide variation across states and localities (Council on Criminal Justice 2020, p. 5).

The Bureau of Justice Statistics reported a 15 percent drop in state prisoners by the end of 2020 (Carson 2021*a*, 2021*b*). Three states were able to decrease their overall prison populations by over a quarter in this first year of the pandemic: West Virginia (33 percent), New Jersey (31 percent), and Connecticut (26 percent; Byrne et al. 2022). However, most of these drops are not the result of prisoner release strategies but rather can be explained by the dramatic 40 percent drop in prison admissions in the first year of the pandemic—a result of crime declines, court delays, and temporary suspension of transfers from local jails (Sawyer and Wagner 2022). Prisoner numbers started to increase again in 19 states between January 2021 and January 2022 (Vera Institute of Justice 2022). The Prison Policy Initiative (2022, p. 1) concluded that US lawmakers have "failed to reduce prison and jail populations enough to slow the spread of Coronavirus" (see also Lemasters et al. 2020; Lockwood 2021).

At the federal level, more systematic attempts were made to decarcerate with mixed success. In March 2020, Attorney General William Barr asked the Bureau of Prisons (BOP) to transfer older and medically vulnerable prisoners to home confinement if they were low risk and convicted of nonviolent crimes (Bagaric, Isham, and Svilar 2021). By April 3, 2020, only 552 prisoners had been released (Prescott, Pyle, and Starr 2020*a*). The CARES Act (2020) authorized federal prisons to release elderly prisoners and those convicted of nonviolent crimes to home confinement (Prison Policy Initiative 2022). Recognizing the limited facilities of the federal probation system, Barr also authorized the BOP to release prisoners to home confinement even if electronic monitoring was unavailable. However, his memo warned against "too liberal releases" and urged continued incarceration of the vast majority of prisoners sentenced for violent offenses (Prescott, Pyle, and Starr 2020*a*, para. 17).

Finally, the Trump Department of Justice announced that released individuals whose terms extended beyond the pandemic must be returned to prison (Bagaric, Isham, and Svilar 2021). The Biden administration rescinded that policy, giving discretion for sentences to be finished at home (Prison Policy Initiative 2022).

In all, between March 2020 and August 2022, over 46,000 federal prisoners were placed on home confinement for part of their sentence as a result of these initiatives (US Bureau of Prisons 2022a). The federal prison population dropped from 177,214 to 155,562 between the end of 2019 and the end of 2020 but had risen again to 158,162 as of August 2022 (US Bureau of Prisons 2022b). As Clear (2021, p. 1419) writes: "These numbers may seem large. They are not. . . . If the aim is to target people in prison who are elderly, infirm, or doing time for less serious crimes, there is plenty of room to release more people from confinement."

C. Impediments to Successful Decarceration

Reflecting back on the first 2 years of the pandemic, the question becomes "what happened to decarceration?" Given the perceived risk of COVID-19 to the public and the extreme protective measures taken in nearly every other sector in society, the lack of substantial decarceration of prisons raises considerable questions.

Stringent eligibility requirements for release initiatives were one major obstacle. Release schemes largely followed IASC (2020) recommendations concerning release of medically vulnerable and elderly prisoners and those nearing the ends of their sentences. However, as Prescott, Pyle, and Starr (2020a, 2020b) point out, two-thirds of people in prison over age 55 in the United States are serving long sentences for offenses considered to be "violent crimes." As such, the majority of older, at-risk prisoners were precluded from COVID-responsive release measures.

Another impediment concerns drug users. The UN Human Rights Office of the High Commissioner highlighted distinct risks faced by drug users because of chronic health problems and socioeconomic marginality and urged consideration of early release for people convicted of nonviolent drug offenses (OHCHR 2020a). Nonetheless, by June 2020, 25 percent of countries undertaking decarceration initiatives "explicitly excluded people incarcerated for drug offences" (HRI 2020, para. 5).

In addition to impeding decarceration efforts, this decision created racial disparities by deeming drug offenders to be riskier than white-collar offenders. In one analysis, Hager (2020) found that only 7 percent of African American prisoners were considered sufficiently low risk for release compared with 30 percent of Whites (non-US citizens with immigration-related offenses were ineligible). Likewise, the Council on Criminal Justice (2020, p. 3) observed that pandemic decarceration efforts in the United States "may have exacerbated some racial and ethnic disparities." As jail populations began to decrease in the early months of the pandemic, the disproportionate confinement of minorities increased (p. 3). Such biases were not limited to the United States. Miranda and colleagues (2021) found in Portugal that public opinion about decarceration was more favorable to early release of White than of Black prisoners. They conclude that documented racial disparities in policing and sentencing may also be "present in the early-release decisions, even when it represents an important measure to address the Covid-19 pandemic" (p. 10).

US policies governing compassionate release of disabled prisoners were also said to be "too narrowly drawn" and were administered "too stringently by the wardens, prosecutors, and judges" (Schotland 2021, sec. 1). Implementation of compassionate release required "ad hoc litigation" and depended too much on criteria for release applied to individuals. Compassionate release applicants usually had no right to counsel; outcomes too often depended on individual prisoners' resources. Nearly 98 percent of release applications by federal prisoners were denied; only 156 were approved (Neff and Blakinger 2020). Similar failings occurred in many countries. The São Paulo Court of Justice in Brazil, often called the "epicenter" of the pandemic in the Global South, for example, also ruled against the vast majority of compassionate release petitioners (Pires de Vasconcelos, Machado, and Wang 2020, p. 1473).

Issues also emerged concerning support and services for safe and secure reintegration of released prisoners. Portuguese reports highlighted that "dozens of inmates were simply given one day's notice and left at the prison gate, with their possessions in a handbag or a bin bag" with no means of transport and restricted public transport (Fróis 2020, p. 26). Fróis asks whether the deficiencies in implementation of release policies heightened COVID-19 risks for those released, "in effect abandoning rather than liberating them—in a global pandemic emergency" (p. 26). Lockdown measures outside of prisons created a "compromised community environment" for released prisoners including diminished reintegration services, lessened socioeconomic activity, and overwhelmed mental health and social security services (Shepherd and Spivak 2020, p. 59). These problems disproportionately affected particular groups, including homeless people and members of indigenous groups (Ricciardelli et al. 2021; Schneider 2021). UN recommendations urged that those released from prison during the pandemic should be provided support with housing and health care (IASC 2020, p. 4; OHCHR 2020a, para. 17). Releasing prisoners without addressing structural inequalities and service deficits can impede reintegration efforts (NASEM 2020).

Overall, implementation of decarceration was neither as widespread nor as efficient as it should have been. Globally, most states not only failed to prevent COVID-19 spread within prison systems but "also did little to prevent the transmission of the virus from prison and jail hotspots to nearby surrounding communities. . . . Ignoring, downplaying, and distorting this systematic failure left communities exposed" (Hooks and Sawyer 2020, para. 3). In the context of a global environment of unprecedented policy initiatives to reduce the spread of COVID, the failings of decarceration became all the more stark. Schotland (2021, sec. 8) concludes that "the neglect of prisoners during the pandemic reflects a combination of racism, classism, disablism and stigma" and that there was "no countervailing public policy justification" for incarceration in such dangerous conditions.

III. The COVID Lockdown

With only a small fraction of incarcerated populations released, prison administrations everywhere were faced with the challenge of containing a highly contagious and deadly disease under near impossible conditions (Pont et al. 2021; Dünkel, Harrendorf, and van Zyl Smit 2022). As in other workplace or residential environments, penal institutions introduced standard mitigation practices, including the use of lateral flow and COVID testing, enhanced sanitization, personal protective equipment, and, beginning in 2021, vaccination (Cloud et al. 2020; Mortaji et al. 2021). Prisons around the world sought to become "Covid responsive" in much the same way as previously they sought to achieve "gender responsivity" or "trauma responsivity" (Bloom, Owen, and Covington 2003; Durr 2020).

The delivery of these measures differed in quality and speed across jurisdictions and between individual prisons. For instance, in July 2021, the World Health Organization reported that more than 84 percent of Spanish prisoners had been fully vaccinated against COVID-19, but only 34.4 percent were vaccinated in Finland (WHO 2021). A number of studies suggest vaccine hesitancy played a role in low rates of uptake, particularly in some US states (but not in California; see Kwan et al. 2022). Prison populations are often overrepresented in clinical trials and, perhaps unsurprisingly, have been found to have high levels of medical mistrust (Chin et al. 2021; Stern at al. 2021).

The most controversial community mitigation measure in most contexts was the introduction of strict policies prohibiting social congregation. Public spaces from nightclubs to children's play parks were closed, and members of the public were urged (sometimes required) to stay in their homes. In what became known as the COVID-19 "lockdown," residents of most countries found their ability to socialize with others outside their household legally curtailed, with nearly unprecedented restrictions imposed on all aspects of social life, including congregating with outsiders inside one's own home. "Lockdowns," in the form of restrictions on out-of-cell time, swiftly became the heart of COVID-responsivity practices in prisons everywhere (Brandon and Dingwall 2022; Dünkel, Harrendorf, and van Zyl Smit 2022). In their comparative survey, Zeveleva and Nazif-Munoz (2022) found that all Council of Europe member states, as well as Belarus and Kazakhstan, implemented "lockdowns" of various severity in the first year of the pandemic. Essentially, prisons did what prisons do best: lock residents away from human contact. In thus section, we explore the "intended and unintended consequences" of these "strict medico-carceral measures" (Durnescu and Morar 2020, pp. 1144–45). We draw in particular on a recently completed case study of the effects of the COVID-19 lockdown in prisons in England and Wales (User Voice and Queen's University Belfast 2022).

A. Locking Down the Locked Up

Before the pandemic, 50,000–80,000 prisoners in the United States were held in solitary on a given day. During the pandemic, this increased by 500 percent to 300,000 (Cipriano 2021). Yet, even ordinary incarceration in the early months of the pandemic could be considered a form of solitary confinement. According to Rule 44 of the United Nations revised Standard Minimum Rules for the Treatment of Prisoners, known as the "Mandela Rules," solitary confinement is defined as confinement for at least 22 hours a day, without meaningful contact. The Mandela Rules proscribe the use of such confinement for more than 15 days at a time. Yet, initial research suggests that prisoners in much of the world were confined to their cells for 23 hours each day for months at a time at the beginning of the pandemic (Cooney 2021; Dünkel, Harrendorf, and van Zyl Smit 2022; Heard and Padfield 2022; Zeveleva and Nazif-Munoz 2022). Informal association time between prisoners, group counseling, workshops and classrooms, gym activity, religious services, family visits, and more were discontinued, and prisons were reduced to something akin to their nineteenth-century origins as places of isolation and solitude. Although this enforced social distancing almost certainly mitigated the spread of the COVID-19, saving lives, it is also unquestionable that "indefinite or prolonged solitary confinement is an inhumane or degrading form of treatment and, in its more extreme manifestations, a form of torture" (Mulgrew and van Zyl Smit 2022, p. 596).

Heard's (2020, 2022) comparative analysis of prison regimes, before and after the onset of the pandemic, provides a rare glimpse into what this change looked like in 10 countries (Australia, Brazil, England and Wales, Hungary, India, Kenya, the Netherlands, South Africa, Thailand, and the United States). Almost all suspended prison visitation for family and friends beginning in March 2020. Before the pandemic, prisoners in South Africa averaged around five visits per month. Those in the Netherlands and Australia averaged one per week, and those in Thailand reported meeting with visitors through an outdoor partition several times each week. For the first months of the pandemic, all visits essentially ended across the surveyed countries except in Thailand, where the time families were allowed was reduced from 20 to 10 minutes (Heard and Padfield 2022). Some jurisdictions sought to compensate for this dramatic shutting down of contact with the outside world. In the United States, the federal BOP facilitated 500 minutes of free calls each month for each prisoner (Federal Bureau of Prisons 2020). In the United Kingdom, in-cell telephones were installed in half of prisons (Heard 2020; Brandon and Dingwall 2022). This acknowledged the inherent difficulties in expecting dozens of prisoners safely to share a single pay phone, especially when each prisoner was allowed out of cell only for an hour (User Voice 2021). In addition, new technology that facilitated online family visits (known as "purple visits") was introduced in many facilities (House of Commons Justice Committee 2020).

Restrictions on visitation were not confined to family but also encompassed legal representatives. Prison-based research essentially came to a halt; thus, the voices of those in prison were largely absent from public debates (Pyrooz et al. 2020; Maycock and Dickson 2021). Of course, some studies captured the views of those who had loved ones in prison (Lockwood 2021; Minson 2021; McDonald et al. 2022), and others drew on data derived from letters and blogs written by prisoners (Armstrong et al. 2020; Prison Reform Trust 2020*a*; Fair Trials 2021; Sorge et al. 2021; Maycock 2022; McDonald et al. 2022). Prison inspections were also suspended in many jurisdictions (Dünkel, Harrendorf, and van Zyl Smit 2022), although in England and Wales the inspectorate carried out interviews with women, men, and children in six prisons between September 30 and November 5, 2020 (HMIP 2021). In 2020, the World Health Organization stated that the pandemic should not be used to prevent external inspection bodies and human rights agencies from obtaining access to prisons, yet research indicates that this recommendation was seldom followed. Charities, human rights agencies, and independent monitoring bodies were denied access in numerous jurisdictions (Heard 2021; Mulgrew and van Zyl Smit 2022).

Although prisoners have a right to the same medical care as those on the outside, this access was sharply curtailed in many jurisdictions during the first years of the COVID pandemic (Pont et al. 2021). Hutchings and Davies (2021) found that prisoners during the pandemic sometimes waited 14 weeks for a doctor's appointment, extending already long waiting times. In many jurisdictions, the suspension of group-based rehabilitation activities had implications for both mental health and progress toward parole release. Heard (2022, p. 627) argues that ending group therapeutic activities denied those in prison "the opportunity to demonstrate good behavior or rehabilitation and made it harder to prepare for release … because there would be nothing to inform the relevant risk assessments or recommendations."

Finally, the lockdown conditions were often elongated as a result of pandemic-related staffing shortages (Akiyama, Spaulding, and Rich 2020; Wang et al. 2020; Nowotny, Kapriske, and Brinkley-Rubenstein 2021; Pont et al. 2021; Vest et al. 2021). In some countries, understaffing and lack of experienced staff worsened conditions experienced by prisoners and resulted in violence, protests, hunger strikes, and riots (Heard and Padfield 2022). Riots were reported to have broken out in more than 22 prisons in Italy over a 2-day period in March 2020 (Sorge et al. 2021). In England, the pandemic caused massive turnover in prison staff with more leaving than could be hired, including the most experienced senior staff. Currently, around a third of officers have been in post for less than 3 years, compared to one in eight in 2010 (Cooney 2021). Staffing issues have also contributed to deteriorating health care with unavailability of prison escorts leading to missed appointments. Like the prisoners they work with, prison staff faced considerable health risks, including mental health risks; absentee levels in prison systems have been extremely high throughout the pandemic (Kothari et al. 2020).

B. Effects of the Lockdown

It is too early to assess the long-term consequences of the pandemic lockdown on the lives of those in prison. Emerging evidence suggests that the extreme isolation, cessation of visits, lack of meaningful activity, and deteriorating relationships with prison staff may be taking an immense toll on the mental health of prisoners (Johnson et al. 2021; Brandon and Dingwall 2022; Kim et al. 2022). Casey and colleagues (2021, p. 481) found: "The experience of lockdown was both traumatising and punitive for people who were already marginalised and subject to criminal justice control. ... In effect, the severity of sentences for people completing custodial sentences and community sentences increased. Crucially, both people in prison and people under supervision suffered extension to and exacerbation of the ways in which punishment suspends and disrupts their lives; their efforts to progress towards a life beyond punishment were often frustrated and stalled."

Prepandemic research suggests that incarceration itself is associated with a 45 percent increase in the odds of suffering major depression (Kessler et al. 2005; Schnittker, Massoglia, and Uggen 2012; Schnittker 2014). These effects are magnified by the experience of long-term solitary confinement, which has been found to have "often devastating psychological consequences" (Wildeman and Andersen 2020, p. 107; see also Smith 2006; Shalev 2011; Haney 2018). Incarcerated people who experience solitary confinement have higher rates of posttraumatic stress disorder (PTSD), self-harm, and suicide (Kaba et al. 2015) and experience long-lasting physical, neurological, and physical health problems (Smith 2006; Haney 2018; Luigi et al. 2020; Jahn et al. 2022). Wildeman and Andersen (2020) found that, compared with the general population, people subjected to solitary confinement in Norway were almost 10 times more likely to die within 5 years of release. Cloud and colleagues (2020, p. 2738) observe: "The hallmarks of solitary confinement—social isolation, physical idleness, and sensory deprivation—lead to immense psychological suffering and lasting trauma, and too often result in self-harm, violence, and suicide, even after only relatively short periods of time."

The cessation of visits from outside is also likely to undermine the precarious mental health of imprisoned people (Sorge et al. 2021). Research since the early 1990s suggests positive effects of family visits on a variety of outcomes for prisoners (Hairston 1988; La Vigne et al. 2005; May, Sharma, and Stewart 2008; Woo et al. 2016; De Claire and Dixon 2017; Turanovic and Tasca 2019). Research findings consistently show positive effects of visits on reduced symptoms of depression in female and adolescent prisoners and positive associations between visits and reduced rule-breaking behavior, reduced recidivism, and improved chances for survival in the community after release (La Vigne et al. 2005; De Claire and Dixon 2017). Hewson et al. (2021, p. 569) argue that the systematic elimination of visits "could lessen the use of social support for mitigating against and coping with mental distress, and the risk of suicide and self-harm. This scarcity of social support might make adjustment to prison more difficult, risking the use of maladaptive coping strategies." Furthermore, suspension of visits in many countries led to dramatic loss of access to essential items often brought in by family, such as medicine, food supplies, clothing, and sanitary products (Heard 2022; Bucerius and Sandberg 2022).

Ironically, the lockdown may have even exacerbated susceptibility to COVID-19. Novisky and colleagues (2021) argue that highly restrictive COVID-responsivity measures can increase vulnerability because of increased cortisol levels resulting from elevated levels of stress associated with isolation. In short, COVID responsivity as practiced in many parts of the world was achieved at considerable cost to the physical and mental health of prisoners. As Lachsz and Hurley (2021, p. 55) conclude: "In light of the well-documented harm that solitary confinement can cause, it is a practice that should be prohibited by law and must not form part of the response to COVID-19. Safer alternatives exist, like reducing the number of people detained in prisons."

IV. A Case Study of the Pandemic Lockdown in England and Wales

Before the onset of the pandemic, HM Prison Service of England and Wales was widely viewed to be in a state of crisis (Brennan 2020; Corker 2020). For a decade, prisons had faced dramatic budget cuts, staff shortages, poor infrastructure, and an overcrowded system that had nearly doubled in size from a population of 44,246 in 1993 (Ministry of Justice 2013) to 83,023 at the end of 2019 (HMPPS 2020). Levels of violence, suicide, and self-harm were at or near record levels in the years leading up to the pandemic (HMPPS 2022*b*). The former Conservative Party minister for prisons Rory Stewart compared the prisons he visited (unfavorably) to war zones he had worked in during his military experience: "Violence had tripled to 30,000 assaults a year, every institution was overcrowded, filthy and rat- and drug-infested" (Cohen 2022, para. 11).

The first COVID-19 infection was reported in HM Prison Manchester in March 2020. Within 2 months, 21 prisoners and seven prison staff died at the high security facility (Heard 2020; Heard and Padfield 2022). Overall, just over 200 people in prisons in England and Wales died having tested positive for COVID-19 between the onset of the pandemic and July 31, 2022 (Ministry of Justice 2022). It could have been much worse. In April 2020, modeling conducted by HM Prison and Probation Service and Public Health England suggested that 800–2,000 more prisoners might die as a result of the pandemic if no action were taken to reduce contact in prisons (Townsend et al. 2020; HMIP 2021).

As terrifying as that possibility was, it also represented an opportunity to make dramatic changes to a prison system that was already in a desperate state. As the chair of the Prison Officers Association for England and Wales stated in August 2020, "Returning to chaos is not an option" (Fairhurst 2020, sec. 2). In other words, British prisons could have followed the lead of other European countries, such as France, Switzerland, and Portugal, and initiated swift decarceration, even seeking to return numbers to 1990s levels in order to close dysfunctional and unsanitary Victorian era prisons.

Decarceration efforts in England and Wales were, however, shambolic. Only a fraction of 1 percent of prisoners were released (Grierson 2020*a*). Scotland and Northern Ireland, which have separate and independent prison systems, fared considerably better (Morrison and Graham 2022; O'Connell et al. 2022). In England and Wales, the prison population did drop from 83,023 at the end of 2019 to 79,092 by the end of 2021 (HMPPS 2020, 2022*b*). For the most part, this resulted from falling crime rates during the COVID period and from courts running at lower capacity, rather than from explicit efforts at decarceration. Indeed, the prison population is now rising again, with 81,274 prisoners in the last week of August 2022 (HMPPS 2022*a*). Moreover, these same court backlogs led to delays in processing cases of remanded defendants, resulting in periods of incarceration longer than the normal "custody time limit" of 6 months, leaving remand imprisonment rates at the highest level since 2010 (Dimsdale and Saunders 2022*b*).

Instead of decarceration, the prison system's primary strategy for mitigating the spread of the virus was a drastic 23-hour lockdown, involving a suspension of visits and almost all out-of-cell activities including workshops, group therapy, and education (House of Commons Justice Committee 2020). These severe conditions were mitigated in some but not all facilities by the introduction of in-cell telephones and technology allowing for online "purple visits" with family members (House of Commons Justice Committee 2020; Brandon and Dingwall 2022; Heard and Padfield 2022).

Although criticized by prison reform groups (e.g., Prison Reform Trust 2020*b*; User Voice 2021), the lockdown was described as a "blessing in disguise" by the head of the Prison Officer Association and some politicians (UK Justice Committee 2020). Proponents touted, in particular, huge drops in levels of violence among prisoners and against prison staff (BBC 2020). These drops from historic highs in 2019 were, however, both predictable and meaningless given that prisoners were allowed out of their cells for only 1 hour per day. More surprisingly, the initial statistics collected by prisons indicated no immediate increase in officially recorded self-harming behaviors in men's prisons in 2020 as might have been expected. (Notably, women's prisons experienced a significant increase in both 2020 and 2021 [HMPPS 2022*a*].) The Prison Officers Association chief observed that "the government should listen to the experts in prisons—the staff—who say the situation is now safer and more stable" as a result of the draconian lockdown (BBC 2020).

In those early days of the pandemic, the government had little choice about whom to listen to, as no external observers were allowed inside the prisons except eventually HM inspectorate of prisons. As a result, for the first several months of the pandemic, prisoners' voices were seldom heard in the media or elsewhere (Prison Reform Trust 2020*a*; User Voice 2021). On September 18, 2020, the *Guardian* newspaper invited submissions: "Tell us: What are pandemic conditions like in UK prisons?" A website where responders could upload their stories was provided, although almost no one in British prisons had access to the internet to respond.

In this context, we and our partner organization User Voice succeeded with a funding application to the UK's Economic and Social Research Council to develop a participatory action research project in 10 prisons (Fine and Torre 2006). Participatory research methods, in which "research participants are regarded as potential collaborators in the co-production of knowledge and become co-researchers" seek to "fundamentally change the dynamic of research" (Schubotz 2019, p. 3). One of our initial premises was more pragmatic: if outside researchers could not get into prisons, then perhaps people in prison could be trained to conduct their own study of prison conditions. This is what we did. During summer 2021, we delivered an accredited 2-day "peer research methods" course to 99 prison residents from 10 facilities, outlining the basics of participant observation, interviewing, and peer surveying. These peer researchers became the "eyes and ears" of the prison, writing field notes, doing one-on-one interviews, and collecting over 1,400 completed surveys from fellow prisoners. We returned to three of the prisons to analyze the anonymized results in collaboration with the peer research volunteers.

The findings painted a striking portrait of the pandemic lockdown from the perspective of the imprisoned. At the time interviews were conducted (summer 2021), nearly 60 percent of survey respondents said they had not had a single in-person visit since the pandemic began. Eighty-five percent said they were out of their cells for an hour or less per day during the first 6 months of the pandemic. Over 80 percent said they were still out of their cells for less than 2 hours per day at the time of the interviews in 2021. Moreover, few agreed with the Prison Officers Association assessment that the lockdown was a "blessing in disguise." Only one in five agreed that the lockdown reduced violence and bullying. Just 8 percent agreed that "this prison is listening to the concerns of residents." Most importantly, over two-thirds agreed that "mental health has never been worse in this prison."

To confirm these assessments, we included two validated mental health measures in the peer survey: the Patient Health Questionnaire-9 (PHQ-9) measure of depression and the Generalised Anxiety Disorder-7 (GAD-7) used to screen for PTSD and related conditions. These two scales are widely used as screening tools in care settings and in epidemiological surveys. They have been used extensively in studies both of the general public during the pandemic and in prison settings before the pandemic, thus allowing for multiple comparisons. A PHQ-9 score between 5 and 9 points indicates "mild depression," 10–14 points indicates "moderate depression," 15–19 points indicates "moderately severe depression," and 20 or more points indicates "severe depression."

The mean PHQ-9 score for our sample of prisoners during the pandemic was 13.9—at the high end of "moderate depression" and more than four times higher than the general population norm of 2.91 (Kocalevent, Hinz, and Brähler 2013). For context, it is useful to compare this score to research findings during the pandemic when mental health suffered throughout most sectors of society. In two studies of the general public in Britain during the pandemic, Shevlin and colleagues (2022) found a mean PHQ-9 score of 5.37, whereas Jia and colleagues (2020) found PHQ-9 scores averaging 7.69. It is also useful to compare our findings to research in prisons before the pandemic. In a large-scale prevalence study of 1,205 male prisoners in England and Wales conducted in 2019, Butcher and colleagues (2021) found that around 20.7 percent scored over 15 on the PHQ-9 (i.e., in the "severe" depression categories). Nearly half (49 percent) of our sample scored over 15.

The statistics on the measurement of anxiety disorder (GAD-7) are equally stark. Like the PHQ-9, the GAD-7 is calculated by aggregating scores on self-reported measures of symptoms such as inability to sleep and inability to control one's worries. The measure is also used for screening three other common anxiety disorders—panic disorder, social anxiety disorder, and PTSD. A score of 10 or more represents the generally accepted cutoff point for identifying potential cases of anxiety disorder, with a score of 15 and above suggesting severe anxiety. The mean GAD-7 score for our sample was 10.67 compared to the population norm of 2.95. In studies of the wider British population, Shevlin and colleagues (2022) found mean GAD-7 scores of 5.15, and Jia and colleagues (2020) found GAD-7 scores of 7.69. The median score for our prison sample was 11, indicating that just over half were reporting symptoms consistent with PTSD and over one-third (34.9 percent) were in the "severe anxiety" category of 15 and up. In a prison survey conducted in 2019, Butcher et al. (2021) found that only around a third of British prisoners (31.4 percent) scored above 10, and only 18 percent above 15. In our research during the lockdown, 52.5 percent scored above 10, and 34.4 percent scored over 15. These comparisons suggest a considerable deterioration in prisoners' mental health over the lockdown period, with measures of severe anxiety nearly doubling.

Although adverse mental health effects of solitary confinement are well established (Shalev 2011; Haney 2018), seeing statistics like these for a sample of over 1,400 ordinary prisoners across 10 British prisons is truly striking. The consequences of this mental health crisis may only be beginning to be understood. In 2021, British prisons saw a record 371 deaths in prison, of which 86 were self-inflicted, representing a 28 percent increase from the previous year (HMPPS 2022b). Remand prisoners accounted for 40 percent of self-inflicted deaths (Dimsdale and Saunders 2022a) despite being only 16 percent of prisoners.

V. Prisons after the Pandemic

The COVID-19 pandemic has exposed the gaps, deficits, and inadequacies of carceral institutions globally in failing to respond adequately to a major public health risk. Despite previous outbreaks ranging from typhus to SARS, few prison systems could be said to have been "sufficiently prepared for a large-scale public health crisis" in 2020 (Council on Criminal Justice 2020, p. 5). At the same time, the prioritization of in-prison mitigation over decarceration strategies demonstrated the robustness and near impenetrability of carceral logic internationally.

In 2020–21, the unthinkable became reality across the world. Whole cities and town centers essentially closed. Schools and workplaces shut their doors; weddings, funerals, sporting events, and other gatherings were cancelled or held without spectators; regulations prohibited socializing in groups and controlled nearly every aspect of social life. In this remarkable and unprecedented context, the prison regime not only remained firm but became more extreme in its punitive form.

This is particularly remarkable considering the historic lack of evidence that prisons actually reduce recidivism. Petrich and colleagues' (2021) meta-analysis of 116 existing studies of the effects of custodial sanctions found no evidence that incarceration reduced recidivism above and beyond community penalties. The authors conclude that "incarceration cannot be justified on the grounds it affords public safety by decreasing recidivism" (p. 353). As such, available evidence suggests that decarceration efforts could be expanded "with no increased threat to public safety" (Byrne et al. 2022, p. 18). For instance, recidivism data for the 7,251 US federal prisoners released under the First Step Act (2018) through September 2020 suggest a reoffending rate of only 11.3 percent (OAG 2020; see also Wegel, Wardak, and Meyer 2022). In August 2022, the US BOP reported that of the 11,000 people released early from federal prisons as party of the CARE Act, only 442 had been returned to prison, and only 17 of those were returned for committing new crimes (most of which were drug related; Johnson 2022). As Clear (2021, p. 1423) writes, fears of a "crime wave" emerging from early release programs appear extremely exaggerated on the basis of existing evidence: "It should be plain that the effects of a handful of moderately earlier releases on public safety are bound to be negligible."

In short, the COVID-19 pandemic proved that mass decarceration and excarceration is feasible, even on a global scale. Even if that process failed to reach its full potential, reducing prison populations by 5 percent worldwide can be seen as something of a success. At the very least, proactive efforts in a minority of prison systems demonstrate that mechanisms are available to address overcrowding and implement decarceration, illuminating pathways for real change (Wegel, Wardak, and Meyer 2022). For example, after struggling for decades to reduce overcrowding in its prison system, Kenya used the impetus provided by COVID to implement rapid decarceration in 2020—described as a "silver lining in the Covid-19 cloud" (Deche and Bosire 2020, p. 921).

However, that these mechanisms exist and many countries nonetheless struggled to decarcerate even chronically overcrowded prison systems represents a warning sign for those hoping the pandemic would be "the catalyst" for mass decarceration (Bagaric, Isham, and Svilar 2021, p. 124). The turn toward a heightened form of solitary confinement occurred notwithstanding the well-documented health risks associated with this kind of forced isolation (Cloud et al. 2015). Even successful decarceration efforts may prove temporary, with reincarceration emerging in numerous countries (HRW 2020a). In India, by December 2020, an estimated 90 percent of those released during COVID had been returned to prison (Dhanuka 2022). Following release of around 35,000 prisoners, Brazilian prisons experienced a 19 percent increase in its prison population by July 2020 (Rodriguez and Khoury 2022). More recent increases can also be seen in Portugal (Rodrigues and Pinto 2022) and France (Herzog-Evans 2022). These returns to the status quo cast real doubt on any expectation that the pandemic will foster "sustained structural changes vital for future pandemic preparedness and public health" (Reinhart and Chen 2020, p. 1412). Herzog-Evans (2022, p. 220) writes: "It has quickly become clear that there will be no Utopian 'day after.' Indeed, no reform is currently being planned to try and draw upon the potentially positive dimensions of the crisis or to learn from the mistakes which have been made." Considering that the contagion risks exposed in the past 2 years are not unique to COVID-19 but have been "reproduced across time and space" (Novisky et al. 2021, p. 1638), this suggests a troubling trend for future outbreaks.

Still, the lessons learned from the COVID pandemic can help inform future decarceration efforts. Amy Fettig (2022, p. 419) of the Sentencing Project, for instance, argues that US efforts were "largely incompetent, inhumane and contrary to public health policy" but nonetheless provide "a roadmap for policy priorities and legal reform in our ongoing need to decarcerate."

Finally, if there is a silver lining, globally, it is that the pandemic may have alerted the wider public health and medical communities to the risks penal institutions pose to public safety. Sivashanker and colleagues (2020, pp. 1–2), in the *British Medical Journal*, observe: "Despite the clear health risks, healthcare organisations have not broadly organised to advance decarceration as a public safety measure. . . . Covid-19 is a call to healthcare workers and organizations to help tackle the deeper sociopolitical root causes of disease, and to intervene before the harm is done. That call is nowhere clearer than in our broken criminal justice system. It's time to pick up our loudspeakers and insist on caring for all." History suggests that such voices can be crucial in shaping penal futures (Simon 2013).

REFERENCES

ACLU (American Civil Liberties Union). 2020. "Mass COVID-19 Model Finds Nearly 100,000 More Deaths than Current Estimates, due to Failures to Reduce Jails." New York: ACLU. https://www.aclu.org/sites/default/files/field_document/aclu_covid19-jail-report_2020-8_1.pdf.

Akiyama, Matthew J., Anne C. Spaulding, and Josiah D. Rich. 2020. "Flattening the Curve for Incarcerated Populations: Covid-19 in Jails and Prisons." *New England Journal of Medicine* 382(22):2075–77.

Altibi, Ahmed M., Bhargava Pallavi, Hassan Liaqat, Alexander A. Slota, Radhika Sheth, Lama Al Jebbawi, Matthew E. George, Allison LeDuc, Enas Abdallah, Luke R. Russell, Saniya Jain, Nariné Shirvanian, Ahmad Masri, and Vivek Kak. 2021. "Characteristics and Comparative Clinical Outcomes of Prisoner versus Non-prisoner Populations Hospitalized with Covid-19." *Scientific Reports* 11(1):1–9.

APM Research Lab. 2021. "The Color of Coronavirus: COVID-19 Deaths by Race and Ethnicity in the U.S." American Public Media, March 5. https://www.apmresearchlab.org/covid/deaths-by-race 03 05-21.

Arambulo, Hannah Kristianne Marie, Caroline Therese Sahagun, and Hazel T. Biana. 2021. "Covid-19: Back to Healthcare Basics in Philippine Prisons." *Journal of Public Health* 43:342–43.

Armstrong, Sarah, et al. 2020. "Left Out and Locked Down: Impacts of COVID-19 for Marginalised Groups in Scotland." Project report. Glasgow: University of Glasgow. http://eprints.gla.ac.uk/236416/.

Arnold, Catharine. 2018. *Pandemic 1918: The Story of the Deadliest Influenza in History*. London: O'Mara.

Bagaric, Mirko, Peter Isham, and Jennifer Svilar. 2021. "The Increased Exposure to Coronavirus (Covid-19) for Prisoners Justifies Early Release: And the Wider Implications of This for Sentencing—Reducing Most Prison Terms due to the Harsh Incidental Consequences of Prison." *Pepperdine Law Review* 48:121–74.

Barnert, Elizabeth, Cyrus Ahalt, and Brie Williams. 2020. "Prisons: Amplifiers of the Covid-19 Pandemic Hiding in Plain Sight." *American Journal of Public Health* 110:964–66.

Baussano, Iacopo, Brian G. Williams, Paul Nunn, Marta Beggiato, Ugo Fedeli, and Fabio Scano. 2010. "Tuberculosis Incidence in Prisons: A Systematic Review." *PLoS Medicine* 7(12):1–10.

BBC. 2020. "Coronavirus: Curbs 'A Blessing in Disguise for Prisons.'" BBC, October 8. https://www.bbc.co.uk/news/uk-politics-54387023.

Belenko, Steven, Richard Dembo, Michael Copenhaver, Matthew Hiller, Holly Swan, Carmen Albizu Garcia, Daniel O'Connell, Carrie Oser, Frank Pearson, and Jennifer Pankow. 2016. "HIV Stigma in Prisons and Jails: Results from a Staff Survey." *AIDS and Behavior* 20(1):71–84.

Bloom, Barbara, Barbara Owen, and Stephanie Covington. 2003. *Gender-Responsive Strategies: Research, Practice, and Guiding Principles for Women Offenders*. Washington, DC: US Bureau of Prisons, National Institute of Corrections. https://nicic.gov/gender-responsive-strategies-research-practice-and-guiding -principles-women-offenders.

Braithwaite, Isobel, Chantal Edge, Dan Lewer, and Jake Hard. 2021. "High Covid-19 Death Rates in Prisons in England and Wales, and the Need for Early Vaccination." *Lancet Respiratory Medicine* 9:569–70.

Brandon, Avril, and Gavin Dingwall. 2022. *Minority Ethnic Prisoners and the COVID-19 Lockdown: Issues, Impacts and Implications*. Bristol: Policy.

Braun, M. Miles, Benedict I. Truman, Barbara Maguire, George T. DiFerdinando Jr., Gary Wormser, Raymond Broaddus, and Dale L. Morse. 1989. "Increasing Incidence of Tuberculosis in a Prison Inmate Population: Association with HIV Infection." *JAMA* 261:393–97.

Brelje, Andrea Berkemeier, and Debra A. Pinals. 2021. "Provision of Health Care for Prisoners during the Covid-19 Pandemic: An Ethical Analysis of Challenges and Summary of Select Best Practices." *International Journal of Prisoner Health* 17:194–205.

Brennan, Pauline K. 2020. "Responses Taken to Mitigate COVID-19 in Prisons in England and Wales." *Victims and Offenders* 15(7–8):1215–33.

Brinkley-Rubinstein, Lauren, Katherine Lemasters, Phuc Nguyen, Kathryn Nowotny, David Cloud, and Alexander Volfovsky. 2021. "The Association between Intersystem Prison Transfers and COVID-19 Incidence in a State Prison System." *PLOS ONE* 16(8):1–6.

Bronson, Jennifer, and Anne E. Carson. 2019. "Prisoners in 2017." Washington, DC: US Department of Justice, Bureau of Justice Statistics. https://www.bjs.gov /content/pub/pdf/p17.pdf.

Bucerius, Sandra, and Sveinung Sandberg. 2022. "Women in Prisons." In *Prisons and Prisoners*, edited by Michael Tonry and Sandra Bucerius. Vol. 51 of *Crime and Justice: A Review of Research*, edited by Michael Tonry. Chicago: University of Chicago Press.

Butcher, Elizabeth, Christopher Packham, Marie Williams, Joanne Miksza, Adarsh Kaul, Kamlesh Khunti, and Richard Morriss. 2021. "Screening Male Prisoners for Depression and Anxiety with the PHQ-9 and GAD-7 at NHS

Healthcheck: Patterns of Symptoms and Caseness Threshold." *BMC Psychiatry* 21(1):1–11.

Byrne, James, Don Hummer, Sabrina S. Rapisarda, and Kimberly R. Kras. 2022. "The United States Government's Response to COVID-19 Outbreaks in Federal, State, and Local Corrections." In *The Impact of COVID-19 on Prison Conditions and Penal Policy*, edited by Frieder Dünkel, Stefan Harrendorf, and Dirk van Zyl Smit. London: Routledge.

Carson, E. Anne. 2021*a*. "Federal Prisoner Statistics Collected under the First Step Act, 2021." Washington, DC: US Department of Justice, Bureau of Justice Statistics. https://bjs.ojp.gov/library/publications/federal-prisoner-statistics -collected-under-first-step-act-2021.

Carson, E. Anne. 2021*b*. "Prisoners in 2020—Statistical Tables." Washington, DC: US Department of Justice, Bureau of Justice Statistics. https://bjs.ojp.gov/library /publications/prisoners-2020-statistical-tables.

Carson, E. Anne, and William J. Sabol. 2016. *Aging of the State Prison Population, 1993–2013*. Washington, DC: US Department of Justice, Bureau of Justice Statistics.

Casey, Ryan, Fergus McNeill, Betsy Barkas, Neil Cornish, Caitlin Gormley, and Marguerite Schinkel. 2021. "Pervasive Punishment in a Pandemic." *Probation Journal* 68:476–92.

Chaddock, Don. 2018. "Unlocking History: 1918 Flu Pandemic Puts Prison Medical Staff to Test." California Department of Corrections and Rehabilitation, October 18. https://www.cdcr.ca.gov/insidecdcr/2018/10/18/1918-flu -pandemic-puts-prison-medical-staff-to-test/.

Chin, Elizabeth T., David Leidner, Theresa Ryckman, Yiran E. Liu, Lea Prince, Fernando Alarid-Escudero, Jason R. Andrews, Joshua A. Salomon, Jeremy D. Goldhaber-Fiebert, and David M. Studdert. 2021. "Covid-19 Vaccine Acceptance in California State Prisons." *New England Journal of Medicine* 385(4):374–76.

Cipriano, Andrew. 2021. "Solitary Increased by 500 Percent during Pandemic." The Crime Report, October 6. https://thecrimereport.org/2021/10/06/solitary -increased-by-500-during-pandemic-report/.

Clear, Todd R. 2021. "COVID-19 and Mass Incarceration." *Rutgers University Law Review* 72:1417–33.

Cloud, David H., Cyrus Ahalt, Dallas Augustine, David Sears, and Brie Williams. 2020. "Medical Isolation and Solitary Confinement: Balancing Health and Humanity in US Jails and Prisons during COVID-19." *Journal of General Internal Medicine* 35(9):2738–42.

Cloud, David H., Ernest Drucker, Angela Browne, and Jim Parsons. 2015. "Public Health and Solitary Confinement in the United States." *American Journal of Public Health* 105(1):18–26.

Cohen, Nick. 2022. "How Many More Charlie Todds Must There Be before Our Prisons Are Reformed?" *Guardian*, January 29. https://www.theguardian.com /commentisfree/2022/jan/29/how-many-more-charlie-todds-must-there-be -before-prisons-reformed?fbclid=IwAR3tXWb6cYlXWhKi8CvZu49 -sCyzFq4MbvivkmrC8uNi2o5E6MFeWmKywhA.

Collica-Cox, Kimberly, and Louis Molina. 2020. "A Case Study of the West-chester County New York's Jail Response to Covid-19: Controlling Covid While Balancing Service Needs for the Incarcerated—a National Model for Jails." *Victims and Offenders* 15:1305–16.

Commissioner for Human Rights. 2020. "Covid-19 Pandemic: Urgent Steps Are Needed to Protect the Rights of Prisoners in Europe." Statement, April 6. Strasbourg: Council of Europe. https://www.coe.int/en/web/commissioner/-/covid-19-pandemic-urgent-steps-are-needed-to-protect-the-rights-of-prisoners-in-europe.

Cooney, Francesca. 2021. "Prisons after Lockdown: Restrictions, Regimes and Re-covery." London: Prisoners Education Trust. https://www.prisonerseducation.org.uk/2021/07/prisons-after-lockdown-restrictions-regimes-and-recovery/.

Corker, Richard. 2020. "Expert Report: Covid-19 and Prisons in England and Wales." London: Howard League for Penal Reform. https://howardleague.org/wp-content/uploads/2020/04/2020_04_01_COKER_Report_HL_PRT.pdf.

Council on Criminal Justice. 2020. "Experience to Action: Reshaping Criminal Justice after Covid-19." Washington, DC: Council on Criminal Justice. https://assets.foleon.com/eu-west-2/uploads-7e3kk3/41697/final_report_-_designed.83f2289da58b.pdf.

Council of Europe. 2022. "Council of Europe's Annual Penal Statistics: Covid-19 Pandemic Helped Reduce Europe's Prison Population." Newsroom, April 5. Strasbourg: Council of Europe. https://www.coe.int/en/web/portal/-/council-of-europe-s-annual-penal-statistics-covid-19-pandemic-helped-reduce-europe-s-prison-population.

CPT (European Committee for the Prevention of Torture and Inhuman or Degrading Treatment or Punishment). 2020. "Statement of Principles Relat-ing to the Treatment of Persons Deprived of Their Liberty in the Context of the COVID-19 Pandemic." March 20. Strasbourg: Council of Europe. https://rm.coe.int/16809cfa4b.

Davis, Angela. 2003. *Are Prisons Obsolete?* New York: Seven Stories.

Deche, Mercy, and Conrad Bosire. 2020. "The Silver Lining in the Covid-19 Cloud: An Appraisal of Accelerated Prison Decongestion in Kenya." *Victims and Offenders* 15:921–32.

De Claire, Karen, and Louise Dixon. 2017. "The Effects of Prison Visits from Family Members on Prisoners' Well-Being, Prison Rule Breaking, and Recid-ivism: A Review of Research since 1991." *Trauma, Violence, and Abuse* 18(2):185–99.

Denney, Matthew G. T., and Ramon Garibaldo Valdez. 2021. "Compounding Racialized Vulnerability: Covid-19 in Prisons, Jails, and Migrant Detention Centers." *Journal of Health Politics, Policy and Law* 46:861–87.

Dhanuka, M. 2022. "India." In *The Impact of COVID-19 on Prison Conditions and Penal Policy*, edited by Frieder Dünkel, Stefan Harrendorf, and Dirk van Zyl Smit. London: Routledge.

Dimsdale, Connie, and Tom Saunders. 2022a. "Delay and Uncertainty Is Killing People as Remand Inmates Account for 40 Percent of Suicides in Prison."

Inews, January 10. https://inews.co.uk/news/delay-and-uncertainty-is-killing
-people-as-remand-inmates-account-for-40-per-cent-of-suicides-in-prison
-1380167.

Dimsdale, Connie, and Tom Saunders. 2022*b*. "'The System Has Collapsed':
Covid Backlog Sees Number of People on Remand in Prison at Highest Level
since 2010." *Inews*, January 10. https://inews.co.uk/news/covid-court-backlog
-remand-prisoners-at-highest-level-since-2010-1368038.

Dolan, Kate, et al. 2016. "Global Burden of HIV, Viral Hepatitis, and Tuberculosis in Prisoners and Detainees." *Lancet* 388:1089–102.

Drucker, Ernest. 2013. *A Plague of Prisons: The Epidemiology of Mass Incarceration
in America*. New York: New Press.

Drucker, Ernest, ed. 2018. *Decarcerating America: From Mass Punishment to Public
Health*. New York: New Press.

Dünkel, Frieder, Stefan Harrendorf, and Dirk van Zyl Smit, eds. 2022. *The Impact of COVID-19 on Prison Conditions and Penal Policy*. London: Routledge.

Durnescu, Ioan, and Ioana Morar. 2020. "An Examination of the Romanian Prison
System during the Covid-19 Pandemic: Are 'Zero Cases' Possible?" *Victims
and Offenders* 15:1133–47.

Durr, Patricia. 2020. "Trauma-Informed Work with People in Contact with the
Criminal Justice System." September 2020. Suffolk: Clinks. https://www.clinks.org
/sites/default/files/2020-09/Clinks%20Evidence%20Library%20Trauma
-informed%20work%20with%20people%20in%20contact%20with%20the
%20criminal%20justice%20system%202020.pdf.

Edge, Chantal, Jake Hard, Lucy Wainwright, Donna Gipson, Verity Wainwright,
and Jenny Anita Mehay. 2021. "Covid-19 and the Prison Population." Working
paper, November. London: Health Foundation. https://www.health.org.uk
/publications/covid-19-and-the-prison-population.

Fair, Helen, and Roy Walmsley. 2021. "World Prison Population List," 13th ed.
World Prison Brief. London: Birkbeck College, University of London, Institute for Criminal Policy Studies. https://www.prisonstudies.org/sites/default
/files/resources/downloads/world_prison_population_list_13th_edition.pdf.

Fair Trials. 2021. "Locked Up in Lockdown: Life on Remand during the Pandemic." Fair Trials, June 24. https://www.fairtrials.org/articles/publications
/locked-in-up-lockdown/.

Fairhurst, Mark. 2020. "National Chair: Returning to Chaos Is Not an Option." London: Prison Officers Association. https://www.poauk.org.uk/news-events/news
-room/posts/2020/august/national-chair-returning-to-chaos-is-not-an-option/.

Farr, Paddy. 2021. "Toward a Critical Race Analysis of the Covid-19 Crisis in
US Carceral Institutions." *Critical Social Policy* 42(2):177–96.

Federal Bureau of Prisons. 2020. "Federal Bureau of Prisons COVID-19 Action Plan." March 13. Washington, DC: Federal Bureau of Prisons. https://
www.bop.gov/resources/news/20200313_covid-19.jsp.

Fettig, Amy. 2022. "Can COVID-19 Teach Us How to End Mass Incarceration?" *University of Miami Law Review* 76:419–46.

Fine, Michelle, and María Elena Torre. 2006. "Intimate Details." *Action Research*
4:253–69.

Franco-Paredes, Carlos, et al. 2020. "Covid-19 in Jails and Prisons: A Neglected Infection in a Marginalized Population." *PLoS Neglected Tropical Diseases* 14:1–4.

Fróis, Catarina. 2020. "Covid-19 Pandemic and Social Distancing in Prisons."
Anthropology Today 36:25–26.

Getaz, L. 2019. "Better Control of Infectious Diseases." *Prison-Info* 2:20–23.

Gough, Ethan, Mirjam C. Kempf, Laura Graham, Marvin Manzanero, Edward W.
Hook, Al Bartolucci, and Eric Chamot. 2010. "HIV and Hepatitis B and C
Incidence Rates in US Correctional Populations and High Risk Groups: A
Systematic Review and Meta-analysis." *BMC Public Health* 10 (177):1–14.

Grierson, Jamie. 2020*a*. "Early-Release Scheme for Prisoners in England and
Wales to End." *Guardian*, August 19. https://www.theguardian.com/society
/2020/aug/19/prisons-inspector-england-wales-warns-of-mental-health-problems
-from-severe-coronavirus-restrictions.

Grierson, Jamie. 2020*b*. "Prison Release Schemes Almost Impossible to Deliver,
Says Watchdog." *Guardian*, May 31. https://www.theguardian.com/society/2020
/may/31/prison-release-schemes-close-to-impossible-to-deliver-says-watchdog
-coronavirus.

Grierson, Jamie. 2020*c*. "UK Coronavirus Prison Plan on Hold after Six Inmates
Freed in Error." *Guardian*, April 18. https://www.theguardian.com/society
/2020/apr/18/uk-coronavirus-prison-plan-suspended-after-six-mistakenly
-released.

Hager, Eli. 2020. "How Bill Barr's Covid-19 Prisoner Release Plans Could Favor White People." March 28. New York: Marshall Project. https://www
.themarshallproject.org/2020/03/28/how-bill-barr-s-covid-19-prisoner-release
-plan-could-favor-white-people.

Hairston, Creasie Finney. 1988. "Family Ties during Imprisonment: Do They
Influence Future Criminal Activity?" *Federal Probation* 52(1):48–52.

Haney, Craig. 2018. "The Psychological Effects of Solitary Confinement: A Systematic Critique." In *Crime and Justice: A Review of Research*, vol. 47, edited by
Michael Tonry. Chicago: University of Chicago Press.

Haugebrook, Sabrina, Kristen M. Zgoba, Tina Maschi, Keith Morgen, and
Derek Brown. 2010. "Trauma, Stress, Health, and Mental Health Issues
among Ethnically Diverse Older Adult Prisoners." *Journal of Correct Health
Care* 16:220–29.

Hawks, Laura, Steffie Woolhandler, and Danny McCormick. 2020. "Covid-19
in Prisons and Jails in the United States." *JAMA Internal Medicine* 180:1041–
42.

Heard, Catherine. 2020. "Commentary: Assessing the Global Impact of the
Covid-19 Pandemic on Prison Populations." *Victims and Offenders* 15:848–
61.

Heard, Catherine. 2021. "Locked in and Locked Down—Prison Life in a Pandemic: Evidence from Ten Countries." London: Institute for Crime and Justice
Policy Research, Birbeck, University of London. https://www.prisonstudies
.org/sites/default/files/resources/downloads/locked_in_and_locked_down.pdf.

Heard, Catherine. 2022. "Prison Population Rates before and during the Pandemic: Lessons from COVID-19 about Overincarceration and Its Consequences

for Health." In *The Impact of COVID-19 on Prison Conditions and Penal Policy*, edited by Frieder Dünkel, Stefan Harrendorf, and Dirk van Zyl Smit. London: Routledge.

Heard, Catherine, and Nicola Padfield. 2022. "England and Wales." In *The Impact of COVID-19 on Prison Conditions and Penal Policy*, edited by Frieder Dünkel, Stefan Harrendorf, and Dirk van Zyl Smit. London: Routledge.

Herzog-Evans, Martine. 2022. "France." In *The Impact of COVID-19 on Prison Conditions and Penal Policy*, edited by Frieder Dünkel, Stefan Harrendorf, and Dirk van Zyl Smit. London: Routledge.

Hewson, Thomas, Louise Robinson, Najat Khalifa, Jake Hard, and Jennifer Shaw. 2021. "Remote Consultations in Prison Mental Healthcare in England: Impacts of Covid-19." *BJPsych Open* 7(2):e49.

HMIP (Her Majesty's Inspectorate of Prisons). 2021. "What Happens to Prisoners in a Pandemic?" London: HMIP. https://www.justiceinspectorates.gov.uk/hmi prisons/wp-content/uploads/sites/4/2021/02/What-happens-to-prisoners-in-a -pandemic.pdf.

HMPPS (Her Majesty's Prison and Probation Service). 2020. "Prison Population Figures, 2019." London: Ministry of Justice. https://www.gov.uk/govern ment/statistics/prison-population-figures-2019.

HMPPS (Her Majesty's Prison and Probation Service). 2022a. "Prison Population Figures, 2021." London: Ministry of Justice. https://www.gov.uk/government /statistics/prison-population-figures-2021.

HMPPS (Her Majesty's Prison and Probation Service). 2022b. "Safety in Custody Statistics, England and Wales: Deaths in Prison Custody to December 2021, Assaults and Self-Harm to September 2021." National statistics. London: Ministry of Justice. https://www.gov.uk/government/statistics/safety-in-custody -quarterly-update-to-september-2021/safety-in-custody-statistics-england-and -wales-deaths-in-prison-custody-to-december-2021-assaults-and-self-harm-to -september-2021.

Hooks, Gregory, and Wendy Sawyer. 2020. "Mass Incarceration, COVID-19 and Community Spread." Prison Policy Initiative. https://www.prisonpolicy.org /reports/covidspread.html.

House of Commons Justice Committee. 2020. *Coronavirus (Covid-19): The Impact on Prisons: Government Response to the Committee's Fourth Report of Session, 2019–21.* London: House of Commons. https://committees.parliament.uk/publications /4074/documents/40487/default/.

HRI (Harm Reduction International). 2020. "Covid-19, Prisons and Drug Policy: Global Scan March–June 2020." June 17. London: HRI. https://www.hri.global /files/2020/07/10/HRI_-_Prison_and_Covid_briefing_final.pdf.

HRW (Human Rights Watch). 2020a. "Announced Releases of Detainees in the Justice System due to Covid-19." https://www.hrw.org/sites/default/files /media_2020/05/announced_releases_detainees_covid19.pdf.

HRW (Human Rights Watch). 2020b. "Covid-19 Prisoner Releases Too Few, Too Slow." May 27. https://www.hrw.org/news/2020/05/27/covid-19-prisoner -releases-too-few-too-slow.

HRW (Human Rights Watch). 2022. "UN: Make Reporting on Covid-19 in Prisons Mandatory." April 22. https://www.hrw.org/news/2022/04/22/un-make-reporting-covid-19-prisons-mandatory.

Hutchings, Rachel, and Miranda Davies. 2021. "Towards a Better Understanding of Health Care Access Challenges for Prisoners." London: Nuffield Trust. https://www.nuffieldtrust.org.uk/files/2021-10/prisoner-health-literature-review.pdf.

Hwang, Seung Joon, Min Ju Kim, and Weldon E. Havins. 2021. "Decreasing Inmate Populations to Mitigate Effects of Covid-19 in State Prisons." *Journal of Legal Medicine* 41:20–21.

IACHR (Inter-American Commission on Human Rights). 2020*a*. "IACHR Concerned about Specific Risks Faced by Persons Deprived of Liberty in the Americas during the COVID-19 Pandemic." Press release, September 9. Washington, DC: Organization of American States. https://www.oas.org/en/iachr/media_center/PReleases/2020/212.asp.

IACHR (Inter-American Commission on Human Rights). 2020*b*. "Pandemic and Human Rights in the Americas." Resolution 1/2020. Washington, DC: Organization of American States. https://www.oas.org/en/iachr/decisions/pdf/Resolution-1-20-en.pdf.

IASC (Inter-agency Standing Committee). 2020. "IASC Interim Guidance on COVID-19: Focus on Persons Deprived of Their Liberty." London: IASC. https://interagencystandingcommittee.org/other/iasc-interim-guidance-covid-19-focus-persons-deprived-their-liberty.

Jahn, Jaquelyn L., Nicolette Bardele, Jessica T. Simes, and Bruce Western. 2022. "Clustering of Health Burdens in Solitary Confinement: A Mixed-Methods Approach." *SSM—Qualitative Research in Health* 2:100036. https://doi.org/10.1016/j.ssmqr.2021.100036.

Jia, Ru, Kieran Ayling, Trudie Chalder, Adam Massey, Elizabeth Broadbent, Carol Coupland, and Kavita Vedhara. 2020. "Mental Health in the UK during the COVID-19 Pandemic: Cross-Sectional Analyses from a Community Cohort Study." *BMJ Open* 10(9):e040620.

Jiménez, Monik C., Tori L. Cowger, Lisa E. Simon, Maya Behn, Nicole Cassarino, and Mary T. Bassett. 2020. "Epidemiology of Covid-19 among Incarcerated Individuals and Staff in Massachusetts Jails and Prisons." *JAMA Network Open* 3:1–4.

Johnson, Carrie. 2022. "Released during COVID, Some People Are Sent Back to Prison with Little or No Warning." National Public Radio, August 22. https://www.npr.org/2022/08/22/1118132380/released-during-covid-some-people-are-sent-back-to-prison-with-little-or-no-warn.

Johnson, Luke, Kerry Gutridge, Julie Parkes, Anjana Roy, and Emma Plugge. 2021. "Scoping Review of Mental Health in Prisons through the Covid-19 Pandemic." *BMJ Open* 11:e046547.

Kaba, Fatos, et al. 2015. "Disparities in Mental Health Referral and Diagnosis in the New York City Jail Mental Health Service." *American Journal of Public Health* 105(9):1911–16.

Kessler, Ronald C., Patricia Berglund, Olga Demler, Robert Jin, Kathleen R. Merikangas, and Ellen E. Walters. 2005. "Lifetime Prevalence and Age-of-Onset

Distributions of DSM-IV Disorders in the National Comorbidity Survey Replication." *Archives of General Psychiatry* 62:593–603.

Kim, Hannah, Emily Hughes, Alice Cavanagh, Emily Norris, Angela Gao, Susan J. Bondy, Katherine E. McLeod, Tharsan Kanagalingam, and Fiona G. Kouyoumdjian. 2022. "The Health Impacts of the COVID-19 Pandemic on Adults Who Experience Imprisonment Globally: A Mixed Methods Systematic Review." *PLOS ONE* 17(5):1–24.

Kinner, Stuart A., Jesse T. Young, Kathryn Snow, Louise Southalan, Daniel Lopez-Acuña, Carina Ferreira-Borges, and Éamonn O'Moore. 2020. "Prisons and Custodial Settings Are Part of a Comprehensive Response to Covid-19." *Lancet Public Health* 5:e188–e189.

Klein, Michael, Melissa A. Kowalski, Youngki Woo, Courtney Solis, Maria Mendoza, Mary K. Stohr, and Craig Hemmens. 2022. "The Novel Coronavirus and Enforcement of the New Separate System in Prisons." *Criminal Justice Policy Review* 33(2):206–30.

Kocalevent, Rüya-Daniela, Andreas Hinz, and Elmar Brähler. 2013. "Standardization of the Depression Screener Patient Health Questionnaire (PHQ-9) in the General Population." *General Hospital Psychiatry* 35(5):551–55.

Kothari, Radha, Andrew Forrester, Neil Greenberg, Natasha Sarkissian, and Derek K. Tracy. 2020. "COVID-19 and Prisons: Providing Mental Health Care for People in Prison, Minimising Moral Injury and Psychological Distress in Mental Health Staff." *Medicine, Science and the Law* 60(3):165–68.

Kwan, Ada, David Sears, Stephano Bertozzi, and Brie Williams, eds. 2022. "California's State Prisons during the COVID-19 Pandemic: A Report by the CalPROTECT Project." San Francisco: CalPROTECT. https://amend.us /wp-content/uploads/2022/05/2022-0501-CalPROTECT-Report.pdf.

Lachsz, Andreea, and Monique Hurley. 2021. "Why Practices That Could Be Torture or Cruel, Inhuman and Degrading Treatment Should Never Have Formed Part of the Public Health Response to the COVID-19 Pandemic in Prisons." *Current Issues in Criminal Justice* 33(1):54–68.

La Vigne, Nancy G., Rebecca L. Naser, Lisa E. Brooks, and Jennifer L. Castro. 2005. "Examining the Effect of Incarceration and In-Prison Family Contact on Prisoners' Family Relationships." *Journal of Contemporary Criminal Justice* 21(4):314–35.

Leibowitz, Abigail I., Mark J. Siedner, Alexander C. Tsai, and Amir M. Mohareb. 2021. "Association between Prison Crowding and Covid-19 Incidence Rates in Massachusetts Prisons, April 2020–January 2021." *JAMA Internal Medicine* 181:1315–21.

Lemasters, Katherine, Erin McCauley, Kathryn Nowotny, and Lauren Brinkley-Rubinstein. 2020. "Covid-19 Cases and Testing in 53 Prison Systems." *Health and Justice* 8(1):1–6.

Link, Bruce G., and Jo Phelan. 1995. "Social Conditions as Fundamental Causes of Disease." *Journal of Health and Social Behavior* 35:80–94.

Lockwood, Kelly. 2021. "'Lockdown's Changed Everything': Mothering Adult Children in Prison in the UK during the COVID-19 Pandemic." *Probation Journal* 689(4):458–75.

Lofgren, Eric, Kristian Lum, Aaron Horowitz, Brooke Madubuonwu, and Nina Fefferman. 2020. "The Epidemiological Implications of Incarceration Dynamics in Jails for Community, Corrections Officer, and Incarcerated Population Risks from COVID-19." MedRxiv. https://doi.org/10.1101/2020.04.08.20058842.

Luigi, Mimosa, Laura Dellazizzo, Charles-Éduardo Giguère, Marie Helene Goulet, and Alexandra Dumais. 2020. "Shedding Light on 'the Hole': A Systematic Review and Meta-analysis on Adverse Psychological Effects and Mortality following Solitary Confinement in Correctional Settings." *Front Psychiatry* 11:840.

Malloy, Giovanni S. P., Lisa Puglisi, Margaret L. Brandeau, Tyler D. Harvey, and Emily A. Wang. 2021. "Effectiveness of Interventions to Reduce Covid-19 Transmission in a Large Urban Jail: A Model-Based Analysis." *BMJ Open* 11:e042898.

Marquez, Neal, Julie A. Ward, Kalind Parish, Brendan Saloner, and Sharon Dolovich. 2021. "Covid-19 Incidence and Mortality in Federal and State Prisons Compared with the US Population, April 5, 2020, to April 3, 2021." *JAMA* 326:1865–67.

Maruschak, Laura M., Marcus Berzofsky, and Jennifer Unangst. 2015. "Medical Problems of State and Federal Prisoners and Jail Inmates, 2011–12." Washington, DC: US Department of Justice, Bureau of Justice Statistics. https://bjs.ojp.gov/content/pub/pdf/mpsfpji1112.pdf.

May, Chris, Nalini Sharma, and Duncan Stewart. 2008. *Factors Linked to Reoffending: A One-Year Follow-Up of Prisoners Who Took Part in the Resettlement Surveys 2001, 2003 and 2004.* London: Ministry of Justice.

Maycock, Matthew. 2022. "'Covid-19 Has Caused a Dramatic Change to Prison Life': Analysing the Impacts of the Covid-19 Pandemic on the Pains of Imprisonment in the Scottish Prison Estate." *British Journal of Criminology* 62(1):21–33.

Maycock, Matthew, and Graeme Dickson. 2021. "Analysing the Views of People in Custody about the Management of the COVID-19 Pandemic in the Scottish Prison Estate." *International Journal of Prisoner Health* 17(3):320–34.

McDonald, Alysha D., Luca Berardi, Justin E. C. Tetrault, Kevin D. Haggerty, and Sandra M. Bucerius. 2022. "More of the Same, Only Worse: COVID-19 and the Administrative Burdens Facing Loved Ones of Incarcerated Men." *British Journal of Criminology* 20:1–17.

Ministry of Justice. 2013. "Story of the Prison Population: 1993–2012 England and Wales." London: Ministry of Justice. https://assets.publishing.service.gov.uk/government/uploads/system/uploads/attachment_data/file/218185/story-prison-population.pdf.

Ministry of Justice. 2022. "HM Prison and Probation Service COVID-19 Official Statistics." London: Ministry of Justice. https://www.gov.uk/government/collections/hm-prison-and-probation-service-covid-19-statistics-monthly.

Minson, Shona. 2021. "The Impact of COVID-19 Prison Lockdowns on Children with a Parent in Prison." Oxford: University of Oxford, Centre for Criminology. https://childhub.org/sites/default/files/library/attachments/the_impact_of_covid-19_prison_lockdowns_on_children_with_a_parent_in_prison.pdf.

Miranda, Mariana P., Rui Costa-Lopes, Gonçalo Freitas, and Catarina L. Carvalho. 2021. "Early Release from Prison in Time of Covid-19: Determinants of Unfavourable Decisions towards Black Prisoners." *PLOS ONE* 16:e0252319.

Morales, Mark. 2021. "Inmates at NYC's Rikers Island Jail in the Midst of 'Emerging Crisis' Related to Omicron Surge." CNN, December 22. https://kyma.com/news/2021/12/22/inmates-at-nycs-rikers-island-jail-in-the-midst-of-emerging-crisis-related-to-omicron-surge/.

Morrison, Katrina, and Hannah Graham. 2022. "Scotland." In *The Impact of COVID-19 on Prison Conditions and Penal Policy*, edited by Frieder Dünkel, Stefan Harrendorf, and Dirk van Zyl Smit. London: Routledge.

Mortaji, Parisa, Michaele Francesco Corbisiero, Michael A. Vrolijk, Andrés F. Henao-Martínez, and Carlos Franco-Paredes. 2021. "Chronicle of Jails and Prisons Covid-19 Deaths Foretold." *American Journal of the Medical Sciences* 361:801–2.

Mulgrew, Roisin, and Dirk van Zyl Smit. 2022. "International Human Rights and COVID-19 in Prisons: Medical Isolation and Independent Oversight." In *The Impact of COVID-19 on Prison Conditions and Penal Policy*, edited by Frieder Dünkel, Stefan Harrendorf, and Dirk van Zyl Smit. London: Routledge.

Murphy, Philip J. 2021. "Unlocking the Means of Covid-19 Spread from Prisons to Outside Populations." *American Journal of Public Health* 111:1392–94.

NASEM (National Academies of Science, Engineering, and Medicine). 2020. *Decarcerating Correctional Facilities during COVID-19: Advancing Health, Equity, and Safety*. Washington, DC: National Academies.

Natoli, Lauren Jeanne, Kathy Linh Vu, Adam Carl Sukhija-Cohen, Whitney Engeran-Cordova, Gabriel Maldonado, Scott Galvin, William Arroyo, and Cynthia Davis. 2021. "Incarceration and COVID-19: Recommendations to Curb COVID-19 Disease Transmission in Prison Facilities and Surrounding Communities." *International Journal of Environmental Research and Public Health* 18:9790. https://doi.org/10.3390/ijerph18189790.

Neff, Joseph, and Keri Blakinger. 2020. "Thousands of Sick Federal Prisoners Sought Compassionate Release: 98 Percent Were Denied." July 10. New York: Marshall Project. https://www.themarshallproject.org/2020/10/07/thousands-of-sick-federal-prisoners-sought-compassionate-release-98-percent-were-denied.

Nellis, Ashley. 2017. "Still Life: America's Increasing Use of Life and Long-Term Sentences." Washington, DC: Sentencing Project. https://www.sentencingproject.org/publications/still-life-americas-increasing-use-life-long-term-sentences/.

Novisky, Meghan A. 2018. "Avoiding the Runaround: The Link between Cultural Health Capital and Health Management among Older Prisoners." *Criminology* 56(4):643–78.

Novisky, Meghan A., Kathryn M. Nowotny, Dylan B. Jackson, Alexander Testa, and Michael G. Vaughn. 2021. "Incarceration as a Fundamental Social Cause of Health Inequalities: Jails, Prisons and Vulnerability to COVID-19." *British Journal of Criminology* 61(6):1630–46.

Nowotny, Kathryn M., Seide Kapriske, and Lauren Brinkley-Rubenstein. 2021. "Risk of Covid-19 Infection among Prison Staff in the United States." *BMC Public Health* 21:1–8.

OAG (Office of the Attorney General). 2020. "The Attorney General's First Step Act Section 3634 Annual Report." Washington, DC: US Department of Justice, OAG. https://www.ojp.gov/Attorney-Generals-First-Step-Act-Section-3634-Annual-Report-December-2020.

O'Connell, Ciara, Mary Rogan, Michelle Martyn, and Shadd Maruna. 2022. "Ireland North and South." In *The Impact of COVID-19 on Prison Conditions and Penal Policy*, edited by Frieder Dünkel, Stefan Harrendorf, and Dirk van Zyl Smit. London: Routledge.

Parsons, Todd L., and Lee Worden. 2021. "Assessing the Risk of Cascading COVID-19 Outbreaks from Prison-to-Prison Transfers." *Epidemics* 37:100532. https://doi.org/10.1016/j.epidem.2021.100532.

Penal Reform International. 2022. "Global Prison Trends 2022." London: Penal Reform International. https://cdn.penalreform.org/wp-content/uploads/2022/05/GPT2022-Exec-summary-EN.pdf.

Petrich, Damon M., Travis C. Pratt, Cheryl Lero Jonson, and Francis T. Cullen. 2021. "Custodial Sanctions and Reoffending: A Meta-analytic Review." In *Crime and Justice: A Review of Research*, vol. 50, edited by Michael Tonry. Chicago: University of Chicago Press.

Phelan, Jo C., and Bruce G. Link. 2015. "Is Racism a Fundamental Cause of Inequalities in Health?" *Annual Review of Sociology* 41:311–30.

Pires de Vasconcelos, Natalia, Maíra Rocha Machado, and Daniel Wei Liang Wang. 2020. "COVID-19 in Prisons: A Study of Habeas Corpus Decisions by the São Paulo Court of Justice." *Revista de Administração Pública* 54:1472–85.

Pitts, Wayne J., and Christopher S. Inkpen. 2020. "Assessing the Effects of COVID-19 in Prisons in the Northern Triangle of Central America." *Victims and Offenders* 15(7–8):1044–61.

Pont, Jörg, Stefan Enggist, Heino Stöver, Stéphanie Baggio, Laurent Gétaz, and Hans Wolff. 2021. "Covid-19: The Case for Rethinking Health and Human Rights in Prisons." *American Journal of Public Health* 111:1081–85.

Prescott, J. J., Benjamin Pyle, and Sonja B. Starr. 2020*a*. "It's Time to Start Releasing Some Prisoners with Violent Records." *Slate News*, April 13. https://slate.com/news-and-politics/2020/04/combat-covid-release-prisoners-violent-cook.html.

Prescott, J. J., Benjamin Pyle, and Sonja B. Starr. 2020*b*. "Understanding Violent-Crime Recidivism." *Notre Dame Law Review* 95(4):1643–98.

Presidential COVID-19 Health Equity Task Force. 2021. "Final Report and Recommendations." Washington, DC: US Department of Health and Human Services, Office of the Assistant Secretary for Health.

Prison Policy Initiative. 2022. "The Most Significant Criminal Justice Policy Changes from the COVID-19 Pandemic." Northampton, MA: Prison Policy Initiative. https://www.prisonpolicy.org/virus/virusresponse.html.

Prison Reform Trust. 2020*a*. "Coronavirus." CAPPTIVE: Covid-19 Action Prisons Project. London: Prison Reform Trust. http://prisonreformtrust.org.uk/project/coronavirus/.

Prison Reform Trust. 2020*b*. "PRT and Howard League Letter to Robert Buckland—Covid-19 and Prisons: The Next Phase." London: Prison Reform Trust. https://prisonreformtrust.org.uk/prt-and-howard-league-letter-to-robert-buckland-covid-19-and-prisons-the-next-phase/.

Prost, Stephanie Grace, Meghan A. Novisky, Leah Rorvig, Nick Zaller, and Brie Williams. 2021. "Prisons and Covid-19: A Desperate Call for Gerontological Expertise in Correctional Health Care." *Gerontologist* 61:3–7.

Pyrooz, David C., Ryan M. Labrecque, Jennifer J. Tostlebe, and Bert Useem. 2020. "Views on COVID-19 from Inside Prison: Perspectives of High-Security Prisoners." *Justice Evaluation Journal* 3(2):294–306.

Reinhart, Eric. 2021. "Mass Incarceration Has Worsened Pandemic." *Jacobin*, February 6. https://jacobinmag.com/2021/06/mass-incarceration-covid-19-pandemic-decarceration-safety-health-prisons.

Reinhart, Eric, and Daniel L. Chen. 2020. "Incarceration and Its Disseminations: Covid-19 Pandemic Lessons from Chicago's Cook County Jail." *Health Affairs* 39:1412–18.

Reutter, David. 2010. "Swine Flu Widespread in Prisons and Jails but Deaths Are Few." *Prison Legal News*, February 15. https://www.prisonlegalnews.org/news/2010/feb/15/swine-flu-widespread-in-prisons-and-jails-but-deaths-are-few/.

Ricciardelli, Rosemary, Sandra Bucerius, Justin Tetrault, Ben Crewe, and David Pyrooz. 2021. "Correctional Services during and beyond COVID-19." *Facets* 69(1):490–516.

Rodrigues, Anabela Miranda, and Inés Horta Pinto. 2022. "Portugal." In *The Impact of COVID-19 on Prison Conditions and Penal Policy*, edited by Frieder Dünkel, Stefan Harrendorf, and Dirk van Zyl Smit. London: Routledge.

Rodrigues, Ellen, and Eduardo Khoury. 2022. "Brazil." In *The Impact of COVID-19 on Prison Conditions and Penal Policy*, edited by Frieder Dünkel, Stefan Harrendorf, and Dirk van Zyl Smit. London: Routledge.

Sawyer, Wendy, and Peter Wagner. 2022. "Mass Incarceration: The Whole Pie 2022." Northampton, MA: Prison Policy Initiative. https://www.prisonpolicy.org/reports/pie2022.html.

Schneider, Luisa T. 2021. "Let Me Take a Vacation in Prison before the Streets Kill Me! Rough Sleepers' Longing for Prison and the Reversal of Less Eligibility in Neoliberal Carceral Continuums." *Punishment and Society*. https://doi.org/10.1177/14624745211010222.

Schnittker, Jason. 2014. "The Psychological Dimensions and the Social Consequences of Incarceration." *Annals of the American Academy of Political and Social Science* 651:122–38.

Schnittker, Jason, Michael Massoglia, and Christopher Uggen. 2012. "Out and Down: Incarceration and Psychiatric Disorders." *Journal of Health and Social Behavior* 53:448–64.

Schotland, Sara. 2021. "Let Them Go! Compassionate Release for Disabled Prisoners with Chronic Health Conditions during the Covid-19 Public Health Emergency." *Disability Studies Quarterly* 41(3). https://doi.org/10.18061/dsq.v41i3.

Schubotz, Dirk. 2019. *Participatory Research: Why and How to Involve People in Research*. London: Sage.

Shalev, Sharon. 2011. "Solitary Confinement and Supermax Prisons: A Human Rights and Ethical Analysis." *Journal of Forensic Psychology Practice* 11(2–3):151–83.

Shepherd, Stephane, and Benjamin L. Spivak. 2020. "Reconsidering the Immediate Release of Prisoners during Covid-19 Community Restrictions." *Medical Journal of Australia* 2(13):58–59.

Shevlin, Mark, et al. 2022. "Measurement Invariance of the Patient Health Questionnaire (PHQ-9) and Generalized Anxiety Disorder Scale (GAD-7) across Four European Countries during the COVID-19 Pandemic." *BMC Psychiatry* 22(1):1–9.

Simon, Jonathan. 2013. "The Return of the Medical Model: Disease and the Meaning of Imprisonment from John Howard to *Brown v. Plata*." *Harvard Civil Rights-Civil Liberties Law Review* 48(1):217–56.

Sims, Kaitlyn M., Jeremy Foltz, and Marin Elisabeth Skidmore. 2021. "Prisons and Covid-19 Spread in the United States." *American Journal of Public Health* 111:1534–41.

Sivashanker, Karthik, Jessie Rossman, Andrew Resnick, and Donald M. Berwick. 2020. "Covid-19 and Decarceration." *British Medical Journal* 369:1–2. https://www.bmj.com/content/bmj/369/bmj.m1865.full.pdf.

Smith, Peter Scharff. 2006. "The Effects of Solitary Confinement on Prison Inmates: A Brief History and Review of the Literature." *Crime and Justice* 34(1):441–528.

Sorge, Antonia, Federica Bassanini, Jennifer Zucca, and Emanuela Saita. 2021. "'Fear Can Hold You, Hope Can Set You Free': Analysis of Italian Prisoner Narrative Experience of the COVID-19 Pandemic." *International Journal of Prisoner Health* 17(3):406–23.

Stanley, Leo L. 1919. "Influenza at San Quentin Prison, California." *Public Health Reports (1896–1970)* 34:996–1008.

Stern, Marc F., Alexandra M. Piasecki, Lara B. Strick, Poornima Rajeshwar, Erika Tyagi, Sharon Dolovich, Priti R. Patel, Rena Fukunaga, and Nathan W. Furukawa. 2021. "Willingness to Receive a COVID-19 Vaccination among Incarcerated or Detained Persons in Correctional and Detention Facilities: Four States, September–December 2020." *Morbidity and Mortality Weekly Report* 70(13):473–77.

Strassle, Camila, and Benjamin E. Berkman. 2020. "Prisons and Pandemics." *San Diego Law Review* 57:1083–125.

Toblin, Robin L., and Liesl M. Hagan. 2021. "Covid-19 Case and Mortality Rates in the Federal Bureau of Prisons." *American Journal of Preventive Medicine* 61:20–23.

Tonry, Michael. 2016. *Sentencing Fragments: Penal Reform in America, 1975–2025*. New York: Oxford University Press.

Townsend, Ellen, Emma Nielsen, Rosie Allister, and Sarah A. Cassidy. 2020. "Key Ethical Questions for Research during the Covid-19 Pandemic." *Lancet Psychiatry* 7:381–83.

Turanovic, Jillian J., and Melinda Tasca. 2019. "Inmates' Experiences with Prison Visitation." *Justice Quarterly* 36(2):287–322.

OHCHR (Office of the High Commissioner for Human Rights). 2020a. "Statement by the UN Expert on the Right to Health on the Protection of People Who Use Drugs during the COVID-19 Pandemic." Geneva: OHCHR.

OHCHR (Office of the High Commissioner for Human Rights). 2020*b*. "Urgent Action Needed to Prevent Covid-19 'Rampaging through Places of Detention'—Bachelet." Geneva: OHCHR. https://www.ohchr.org/en/statements/2020/03/urgent-action-needed-prevent-covid-19-rampaging-through-places-detention.

UK Justice Committee. 2020. *Oral Evidence: COVID-19: The Impact on Prison, Probation and Court Systems*. HC 299, June 23. London: UK Justice Committee. https://committees.parliament.uk/oralevidence/565/html/.

UNODC (United Nations Office on Drugs and Crime). 2015. "United Nations Standard Minimum Rules for the Treatment of Prisoners (the Nelson Mandela Rules)." UN Doc A/RES/70/175 (17 December 2015) annex. Vienna: UNDOC. https://www.unodc.org/documents/justice-and-prison-reform/Nelson_Mandela_Rules-E-ebook.pdf.

UNODC (United Nations Office on Drugs and Crime). 2021. "Mitigating the Disruptive Impact of Infection Prevention and Control Measures in Prisons: Core Principles and Recommendations." COVID-19 Guidance Note. Austria: UNODC. https://www.unodc.org/res/justice-and-prison-reform/nelsonmandelarules-GoF_html/COVID_19_Guidance_Note_IPC_ebook.pdf.

US Bureau of Prisons. 2022*a*. "Frequently Asked Questions Regarding Potential Inmate Home Confinement in Response to the COVID-19 Pandemic." Washington, DC: US Department of Justice, Bureau of Prisons. https://www.bop.gov/coronavirus/faq.jsp.

US Bureau of Prisons. 2022*b*. "Population Statistics." September 1. Washington, DC: US Department of Justice, Bureau of Prisons. https://www.bop.gov/mobile/about/population_statistics.jsp#bop_pop_table.

User Voice. 2021. "The User Voice of Lockdown." London: User Voice. https://www.uservoice.org/wp-content/uploads/2020/07/The-user-voice-of-lockdown.pdf.

User Voice and Queen's University Belfast. 2022. *Coping with Covid in Prison: The Impact of the Prisoner Lockdown*. London: User Voice. https://www.uservoice.org/wp-content/uploads/2022/08/User-Voice-QUB-Coping-with-Covid.pdf.

Valway, Sarah E., Sonia B. Richards, Joan Kovacovich, Robert B. Greifiger, Jack T. Crawford, and Samuel W. Dooley. 1994. "Outbreak of Multi Drug-Resistant Tuberculosis in a New York State Prison, 1991." *American Journal of Epidemiology* 140:113–22.

Vera Institute of Justice. 2022. "People in Prison in Winter 2021–22." New York: Vera Institute of Justice. https://www.vera.org/downloads/publications/People_in_Prison_in_Winter_2021-22.pdf.

Vest, Noel, Oshea Johnson, Kathryn Nowotny, and Lauren Brinkley-Rubinstein. 2021. "Prison Population Reductions and Covid-19: A Latent Profile Analysis Synthesizing Recent Evidence from the Texas State Prison System." *Journal of Urban Health: Bulletin of the New York Academy of Medicine* 98:53–58.

Wang, Jiao, Wenjing Yang, Lijun Pan, John S. Ji, Jin Shen, Kangfeng Zhao, Bo Ying, Xianliang Wang, Liubo Zhang, Ling Wang, and Xiaoming Shi. 2020. "Prevention and Control of Covid-19 in Nursing Homes, Orphanages, and Prisons." *Environmental Pollution* 266:1–6. https://doi.org/10.1016/j.envpol.2020.115161.

Wegel, Melanie, Sabera Wardak, and Darleen Jennifer Meyer. 2022. "Special Challenges in Dealing the COVID-19 Pandemic in Swiss Prisons." *SAGE Open.* https://doi.org/10.1177/21582440221079789.

WHO (World Health Organization). 2021. "Europe Shows High Rates of COVID-19 Vaccination in Prisons." News release, July 15. Geneva: WHO.

Wildeman, Christopher, and Lars H. Andersen. 2020. "Solitary Confinement Placement and Post-release Mortality Risk among Formerly Incarcerated Individuals: A Population-Based Study." *Lancet Public Health* 5(2):e107–e113.

Williams, Brie A., James S. Goodwin, Jacques Baillargeon, Cyrus Ahalt, and Louise C. Walter. 2012. "Addressing the Aging Crisis in U.S. Criminal Justice Health Care." *Journal of the American Geriatrics Society* 60:1150–56.

Woo, Youngki, Mary K. Stohr, Craig Hemmens, Faith Lutze, Zachary Hamilton, and Ok-Kyung Yoon. 2016. "An Empirical Test of the Social Support Paradigm on Male Inmate Society." *International Journal of Comparative and Applied Criminal Justice* 40(2):145–69.

Young, L. C., D. E. Dwyer, M. Harris, Z. Guse, V. Noel, and M. H. Levy. 2005. "Summer Outbreak of Respiratory Disease in an Australian Prison due to an Influenza A/Fujian/411/2002(H3N2)-Like Virus." *Epidemiology and Infection* 133:107–12.

Zeveleva, Olga, and José Ignacio Nazif-Munoz. 2022. "Covid-19 and European Carcerality: Do National Prison Policies Converge When Faced with a Pandemic?" *Punishment and Society* 24(4):642–66.

Robert D. Crutchfield

The Peculiar Journey: Race, Racism, and Imprisonment in American History

ABSTRACT

"The problem of the twentieth century is the problem of the color-line" wrote W. E. B. Du Bois in *The Souls of Black Folk*. That remains true in twenty-first-century America, especially in criminal justice systems generally and particularly in prisons. Racial disparities in sentencing and in imprisonment have declined slightly from historic peaks in the 1980s and 1990s but remain stubbornly high. Differential criminal justice system treatment of Blacks and Whites has changed form since the Civil War but endured as convict labor, prison farms, imprisonment rate disparities, contemporary tough-on-crime laws, and police practices that target members of minority groups, places they frequent, and behaviors for which they are disproportionately often arrested. In earlier times, differential treatment was often openly invidious. In more recent times it is nominally color-blind but produces similarly skewed results. We need to understand why and how differential treatment of Black people has persisted through a century and a half of fundamental changes in criminal justice system policies and practices and how this has happened within the context of shifting notions of what race is and what constitutes racism.

Any number of books and articles on race in America begin with W. E. B. Du Bois's words in *The Souls of Black Folk* (2015), "The problem of the twentieth century is the problem of the color-line" (see, e.g., Anderson and Massey 2001; Lee and Bean 2007; Appiah 2015). As important as that

Robert D. Crutchfield is professor emeritus of sociology, University of Washington.

Electronically published October 6, 2022

Crime and Justice, volume 51, 2022.
https://doi.org/10.1086/722510

line is, it is useful to consider the complete opening paragraph of his chapter 2:

> The problem of the twentieth century is the problem of the color-line—the relation of the darker to the lighter races of men in Asia and Africa, in America and the islands of the sea. It was a phase of this problem that caused the Civil War; and however much they who marched South and North in 1861 may have fixed on the technical points, of union and local autonomy as shibboleth, all nevertheless knew, as we know, that the question of Negro slavery was the real cause of the conflict. Curious it was, too, how this deeper question ever forced itself to the surface despite effort and disclaimer. No sooner had Northern armies touched Southern soil than this old question, newly guised, sprang from the earth—What shall be done with Negroes? Peremptory military commands this way and that, could not answer the query; the Emancipation Proclamation seemed but to broaden and intensify the difficulties; and the War Amendments made the Negro problems of to-day. (Du Bois 2015, p. 7)

So it was when Du Bois wrote in 1903, and so it is two decades into the twenty-first century as the United States confronts problems of police killings of Black people, disproportionate imprisonment of people of color, and mass incarceration. In few spheres is it more obvious that America continues to struggle with the question, "What shall be done with Negroes?" than in relation to crime and justice and especially to imprisonment. Central to debates about race and justice, even when some assert that race is irrelevant—"justice is blind after all" they say—are our conceptions of what "race" means and what constitutes racism.

There have been two important intellectual changes concerning race since the United States opened its first penitentiaries in the early nineteenth century. Together they highlight a fundamental tension between perceptions of and ongoing racial disparities in American imprisonment. First, we have come to understand that race is a social construct not a biological fact. Second, we understand now that there are important differences between classic or traditional racism—old-fashioned bigotry and prejudice—and contemporary "color-blind" racism. The former was overt and explicitly expressed in word and deed. The latter occurs when people are aware of historical and contemporary inequities based on race but evaluate Blacks and other people of color as if all people play on an equal playing field.

Why "The Peculiar Journey" as a title? In 1956, historian Kenneth Stampp published *The Peculiar Institution: Slavery in the Ante-bellum South*

(Stampp 1956). He rejected the view of slavery promulgated by some historians, slavers, plantation owners, and others who characterized antebellum slavery as a benign institution that benefited Blacks. Description of slavery as the "peculiar institution" is said to have begun with John C. Calhoun, the then respected but now reviled member of Congress and successively vice president to John Quincy Adams and Andrew Jackson. The experience of slavery has affected everything (or nearly everything) about the experience of Black people in America. And, it has especially profoundly affected Black imprisonment. As with those who defended slavery, the predominant view of American prisons from their inception until very recently has been that, even if harsh, they are for the most part, fair, just, and appropriate and that Black people confined in them are there justly.[1] Many people to this day hold that view. But, as was true of slavery, imprisonment in America is confounded by Whites' negative views of Black people, association of African Americans with violence and savagery, and belief in a need for control.

To be sure, conceptions of race and views about Blackness have changed since the early nineteenth century when Eastern State Penitentiary was founded in Philadelphia and Auburn Penitentiary opened its doors in New York. This peculiar intellectual journey follows the evolution in the United States in thinking about Black people, their history, and their circumstances in contemporary America and, with that, about race and imprisonment. Racism has changed. In America's early years the concept is likely seldom if ever to have been used. Now we use it, some arguing that it no longer exists and others believing it was a powerful historical force and also in contemporary life.

In this essay, I briefly summarize the history of race and imprisonment in the United States. A rich and rapidly growing literature documents and analyzes that history. I cannot and do not try to do justice to that work here (cf. Muhammad 2011; Muller 2012, 2018; Muller and Schrage 2021). Here I simply note important patterns in that history. Then I describe shifts that have occurred in scholarly thinking about race and racism, noting in particular contrasts between those changes and popular thinking. Finally, I take on the "Who cares?" question and explain why these changes matter.

---

[1] It should be noted that some early twentieth-century researchers and writers asked and tried to find out whether disproportionate incarceration of Blacks was due to discrimination (Spohn 2015).

I. Race and American Imprisonment

In thinking about racial differences in imprisonment, it is important to distinguish between two accounts of paths to imprisonment. The first, the one the general public assumes, is focused on crime. People who commit crimes increase their likelihood of being incarcerated. Racial differences in imprisonment that result from racial differences in criminal involvement are, on this account, legally justifiable. The second account focuses on decisions, policies, and practices that are either explicitly racist or implicitly based on considerations that deny equal treatment to Black people, rather than on racial differences in crime. Both accounts describe things that influence observable racial differences in imprisonment. The critical question, as Alfred Blumstein (1982, p. 1261) succinctly put it, is "the degree to which [those differences are] likely to have emerged as a consequence of racial discrimination in the criminal justice system compared to the alternative explanation that the racial disproportionality might have emerged as a consequence of disproportionate involvement in criminal activity."

Over the course of American history, the nation has gone from there being comparatively few Blacks in prison in the seventeenth, eighteenth, and early nineteenth centuries, especially in the South, to there being a great many today. For the past 40 years, Black imprisonment rates have been five to seven times higher than White rates (Tonry 2011). Racial disparities in sentencing and imprisonment have declined somewhat from historic peaks in the 1980s and 1990s but remain extreme (Carson 2021). The early patterns were driven by economic considerations; some would still say that (Muller 2021), but the economic bases for contemporary penal policy are today more contested. Even after the "invention" of the penitentiary in the early nineteenth century, few Blacks were incarcerated in southern prisons; state officials did not want to deprive White slaveholders of the economic value of their property without due process. Punishment for most slaves' "offenses," such as being where they did not belong, malingering, or running away, was at the discretion of owners. Pre–Civil War imprisonment of Blacks had little to do with offenses and everything to do with their legal definition as being subhuman chattels. They were economic tools, and the state treated them as such.

A. Reconstruction, Jim Crow, and Southern Imprisonment

After the federal capitulation to southern politics that ended Reconstruction, imprisonment in the South continued to be based on economic considerations, although maintenance of White supremacy was also important (Richardson 2004; Muller and Schrage 2021). Comparatively few prisons existed in the South in the decades after the Civil War (Mancini 1996), and those that did housed primarily Whites (Cable 1899). Black prisoners were typically leased out or assigned to work gangs.

It is popularly believed that convict leasing was a replacement for slavery, but this is not quite right. Convict leasing was part of a larger project to oppress Black people and maintain a stable, cheap workforce (Cable 1899; Adamson 1983; Hawkins 1985; Mancini 1996). Convict leasing buttressed tenant farming, sharecropping, and vagrancy laws that authorized arrests of Blacks who could not prove they were employed. Vagrancy arrests were an ever-present threat if freedmen dared leave the near slavery of work as a tenant farmer or in a sharecropping arrangement on a White person's land. Muller (2018) shows that the leasing of Black prisoners was most pronounced in locations where elite White landowners had not managed fully to resubjugate the previously enslaved population. The leasing system also provided workers for dangerous jobs such as railroad building and mining. Even in the open spaces of the Great Plains, building railroads was dangerous work. Black people worked on new railroads in the South and on replacement of those destroyed during the Civil War. Southern tracks needed to be laid in mountains and swamps; both were deadly places to work. Black convict labor was disposable.

When federal troops abandoned southern freedmen, leaving them vulnerable to White southerners' negative views about "their Africans," Blacks were viewed as a problem population, a source of cheap labor that needed to be controlled. Beliefs about and attitudes toward Black people were little if at all different after the war from what they were before. Many Whites throughout the country may have believed it wrong to buy, sell, and possess other humans as chattels, but few believed Blacks were equal to Whites and entitled to the same rights and privileges. Even Abraham Lincoln, the Great Emancipator, believed Blacks to be inherently inferior (Fredrickson 1975). These beliefs allowed White southerners to exploit Black labor and imprison Black people in order to control their labor. These beliefs also long served to divide working class Blacks and Whites (Alexander 2010). The social structure put into place and the accompanying belief systems assured White elite supremacy.

B. In the North

After the war, the African American population remained mostly rural and southern. Comparatively few Blacks lived in the North and there mostly in cities. They were too few to be seen as a threat to the White racial order. Like southern Whites, northerners tended to have negative views about Blacks and to believe them prone to violence and criminality. That northern prisons held disproportionate numbers of Blacks was not seen as a problem but as validation of northerners' preconceptions about their Black neighbors (Hawkins 1995; Du Bois 2007).

Philadelphia, with the largest urban Black population outside the South before the Civil War, had 22,000 Black residents by 1869, according to the federal census.[2] This was long before the Great Migration, the twentieth-century movement by large numbers of Black people from the rural south to urban areas of the east, Midwest, and later the west (Lemann 1991; Tolnay 2003). Philadelphia, with its comparatively large African American presence, was the birthplace of the penitentiary movement. The historically important Walnut Street Jail, later the Eastern State Penitentiary, was in Philadelphia. Black residents mostly lived in the major cities, making it fair to guess that most Black inmates at Eastern State Penitentiary were from Philadelphia even though the penitentiary could be expected to draw inmates from throughout the mostly White Commonwealth. In its early years, the prison admitted 209 inmates, of whom 153 were White and 54 Black (four are described as Black women, implying that there were no White women; Johnston 1994). More than a fourth of the inmates were Black, compared with 20 percent of the 80,462 residents of the city and surrounding suburbs. Lest that disproportion seem not so bad, the Black imprisoned percentage nearly doubled between 1830 and 1839.[3] Black imprisonment in the North grew during the twentieth century as the African American population increasingly migrated out of the rural South (Muller 2021).

II. Shifting Conceptions of Race

The concept of "race" has been pliably used for centuries, primarily to denote the "other." Roman conquerors described the tribes of northern Europe as racially inferior (McCoskey 2021). The English frequently referred to the Irish as an inferior race (Ignatiev 1995). Jews were widely considered to be a distinct racial group, with distinctive social, cultural, and physical features, well into the twentieth century (Singer and Adler

---

[2] By 1880, 32,000, and by 1900, 63,000.

[3] For a description of the racial and ethnic background of Eastern State Penitentiary's population, see https://esp2018.humspace.ucla.edu/uncategorized/ethnicity/

1907), and in some circles still are. Throughout human history, some racial distinctions, particularly in their cruder forms, broke down, usually as a result of increased intergroup contact (Allport 1954; Pettigrew et al. 2011). During the Age of Discovery when Europeans began to encounter Asians, Africans, and Americans often (Arnold 2002), they developed essentialist conceptions of race and built a pseudoscience that purported to explain European superiority and justify genocide, enslavement, and colonization.

A. Race as a Biological Fact

Those conceptions of race were largely biological, focusing on easily observable physiological traits such as skin color, hair texture, and facial features. Their creators knew, or perhaps cared less, about other observable features that could have led to very different categorical groupings. Most people, perhaps nearly all, understood the existence of distinct human races to be a fixed, biological fact, paralleling recognition of differences between species among other animals. The races were conventionally characterized as Caucasoid, Negroid, or Mongoloid (Rushton 1987). Some people, such as Indigenous Americans, did not quite fit, and never mind that a large portion of African Americans were and are (using the old categories) of mixed racial heritage. Cultural traits were ascribed to racial groups, but the social positioning of the races in a hierarchical stratification, with White Europeans on top, was justified by claims and beliefs about each group's biological inheritance. Only late in the twentieth century has it become generally recognized in the social sciences that the concept of race is socially constructed (Omi and Winant 2014). Even so, much of the wider public, including many policy makers, public officials, and criminal justice practitioners, neither accept nor understand that race is not a biological category. For many Americans, maybe even most citizens of Western nations, race is still seen as a set of biological categories. And, with biology come behavioral differences that to many explain why people of color are often marginalized by dominant groups. People who insist they are neither racist nor otherwise bigoted nonetheless argue that inherent differences interact with social conditions disproportionately to increase crime by people of color and immigrants, which is then said to justify their higher rates of imprisonment in the United States and elsewhere (Tonry 1997).

B. The Emergence of Race as a Social Construct

Conceptions of race have changed over time, especially after biologists and other scientists compellingly showed that race is not a biological category but a social construction. Not only have conceptions of race changed; how racism is viewed and practiced has also changed. Appreciating how race and racism are understood is important for understanding long running debates about race, crime, and justice.

Views about race have changed in large part because of advances made by social and biological scientists. These changes were no doubt influenced by substantial increases in the number of scholars of color in all disciplines since late in the twentieth century. I titled this essay "The Peculiar Journey" to emphasize that changes were occurring in understanding of and views about race and in prevailing views about civil rights at the same time as massive increases in racial disparity in imprisonment were occurring. It would have been reasonable to expect the prevalence of racial injustice to decline as belief in inherent racial differences declined and support for civil rights increased. Didn't happen!

Those concurrent changes can be seen as two parts of a meandering national intellectual journey. Controversies about race and imprisonment reflect an unresolved tension between unchanged views about race held by many in the public, many policy makers, and many jailers and the scientific refutation of the reality of "race" (e.g., Gould and Gold 1996). That tension has played out historically and, in our time, in the locking up of disproportionate numbers of people of color, especially Black people.

There is nothing new in the idea that race is a social construct. Du Bois objected early in the last century to the notion that race is biological and insisted that discrete categories—Black and White—obscure the range of human diversity (Gannon 2016). Du Bois's views, however, were not widely shared among scholars. Muhammad (2011) observed that in the early twentieth century not just the general public but also scholars typically believed in the inherent inferiority and criminality of Blacks, which provided a rationale to justify racial residential segregation. Muhammad also observed that some White progressives (such as Jane Addams and Mary White Ovington) rejected these notions in favor of cultural explanations of Blacks' involvement in crime that were advanced by anthropologist Franz Boas. Later in the twentieth century, social scientists returned to cultural and subcultural explanations and replaced notions of Black individuals' inferiority with notions of collective inferiority. Beliefs and attitudes about Black inferiority among the general public, policy makers, and criminal justice practitioners persist relatively unchanged from those widely held views in the early part of the last century.

It is safe to say that an evolution in views of race has not yet broadly taken hold within the American general public. Anyone who has taught undergraduate courses that deal with race knows this. When told that race, biologically speaking, does not exist, undergraduates often look dumbfounded or dismissive. "Of course race is real," many people say. "Racial differences are biological facts," they say; "Race is inherited." To most such people, racial differences imply different capacities, proclivities, behavioral traits, and maybe even abilities (Rushton 1987). Little wonder then that some elected officials and criminal justice practitioners hold these views: if Blacks are less intelligent, more aggressive, and more crime prone than Whites, then naturally they disproportionately wind up in jails and prisons.

The views of many, but by no means all, contemporary scholars are more consistent with Du Bois's a century ago. However, the shift from conceptualizing race as essentially biological to recognizing it to be a social construct has been neither monotonic nor smooth. Substantial diversity in conceptions of race endures, including among scholars (Gannon 2016).

Some prominent scholars (e.g., Wilson and Herrnstein 1985; Herrnstein and Murray 1994) have been less explicit in endorsing ideas about racial essentialism but fall within the tradition that Gould and Gold (1996) characterized as "scientific racism." Their writings are more sensitive to contemporary standards of how we talk about race, but their views are not unlike those held long ago by slavers and apologists for Jim Crow. It oversimplifies only slightly to say that they argue that Black crime is attributable to Blackness. Those views are not widely shared, at least among scholars. For several decades now, most have concluded, and believed, that definitions and divisions based on race are social constructs, fictions (Omi and Winant 2014).

Some scholars emphasize that care is needed when talking about social constructs because, even if race is one, as a social and political matter many people believe race to be real and to have real consequences (Smaje 1997). Attributions of race determine where people live, their opportunities, the doors that are open to them, and the probabilities that they will be perpetrators or victims of crime. So, even though race is a social construct, its perception is an important determinant of whether individuals spend time in jail or prison. It is both a correlate of racial differences in crime and imprisonment rates and a cause of racial differences in both. Race as it has been and continues to be socially constructed is criminogenic.

Contemporary Black imprisonment rates in the United States are a direct consequence. High levels of Black imprisonment increase the deprivation suffered by Black people and Black communities and thus shape criminogenic conditions (Western 2006; Clear 2009; Western and Pettit 2010; Western and Harding 2022). Is that racist? An answer requires that we consider how conceptions of racism shifted between the time when John C. Calhoun defended the South's peculiar institution and today.

III. Old-Fashioned Prejudice, Modern Racism, and Color-Blind Racism

Old-fashioned racial prejudice, what some call "redneck racism" (Sears and Jessor 1996), is simple to describe. Racially prejudiced people establish, maintain, and defend institutional and social structure arrangements that benefit some people and hinder others on the basis of racial categories. Those arrangements are justified by the innate superiority of White people and the innate inferiority of Black people and other people of color. People who embrace old-fashioned prejudice have no motivation to challenge racial hierarchies, inequalities, or differences within the criminal justice system. They and the institutions they created hum along benefiting Whites and harming people of color, even though many Whites do not consciously intend to discriminate. Racist institutions and social structures can function and flourish without conscious efforts of prejudiced people to maintain them. Those who practice old-fashioned prejudice argue that Black crime is a product of inherent Black inferiority and Black characteristics. Disproportionate Black imprisonment can thus be seen as a consequence of Black inferiority.

Modern racism, sometimes called symbolic racism, is premised on beliefs that Black people no longer suffer from discrimination, whatever may have happened in the past; disadvantages experienced today result from their own personal failings (Henry and Sears 2002). Those who hold such views tend to believe that Black people ask too much from government and society. Failure to socialize children properly, to work hard in school, and to strive in the labor market are believed to lead to higher Black involvement in crime and cause Blacks to live in distressed criminogenic neighborhoods. Responsibility for reducing disproportionate Black imprisonment, according to adherents to modern racism, rests with Black people.

Bonilla-Silva offers a third option, which he called "color blind racism." His *Racism without Racists* begins by describing how things are different now and yet in many ways remain the same (Bonilla-Silva 2006, p. 1):

Nowadays, except for members of white supremacist organizations, few whites in the United States claim to be "racist." Most whites assert they "don't see any color, just people"; that although the ugly face of discrimination is still with us, it is no longer the central factor determining minorities' life chances; and, finally, that like Dr. Martin Luther King Jr., they aspire to live in a society where "people are judged by the content of their character, not by the color of their skin." More poignantly, most whites insist that minorities (especially blacks) are the ones responsible for whatever "race problem" we have in this country. They publicly denounce blacks for "playing the race card," for demanding the maintenance of unnecessary and divisive race-based programs, such as affirmative action, and for crying "racism" whenever they are criticized by whites. Most whites believe that if Black and other minorities would just stop thinking about the past, work hard, and complain less (particularly about racial discrimination), then Americans of all hues could "all get along."

This view gained strength after Barack Obama's election as president; after all, how can racism persist if a Black man was elected president? On this account, efforts to explain differentially higher criminal involvement by Blacks are excuses for individuals who make bad choices. Blacks are imprisoned because of their actions; that is justifiable because they victimized others.

As with conceptions of race, most scholars' views of racism differ from those held by much of the general public. Scholars quibble about what it means to say that race is socially constructed but biological conceptions of race have generally been discarded. Many who study crime and justice have demonstrated analytically, and empirically, that disproportionate Black involvement in some kinds of crime is a consequence of historical racism and contemporary patterns of racialized disadvantage. The evidence that social and economic disadvantage explains racial differences in crime is compelling (Wilson 1987; Sampson 2012; Sharkey 2013; Sampson and Wilson 2020; Sharkey and Marsteller 2022). The evidence that residential segregation is a criminogenic feature of African American life is equally compelling (Massey and Denton 1993; Peterson and Krivo 2010; Krivo et al. 2015). The importance of social structural inequality as an explanation of racial differences in criminal involvement is incontrovertible. The necessary conclusion is that racial disproportionality in imprisonment results primarily from two things: racial inequality that produces differential patterns of involvement in crime, and legally unjustifiable differential treatment of Black people from first police contact through reentry into society from jail or prison.

This understanding is not a central consideration in development of laws and policies that shape American patterns of imprisonment. Of course, some legislators and members of their staffs, people in police departments and prosecutors' offices, judges, parole board members, and people running prisons "get it." But, it is fair to say that federal and state policies and practices have not fundamentally changed, even if twenty-first-century imprisonment reflects different assumptions or beliefs about race and imprisonment than were common when the penitentiary was long ago viewed as a positive institution. How have we collectively made this peculiar intellectual journey? How can we have learned so much and our practices changed so little?

IV. Race, Racism, Crime and Imprisonment in Contemporary America

Tracing changes in the racial or ethnic distributions of inmates in US prisons before the early twentieth century is difficult because the groups of "others" who were tracked differed depending on who was counting, who were seen as members of a "problem population," and what state or county politics looked like. Disproportionate numbers of prisoners, however, have always been members of racial or ethnic minority groups or immigrants (Cahalan 1979; Tonry 1997).

Twentieth-century data are available. Now as in earlier times, Black people are everywhere disproportionately imprisoned compared with their presence in the general population (Muhammad 2011). Racial disparities increased steadily from the 1960s through the early 1990s, when half of all inmates were Black (Tonry and Melewski 2008); disparities have since somewhat diminished but remain at historically high levels. While there was racial disproportionality in the North before the Great Migration in the 1910s and 1920s, this major population movement was accompanied by increasing Black imprisonment outside of the South (Muller 2012). Muhammad (2011) notes that liberals and even social reformers in the North, not only old-fashioned bigots, were responsible for high arrest and imprisonment rates for Blacks. Liberals and reformers did not attribute Black criminality so much to inherent traits but to pathological cultures. This shift in thinking did not change enforcement patterns. There seems to have been little or no critical debate about these views in popular writings or in the scholarly literature. Presumably this was because it was widely assumed that high levels of Black imprisonment necessarily resulted from high levels of criminality. Essentially, it was "understood" that racial disparities in prison populations and arrests reflect racial differences in criminality.

Well into the 1960s social scientists commonly viewed police arrest statistics as reasonably accurate representations of the distribution of crime involvement, even though some criminologists in the early twentieth century challenged that view (Spohn 2015, pp. 72–74). The 1967 report of the President's Commission on Law Enforcement and Administration of Justice (PCLEAJ 1967), President Johnson's crime commission, for example, used arrest statistics uncritically to discuss racial differentials in criminal involvement. Because Black arrest rates substantially exceeded White rates, the commission concluded that Black criminality substantially exceeded that of Whites. So, of course more Blacks were locked up. Members of the president's commission accepted the "opportunity structure" explanations of crime distribution developed by Richard Cloward and Lloyd Ohlin (1960). Other people's views continued to reflect conceptions of race not so different from those that justified slavery: Blacks were inherently more aggressive, more violent, and more in need of control and regulation, a view that drove policing and crime control policies (Hinton and Cook 2021). It was widely believed that Black traits produced higher levels of criminality, more arrests, and disproportionately high imprisonment rates.

Such things were not said out loud in polite society, and sociologists and criminologists did not often write about them. Academics did, however, use and in some instances continue to use versions of Black inferiority/ aggressiveness/inherently criminal tropes. Examples include analyses of subcultures of violence (Ferracuti and Wolfgang 1969; Curtis 1975), subcultures of poverty (Banfield 1970; Murray 1984), and pseudogenetic or behaviorist theories (Wilson and Herrnstein 1985). By all these accounts, racial differences in crime rates resulted from racial differences in criminal involvement that justified higher rates of Black imprisonment. Too often these propositions were neither questioned nor tested critically.

Twentieth-century scholars recognized that African Americans then and in the past faced structural disadvantages. It is common today in some political circles to deny that continuing racial inequality results from structural disadvantages. But few serious scholars deny that, compared to Whites, contemporary Blacks are substantially economically and socially disadvantaged. Slavery played a pivotal historical role in shaping those disadvantages, but neither the Emancipation Proclamation nor the Thirteenth Amendment to the US Constitution that abolished slavery made things right. Too many Americans nonetheless appear to continue to believe that emancipation ended Black oppression. Many, when protesting remedial efforts such as affirmative action, insist, "My parents didn't own slaves."

Whites of European heritage sometimes argue that their immigrant ancestors were discriminated against, but they pulled themselves up on their own, without government handouts. Some academics have made this argument (e.g., Sowell 1981). It is fundamentally misconceived. Stanley Lieberson in *A Piece of the Pie* (1981) demonstrated its fallaciousness. He documented the paths followed by successive waves of European immigrants and showed that their advancement, although at times difficult, was enhanced by being able to fill occupational niches in a growing nation within an economy that was usually growing. Most immigrant groups were soon slotted in above Blacks in America's racial hierarchy. Lieberson also showed that Blacks moving north as part of the Great Migration encountered extensive discrimination in employment and housing and that their children commonly received substandard educations, rationalized on the basis that they inherently lacked the talent required for academic success.

The experience of African American internal migrants was starkly different from that of immigrants from Europe. That reality is dramatically shown by patterns of residential discrimination. Massey and Denton (1993, pp. 32–33) compared residential segregation affecting African Americans to what White immigrants experienced: "Migration and industrial development also segregated the 'new' European immigrant groups, of course, but recent studies have made it clear that immigrant enclaves in the early twentieth century were in no way comparable to the Black ghetto that formed in most northern cities by 1940. To be sure, certain neighborhoods could be identified as 'Italian,' 'Polish,' or 'Jewish'; but these enclaves differed from Black ghettos in three fundamental ways."

The three fundamental differences are as follows: immigrant enclaves were not homogenous; most European immigrants did not live in ghettos; and, unlike Black ghettos, immigrant enclaves did not become permanent. Federal, state, and local housing officials, conspiring with private citizens and corporations, created permanent ghettos in which a large portion of the Black population lived for most of the twentieth century. In large measure that continues to be true. By "conspired" I do not claim that explicit agreements were made that effectively forced Blacks into ghettos. Rather, the effects of their actions, working together and separately, created the patterns of racial residential segregation that continue to characterize most American cities and towns.

Other policies were put into place—we cannot say with this purpose—that perpetuated conditions that kept Black Americans from developing wealth and opportunities comparable to those of Whites. It is, however, very, very difficult to imagine any credible alternative explanations. Native-born Whites and countless immigrants, for example, benefited from the Homestead Acts that enabled western expansion during and after the Civil War; Blacks were by law ineligible to establish homesteads until the Four-teenth Amendment was enacted in 1868 (Bowles and Gintis 2002). One of the founders of the Washington Territory (later Washington state), George Bush, a Black man, was permitted to establish a legal claim to land he farmed, near a town he and his family founded, only because the Terri-torial Legislature passed a special act asking the federal government to make an exception for him (Oldham 2004).[4] After World War II, White former soldiers and sailors received generous GI Bill benefits that allowed them to buy houses and obtain college educations. The GI Bill is widely credited for the considerable expansion of the White middle class that was a hallmark of the 1950s and '60s. Black GIs and sailors often lost out because GI Bill programs were administered by state agencies, which often denied benefits to veterans of color.

When White members of the public explain racial patterns of wealth and income, they often ignore or do not know about these and similar federal, state, and local government (e.g., racially restrictive deed covenants) poli-cies and practices that have caused those patterns that helped Whites and hindered Blacks. Ownership of real property, the principal wealth of Amer-ican families today, was systematically facilitated for Whites and systemat-ically obstructed for Blacks. Contemporary gaps in wealth and income do not result from racial differences in willingness to work hard or in the ca-pacity to save or defer gratification.[5] They are the foreseeable results of de-liberate, racist government policies. Countless other actions and practices of individuals, businesses, unions, and corporations forced African Amer-icans to live in substandard segregated housing, to work in low end jobs

---

[4] An Act for the Relief of George Bush, of Thurston County, Washington Territory, Pvt. L. 33-63, 33rd Cong. (February 10, 1855).

[5] A central component of Banfield's argument in the *Unheavenly City* (1970) is that peo-ple of the lowest class have less capacity to defer gratification.

or not at all, and to send their children to subpar schools. A more complete modern package of racial oppression could not have been imagined until South African Whites established Apartheid, explicitly patterning it on American laws and practices.

No honest, informed observer can fail to recognize that America's regularly recurring "wars" on crime and drugs began not long after the Great Migration when migrants' children experienced the frustrations and disappointments of the northern Promised Land (Lemann 1991).[6] The effects of historical discrimination, like racial oppression, persist today. Black Americans disproportionately live in socially and economically disadvantaged, criminogenic neighborhoods because of their historical marginalization; because social policy, economic, and residential patterns shaped by that marginalization continue; and because discrimination continues. Those realities make it easy to understand—for anyone paying attention— why African American crime rates are higher for some, but by no means all, crimes.

V. Explaining Racial Differences in Crime and Imprisonment

Few social scientists before the late 1960s critically evaluated criminal justice system statistics. Even then, factors widely known to be criminogenic—poverty, inequality, unemployment, subpar schooling—received little attention (Russell 1992; Unnever and Gabbidon 2011). The President's Commission on Law Enforcement and Administration of Justice naively documented racial differences in crime and delinquency using police arrest data reported in the *Uniform Crime Reports*. Now we know better. We know, for example, that there are biases in arrest rates for all crimes but that degrees of error vary widely, least for the most serious crimes such as homicide, more for lesser crimes, and most for drug arrests and public order offenses (Tonry and Melewski 2008). Distortions are even greater when arrest statistics are used to measure racial differences in criminal involvement by juveniles (Hindelang, Hirschi, and Weis 1981).

Labeling and conflict theories that became popular in the 1960s, but were elaborated decades earlier, help explain racial arrest patterns. Those

---

[6] See Muller (2021) for a political economy explanation of the patterning of Black imprisonment in the nineteenth and twentieth centuries.

theories and, not coincidentally, social movements for civil rights, opposition to the Vietnam War, women's rights, environmental protection, and slightly later gay rights marked leftward political shifts among researchers and scholars. Frank Tannenbaum (1938) first promoted what later became known as labeling theory, and Willem Bonger (1916) proposed a Marxist criminology that focused on poverty, work, and welfare as causes and antidotes of crime. The reemergence of these perspectives in the 1960s challenged uncritical acceptance of conventional wisdom and official data about racial differences in crime and delinquency (Becker 1963; Quinney 1970; Chambliss 1973). Today, nearly all social scientists agree that there are important biases in arrest data. This means, because arrests and arrest data lay foundations for all subsequent criminal justice system processes, that there are systematic biases in all criminal justice statistics. They measure criminal justice system activities and do not provide objective measures of crime. This does not mean they cannot be used for some purposes, but only with nuance. An article by Blumstein and Beck (2012) illustrates problems in using official data to develop generalizations about race and criminality. They found that racial differences apparent in homicide arrest data closely parallel racial differences in imprisonment for murder. And they found just the opposite—little relation between racial patterns of involvement in drug offenses and of incarceration for drug possession or sale. Other major crimes, including some serious violent offenses, fell between those poles. The takeaway is that, except for the most serious crimes, there are enormous differences between patterns of racial difference in committing crimes and racial patterns of imprisonment (and, necessarily, of arrest, prosecution, and sentencing).

A. Contemporary Discussions of Race, Crime, and Imprisonment

Hinton (2016) traces the roots of mass incarceration and increased racial disproportionality in imprisonment not to President Reagan's War on Drugs in the early 1980s but to earlier federal legislation as part of President Johnson's War on Crime that began in 1965. Scholarly efforts to understand racial patterns of imprisonment began with Christianson's (1980, 1981) examinations of disproportionality in the 50 states. A growing literature since then has sought to document, understand, and explain racial disparities throughout the American criminal justice system (see Spohn [2015] for a review). Two features of this literature are pertinent. First, nearly all studies are quantitative (this is important because they measure some things well and other things, e.g., discrimination, not at all or at least not well). Second, little attention has been paid by criminologists to shifting conceptions of race and racism in other social science literatures. Racism, to be sure, has usually been a subtext of race and imprisonment research. The question usually asked—How much of observed racial differences in imprisonment can be accounted for by legally relevant criteria (crime severity and criminal history)?—essentially acknowledges that some portion, large or small, is associated with race. The crucial follow-up question—How much?—cannot be answered without acknowledging what is being asked about is racism. These inquiries do not take into account the possibility that differences in criminal involvement are products of the racially structured lives of people who are prosecuted or result from racially skewed police and prosecution practices.

Scholars who have written about disparities no doubt conceive of race and racism in different ways. Many can be criticized, and some have been, for not addressing these concepts head on. Unnever and Gabbidon (2011), calling for a theory of African American offending, criticize major theorists for failing to take account of the unique experience and positions of Blacks in American society adequately (see also Russell 1992).[7] Whether or not a distinct theory of Black offending is needed, it is hard not to agree that criminologists have seldom adequately accounted for the historical experience and contemporary circumstances of Black Americans. Historians (Muhammad 2011; Hinton 2016), demographers (Lieberson 1981; Massey and Denton 1993), and sociologists (Peterson and Krivo 2010; Sampson and Wilson 2020) convincingly demonstrate that African Americans as a group have experienced a uniquely difficult history and unequal contemporary circumstances that are criminogenic to an extent unmatched in American life by any other group.

Early twentieth-century researchers concluded that there was substantial racial discrimination in sentencing. Later scholars, who criticized major methodological flaws in that work, did not find widespread evidence of systematic discriminatory sentencing (Spohn [2015] tells that story). In

---

[7] The counter position, referred to as the racial invariance thesis, holds that racial differences in crime do not need a theory specific to Black Americans, but rather factors such as extreme poverty and racial residential segregation explain observable racial differences in criminal involvement (Peterson and Krivo 2010; Sampson and Wilson 2020).

an oft-cited article examining sentencing in multiple jurisdictions, Kleck (1981) concluded that there was not a consistent statistically significant difference in sentencing. In contrast, Chiricos and Crawford (1995) concluded that race explained a substantial part of observed racial differences in imprisonment. Hagan and Bumiller (1983), writing for a National Academies of Sciences report, observed that recent work had overlooked isolated pockets of discrimination that no doubt existed and disregarded the likelihood that individual judges discriminate against Black people. Overall, they agreed with sentencing studies through the mid-1970s that found little evidence of systematic anti-Black bias.

None of those studies dealt with selection bias, the possibility (the likelihood) that earlier racial differences in case processing—discriminatory arrests, bail decisions, prosecutions, charges, plea bargains, convictions—washed out observable racial differences at sentencing. The research evidence is thus far thin, but there is reason to believe that low-level racial differences in criminal justice processing have important cumulative effects that negatively affect Blacks (Zatz 1987; Crutchfield, Fernandes, and Martinez 2010; Kurlychek and Johnson 2019). Hagan (1974) long ago argued that studies that simply examine one single stage of the process, such as sentencing, imprisonment, or parole release, risk missing important cumulative effects that occur as defendants move through the system. Studying the process stage by stage is essential to understanding how and how much race matters. Decisions at each stage influence subsequent stages (this is the crux of the selection bias problem). Crutchfield, Fernandes, and Martinez (2010), reviewing studies of race and case processing in both juvenile and adult systems, demonstrate the importance of accumulating racial differences. Spohn (2015, p. 92), after exhaustively reviewing work on racial differences from arrest to imprisonment, concluded: "We know that disparities in incarceration result 'to some extent' from racially discriminatory decision making in the criminal justice system and 'to some extent' from policies and practices that have racially disparate effects."

Some scholars, however, had earlier begun to examine aggregate racial differences in imprisonment patterns rather than individual-level sentencing decisions. Christianson (1980, 1981), who looked at racial disparities in state prisons, was criticized (e.g., Blumstein 1982) for comparing racial patterns in state prisons with racial patterns in state populations. The critics argued that imprisonment patterns should instead be compared with patterns of criminal involvement. The entire population is not at risk of imprisonment, the argument went, only people who commit crimes. This may to an extent be a fair comment, but it may also miss a much larger point. Christianson's comparison may be the right one if the aim is to investigate not just case processing but comparative life chances of Blacks and Whites, which are shaped not only by arrests and imprisonment but also by criminogenic conditions of their lives.

Blumstein (1982) treated fair functioning of the justice system as the important issue. Focusing on arrests for violent crimes reported in the *Uniform Crime Reports*, he compared patterns of criminal involvement (as shown by arrest rates, subject to selection bias problems) to imprisonment patterns. He reasoned that people committing violent crimes were most likely to wind up in prison. Blumstein's data, like Christianson's, were compiled during the 1970s, when some early sentencing law changes that produced mass incarceration were in place but before mass incarceration became endemic (Travis, Western, and Redburn 2014). President Reagan's War on Drugs, which massively increased prison populations, did not begin until 1984.[8] Blumstein's logic was not unreasonable, but his analyses disregarded people incarcerated for nonviolent offenses, especially repeat offenders. His logic was, however, supported by notable earlier research (Curtis 1975; Hindelang 1978).

Blumstein concluded that about 80 percent of Black/White imprisonment disparities can be accounted for by higher levels of Black involvement in violent crime. This finding is important but begs several questions. First, 20 percent of racial differences in imprisonment, a large amount that if correct affects hundreds of thousands of people, cannot be accounted for. Much disparity remains legally unexplained. The explanation may include criminal history considerations (not part of the analysis) but inevitably also includes considerations of race. Especially in 1970s data, from a time when many Americans acknowledged beliefs in racial superiority and inferiority, racism no doubt played a part.

Second, Blumstein uses arrest statistics to measure criminal involvement. Arrest statistics, however, measure police decisions to arrest particular people rather than crimes that have been committed. Blumstein is likely correct in assuming police use less discretion when making violent crime arrests. Nonetheless, arrest rates primarily measure police behavior.

---

[8] An earlier war on drugs was instituted during the Nixon administration in 1970 (Musto 1999), but it did not contribute to anything like the substantial increases in imprisonment that the Reagan era policies would. One might argue that the federal Harrison Act of 1914 and Marijuana Tax Act of 1937 were also wars on drugs, but neither had the level of effects on imprisonment levels or racial disparities that the Reagan era policies had.

This is starkly evident in drug arrests. Evidence from a wide variety of credible sources, including decades of federally funded national drug use surveys, shows that fewer Blacks than Whites use or sell illegal drugs, but for at least 40 years large majorities of people arrested for drug offenses have been Black. At their height, Black arrest rates were six times those for Whites (Tonry 2011). Blumstein's subsequent work with Beck (2012) drives this point home when they report that even drug arrest patterns cannot legally explain the dramatic racial disparity for imprisonment for drug offenses. Langan (1985) replicated Blumstein's study using reports by victims of personal crimes contained in the National Crime Victimization Survey rather than arrest statistics. Like Blumstein, he concluded that involvement in violent crime explains much but not all racial differences in imprisonment. Neither study can refute hypotheses that racism, unconscious bias, and racial differences in criminal justice processing explain racial differences in imprisonment.

Two additional studies replicating Blumstein's analysis, but for each state rather than for the entire country, confirmed Hagan and Bumiller's speculation that averages camouflage large local variations (Hawkins and Hardy 1989; Crutchfield, Bridges, and Pitchford 1994). Both found substantial differences between states, with higher levels of unexplained racial imprisonment disparity in a number of northern, midwestern, and western states; the lowest unexplained differences were in the South. In some states, differences in Black and White violent crime arrests explained much lower proportions of prison disparities than Blumstein's 80 percent (e.g., in Massachusetts and Washington only 40 percent).

This body of research treats the link between race and imprisonment as problematic. That is, unlike earlier writers who were essentially silent about the nature of race and why Black people were disproportionately incarcerated, and certainly unlike many nineteenth-century Americans who saw Blacks as inherently aggressive and crime prone, recent research has investigated the extent to which Black imprisonment reflects Black criminality and the extent to which other factors are at play. That work, however, is mostly silent about discrimination and racism. These aggregate studies do not measure either of these crucial concepts and thus cannot conclude whether small or large unexplained racial differences result from racial discrimination or racism. They also do not dismiss the possibilities of implicit bias, structural racism, or systemic discrimination.

These studies should be read in the context of shifts occurring in criminology since the social and political upheavals of the 1960s. These developments reject old-fashioned prejudice and "redneck racism." Research on the causes of crime has increasingly shown that traditional, modern, and color-blind racisms' takes on crime are incompatible with growing evidence that observable racial differences in crime do not result from inherited traits or unwillingness of Black people to "be better." Crime differences result from well-documented racial differences in education, employment, social and economic disadvantage, and residential segregation.

This is the intellectual context in which recent racial disparities studies have been conducted. A large portion of racial disproportionality in imprisonment that appears to be accounted for by arrest rate differences is likely instead to be the effects of structural racism that affect people in ways that produce differential rates of involvement in crime. The debate then should be about the proportion of observed racial disproportionality attributable to structural racism in society and the proportion attributable to racial inequality in case processing.

A new recent line of research examines how disproportionate incarceration of African Americans affects them personally and how it affects the communities from which they come. Western (2006), for example, concluded that mass incarceration did little to reduce crime but increased racial inequality in the broader society. The negative effects of imprisonment, especially for young, Black, poorly educated men, have become particularly onerous and handicapping. Mass incarceration, by removing Black males from labor market analyses, has distorted racial patterns of employment that as a result misleadingly indicate that labor market gaps between Whites and Blacks have narrowed. Prisoners are omitted from the analyses, which effectively compare employment and labor market participation rates for nonincarcerated Whites and nonincarcerated Blacks. When incarcerated people are taken into account, "progress" in reducing racial labor market differences has been very limited (Pettit and Lyons 2009; Lyons and Pettit 2011; Pettit 2012).

Michelle Alexander's bestselling book *The New Jim Crow* (2010) brought mass incarceration, its evils, and its negative effects to the attention of the general public. She argues compellingly that the criminal justice system and mass incarceration damn and damage Black communities in much the same ways as did the South's Jim Crow laws. She largely attributes mass incarceration to the disproportionate focus of the War on Drugs on Black communities even though there are no substantial racial differences in drug use or sales (Tonry 2011). Rose and Clear (1998) and Clear (2009) used the term "coercive mobility" to describe the population churning of people moving from Black communities into prisons and returning after release to the same or similar communities. Those reentering prisoners are usually more handicapped competing in the labor market than before they were locked up (Pager 2003, 2008). Coercive mobility is criminogenic and worsens people's chances of achieving law-abiding lives. This pattern is consistent with overwhelming evidence that mass incarceration has failed as an effective crime control policy but increased distress in communities of color (Travis, Western, and Redburn 2014).

The National Academies of Sciences' Committee on the Causes and Consequences of High Rates of Incarceration (Travis, Western, and Redburn 2014) attributed the immense growth in American imprisonment that began in 1973 to enactment of unprecedentedly severe sentencing laws and the successive "wars" on drugs. Both dramatically increased racial disproportionality in state and federal prisons. The War on Drugs hit Black communities especially hard.

B. What Were They Thinking?

It is impossible to know what the people who enacted the laws that led to high rates of imprisonment for people of color were thinking about race: how they defined it; whether they were influenced by old-fashioned prejudice, symbolic racism, or color-blind racism; or whether they understood how historic and current structural racism affect both crime and criminal justice. Nor can we know how lawmakers and practitioners of bygone days, or academics who wrote about race and crime in the twentieth century, thought about these things. It is reasonable, however, to speculate, on the basis of past and present prevailing views and the laws and practices that were put into place, about how these folks thought about race and racism. For many, the answer to Du Bois's question, "What shall be done with Negroes?" was, clearly, imprisonment.

Many Americans still refuse to acknowledge centuries of racial oppression and structured inequality and contemporary structured racial inequality. How else can we explain current obsessions with banning critical race theory, a framework that posits that slavery, Jim Crow, segregation, and continuing oppression and marginalization of Black people are important parts of America's story and powerfully influence contemporary life (Bell 1995; Crenshaw 2011)?

Some scholars throughout the twentieth century pointed to social inequality as the explanation for racial differences in criminal involvement. As early as the 1920s, some argued that imprisonment differences resulted from discriminatory sentencing (Spohn 2015). Only recently though have discriminatory policies and practices, racial disproportionality in imprisonment, and racial inequality as an underlying cause of crime been adequately linked. "Well, of course," some might say, but what is important is that "well, of course" is much more likely mostly to be said by scholars than by policy makers and practitioners. Until they come to understand that race is a social construct and that no group is inherently criminal, and abandon not only old-fashioned prejudice but modern and color-blind racism, America's criminal justice system and prisons will continue to be instruments of racial oppression.

The products of this failure to take account of the history of racism and of contemporary structural racism have been heavy-handed in the form of "broken windows" policing, proactive strategic policing that depends too heavily on data gathered from biased policing, and excessive deaths of people of color at the hands of police. These failures led to "wars" on crime and drugs that overemphasized violations in communities of color and to mass incarceration that exacerbated racial disproportionality in American prisons. They produced moral panics about "crack babies" and "super predators" that in retrospect did not exist.

There are two inconvenient and uncomfortable truths about crime in America. First, there are not substantial racial differences in who commits most types of crime, but there are some. African Americans are substantially more likely to be the victims of homicide, and, more often than not, their killers are black too. Second, racism causes crime. Racism is complicit in the crimes of Black offenders. Policy makers, criminal justice administrators, and practitioners who continue to be influenced by John C. Calhoun-esque prejudice and old-fashioned racism are complicit in this criminality, as are moral entrepreneurs who insist that they are not prejudiced but instead practice color-blind racism. They have the responsibility to know better, to acknowledge the effects of history, and to understand the consequences of ongoing structured inequality of which they are a part. Practicing color-blind racism makes them complicit in the victimization of both crime victims and perpetrators.

C. A Note on Agency

To say that structural inequality leads to higher levels of criminal involvement is not to say that African American individuals lack agency, the capacity to make choices, or that they are not responsible for their criminal actions. Most Black people, although their lives are affected by structural racism, do not commit crimes. Racism causes crime, but it also causes victimization. The likeliest victims of Black people's crimes are other Black people (Lauritsen and Heimer 2010). America needs a system of justice that responds to crime and victimization but neither racially victimizes perpetrators nor revictimizes victims.

VI. Reflections

How can the United States reduce or eliminate racial disproportionality in imprisonment? There is a simple answer: eliminate structured racial inequality. But what of history? Would becoming a truly egalitarian society eliminate or fundamentally ameliorate the negative effects of slavery, Jim Crow, segregation, and oppression? Likely not, but that question is largely theoretical. The United States is not likely any time soon to undertake really serious efforts to eliminate racial inequality. Are we stuck? Has this peculiar journey brought the United States to a point at which we know that racial inequality is of our own making but are doomed to live with it? Perhaps.

The upheaval that rocked the United States after the murder of George Floyd drew attention to people who advocate abolition of the criminal justice system as it now exists. Possible paths to improvement may be found in the shouts of those activists and in the efforts of reformers. Whether one embraces abolition of the existing system, believes such radical change is "crazy thinking," or falls somewhere in between, it is clear that many more people want to see things done differently. There are at least some ways things can be made better. One, requiring preparation of racial impact statements when criminal laws are changed, is being adopted in a growing number of states. They require careful analyses of intended and unintended racial effects of proposed new laws and changes in existing laws. Some jurisdictions are exploring dramatic changes in drug laws that inappropriately and disproportionately lead to the incarceration of people of color. The get-tough sentencing reforms of the 1980s and 1990s should be reconsidered. And, just maybe, we as a society can get serious about racial equality.

Scholars have long been on the peculiar journey required to understand and address problems of race, racism, and imprisonment, but there is a long way to go. It is doubtful many members of the general public, politicians, or practitioners have even begun the journey that will take them beyond old-fashioned, modern, and color-blind racism.

Social scientists, especially criminologists, face challenges not unlike those facing public health experts in the COVID era: their knowledge is doubted, questioned, and often rejected simply because many people neither accept the science nor want to learn from it. If American criminal justice is to accomplish more that is good for everyone and less that is harmful to African Americans and other people of color, social scientists need to push others to set out on the peculiar journey and not simply wait for them to "get it." The public, policy makers, and practitioners need to understand that America has for too long been on a peculiar journey. Americans' thinking about race and racism should long ago have changed.

REFERENCES

Adamson, Christopher R. 1983. "Punishment after Slavery: Southern State Penal Systems, 1865–1890." *Social Problems* 30(5):555–69.

Alexander, Michelle. 2010. *The New Jim Crow: Mass Incarceration in the Age of Colorblindness*. New York: New Press.

Allport, Gordon Willard. 1954. *The Nature of Prejudice*. Introduction by Kenneth Clark; foreword by Thomas Pettigrew. New York: Perseus.

Anderson, Elijah, and Douglas Massey, eds. 2001. *Problem of the Century: Racial Stratification in the United States*. New York: Russell Sage.

Appiah, Kwame Anthony. 2015. "Race in the Modern World: The Problem of the Color Line." *Foreign Affairs* 94(2):1–8.

Arnold, David. 2002. *The Age of Discovery, 1400–1600*. New York: Routledge.

Banfield, Edward C. 1970. *The Unheavenly City: The Nature and Future of Our Urban Crisis*. Boston: Little, Brown.

Becker, Howard S. 1963. *Outsiders: Studies in the Sociology of Deviance*. New York: Free Press.

Bell, Derrick A. 1995. "Who's Afraid of Critical Race Theory?" *University of Illinois Law Review* 1995(4):893–910.

Blumstein, Alfred. 1982. "On the Racial Disproportionality of United States' Prison Populations." *Journal of Criminal Law and Criminology* 73(3):1259–81.

Blumstein, Alfred, and Allen J. Beck. 2012. "Trends in U.S. Incarceration Rates (1980–2010)." Presentation to the National Research Council Committee on Causes and Consequences of High Rates of Incarceration. Unpublished manuscript. School of Urban and Public Affairs, Carnegie-Mellon University. (Cited in *The Growth of Incarceration in the United States: Exploring Causes and Consequences*, edited by Jeremy Travis, Bruce Western, and Steve Redburn. Washington, DC: National Academies.)

Bonger, Willem Adriaan. 1916. *Criminality and Economic Conditions*. Boston: Little, Brown.

Bonilla-Silva, Eduardo. 2006. *Racism without Racists: Color-Blind Racism and the Persistence of Racial Inequality in the United States*. Lanham, MD: Rowman & Littlefield.

Bowles, Samuel, and Herbert Gintis. 2002. "The Inheritance of Inequality." *Journal of Economic Perspectives* 16(3):3–30.

Cable, George W. 1899. *The Silent South, Together with the Freedman's Case in Equity and the Convict Lease System*. New York: Scribner.

Cahalan, Margaret. 1979. "Trends in Incarceration in the United States since 1880: A Summary of Reported Rates and the Distribution of Offenses." *Crime and Delinquency* 25(1):9–41.

Carson, E. Ann. 2021. *Prisoners in 2020: Statistical Tables*. Washington, DC: US Department of Justice, Bureau of Justice Statistics.

Chambliss, William J. 1973. "The Saints and the Roughnecks." *Society* 11(1):24–31.

Chiricos, Theodore G., and Charles Crawford. 1995. "Race and Imprisonment: A Contextual Assessment of the Evidence." In *Ethnicity, Race, and Crime: Perspectives across Time and Place*, edited by Darnell F. Hawkins. Albany, NY: SUNY Press.

Christianson, Scott. 1980. "Corrections Law Developments: Racial Discrimination and Prison Confinement—a Follow-Up." *Criminal Law Bulletin* 16:616–17.

Christianson, Scott. 1981. "Our Black Prisons." *Crime and Delinquency* 27(3): 364–75.

Clear, Todd R. 2009. *Imprisoning Communities: How Mass Incarceration Makes Disadvantaged Neighborhoods Worse*. New York: Oxford University Press.

Cloward, Richard A., and Lloyd E. Ohlin. 1960. *Delinquency and Opportunity: A Theory of Delinquent Gangs*. Glencoe, IL: Free Press.

Crenshaw, Kimberlé Williams. 2011. "Twenty Years of Critical Race Theory: Looking Back to Move Forward." *Connecticut Law Review* 43(5):1253–354.

Crutchfield, Robert D., George S. Bridges, and Susan R. Pitchford. 1994. "Analytical and Aggregation Biases in Analyses of Imprisonment: Reconciling Discrepancies in Studies of Racial Disparity." *Journal of Research in Crime and Delinquency* 31(2):166–82.

Crutchfield, Robert D., April Fernandes, and Jorge Martinez. 2010. "Racial Disparity in the Criminal Justice System: How Much Is Too Much?" *Journal of Criminal Law and Criminology* 100(3):903–32.

Curtis, Lynn A. 1975. *Violence, Race, and Culture*. Lexington, MA: Lexington.

Du Bois, W. E. B. 2007. *The Philadelphia Negro*. New York: Oxford University Press. (Originally published 1899. Philadelphia: University of Pennsylvania.)

Du Bois, W. E. B. 2015. *The Souls of Black Folk*. New Haven, CT: Yale University Press. (Originally published 1903. Chicago: McClurg.)

Ferracuti, Franco, and Marvin E. Wolfgang. 1969. *Subculture of Violence*. London: Routledge.

Fredrickson, George M. 1975. "A Man but Not a Brother: Abraham Lincoln and Racial Equality." *Journal of Southern History* 41(1):39–58.

Gannon, Megan. 2016. "Race Is a Social Construct, Scientists Argue." *Scientific American*, February 5. https://www.scientificamerican.com/article/race-is-a-social-construct-scientists-argue.

Gould, Stephen Jay, and Steven James Gold. 1996. *The Mismeasure of Man*. New York: Norton.

Hagan, John. 1974. "Extra-legal Attributes and Criminal Sentencing: An Assessment of a Sociological Viewpoint." *Law and Society Review* 8(3):357–83.

Hagan, John, and Kristin Bumiller. 1983. "Making Sense of Sentencing: A Review and Critique of Sentencing Research." In *Research on Sentencing: The Search for Reform*, vol. 2, edited by Alfred Blumstein, Jacqueline Cohen, Susan E. Martin, and Michael H. Tonry. Washington, DC: National Academies.

Hawkins, Darnell F. 1985. "Trends in Black-White Imprisonment: Changing Conceptions of Race or Changing Patterns of Social Control?" *Crime and Social Justice* 24:187–209.

Hawkins, Darnell F. 1995. "Ethnicity, Race, and Crime: A Review of Selected Studies." In *Ethnicity, Race, and Crime: Perspectives across Time and Place*, edited by Darnell F. Hawkins. Albany, NY: SUNY Press.

Hawkins, Darnell F., and Kenneth A. Hardy. 1989. "Black-White Imprisonment Rates: A State-by-State Analysis." *Social Justice* 16(4):75–94.

Henry, Patrick J., and David O. Sears. 2002. "The Symbolic Racism 2000 Scale." *Political Psychology* 23(2):253–83.

Herrnstein, Richard J., and Charles Murray. 1994. *The Bell Curve: Intelligence and Class Structure in American life*. New York: Free Press.

Hindelang, Michael J. 1978. "Race and Involvement in Common Law Personal Crimes." *American Sociological Review* 43(1):93–109.

Hindelang, Michael J., Travis Hirschi, and Joseph G. Weis. 1981. *Measuring Delinquency*. Beverly Hills, CA: Sage.

Hinton, Elizabeth. 2016. *From the War on Poverty to the War on Crime*. Cambridge, MA: Harvard University Press.

Hinton, Elizabeth, and DeAnza Cook. 2021. "The Mass Criminalization of Black Americans: A Historical Overview." *Annual Review of Criminology* 4:261–86.

Ignatiev, Noel. 1995. *How the Irish Became White*. New York: Routledge.

Johnston, Norman. 1994. *Eastern State Penitentiary: Crucible of Good Intentions*. Philadelphia: Museum of Art.

Kleck, Gary. 1981. "Racial Discrimination in Criminal Sentencing: A Critical Evaluation of the Evidence with Additional Evidence on the Death Penalty." *American Sociological Review* 46:783–805.

Krivo, Lauren J., Reginald A. Byron, Catherine A. Calder, Ruth D. Peterson, Christopher R. Browning, Mei-Po Kwan, and Jae Yong Lee. 2015. "Patterns of Local Segregation: Do They Matter for Neighborhood Crime?" *Social Science Research* 54:303–18.

Kurlychek, Megan C., and Brian D. Johnson. 2019. "Cumulative Disadvantage in the American Criminal Justice System." *Annual Review of Criminology* 2:291–319.

Langan, Patrick. 1985. "Racism on Trial: New Evidence to Explain the Racial Composition of Prisons in the United States." *Journal of Criminal Law and Criminology* 76(3):666–83.

Lauritsen, Janet L., and Karen Heimer. 2010. "Violent Victimization among Males and Economic Conditions: The Vulnerability of Race and Ethnic Minorities." *Criminology and Public Policy* 9(4):665–92.

Lee, Jennifer, and F. D. Bean. 2007. "Redrawing the Color Line?" *City and Community* 6(1):49–62.

Lemann, Nicholas. 1991. *The Promised Land: The Great Black Migration and How It Changed America*. New York: Vintage.

Lieberson, Stanley. 1981. *A Piece of the Pie: Blacks and White Immigrants since 1880*. Berkeley: University of California Press.

Lyons, Christopher J., and Becky Pettit. 2011. "Compounded Disadvantage: Race, Incarceration, and Wage Growth." *Social Problems* 58(2):257–80.

Mancini, Matthew J. 1996. *One Dies, Get Another: Convict Leasing in the American South, 1866–1928*. Columbia: University of South Carolina Press.

Massey, Douglas S., and Nancy Denton. 1993. *American Apartheid: Segregation and the Making of the Underclass*. Cambridge, MA: Harvard University Press.

McCoskey, Denise Eileen. 2021. *Race: Antiquity and Its Legacy*. London: Bloomsbury.

Muhammad, Khalil Gibran. 2011. *The Condemnation of Blackness: Race, Crime, and the Making of Modern Urban America*. Cambridge, MA: Harvard University Press.

Muller, Christopher. 2012. "Northward Migration and the Rise of Racial Disparity in American Incarceration, 1880–1950." *American Journal of Sociology* 118:281–326.

Muller, Christopher. 2018. "Freedom and Convict Leasing in the Postbellum South." *American Journal of Sociology* 124(2):367–405.

Muller, Christopher. 2021. "Exclusion and Exploitation: The Incarceration of Black Americans from Slavery to the Present." *Science* 374(6565):282–86.

Muller, Christopher, and Daniel Schrage. 2021. "The Political Economy of Incarceration in the Cotton South, 1910–1925." *American Journal of Sociology* 127(3):828–66.

Murray, Charles. 1984. *Losing Ground: American Social Policy, 1950–1980*. New York: Basic.

Musto, David F. 1999. *The American Disease: Origins of Narcotic Control*, 3rd ed. New York: Oxford University Press.

Oldham, Kit. 2004. "George Bush Settles with His Family at Bush Prairie Near Tumwater in November 1845." HistoryLink, February 1. https://www.history link.org/File/5646.

Omi, Michael, and Howard Winant. 2014. *Racial Formation in the United States*, 3rd ed. New York: Routledge.

Pager, Devah. 2003. "The Mark of a Criminal Record." *American Journal of Sociology* 108(5):937–75.

Pager, Devah. 2008. *Marked: Race, Crime, and Finding Work in an Era of Mass Incarceration*. Chicago: University of Chicago Press.

PCLEAJ (President's Commission on Law Enforcement and Administration of Justice). 1967. *The Challenge of Crime in a Free Society*. Washington, DC: US Government Printing Office.

Peterson, Ruth D., and Lauren J. Krivo. 2010. *Divergent Social Worlds: Neighborhood Crime and the Racial-Spatial Divide*. New York: Russell Sage.

Pettigrew, Thomas F., Linda R. Tropp, Ulrich Wagner, and Oliver Christ. 2011. "Recent Advances in Intergroup Contact Theory." *International Journal of Intercultural Relations* 35(3):271–80.

Pettit, Becky. 2012. *Invisible Men: Mass Incarceration and the Myth of Black Progress*. New York: Russell Sage.

Pettit, Becky, and Christopher J. Lyons. 2009. "Incarceration and the Legitimate Labor Market: Examining Age-Graded Effects on Employment and Wages." *Law and Society Review* 43(4):725–56.

Quinney, Richard. 1970. *The Social Reality of Crime*. Boston: Little, Brown.

Richardson, Heather Cox. 2004. *The Death of Reconstruction: Race, Labor, and Politics in the Post–Civil War North, 1865–1901*. Cambridge, MA: Harvard University Press.

Rose, Dina R., and Todd R. Clear. 1998. "Incarceration, Social Capital, and Crime: Implications for Social Disorganization Theory." *Criminology* 36(3): 441–80.

Rushton, J. Philippe. 1987. "Race Differences in Behaviour: A Review and Evolutionary Analysis." *Personality and Individual Differences* 9(6):1009–24.

Russell, Katheryn K. 1992. "Development of a Black Criminology and the Role of the Black Criminologist." *Justice Quarterly* 9(4):667–83.

Sampson, Robert J. 2012. *Great American City: Chicago and the Enduring Neighborhood Effect*. Chicago: University of Chicago Press.

Sampson, Robert J., and William J. Wilson. 2020. "Toward a Theory of Race, Crime, and Urban Inequality." In *Crime and Inequality*, edited by John Hagan and Ruth Peterson. Stanford, CA: Stanford University Press.

Sears, David O., and Tom Jessor. 1996. "Whites' Racial Policy Attitudes: The Role of White Racism." *Social Science Quarterly* 77(4):751–59.

Sharkey, Patrick T. 2013. *Stuck in Place: Urban Neighborhoods and the End of Progress toward Racial Equality*. Chicago: University of Chicago Press.

Sharkey, Patrick T., and Alisabeth Marsteller. 2022. "Neighborhood Inequality and Violence in Chicago, 1965–2020." *University of Chicago Law Review* 89(2): 349–82.

Singer, Isidore, and Cyrus Adler. 1907. *The Jewish Encyclopedia: A Descriptive Record of the History, Religion, Literature, and Customs of the Jewish People from the Earliest Times to the Present Day*, vol. 1. New York: Funk & Wagnalls.

Smaje, Chris. 1997. "Not Just a Social Construct: Theorizing Race and Ethnicity." *Sociology* 31(2):307–27.

Sowell, Thomas. 1981. *Ethnic America: A History*. New York: Basic.

Spohn, Cassia. 2015. "Race, Crime, and Punishment in the Twentieth and Twenty-First Centuries." In *Crime and Justice: A Review of Research*, vol. 44, edited by Michael Tonry. Chicago: University of Chicago Press.

Stampp, Kenneth M. 1956. *The Peculiar Institution: Slavery in the Ante-bellum South*. New York: Knopf.

Tannenbaum, Frank. 1938. *Crime and the Community*. New York: Columbia University Press.

Tolnay, Stewart E. 2003. "The African American 'Great Migration' and Beyond." *Annual Review of Sociology* 29:209–32.

Tonry, Michael. 1997. "Ethnicity, Crime, and Immigration." In *Ethnicity, Crime, and Immigration: Comparative and Cross-National Perspectives*, edited by Michael Tonry. Vol. 21 of *Crime and Justice: A Review of Research*, edited by Michael Tonry. Chicago: University of Chicago Press.

Tonry, Michael. 2011. *Punishing Race*. New York: Oxford University Press.

Tonry, Michael, and Matthew Melewski. 2008. "The Malign Effects of Drug and Crime Control Policies on Black Americans." In *Crime and Justice: A Review of Research*, vol. 37, edited by Michael Tonry. Chicago: University of Chicago Press.

Travis, Jeremy, Bruce Western, and Steve Redburn. 2014. *The Growth of Incarceration in the United States: Exploring Causes and Consequences*. Washington, DC: National Academies.

Unnever, James D., and Shaun L. Gabbidon. 2011. *A Theory of African American Offending: Race, Racism, and Crime*. New York: Routledge.

Western, Bruce. 2006. *Punishment and Inequality in America*. New York: Russell Sage.

Western, Bruce, and David J. Harding. 2022. "Careers in Criminalization: Reentry, Recidivism, and Repeated Incarceration." In *Prisons and Prisoners*, edited by Michael Tonry and Sandra Bucerius. Vol. 51 of *Crime and Justice: A Review of Research*, edited by Michael Tonry. Chicago: University of Chicago Press.

Western, Bruce, and Becky Pettit. 2010. "Incarceration and Social Inequality." *Daedalus* 139(3):8–19.

Wilson, James Q., and Richard J. Herrnstein. 1985. *Crime and Human Nature*. New York: Simon & Schuster.

Wilson, William Julius. 1987. *The Truly Disadvantaged: The Inner City, the Underclass, and Public Policy*. Chicago: University of Chicago Press.

Zatz, Margaret S. 1987. "The Changing Forms of Racial/Ethnic Biases in Sentencing." *Journal of Research in Crime and Delinquency* 24(1):69–92.

Sandra Bucerius and Sveinung Sandberg

Women in Prisons

ABSTRACT

Before being locked up, incarcerated women are more marginalized, have higher rates of mental illness and substance misuse, and have more often experienced physical or sexual victimization than incarcerated men. Women experience prison differently. However, much of what we know about women's experiences comes from research in the United States and the United Kingdom, providing little insight into women prisoners' experiences elsewhere. This is unfortunate for many reasons; policy makers wishing to develop evidence-based initiatives, for example, cannot know whether what seems to work in one place is appropriate in another. Case studies from Canada, Norway, and Mexico reveal similarities and substantial differences in women's experiences. Incarcerated women in all three places have histories of victimization and identify their children as their primary motivator to desist from crime and drug use. However, how they relate to programming, prison work, accommodation, and prison food varies greatly. How women in these three different countries experience imprisonment is related to conditions of their lives outside of prison and to the nature, extent, and quality of available social welfare services. Researchers need to pay much closer attention to geographical and contextual differences when assessing the conditions, challenges, and prospects of women in prisons.

Scholars have mostly studied men's prisons and male prisoners (e.g., Sykes 1958; Irwin and Cressey 1962; Jacobs 1977). This is not surprising. Men's prisons far outnumber those for women, and men make up 90–95 percent of prisoners in most countries. Rises in female incarceration

Sandra Bucerius is Henry Marshall Tory Chair and professor of sociology and criminology, University of Alberta. Sveinung Sandberg is professor of criminology, University of Oslo.

Electronically published September 30, 2022

Crime and Justice, volume 51, 2022.

rates and increases in female fractions among prison populations in many countries in recent years have fueled interest in understanding more about women's incarceration, the challenges women prisoners face, and the effects of incarceration on them and their families and loved ones (e.g., Bloom 1995; Owen 1998; Kruttschnitt and Gartner 2005, 2008; DeHart 2008; Wright and Cain 2017; Beckett and Goldberg 2022; Wakefield 2022).

Most English-language research on women in prison concerns the United States or, to a lesser extent, the United Kingdom.[1] While there may be understandable reasons for this—language proficiency, delimitation of focus, and time and space concerns—it is regrettable. Context always matters, and there is no good reason to doubt that is true of women's prisons (Bloom et al. 2003). Limited work in other countries and a near absence of comparative work obstruct development of a more general understanding.[2] It has been consistently shown that how people experience imprisonment depends on the challenges, opportunities, and life circumstances they experience in the community (e.g., Comfort 2012; Crewe and Levins 2020; Bucerius, Haggerty, and Dunford 2021; Schneider 2021).

In this essay, we present findings from qualitative studies of women's experiences of imprisonment in Canada, Mexico, and Norway. In all three countries, incarcerated women experienced victimization throughout their lives; the overwhelming majority have initial victimization experiences in childhood. Prison administrations need to create and operate trauma-informed approaches and programs to address these experiences while at the same time offer programs addressing the more immediate

[1] Netherlands (e.g., Slotboom et al. 2011; Kruttschnitt et al. 2013) and Canadian studies (e.g., Jones, Bucerius, and Haggerty 2019; Bucerius, Berardi, and Haggerty 2022) are notable exceptions.

[2] Candace Kruttschnitt's and Catrien Bijleveld's (2011) edited collection brought together works on the lives of incarcerated women in different countries and illuminated how different social contexts aggravate or mitigate women's vulnerabilities and their pathways to imprisonment. The collection, however, offers no systematic comparisons between countries. Instead, it provides deep insights into some aspects of the lives of incarcerated women in one country and on other aspects in another (e.g., on the relationship between imprisoned mothers and their children in Denmark and on the institutionalization of boys and girls in the Netherlands). Another exception is Ben Crewe's project "Penal Policy Making and the Prisoner Experience: A Comparative Analysis," which includes comparative ethnographic work on women's experiences in England, Wales, and Norway (e.g., Crewe et al. 2022).

factors that may have led to incarceration (such as substance misuse or lack of economic opportunities). In Canada, but not significantly in Norway and Mexico, many women prisoners regarded prisons as refuges from their harsh lives outside. In Canada and Mexico, but not in Norway, many women prisoners believed that welfare programs and treatment programs were more accessible and useful in prison than in the community. Women prisoners in all three countries describe missing their children as their primary motivation to change their lives and desist from crime, stressing the importance of visits and cohousing options. Prisons vary greatly between and within countries, as do the societal positions of women inside and outside prison and the nature of social welfare services in prisons and in the outside community. Local and contextual dynamics in women's position in society and their incarceration experiences need to be foregrounded when developing policies and programs. Variabilities that exist within groups of incarcerated women, such as diverse racial and ethnic backgrounds, social class, sexual orientation, gender identity, and citizenship status, need to be attended to as well.

Here is how this essay is organized. In Section I we set the stage with a brief overview of past research on prisoners' lives inside prisons. We pay particular attention to women's incarceration, women's pathways into prison, and inequalities and challenges in women's incarceration experiences. In Section II, we describe overriding problems in women offenders' lives—sexual and physical abuse, mental health problems, drug dependence—and identify five fundamental challenges that confront women in prison: accommodation and food, victimization, programming and treatment, work, and motherhood. In Section III, organized around those five challenges, we examine similarities and differences in women's incarceration in Canada, Norway, and Mexico. We emphasize local particularities to show how conventional wisdom about women's imprisonment can be challenged by findings from different societal, cultural, and national contexts.

I. Imprisonment of Women

The imprisonment of women varies between and within countries, although incarceration of women has increased in recent years in many countries (see, e.g., Wright and Cain 2017). Incarceration rate increases for women outpaced those for men in several countries, including Australia and Canada (Bucerius and Urbanik 2015; Walmsley 2017).[3] More than 714,000 women and girls were incarcerated globally in 2017 (Walmsley 2017, p. 2), a number that increased on all continents between 2000 and 2019 (when the COVID-19 pandemic emerged).[4] Two patterns stand out globally: the United States incarcerates by far the greatest number of women and girls; incarceration of women is shaped by larger racial and ethnic patterns.

A. Women's Incarceration and US Exceptionalism

The increase in female prisoners was nowhere more pronounced than in the United States. Internationally, about a third of all female prisoners are in the United States (Kajstura 2018; Fair and Walmsley 2021). Table 1 provides data on Canada, Mexico, and Norway and, for contrast, the United States and England and Wales. Women make up relatively small fractions of prisoners (although nearly twice as large in the United States as elsewhere), and US women's imprisonment rates are about 10 times higher than those elsewhere.

Criminologists in the United States have tried to explain why women's rate of incarceration has recently increased faster than men's and why their proportion of the prison population has been increasing. Women appear by and large to engage in the same types of crimes as in earlier times and are less violent than men (e.g., Bloom, Owen, and Covington 2004; Kruttschnitt and Gartner 2008). Instead, analysts argue that women's criminal involvement must be understood in the context of larger societal and political shifts in drug law enforcement (Garland 2001). Emergence of "get tough" policies, stiffer penalties for drug crimes and mandatory minimum sentences, three strikes, and similar laws generated huge increases in incarceration generally (e.g., Javdani, Sadeh, and Verona 2011). The war on drugs led to the introduction of mandatory minimum sentences for sales, possession, and conspiracies involving drugs. These changes were "gender neutral," affecting both men and women and targeting both high-level distributors and street-level dealers. However,

---

[3] This is not true universally, however, or over longer periods. In the United Kingdom, for example, men's incarceration rates increased more rapidly than women's over 100 years (Ministry of Justice 2020).

[4] Numbers for both men and women have declined in some jurisdictions since the COVID-19 pandemic began (Maruna, McNaull, and O'Neill 2022). For example, the number of women sentenced and convicted in criminal courts in the United States fell by 30 percent from 2019 to 2020, largely due to the COVID-19 pandemic. The courts significantly altered operations in 2020, leading to delays in trials, sentencing, or both (Carson 2021, p. 1).

TABLE 1
Female Prison Population, Selected Countries

Country	Female Prison Population	Prison Popula-tion Percentage	Estimated National Population (Millions)	Imprisonment Rate per 100,000
Canada	2,727	5.6	35.40	7.7
Mexico	10,832	5.2	123.75	8.8
Norway	238	6.1	5.29	4.5
England and Wales	3,974	4.6	59.00	6.7
United States	211,870	9.8	322.30	65.7

SOURCE.—Based on Walmsley (2017).

women are more likely to be involved in lower-level drug dealing than other types of crime (also to address their substance misuse habits) and were therefore disproportionately affected by increased street-level drug law enforcement (Heimer, Wittrock, and Unal 2006).

B. Racial and Ethnic Patterns

The incarceration of women varies between countries and both reflects and is shaped by broader racial, cultural, and classed inequalities. Differences reveal a great deal about prisons and the societies in which they are located. Incarceration of women at national levels reflects patterns of racial inequality, with members of some groups incarcerated at much higher rates than members of others. In the United States, Black and Latino women are disproportionately incarcerated (Sentencing Project 2020). In Canada, the most extreme disparities affect Indigenous women (Bucerius, Berardi, and Haggerty 2022). In some European countries, citizenship status seems to be a key determining factor. For example, 71.5 percent of prisoners in Switzerland in 2020 were foreign nationals. Switzerland is an extreme case, but foreign nationals are overrepresented in all other Western European countries (Prisonwatch 2022, p. 6). The main lesson is that members of particular racial, ethnic, or nationality groups are often incarcerated disproportionately in every country.

General patterns of racial and ethnic disparity affect both men and women. Trends, however, differ, depending on the context. For example, incarceration of Black American women fell by 60 percent in the United States between 2000 and 2019, but their incarceration rate continues to be higher than those of White and Latino women (Sentencing Project 2020). During those years, incarceration rates of White and Latino women increased by 41 percent and 5 percent respectively, while rates for men in all three groups decreased.[5] Racial and ethnic backgrounds also influence sentence lengths in England and Wales (Ministry of Justice 2020, p. 40). Overall then, while the specifics vary from country to country, race and ethnic background generally influence custody rates and sentencing outcomes.

C. Why Are Women Imprisoned?

Women's pathways to incarceration are different from those of men. Victimization, mental health, and substance misuse problems are widely seen as major contributing causes; this has led to development and implementation of "gender-responsive" assessment tools and programing in the United States, England, and elsewhere (Daly 1992; Bloom et al. 2003). The pertinent scholarship, however, is mostly based on female-only samples and was conducted primarily in the United States. It ignores geographical contexts. It also often fails to acknowledge that many characteristics described as unique to women can also apply to men. Prior victimization, for example, is a common element in male prisoners' lives (Kruttschnitt 2016; Bucerius et al. 2020). Gender-responsive assessment tools often ignore race, class, age, and other important differences. Newer research has drawn attention to more immediate factors that lead to women's incarceration, such as lack of employment, troubled relationships, and addiction (Kruttschnitt, Joosen, and Bijleveld 2019). This literature urges that contextual differences in women's lives be taken into account and that it cannot be assumed that victimization experiences are the most critical contributors to a woman's pathway into prison.

1. *Victimization and Mental Health.* Women's characteristics influence their pathways to incarceration. Feminist scholars have drawn attention to the effects of early childhood victimization and mental health issues on later-in-life incarceration (Bloom et al. 2003; Corston 2007).

---

[5] The reasons for the simultaneous increase for White women and decrease for Black women are not well understood. White women are disproportionately affected by the opioid crisis and more engaged in methamphetamine offenses than women of other racial backgrounds. Harsh sentencing policies for methamphetamine and opioid offenses have led to higher incarceration rates for White women (Mauer 2013). An additional explanation may be that broader socioeconomic trends that have contributed to a decline in life expectancy for low-income White women have affected offending rates (p. 10).

Others have shown that these experiences may not be unique to women (Kruttschnitt 2016; Bucerius et al. 2020). After all, both men and women prisoners disproportionately come from socially and economically marginalized backgrounds (Keene, Smoyer, and Blankenship 2018). Incarcerated men and women both have higher rates of substance misuse and mental illness than the general population, although rates are higher for incarcerated women (Binswanger et al. 2010; Wright et al. 2012; Jones, Bucerius, and Haggerty 2019; Bucerius, Berardi, and Haggerty 2022). It is also well established that both incarcerated women and men have much higher prevalence of sexual and physical victimization than does the general public (Bucerius et al. 2020). However, women experience serious sexual and serious domestic violent victimization at higher rates than men (Tjaden and Thoennes 2000).

2. *Substance Misuse.* Women are more likely to use alcohol excessively, to develop drug-induced mental issues, and to develop serious mental health problems. Posttraumatic stress disorder and substance misuse are highly correlated for women, whereas men are more likely to use drugs and excessive alcohol to alter their moods. Drug use affects women differently from men: biological differences make women reach dependency faster even though women typically initiate drug use at later ages (O'Brien 2001; Young and Reviere 2006). Patterns of substance misuse may result from women's efforts to self-medicate, often to cope with mental health issues and previous traumas (Anderson, Rosay, and Saum 2002; Jones, Bucerius, and Haggerty 2019). Women also experience negative effects—such as social isolation and family breakdown—more quickly than men. Unsurprisingly then, women are more likely than men to have used illicit drugs or alcohol at the time of arrest. Women's drug use also plays a role in their involvement in crime and in their punishments. In the United States, women are disproportionately involved in drug and property offenses that result in two-thirds of women's incarceration (West and Sabol 2008).

3. *Relationships.* Intimate and biological relationships have profound and paradoxical effects on women's arrest and incarceration experiences and on their pathways into crime. Familial relationships can be why women engage in crime in the first place, but these relationships also provide reasons to desist from crime. Women sometimes commit crimes to provide material resources for their families and children, and other times women avoid crime to protect their loved ones (O'Brien 2001).

Relationships with women have a mitigating effect on men's criminality (Sampson and Laub 1993; Zoutewelle-Terovan et al. 2014), while men often introduce or coerce women into crime (Maher 1997; Jones 2008; Barlow 2016; Barlow and Weare 2018). Diaz Cotto (2006) and Vernetta Young and Rebeccah Reviere (2006) found that women of color are disproportionately arrested and convicted, often because of relationships with men involved in drug dealing. In the American War on Drugs, for example, conspiracy, possession, and trafficking charges often ensnared intimate partners of drug dealers, even if they were not themselves involved in sales (Feld 2009). Intimate relationships also influence sentence lengths. Women often lose out on available sentence reductions because they lack substantial information to divulge to prosecutors or are silenced by threats of violence from intimate partners (Young and Reviere 2006).

4. *Connection between These Factors and Prison Programming.* The links between these characteristics and incarceration are murky and have affected how scholars think about prison programming for women. For example, gender-responsive programming—based on the pathways scholarship described above—aims to understand women's incarceration experiences in relation to trauma and victimization. Candace Kruttschnitt, Katharina Joosen, and Catrien Bijleveld (2019), by contrast, argue that other factors such as drug use, lack of economic opportunities, and intimate relationships before incarceration have more immediate effects on women's incarceration. They call for programming addressing women's immediate needs for employment or substance misuse treatment.

These two lines of thought are not necessarily at odds. While early childhood victimization, for example, may not have a direct influence on later-in-life incarceration, it may influence later-in-life drug use that, in turn, may lead to incarceration and reoffending. Ideally, prison programming should take the individualized needs of women or men into account. This may mean for some prisoners addressing the root causes of their substance misuse and for others working only on their substance misuse.

The characteristics of incarcerated men and women are not necessarily as different as the early pathways literature assumed, even if past victimization, mental health problems, and substance misuse rates are more pronounced among incarcerated women. Women's victimization experiences and mental health challenges often intersect with their substance misuse. In turn, these influence arrest and incarceration experiences. Other intersecting factors, such as race, citizenship status, and sexual orientation, may have compounding effects. Likewise, children and intimate partners influence why women engage in crime and why they get arrested.

II. Experiences of Women in Prison

Women and men experience prison differently. Historically, research on women mostly focused on how their experiences reinforce dominant gender relations (Bosworth 2000), although there are few in-depth accounts of women's experiences in prison. The few observational and qualitative studies that do exist were almost exclusively conducted in the United States.

A. The Literature

David Ward and Gene Kassebaum (1965) and Rose Giallombardo (1966) published the first serious sociological inquiries into women's prisons. Ward and Kassebaum offered an in-depth account of how women's adaptations to prison life differed from men's, especially with respect to "inmate roles" laid out in Sykes's (1958) pivotal study. They concluded that the inmate role model did not apply to women. Instead, heavily relying on functionalist sex role theory, they found that relationships among women inmates were predominately based on sexual relationships and conditioned by gender roles women hold in society, particularly being a mother and wife. Giallombardo's (1966) ethnographic study similarly made essentialist claims about sex roles and gender norms to show that women form relationships in prison that mimic those outside prison walls. Neither early study adequately accounted for the effects of power and domination in explaining gender roles in prison or paid attention to class, race, and other characteristics that shape relationships. Heffernan (1972) provided additional nuance to understanding of how women "do time." Rejecting the existence of a monolithic "inmate code," Heffernan found that women draw on diverse individual strategies to adapt to prison life, such as by relying on established networks developed during prior prison stints or on the streets or by enrolling in religious programs.

Two decades later, Owen (1998) moved away from the early emphasis on sex roles. She drew attention to how women's prison experiences are shaped by economic marginalization, substance misuse, personal victimization, and relationships with children—a focus that continues to shape contemporary research.

Two additional studies—by Candace Kruttschnitt and Rosemary Gartner (2005) and Jill McCorkel (2013)—showed how mass incarceration affected women's prison experiences in light of the collapse of the "rehabilitative ideal." Kruttschnitt and Gartner (2005) found that women took more responsibility for their own rehabilitation. With institutional support for and involvement in women's rehabilitation declining, women became highly suspicious of each other and of staff, creating a socially fractured dynamic.

McCorkel's multiyear ethnographic study focused on how the increase in the number of incarcerated women at the end of the century destabilized established governance structures. She demonstrated that women adapted to the "new penology" that emerged as a consequence of the War on Drugs and was exacerbated by a lack of staff and housing for women and by deeply racialized and gendered forms of punishment. One of the effects of the gender, race, and class politics of the War of Drugs was a new way of thinking about women offenders, who became pathologized as deeply criminal, drug addicted, and violent and needing radical intervention to change into their "respectable" selves. McCorkel described in detail how women prisoners resisted efforts to transform them into "respectable beings."

Quantitative studies have also contributed to understandings of the characteristics that shape women's experiences in prison, including co-occurrence of victimization, substance misuse, homelessness, poor health, and mental health issues (Peters, Bartoi, and Sherman 2008; Houser, Belenko, and Brennan 2012; Jones, Bucerius, and Haggerty 2019). These studies, like their qualitative counterparts, mostly concern the United States—often, particular state prisons—making the generalizability of findings difficult to ascertain.

B. Facets of Women's Incarceration

Details of prison life matter. Conditions—such as accommodation and food, victimization, programming and treatment, prison work, and motherhood—influence women's experiences. These differ, sometimes enormously, depending on the societal context. Below, we identify five facets of women's imprisonment around which we organize our comparative analysis in Section III.

1. *Accommodation and Food.* Gresham Sykes's (1958) foundational study of a New Jersey prison highlighted a lack of access to goods and services, including food and proper accommodation, as one of five fundamental deprivations of imprisonment. Accommodation in prison varies considerably, within and across national contexts, and depends on security levels and whether women are housed in mixed-gender or women-only prisons. Generalizations are, thus, difficult to make, although prisons in

Western Europe and, to a greater extent, Scandinavia seem to offer comparatively comfortable living accommodations for both men and women. In contrast, Canadian, UK, and US prisons generally offer sparse housing conditions. In Latin America and other parts of the world, prisons are even more underfunded and overcrowded.

Food quality and particularities of consumption and preparation also vary widely. Criminologists have not paid much attention to the subject; a recent scoping review (Smoyer 2019) found only 38 articles of varying quality and focus written on the topic over 20 years. Many frame practices concerning food as ways for prisoners to resist oppressive conditions and fashion distinctive identities (e.g., Earle and Phillips 2012; Smoyer 2015, 2019; Smoyer and Lopes 2017; Gibson-Light 2018; Einat and Davidian 2019). These studies illustrated how the acquisition, preparation, and consumption of food becomes particularly important in an environment characterized by extreme material deprivation (Valentine and Longstaff 1998). The few works on women foreground identity work and emphasize how women use their relationship with food to present themselves as "good" and "healthy," constructing themselves as "caring empathetic, generous people who would go out of their way to help others" (Smoyer 2014, p. 530) by sharing food, sometimes violating prison rules.

2. *Victimization.*   Women's incarceration experiences cannot be understood without considering their abuse histories (Liebling 2009). Many prison experiences can retraumatize women (e.g., strip searchers; Davis 2003; George and McCulloch 2008; Hutchison 2019) and trigger coping mechanisms forged in response to childhood abuse (Dirks 2004). Both incarcerated men and women have disproportionate histories of prior sexual and physical abuse (Belknap and Holsinger 2006; Bucerius et al. 2020). Women have different, "gender-responsive" reactions including engaging in illegal activities (e.g., Gilfus 1992; Giarratano, Ford, and Nochajski 2020) and substance misuse (Grella, Stein, and Greenwell 2005; Widom, Marmorstein, and White 2006) and developing mental health problems (Tripodi and Pettus-Davis 2013). Consequently, women prisoners' levels of mental illness and poor health are higher than among the general public or compared with male prisoners' (Maruschak 2008; Zlotnick et al. 2008). Almost twice as many incarcerated women suffer from serious mental illnesses than do incarcerated men (17.4 percent in comparison to 9.6 percent; Magletta et al. 2009). Incarcerated women also have a higher likelihood of self-harm or attempted suicide (Bloom et al. 2003; Covington 2008; Tripodi, Onifade, and Pettus-Davis 2014), although this varies with prison conditions

and social contexts (Kruttschnitt and Vuolo 2007).[6] These concerns need to be understood in the context of their victimization experiences, often starting in early childhood (Bucerius, Haggerty, and Dunford 2021). Incarceration does not necessarily end victimization. While some women speak of prison as a safe place that allows them physical distance from abusive people, who are mostly men (Schneider 2021; Bucerius, Berardi, and Haggerty 2022), others continue to experience physical and sexual victimization in prison (e.g., Morash and Schram 2002; Davis 2003).

3. *Programming.* Programming for women in prison should focus on rehabilitation and trauma-informed services that address trauma, mental health challenges, victimization, and abuse (Wright et al. 2012; Giarratano, Ford, and Nochajski 2020). Programs should be nonpunitive, relational, and based on cognitive behavioral models that aim to restructure attitudes, thoughts, and behaviors (Van Voorhis, Braswell, and Lester 2009). Such efforts can target cognitive changes by considering women's strengths, such as positive relationships with counsellors and children. Programs for women must address comorbidity between substance misuse, victimization, and mental health and provide access to substance misuse programs (without mandating sobriety; Covington 2008).

Many jurisdictions have developed such programs, but whether they are offered in specific prisons is a different question. Our fieldwork has shown that there is often a discrepancy between the programs correctional ministries announce and those that are offered. Program spaces are often severely limited in number, admitting only a few selected participants (Bucerius, Berardi, and Haggerty 2022). In assessing programs, researchers need to pay close attention to on-the-ground realities. General health care and other program needs are not met in many prisons (Belknap 2010). In addition, how women experience and evaluate available programs depends on their opportunities and access to similar programs in the community (Bucerius, Haggerty, and Dunford 2021; Schneider 2021).

4. *Work.* Lack of access to employment shapes criminal careers and is a major obstacle to desistance from crime (e.g., Sampson and Laub 1993). No wonder, then, that prison work programs are high on reform agendas. Prison labor, in one form or another, is present in most prison systems (Van zyl Smit and Dunkel 2018). It is diversely described as an element

---

[6] Men in the general population are more likely than women to commit suicide, but in prison women are as likely as men to kill themselves (Fazel et al. 2011).

of punishment, moralistic coercion, rehabilitation, discipline, or a way to keep prisoners busy and as regular but cheap labor. Prison work programs in the United States usually include institutional maintenance, traditional correctional industry jobs, or employment by private businesses (Nur and Nguyen 2022). These prison work programs are usually described as reducing idleness, upholding order, reducing operations costs, promoting the work ethic, and preparing incarcerated people for later employment (Crittenden, Koons-Witt, and Kaminski 2018; Nur and Nguyen 2022). Such programs, however, are criticized for not being translatable to work outside of prison (Nur and Nguyen 2022) and for being exploitative (DelSesto 2021).

Women work in prison for several reasons including being required to (e.g., in Germany, where prison work is mandatory), to learn a work ethic in an environment in which idleness is disparaged, to forget about prison life, or to make money (Buck 2004). Women prisoners' work and training opportunities are often highly gendered. Prisoners are often "grouped into work areas based on what are perceived to be 'appropriate tasks' for certain gender and racial groupings," such as sewing, cooking, and domestic tasks for women and public works and farming for men (Crittenden, Koons-Witt, and Kaminski 2018, p. 360). Racial and gender stereotypes seem to influence work assignments in the United States (Crittenden, Koons-Witt, and Kaminski 2018). There is little reason to believe this is different elsewhere.

5. *Parenting and Childbirth.* Being pregnant in prison raises challenging issues, especially if women are shackled during childbirth (Ocen 2012) or must immediately surrender newborns to the authorities (Rowe 2012). Whether women must surrender newborns depends on the national context and on the security levels of the prison and prisoner. Some prisons have nurseries in which women are allowed to care for their children.[7] Critical scholars acknowledge the good intentions behind such programs but emphasize that institutional realities and being a prisoner are so constraining that they may turn "motherhood into a technique of control and a means to a punitive end" (Haney 2013, p. 107).

---

[7] Depending on the country and jurisdiction, nurseries can be controversial. Some argue that prison is not an appropriate place for babies and toddlers. If a woman is serving a lengthy sentence, a child raised in prison may have attachment issues if later forced to separate. However, a study of long-term effects of growing up alongside their mothers in prison did not find different levels of attachment (Byrne, Goshin, and Joestl 2010).

An additional challenge for parents in general is that imprisonment interrupts and makes parents "miss out" on their relationships with children (Chen 2009; Collica 2010; Foster 2012). Both men and women indicate that being separated from children is an especially painful aspect of incarceration (Arditti and Few 2008; Loper et al. 2009; Schultz, Bucerius, and Haggerty 2021). "Missing out" on relationships with their children, which often involves being absent for many of their children's "firsts" (Foster 2012), is a central theme in the literature on incarcerated women.[8] Some researchers suggest that the prevalence of mental illness, attempted suicide, and substance misuse among incarcerated women (Bloom et al. 2003; Binswanger et al. 2010) is partly attributable to interruption of women's relationships with their children (Chen 2009; Collica 2010). Women also experience additional stress and anxiety because they are more likely than men to be primary caregivers before and after incarceration. While children can provide inspiration and motivation for a life without crime, women might also engage in criminal behavior to provide for their children. Being incarcerated and away from children not only causes emotional pain but can cause additional anxiety because of the women's limited abilities to provide financially for their children while incarcerated.

III. Developing an International, Qualitative, and Comparative Perspective

In sum, although there is a sizable literature on women in prison from the United States and Britain, our own research makes us hesitant to generalize from its findings. Countries and individual facilities vary widely in how they deal with accommodation and food, programming and treatment, work, and motherhood. There seem to be more similarities concerning responses to victimization. Comparing the prison experiences of women in diverse settings allows us to consider whether phenomena are generalizable or context specific. Inequalities relating to incarceration, for example, operate in various ways in different places. Inequalities of gender, race, class, sexual orientation, and physical ability interact to influence who gets imprisoned (and how people experience imprisonment; Owen, Wells, and Pollock 2017). How these intersectional dynamics play out, then, can

---

[8] This considers only effects of separation on mothers. Parental incarceration has heterogeneous effects on children and can be beneficial (Turanovic, Rodriguez, and Pratt 2012; Turney and Wildeman 2015).

depend on societal context. Class differences, for example, vary considerably in different countries and manifest differently in local and national contexts. Similarly, race may be vitally important in some countries, while ethnicity or religious affiliation matter more elsewhere.

Below, we point out insights that emerge from qualitative exploration of conditions and challenges of women in prison outside the United States and the United Kingdom. Understanding specific contexts, however, is a prerequisite. We focus on three locations—Canada, Mexico, and Norway—because we have done research there. A more truly global and more southern perspective would have been better, but we hope evidence from these countries demonstrates the benefits of a more international, qualitative, and comparative approach.

A. Canada, Mexico, and Norway

These countries have different social, economic, and crime policies, including in relation to corrections. Norway is one of the world's most advanced social welfare states and has a long history of social democracy, providing, among other social benefits, free education—including university—and health care for all citizens. Income disparities are less pronounced than in more purely capitalist societies. Norway has the lowest poverty rate among the three countries we discuss; Canada is in the middle, and Mexico is highest (OECD 2021b). Norway has the highest employment rate of the three, with Canada in the middle and Mexico the lowest (OECD 2021a). Norway ranks highest in world happiness surveys among the three, followed by Canada, and then Mexico (Helliwell et al. 2021).

Canada is more explicitly capitalist, with an economy largely driven by private enterprise and free markets. Although, compared with the United States, Canada has well-developed social welfare programs, they fall well below Scandinavian standards. For example, while Canada has free education for school-age children and publicly funded universal health care, university education and preschool childcare costs are expensive. Social inequality is particularly stark in relation to Indigenous people (Tetrault 2022).

Mexico, by stark contrast, is a developing country, even though its economy is fifteenth largest globally based on nominal gross domestic product. In social policies, Mexico runs lowest among the three countries (forty-first in the most recent set of Sustainable Governance Indicators;

Norway ranked first and Canada seventh).[9] Income inequality is stark, comparable to other Latin American countries, and considerably higher than in other Organization for Economic Cooperation and Development countries and emerging economies (Lambert and Park 2019, p. 1). Poverty among Indigenous and rural populations is particularly severe. Health care quality varies widely; public health care and education systems are underfunded, and outcomes are generally poor. While Mexico has free education and health care options, they tend to be of poor quality. People who can afford it typically opt out in favor of private alternatives.

Canada, Norway, and Mexico have starkly different incarceration rates: Mexico's incarceration rate in 1921 was 169 per 100,000, Canada's 104, and Norway's 59. Women make up roughly the same proportions of total prisoner populations: 5.4 percent in Norway in 2021, 5.6 percent in Canada in 2018, and 5.7 percent in Mexico in 2021 (Fair and Walmsley 2021).

Canadian incarceration rates are decreasing overall, but incarceration of Indigenous women continues to rise (Sandulescu 2021; Statistics Canada 2018). Indigenous women constitute only 4 percent of the general population, but 43 percent of female prison admissions nationally (26 percent for Indigenous men; Maleakieh 2018; Zinger 2019).

Federal prisons in Canada detain individuals serving sentences of 2 years or more; on average in 2018–19 683 women were in federal custody. They were held in five federal women's prisons or the federal healing lodge designed for Indigenous women (Correctional Service Canada 2022). Six thousand women were in custody in provincial and territorial prisons that house remand prisoners and people serving sentences up to 2 years.[10]

Incarceration of women and men increased in Norway between 2002 and 2012 but has since decreased. Changes in imprisonment patterns for men and women have been broadly similar (Fair and Walmsley 2021). Most incarcerated women serve their sentences in women's prisons, but some are housed in mixed-gender prisons. A disproportionate number are foreign nationals who constituted 25 percent of women prisoners in 2020 but only 16.8 percent of the female population (Kriminalomsorgen 2021).

In Mexico, total incarceration rates increased from 77 per 100,000 population in 1972 to 212 in 2014. The rate was 169 in 2021 (World Prison

---

[9] See https://www.sgi-network.org/2020/Mexico.

[10] See https://www.womensprisonnetwork.org/Facts.htm.

Network 2021). In absolute numbers, the number of women prisoners has increased more than for men (Bergman and Fondevila 2021); this is linked to broader processes of mass incarceration in the region and to women's increasing role in the illegal drug economy. There are only a few women-only prisons; women usually serve their sentences in separate wards or centers within men's prisons. Except for sharing school and health facilities, women in shared prisons are usually housed completely separately.[11] Living conditions and programs are usually better for women than for men in Latin American prisons (Bergman and Fondevila 2021).

The structure and operation of prisons in each country can vary widely, which makes generalizing particularly challenging. Nonetheless, Scandinavian prison conditions are often described as comparatively humane and progressive (so-called Nordic exceptionalism; Pratt and Eriksson 2013; cf. Uglevik and Dullum 2012). Such depictions tend to be exaggerated and gloss over considerable differences between prisons in Scandinavia, but most observers agree that Nordic prisons tend to be smaller, relations between incarcerated people and correctional officers more egalitarian and respectful, and the quality of prison life better for incarcerated people than in most other countries (Pratt and Eriksson 2013).

In Canada, remand prisons especially suffer from overcrowding and are probably more like US than Scandinavian prisons. Cells are typically designed for two people and contain a bed, a toilet, and perhaps a desk and chair. It is not uncommon for a third person to sleep on a mattress on the floor.

In Mexico, a huge increase in the prison population in recent decades produced overcrowded prisons and comparatively poor conditions (Bergman and Fondevila 2021). The ratio between incarcerated people and correctional officers is higher than in the other two countries, and overcrowded cells, cells with numerous prisoners, and sleeping on mattresses on the floor are common. Organization and daily life of Mexican prisons is largely dictated by the most powerful incarcerated people, which contributes to considerable levels of interpersonal violence. Surprisingly, one study shows that this is truer for women than for men (Bergman and Fondevila 2021). In most Mexican prisons, prisoners depend on work within the prisons or support from family on the outside to pay for basic

[11] This is also true in Canada. Men and women in mixed-gender prisons typically meet only during school, in chapel, at health facilities, or when escorted to court.

supplies and resources (CNDH Mexico 2019; Agoff, Sandberg, and Fondevila 2020). Given these different contexts, we would expect prison experiences for incarcerated women to differ substantially in the three countries.

B. Three Studies

Qualitative data show commonalties and differences in women's incarceration. The three projects were not developed to be comparative and have different designs and addressed prison conditions differently. However, because the projects interviewed incarcerated women, we use the data together, along with other sources, to illustrate similarities and differences. The Canadian project developed the largest, most comprehensive data set, so we devote more attention to it and draw on the other two projects to highlight differences and similarities. Before outlining women's experiences, we briefly describe methodologies.

1. *Methodologies.* The Canadian data were collected as part of the University of Alberta Prison Project—a multimethod examination of prison life in Western Canada organized by Sandra Bucerius and Kevin D. Haggerty.[12] Nearly 800 incarcerated people in four provincial and two federal prisons have been interviewed along with nearly 190 prison staff. The methodology included a quantitative survey in four institutions of prisoners' victimization histories. For this essay, we draw on interviews and surveys conducted with 63 women incarcerated in a federal women's prison in 2019 and 88 interviews with women in three different provincial prisons conducted between 2016 and 2018. The federal prison, the only federal women's prison in Western Canada, has three security areas: minimum, medium, and maximum. At the time of our interviews, 18 participants were in minimum security, 39 in medium, and four in maximum. Of the 88 women in provincial facilities, 59 were remand prisoners and held in a maximum-security prison. The 29 sentenced women were housed in a medium-security prison. The participants in the federal sample were between 22 and 69 years old, with an average age of 37. Participants in the provincial sample were between ages 19 and 58, with an average age of 31. Indigenous participants were, on average, younger in both data sets. All women interviewed had children—slightly more than two, on average. They were

---

[12] More information can be found at https://www.canadiancriminology.com/projects/uapp.

sentenced or awaiting trial for a variety of offenses, with drug possession, trafficking, theft, robbery, and violent offenses (including manslaughter and homicides) making up the majority. Some women were sentenced or awaiting trial for financial frauds and sexual crimes.

Sveinung Sandberg is organizing the Crime in Latin America (CRIMLA) project together with Gustavo Fondevila; it will interview 300 imprisoned women (and men) in Mexico, Honduras, Colombia, Brazil, Argentina, and Chile. As part of that initiative, Sandberg was part of a research group that interviewed 12 incarcerated women in Mexico in 2019. These women serve as our sample of incarcerated Mexican women. Interviews were conducted in a medium-security prison in Mexico City for people convicted of common (nonfederal) crimes (Sandberg, Agoff, and Fondevila 2021). All were Mexican nationals between 18 and 50 years old, with an average age of 24. They had been in prison between 3 and 16 years, with an average of 8 years, and had been sentenced for crimes including theft, robbery, homicide, manslaughter, sexual crimes, and kidnapping. Their sentences ranged from 4 to 60 years, with an average sentence of 22. All had children (slightly more than two on average). At the time of the interviews, five women were living with their children in prison.

As part of a larger study of drug markets, Sandberg also organized life-history interviews with 30 women in Norwegian prisons between 2011 and 2012. Participants' ages ranged from 20 to 50, with a median of 36. The women were Norwegian citizens or spoke Norwegian, and all had extensive substance misuse histories. All were criminally involved in illegal hard-drug markets. The vast majority came from low-socioeconomic-status families; 21 had children. Twelve had one child, seven had two, and two had three. Interviews were conducted in three different prisons that housed both people serving sentences and remand prisoners. All interview participants had been convicted and were serving sentences (Grundetjern 2015).

These studies differ in significant respects, but there are notable similarities. In all three, interviews were conducted one on one with a researcher in a "private" location (visiting room, cell, workshop area, classroom) at a time convenient for the participants and not in the presence of correctional officers. In all three studies, interviews were semistructured and organized as "life stories" (Atkinson 1998) or in-depth conversations that took between 1.5 and 3 hours. This allowed participants' perspectives and experiences to shape the conversations (Maxwell 2013; Charmaz 2014), resulting in a broad range of insights into their biographies and day-to-day realities of prison life. In the Canadian study, most participants were interviewed once, with a handful asking for follow-up conversations. Four of the Norwegians were interviewed twice, and most of the Mexicans were interviewed three times—the approach of the larger CRIMLA study. Participants were promised strict confidentiality and anonymity, and the interviewers requested permission to record the interviews digitally. Interviews were later transcribed and thematically coded.

The Canadian interviews were combined with a survey collecting systematic demographic information and data on prior sexual and physical victimization. Given the smaller numbers of participants in Mexico and Norway, we combine interviews with a review of the relevant literature to provide background for a fuller understanding of women's imprisonment in these countries. The three settings vary, and our characterizations do not apply equally to all of the women. The quotes used in this essay reflect the dominant views of our participants, unless indicated otherwise. Qualitative data cannot be generalized to the entire population in question but should be seen as indicative of possible trends and experiences. They serve well, however, to explore topics in-depth, for example, paying attention to details and nuances pertaining to how prison contexts differ and are experienced.

2. *Perceptions of Incarceration.* Early prison scholars placed considerable emphasis on how incarcerated individuals adapt to the deprivations of prison life. However, this "deprivation model" missed the influences of broader biographical and sociopolitical factors that prisoners "import" into the prison.

Our discussions with women show that hardships are not singular or uniform and do not operate in the same way in different settings or groups. They are best approached as multidimensional and multifaceted, experienced in different ways by different groups. This counsels against speaking uniformly about "prison experiences" and emphasizes the need to pay close attention to contextual differences. The three studies identify hardships associated with incarceration, but the women in the three countries had different views on whether a particular prison hardship is more agreeable than the viable alternatives available to them in the community.

3. *Accommodation and Food.* The women in the Canadian sample often observed that being in prison could be safer or healthier than the options available to them outside (see also Jones, Bucerius, and Haggerty 2019). With 64 percent of the federal sample having been homeless at some point in their lives, it is not surprising that a subset regularly indicated that one

immediate consequence of being incarcerated was that they did not need to worry about finding a place to sleep at night, especially in subzero temperatures that are common in Western Canada.[13] While most large Canadian cities have shelters, Kerry explained that "shelters aren't always safe. There is lots of beef [fights]." Women who avoided shelters often ended up sleeping on the streets or in city parks or in transient arrangements in other people's homes. Such practices could be taxing and dangerous over longer periods and often coincided with extensive patterns of drug use: "Like sometimes we have to . . . use pint [crystal methamphetamine] to stay up [awake]. You have to do the drugs to stay up, cause you can't fall asleep on the streets, you'll get raped, you know what I mean. The guys would take advantage of you or something. . . . Yeah, like it's a bit of a relief coming to jail."

Consequently, these women emphasized that prison provided them with an opportunity to sleep safely and gain access to basic amenities such as showers. As Mindy says: "Before I got arrested this last time I . . . wanted to come back to jail because I didn't have a house. I didn't have a shelter. I didn't know when I was going to eat. I didn't know where I was going to shower." Some women would remain in unsafe living situations because they did not want to be homeless. For example, Kelsi told us about a previous violent relationship she had been in: "I went to start datin' him, and kept going back because . . . it was him or homeless. *And I know how to be in an abusive relationship. I don't know how to be homeless.*"

Canada's reputation as a social welfare state can contribute to the assumption that people in need can get access to safe housing and shelters. The Canadian women in our sample starkly refuted this belief, something that was also reinforced by the correctional staff. As one of our correctional officer participants explained: "In the wintertime, we have women lining up at the door. They think they can check in like into a hotel. We have to turn them away. But this is the place they know is safe for them. So, they want to check in because it's cold. So, as a society . . . society forces them to re-offend so that they can be here."

Relatively safe accommodation was only one of the basic necessities that prison could offer. Other important attributes included regular meals

[13] Three weeks each year temperatures reach −30°C during the day in the region where we conducted our research. Nighttime temperatures are lower. Snowfall during the summer is not uncommon; snow typically covers the ground for 7 months each year.

and finding a sense of community with other women. Tanya explained this in greater detail:

> *Tanya:* Ya it's a safe spot for us. Ya. For ya, we feel safe when we come here. We're not in survival mode, ya. We get three meals a day and stuff like that, it's almost kind of we're living the dream but we're not you know, we're not right.... We laugh a lot here, you know what I mean, it's honestly I feel like, the last couple times I came into jail, I had a lot more fun here than I did out there.

> *Interviewer:* You're kidding.

> *Tanya:* Ya just cause you're safe, you don't have to worry about drugs, you don't have to worry about survival. You have three meals a day.

In Mexico the situation is very different. Prisons are severely underfunded, providing few amenities and little programming. The prison system often does not provide incarcerated people even with necessities. For example, only a few participants reported receiving clothing (25 percent), blankets (21 percent), footwear (8.9 percent), and personal hygiene items (7.6 percent) from the correctional institutions (ENPOL 2016). Consequently, incarcerated people must rely on their own income for necessities (CNDH Mexico 2019). One participant, Rita, said that "everything we need can be bought in prison, food, shoes or other things we lack." Other participants mentioned purchasing toilet paper, blankets, cooking pans—all things routinely provided to women in Canada and Norway.

To acquire these resources, prisoners need to earn money from the work they perform inside the prisons or rely on resources provided by visitors. Semiri explained that to secure extra money she sometimes worked for other prisoners: "Here in the institution, they also ask us to do cleaning, we are assigned certain cleaning areas. There are girls who obviously have money and they don't get their hands dirty, so I come in there, I get them dirty for them. They pay me for that, and I live on that, thank God. It's not a lot of money but at least I have something to give to my mom and my son."

Note how Semiri had to pay for her own necessities and was expected to provide for her family outside of prison (Agoff, Sandberg, and Fondevila 2020). This challenge is unique among the three studies but appears to be common among incarcerated people in Latin American—a challenge that has largely been ignored by the English-language literature on incarcerated women. Unlike sentiments reported by incarcerated Canadian women, the incarcerated Mexican women did not describe prison as a temporary refuge providing basic material resources. For them, the daily struggles related to securing rudimentary basics of existence were comparable inside and outside.

The incarcerated women in Norway did perceive incarceration as a form of temporary refuge, but not concerning food and shelter. Norway provides greater access to housing and food in the community for marginalized populations than does Canada. The Norwegian women had regular and predictable access to food and accommodation with no marked differences between life outside and inside. To the extent that Norwegian women saw the prison as a refuge, it was because they could avoid the consequences of excessive drug use and nomadic lifestyles, while being protected from abuse and gaining a sense of community with other women. And while the Norwegian women certainly had complaints about the prison regime, they were also aware that they were better off than people in other countries, both inside and outside of prison. Marta, for example, said that "it's a lot better here than in other countries. It's better for us than for other people that are imprisoned in England, USA, Brazil, right. They have it three times worse than us. Sometimes I have to remind myself."

The three studies show that how women perceive prison in relation to accommodation and food is closely related to life outside of prison (Bucerius, Haggerty, and Dunford 2021; Schneider 2021; Bucerius, Berardi, and Haggerty 2022). While Canadian women often saw prison as a relief from difficult lives in the community, Mexican women emphasized that prison was not a refuge because securing necessities was difficult both inside and outside. The Norwegian women said they had regular access to food and accommodation wherever they were and that prison played no distinctive role in providing them with basic necessities.

4. *Victimization.* Many prisoners had been victims (Sampson and Laub 1997; Wood et al. 2002), oftentimes during childhood (e.g., Currie and Tekin 2011; Watts and McNulty 2013).[14] Our projects confirm that victimization played a central role in women's lives in all three countries. The vast majority of the Canadian women had previously been physically and sexually abused. Ninety percent of incarcerated women in the federal

---

[14] Importantly, not all victims of sexual and physical child abuse will perpetrate violence in their future (Jaffee et al. 2007).

sample had been physically victimized; on average they were 10 years old the first time. Eighty-four percent had been sexually victimized, averaging 7 years old the first time. Overall, 95 percent of the federal women had been victimized sexually, physically, or both. Their victimization profiles and often prolonged histories of violence—predominately at the hands of men—contributed to their seeing prison as a safe place.

For example, Elisabeth had been physically and sexually abused throughout her life. She had been assaulted by foster parents, foster siblings, residential schoolteachers, family friends, and her spouse.[15] Twice, she told family and social welfare services about the abuse she was experiencing—twice she was ignored. Elisabeth's community life had been characterized by so many violent, dangerous, and unhealthy incidents that she reported: "I like it here [in prison]. I cook for everyone, and I know where to do my laundry. I don't have to fear for my safety."

Elisabeth's relationship to prison must be understood in relation to her upbringing. She had attended residential school and bounced between schools and abusive foster homes, ultimately living in 27 foster homes. She never had what she characterized as a safe living situation before being incarcerated. And while there were undeniably risks in prison, she articulated a view shared by many women that, relatively speaking, prison was safer than the alternatives in the community where she and other women experienced more victimization than in prison. Only 14 percent of the federal sample had been physically victimized during their, often lengthy, terms of incarceration, and none had been sexually victimized in prison, providing support for the assessment that prison could be a safer space.

Widespread victimization was also common for the Mexican women. All had experienced severe sexual and physical abuse before incarceration, often from a young age. Tatiana was abused by her father as a child and youth. Once she was violently beaten because she was observed with a boyfriend: "My dad hit me, he hit me with a thick stick, he cut my hair, his knees were on my shoulders, he hit me with a clenched fist, he broke

---

[15] The residential school system, initiated in 1880, systematically removed Indigenous children from their families, homes, and communities—stripping them of culture and language to absorb them into the White settler society. Given that the last residential school was closed only in 1996, many Indigenous people in Canada either have attended them or have relatives who did. It is now well documented that the staff at these schools often physically, sexually, and psychologically abused students (Stout and Kipling 2003; Regan 2010), producing intergenerational trauma in Indigenous communities (Regan 2010; Truth and Reconciliation Commission of Canada 2015).

my nose. . . . I said not to hit me, and I wanted him to let me explain why, that it was gossip. And then he hit me, and from there I hated him, I wanted him to die."

Many of the women grew up with controlling fathers and, as they became adults, continued to live with their abusive families or exchanged abusive fathers for abusive partners and husbands (Sandberg, Agoff, and Fondevila 2021). Kaly, for example, was repeatedly assaulted by her partner, stating: "I always wondered why do people who are abused remain silent? It's as if you, like the butterflies you put in a glass, they stay there and they stay days, without shouting, without anything, all I wanted was to run away from that place."

Many of the Mexican participants became mothers at young ages, often between 13 and 16. This pattern was shaped by a lack of access to abortion— an illegal procedure in most Mexican states—and a moral and religiously informed opposition to abortion. For many of the women in all three countries, having children could bind them to their abusive partners. Maria, in Canada, talked at length about trying to leave her abusive partner, a challenging prospect given that he financially supported her children. Maria was incarcerated because she killed him during a particularly violent incident: "It came down to me or him. That night, only one of us could survive. It was me or him." When asked why she could not have left him earlier, she stated: "I tried everything. Shelters don't always take kids. I could not leave my babies with him. And when I went to family or friends . . . he always found me. I asked for help. . . . I had no choice. I needed the money for the kids and a roof over their heads. I was trapped. Now I lost everything. *His* family has the kids."

In Norway too, most of the women had been in abusive relationships. Kari, for example, said that her boyfriend started to become violent when his drug use escalated: "There was great difference when he used that and when he used other things. He became two personalities. Very violent, I had to go back and forth to the hospital. . . . Once he locked me up in the apartment for several hours. Came in with a knife and a scissor and accused me of all sorts of things. . . . Fortunately, I managed to escape. I ran to a gas station and called the police."

Two-thirds of the Norwegian women had children, but they became mothers a little later in life than in Canada and much later than in Mexico. Although they could undoubtedly find themselves in abusive relations, staying in such relationships was not typically couched in language about financial stability for children. In Mexico, 59 of every 1,000 pregnancies occur among girls and adolescents ages 15–19, compared to eight in Canada and five in Norway (World Bank 2019). These are dramatic structural differences. The comparably lower ages at first childbirth among the incarcerated Mexican women, and the associated emotional immaturity, may help explain their greater economic dependence on the child's father, which also occurs, to some extent, in Canada. Economically, life as a single mother is easier in Norway than in Canada or Mexico. In Mexico, single motherhood is particularly difficult because the extended family typically takes on the role of the welfare state, often making it difficult to leave abusive relationships.

The women's accounts were similar in the three countries. The vast majority experienced abuse during childhood and adolescence. For many, victimization continued into adulthood. Views on how prison could protect them from victimization were strikingly similar. In all three countries, women experienced prison as a "safe place" in relation to physical, sexual, and emotional abuse.

5. *Programming and Treatment.* Prison administrators in many places have implemented programs and treatment options to address the needs of women (Covington 1998). Correctional Service Canada emphasizes therapeutic programming for incarcerated women. At the same time, women serving time in provincial remand centers are in gender-mixed prisons and do not receive programming especially designed for women. Similar differences probably exist in most countries, meaning that programming is less likely to be based on national ideas about women prisoners than on other considerations.

Many women in both federal and provincial prisons in Canada pointed to difficulties in accessing programming or obtaining treatment in the community. Relevant social programs either did not exist or were not available when women needed them. Natasha, for example, who started using drugs and drinking alcohol as a young teenager, told us she purposefully got herself arrested to get a break from the challenges and dangers of street life and to sober up in prison. When asked whether there might have been a better solution, such as obtaining treatment or counselling in the community, she replied: "Fuck no. I was too messed up. I needed a real break." She explained that she could not check into the treatment center because participants must be sober to be admitted—something that is true for many treatment centers in Canada. Almost all of our participants indicated that this requirement was difficult or impossible to meet. As Terra explained, prison could serve as a lifeline for women struggling with addictions: "This place saved my life. ... I would've been a junkie or instead of showing up in shackles and handcuffs I'd probably would've been in a body bag, you know."

The Canadian women also spoke positively about other services in prison, including educational programs, psychological services, and cultural programs. Some women took part in or got introduced to Indigenous cultural programming. While some scholars have raised concerns about the cultural authenticity of such programming (e.g., McGuire and Murdoch 2021), the women overall spoke extremely highly about it (Tetrault 2022), criticizing mainly its limited availability. Because many of the Indigenous women were raised outside their traditional communities and spent years living precariously on the streets, such programming was often their first exposure to their culture. As Casey made clear: "This place, though, is like ... I learned my spirituality here. I learned a lot about my culture. Like a lot. I learned so much. ... But now, like, I've gained friendships—like close, like sister close—that I've never even thought I would be able to have. Umm ... And just connection to my culture and the creator."

The Indigenous women identified other beneficial services they could access in prison but not in the community. Marie, for example, struggled with substance misuse on the outside; she was one of many who spoke glowingly about the dialectical behavior therapy (DBT) program in prison. When asked about programming that might help her not reoffend, she quickly said: "The DBT program. I was able to take that, and I gotta say it is absolutely life changing. Umm, just on so many levels, the dialectical behavioral therapy was phenomenal. It's like a cognitive program, like just changing your thinking and being able to handle different ways of handling stressors and different ways of handling emotions and just separating levels of emotions. ... It really helps."

Marie attributed being better able to manage her emotions, most notably regulating her anger, to this program. She said it was "absolutely life-changing." Despite Canada's reputation as a social welfare state, there are simply not enough governmental or community-based programs to serve existing needs outside of prison. There are usually long waiting lists.

In Mexico, access to treatment and programming varies so greatly that it is difficult to generalize across states or prisons within one state. As in Canada, many Mexican prisons offer personal development courses and programs. They are often taught by nongovernmental organizations and include drug treatment, anger management, and job training (Sandberg,

Agoff, and Fondevila 2021). The Mexican women spoke positively about the programs. Ana, for example, stated: "It has helped me right now, so I am grabbing it like a catharsis, for when I get out. And the truth is that I'm just waiting for the moment when I can show my changes to my parents." Karen offered a similar assessment, noting: "Everything I know and everything I've tried to learn has been from here [prison]. . . . I have courses in psychology, criminology. I have support, I have a school, I have everything I need." Karen had also been in drug treatment but was removed because she continued to use drugs. Such positive appraisals of Mexican prison programming, however, need to be understood in a context in which such options are often unavailable on the outside.

The programming options in Mexico are distinctive. First, they are highly gendered in many programs, for example, focusing on being a mother, but with few addressing being a father—or a "parent," as in Canadian institutions. Similar gendered dynamics can also be seen in physical exercise programs (Britton 1997) or sports (Baumer and Meek 2018), which are often available only in men's prisons. Programming is often religious themed, which may raise religious freedom issues, but in a country in which over 80 percent of people identify as Catholic, it was appreciated by several women. For Ximena, religion provided her with meaning and helped her serve her time and initiate personal changes: "I knew that God existed. I knew that he loved me very much, and whenever I had problems, I went and cried and prayed to him. He's really with me, telling me how beautiful I am. It makes it easier to live with how bad I have been. . . . I don't have to fall when I have that."

Contrary to outsiders' probable assumptions about Scandinavian countries, the Norwegian women did not have particularly ready access to relevant programming and treatment in prison (see, e.g., Kristoffersen 2019; Hellebust et al. 2021). Some felt in-prison programs were inadequate and worse than those in the community. Randi, for example, said it was "really sad that we don't get help while doing time, when we want to quit drugs. That's really sad." And while Scandinavia is famous for gender equality, many prison programs and work opportunities were deeply gendered, including programs exclusively available to women on knitting and handicrafts (Karlsen 2018).

More than any particular program or treatment initiative, Kristin appreciated the general support offered by staff. As she observed: "There are very good prison guards around me, and psychologists and nurses, all kinds of people that support me in a good way—and want me not to come back. Right, because the prison guards are really like, especially when it comes to young girls 'you're not coming back. We will do anything so that you don't come back.'"

Anna, in prison for the first time, emphasized that her stay was better than she expected, although she was unclear why. She echoed Kristen's observations about supportive staff and people she could talk to. She did not, however, as in Canada, describe this support as being better than what she believed was available in the community. She underlined that "I've been going to a psychologist the last six years (outside of prison). So, I have understood that it is good to get things out in the open. Not be stuck with it on your own."

Among the three countries, Canada again stands out for incarcerated women's views about the availability and quality of programming inside and outside prisons. Canadian participants were much more satisfied with prison programs and treatments than were women in Mexico or Norway. In Mexico, women's appreciation for having some access to treatment and programs must be understood in relation to the poor level of services provided outside of prison and the women's low expectations.

Norway presents a different picture altogether, with participants stating that in-prison programs were not offered frequently enough and were not necessarily of high quality. This lower level of programming is probably because Norway is a small country that incarcerates few women. Catering to "the few" has not become a priority. The lack of programming is regrettable, but negative effects are mediated by comparatively short prison sentences and relatively generous access to treatment and programs upon release. Incarcerated women in Norway are mostly highly marginalized people with pronounced patterns of substance misuse. Some have indicated that their most pressing need is for "rest" (Hellebust et al. 2021).

When looking at how women in prison experience and evaluate programming and treatment, it is important to consider how easily they can gain access to similar programs on the outside. It is also important to consider how prison populations differ from place to place. In Canada and Norway, the female prison population consists mainly of highly marginalized women with substance misuse issues and a multitude of psychological and health-related problems (Jones, Bucerius, and Haggerty 2019; Hellebust et al. 2021). In Mexico, however, while some women belong to marginalized groups, most are incarcerated for petty crimes, often related to trying to meet subsistence needs for themselves or their children or families (Bergman and Fondevila 2021). Because the prison population in Mexico is less vulnerable concerning substance misuse issues and psychological needs, programming and treatment do not play a prominent role when reflecting on what women need in prison. Women view them as a potential benefit but not as a necessity as in Norway and Canada.

6. *Prison Work.* Because Mexican women often lack necessities, paid work inside prison was more important to them than access to programs and treatment options. This is quite different from Canada and Norway. For the Mexican women, work could be formally organized by prison authorities in collaboration with private actors, working in industries, usually factories, with economic profits (e.g., maquiladora). Prison authorities could also assign women to work in the kitchen or laundry or to take on janitorial work. Ximena, for example, recounted how 7 days a week she made boxes in a workshop from 8:00 in the morning until 6:00 in the afternoon. She was paid 500 pesos (25 dollars) a week, well below Mexico's minimum wage of 140 pesos per day.

Ainhoa described working from 9:00 to 6:00 every day making jewelry to earn 409 pesos a week. Although masks alleviated the smell of this process, women complained about poor working conditions: "The sight and smell are a problem, because there are pieces that are enameled. It smells of solvent and hurts the nose a lot. There is another material too, *cyano*, which is like a crazy glue. ... When I went to sleep at night I felt it in my chest a lot, and in the throat a lot."

Access to cheap prison labor may attract outside business interests that are little concerned about the welfare of their incarcerated workforce. Working conditions were poorly regulated, and the work was often difficult. Incarcerated women, however, depended on the income from work that was stable and reliable, even if poorly paid.

Prisons had an informal economy. By choice or because it was the only work available, women took part in informal arrangements such as setting up food stands or doing chores for wealthier prisoners (Agoff, Sandberg, and Fondevila 2020). Ximena, for example, after having worked in the formal industries, concluded that "I will not kill myself for just 80 pesos a day." Like other Mexican prisoners, however, she needed an income or financial assistance. She believed God steered such support to her via the informal economy: "I have always believed that God is great. He does not give me more than I need, but if he does not give me money, he gives me people who needs me to wash their clothes, bring them something. And if they don't give me money they can give me toilet paper, a soap, a shampoo, and with that my basic needs are covered." The women performed countless informal jobs, including washing other prisoners' clothes, hauling water, cooking, or writing love letters for other prisoners.

The authorities also allowed the women to run small informal businesses. This is a common feature of Mexican prisons. Some prisoners made tacos, *chicharrones*, or other food from ingredients that friends or relatives bring them; they are then sold to other prisoners. Others used supplies from outside to make crafts or artifacts that relatives would sell outside. Marta, who became pregnant in prison, said she always worked in prison: "since I arrived, I sewed." Antonia noted that her boyfriend sent her things to sell. When we asked Sophia how she survived, she said she relied on her boyfriend, Javier, who "sometimes brings me cigarettes. He brings me nine packs of cigarettes. Of those I just keep one, and all the others I sell." On a good day, she could make 40 pesos, which she used to purchase necessities and more supplies to sell. Renata's business was even more professional. She had a boss and worked hard, selling commodities to other incarcerated women: "My way out, and my way to relax is to sell. To see that I'm good for other things that selling myself makes me happy."

This constant drift of money, materials, and commodities was crucial to Mexican prisoners and, by extension, to some of their families (Agoff, Sandberg, and Fondevila 2020). The more food, hygiene products, and the like they received from outside, the less they had to work inside. Some women were able to give money from their prison-based labor to their families, which was a considerable source of pride (Agoff, Sandberg, and Fondevila 2020).

The relative freedom means that prisoners in Latin American prisons organize a considerable portion of their daily routines and economic lives (e.g., Fleetwood 2014). This has advantages and disadvantages. Prisoners will not starve, but the system is based on prisoners paying for a considerable part of prison expenses (ENPOL 2016). However, access to work and the prisons' informal economy mean that life inside and outside are more comparable than in other places. This is particularly true since Mexico has a well-established informal economy that appears to make reintegration after release somewhat easier.

The Mexican situation was, thus, starkly different from those in Canada or Norway where prisoners might be allowed—or required—to work but were not expected to pay for meals and basic necessities. The women in Canada and Norway typically did not need to provide financially for their children on the outside or to pay for personal necessities on the inside. In many cases, women in Canada and Norway did not have financial obligations related to children because they had lost primary care responsibilities for children who were being cared for by relatives or had been placed with foster families (see below).

For Canadian and Norwegian women, only small financial rewards were associated with prison work, and these funds were mostly used to buy canteen items, such as chocolate bars, soda, and toiletries (Iefonu, Haggerty, and Bucerius 2022). Dorothy, who had been incarcerated several times, emphasized that prison work let her pay for small things that brought personal enjoyment. The focus is not on accumulating money but on paying for everyday items: "I got here like late at night, I got here at like 6:30, 7:00 in the evening, and then the next day I already had a job working in the stores here, like so I made myself, got myself a job and y'know, so I can make a little bit of money so I could buy myself some, just some normal hair shampoo and conditioner, a little bit of makeup or what have you, just y'know, have a little bit of homey things right?"

Women incarcerated in Canada's federal system had to pay a nominal fee for room and board and other amenities. As Maria pointed out, a portion of their income was retained by the prison administration: "We have to pay for food, we have to pay for accommodation, we have to pay for cable, we have to pay for our phone and then we have to pay for inmate welfare committee money. You know and like, man we have basic cable. You charge us all like, 14 dollars every two weeks."

To the extent that prison work was important, it gave the women "something to do" in an environment in which time dragged and boredom was a constant challenge. Rather than fixate on earning an income, the Canadian women wanted prison work to socialize and pass the time. One reason they saw Canada's provincial remand facilities as particularly harsh was that they provided only limited work opportunities. As Stella points out: "The feds [federal system] are killing it in comparison to provincial. It's so much better when you have work and programs." She described how she took jobs to engage with others and pass time: "I usually try to keep busy like with whatever I can and try to work, find work, um, ... I dunno, for the first little while like it was jus' like really hard tryin' to like learn to live with strangers. And then, ... you work with them and get to know them and like where they came from." Norway was like Canada, with work playing a minor role in the narratives of the incarcerated women.

Understanding women's needs and responsibilities inside and outside prison helps explain differences between countries. Mexican women are more dependent on prison work, both to provide for their families outside and to buy necessities inside. Because they are less affected by substance misuse issues and psychological and health-related problems than Canadian and Norwegian women (Jones, Bucerius, and Haggerty 2019; Hellebust et al. 2021), they may be better placed to take on paid labor within the prison.

7. *Children and Mothering.* Having a family member incarcerated can be detrimental to the family (e.g., Comfort 2007), particularly for children of incarcerated parents (Wakefield 2022). While some children may be in a safer or more stable environment because they are physically separated from a parent, having an incarcerated parent is an "adverse childhood experience" associated with unfavorable outcomes such as criminality, health issues, and higher suicide risk later in life (Murray, Farrington, and Sekol 2012). Such children are themselves collateral victims of the correctional system (Smith 2014).

At the same time, research has consistently shown that incarcerated people suffer as a result of family separation (Turney and Wildeman 2013; Haney 2018; Schultz, Bucerius, and Haggerty 2021). Women in all three samples uniformly observed that missing their children was one of the hardest—often *the* hardest—aspects of being incarcerated (Crewe, Hulley, and Wright 2017). They often told poignant stories about suffering and anomie arising from being disconnected from their family and missing their children.[16]

In all three countries the women said that having children helped them deal with the painful reality of incarceration. Many framed their incarceration as "necessary" or "an opportunity" to improve themselves for the sake of their children. To get better "for the children" was the prime motivation for personal change expressed by the great majority of women in all three countries. They talked extensively about addressing their substance misuse and moving out of a criminal lifestyle for the benefit of

---

[16] The three studies are paralleled by studies of male prisoners. Fatherhood narratives among men incarcerated in Canada (Schultz, Bucerius, and Haggerty 2021), Mexico (Sandberg, Agoff, and Fondevila 2020), and Norway (Grundetjern, Copes, and Sandberg 2021) show that men also profoundly missed their children. They talked extensively about their desire to "get better," to get substance misuse treatment, and to quit crime to become better fathers.

their children. Jody, in Canada, articulated what most women in all three countries repeatedly observed: "Right now, I'm trying to do my own thing and get out. I'm trying to go to treatment and trying to straighten out for my kids."

Whereas Jody was in the process of self-improvement, Martha said she had "turned her life around" to the point that she had been granted visitation rights and expected to be with her daughter after she was released. As she stated, "change" was possible because she was longing to see her daughter:

> *Martha:* I was always fucked up. On drugs. That was like my life. Until my daughter came. Yeah. She prompted me to clean up cuz without that there would probably no point of me, of change. Now, it's like: Kay go do your time, get out, be clean. I've been clean since 2018 July.

> *Interviewer:* Good for you. Do you find that's hard in here?

> *Martha:* It's easy, knowing that I get drug tested and like in order for me to see my child like I have to be clean right, so it's easy with motivation.

There was considerable variability in the three countries regarding women's relationships with their children. Some had no contact, others occasionally received visits, and others were raising their children in prison. Regardless of the nature of the relationship, women in all three countries offered moral arguments justifying their relations with their children and engaged in boundary work (Lamont and Molnár 2002) to emphasize that particular parental arrangements made them "good mothers" (Grundetjern 2015).[17] Some women did not see themselves as adequate or suitable parents, but when talking about desistance the women in all three countries said they were committed to changing for their children. Lisa in Canada explained, "I want to change for him. Get my shit together. Maybe one day he can be proud of me."

Norwegian and Canadian women had few opportunities to have their children with them. In Mexico, children are generally allowed to live with their incarcerated mother until they are 4 or 6 years old, depending on the

---

[17] They were good mothers either because they did not want to expose their children to the prison environment or because they insisted on seeing their children as much as possible.

region; in Norway, children cannot live in prison but can visit up to three times a week. In Canada, the federal prison allowed some women to have children with them full time to age 4. Welfare states such as Norway and Canada are readier to remove children whose parents are deemed unfit (Ystandes and Uglevik 2020). Consequently, the Norwegian women talked extensively about the threat of having their children removed or losing custody altogether. Similar fears afflicted Canadian mothers (Smith and Uglevik 2017). This was not a particular concern for the Mexican women.

Some women in Norway and Canada had lost access to their children when they were taken into government care, as Naomi explains: "Yeah, and if they're in child welfare, they don't bring your kids here at all. That's something that I'm dealing with, cuz my kids are in child welfare, right? And they don't, I haven't seen my kids in almost a year."

Such situations provided an additional motivation for self-improvement.[18] To stand a chance of gaining visitation rights or regain guardianship, they had to satisfy a long list of conditions such as courses they needed to take in prison and becoming sober. As Dorothy in Canada explained, they also depended on the good will of parole workers and other staff to forge connections with their children: "My daughter was removed by Child and Family Services. My PW [parole worker] phoned Child and Family Services and talked to them until she ended up getting my daughter's phone number. If my PW had not done that, I still would not have access to my daughter to this day. I had no idea where she is. I've now been talking to my daughter since Christmas."

In Norway, many women had experiences with child welfare services. Some believed it was easier to deal with prison authorities than with welfare agencies. Non-Norwegian mothers in prison especially felt, as Ystanes and Ugelvik (2020, p. 892) put it, that "the state's welfare-oriented left hand was tighter and more punitive than the right hand."

Like some Canadian women prisoners, Norwegian mothers often did not see themselves as good parents. Sara, for example, said she hoped her children had "been scared straight" by her behavior and was glad that they were "anti-drugs." When asked whether she thought they had troubled childhoods, she said "they've had that. I've been gone for long periods

---

[18] For example, Janne in Norway said she did not want to look like a "drug user" because of her children and "[doesn't] want them to suffer because of [her]." Dorte stated she quit using drugs "for me, my family and my son."

of time, and it's not cool to have a mother that is in prison. They have struggled with that."

Mexican women, by contrast, did not fear losing their children. Living in a weak social welfare state meant that they were less likely to encounter the state's coercive soft power. Having children grow up with extended family was a common practice that was arranged informally (Sandberg, Agoff, and Fondevila 2021). This made the transition from life on the outside to life inside easier as children need not face massive family disruptions. Instead, they continued to live with relatives as they had before incarceration.[19] Some Canadian women had their children raised by relatives, but these arrangements were usually formalized.

There were big differences in the three countries in women's experiences with state interventions, but there were many similarities. Mothers stressed how much they loved their children. Motherhood ideals were aspirational, motivating efforts toward sobriety and desistance. "Changing" for ones' children and viewing incarceration as an opportunity to improve parenting skills through prison-based programming helped women give positive meaning to their incarceration. Such ideals were not necessarily fulfilled in practice, but for almost all incarcerated mothers their children were a source of hope.

8. *Connecting Life Inside and Outside.* Examination of dynamics of women's incarceration in three countries makes clear that context matters. Observed differences are likely related to life outside of prisons. Norway, an exemplar of the Scandinavian welfare state, provides considerable resources and programs to struggling citizens outside of prison. Canada also provides social welfare resources and assistance but not at Scandinavian levels of quality or accessibility. For some of Canada's most vulnerable individuals, it can be less expensive or burdensome to access certain services and programs in prison (Bucerius, Haggerty, and Dunford 2021; Tetrault 2022). In Mexico, programing and resources in prison are sparse. While the existing programs are viewed positively, they do not address the most immediate

---

[19] This practice of child raising in extended family networks is sometimes challenged when Mexican women participate in motherhood programs in prison. They often learned other ideals for mothering that became their goals after imprisonment (Sandberg, Agoff, and Fondevila 2021). These programs often teach Western parenting ideals, urging mothers to take primary responsibility for their children. Paradoxically, these ideals sometimes worked against traditional Mexican child-rearing practices involving the extended family. In this way, by introducing new norms and ideals of motherhood the correctional system sometimes helped mothers connect better to their children and at other times undermined beneficial traditional forms of child raising.

concerns of Mexican prisoners (such as the need to provide financial support for their children and families). Further, Mexican women do not seem to have the same need for programming on substance misuse or mental health issues as do prisoners in Canada and Norway. This lessens the prospect that prisons be seen as offering useful programs or refuge from harsh conditions outside.

In Canada, many women identified prison as a place of temporary refuge (Pyrooz et al. 2020; Bucerius, Haggerty, and Dunford 2021). While they frequently mentioned "advantages" or "benefits" to being in prison, these should not be understood as "pro-prison" sentiments. Instead, prisons often provided them with material and emotional resources that were unavailable outside: basic subsistence, help with substance misuse, protection from domestic violence, a relatively safe sleeping space, community with other women, some access to basic health and dental care, a connection to their culture, and some basic educational or psychological programming. This supports Wacquant's (2002, p. 388) assertion that prison is "woven deep into the fabric and life course of the lower classes across generations" and is not necessarily "distortive and wholly negative" for incarcerated individuals. Instead, prison within limits can be a place of refuge and a space that offers rudimentary social services and other benefits.

The women do not necessarily endorse carceral institutions. That they sometimes frame their experiences positively is instead an implicit denunciation of conditions they endure in "free society." For the Indigenous women, it is further testament to the lingering injuries and injustices of colonialism (for similar findings in Australia, see Baldry and Cunneen [2014]). For many Indigenous people, Canadian society continues to be associated with removal from their homes and parents, shuffling between foster homes, subjection to physical and sexual abuse, inadequate housing or being homeless, and being forcibly separated from children.[20]

Incarcerated Mexican women expressed some positive views about prison, but they did not characterize it as a temporary refuge. Incarceration for Mexican women was an opportunity to escape abusive husbands, relatives, and other acquaintances and become involved in programs and courses, particularly parenting classes (Sandberg, Agoff, and Fondevila

---

[20] For a detailed summary, see Tetrault (2022).

2020). However, the women described these programs as limited and did not view prison programming as a reason to view imprisonment itself as beneficial.

Unlike the Canadian women, Mexican women typically did not have extensive histories of homelessness but had lived with extended family or people in their broader social networks (often in humble conditions). Mexican women did not face the prospect of freezing to death on the streets. Accordingly, prison was not seen as fulfilling pressing housing needs. However, the Mexican women were distinctive in the strong emphasis they placed on economic opportunities in prison. They took on work that provided meagre but vital income and allowed some to help support their children.

The Norwegian women also did not characterize prisons as places of refuge. Some Norwegian studies suggest that prisons might provide health-related benefits to prisoners, particularly concerning substance misuse (Hellebust et al. 2021), but such views were expressed only by vulnerable women with pronounced health and substance misuse concerns. Food and shelter were minor concerns for the Norwegian women.

The women's cultural expectations and frames of reference also differed substantially. In more traditional and conservative Mexico, women prisoners drew on the ideology of familism or religious frameworks to make sense of their imprisonment. Some tended to value prison as a place for reflection and an opportunity to seek out programs that deepened their spirituality or religious knowledge. In Norway, incarcerated women might have access to a priest, but religious and cultural programs otherwise played little role. In Canada, participants tended to adopt the neolib eral ethos of "taking responsibility" and showing agency. Unsurprisingly, the Canadian women tended to focus on initiatives aimed at self-awareness and self-improvement. Indigenous participants were attracted to programs that taught them about their heritage and cultural background in a way that increased their pride, self-respect, and resiliency.

In all countries, the women said they were motivated by love for their children, regardless of whether they tried to "protect" their children by minimizing contact or sought as much contact as possible. Perhaps the most consistent finding in all three studies was that the relationship with children served as motivation for desistance from drugs and crime.

Two crucial differences distinguished parental dynamics. The first was that Mexican women often leave their children with extended family for long period of times before going to prison (because of work or to pursue a criminal lifestyle), which helped reduce differences between mother-hood roles inside and outside prison. Second, unlike in Norway and Canada, Mexican women did not fear governmental removal of their children. Women detained in Canada and Norway were often afraid they would lose their children. In both countries that scenario often happened.

IV. Conclusion

We draw six lessons from this excursus into findings from qualitative studies of women's experiences of imprisonment in three countries. First, how women experience prison is related to their situations outside of prison. Analysts should be cautious in offering sweeping generalizations about "women's incarceration" based on experience in one country, re-gion, or prison. Local conditions and women's overall social standing in particular shape how they experience imprisonment.

Second, in places where prison sometimes serves as a temporary refuge for the most vulnerable, successful reintegration depends on resources and programs outside the prison. In several Canadian provinces, for exam-ple, obtaining health care and medicine after release is often difficult: for-mer federal prisoners cannot apply for health care coverage until they le-gally acquire a residence address.

Third, policy recommendations and program development must be sensitive to variability among women prisoners, including racial and ethnic backgrounds, socioeconomic status, sexual orientation, gender identity, and citizenship status. In the past, for example, reform activists encouraged de-velopment of "gender-responsive" programming tailored to the needs of incarcerated women. Those recommendations stemmed from a time when feminists were mostly concerned with dichotomous differences between men and women, largely ignoring gender-fluid identities and whether programming is culturally appropriate or addresses distinctive needs of members of racial and ethnic minority groups.

Fourth, because majorities of women prisoners seemingly everywhere have experienced sexual and violent victimization, prison administrations should adopt trauma-informed approaches and programs. Canadian data show that incarcerated women experience the overwhelming majority of their victimization long before being in contact with the criminal justice system. Whether a woman wishes to partake in such programming, how-ever, should be based on her needs and wishes. Prior victimization often does not play a direct role in women's offending; substance misuse, lack of economic opportunities, and intimate partners play more immediate roles. Programming, thus, must also address those realities.

Fifth, children are primary motivators of women's desistance from crime and drug use. Administrators of women's prisons everywhere, always taking children's best interests into account, should work to facilitate visits by children and to provide cohousing options.

Finally, women's experiences of imprisonment vary greatly between and within countries. The scholarly literature continues to be dominated by findings from the United States and the United Kingdom. Much more work, especially qualitative research, is needed in other places to unearth the local and contextual dynamics of women's incarceration. Qualitative research on prisons stands a much better chance to uncover how on-the-ground dynamics and specifics differ from how ministries describe their institutions and programs. Equally importantly, qualitative work gives incarcerated people the opportunity to express what truly matters to them and allows researchers to examine contextual differences between correctional facilities and national contexts. This is ultimately key for policy and program development: what's important to incarcerated women in one context may be trivial to incarcerated women in another.

REFERENCES

Agoff, Carolina, Sveinung Sandberg, and Gustavo Fondevila. 2020. "Women Providing and Men Free Riding: Work, Visits and Gender Roles in Mexican Prisons." *Victims and Offenders* 15(7/8):1086–104.

Anderson, Tammy L., Andre B. Rosay, and Christine Saum. 2002. "The Impact of Drug Use and Crime Involvement on Health Problems among Female Drug Offenders." *Prison Journal* 82(1):50–68.

Arditti, Joyce, and April Few. 2008. "Maternal Distress and Women's Re-entry into Family and Community Life." *Family Process* 47(3):303–21.

Atkinson, Robert. 1998. *The Life Story Interview*. Thousand Oaks, CA: Sage.

Baldry, Eileen, and Chris Cunneen. 2014. "Imprisoned Indigenous Women and the Shadow of Colonial Patriarchy." *Australian and New Zealand Journal of Criminology* 47(2):276–98.

Barlow, Charlotte. 2016. *Coercion and Women Co-offenders: A Gendered Pathway into Crime*. Bristol: Policy.

Barlow, Charlotte, and Siobhan Weare. 2018. "Women as Co-offenders: Pathways into Crime and Offending Motivations." *Howard Journal of Crime and Justice* 58(1):86–103.

Baumer, Hannah, and Rosie Meek. 2018. "Sporting Masculinities in Prison." In *New Perspectives on Prison Masculinities*, edited by Matthew Maycock and Kate Hunt. New York: Springer.

Beckett, Katherine, and Allison Goldberg. 2022. "The Effects of Imprisonment in a Time of Mass Incarceration." In *Prisons and Prisoners*, edited by Michael Tonry and Sandra Bucerius. Vol. 51 of *Crime and Justice: A Review of Research*, edited by Michael Tonry. Chicago: University of Chicago Press.

Belknap, Joanne. 2010. "Offending Women: A Double Entendre." *Journal of Criminal Law and Criminology* 100(3):1061–98.

Belknap, Joanne, and Kristi Holsinger. 2006. "The Gendered Nature of Risk Factors for Delinquency." *Feminist Criminology* 1:48–71.

Bergman, Marcelo, and Gustavo Fondevila. 2021. *Prisons and Crime in Latin America*. Cambridge: Cambridge University Press.

Binswanger, Ingrid, Joseph O. Merrill, Patrick M. Krueger, Mary C. White, Robert E. Booth, and Joann G. Elmore. 2010. "Gender Differences in Chronic Medical, Psychiatric, and Substance-Dependence Disorders among Jail Inmates." *Research and Practice* 100(3):476–82.

Bloom, Barbara. 1995. "Imprisoned Mothers." In *Children of Incarcerated Parents*, edited by Katherine Gabel and Denise Johnston. New York: Lexington.

Bloom, Barbara, Barbara Owen, and Stephanie Covington. 2004. "Women Offenders and the Gendered Effects of Public Policy." *Review of Policy Research* 21(1):31–48.

Bloom, Barbara, Barbara Owen, Stephanie Covington, and Myrna Raeder. 2003. *Gender-Responsive Strategies for Women Offenders: A Summary of Research, Practice, and Guiding Principles for Women Offenders*. Washington, DC: US Bureau of Prisons, National Institute of Corrections.

Bosworth, Mary. 2000. "Confining Femininity: A History of Gender, Power and Imprisonment." *Theoretical Criminology* 4(3):265–84.

Britton, Dana. 1997. "Gendered Organizational Logic: Policy and Practice in Men's and Women's Prisons." *Gender and Society* 11(6):796–818.

Bucerius, Sandra, Luca Berardi, and Kevin D. Haggerty. 2022. "'I'm in a Federal Prison, and I've Never Felt More Free': The Multi-Faceted Pains Experienced by Incarcerated Indigenous Women in Canada." In *Power and Pain in the Modern Prison: The Society of Captives Revisited*, edited by Ben Crewe, Andrew Goldsmith, and Mark Halsey. Oxford: Oxford University Press.

Bucerius, Sandra, Kevin D. Haggerty, and David T. Dunford. 2021. "Prison as Temporary Refuge: Amplifying the Voices of Women Detained in Prison." *British Journal of Criminology* 61(2):519–37.

Bucerius, Sandra, Dan Jones, Ashley Kohl, and Kevin D. Haggerty. 2020. "Addressing the Victim-Offender Overlap in Prisons and Police Organizations: Advancing Evidence-Based Research to Better Service Criminally-Involved People with Victimization Histories." *Victim and Offender* 16(1):148–63.

Bucerius, Sandra, and Marta Urbanik. 2015. "Crime and Punishment in Canada." In *The Encyclopedia of Crime and Punishment*, edited by Wesley G. Jennings, George E. Higgins, David N. Khey, and Mildred Maldonado-Molina. New York: Wiley-Blackwel.

Buck, Marilyn. 2004. "Women in Prison and Work." *Feminist Studies* 30(2):451–55.

Byrne, M. W., L. S. Goshin, and S. S. Joestl. 2010. "Intergenerational Transmission of Attachment for Infants Raised in a Prison Nursery." *Attachment and Human Development* 12(4):375–93.

Carson, Ann E. 2021. "Prisoners in 2020." Washington, DC: US Department of Justice, Bureau of Justice Statistics.

Charmaz, Kathy. 2014. *Constructing Grounded Theory*. Newbury Park, CA: Sage.

Chen, Gila. 2009. "Patterns of Crime and Substance Abuse among Israeli Ex-addict Female Inmates." *Asian Criminology* 4:47–60.

CNDH Mexico. 2019. "Diagnóstico Nacional de Supervisión Penitenciaria." https://www.cndh.org.mx/sites/all/doc/sistemas/DNSP/DNSP_2019.pdf.

Collica, Kimberley. 2010. "Surviving Incarceration: Two Prison-Based Peer Programs Build Communities of Support for Female Offenders." *Deviant Behavior* 31(4):314–47.

Comfort, Megan. 2007. "Punishment beyond the Legal Offender." *Annual Review of Law and Society* 3:271–96.

Comfort, Megan. 2012. "'It Was Basically College to Us': Poverty, Prison, and Emerging Adulthood." *Journal of Poverty* 16(3):308–22.

Correctional Service Canada. 2022. "Women's Facilities." https://www.csc-scc.gc.ca/women/002002-0003-en.shtml.

Corston, Jennifer. 2007. "The Corston Report: A Review of Women with Particular Vulnerabilities in the Criminal Justice System." London: Home Office.

Cotto, Diaz. 2006. *Chicana Voices and Criminal Justice*. Austin: University of Texas Press.

Covington, Stephanie. 1998. "Women in Prison." In *Breaking the Rules: Women in Prison and Feminist Therapy*, edited by Judy Hardy and Marcia Hill. New York: Routledge.

Covington, Stephanie. 2008. *Helping Women Recover: A Program for Treating Substance Abuse*. San Francisco: Jossey-Bass.

Crewe, Ben, Susie Hulley, and Serena Wright. 2017. "The Gendered Pains of Life Imprisonment." *British Journal of Criminology* 57(6):1359–78.

Crewe, Ben, and Alice Levins. 2020. "The Prison as a Reinventive Institution." *Theoretical Criminology* 24(4):568–89.

Crewe, Ben, Alice Levins, Simon Larmour, Julie Laursen, Kristian Mjåland, and Anna Schliehe. 2022. "Nordic Penal Exceptionalism: A Comparative, Empirical Analysis." *British Journal of Criminology*. https://doi.org/10.1093/bjc/azac013.

Crittenden, Courtney, Barbara Koons-Witt, and Robert Kaminski. 2018. "Being Assigned Work in Prison: Do Gender and Race Matter?" *Feminist Criminology* 13(4):359–81.

Currie, Janet, and Erdal Tekin. 2011. "Understanding the Cycle: Childhood Maltreatment and Future Crime." *Journal of Human Resources* 47(2):509–49.

Daly, Kathy. 1992. "Women's Pathways to Felony Court: Feminist Theories of Law-Breaking and Problems of Representation." *Southern California Review of Law and Women's Studies* 2(1):11–52.

Davis, Angela. 2003. *Are Prisons Obsolete?* New York: Seven Stories.

DeHart, Dana. 2008. "Pathways to Prison: Impact of Victimization in the Lives of Incarcerated Women." *Violence against Women* 14(12):1362–81.

DelSesto, Matthew. 2021. "Contested Theories of Prison Labor Practice." *Sociology Compass* 15(7). https://doi.org/10.1111/soc4.12888.

Dirks, Danielle. 2004. "Sexual Revictimization and Retraumatization of Women in Prison" *Women's Studies Quarterly* 32(3/4):102–15.

Earle, Rod, and Coretta Phillips. 2012. "Digesting Men? Ethnicity, Gender and Food: Perspectives from a 'Prison Ethnography.'" *Theoretical Criminology* 16(2):141–56.

Einat, Tomer, and Moran Davidian. 2019. "'There Is No Sincerer Love than the Love of Food': The Meaning of Food and Its Uses in Prison Subculture." *European Journal of Criminology* 16(2):127–46.

ENPOL (Encuesta Nacional de Población Privada de la Libertad). 2016. "Principales Resultados." INEGI. https://www.inegi.org.mx/programas/enpol /2016/Ennúmeros.

Fair, Helen, and Roy Walmsley. 2021. *World Prison Brief*, 13th ed. London: Birkbeck College, University of London, Institute for Criminal Policy Studies.

Fazel, Seena, Martin Grann, Boo Kling, and Keith Hawton. 2011. "Prison Suicide in 12 Countries: An Ecological Study of 861 Suicides during 2003–2007." *Social Psychiatry and Psychiatric Epidemiology* 46:191–95.

Feld, Barry. 2009. "Violent Girls or Relabeled Status Offenders? An Alternative Interpretation of the Data." *Crime and Delinquency* 55(2):241–65.

Fleetwood, Jennifer. 2014. *Drug Mules: Women in the International Cocaine Trade*. New York: Springer.

Foster, Holly. 2012. "The Strains of Maternal Imprisonment: Importation and Deprivation Stressors for Women and Children." *Journal of Criminal Justice* 40(3):221–29.

Garland, David. 2001. *The Culture of Control: Crime and Social Order in Contemporary Society*. Chicago: University of Chicago Press.

George, Amanda, and Jude McCulloch. 2008. "Naked Power: Strip Searching in Women's Prisons." In *The Violence of Incarceration*, edited by Phil Scraton and Jude McCulloch. Abingdon: Routledge.

Giallombardo, Rose. 1966. *Society of Women: A Study of Women's Prisons*. New York: Wiley.

Giarratano, Paulette, Julian Ford, and Thomas Nochajski. 2020. "Gender Differences in Complex Posttraumatic Stress Symptoms, and Their Relationship to Mental Health and Substance Abuse Outcomes in Incarcerated Adults." *Journal of Interpersonal Violence* 35(5–6):1133–57.

Gibson-Light, Michael. 2018. "Ramen Politics: Informal Money and Logics of Resistance in the Contemporary American Prison." *Qualitative Sociology* 41(2):199–220.

Gilfus, Mary. 1992. "From Victims to Survivors to Offenders: Women's Routes of Entry and Immersion into Street Crime." *Women and Criminal Justice* 4:63–90.

Grella, Christine, Judith A. Stein, and Lisa Greenwell. 2005. "Associations among Childhood Trauma, Adolescent Problem Behaviors, and Adverse

Adult Outcomes in Substance-Abusing Women Offenders." *Psychology of Addictive Behaviors* 19(1):43–53.

Grundetjern, Heidi. 2015. "Women's Gender Performances and Cultural Heterogeneity in the Illegal Drug Economy." *Criminology* 53(2):253–79.

Grundetjern, Heidi, Heith Copes, and Sveinung Sandberg. 2021. "Dealing with Fatherhood: Paternal Identities among Men in the Illegal Drug Economy." *European Journal of Criminology* 18(5):643–59.

Haney, Lynn. 2013. "Motherhood as Punishment: The Case of Parenting in Prison." *Signs: Journal of Women in Culture and Society* 39(1):105–30.

Haney, Lynn. 2018. "Incarcerated Fatherhood: The Entanglements of Child Support Debt and Mass Imprisonment." *American Journal of Sociology* 124(1): 1–48.

Heffernan, Esther. 1972. *Making It in Prison*. New York: Wiley.

Heimer, Karen, Stacey Wittrock, and Halime Unal. 2006. "The Crimes of Poverty: Economic Marginalization and the Gender Gap in Crime." In *Gender and Crime: Patterns in Victimization and Offending*, edited by Karen Heimer and Candice Kruttschnitt. New York: New York University Press.

Hellebust, Marion, Peter Scharff Smith, Ingrid Lundeberg, and May-Len Skilbrei. 2021. *Lengst inne i fengselet: Kvinnelige innsatte med behov for helsehjelp*. Oslo: University of Oslo Press.

Helliwell, John, Richard Layard, Jeffrey Sachs, and Jan De Neve. 2021. *World Happiness Report, 2021*. New York: Sustainable Development Solutions Network.

Houser, Kimberley, Steven Belenko, and Pauline Brennan. 2012. "The Effects of Mental Health and Substance Use Disorders on Institutional Misconduct among Female Inmates." *Justice Quarterly* 29(6):799–828.

Hutchison, Jessica. 2019. "'It's Sexual Assault. It's Barbaric': Strip Searching in Women's Prisons as State-Inflicted Sexual Assault." *Affilia* 35(2):160–76.

Iefonu, Collins, Kevin Haggerty, and Sandra Bucerius. 2022. "Calories, Commerce, and Culture: The Multiple Valuations of Food in Prison." *Punishment and Society*. https://doi.org/10.1177/14624745221097367.

Irwin, John, and Donald Cressey. 1962. "Thieves, Convicts and the Inmate Culture." *Social Problems* 10(2):142–55.

Jacobs, Jim B. 1977. *Stateville: The Penitentiary in Mass Society*. Chicago: University of Chicago Press.

Jaffee, Sara, Avshalom Caspi, Terrie E. Moffitt, Monica Polo-Tomás, and Alan Taylor. 2007. "Individual, Family, and Neighborhood Factors Distinguish Resilient from Non-resilient Maltreated Children: A Cumulative Stressors Model." *Child Abuse and Neglect* 31(3):231–53.

Javdani, Shabnam, Naomi Sadeh, and Edelyn Verona. 2011. "Gendered Social Forces: A Review of the Impact of Institutionalized Factors on Women and Girls' Criminal Justice Trajectories." *Psychology, Public Policy, and Law* 17:161–211.

Jones, Dan, Sandra Bucerius, and Kevin Haggerty. 2019. "Voices of Remanded Women in Western Canada: A Qualitative Analysis." *Journal of Community Safety and Well-Being* 4(3):44–53.

Jones, Stephen. 2008. "Partners in Crime: A Study of the Relationship between Female Offenders and Their Co-defendants." *Criminology and Criminal Justice* 8(2):147–64.

Kajstura, Alex. 2018. "States of Women's Incarceration: The Global Context." Northamptopn, MA: Prison Policy Initiative.

Karlsen, M. L. 2018. "Feminiteter i fengslet: Kvinnelige innsattes soningsforhold." In *Fengslende sosiologi: Makt, straff og identitet i Trondheims fengsler*, edited by J. F. Rye and I. R. Lundeberg. Oslo: Cappelen Damm Akademisk.

Keene, Danya, Amy Smoyer, and Kim Blankenship. 2018. "Stigma, Housing and Identity after Prison." *Sociological Review* 66(4):799–815.

Kriminalomsorgen. 2021. "Annual Report, 2020." Norwegian Correctional Service. https://www.kriminalomsorgen.no/informasjon-paa-engelsk.536003.no.html.

Kristoffersen, Ragnar. 2019. "Discrimination against Women Sentenced to Prison in Norway Is a Myth." Institute of Criminology. https://www.compen.crim.cam .ac.uk/Blog/blog-pages-full-versions/discrimination-against-women-sentenced -to-prison-in-norway-is-a-myth.

Kruttschnitt, Candace. 2016. "The Politics, and Place, of Gender in Research on Crime." *Criminology* 54(1):8–29.

Kruttschnitt, Candace, and Catrien Bijleveld. 2011. *Lives of Incarcerated Women*. Abingdon: Routledge.

Kruttschnitt, Candace, and Rosemary Gartner. 2005. *Marking Time in the Golden State: Women's Imprisonment in California*. New York: Cambridge University Press.

Kruttschnitt, Candace, and Rosemary Gartner. 2008. "Female Violent Offenders: Moral Panics or More Serious Offenders?" *Australian and New Zealand Journal of Criminology* 41(1):9–35.

Kruttschnitt, Candace, Katharina Joosen, and Catrien Bijleveld. 2019. "Research Note: Re-examining the Gender Responsive Approach to Female Offending and Its Basis in the Pathways Literature." *Journal of Offender Rehabilitation* 58(6):485–99.

Kruttschnitt, Candace, Anne-Marie Slotboom, Anja Dirkzwager, and Catrien Bijleveld. 2013. "Bringing Women's Carceral Experiences into the 'New Punitiveness' Fray." *Justice Quarterly* 30(1):18–41.

Kruttschnitt, Candace, and Mike Vuolo. 2007. "The Cultural Context of Women Prisoners' Mental Health: A Comparison of Two Prison Systems." *Punishment and Society* 9(2):115–50.

Lambert, Frederic, and Hyunmin Park. 2019. "Income Inequality and Government Transfers in Mexico." IMF Working Paper 19/148. Washington, DC: International Monetary Fund.

Lamont, Michèle, and Virág Molnár. 2002. "The Study of Boundaries in the Social Sciences." *Annual Review of Sociology* 28(1):167–95.

Liebling, Alison. 2009. "Women in Prison Prefer Legitimacy to Sex." *British Society of Criminology Newsletter* 63:19–23.

Loper, Ann, Wrenn Carlson, Lacey Levitt, and Kathryn Scheffel. 2009. "Parenting Stress, Alliance, Child Contact and Adjustment of Imprisoned Mothers and Fathers." *Journal of Offender Rehabilitation* 48(6):483–503.

Magletta, Phillip R., Pamela M. Diamond, Erik Faust, Dawn M. Daggett, and Scott D. Camp. 2009. "Estimating the Mental Illness Component of Service Need in Corrections: Results from the Mental Health Prevalence Project." *Criminal Justice and Behavior* 36(3):229–44.

Maher, Lisa. 1997. *Sexed Work.* New York: Oxford University Press.

Maleakieh, Jamil. 2018. "Adult and Youth Correctional Statistics in Canada, 2016/17." Ottawa: Canadian Centre for Justice Statistics.

Maruna, Shadd, Gillian McNaull, and Nina O'Neill. 2022. "The COVID-19 Pandemic and the Future of the Prison." In *Prisons and Prisoners,* edited by Michael Tonry and Sandra Bucerius. Vol. 51 of *Crime and Justice: A Review of Research,* edited by Michael Tonry. Chicago: University of Chicago Press.

Maruschak, Laura. 2008. *Medical Problems of Prisoners.* Washington, DC: US Department of Justice, Bureau of Justice Statistics.

Mauer, Marc. 2013. *The Changing Racial Dynamics of Women's Incarceration.* Washington, DC: Sentencing Project.

Maxwell, Joseph. 2013. *Qualitative Research Design: An Interactive Approach.* Thousand Oaks, CA: Sage.

McCorkel, Jill. 2013. *Breaking Women: Gender, Race, and the New Politics of Imprisonment.* New York: New York University Press.

McGuire, Michaela, and Danielle Murdoch. 2021. "(In)-justice: An Exploration of the Dehumanization, Victimization, Criminalization, and Over-incarceration of Indigenous Women in Canada." *Punishment and Society* 24(4):529–50.

Ministry of Justice. 2020. "Statistics on Women and the Criminal Justice System, 2019." Ministry of Justice, England and Wales. https://assets.publishing.service .gov.uk/government/uploads/system/uploads/attachment_data/file/938360/sta tistics-on-women-and-the-criminal-justice-system-2019.pdf.

Morash, Merry, and Pamela Schram. 2002. *The Prison Experience: Special Issues of Women in Prison.* Prospect Heights, IL: Waveland.

Murray, Joseph, David Farrington, and Ivana Sekol. 2012. "Children's Antisocial Behavior, Mental Health, Drug Use, and Educational Performance after Parental Incarceration: A Systematic Review and Meta-analysis." *Psychological Bulletin* 138(2):175–210.

Nur, Alexandra, and Holly Nguyen. 2022. "Prison Work and Vocational Programs: A Systematic Review and Analysis of Moderators of Program Success." *Justice Quarterly.* https://doi.org/10.1080/07418825.2022.2026451.

O'Brien, Patricia. 2001. *Making It in the Free World.* Albany, NY: SUNY Press.

Ocen, Priscilla. 2012. "Punishing Pregnancy: Race, Incarceration, and the Shackling of Pregnant Prisoners." *California Law Review* 100(5):1239–311.

OECD (Organization for Economic Cooperation and Development). 2021a. "Employment Rate." https://data.oecd.org/emp/employment-rate.htm.

OECD (Organization for Economic Cooperation and Development). 2021b. "Poverty Rate." https://data.oecd.org/inequality/poverty-rate.htm.

Owen, Barbara. 1998. *In the Mix: Struggle and Survival in a Women's Prison.* Albany, NY: SUNY Press.

Owen, Barbara, James Wells, and Joycelyn Pollock. 2017. *In Search of Safety.* Berkeley: University of California Press.

Peters, Roger H., Marla G. Bartoi, and Pattie B. Sherman. 2008. *Screening and Assessment of Co-occurring Disorders in the Justice System.* Delmar, NY: Center for Mental Health Services National GAINS Center.

Pratt, John, and Anna Eriksson. 2013. *Contrasts in Punishment: An Explanation of Anglophone Excess and Nordic Exceptionalism.* New York: Routledge.

Prisonwatch. 2022. "Foreign Prisoners." https://prisonwatch.org/foreign-prison ers/#publications.

Pyrooz, David, Ryan M. Labrecque, Jennifer J. Tostlebe, and Bert Useem. 2020. "Views on COVID-19 from Inside Prison: Perspectives of High-Security Prisoners." *Justice Evaluation Journal* 3(2):294–306.

Regan, Paulette. 2010. *Unsettling the Settler Within: Indian Residential Schools, Truth Telling, and Reconciliation in Canada.* Vancouver: University of British Columbia Press.

Rowe, Abigail. 2012. "Women Prisoners." In *The Prisoner*, edited by Ben Crewe and Jamie Bennett. Abingdon: Routledge.

Sampson, Robert, and John Laub. 1993. *Crime in the Making: Pathways and Turning Points through Life.* Cambridge, MA: Harvard University Press.

Sampson, Robert, and John Laub. 1997. "A Life-Course Theory of Cumulative Disadvantage and the Stability of Delinquency." *Developmental Theories of Crime and Delinquency* 7:133–61.

Sandberg, Sveinung, Carolia Agoff, and Gustavo Fondevila. 2020. "Stories of the 'Good Father': The Role of Fatherhood among Incarcerated Men in Mexico." *Punishment and Society* 24(2):241–61.

Sandberg, Sveinung, Carolia Agoff, and Gustavo Fondevila. 2021. "Doing Marginalized Motherhood: Identities and Practices among Incarcerated Women in Mexico." *International Journal for Crime, Justice and Social Democracy* 10(1):15–29.

Sandulescu, Ally. 2021. "Indigenous Peoples in the Canadian Criminal Justice System: Over-Representation and Systemic Discrimination." *York University Criminological Review* 3(1):65–89.

Schneider, Luisa. 2021. "Let Me Take a Vacation in Prison before the Streets Kill Me! Rough Sleepers' Longing for Prison and the Reversal of Less Eligibility in Neoliberal Carceral Continuums." *Punishment and Society.* https://doi.org/10 .1177/14624745211010222.

Schultz, William, Sandra Bucerius, and Kevin D. Haggerty. 2021. "'I Don't Want to Be That Dad to My Kids': The Narrative Uses of Fatherhood in Prison." *Punishment and Society.* https://doi.org/10.1177/14624745211018760.

Sentencing Project. 2020. "Fact Sheet: Incarcerated Women and Girls." Washington, DC: Sentencing Project.

Slotboom, Anne-Marie, Candace Kruttschnitt, Catrien Bijleveld, and Barbara Menting. 2011. "Psychological Well-Being of Incarcerated Women in the Netherlands: Importation or Deprivation?" *Punishment and Society* 13(2):176–97.

Smith, Peter Scharff. 2014. *When the Innocent Are Punished.* London: Palgrave Macmillan.

Smith, Peter Scharff, and Thomas Uglevik. 2017. *Scandinavian Penal History, Culture and Prison Practice.* London: Palgrave Macmillan.

Smoyer, Amy. 2014. "Good and Healthy: Foodways and Construction of Identity in a Women's Prison." *Howard Journal of Criminal Justice* 53(5):525–41.

Smoyer, Amy. 2015. "Feeding Relationships: Foodways and Social Networks in a Women's Prison." *Affilia* 30(1):26–39.

Smoyer, Amy. 2019. "Food in Correctional Facilities: A Scoping Review." *Appetite* 141. https://doi.org/10.1016/j.appet.2019.06.004.

Smoyer, Amy, and Geza Lopes. 2017. "Hungry on the Inside: Prison Food as Concrete and Symbolic Punishment in a Women's Prison." *Punishment and Society* 19(2):240–55.

Statistics Canada. 2018. "Adult and Youth Correctional Statistics in Canada, 2016/2017." Ottawa: Canadian Centre for Justice Statistics.

Stout, Madeleine, and Gregory Kipling. 2003. *Aboriginal People, Resilience and the Residential School Legacy*. Ottawa: Aboriginal Healing Foundation.

Sykes, Gresham. 1958. *The Society of Captives: A Study of a Maximum Security Prison*. Princeton, NJ: Princeton University Press.

Tetrault, Justin. 2022. "Indigenizing Prisons: A Canadian Case Study." In *Prisons and Prisoners*, edited by Michael Tonry and Sandra Bucerius. Vol. 51 of *Crime and Justice: A Review of Research*, edited by Michael Tonry. Chicago: University of Chicago Press.

Tjaden, Patricia, and Nancy Thoennes. 2000. "Prevalence and Consequences of Male-to-Female and Female-to-Male Intimate Partner Violence as Measured by the National Violence against Women Survey." *Violence against Women* 6(2):142–61.

Tripodi, Stephen J., Eyitayo Onifade, and Carrie Pettus-Davis. 2014. "Nonfatal Suicidal Behaviors among Women Prisoners: The Predictive Roles of Childhood Victimization, Childhood Neglect, and Childhood Positive Support." *International Journal of Offender Therapy and Comparative Criminology* 58(4): 394–411.

Tripodi, Stephen J., and Carrie Pettus-Davis. 2013. "Histories of Childhood Victimization and Subsequent Mental Health Problems, Substance Use, and Sexual Victimization for a Sample of Incarcerated Women in the US." *International Journal of Law and Psychiatry* 36:30–40.

Truth and Reconciliation Commission of Canada. 2015. *Honoring the Truth, Reconciling for the Future: Summary of the Final Report of the Truth and Reconciliation Commission of Canada*. Winnipeg: Truth and Reconciliation Commission of Canada.

Turanovic, Jillian, Nancy Rodriguez, and Travis Pratt. 2012. "The Collateral Consequences of Incarceration Revisited." *Criminology* 50(4):913–59.

Turney, Kristin, and Christopher Wildeman. 2013. "Redefining Relationships: Explaining the Countervailing Consequences of Paternal Incarceration for Parenting." *American Sociological Review* 78:949–79.

Turney, Kristin, and Christopher Wildeman. 2015. "Detrimental for Some? Heterogeneous Effects of Maternal Incarceration on Child Wellbeing." *Criminology and Public Policy* 14(1):125–56.

Uglevik, Thomas, and Jane Dullum. 2012. *Penal Exceptionalism? Nordic Prison Policy and Practice*. Abingdon: Routledge.

Valentine, Gill, and Beth Longstaff. 1998. "Doing Porridge: Food and Social Relations in a Male Prison." *Journal of Material Culture* 3(2):131–52.

Van Voorhis, Patricia, Michael Braswell, and David Lester. 2009. *Correctional Counseling and Rehabilitation*, 7th ed. Cincinnati: Anderson.

Van zyl Smit, Dirk, and Frieder Dunkel. 2018. *Prison Labour: Salvation or Slavery? International Perspectives*. New York: Routledge.

Wacquant, Loic. 2002. "Scrutinizing the Street: Poverty, Morality, and the Pitfalls of Urban Ethnography." *American Journal of Sociology* 107(6):1468–532.

Wakefield, Sara. 2022. "Incarceration, Families, and Communities: Recent Developments and Enduring Challenges." In *Prisons and Prisoners*, edited by Michael Tonry and Sandra Bucerius. Vol. 51 of *Crime and Justice: A Review of Research*, edited by Michael Tonry. Chicago: University of Chicago Press.

Walmsley, Roy. 2017. *World Female Imprisonment List*, 4th ed. London: Birkbeck College, University of London, Institute for Criminal Policy Research.

Ward, David, and Gene Kassebaum. 1965. *Women's Prison: Sex and Social Structure*. Chicago: Aldine.

Watts, Stephen, and Thomas McNulty. 2013. "Childhood Abuse and Criminal Behavior: Testing a General Strain Theory Model." *Journal of Interpersonal Violence* 28(15):3023–40.

West, Heather, and William Sabol. 2008. *Prisoners in 2007*. Washington, DC: Bureau of Justice Statistics.

Widom, Cathy, Naomi Marmorstein, and Helene White. 2006. "Childhood Victimization and Illicit Drug Use in Middle Adulthood." *Psychology of Addictive Behaviors* 20(4):394–403.

Wood, Jennifer, David Foy, Christopher Layne, Robert Pynoos, and James Boyd. 2002. "An Examination of the Relationships between Violence Exposure, Posttraumatic Stress Symptomatology, and Delinquent Activity: An 'Eco-pathological' Model of Delinquent Behavior among Incarcerated Adolescents." *Journal of Aggression, Maltreatment and Trauma* 6(1):127–47.

World Bank. 2019. "Adolescent Fertility Rate." https://data.worldbank.org/indicator/SP.ADO.TFRT.

World Prison Network. 2021. "Country Report, Mexico." Prison Insider. https://www.prison-insider.com/en/countryprofile/mexique-2021.

Wright, Emily, and Calli Cain. 2017. "Women in Prison." In *Oxford Handbook of Prisons and Imprisonment*, edited by John Wooldredge and Paula Smith. New York: Oxford University Press.

Wright, Emily, Patricia Van Voorhis, Emily Salisbury, and Ashley Bauman. 2012. "Gender Responsive Lessons Learned and Policy Implications for Women in Prison: A Review." *Criminal Justice and Behavior* 39(12):1612–32.

Young, Vernetta, and Rebeccah Riviere. 2006. *Women Behind Bars: Gender and Race in U.S. Prisons*. Boulder, CO: Rienner.

Ystanes, Vilde, and Thomas Ugelvik. 2020. "'They Tell Me I'm Dangerous': Incarcerated Mothers, Scandinavian Prisons and the Ambidextrous Penal Welfare State." *British Journal of Criminology* 60(4):892–910.

Zinger, Ivan. 2019. *Office of the Correctional Investigator 2018–2019 Annual Report*. Ottawa: Office of the Correctional Investigator. https://oci-bec.gc.ca/cnt/rpt/annrpt/annrpt20182019-eng.aspx.

Zlotnick, Caron, Jennifer Clarke, Peter Friedmann, Mary Roberts, Stanley Sacks, and Gerald Melnick. 2008. "Gender Differences in Comorbid Disorders among Offenders in Prison Substance Abuse Treatment Programs." *Behavioral Science and the Law* 26:403–12.

Zoutewelle-Terovan, Mioara, Victor van der Geest, Aart Liefbroer, and Catrien Bijleveld. 2014. "Criminality and Family Formation: Effects of Marriage and Parenthood on Criminal Behavior for Men and Women." *Crime and Delinquency* 60(8):1209–34.

Justin E. C. Tetrault

Indigenizing Prisons: A Canadian Case Study

ABSTRACT

Mass incarceration of Indigenous peoples is a fundamental Canadian human rights problem. One response since the 1970s has been to "Indigenize" prisons by teaching Indigenous culture and history, facilitating spirituality, involving Elders and communities in rehabilitation, and creating special prisons called "healing lodges." Criminologist proponents of "critical prison studies" are widely dismissive of these programs, with some arguing that Indigenized programming advances cultural genocide. They are wrong. University of Alberta Prison Project researchers interviewed nearly 600 prisoners in six prisons across western Canada, of whom 40 percent self-identified as Indigenous. Respondents generally praised Indigenizing initiatives for teaching them about their history and culture and helping them feel empowered and proud of their Indigenous identity. They said the initiatives helped them feel better able to cope with colonial traumas, including residential school and foster care system experiences; created a support network between Elders and fellow prisoners; and facilitated basic religious accommodation. Respondents' criticisms focused on prison management, particularly security restrictions and staff prejudice that can prevent access to Indigenized resources. Indigenized programming supports the dignity and religious rights of incarcerated Indigenous peoples. Participants wanted expanded, more easily accessible cultural programming.

Indigenous peoples are grossly overrepresented in prisons in Canada, the United States, Australia, New Zealand, and other nations, representing

Justin E. C. Tetrault is assistant professor of sociology at the University of Alberta, Augustana; senior researcher and project manager of the University of Alberta Prison Project; and a proud member of the Manitoba Métis Nation. I thank the incarcerated men and women for their time and insights; Sandra Bucerius, Kevin Haggerty, Ashley Kohl, Luca

Electronically published September 12, 2022

Crime and Justice, volume 51, 2022.
https://doi.org/10.1086/720943

failures by these countries to address the ongoing effects of colonization. In Canada, Indigenous adults account for 28 percent of admissions to provincial and territorial prisons and 28 percent of federal admissions, despite constituting only 5 percent of the adult population (Maleakieh 2018). The Indigenous Māori make up 16 percent of New Zealand's national population but 52 percent of its prison population (Harper 2020). In the United States, the Bureau of Justice Statistics reports that Native Americans are incarcerated in local jails at twice the rate of both white and Hispanic Americans (Zeng 2020, p. 4). In Australia, Indigenous people make up 3 percent of the population but more than 29 percent of prison inmates (Australian Bureau of Statistics 2021).

Overrepresentation is even more pronounced for Indigenous women. In Canada, Indigenous women account for 43 percent of female admissions to provincial prisons nationally (vs. 26 percent for Indigenous men; Maleakieh 2018) and half of all federally sentenced women (Jacobs 2022). In the federal system, Indigenous women account for 31 percent of admissions to sentenced custody (vs. 23 percent for Indigenous men; Reitano 2017, p. 5). One study found that Native American women were admitted to US prisons at a rate 6.7 times higher than white women (Hartney and Vuong 2009, p. 16). In 2016, Indigenous women in Australia were 21.2 times more likely to be imprisoned than non-Indigenous women (ALRC 2017, p. 41).

Indigenous peoples in Canada have long struggled for self-determination, sovereignty, and improved material well-being—sometimes called "decolonization." Activists and communities have attempted to "decolonize" Canada's criminal justice system by increasing Indigenous cultural influence; activists and scholars refer to this as "Indigenization" (Gaudry and Lorenz 2018). Put another way, we Indigenize aspects of society with the intent of fostering decolonization by increasing Indigenous sovereignty, self-determination, and material well-being. However, Indigenizing spaces does not always lead to decolonization. Since the 1970s, Canada has been at the forefront of Indigenizing prisons—one of many governmental responses to mass incarceration of Indigenous peoples (Martel, Brassard, and Jaccoud 2011, p. 237). Initiatives include cultural programming using Indigenous teachings, facilitating and encouraging spirituality, involving Indigenous Elders and communities in rehabilitation efforts, and creating special Indigenized prisons called "healing lodges." Settler colonial

Berardi, and William Schultz for their support and camaraderie; and Seth Adema, Michael Granzow, Michael Tonry, and anonymous reviewers for their guidance.

states such as New Zealand and Australia have introduced similar initiatives (Waitangi Tribunal 2017). Scholars disagree as to whether Indigenizing prisons is decolonial.

Some criminologists, in light of the Canadian government's history of violence and cultural genocide toward Indigenous peoples and incarceration rates for them that increased more than 43 percent in the last decade, have been rightfully skeptical of the benefits and decolonial nature of Indigenized prison programming (Zinger 2020).[1] However, in recent years, a more strident intellectual certainty has supplanted healthy skepticism of Indigenizing prisons. While ethnographic research shows that Indigenous peoples value cultural programming, critics are dismissive, portraying these initiatives as a colonial endeavor. Sometimes described as proponents of "critical prison studies," they argue that Indigenized programming is forced assimilation, that Canadian prisons are genocidal, and that only abolition counts as decolonial (Nichols 2014; Struthers Montford and Moore 2018; Marques and Monchalin 2020; McGuire and Murdoch 2021). Those assertions are an oversimplification. In a separate article, I show that the "critical prison studies" critiques can be a disservice to the interests, needs, and preferences of incarcerated Indigenous people.

Working as part of a research team from the University of Alberta Prison Project, I draw from almost 600 interviews with incarcerated men and women inside four provincial and two federal prisons in western Canada. A significant number of our interviewees (almost 40 percent) identified themselves as Indigenous. Indigenous women constituted 73 percent of the population of the women's prison we studied and 53 percent of our sample of women. Our findings complicate the idea that Indigenizing prisons is mostly a colonial project. Participants instead almost universally celebrated these initiatives for teaching many incarcerated Indigenous people their history and culture for the first time, helping them feel empowered and proud of their culture and heritage, helping them cope with traumas (including from residential school and foster care system experiences), creating a support network between Elders and fellow prisoners (rather than being a coercive and top-down imposition), and facilitating basic religious accommodation in prison.

---

[1] Zinger (2020) found, in stark contrast, that the incarceration of non-Indigenous people decreased by 14 percent in the past decade.

Our participants were critical of some aspects of Indigenized programming but generally not its content. Their concerns focused almost exclusively on prison management, particularly ways that security restrictions and staff prejudice prevent people from accessing Indigenized services (Acoose and Charlton 2018; Correctional Investigator 2021, p. 37). Altogether, our findings suggest that Indigenized programming can advance the dignity, cultural pride, and religious rights of incarcerated people. Participants want cultural programming to be expanded and made more widely accessible.

Many arguments against Indigenizing prisons are premised on abolitionist theory rather than empirical evidence. This is unfortunate; incarcerated Indigenous people and communities who participate in prison-community partnerships over whelmingly support Indigenized programming in Canada, despite its many flaws and limitations.

Indigenized programming was born out of advocacy and resistance by the inmate-led Native Brotherhood and Sisterhood movement and fought for by Elders and community members (Adema 2014, 2018). Canada's Truth and Reconciliation Commission (TRC) and the National Inquiry into Missing and Murdered Indigenous Women and Girls (MMIWG) advocate for improving and expanding Indigenized prison services.[2] The TRC report is based on interactions with over 70 Indigenous communities over 5 years, and the final report of the MMIWG inquiry is based on over 2,300 recorded experiences of Indigenous peoples over 2 years (TRC 2015c; NIMMIWG 2019). Decolonial prison research must engage with Indigenous peoples affected by prisons to help identify and address their needs, attempt to introduce and improve decolonial efforts and reject absolutist thinking and prescriptions, and promote concrete material outcomes for Indigenous people.

---

[2] As part of the Indian Residential Schools Settlement Agreement, the Canadian government created the TRC; it had a 5 year mandate to gather information and educate Canadians about Indian residential schools and their harmful legacy. The TRC's 2015 report contained 94 "calls to action" to help address these problems (TRC 2015a). In 2016, the government launched the MMIWG, responding to the TRC's call to action 41, addressing the "causes of, and remedies for, the disproportionate victimization of Aboriginal women and girls." The MMIWG inquiry introduced 18 "calls for justice" (including 231 recommendations) concerning health and wellness, security, media representation, transportation, policing, prisons, and social work as they affect Indigenous women, children, and the LBTQ2S community. See calls to action 35, 36, and 37 and calls for justice 14.6, 14.8, 14.10, 14.12, 16.30, 17.27, and 18.22.

This essay has four sections. In Section I, I outline the social problems associated with mass incarceration of Indigenous peoples, showing how Canada's colonial history impoverished and criminalized them. I review contemporary scholarship on Indigenizing prisons in Canada. In Section II, I outline my analytical framework, explain my approach to decolonial research, and describe my methodology as part of the University of Alberta Prison Project. In Section III, I summarize our findings on Indigenized prison programming. In Section IV.A, I demonstrate the limitations of arguments against Indigenizing prisons in light of current knowledge. In Section IV.B, I argue that decolonial research inside prisons is possible but must include input from incarcerated Indigenous peoples or Indigenous communities to generate concrete material outcomes, and I offer recommendations for improving Indigenized services.

In drawing attention to how Indigenized programming can help people, I do not dismiss or downplay the harms of imprisonment or the effects of colonization. Our research team, as a result of our professional relationships with Indigenous activists, practitioners, and community leaders and having interviewed hundreds of incarcerated men and women, is acutely aware of such issues.

For me, these are personal issues. I am Red River Métis and a direct descendent of Eulalie Gladu (Riel), sister to Métis leader Louis Riel. Social workers abducted my father, aunts, and uncles from their family farm during the Sixties Scoop, separating them in foster care homes across the country.[3] I have family members who have been incarcerated and lost others to trauma and substance abuse traceable to Canada's colonial policies.

I. Social Context

Canada's colonial policies have negatively affected Indigenous peoples; they suffer from high rates of poverty and mental health struggles, as well as stereotyping and discrimination—factors that contribute to higher incarceration rates. Incarcerated Indigenous people, activists, and communities pushed for Canadian prisons to recognize the unique cultural needs of

---

[3] I elaborate on the Sixties Scoop below. Provincial governments in 1951 were given power over Indigenous child welfare. One consequence was the Sixties Scoop: the systematic mass removal of Indigenous children from their families, often without the knowledge or consent of family members or of communities (Johnston 1983; Sinclair 2007).

Indigenous peoples, leading the Canadian government to "Indigenize" prisons.

A. A Background to Cultural Genocide in Canada

While Indigenous people are often analyzed together within and across countries, they are—like all racialized populations—made up of diverse cultures. In Canada, there are more than 630 distinct Indigenous communities encompassing more than 50 Nations and over 70 Indigenous languages (Government of Canada 2017b; Statistics Canada 2017).[4] The differences between these communities and cultures can be as prominent and pronounced as the similarities between them. Despite their diverse identities and ways of life, popular media and Canadian institutions (including prisons) often caricature Indigenous peoples and cultures as if they are homogenous.

Contemporary struggles faced by Indigenous people in Canada are inseparable from the country's colonial foundation and overtly anti-Indigenous policies that many argue amounted to "cultural genocide" (TRC 2015c, p. 48). Indigenous peoples lived in the northern region of Turtle Island continent (North America) for 12,000–14,000 years predating contact with the French and British in the sixteenth century (Fagan 2016, p. 124; RCGS 2018). While extensive commercial trading and peace treaties were common between Indigenous communities and European settlers, settler colonies expanded and increasingly used state violence to manage and relocate Indigenous populations while breaking treaty promises (Miller 2009). Settlers often tricked or forced Indigenous peoples into surrendering their lands. Settlers justified violent seizures of land through interlocking discourses of Christian imperialism, liberalism, and white supremacism, which constructed Indigenous peoples as a godless race with no right to property. European colonizers also transmitted foreign diseases such as smallpox to Indigenous peoples, devastating many communities, in some cases killing over half their populations (Carlson 1997; Daschuk 2013).[5]

---

[4] The Canadian Constitution recognizes three groups of Indigenous peoples: Indians (often referred to as First Nations), Inuit, and Métis (sec. 35).

[5] Some Plains Indigenous communities lost over 75 percent of their members to smallpox. Historians estimate that half of First Nations people living along the Saskatchewan

With the founding of Canada in 1867, Indigenous peoples became subject to government control and assimilationist policies designed to eradicate their culture. Such efforts were numerous. I limit this discussion to prominent late nineteenth- and early twentieth-century examples including the Indian Act, residential schools, and the Scoops.

The Canadian government introduced the Indian Act in 1876, imposing greater controls on Indigenous life while bureaucratically and legally delineating who qualified as "Indian." The Act was premised on the belief that Indigenous peoples could not govern themselves and that assimilationist policies such as banning cultural and religious ceremonies such as potlatches and Sun Dances were in their best interest. The Act awarded white government agents ultimate power in community decision-making, denied Indigenous women Indian status and participation in governing, and prevented Indigenous communities from purchasing land (Miller 2000; Government of Canada 2017a; Joseph 2018). Amendments to the Act in 1951 allowed provincial governments to identify "mentally incompetent Indians" for forced sterilization under Alberta and British Columbia's Sexual Sterilization Acts (Stote 2012, p. 121).

Establishment of the residential school system in 1870 was another major assimilationist policy. Canadian politicians designed residential schools, administered by various churches and religious organizations, to assimilate Indigenous children into Euro-Canadian culture. The Royal Canadian Mounted Police enforced residential school compliance by forcibly removing Indigenous children from their families, fining parents, and policing truants (LeBeuf 2011). Teachers punished children for practicing their culture, including speaking their language. It is well documented that many school staff abused students physically, mentally, and sexually (TRC 2015b). In 1913, Duncan Campbell Scott became deputy superintendent general of the Department of Indian Affairs and expanded the residential school system by amending the Indian Act, forcing children between the ages of 7 and 15 to attend. He described his department's role as "geared towards the final solution of our Indian Problem."[6]

By the 1940s, residential schools attracted critical public scrutiny, and government officials largely accepted that the program was a failure, leading

---

River died of smallpox or epidemic-related starvation. The Huron-Wendat lost 60 percent of its population due to smallpox and other diseases (Carlson 1997; Daschuk 2013).

  [6] Superintendent D. C. Scott to Indian Agent General Major D. McKay, April 12, 1910, Library and Archives of Canada, Department of Indian Affairs, R.G. I.

Indian Affairs to begin closing some schools (RCAP 1996a, pp. 344–53).[7] However, as the government gradually phased out the residential school system (a process that took decades),[8] amendments to the Indian Act in 1951 granted provincial governments power over Indigenous child welfare, leading to what is now widely referred to as the Sixties Scoop (Johnston 1983). These new provisions authorized the systematic mass removal of Indigenous children from their families, often without the knowledge or consent of family members or of communities (Sinclair 2007, p. 66). This included "scooping" newly born babies for placement in the child welfare system without their parents' consent (Sinclair 2007). As part of the ongoing effort to extinguish Indigenous culture, child services assigned "scooped" children to predominantly white families across Canada and sometimes in the United States and Europe. By 1970, one in three Indigenous children had been removed from their families (Johnston 1983; Fournier and Crey 1997; Sinclair 2007, p. 66).

Today, Indigenous peoples in Canada are disproportionately affected by poverty, hunger, poor health, and substandard living conditions. Compared to other Canadians, they have higher rates of unemployment and suicide and lower rates of education, wealth, and income (Bourassa 2008; Dickason and Long 2011; Howard and Proulx 2011; Gordon and White 2014; Bourassa et al. 2015; Statistics Canada 2019). Indigenous women and children fare even worse on almost every possible measure. First Nations children on reserve and off experience poverty rates of 53 percent and 41 percent, respectively, while 32 percent of nonstatus First Nations children, 25 percent of Inuit children, and 22 percent of Métis children live in poverty (Sarangi 2020).[9] Indigenous women and girls are five times more likely to experience violence than any other female population groups in Canada (Assembly of First Nations 2021). From 2001 to 2014, the homicide rate for Indigenous women was four times higher than for non-Indigenous women (Assembly of First Nations 2021).

---

[7] This varied by province. Some provinces saw brief periods of expansion, such as the residential school system in northern Quebec (TRC 2015b, pp. 10–11).

[8] This phasing out also led to decreased funding in existing schools, worsening already harmful conditions (Milloy 1999).

[9] "First Nations children" means those registered as Indian under Canada's Indian Act. "Nonstatus" refers to First Nations people who are not registered with the federal government.

Historians, social scientists, medical professionals, and other experts have empirically demonstrated that modern Indigenous struggles with matters ranging from income inequality to substance abuse emanate directly from colonial policies. For instance, in the late 1990s, social scientists in Canada and the United States sought to explain why Indigenous people disproportionately suffer from mental health struggles. Examining "intergenerational trauma" (also called transgenerational or historical trauma), they demonstrated that the violence of assimilationist policies (including abuse in residential schools and forcible separation from one's family) can lead to posttraumatic stress disorder in Indigenous persons that can be transmitted to subsequent generations (Menzies 2010, pp. 67–70). This trauma can manifest in anxiety, depression, low self-esteem, domestic violence, substance abuse, emotional detachment, and suicidal and homicidal thoughts (Aguiar and Halseth 2015, pp. 7–8).

While experts have for decades provided robust sociohistorical explanations for Indigenous struggles (as have Indigenous advocates for much longer), such accounts have yet to displace pervasive stereotypes about Indigenous peoples in broader Canadian society. Over a century of Eurocentric nation-building and meritocratic ideology taught in Canadian public schools (Schick and St. Denis 2005; Robson 2013), and broader ignorance of Indigenous cultures and colonial history (Godlewska, Moore, and Bednasek 2017), have caused many Canadians to demonstrate anti-Indigenous prejudices and interpret Indigenous struggles and trauma through racist caricatures, such as the "drunken Indian" stereotype or the discredited "culture of poverty" thesis (RCAP 1996*b*, p. 581; Harding 2005, p. 326; Vowel 2016, p. 151; McDermott and Vossoughi 2020). Wylie and McConkey (2019) show that Indigenous peoples face abusive treatment, stereotyping, and reduced quality of care in Canada's health care system, which discourages them from accessing needed services. Education scholars similarly show that Indigenous students face mockery and racial bias in public schools, including lowered expectations by teachers, which has well-documented negative effects on student outcomes (Riley and Ungerleider 2012; Clark et al. 2014). Indigenous peoples are subject to housing discrimination (Cohen and Corrado 2004; Motz and Currie 2019) and racial profiling by police (Smith 2006), are denied bail more frequently than other groups when charged with crimes, and are sentenced to custody in greater proportions than non-Indigenous offenders, despite initiatives designed to address sentencing disparities (Clark 2019; see also Turnbull 2014; Cunneen and Tauri 2017; Cardoso 2020).

Despite massive racial inequalities in imprisonment on par with the United States (Gilmore 2015), Canada is widely celebrated for its racial politics and enjoys a reputation as a "political utopia" or "progressive paradise" (Beauchamp 2016; *Deconstructed* 2019), an identity that many Canadians take pride in (Reitz 2011, pp. 18, 21; see also Stewart 2014; Tetrault, Bucerius, and Haggerty 2020). While attitudes toward Indigenous peoples have slightly improved (Neuman 2016, p. 12) and the Canadian government has taken steps to highlight and address some Indigenous issues, little progress has been made overall regarding the material well-being of Indigenous people concerning housing and poverty. In some instances, Indigenous peoples fare worse than a decade ago, such as with increased unemployment, worsening morbidity and mortality rates, and rising incarceration rates (Friesen 2019; OECD 2020, chap. 2; Zinger 2020).

B. *What Do We Know about Indigenizing Prisons?*

Much is written on the broader issue of mass incarceration in Canada on subjects such as how policing and sentencing and nonpunitive institutions affect Indigenous people's entrance into the criminal justice system (Chartrand 2019). There is also a growing body of work examining Indigenous justice alternatives, such as Hansen's (2015) study of the Saskatoon Tribal Justice Program, a restorative justice initiative for Indigenous youth, and Murdocca's (2020) study on section 81 agreements that help Indigenous people return to their communities, focusing on the experiences of women.[10] However, scholarship centered on Indigenous peoples' experiences inside prison is extremely limited and almost always centers on Indigenized prison programming.

Historian Seth Adema (2012, 2014, 2018) documents the history of Indigenizing prison efforts in Canada. They emerged from the inmate-led Native Brotherhood movement that started in 1958 in Stony Mountain Penitentiary in Manitoba. The movement initially raised awareness of Indigenous issues and challenged the notion that Christian theology could heal Indigenous prisoners.[11] The Native Brotherhood—and later,

[10] Section 81 agreements authorize Indigenous communities to take on the "care and custody" of Indigenous people who would otherwise be imprisoned.

[11] As Adema (2012, p. 41) notes, the Brotherhood did not absolutely reject everything "western" and did not reject Christianity outright. Most incarcerated Indigenous people—including Elders—at the time had Christian backgrounds.

Sisterhood—grew and pressured prison administrators to recognize and sanction sweat and pipe ceremonies. Another key objective was to recognize how colonization affects Indigenous people at a personal level, especially concerning childhood trauma and feelings of shame relating to Indigenous identity. As Adema (2012, pp. 40, 45) explains, the movement sought to confront the "colonized personality" by celebrating Indigenous culture and engaging in spiritual healing through ceremony, group therapy, support networks, and cultural handicrafts (such as bead- and leatherwork). Organizing around commonalities and shared traumas necessitated creating a "Pan-American" or "ethnic" Indigenous identity to unify diverse incarcerated Indigenous people (pp. 43–44). The Brotherhood and Sisterhood also advocated for Indigenous alcohol and drug treatment programs and used hunger and labor strikes to protest prison conditions (Adema 2016).

The movement gradually became more formal, and in 1975, as part of the National Conference on Native Peoples and the Criminal Justice System, advanced a series of recommendations, including advocating for Indigenous rights to culture and ceremonies, Indigenous employment in the criminal justice system, and culturally relevant programming (Adema 2014, p. 252).[12] These recommendations are the foundation of what later became modern Indigenized prison programs.

Since the 1960s, Indigenous Elders have also fought to have a presence in the prison system and advocated nearly identical initiatives. Perhaps most famous is the work of Elder Arthur Solomon, who condemned prisons as an "abomination" and "evil empire" while also working inside the CSC with the mission of using spiritual healing to give incarcerated Indigenous people a sense of self-worth and dignity (Solomon 1994; Adema 2018, pp. 51–52). The prison Elders began as community volunteers who operated with little oversight from the prison administration (Adema 2014, 2018). By the late 1980s, however, Indigenous communities and prison Elders lost control of the program when Canadian corrections institutionalized "prison Elders." Elders became paid employees more strictly bound by institutional rules. As of 2013, CSC hires Indigenous people to serve as Elders through

[12] Part of this recommendation was related to nearly complete ignorance of Indigenous cultures by criminal justice staff, especially in prisons. As the Native Brotherhood put it, an early major challenge was addressing the "complete lack of awareness of the Native inmate" (Adema 2018, p. 253). Waldram (1997) similarly argues that the Correctional Service Canada (CSC) never understood Indigenous spirituality and the role of Elders (pp. 16–17, 38–41).

a process involving formal job postings and consultation with Indigenous communities, advisory committees, and Councils of Elders (Adema 2014, p. 262; Vecchio 2018, p. 105). In other words, "Eldership" is determined by CSC, rather than by Indigenous communities.

We know remarkably little about how incarcerated Indigenous people relate to these changes, as there are few empirical studies of contemporary Indigenized prison programming, and prison scholars rarely engage with incarcerated or formerly incarcerated Indigenous people and communities. Yuen and Pedlar (2009) provide one rare qualitative study of the experiences of incarcerated Indigenous women. Their findings inside a federal prison show that Indigenized cultural programming helped participants connect to or discover their culture, resist shame and perceived stigma associated with Indigenous identity, and heal emotionally and spiritually. Martel and Brassard (2008) are more critical, arguing that Canadian prisons construct an "oversimplified" and "over-generalized" "master narrative" of pan-Indigenous identity that serves the interests of the Canadian state while ignoring the diversity of Indigenous communities (pp. 344, 357). They assert that prisons "impose" pan-Indigenous identity on prisoners, as engaging in cultural programming is sometimes required as a term of the sentence and a consideration for release (p. 357). They found, on the basis of 25 interviews with formerly incarcerated women across Canada, that some participants resisted this pan-Indigenous identity, while others mobilized it to increase their chances of potential release.

More recent empirical findings include public health research by Timler, Brown, and Varcoe (2019) and Varcoe et al. (2020).[13] Those studies investigate partnerships between prisons and Indigenous communities. Timler, Brown, and Varcoe's (2019, pp. 449, 458) research on a prison-community gardening program shows that incarcerated men, mostly Indigenous, experienced "substantial benefits" from the experience, such as improved dietary health, reduced stress, and increased self-esteem and self-worth; it allowed them to imagine a meaningful future postrelease. Similar findings come from Varcoe et al.'s (2020) study of a multi-institutional and multicommunity program called Work 2 Give, in which incarcerated men build toys, furniture, and Indigenous cultural items and grow food to donate to disadvantaged First Nations communities. The initiative benefited

---

[13] See also Boyer et al. (2019), who interviewed health experts, prison staff, and community leaders about how the prison health care system affects Indigenous prisoners.

both parties: it helped reduce the stigma around being incarcerated,[14] fulfilled incarcerated men's desire to "do good" through meaningful work, and created positive relationships between prisoners and the community, fostering potential future collaborations. As Varcoe et al. (2020) explain, while such programs are limited and cannot rectify broader social injustices, they can lead to better outcomes for incarcerated people and Indigenous communities.

II. Analytical Framework and Method

"Decolonization" and "decolonial research" are ideas that constitute my analytical framework and are based on my work as part of the University of Alberta's Truth and Reconciliation Calls to Action committee from 2019 to 2022, including conversations with Elders and Indigenous community leaders. Decolonial research should be empirical because it must involve interactions with Indigenous people or communities to help identify and address their needs. I outline my method as part of the University of Alberta Prison Project, involving 587 interviews with incarcerated men and women across six prisons in western Canada. Nearly half of our participants self-identified as Indigenous.

A. Analytical Framework: What Are Decolonization and Decolonial Research?

Some Indigenous people in Canada believe their communities have been overresearched or "researched to death" (Schnarch 2004, p. 82; Goodman et al. 2018). Indeed, there is a long history of colonial scientists studying Indigenous peoples for the purposes of advancing social control and settler expansion. More recently, Indigenous peoples have experienced at best minimal improvement in their material well-being despite ongoing academic and government research and reports (Wolfe 2006; Smith 2008). While skepticism about the value of research is understandable, decolonial research is a growing subfield in sociology and other disciplines that attempts to remedy the ethical failures of the social sciences (Connell 2018).

My analysis, critique, and research are informed by decolonial theory, borrowing from existing scholarship, and by my work on the University

---

[14] Many Indigenous people face stigma in their own communities for having been imprisoned.

of Alberta's Truth and Reconciliation Calls to Action committee. I was the principal author of an evolving "living document" on decolonizing sociology, which, to date, has been developed over almost 2 years with guidance from Elders and Indigenous community leaders in Treaty 6 territory (Alberta), as well as help from other committee members including Indigenous and non-Indigenous graduate students and sociologists. The document details the dynamics of decolonization and how it relates to sociological research and pedagogy. The committee organized events in 2020 and 2021 to receive feedback on the document from students, sociologists, Indigenous community members, and Elders. The following definition of decolonization (and by extension, decolonial research) is based on the most recent version of that document.

B. *What Is Decolonization?*

While decolonization is a global project, it proposes action and change within specific lands and among specific peoples. Consequently, decolonization necessitates attention to context, especially the histories and material legacies of nation-states. In Canada, decolonization is a long-term process involving two major components.

1. *Visibility.* Decolonization acknowledges Indigenous peoples' land and sovereignty and the myriad ways that imperialism and colonialism continue to manifest in contemporary Canada and disproportionately harm Indigenous peoples. A key feature of colonialism is that Indigenous peoples are made invisible. Decolonization elevates Indigenous perspectives and knowledge while drawing attention to issues affecting Indigenous peoples. This includes taking account of the effects of intergenerational trauma from residential schools and the Sixties Scoop, ongoing struggles against corporate threats to Indigenous lands, such as pollution and pipeline expansion. It challenges the ways racist thinking and stereotypes about Indigenous peoples permeate Canadian education, government, popular media, and "common sense" and foregrounds how Indigenous poverty and overrepresentation in the criminal justice system stem from colonialism. Colonialism also imposed European patriarchy upon Indigenous peoples, manifested in laws such as the Indian Act, which denied Indigenous women certain rights, and political power, and allowed for the removal of women's Indian status. Decolonization recognizes that gendered inequalities continue into the present and involves empowering Indigenous women. For both Indigenous and non-Indigenous people, the first step toward decolonization is to reckon with how we are personally

implicated in processes that can reproduce ideas and practices harmful to Indigenous peoples.

2. *Action.* Decolonization involves Indigenous-led collaborations with non-Indigenous people to advance material change by restoring Indigenous culture, language, and history and addressing power imbalances. If the first step of decolonization is recognizing the problem, the second is working to dismantle that discourse, practice, or process and rebuild anew to advance Indigenous self-determination, sovereignty, and material well-being. Without this second step, decolonization is little more than a symbolic gesture or tokenism. Acting on decolonization involves cooperation between Indigenous and non-Indigenous people. Such initiatives must be Indigenous led. The practice of introducing or increasing Indigenous influence is sometimes called "indigenization" or "indigenizing" (Gaudry and Lorenz 2018).

For action to occur, paying attention to context is central; Indigenous peoples are not homogenous, nor are their struggles. There is no single or obvious approach to decolonization and indigenization. Instead, acting requires constant local engagement between Indigenous and non-Indigenous people, communities, and institutions. In short, decolonial action must be open-ended and dictated by the needs of Indigenous people and communities.

Altogether, decolonization involves developing contextual, practical, and realistic goals and recognizing the barriers and challenges to achieving those goals. Meaningful action must also demonstrate how certain decolonial practices have worked or explain why they have not worked.

There are many competing views about decolonization, but there tends to be agreement that, through action and collaboration, change is possible (Sium, Desai, and Ritskes 2012). Decolonization must be an ongoing process, rather than an end product. In other words, we cannot "arrive" at decolonization or a "postcolonial" institution or society. Just as colonialism is a permanent fixture of our collective histories and identities, conversations and collaborations to decolonize must also be permanent.

C. Decolonial Research

How does decolonization apply to research? Decolonial research, sometimes called "Indigenous research methods," is inherently critical of colonialism, Eurocentrism, and colonial societies; makes Indigenous peoples, knowledge, and issues visible; and works with Indigenous peoples to advance their material well-being, such as by engaging directly with recommendations from the TRC and MMIWG (see Smith 2008; Ormiston 2010; Sium, Desai, and Ritskes 2012; Gaudry and Lorenz 2018).[15] While many studies use decolonial theory and draw attention to Indigenous issues, far less critical research engages with Indigenous peoples or directly furthers concrete change. Ideally, decolonial research takes an "activist-scholarship" approach in which the researcher works with Indigenous people to advance concrete political outcomes (see Juris 2007; Gillan and Pickerill 2012; Cunneen and Tauri 2017, pp. 30–31). Put another way, decolonial research ideally has a qualitative or quantitative empirical component; this is not common as broader decolonial scholarship is dominated by political theory and social commentary. While theoretical works can sometimes lead to meaningful change, this is never a guarantee. Consequently, even scholarship advancing decolonial theory and highlighting Indigenous issues is not inherently decolonial research. Decolonial commentary does not have intrinsic usefulness or relevance to Indigenous people, most of whom are profoundly aware of the problems facing their communities.

Decolonial prison research views prisons as reproducing dominant colonial power relations, while acknowledging that they can contain contradictory decolonial elements in the form of Indigenized programming. In other words, this approach rejects arguments that prisons are absolutely colonial spaces, a position advanced or implied by many critical prison studies scholars. This method also rejects Tuck and Yang's (2012, p. 3) popular argument that decolonization is "distinct" from "civil and human rights-based social justice projects." Instead, I argue that decolonial action always occurs in the context of colonial structures, such as oppressive institutions and discourses, including human rights discourse. Ideally, decolonial prison research works with Indigenous peoples to better their material well-being, while recognizing that addressing mass incarceration will require radical solutions. Indigenous peoples in Canada are often represented in official statistics, government reports, and critical academic studies, but decolonial research is severely lacking, including in the study of incarcerated Indigenous people.

---

[15] Murdocca's (2020) study on section 81 agreements is an excellent contemporary example of decolonial research (although she disagrees with the "decolonial" label, citing Tuck and Yang [2012, p. 36]). Murdocca (2020) adopts a critical lens, engages directly with Indigenous people about their experiences in the system, and explains how her work advances the MMIWG's calls for justice and the TRC's calls to action. She adopts abolitionist politics while recognizing that attempts to decolonize the criminal justice system are necessary for helping Indigenous people.

D. Method

My data come from the University of Alberta Prison Project, a multi-year study of life experiences inside western Canadian prisons. I draw from semistructured interviews with 587 incarcerated men and women held in four provincial prisons and two federal prisons in western Canada (see table 1). Provincial prisons detain individuals sentenced to a term of incarceration of up to 2 years. Two of the provincial prisons in our study were pretrial "remand" prisons, another was a sentenced facility, and the fourth was a mixed facility (half remand, half sentenced). In Canada, remand prisons largely detain legally innocent people who are awaiting trial

TABLE 1
Survey Statistics

Prison Type	Indigenous			All Ethnicities		
	Women	Men	All	Women	Men	All
	Race/Ethnicity of Participants (Survey Sample)					
Federal	38	14	52	63	84	147
Provincial	16	92	108	38	228	266
All	54	106	160	101	312	413
	Participants Who Attended Residential School or Had Family Who Did (Survey Sample)					
Federal	27	11	38	29	11	40
	Indigenous Participants Who Live on Reserve (Survey Sample)					
Federal	9	7	16			
Provincial	6	32	38			
All	15	39	54			
	Participants Who Were in the Foster Care System (Survey Sample)					
Federal	18	5	23	19	11	30
Provincial	4	27	31	5	46	51
All	22	32	54	24	57	81
	Participant Type					
	No Survey	Survey	All			
Federal	0	147	147			
Provincial	174	266	440			
All	174	413	587			

NOTE.—We do not have demographic information for 174 provincially incarcerated participants and did not include a survey question about residential schools until the fifth prison.

in custody rather than in the community. Remand prisoners are a diverse population of people charged with or convicted of minor offenses, such as having failed to pay outstanding fines, and others charged with or convicted of serious crimes, such as murder. Those convicted of serious crimes ultimately serve their sentence in federal prison but sometimes await relocation in remand prisons. Remand prisoners generally have little to no programming, and one institution locked them in their cells for 23 hours per day. The provincial prisons, except for the sentenced facility, housed men and women. One of the two federal prisons housed only men and the other only women. Two of the six prisons were severely overcrowded, requiring three people to share cells designed for two (with one sleeping on a thin mattress on the floor).

Data collection at each institution lasted 3–4 weeks, with a research team composed of the two principal investigators, Sandra Bucerius and Kevin Haggerty, and six to eight graduate students. I was a senior PhD student during most of this fieldwork from 2016 to 2020 and eventually became project manager, training research assistants to interview participants inside prisons and to transcribe and code interviews. The fieldwork team consisted of 10 interviewers, split evenly by gender. The interviewer's gender had noticeable effects on how participants responded; incarcerated men tended to prefer women interviewers. Team members had varying ethnic backgrounds, although all could be perceived as white (one was half Indigenous, one half Iranian). As a researcher's positionality and background can influence building rapport with research participants, it is possible a more ethnically diverse research team might have garnered more varied answers regarding race and other issues (see Phillips and Earle 2010). That said, the racial composition of the research team did not appear to affect our participation rate or the interview dynamics meaningfully— participants were largely candid about their experiences with racial prejudice and discussions about culture.

To recruit participants, we made announcements on the individual living units of each prison. To our surprise, many incarcerated people signed up, either out of intrinsic interest or because the study offered something to do in institutions with little programming and few recreational opportunities. Our interviews were semistructured and used a generalized prompt guide. While our interview questions centered on daily prison life and personal experiences with other prisoners and staff, we allowed individuals' unique accounts to drive the discussion. We commenced each interview by inviting participants to "tell us whatever you would like us to know about yourself," letting them decide what they wanted to share. Nearly all participants discussed programming (or its absence), and Indigenous participants often discussed their culture. When programming and Indigenized services came up as topics, we asked participants their opinions on what could be improved. At four of the six prisons (413 participants), we concluded interviews with a survey of 57 questions focusing on background information about participants' personal history, demographic characteristics, victimization history, and involvement in criminalized acts.[16] All interviews were audio recorded and took place in private interview rooms. They typically lasted around 90 minutes. We transcribed all recorded interviews verbatim and coded the documents using Nvivo Pro 11.

III. Findings

This section outlines our participants' perceptions of Indigenized programming. Section III.A details the demographic makeup of our sample and explains the different forms Indigenized programming takes; it can be structured, semistructured, or unstructured. Section III.B outlines how Indigenized programming helped participants connect to their culture and feel empowered and proud of their Indigenous identity and heritage. Section III.C outlines our findings on participants' victimization history. Indigenized programming can have therapeutic or healing components that can create valuable support networks and help incarcerated Indigenous people cope with past victimization and colonial traumas including residential school and foster care system experiences. Our findings suggest that Indigenous people desire help and encouragement for improving their mental and physical health and overall well-being (rather than have rehabilitation be mostly coercive and top-down). Section III.D outlines participants' criticisms of Indigenized services. This did not concern the content of the programs. Instead, participants criticized security restrictions preventing them from accessing Indigenized services. Medium and high security prisoners struggle with access the most. The second major criticism concerned the racial prejudice of some staff. Our participants

---

[16] Two federal prisons and two provincial prisons comprised these four prisons. We documented age at the time of victimization, where victimizations occurred (such as home or school), and types of offender (such as parent, religious figure, family friend). We also asked whether the prisoners reported their victimization to the police and whether they were offered or received assistance from Victim Services (for a more detailed analysis, see Bucerius, Haggerty, and Dunford [2020]).

explained that prison staff (especially correctional officers) have considerable power over programming and resources, allowing some staff to deny Indigenized resources because of their racist attitudes or perceptions.

A. Sample Demographics and Indigenized Programming

We conducted demographic surveys at four of the six prisons (see table 1). Among our survey sample, 39 percent of participants identified as Indigenous (160 people), with Indigenous women being the most severely overrepresented racialized group in our study, making up 53 percent of our sample population of incarcerated women.[17] Of our Indigenous survey participants, 25 percent (40 people) attended residential schools or had family members who did,[18] 34 percent lived on reserves, and 34 percent experienced the foster care system. Considering these demographics, discussions about Indigeneity were prominent in our findings. Many Indigenous participants discussed their history with the foster care system and outlined their home life on reserves and, for a considerable number of individuals, their experiences with homelessness. Participants almost always connected their Indigeneity to their experiences with Indigenized prison initiatives.

Critiques of Indigenizing prisons tend to center on the course-based programs involving instructors teaching Indigenous culture and history. Indigenizing prisons cannot be reduced to a single initiative but instead encompasses diverse practices that vary by institution, are often connected to constitutionally protected rights of religious accommodation,[19] and are distinct between the federal and provincial system. In Canada, federal prisons detain people with longer sentences (more than 2 years) and, consequently, tend to facilitate more robust and long-term programming, such as Indigenized living units—the Pathways program—in which participants can

[17] As we have detailed elsewhere (Tetrault, Bucerius, and Haggerty 2020), western Canadian prisons are not racially segregated like their American counterparts and more closely resemble the prison politics of Western European countries. While racialized gangs are prominent in Canadian prisons, race plays a comparatively marginal role in daily interactions. Incarcerated people of all ethnic or racial backgrounds intermingle in the living units, and racial prejudice from staff or between prisoners was not identified by our participants as a significant issue.

[18] This number is likely higher among our survey sample, as we did not include this survey question until our fifth prison.

[19] See specifically the Canadian Charter of Rights and Freedoms (secs. 2 and 15), Canadian Human Rights Act (sec. 3(1)), and the Corrections and Conditional Release Act (secs. 75 and 83). See also Reid (2020).

partake in daily Indigenous cultural practices, spiritual events, and classes. By contrast, provincial prisons detain pretrial detainees and people sentenced for 2 years or less, making the programming more short term. We spoke to many provincial prisoners, for instance, who had to leave courses early because they completed their sentences or who never got off the wait list for such programming.[20]

Indigenized programming can take a structured, semistructured, or unstructured form. Structured Indigenized programming, for instance, includes courses taught in a classroom setting, which typically centers on teaching about historical inequality with therapeutic and self-help elements related to cultural teachings. Indigenized programming also takes a more fluid or unstructured form, including initiatives led by prisoners. For example, most prison units we studied allowed regular access to ceremonial materials, such as sage, sweetgrass, and drums, which incarcerated men and women could use for personal prayer or group ceremony (such as smudging; however, see Sec. III.C).[21] Elder visits can also be considered a semistructured form of programming, as Elders have more discretion than program instructors and provide personalized guidance to incarcerated men and women. Unstructured programming is often inseparable from incarcerated peoples' right to religious accommodation.

The most substantive and celebrated Indigenized programming initiative among our sample was the Pathways program, which contains both structured and unstructured elements. Pathways units are based on Indigenous ideas about "healing," which is viewed as holistic and must therefore be a total process that occupies a person's daily life (Adema 2018, p. 50). Here incarcerated people spend multiple months on an Indigenized living unit, taking lessons on Indigeneity in Canada, combined with one-on-one counselling with Elders, and group therapy and rehabilitation using cultural

---

[20] For example, some participants told us they were being released the following week, despite being about to start a program or having weeks of programming left to finish.

[21] Smudging is a ritual involving the burning of sacred herbs, especially sweetgrass or sage. Most commonly, the smoke is intended to bless or spiritually cleanse people, objects, or spaces. A participant, Layne, explains smudging: "there's usually about 10 of us; ... it's cleansing right? We pray for everything. Like smudging, to me, the old traditional way, is you give thanks to the Creator for your life. You give them thanks for the food that we get every day, and our health, that we're healthy. Those are the three things you have to give thanks for every time you smudge. ... I always three to my heart [gesture] all the time, like thank you for my health, my food, and my life. I'm happy that I'm here every day, you know? Sometimes, you know, when I do that every day . . . I know I'm having a good day, because I know he watches."

teachings. Prisoners can also engage in smudging and sweats.[22] CSC offers different types of Pathways programs at 23 sites for men and three sites for women across Canada (Morin 2018).[23] While CSC restricts Pathways to minimum and medium security federal prisoners, most incarcerated men and women in western Canada have access to similar cultural resources, albeit in a limited and intermittent capacity (as I discuss below).

B. Connecting with Culture and Identity through Indigenized Programming

Incarcerated Indigenous people tend to have a complicated relationship to education or learning. Many participants grew up in environments where education was not attainable because of life circumstances such as extreme poverty. Others attended residential schools (or had family members who did), where education was intimately connected to emotional, physical, and sexual abuse. Despite such past circumstances, Indigenous interviewees universally celebrated Indigenized prison courses and other forms of structured learning.

Many Indigenous participants explained that programming taught them Indigenous history and helped them connect to their culture for the first time (see also Waldram 1993). Irene was a 30-year-old Indigenous woman who spent most of her life in and out of group homes and treatment centers when not imprisoned. She was sexually abused as a child, and both of her parents attended residential schools. Irene's life story was familiar among our sample of women, and her experience with federal Indigenized courses also reflects the broader orientation of our participants:

> I was 19 when I first got in trouble. . . . It was my first charge as an adult, [and] I have been incarcerated each year since. I wasn't aware of much of my history, my Aboriginal social history, I've only learned about all that this past year through the new incorporated programs here.
>   I am Native, I am Cree, I am from Alberta. I have participated in almost all the programs here. . . . I've come from a really high-risk

---

[22] A sweat is a cleansing ritual typically involving a dome-shaped structure (sweat lodge). Heat is generated by pouring water onto steaming rocks. The intent is for participants to sweat out toxins and negative energy. Canada's Indian Act banned sweat lodges (among many cultural practices) until 1951. Consequently, the practice also serves as a symbol of resistance and resilience today (McAdam 2015).

[23] This initiative varies by institution and security level. The Pre-pathways Initiatives, for instance, is a day-long program for maximum security prisoners. There are also Pathways transition houses (Correctional Service Canada 2019).

lifestyle, violence, you name it—I've got nothing but guns and violence on my record. I completely turned my life around. I'm now in a traditional Pathways [Indigenized] unit here living a traditional life [following cultural teachings] so ... I basically learned about my history and understood about colonization and residential schools and the impact thereof. I just needed to really understand how much [it impacted me] as a Native American and um, I just don't wanna be defined by [my past] so, I made the choice to change my ways and sober up and leave all that behind and things have been really good for me.

Like Irene, other participants tended to cite their "lifestyle" as the primary reason for not engaging with their culture before being incarcerated, such as being surrounded by drugs and violence or gangs or being homeless—conditions typically related to poverty. For instance, among federally incarcerated people, 82 percent of Indigenous women and 36 percent of Indigenous men we interviewed experienced homelessness at some point in their lives (see fig. 1). Additionally, 100 percent of federally sentenced Indigenous women used illicit drugs outside of prison, as did 79 percent of Indigenous men (Bucerius, Oriola, and Jones 2021, p. 6; see fig. 2). Drug use in Canadian prisons is widespread, and prisoners strongly discouraged others from participating in cultural practices or ceremonies while under the influence of alcohol or drugs—a rule among most Indigenous cultures in Canada. As Amy explained: "I wasn't raised in it [Indigenous culture] because I went from home to home, you know? And then

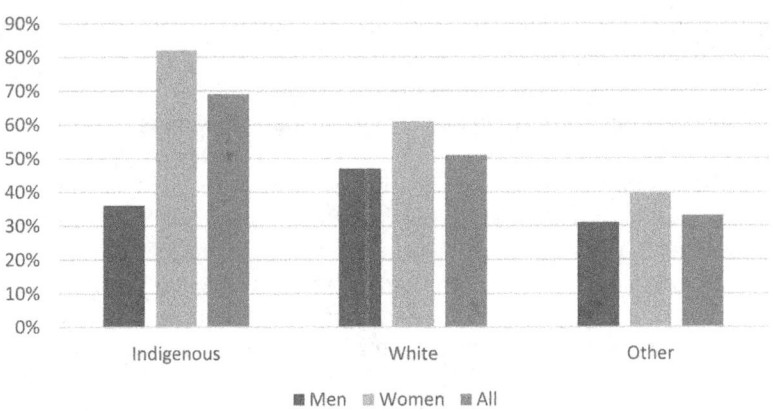

Fig. 1.—Homelessness

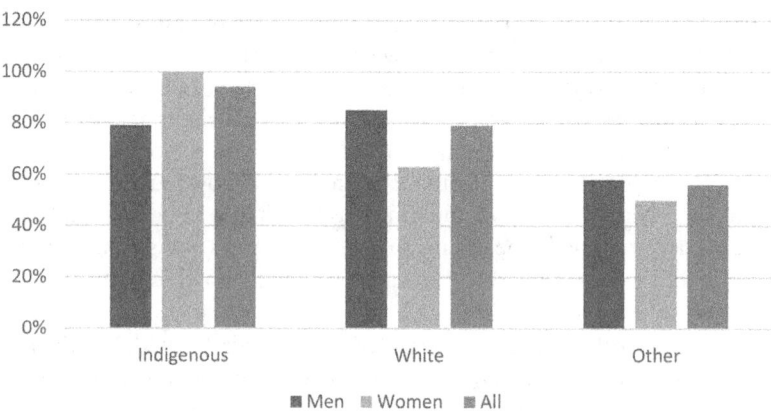

FIG. 2.—Illicit drug use

living life on the streets they don't teach that, at all. Like nobody's gonna be smudging while they're getting high (chuckles). That's just sacrilegious." Barney echoed this view: "I never really knew [my culture] until I came here my last sentence. And then … if I'm sober, I'm really, I really try to practice it. I … it's the only thing I think that really helps me."

Those with more limited access to programming offered nearly identical responses. Ryan was a young Indigenous man from the Northwest Territories, and as a "high risk inmate" in a provincial prison, he did not have access to Indigenized courses.[24] Nonetheless, Ryan could participate in unstructured programming and shared his experiences with prisoner-led ceremonies and Elder visits:

Interviewer: So do they have Aboriginal programming?[25]

Ryan: Oh yeah, there's drumming, you could go smudge, you know what smudging is, yeah? With the sweet grass. They do sweats in the summer out here, yeah there's some Aboriginal programming. That's what's making me think about following my culture, is that I went to the drum circle and, I am enjoying the sweet grass praying circles and it makes me want to follow the

---

[24] Programming is not offered on some prison units that house "high risk inmates."

[25] Participants almost never used the term "Indigenous"—many not knowing its meaning. Nearly all participants used "Aboriginal" or "Native."

culture. 'Cause an Elder comes in and talks about how the Creator is helping her [help us]. And she goes to programs and she makes new friends, and she has a good time and she's teaching her grandkids about it.

I don't know, it just makes me ... just cause, I don't know, I never had the opportunity to follow my culture, right? Cause my parents are always drinking and my real grandfather passed away and my grandmother died when I was—just before I ran away. That's what made me lose it. I started not caring, so I fucked up [committed a crime]. So yeah, I never really had the opportunity to follow my culture until I went to, I came to jail. And my first sweat was in jail, my first time enjoying sweet grass was in jail, first time drumming was in jail.

Other participants recounted that they did not learn their culture because of their experience in the foster care system. Nathan was a 34-year-old half-Vietnamese, half-Cree man who lived in multiple foster homes where he was physically and sexually abused throughout his childhood. One set of foster parents locked him in their basement when attending church, telling him they did not want their reputation "tarnished" by bringing an "Indian."[26] Another set of parents threatened Nathan with violence unless he told other people he was half Spanish or "anything but Indian." He outlined how Indigenized programming helped him to eliminate that stigma and be proud of his identity:

I went to the federal system ... and I really hated ... identifying myself as Aboriginal, because of the trauma that I've been through in my early years. But once I went to the federal system ... they have an amazing ... Aboriginal community in there. An amazing Aboriginal community. And they took me in and they showed me how to appreciate, how to love myself, and they showed me my roots, and they showed me [sniffs] how Native people really are, the magic, and uh, the-the-the [Native] Brotherhood, I mean the way that the Native people can unite, and be like the-the magic of it, just like the way they appreciated everything. Like each of the plants, the animals, like they feel like—I mean, it's such a beautiful culture. I now today, I have no problem being proud to say I'm part Native.

[26] In Canada, "Indian" is a now antiquated term for Indigenous peoples that is seen as a slur in many communities.

For nearly all interviewees, Indigenized programming served as one of the few opportunities encouraging personal and collective empowerment in prison. Some even contrasted Indigenized programming to residential schools. Samantha grew up on a poor reserve affected by the opioid crisis that escalated dramatically in 2016. Most of her eldest family—including her parents, uncles, cousins, and both sets of grandparents—attended residential schools. She explained how most of her peers were learning and celebrating their culture in prison, contrasting it to how residential schools attempted (and failed) to assimilate her grandparents:

> I was thinking about it and lotsa these girls, they sing [and drum], they do beading—who had never even done that, or like, thought of doing that before coming here, yeah ... in the past few decades it's been assimilation, you know? Termination kinda thing. That's like, our culture was pretty much beaten out of us, strictly forbidden right? For a lot of years, and like my grandparents are all residential school survivors. And they managed to come back from that and, you know, managed to remember all of the songs and all the practices—like the ceremonies that they did when they were younger, that's pretty amazing, I think.

Other interviewees echoed viewpoints similar to Samantha's, viewing prison-based Indigenized programming as a foil to their experience in the residential school system. Chester was a 51-year-old Cree man who attended residential schools during the mid-1970s and explained how access to sweetgrass provided in prison helped him cope with his trauma from that experience:

> *Interviewer:* What was [attending residential schools] like for you?
>
> *Chester:* Oh, terrible ... I took off [ran away], three or four times, I was brought back. But when I did take off ... I went to my Elders and I learnt Cree.[27] My band is very tough, Cree, the protocols and the prayers in Cree. That's my strength and I've been consistent with my language ... but I still struggle through that [trauma], you know. The abuse you go through, some of the things that happened [at the school], *oh man* [emphasis]. ... The sweetgrass here helps a lot for that, being in residential school, it helps me relax. You know, to have that. ... I wish we had

---

[27] Residential schools punished Indigenous children for speaking their language.

sweet grass [right now]... you know what I mean? Because ... [my past] kind of overwhelms me sometimes.... But I'm looking forward to the pipe ceremony next Wednesday.

Altogether, Indigenized programming serves a multitude of purposes. These initiatives can help incarcerated Indigenous people connect to their culture and heritage, destigmatize, feel empowered and proud of their identity, encourage self-expression, and serve therapeutic or healing purposes.

C. Trauma, Learning, Therapy, and Support Networks

Indigenized programming often has a therapeutic component that can help incarcerated Indigenous people work through their traumas, as their victimization rates tend to be more prominent and severe when compared to those of other incarcerated populations. Among our sample, 95 percent of federally sentenced women and 87 percent of federally sentenced men have experienced either physical or sexual victimization or both (Bucerius, Haggerty, and Dunford 2020; Bucerius, Oriola, and Jones 2021; see fig. 3).[28] When looked at separately, 84 percent of federally sentenced women had been sexually victimized (e.g., unwanted touching and sexual assault), while 90 percent were physically victimized (e.g., hitting, getting beaten up, had weapons used against them).[29] Among men, 48 percent were sexually victimized and 79 percent physically victimized. These numbers are significantly higher for Indigenous men, of whom 71 percent experienced sexual victimization, and 86 percent experienced physical victimization. Federally sentenced Indigenous people are also more likely to have been victimized at a younger age than whites. The average age for the first violent victimization among federally sentenced Indigenous women in our sample is 9.8 years (compared to 11.2 years for white women) and 8.8 years for Indigenous men (compared to 13.1 years for white men). For sexual victimization, the average age when first victimized is 7.3 years for Indigenous women (8.2 years for white women) and 8.8 years for Indigenous men (9.7 years for white men; Bucerius, Oriola, and Jones 2021, pp. 5–6). Today's Indigenized programming recognizes that such

---

[28] These studies are based on the same data set.

[29] The great majority experience both childhood abuse and abuse throughout their lives (Bucerius, Haggerty, and Dunford 2020).

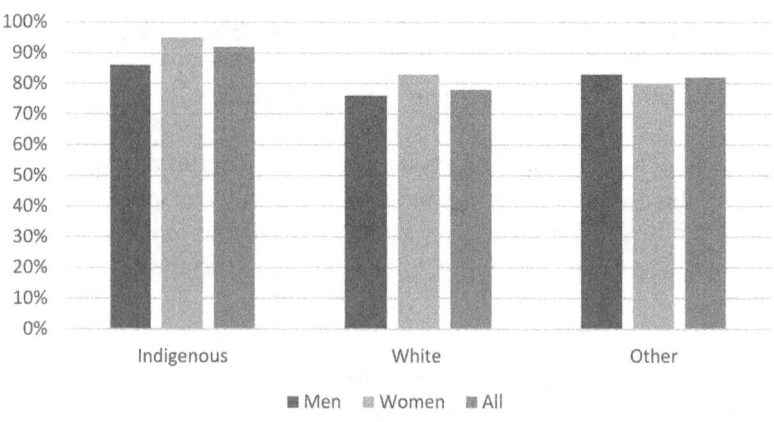

FIG. 3.—Victimization and race/ethnicity

experiences have significant influence on the mental, social, and physical health of incarcerated people.

Contrary to critics' claims that rehabilitative programming is essentially coercive, remarkably few of our participants expressed this sentiment.[30] Instead, the great majority explained that they desire help and encouragement for improving their mental and physical health and overall well-being. People suffering from trauma (the great majority of our participants) often use drugs or alcohol to deal with it; among our sample, this was more pronounced among Indigenous people. Many Indigenous prisoners viewed drug rehabilitation—or "getting clean"—as an essential part of their personal "healing journey." Irene explained how Indigenized programming attempted to address trauma and its relationship to drug use:

> And working on programs ... [they] go back to where everything started and explain how these cycles of violence or cycles of addiction or cycles of oppression—whatever it is that we were affected by—and go from there, and install those alternatives that are going to give us a way to live healthy and not, you know, ways to cover up your problems. ...
> I know people need medicine [prescription drugs] and other stuff [illicit

---

[30] At worst, participants complained about having to take mandatory programs as part of their correctional plan, which they viewed as unhelpful or boring. However, these complaints were never in the context of Indigenized programming. Incarcerated people with higher education and income tended to find less value in prison programming.

drugs] for their mentality [coping with trauma], but there's other ways that you can [help that]. . . .

I think traditional ways [following Indigenous teachings] is something that helps girls especially. It's not an "only-Native program" [either,] it's welcoming to all people who want to heal. So more cultural programs and more access to that is something that would benefit and take girls' minds off using that kind of alternative [illicit and prescription drugs,] big time.

The most marginalized among our sample—who tended to be Indigenous—found the most value in programming's rehabilitative elements. Jamie, for instance, was a 20-year-old Indigenous woman who had been homeless since she was 14 after running away from a group home in which she was sexually abused. As she put it: "programming? Right now I'm thinking they're all gonna be useful. I literally haven't learned [been taught] anything in life. I done it all on my own." For the most vulnerable men and women like Jamie, programming was seen as being essential for developing confidence, as many incarcerated people struggle with self-worth related to childhood trauma—especially Indigenous women.[31] Reita explained how sexual abuse affected her self-worth:

[Being sexually abused] made me angry, and I felt useless. I felt it was a dirty thing. I felt dirty. Like it was my fault. I had a lot of anger. And I was really disappointed in myself. I felt like a failure. Like I was just like a nobody. I didn't deserve anything . . . cause when you feel like you're worth nothing, it doesn't matter. It's not gonna matter anyway, cuz I'm not worth anything, what difference would it make? Who cares? And I wish there was someone there to say, you know, [Reita], you are worth it. You. Like, just something, give me kick in the ass, "get to school, go to school [Reita]."

As Reita suggests, having external support is important for developing self-respect. This sentiment is echoed by Clayton, a federally sentenced Ojibwe man and victim of extreme violence as a child. He outlined how Indigenized rehabilitation in prison helped build his confidence:

---

[31] It also may be that men struggle just as much with self-worth, but hypermasculine prison culture may have prevented some male participants from expressing that to us.

Clayton: I'm going to AA [Alcoholics Anonymous] and NA [Narcotics Anonymous] every week, and I'm taking Aboriginal moderate intensity program.[32]

Interviewer: And which one of these three do you find the most helpful?

Clayton: Mmm, I think the Aboriginal moderate intensity program, because they get right in-depth, whereas NA and AA seem to talk about, like, God and things like that. . . . [Aboriginal moderate intensity program] talks about colonization and how we were hurt as [Indigenous] people. And how it makes us wanna turn to substance abuse more. . . .

It teaches us how to deal with our emotions and, umm, how to cope [with trauma], you know? . . . I find that it actually does help. Because before, I looked at things in a really pessimistic way, like telling myself that I couldn't do it, or that I was a failure. But with all these people [a support network] . . . and now I'm able to, like, redirect myself to . . . like: "*I can do this.*" You know? "*I am worth it. . . .*" You know? If I just try sometimes, there's a road bump in the road—but I can get over it. Seems like this place likes to try to set you up for like, you know, success, for when you get out. They direct you in, in ways towards, you know, healing and stuff, and schooling. They help you with school.

Like Clayton, many participants did not have a support network throughout their lives. This situation was particularly pronounced among the most marginalized of our sample, who grew up in unstable or chaotic situations and lacked the institutional and social resources necessary for social mobility. Some living on impoverished reserves, for instance, explained that there was no upward social mobility in their community, often creating an atmosphere of hopelessness and abandonment. We interviewed Hannah, a 24-year-old federally sentenced Jamaican-Cree woman housed on a maximum security unit. Programming introduced Hannah to Indigenous teachings for the first time and she explained how it was also her first experience in a supportive environment: "I never had that positive role model in my life. Like I grew up on a reserve where

---

[32] According to our findings, Alcoholics Anonymous and Narcotics Anonymous are voluntary programs led by prisoners.

there was drinking, violence, I think that's what led me to where I am today. But in here we have positive people who really are trying to help us, instead of just like, wanting to see us in here for a long time [compared to my experience in provincial prisons]. And [they] actually take the time to listen to us and help us."

Respondents often said that programming—particularly Indigenized programming—could foster a support network, such as having peers, program instructors, or Elders encouraging them to succeed, in contrast to the stereotype that prison rehabilitation is mostly imposed on incarcerated people in a top-down manner. Interviewees often emphasized that positive reinforcement from peers can be just as important as the program content itself, as Irene outlined here:

> [On the Pathways unit] we're about lifting each other up and not trying to break you down when you're getting ahead. It's actually, things are changing the way people view [one another] because they weren't very empowering [in the past] you know? ... People [were stuck] in one mindset [where you couldn't] heal yourself and actually, feeling good about yourself, you know? [Because if you improved] people [would] think well, "she thinks she's better than me." You know? [They would judge you] ...
>
> I haven't been the best inmate, like you know, in the beginning, but this time around, things have been different and a lot of girls look up to me because of my reputation on the street or in jail, you know? So like, I'm using that [to help and support others] and I'm just using it in a positive way.

Some participants cited certain staff members (including correctional officers) as exerting a significant influence on their positive personal growth, although this was not common. Samantha, for instance, explained that she pursued education through the help and encouragement of her parole officer:

> I never realized how important [education] was. I sat down with one of the staff [case worker] here—who was actually my parole officer my first bit [first time being imprisoned]—and she said "well what do you wanna do?" Like whatever it is you wanna do. She said "I'll help you. I'll get you as much courses as I can get you to do," right?
>
> So I thought about it and I said: okay, well before I go home I wanna make sure I'm, for one, educated. ... I wasn't the best band [Indigenous

community] member, so I don't wanna go back there unhealthy. ...
So they [case worker] helped me pick the courses, and I put my mind to
something and I surprised myself! So I see now, how, you know,
I'm really grateful that I have this mentality, that I still have my mind
and a really good head on my shoulders. Because I've done a lot of
drugs, I've done a lot of damage to my body, you know? And, I just,
I'm taking full advantage of that [programs], and I'm grateful for
that. Like I don't even smoke anymore.

And I mean, we're in the pen [penitentiary] but, it's not like we
don't have access [to help], right? So, it shows me a lot, how much
[further] I've come. Especially to respect my body and ... it's a lot. I
know that education is key to gaining back a lot of what our people
lost, you know?

While participants such as Samantha reported extremely positive experiences with her case worker, most said that the attitudes of prison staff
(those not affiliated with programs) were highly inconsistent across prison
units and institutions, which I explore further in the following section.

D. Criticisms: Indigenized Programming Access and Needs

Criticisms of Indigenized programming (such as course content) were
nearly nonexistent among our sample. Instead, critical concerns almost
exclusively centered on issues of accessibility related to staff and prison
management. While those living on Pathways units have consistent access to ceremonial materials, Indigenized courses, and Elders, the great
majority of incarcerated people have inconsistent and limited access. Incarcerated people are often deprived of Indigenized programming (including religious accommodations) because of security restrictions and
prejudice combined with considerable discretion exercised by officials
in prison.

1. *Security Restrictions.*   In all six prisons we studied, access to Indigenized programming was highly inconsistent for medium and high security
prisoners—especially those in the provincial system. Some provincially
sentenced respondents explained that security protocols barred access
to basic cultural and religious resources for weeks or months at a time—
some claimed to have no access at all. Gideon was a provincially sentenced
45-year-old Indigenous man who had been in and out of prison since he
was 18. He explained that his medium security unit at Silverside Correctional Centre (pseudonym) had restricted access to nearly all Indigenized
programming offered by the institution:

We used to be able to go out to that yard, do our ceremonies, our smudges, sweat lodge, and everything. [Today] we get nothing. Nothing. We get fuck-all here. We get nothing here [on this unit]. We go into this little yard [gestures to window, outside] and we burn our sage—well, not even sage—we burn sweet-grass. There ain't no Elder [that] comes with us and sits down and prays with us or anything. Nothing. We get nothing. We got a sweat lodge that's been out there for 20-some years, and we don't get to use that. Protective custody gets to use it because they're minimum security. Ten guys.

According to Gideon and others at Silverside, prison management restricted access to the sweat lodge and other Indigenized programming to minimum security prisoners after a security breach 5 years earlier. Dennis was a remanded prisoner at a maximum security institution, and his experience represents a commonly expressed criticism of how staff justify program restrictions with security:

> *Dennis:* They don't let Aboriginal people express themselves, don't let us smudge. They finally gave us a drum group to where we can go and drum and sing with each other. That's basically the extent of it. They give us sweet grass, but they won't give us our herbal medicines like bark, roots, and stuff. They won't let us wear our medicine pouches to where it wards of bad energy, bad spirits, all that stuff. They don't let us have those things in here.

> *Interviewer:* Are you guys asking for that?

> *Dennis:* We've requested it. They said that they could be abused in many ways: "they [inmates] could use that pouch to pocket stuff [hide contraband]." It's not like they wouldn't search it; they wouldn't look through it. . . . And they don't let us smudge when we feel like it [you have to send a request]. They don't let us burn our sweet grass unless it's "approved" [by paperwork], like once a week, if we're lucky.

> *Interviewer:* Do you do a lot of that cultural stuff at home?

> *Dennis:* I do. I believe in it strongly. It makes me feel better. It makes me feel more confident in going out there and doing something positive. You can't do negative things when you smudge. You can't. You have to do positive things. You have to

have positive energy. You have positive output, and it just brings that spirituality. The spirituality alone in here strengthened me so much to where I don't worry about politics [drugs and gangs]. I don't worry about anything. I just worry about bettering myself so when I get out of here, I have something to focus on. I have something to look forward to. Then, it just puts me on a straight path.

As Dennis outlined, prison units often require incarcerated people to submit paperwork requests for hosting ceremonies and using spiritual materials and services. As Juliet puts it: "you have to put in a request to smudge, if you wanted to smudge, you have to plan it in advance."[33] Prisoners often criticized this process as needlessly bureaucratic and alien to their culture and experiences back home.

Participants at all prisons pointed to unit "lockdowns" as a constant source of frustration, a practice that prison staff use as a security measure or, more often, as punishment.[34] On a typical general population unit, lockdowns dramatically increase the time that prisoners are locked inside their cell, reducing their time in the larger common area ("room time"), where they can socialize, make phone calls, shower, play games, watch TV, etcetera.[35] At the time we interviewed Chester, correctional officers were punishing his living unit with a week-long lockdown, which suspended certain privileges and programming, including courses, Elder visits, and access to ceremonial materials such as sweetgrass: "They keep the drum behind the counter, plus the sweetgrass and the matches. [Using sweetgrass] helps [me] out, because being in residential schools . . . [I] went through a lot of shit man, and being in here [during a lockdown] is kind of like 'wow,' [not being able to use them] brings it back [triggers memories] all the time, you know what I mean? Cause they [residential schools] took away everything from us. You know, no sweetgrass, no drums, you know. No pipe ceremonies, nothing."

[33] This is not the case for those on Pathways units and those on minimum security units.

[34] Correctional officers typically have the power to lock down a unit even if misconduct was committed by a single person (which is often the case). Misconduct can include being late for head counts, fighting, talking back to staff, having drugs in a cell, and stealing objects from staff. Unit lockdowns were a common punishment tactic by staff at all six prisons.

[35] For example, provincial prisoners typically have 8–10 hours per day out of their cell, although this is extremely variable across institutions and individual living units. Lockdown restrictions are also highly variable and dependent on staff discretion. Some staff members, for instance, allow prisoners to leave the unit to attend classes during lockdowns.

Chester explained that being denied access to ceremonial materials triggered traumatic memories of residential schools. For him, spiritual practices are a normative part of his life and identity, somewhat in contrast to Indigenous people who are new to their culture in prison. Put another way, incarcerated men and women like Chester, who had prior experiences with their cultural practices were not accustomed to having these actions regulated. Consequently, restricting programming is arguably more detrimental for the mental health of Indigenous people who have a longer history with their culture.

2. *Staff Prejudice and Discretion.* Accessing certain kinds of Indigenized programming is highly dependent on staff discretion. On most prison units we studied, staff are essential to facilitating cultural practices (such as smudging or drum circles), as correctional officers often need to accompany prisoners outdoors or supervise the event. They also control access to ceremonial materials on the living unit. Without staff support, Indigenous programming is often impossible.

Most incarcerated people must register to use ceremonial materials; requests are typically submitted to correctional officers. While some officers allow prisoners to do ceremony without paperwork, staff can also outright deny these requests, which our participants attributed to racial prejudice, interpersonal grudges, or "if they're in a bad mood." Rory was a remanded prisoner who explained how some staff disrespect Indigenous culture and do not facilitate ceremonies:

> *Rory:* Sometimes we run out of sweet grass, we run out of our BBQ lighter, you know? [And we need more, but] they [correctional officers] don't care. And that, too, is a big problem here, is when we want to go out and smudge a lot of the guards won't let us. . . . Some of them look down on us like: "fuck you guys, you don't need to do that shit." And I've actually heard them say that. And I'm like "excuse me?" I was like, "I'm Aboriginal, you cannot take that from me," right? How dare you even talk about my heritage like that. Like that's totally disrespectful, you know? Some of them don't care.
>
> *Interviewer:* So what do you do in that situation, you just have to wait?
>
> *Rory:* You just bite your tongue, right? And just do whatever you can. Here it [practicing culture] is a "privilege," so we just have to

treat it like that.... Last time I said [to them] "this isn't a residential school, man."

Others explained that they were denied access to materials because
correctional officers questioned their Indigeneity, as many incarcerated
Indigenous people are white passing. Regardless of who makes these requests, CSC policy states that non-Indigenous prisoners have access to
ceremonial materials. Many provincial prisoners, such as Julian, a 35-year-
old remanded Indigenous man, attribute these prejudices to a lack of basic
knowledge of Indigenous culture and Canadian history: "They need [more
cultural] sensitivity training. Like, the guards need to know how us Ab-
originals have been through a lot of shit. And they need to actually learn
some fuckin history too.... Not only that, they need to know like, when
we try to tell them that we're on [Treaty Six] territory—they don't even
know what the hell that is! They have no idea what [Treaty Six] is, they
have no idea what the treaties are, or anything like that."

Participants' concerns about racial prejudice among staff were more
prominent in the provincial system and almost always focused on certain
individuals, rather than on correctional officers or prison staff as a whole.
Respondents were surprisingly nuanced in their perceptions of officers
and just as likely to praise individual staff members for their behavior or
support as they were to criticize them. The great majority of respondents
expressed their views of staff as Dale does: "They're just people doing their
job. Just like in real life, some are bad racist bastards, and some are good
people."

IV. Implications

In this section I discuss implications of our findings. Section IV.A addresses the critiques that portray Indigenized programming as advancing
colonialism or cultural genocide. Our findings directly challenge or complicate these criticisms. Section IV.B reviews the arguments and findings
summarized here and offers practical recommendations for decolonizing
Canadian prisons. I also advocate for research that directly engages with
Indigenous people and communities affected by prisons.

A. Criticisms of Indigenized Programs

Academic discussions about decolonization and prisons, especially in
Canada, are increasingly dominated by critics who dismiss the value

and potential of Indigenized programming. Our findings from the University of Alberta Prison Project directly challenge their three primary criticisms.

1. *Forced Assimilation.* The critics correctly observe that prisons and prison programming have an inherently coercive element. This is true whether incarcerated people engage in programs voluntarily or as a condition of their release. However, the degree to which Indigenized teachings are "imposed" is highly questionable (Martel and Brassard 2008; Struthers Montford and Moore 2018; McGuire and Murdoch 2021), as the word "imposed" suggests that such initiatives are unwanted and implemented in a top-down fashion. Our participants, in contrast, explained that learning about their identity and history was a welcome dynamic and collective process involving support networks that include staff, Elders, and fellow prisoners. Indigenized teachings in prison take a multitude of forms. While some may view these dynamics as "coercive," no participants framed the situation that way. Rather than its being unwanted or burdensome, nearly all participants (Indigenous and non-Indigenous) praised programming and wanted expanded resources, especially Indigenized resources.

2. *Prisons as Genocide.* Arguments that essentialize prisons as exclusively colonial institutions advancing genocide deny incarcerated Indigenous people their agency, personal truths and accomplishments, and history of resistance. As Adema (2012, 2014, 2018) and others have shown, Indigenous people constantly fight for self-determination and recognition in the Canadian prison system. To present prisons and, by extension, prison programming, as absolutely colonial implies that connecting to one's Indigeneity through prison initiatives is illegitimate, insincere, or an expression of false consciousness. For some participants (especially those from the foster care system), Indigenized resources helped them overcome feelings of shame related to their identity and feel empowered about being Indigenous. Other participants used these resources to cope with traumas resulting from colonial violence and contrasted Indigenized programming with cultural genocide.

3. *Prison Abolition.* Some critics see the prison as a uniquely and absolutely colonial institution that cannot be decolonized, portraying imprisonment and prison abolitionism as polar opposites, with prisons being totally colonial and abolitionism totally decolonial (see Nichols 2014; Struthers Montford and Taylor 2021). This implies that therapeutic prison initiatives or reforms are by definition meaningless (if not genocidal). This is unsettling, as both the TRC and MMIWG stress the importance

of mental health resources for those affected by colonial violence. Moreover, many Indigenous spiritualities have a "therapeutic" element, hence the prominent language of "healing" in most Indigenous cultures (see also Cunneen and Tauri 2017, p. 128). Lavallée and Poole (2010) outline the teachings of the medicine wheel in which, for many Indigenous cultures (such as the Algonquin and Ojibwe Nations), a "healthy state" is based on balance between the four interconnected realms: physical, mental, emotional, and spiritual (see also NAHO 2005; Anishnawbe Health Clinic 2006; Stewart 2008). Cunneen and Tauri (2017) explain that for many Indigenous cultures, healing is a collective process involving connection with self-identity and promotion of community bonds. Waldram (1997) argues that Canadian prisons have long overlooked the practical therapeutic or "healing" value of Indigenous culture by reducing spirituality to "religion." Adema (2018) similarly observes that for most Indigenous cultures, decolonization and healing from colonial traumas are inseparable (see also Cunneen and Tauri 2017).

B. Conclusion and Recommendations

Elder Arthur Solomon (1993, 1994) condemned the Canadian prison system as a "crime," "abomination," "evil empire," and "white racist institution." He also emphasized the importance of helping incarcerated Indigenous people live dignified lives and devised a curriculum for incarcerated Indigenous people in Ontario (Solomon 1994; Adema 2018). Like many modern institutions, Canadian prisons encompass contradictory colonial and decolonial elements characteristic of liberalism.

Colonialism is a structure of settler societies, meaning all institutions are informed by colonial history and thus have colonial elements (Wolfe 2006). Decolonial action always occurs within the limits of modern colonial structures and, at best, pushes those limits. Critical prison scholars tend to represent prison abolition as the only legitimate way to decolonize prisons. However, just as one cannot exist outside of history, no person or politics—including abolitionism—is outside of colonialism. There is no pure decolonial theory or action. Different from the moral and intellectual certainty displayed by much prison abolitionist discourse on decolonization, Sium, Desai, and Ritskes (2012) argue that decolonization is a "tangible unknown": we can be certain about the present issues facing Indigenous people, but the future pathways to healing, restoration, and reclamation are uncertain. How best to decolonize is never obvious, fixed, or predetermined. There is no grand theory or one-size-fits-all approach to decolonial action; Indigenous struggles are diverse and vary by place and scope. Consequently, while we must critique Indigenized programming, we cannot reduce decolonizing prisons to a single set of preordained ideas or ambitions. Indigenous peoples' needs are not homogenous. What constitutes decolonial action must be decided by Indigenous people, not dictated or prescribed by academic outsiders. Decolonial action is a necessarily open, exploratory, and fluid process meant to address the issues affecting Indigenous people and communities with responses differing based on different needs, urgency, places, and times.

Decolonial prison research involves identifying and prioritizing the needs of Indigenous people affected by prisons, and, ideally, researchers collaborate with participants to improve their immediate material well-being through advocating for policy changes, such as the recommendations advanced by the TRC and the National Inquiry into MMIWG, or through working alongside Indigenous communities or organizations. Prison scholars can show that prisons are harmful and colonial and ought to be minimized or abolished while also advocating for improved programming, as Elders and Indigenous advocates have long been doing (Adema 2014, 2018). Indigenized prison programming cannot be a panacea. It is a limited and flawed but still defensible form of harm reduction that can help meet the basic cultural and spiritual needs of incarcerated Indigenous people.

Our interviews with incarcerated Indigenous people show that Indigenized programming can help empower, heal, and foster community among prisoners and is necessary to basic (and legally mandated) religious and cultural accommodation in prison. Many incarcerated Indigenous people use Indigenized resources to cope with colonial traumas, such as residential schools, foster care system abuse, and the Sixties and millennium Scoops. Our participants' criticisms of these resources focused almost exclusively on their accessibility. Given these findings, I offer the following recommendations, which align with the TRC's calls to action and the National Inquiry into MMIWG's calls for justice.

Give power to Indigenous community leaders and Elders in all decision-making related to Indigenized programming.—Canadian prison administrators have a history of ignorance of Indigenous cultures. For instance, designing Inuit-specific services must be Indigenous led, involving collaboration with Inuit community leaders. Development of Indigenous-led prison program oversight committees will help encourage and facilitate Indigenous control of Indigenized resources and initiatives, thereby addressing the dynamic and changing interests of Indigenous people and communities.

Minimize the imprisonment of Indigenous peoples.—Maximize the *Gladue* principles in all decision making concerning Indigenous people in the criminal justice system. The *Gladue* principles require officials to acknowledge the unique circumstances of Indigenous peoples in Canada when determining bail, sentences, appeals, and parole release.

Encourage and maximize use of the Corrections and Conditional Release Act, particularly sections 81 and 84. Section 81 allows Indigenous communities to take on the "care and custody" of Indigenous people who would otherwise be imprisoned by CSC. Section 84 allows for the release of incarcerated Indigenous people into an Indigenous community or supervision by an Indigenous organization.

Ensure adequate transportation is available to Indigenous people released from prison, such as for those who live in remote communities and reserves.

Assess and reduce unnecessary barriers to programming and spiritual services.—Many if not most prisoners struggle to access Indigenized programming. This is especially a problem concerning religious services. Prisons are required to meet incarcerated peoples' religious needs under the Canadian Charter of Rights and Freedoms and the Corrections and Conditional Release Act. Regular access to spiritual materials is a human right. Prisons must also assure that Indigenized programming is readily and easily accessible to medium and high security prisoners.

Foster a trauma-informed environment.—The great majority of incarcerated people are victims of physical or sexual violence, which is more common and intense among Indigenous people. Trauma-informed approaches create awareness of the psychological and sociological effects of being victims of sexual or violent crimes. These approaches incorporate Indigenous teachings around mental and physical healing to support those suffering from unresolved trauma.

Include more opportunities for person-centered trauma-informed programs, such as group sessions that address posttraumatic stress, personal healing, and group healing.

Ensure that general cultural programming for incarcerated Indigenous individuals is trauma informed to better aid healing and avoid retraumatization. This may involve training program coordinators and designers.

Train staff to be person centered and trauma informed, drawing attention to how incarcerated Indigenous people are disproportionately and more severely affected by victimization. If possible, involve Indigenous staff members in training processes and explain why cultural and trauma-informed programming for Indigenous persons is necessary.

Ceremony can help Indigenous and non-Indigenous people reduce stress and cope with traumas. Train or encourage staff to allow for more frequent smudging (led by incarcerated people) and ensure that Indigenous ceremonial materials, such as drums, sweetgrass, pipes, and lighters or matches, are always available.

Create or designate a space as a "healing range," where Indigenous religious and healing practices can occur.

Educate all prison staff (including health care workers and program instructors) on historical and contemporary Indigenous issues and develop skills-based training on intercultural competency, conflict resolution, human rights, and antiracism.—Indigenized programming is impossible without staff cooperation and facilitation. This training must be trauma informed.

Create and expand programming for men and boys that confronts domestic violence against Indigenous women, girls, and LGBTQ2S people.—The great majority of federally sentenced women (84 percent) are victims of sexual violence; victimization is more frequent and severe for Indigenous women.

Create more federal healing lodges, without increasing the number of incarcerated Indigenous people.—Our participants nearly universally celebrated Indigenized living units or the Pathways program. Federal healing lodges are a robust form and were praised by participants who had experience with them. Healing lodges should be run by Indigenous communities.

Assess how Indigenized programming can better meet the region-specific needs of Indigenous peoples.—Indigenous peoples are diverse. Current programming may not address the unique cultural needs of some groups, such as the Inuit and Métis.

Evaluate, update, and develop security classification scales and tools that are sensitive to Indigenous backgrounds and realities.—For instance, the maximum security classification disproportionately constrains federally sentenced Indigenous women from gaining access to services, support, and programs required to facilitate their safe and timely reintegration into society.

Ensure incarcerated Indigenous people have access to legal services to support and assert their human rights and Indigenous rights.—Even the best programs are sometimes poorly managed. Access to programming is wrongly denied.

Ensure that all persons involved in provision of health services to Indigenous people receive ongoing training and education.—Subjects covered should include, but not be limited to, the history of colonialism in the oppression and genocide of Inuit, Métis, and First Nations Peoples; antibias and antiracism; local language and culture; and local health and healing practices.

Our study focuses on Canada, but its findings and methodology are almost certainly applicable to other settler-colonial countries including Australia, New Zealand, Mexico, Greenland, and the United States (Burt 2011; Baldry and Cunneen 2014; Nielsen 2020; Castillo 2021). The United States has "tribal jails" managed by tribal authorities or the Bureau of Indian Affairs. These institutions provide some cultural programming but suffer from overcrowding and other major inadequacies. Mainstream US prisons have also introduced Indigenized programming, including sweat lodges. Australia has designed prisons with Indigenous community consultation, resembling Canada's healing lodges. Some mainstream Australian prisons have cultural gathering spaces and others take the form of rural work camps, which are structured like a community center and teach working skills for postrelease. New Zealand has specialized Maori Focus Units and cultural centers in some prisons. Grant (2016) reports that a major issue across these initiatives is access, as most incarcerated Indigenous people struggle to gain security clearance for Indigenized programming and spaces.

There is strong research in all those countries that encourages policy changes to reduce mass incarceration, but scholarship dealing with Indigenous people in prisons remains scant. There is little research on Indigenized prison programming generally, despite growing demand for such initiatives among criminal justice practitioners and Indigenous communities. Building on the Canadian case study, I have proposed a basic foundation for decolonial prison research, which requires collaboration with incarcerated Indigenous peoples to identify and help address their needs. Some forms of cultural programming can help enrich the lives of those in prison, especially the most marginalized (see also Bucerius, Haggerty, and Dunford 2020).

Critiques of Indigenizing prisons are needed but should be based on the experience of the full range of participants and encourage improvement of such initiatives, rather than discourage them or denounce their value. No amount of academic theorizing or ideological posturing can substitute for speaking and listening to Indigenous people. There is no contradiction between advocating for harm reduction through more humane and culturally sensitive prison programming and for shrinking the prison system.

REFERENCES

Acoose, Sharon L., and John E. Charlton. 2018. "They Stole My Thunder: Indian Women and Post-incarceration Health." In *Global Indigenous Health: Reconciling the Past, Engaging the Present, Animating the Future*, edited by Robert Henry, Amanda Lavallee, Nancy Van Styvendale, and Robert Alexander Innes. Tucson: University of Arizona Press.

Adema, Seth. 2012. "'Our Destiny Is Not Negotiable': Native Brotherhoods and Decolonization in Ontario's Federal Prisons, 1970–1982." *Left History* 16(2):37–54.

Adema, Seth. 2014. "Tradition and Transitions: Elders Working in Canadian Prisons, 1967–1992." *Journal of the Canadian Historical Association* 25(1):243–75.

Adema, Seth. 2016. "More than Stone and Iron: Indigenous History and Incarceration in Canada, 1834–1996." PhD dissertation, Department of History, Wilfrid Laurier University.

Adema, Seth. 2018. "Helping His Brothers and Sisters Heal: Arthur Solomon and Penal Reform in Canada." In *Global Indigenous Health: Reconciling the Past, Engaging the Present, Animating the Future*, edited by Robert Henry, Amanda Lavallee, Nancy Van Styvendale, and Robert Alexander Innes. Tucson: University of Arizona Press.

Aguiar, William, and Regine Halseth. 2015. *Aboriginal Peoples and Historic Trauma: The Processes of Intergenerational Transmission*. Prince George: National Collaborating Centre for Aboriginal Health.

ALRC (Australian Law Reform Commission). 2017. *Pathways to Justice: An Inquiry into the Incarceration Rate of Aboriginal and Torres Strait Islander Peoples*. Canberra: Australian Law Reform Commission.

Anishnawbe Health Clinic. 2006. *Anishnawbe Health Brochure*. Toronto: Anishnawbe Health.

Assembly of First Nations. 2021. "Missing and Murdered Indigenous Women and Girls and Ending Violence." https://www.afn.ca/policy-sectors/mmiwg-end-violence/.

Australian Bureau of Statistics. 2021. "Corrective Services, Australia." Australian Bureau of Statistics, Canberra. https://www.abs.gov.au/statistics/people/crime-and-justice/corrective-services-australia/latest-release#key-statistics.

Baldry, Eileen, and Chris Cunneen. 2014. "Imprisoned Indigenous Women and the Shadow of Colonial Patriarchy." *Australian and New Zealand Journal of Criminology* 47(2):276–98.

Beauchamp, Zack. 2016. "Justin Trudeau, Canada's Dreamy Prime Minister, Explained for Americans." *Vox*, March 10. https://www.vox.com/2016/3/10/11193958/justin-trudeau-canada.

Bourassa, Carrie A. 2008. *Destruction of the Métis Nation: Health Consequences*. Regina: University of Regina.

Bourassa, Carrie A., Melissa Blind, Devin Dietrich, and Eric Oleson. 2015. "Understanding the Intergenerational Effects of Colonization: Aboriginal Women with Neurological Conditions—Their Reality and Resilience." *International Journal of Indigenous Health* 10(2):3–20.

Boyer, Yvonne, Jade Fletcher, Katherine Sutherland, and Drew T. Spicer. 2019. "First Nations, Métis, and Inuit Prisoners' Rights to Health within the Prison System: Missed Opportunities." *McGill Journal of Law and Health* 13(1):27–72.

Bucerius, Sandra M., Kevin D. Haggerty, and David T. Dunford. 2020. "Prison as Temporary Refuge: Amplifying the Voices of Women Detained in Prison." *British Journal of Criminology* 61(2):519–37.

Bucerius, Sandra M., Temitope B. Oriola, and Daniel J. Jones. 2021. "Policing with a Public Health Lens—Moving towards an Understanding of Crime as a Public Health Issue." *Police Journal.* https://doi.org/10.1177/0032258X211009577.

Burt, Gregory. 2011. "What about the Wähine? Can an Alternative Sentencing Practice Reduce the Rate That Maori Women Fill Our Prisons? An Argument for the Implementation of Indigenous Sentencing Courts in New Zealand." *Waikato Law Review* 19(1):206–18.

Cardoso, Tom. 2020. "Bias Behind Bars: A *Globe* Investigation Finds a Prison System Stacked against Black and Indigenous Inmates." *Globe and Mail*, October 24. https://www.theglobeandmail.com/canada/article-investigation-racial-bias-in-canadian-prison-risk-assessments/.

Carlson, Keith T. 1997. "First Contact: Smallpox, 'A Sickness That No Medicine Could Cure, and No Person Escape.'" In *You Are Asked to Witness: The Stó:lō in Canada's Pacific Coast History*, edited by Keith T. Carlson. Chilliwack: Stó:lō Heritage Trust.

Castillo, R. Aida H. 2021. "Prison as a Colonial Enclave: Incarcerated Indigenous Women Resisting Multiple Violence." In *Indigenous Women and Violence: Feminist Activist Research in Heightened States of Injustice*, edited by Lynn Stephen and Shannon Speed. Tucson: University of Arizona Press.

Chartrand, V. 2019. "Unsettled Times: Indigenous Incarceration and the Links between Colonialism and the Penitentiary in Canada." *Canadian Journal of Criminology and Criminal Justice* 61(3):67–89.

Clark, D. Anthony, Sela Kleiman, Lisa B. Spanierman, Paige Isaac, and Gauthamie Poolokasingham. 2014. "'Do You Live in a Teepee?' Aboriginal Students' Experiences with Racial Microaggressions in Canada." *Journal of Diversity in Higher Education* 7(2):112–25.

Clark, Scott. 2019. *Overrepresentation of Indigenous People in the Canadian Criminal Justice System: Causes and Responses*. Ottawa: Department of Justice, Research and Statistics Division.

Cohen, Irwin M., and Raymond R. Corrado. 2004. "Housing Discrimination among a Sample of Aboriginal People in Winnipeg and Thompson, Manitoba." *Aboriginal Policy Research Consortium* 1:115–26.

Connell, Raewyn. 2018. "Decolonizing Sociology." *Contemporary Sociology* 47(4):399–407.

Correctional Investigator. 2021. "Annual Report, 2020–21." Office of the Correctional Investigator, Ottawa. https://www.oci-bec.gc.ca/cnt/rpt/pdf/annrpt/annrpt20202021-eng.pdf.

Correctional Service Canada. 2019. "Correctional Programming for Indigenous Offenders." Correctional Service Canada, Ottawa. https://www.csc-scc.gc.ca/002/003/002003-0002-en.shtml.

Cunneen, Chris, and Juan Tauri. 2017. *Indigenous Criminology*. Bristol: Policy.

Daschuk, James. 2013. *Clearing the Plains: Disease, Politics of Starvation, and the Loss of Aboriginal Life*. Regina: University of Regina Press.

Deconstructed. 2019. "Deconstructed Live from Toronto: Is Canada Really a Progressive Paradise?" Intercept, November 14. https://theintercept.com/2019/11/14/deconstructed-live-from-toronto-is-canada-really-a-progressive-paradise/.

Dickason, Olive P., and David Long. 2011. *Visions of the Heart: Canadian Aboriginal Issues*, 3rd ed. Oxford: Oxford University Press.

Fagan, Brian M. 2016. *World Prehistory: A Brief Introduction*, 8th ed. London: Routledge.

Fournier, Suzanne, and Ernie Crey. 1997. *Stolen from Our Embrace: The Abduction of First Nations Children and the Restoration of Aboriginal Communities*. Vancouver: Douglas & McIntyre.

Friesen, Joe. 2019. "Mortality Rates for First Nations Young Women and Girls May Have Worsened: Study." *Globe and Mail*, May 26. https://www.theglobeandmail.com/canada/article-mortality-rates-for-first-nations-young-women-and-girls-may-have/.

Gaudry, Adam, and Danielle Lorenz. 2018. "Indigenization as Inclusion, Reconciliation, and Decolonization: Navigating the Different Visions for Indigenizing the Canadian Academy." *AlterNative* 14(3):218–27.

Gillan, Kevin, and Jenny Pickerill. 2012. "The Difficult and Hopeful Ethics of Research on, and with, Social Movements." *Social Movement Studies: Journal of Social, Cultural and Political Protest* 11(2):133–43.

Gilmore, Scott. 2015. "Canada's Race Problem? It's Even Worse than America's." *Maclean's*, January 22. https://www.macleans.ca/news/canada/out-of-sight-out-of-mind-2/.

Godlewska, Anne, Jackie Moore, and C. Drew Bednasek. 2017. "Cultivating Ignorance of Aboriginal Realities." *Canadian Geographer* 54(4):417–40.

Goodman, Ashley, Rob Morgan, Ron Kuehlke, Shelda Kastor, and Kim Fleming. 2018. "'We've Been Researched to Death': The Research Experiences of Urban Indigenous Peoples in Vancouver, Canada." *International Indigenous Policy Journal* 9(2):1–20.

Gordon, Catherine E., and Jerry P. White. 2014. "Indigenous Educational Attainment in Canada." *International Indigenous Policy Journal* 5(3):1–25.

Government of Canada. 2017*a*. "First Nations in Canada." Government of Canada, Ottawa. https://www.rcaanc-cirnac.gc.ca/eng/1307460755710/1536862806124.

Government of Canada. 2017*b*. "Indigenous Peoples and Communities." Government of Canada, Crown-Indigenous Northern Affairs Canada, Ottawa. https://www.rcaanc-cirnac.gc.ca/eng/1100100013785/1529102490303.

Grant, Elizabeth. 2016. "Designing Carceral Environments for Indigenous Prisoners: A Comparison of Approaches in Australia, Canada, Aotearoa New Zealand, the US, and Greenland (Kalaallit Nunaat)." *Advancing Corrections Journal* 1:26–47.

Hansen, John G. 2015. "Indigenous-Settler Incarceration Disparities in Canada: How Tribal Justice Programming Helps Urban Indigenous Youth." *Indigenous Policy Journal* 25(3):1–16.

Harding, Robert. 2005. "The Media, Aboriginal People, and Common Sense." *Canadian Journal of Native Studies* 25(1):311–35.

Harper, Jendy. 2020. "Why Does NZ Imprison So Many Māori?" *Newsroom*, August 29. https://www.newsroom.co.nz/why-does-nz-imprison-so-many-maori.

Hartney, Christopher, and Linh Vuong. 2009. *Created Equal: Racial and Ethnic Disparities in the US Criminal Justice System*. Madison, WI: National Council on Crime and Delinquency.

Howard, Heather A., and Craig Proulx. 2011. *Aboriginal Peoples in Canadian Cities: Transformations and Continuities*. Waterloo: Wilfrid Laurier University Press.

Jacobs, Emma. 2022. "Half of the Women in Canada's Federal Prisons Are Indigenous." NPR, May 10. https://www.npr.org/2022/05/10/1098014745/nearly-half-the-women-in-canadas-federal-prisons-are-indigenous.

Johnston, Patrick. 1983. *Native Children and the Child Welfare System*. Toronto: Lorimer.

Joseph, Bob. 2018. *21 Things You May Not Know about the Indian Act: Helping Canadians Make Reconciliation with Indigenous Peoples a Reality*. Toronto: CBC Press.

Juris, Jeffrey S. 2007. "Practicing Militant Ethnography with the Movement for Global Resistance in Barcelona." In *Constituent Imagination: Militant Investigations/Collective Theorization*, edited by Stevphen Shukaitis, David Graeber, and Erika Biddle. Oakland, CA: AK Press.

Lavallée, Lynn F., and Jennifer M. Poole. 2010. "Beyond Recovery: Colonization, Health and Healing for Indigenous People in Canada." *International Journal of Mental Health and Addiction* 8(2):271–81.

LeBeuf, Marcel-Eugene. 2011. *The Role of the Royal Canadian Mounted Police during the Indian Residential School System*. Ottawa: Royal Canadian Mounted Police.

Maleakieh, Jamil. 2018. *Adult and Youth Correctional Statistics in Canada, 2016/17*. Ottawa: Canadian Centre for Justice Statistics.

Marques, Olga, and Lisa Monchalin. 2020. "The Mass Incarceration of Indigenous Women in Canada: A Colonial Tactic of Control and Assimilation." In *Neo-Colonial Injustice and the Mass Imprisonment of Indigenous Women*, edited by Lily George, Adele N. Norris, Antje Deckert, and Juan Tauri. London: Palgrave Macmillan.

Martel, Joane, and Renee Brassard. 2008. "Painting the Prison 'Red': Constructing and Experiencing Aboriginal Identities in Prison." *British Journal of Social Work* 38(2):340–61.

Martel, Joane, Renee Brassard, and Mylene Jaccoud. 2011. "When Two Worlds Collide: Aboriginal Risk Management in Canadian Corrections." *British Journal of Criminology* 51(2):235–55.

McAdam, Sylvia. 2015. *Nationhood Interrupted: Revitalizing Nêhiyaw Legal Systems*. Saskatoon: Purich.

McDermott, Ray, and Shirin Vossoughi. 2020. "The Culture of Poverty, Again." *Diaspora, Indigenous, and Minority Education* 14(2):60–69.

McGuire, Michaela M., and Danielle J. Murdoch. 2021. "(In)-justice: An Exploration of the Dehumanization, Victimization, Criminalization, and Over-incarceration of Indigenous Women in Canada." *Punishment and Society*. https://doi.org/10.1177/14624745211001685.

Menzies, Peter. 2010. "Intergenerational Trauma from a Mental Health Perspective." *Native Social Work Journal* 7:63–85.

Miller, James R. 2000. *Skyscrapers Hide the Heavens: A History of Indian-White Relations in Canada*, 3rd ed. Toronto: University of Toronto Press.

Miller, James R. 2009. *Compact, Contract, Covenant: Aboriginal Treaty-Making in Canada*. Toronto: University of Toronto Press.

Milloy, John S. 1999. *A National Crime: The Canadian Government and the Residential School System, 1879 to 1986*. Winnipeg: University of Manitoba Press.

Morin, Brandi. 2018. "How a Cree Grandmother Helps Dangerous Offenders Find Their Path to Rehabilitation." CBC News, March 19. https://www.cbc.ca/news/indigenous/how-a-cree-grandmother-helps-dangerous-offenders-find-their-path-to-rehabilitation-1.4560521.

Motz, Takara A., and Cheryl Currie. 2019. "Racially-Motivated Housing Discrimination Experienced by Indigenous Postsecondary Students in Canada: Impacts on PTSD Symptomology and Perceptions of University Stress." *Public Health* 176:59–67.

Murdocca, Carmela. 2020. "Re-imagining 'Serving Time' in Indigenous Communities." *Canadian Journal of Women and the Law* 32(1):31–60.

NAHO (National Aboriginal Health Organization). 2005. *First Nations Regional Longitudinal Health Survey*. Ottawa: NAHO.

Neuman, Keith. 2016. *Canadian Public Opinion on Aboriginal Peoples: Final Report*. Toronto: Environics Institute for Survey Research.

Nichols, Robert. 2014. "The Colonialism of Incarceration." *Radical Philosophy Review* 17(2):435–55.

Nielsen, Marianne O. 2020. "How Indigenous Justice Programs Contribute to Indigenous Capacity-Building and Achieving Human Rights." In *Traditional, National, and International Law and Indigenous Communities*, edited by Marianne O. Neilsen and Karen Jarratt-Snider. Tucson: University of Arizona Press.

NIMMIWG (National Inquiry into Missing and Murdered Indigenous Women and Girls). 2019. *Reclaiming Power and Place: Final Report of the National Inquiry into Missing and Murdered Indigenous Women and Girls*. Vancouver: Privy Council Office.

OECD (Organization for Economic Cooperation and Development). 2020. *Linking Indigenous Communities with Regional Development in Canada*. Paris: OECD.

Ormiston, Naadli T. 2010. "Re-conceptualizing Research: An Indigenous Perspective." *First Peoples Child and Family Review* 5(1):50–56.

Phillips, Coretta, and Rod Earle. 2010. "Reading Difference Differently: Identity, Epistemology and Prison Ethnography." *British Journal of Criminology* 50(2): 360–78.

RCAP (Royal Commission on Aboriginal Peoples). 1996a. *Report of the Royal Commission on Aboriginal Peoples*. Vol. 1, *Looking Forward, Looking Back*. Ottawa: Canada Communication Group.

RCAP (Royal Commission on Aboriginal Peoples). 1996b. *Report of the Royal Commission on Aboriginal Peoples*. Vol. 3, *Gathering Strength*. Ottawa: Canada Communication Group.

RCGS (Royal Canadian Geographical Society). 2018. *The Indigenous Peoples Atlas of Canada*. Ottawa: Canadian Geographic.

Reid, Andrew A. 2020. "Reducing the Use of Imprisonment: Lessons from 20 Years' Experience in Canada." *British Journal of Criminology* 60:1480–501.

Reitano, Julie. 2017. "Juristat: Adult Correctional Statistics in Canada." Statistics Canada, Canadian Centre for Justice Statistics, Ottawa. https://www150.statcan .gc.ca/n1/pub/85-002-x/2017001/article/14700-eng.pdf.

Reitz, Jeffrey G. 2011. *Pro-immigration in Canada: Social and Economic Roots of Popular Views*. Institute for Research on Public Policy Study no. 20. Montreal: Institute for Research on Public Policy.

Riley, Tasha, and Charles Ungerleider. 2012. "Self-Fulfilling Prophecy: How Teachers' Attributions, Expectations, and Stereotypes Influence the Learning Opportunities Afforded Aboriginal Students." *Canadian Journal of Education* 35(2):303–33.

Robson, Karen L. 2013. *Sociology of Education in Canada*. Toronto: Pearson Canada.

Sarangi, Leila. 2020. "2020: Setting the Stage for a Poverty-Free Canada." Campaign 2000, Toronto. https://campaign2000.ca/wp-content/uploads/2020/01 /campaign-2000-report-setting-the-stage-for-a-poverty-free-canada-updated -january-24-2020.pdf.

Schick, Carol, and Verna St. Denis. 2005. "Troubling National Discourses in Anti-racist Curricular Planning." *Canadian Journal of Education* 28(3):295–317.

Schnarch, Brian S. 2004. "Ownership, Control, Access, and Possession (OCAP) or Self-Determination Applied to Research: A Critical Analysis of Contemporary First Nations Research and Some Options for First Nations Communities." *Journal of Aboriginal Health* 1:80–95.

Sinclair, Raven. 2007. "Identity Lost and Found: Lessons from the Sixties Scoop." *First Peoples Child and Family Review* 3(1):65–82.

Sium, Aman, Chandni Desai, and Eric Ritskes. 2012. "Towards the 'Tangible Unknown': Decolonization and the Indigenous Future." *Indigeneity, Education, and Society* 1(1):1–8.

Smith, Charles. 2006. "Racial Profiling in Canada, the United States and the United Kingdom." In *Racial Profiling in Canada: Challenging the Myth of a Few Bad Apples*, edited by C. Tator and F. Henry. Toronto: University of Toronto Press.

Smith, Linda T. 2008. *Decolonizing Methodologies: Research and Indigenous Peoples*. New York: Zed.

Solomon, Arthur. 1993. *Introduction to the American Indian in the White Man's Prisons: A Story of Genocide*, edited by Little Rock Reed. Taos, NM: Uncompromising.

Solomon, Arthur. 1994. *Eating Bitterness: A Vision beyond the Prison Walls: Poems and Essays of Arthur Solomon*, edited by Cathleen Kneen and Michael Posluns. Toronto: NC Press.

Statistics Canada. 2017. "The Aboriginal Languages of First Nations People, Métis and Inuit." Census in Brief. Statistics Canada, Ottawa. https://www12.statcan .gc.ca/census-recensement/2016/as-sa/98-200-x/2016022/98-200-x2016022-eng .cfm.

Statistics Canada. 2019. "Suicide among First Nations People, Métis and Inuit (2011–2016): Findings from the 2011 Canadian Census Health and Environment Cohort." Statistics Canada, Ottawa. https://www150.statcan.gc.ca/n1/en/catalogue/99-011-X2019001.

Stewart, Anthony. 2014. *Visitor*. Halifax: Fernwood.

Stewart, Suzanne L. 2008. "Promoting Indigenous Mental Health: Cultural Perspectives on Healing from Native Counsellors in Canada." *International Journal of Health Promotion and Education* 46(2):49–56.

Stote, Karen. 2012. "The Coercive Sterilization of Aboriginal Women in Canada." *American Indian Culture and Research Journal* 36(3):117–50.

Struthers Montford, Kelly, and Dawn Moore. 2018. "The Prison as Reserve: Governmentality, Phenomenology, and Indigenizing the Prison (Studies)." *New Criminal Law Review* 21(4):640–63.

Struthers Montford, Kelly, and Chloë Taylor. 2021. "Introduction: Doing Abolition." In *Building Abolition*, edited by Kelly Struthers Montford and Chloë Taylor. Abingdon: Routledge.

Tetrault, Justin E. C., Sandra M. Bucerius, and Kevin D. Haggerty. 2020. "Multiculturalism under Confinement: Prisoner Race Relations Inside Western Canadian Prisons." *Sociology* 54(3):534–55.

Timler, Kelsey, Helen Brown, and Colleen Varcoe. 2019. "Growing Connection beyond Prison Walls: How a Prison Garden Fosters Rehabilitation and Healing for Incarcerated Men." *Journal of Offender Rehabilitation* 58(5):444–63.

TRC (Truth and Reconciliation Commission of Canada). 2015*a*. *Calls to Action*. Winnipeg: TRC.

TRC (Truth and Reconciliation Commission of Canada). 2015*b*. "Canada's Residential Schools: The History, Part 2 1939 to 2000." Final Report of the Truth and Reconciliation Commission of Canada, vol. 1. Montreal: McGill-Queen's University Press.

TRC (Truth and Reconciliation Commission of Canada). 2015*c*. "Canada's Residential Schools: Reconciliation." Final Report of the Truth and Reconciliation Commission of Canada, vol. 6. Montreal: McGill-Queen's University Press.

Tuck, Eve, and K. Wayne Yang. 2012. "Decolonization Is Not a Metaphor." *Decolonization: Indigeneity, Education and Society* 1(1):1–40.

Turnbull, Sarah. 2014. "Aboriginalising the Parole Process: Culturally Appropriate Adaptations and the Canadian Federal Parole System." *Punishment and Society* 16(4):385–405.

Varcoe, Colleen, Helen Brown, Kelsey Timler, Melissa Taylor, and Elizabeth Straus. 2020. "'Healing on Both Sides': Strengthening the Effectiveness of Prison–Indigenous Community Partnerships through Reciprocity and Investment." *International Indigenous Policy Journal* 11(3):1–26.

Vecchio, Karen. 2018. "A Call to Action: Reconciliation with Indigenous Women in the Federal Justice and Correctional Systems." Report of the Standing Committee on the Status of Women. House of Commons. http://www.ourcommons.ca/DocumentViewer/en/42-1/FEWO/report-13.

Vowel, Chelsea. 2016. *Indigenous Writes: A Guide to First Nations, Métis, and Inuit Issues in Canada*. Winnipeg: HighWater.

Waitangi Tribunal. 2017. *Tū Maite Rangi! Report on the Crown and Disproportionate Reoffending Rates*. Lower Hutt: Legislation Direct.

Waldram, James B. 1993. "Aboriginal Spirituality and Symbolic Healing in Canadian Prisons." *Culture, Medicine and Psychiatry* 17:345–62.

Waldram, James B. 1997. *The Way of the Pipe: Aboriginal Spirituality and Symbolic Healing in Canadian Prisons*. Toronto: University of Toronto Press.

Wolfe, Patrick. 2006. "Settler Colonialism and the Elimination of the Native." *Journal of Genocide Research* 8(4):387–409.

Wylie, lloy, and Stephanie McConkey. 2019. "Insiders' Insight: Discrimination against Indigenous Peoples through the Eyes of Health Care Professionals." *Journal of Racial and Ethnic Health Disparities* 6:37–45.

Yuen, Felice, and Alison Pedlar. 2009. "Leisure as a Context for Justice: Experiences of Ceremony for Aboriginal Women in Prison." *Journal of Leisure Research* 41(4):547–64.

Zeng, Zhen. 2020. "Jail Inmates in 2018." US Department of Justice, Bureau of Justice Statistics, Washington, DC.

Zinger, Ivan. 2020. "Indigenous People in Federal Custody Surpasses 30%: Correctional Investigator Issues Statement and Challenge." News release, January 21. Office of the Correctional Investigator, Government of Canada. https://www.oci-bec.gc.ca/cnt/comm/press/press20200121-eng.aspx.

David C. Pyrooz

The Prison and the Gang

ABSTRACT

A prison gang is a durable group that shares a collective identity, maintains a
locus of custodial influence, exhibits collective behavior, and engages in a pattern
of illegal activity. Prison gangs proliferated in recent decades for reasons that
remain unclear. The classic view of prison gangs—conspiratorial, hierarchical,
monolithic, predatory, and rule bound—is outdated; contemporary research
reveals far greater heterogeneity in forms and functions. There is a nascent
micro-macro paradox about gangs and (dis)order. Misconduct, especially violence, is concentrated disproportionately among gang populations, attributable
to group processes rather than to individual propensities. Countervailing
claims that gangs bring order and disorder remain at best speculative and await
more rigorous research. About 15 percent of US prisoners are affiliated with
gangs; a much larger proportion maintain associations by virtue of homophily
and institutional constraints. Emerging evidence suggests that prisoners
enter and exit gangs while incarcerated. Prison officials have constructed
intelligence apparatuses to document and manage gang populations. There
is no consensus whether concentration or dispersion strategies produce safer
prisons, although gang affiliates are overrepresented in solitary confinement.
Evidence is too sparse to reach any conclusions about the effectiveness of
promising liabilities- and obligations-based rehabilitative programs.

Tom Clements was watching television with his wife on March 19, 2013,
when the doorbell rang. When he opened the door, a man in a pizza

David C. Pyrooz is associate professor of sociology at the University of Colorado. I thank
Sandra Bucerius, *Crime and Justice* reviewers, Scott Decker, James Densley, John Hagedorn,
John Leverso, and Michael Tonry for helpful suggestions. The original research discussed
was supported by funding from the National Institute of Justice (grant 2014-MU-CX-0111)
and coordination with the Texas Department of Criminal Justice (723-AR15). Opinions,
findings, and conclusions are mine and do not necessarily reflect those of the supporting
agencies.

Electronically published September 8, 2022

Crime and Justice, volume 51, 2022.
https://doi.org/10.1086/720944

delivery uniform shot him twice with a 9 mm handgun. He was pronounced dead within 30 minutes, making him one of 145 homicide victims
in Colorado that year. All homicides are tragic, but this one was different.
Clements was the executive director of the Colorado Department of
Corrections. The killer, Evan Ebel, had been released 7 weeks earlier. Classified as a member of the 211 Crew, a notorious White prison gang, Ebel
spent the bulk of his 8-year sentence in solitary confinement. After nearly
10 years, it remains unclear whether the killing was a gang-ordered assas-
sination or an act of personal vengeance.

A few months later, another event attracted international attention to
prisons and prison gangs. Beginning July 8, around 30,000 California
prisoners refused meals. The hunger strike was orchestrated by purported
affiliates of four leading prison gangs in a security housing unit corridor
in Pelican Bay who set aside gang, racial, and prison politics to unite
in protest against the conditions of their confinement. Their core motivation was California's policy of housing prisoners affiliated with gangs indeterminately in solitary confinement, running counter to protections of
due process and prohibitions against cruel and unusual punishment. The
strike ended within 2 months, after state legislators promised to hold
hearings. A federal class action lawsuit, *Ashker v. Governor of the State of
California*,[1] was settled in 2015 and resulted in sweeping changes to restrictive housing policy.

Outside of extreme events, such as violence, lawsuits, riots, and unrest,
prison gangs and gang members rarely attract the interest of mainstream
media. To the general public what happens behind bars is "out of sight,
out of mind." Social scientists have likewise shown little interest. Many
topics relating to incarceration deserve scholarly inquiry, as this volume
of *Crime and Justice* makes clear, but as Jacobs (2001, p. vi) remarked
two decades ago: "It is hard to understand why the prison gang phenomenon does not attract more attention from the media, scholars, and policy
analysts. One would think it would be big news that powerful race and
ethnically based gangs are an entrenched feature of many American (and
foreign) prisons and that this phenomenon has only gotten bigger and
more entrenched." Jacobs was correct. At the turn of the century, popular
and academic interest in prison gangs was meager, as the trajectories

---

[1] No. C 09-5796 CW (N.D. Cal. September 1, 2015). For an overview of the lawsuit's
origins and evolution, consult the Center for Constitutional Rights: https://ccrjustice.org
/home/what-we-do/our-cases/ashker-v-brown.

reported in figure 1 show. The dashed trajectory is based on data from the Google Ngram Viewer, which plots the relative frequency, expressed as a percentage, of the annual appearance of the bigram prison + gangs in the American English corpus. The solid trajectory plots the annual output in academic scholarship—books, articles, chapters, and reports—concerning gangs in incarcerated settings (Pyrooz and Mitchell 2015; Gravel, forthcoming). Both trajectories reveal that interest in prison gangs grew in the 1980s but was flat in the 1990s. There was a surge of interest in the new millennium. For the Google Ngram trajectory, the frequency of appearance of the bigram doubled in the first decade and then again in the second. For the scholarly works trajectory, the average annual output increased by 19 percent in the 2000s relative to the 1990s and by 52 percent in the 2010s relative to the 2000s. Of course, these numbers pale in comparison to the amount of popular and scholarly interest in gangs on the street, but they reflect an evolving landscape of scholarship. And with such growth comes a need to take stock of what has been learned.

In this essay I provide a comprehensive overview of research on gangs in prison. Four qualifications are in order. First, the research covered is

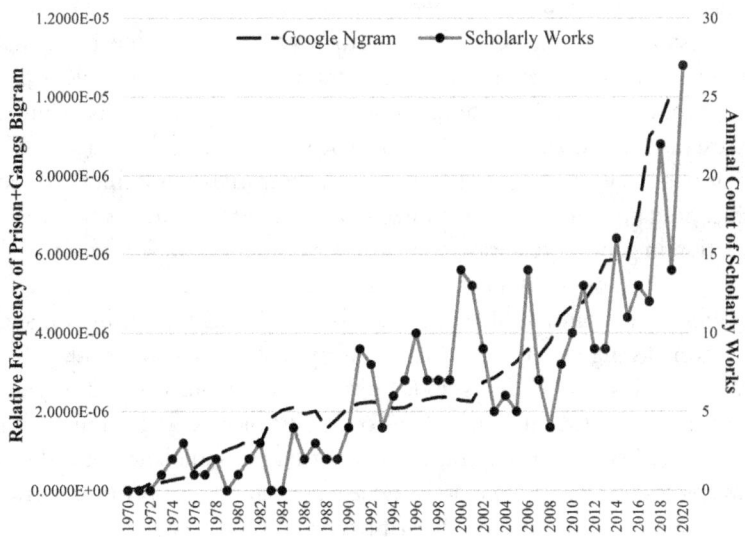

Fɪɢ. 1.—Google NGram and scholarly output on prison gangs. Google NGram refers only to relative frequency of prison + gangs bigram appearances in the American English corpus. The annual count of scholarly works includes research conducted in all incarcerated settings.

based primarily in US prisons. This reflects the state of scholarship, not my preference; relevant research outside the United States is discussed. Even in the United States there is uneven coverage across the 51 state and federal systems. Second, I focus mostly on gangs in prisons rather than in juvenile or jail settings. Age and incarceration length distinguish prisons from people confined in the other settings. Still, research conducted in juvenile and jail settings is covered to the extent it is relevant. Third, I draw on precepts established in the wider literature on gangs to inform the substantive areas covered. Finally, although I do not devote standalone space to research methodologies, it warrants mention that official descriptions of gangs are more common sources of data than are ethnographic observations, in-depth interviews, and surveys of prisoners. Access to prisons is difficult to secure, and original data collection is challenging to conduct, especially on gangs. The most reliable conclusions are reached when the evidence is corroborated by multiple sources of data, although I privilege the research conducted with incarcerated people over the views of prison authorities on most issues since my concern is primarily with behaviors and experiences of prisoners.

Gangs occupy a central place in the social order of prisons. Far too little social scientific attention has been aimed at collectives of prisoners who are considered or consider themselves to be gangs. This is due to the challenges of gaining access to prison and other pressing substantive topics, but not entirely. Inconsistent definitions of gangs, which have been either too exclusive or too inclusive, have also been a source of obfuscation. The traditional view of gangs in prison as conspiratorial, hierarchical, monolithic, predatory, and rule-bound groups is outdated. There is far greater variation in gangs—represented by ideal types of informal diffuse and instrumental rational—than the field has been led to believe. I address this by offering a definition of gangs in prison capable of accounting for such variation, distinguishing between defining properties and descriptive characteristics. Two conclusions about forms and functions of prison gangs seem universal, the first being the centrality of race and ethnicity and the second being that they bring about at least a semblance of order. It remains unclear whether gangs provide a net value to the prison generally or to their members specifically that overcomes formal and informal negative consequences of their presence.

The widespread emergence of prison gangs occurred concomitant with the rise of mass incarceration—the quadrupling of the imprisonment rate from the early 1970s to 2010. Predominant theories of prison social organization, including deprivation, importation, and management, offer the scaffolding to understand gang emergence in prison, although the lack of empirical testing undermines reaching any firm conclusions about the validity of the theories. Studies of individuals reveal the contours of gang membership in prison; many people bring their gang affiliations with them, while many others join for the first time while imprisoned, and still others, despite popular perception, disengage while behind bars, making developmental and life-course theories and methods quite appealing. Misconduct and violence are higher among gang populations than among other prisoners, but this is attributable to the group processes of gangs and not to individual deficiencies of members. How to respond to gangs remains the subject of much debate. In general, prison systems seek to manage gang populations rather than to offer meaningful interventions designed to target liabilities and obligations. Evaluations of responses to street gangs have flourished over the last two decades—both in rigor and volume—but that is not true of prison gangs. The evidence base is far too sparse to support any firm conclusions about how to best manage or intervene with gangs in prison.

This essay has six sections. Section I offers a definition of gangs in prison that overcomes the limitations of prior definitions. I draw on historical accounts of the rise of gangs in prison and the leading theoretical accounts of their emergence and existence. Section II focuses on forms and functions. I highlight the group-level characteristics of gangs and their variation and the meaning, purpose, and utility of gangs in prison. Section III concentrates on what attracts the attention of academics, policy makers, and practitioners (and the public): misconduct and violence. I take stock of the leading empirical evidence on the consequences in prisons of gangs and gang affiliations. Section IV examines the contours of gang involvement, including joining and leaving in prison, and highlights the importance of embeddedness in gangs. Section V outlines responses to gangs in prison, including management and intervention strategies. In each section I express my degree of confidence in the conclusions reached and identify subjects worthy of future attention from social scientists. An agenda for advancing the current state of knowledge is offered in Section VI.

I. Origins

"I very much fear that the gang has been the theoretician's Rorschach in criminology—one can easily find what he seeks." Klein (1971, p. viii) wrote this 50 years ago in the opening to *Street Gangs and Street Workers*, a pivotal book that marked a transition from the playgroup orientation of studies of neighborhood youth groups (Puffer 1912; Thrasher 1927) to the "social problems" era (Pyrooz and Mitchell 2015). There is no shortage of researchers' definitions of street gangs. Bjerregaard (2002) identified 15 that have obtained prominence.[2] Few issues spark debates as animated and spirited as the definition of gangs for the reasons Klein feared. Gangs are portrayed as anything from resistance movements to loosely coupled youth with poor self-control (Brotherton and Barrios 2004; Pyrooz, Melde, et al. 2021), reflecting disciplinary orientations and theoretical preferences as much as the data on which the portrayals are based. This led Katz and Jackson-Jacobs (2004, p. 102) to describe a "multi-theory interpretive feast" that involves a "tacitly shared agreement to treat gangs as windows" through which researchers see the world. These issues have escaped sustained discussion in incarceration settings generally and in prisons specifically.

What is a gang in prison? When did they emerge? And what explains their existence? This section provides a foundation for what follows, by addressing core questions that are fundamental to understanding and responding to gangs in prison.

A. Defining Gangs in Prison

It is not feasible to apply definitions of street gangs to the custodial context despite their being the closest corollary to prison gangs. Maxson (2012, p. 113) learned this when trying to apply the Eurogang definition—"street gang (or troublesome youth group) is any durable, street-oriented youth group whose involvement in illegal activity is part of their group identity"—to youth gangs incarcerated in California's Division of Juvenile Justice. The problem is that there is no "street" in prison. That led Maxson to propose an adaptation emphasizing "visibility" of collective behavior, as when members spend time together in day rooms, recreation areas, and other public settings. Yet even that proved not viable since the monolithic schedule of youth activities prevented unstructured, public-facing socialization.

---

[2] Forty-five states and the federal government maintain statutory definitions of a gang (Decker, Pyrooz, and Densley 2022). There is more consistency across legal than academic definitions (Barrows and Huff 2009), a likely consequence of isomorphic adoption of California's definition introduced in 1988.

Even leading definitions developed with prisons in mind are problematic because they are too exclusive or too inclusive. Lyman (1989, p. 48), using his work on crime groups that traffic in drugs, offered the first definition: "an organization which operates within the prison system as a self-perpetuating criminally oriented entity, consisting of a select group of inmates who have established an organized chain of command and are governed by an established code of conduct." Skarbek's (2014, p. 9) more recent definition is similar: "an inmate organization that operates within a prison system, that has a corporate entity, exists into perpetuity and whose membership is restricted, mutually exclusive, and often requires a lifetime commitment." Both definitions are inadequate because they are too exclusive: only corporatized groups satisfy them. Miller's (1975) proposed definition faltered because of an overemphasis on gang organization and structure; so do Lyman's and Skarbek's, as I explain below.

The FBI's definition, while more detailed, suffers from similar limitations: "Prison gangs are criminal organizations that originated within the penal system and operate within correctional facilities throughout the United States, although released members may be operating on the street. Prison gangs are also self-perpetuating criminal entities that can continue their criminal operations outside the confines of the penal system" (NGIC 2011). Not only must the gang maintain corporatized features, but it must also have originated in prison. While possibly useful for defining a type of gang, it is too restrictive to characterize the universe of gangs in prison because of the importation of groups and culture from the street (Jacobs 1974; Pyrooz and Decker 2019). Maitra (2020, p. 133) offered a definition based on field research in English prisons that offers a rare inductive approach. He defined prison gangs as any collective whose identity within prison involves "identifying with their 'home' area; exclusivity in membership; and engaging in violent conflicts with other gangs/groups within prison," avoiding the organizational limitations of prior research but unnecessarily imposing violence and hometown identification as definitional properties, potentially excluding gangs united by race or other factors.

Other definitions are too inclusive. With a focus primarily on criminal organizations found in Latin American prisons, Lessing (2010, p. 159) contended that even defining prison gangs as a "somewhat informal group dedicated to self-preservation and perhaps predatory or illegal activities" was too narrow. Instead, he considered "all self-identifying associations of inmate groups that exhibit some form of collective behaviour" to fit within his review. This includes just about every group of prisoners. Using research in nine prisons in England and Wales, Wood (2006, p. 606) defined a gang as "a group of three or more prisoners whose negative behaviour has an adverse impact on the prison that holds them." This includes too wide a swath of prisoner associations, including especially fleeting collectives. Knox (2005, p. 1) took a similar approach, claiming that "any group of three (3) or more persons with recurring threatening or disruptive behavior" were gangs, which ignores collective identity and conflates co-offending with gangs. Others have ducked the issue altogether (Pyrooz and Decker 2019, p. 18), appealing instead to self-nomination and the common understanding of gangs in an individual-level study of prisoners.

Obtaining a reliable and valid definition is essential. Common definitions are foundational to the scientific enterprise, and the study of gangs is no exception (Klein 2012). In defining street gangs, Ball and Curry (1995, p. 239) observed: "Definitions tend to be based on those aspects of the phenomena in question that were most visible and most salient at the time. As the relative visibility of various phenomenal features changes with research progress, and the salience of these various features shifts with new perspectives and purposes, redefinition often becomes necessary." This is a fitting characterization of the state of prison gang definitions. While the earliest stages of mass incarceration yielded representations of gangs that permitted definitions with corporate and indigenous properties, as discussed below, more recent research has shown that is not the case. Variation in gangs has always been the norm, not the exception. Informal-diffuse gangs have likely long existed in prison but were overshadowed by interest in gangs with instrumental-rational features (Camp and Camp 1985; Decker, Bynum, and Weisel 1998). What is needed is a definition that captures the full spectrum of gangs in custodial settings. Correctional agencies and researchers recognize that a variety of types of gangs exist in such settings, and a definition should be able to account for this.[3]

Drawing on precepts from the wider gang literature generally and findings from the corrections literature specifically, I propose the following

---

[3] This is perhaps best reflected in terminology that runs the gamut of security threat groups (STGs), security risk groups, disruptive groups, cliques, institutional gangs, and incarcerated street gangs. Some agencies ignore group distinctions altogether, while others use the level of threat and organizational structure to create tiers of gangs.

TABLE 1

Defining Properties versus Descriptive Statistics of Institutional Gangs

Defining Property	Descriptive Characteristic
Durability across time	Organization and structure
Collective identity	Group demographics
Locus of custodial influence	Institutional origins and street-based activity
Collective behavior	Membership fluidity and relational boundaries
Illegal activity	Criminal specialization and violence

definition of an institutional gang: "a durable group that shares a collective identity, maintains a locus of custodial influence, exhibits collective behavior, and engages in a pattern of illegal activity." Following the logic outlined by Ball and Curry (1995), this is primarily a definition by analysis that lists core properties, but to a lesser extent it is also a definition by synthesis that is in part correlative. Using the strategy of Eurogang, an international research group that reached a consensus definition (Weerman and Decker, forthcoming), I differentiate between definers, essential properties, and descriptors, qualities yielding variation across gangs; this is reflected in table 1. The five salient properties require elaboration.

Durability refers to temporal persistence. The Eurogang definition specifies 3 months (Weerman et al. 2009), but time in prison marches to a different beat than on the street (Crewe, Hulley, and Wright 2020). Integration likely requires a longer embryonic period. Six months seems sufficient to avoid conflating fleeting prisoner associations with more persistent ones. Whether a gang outlasts turnover in membership—including, should it exist, leadership—is an empirical question.

Collective identity captures the common interests of members and group consciousness. Common or shared geography, experiences, ideology, race or ethnicity, or other affinities unite the group, which should manifest as names, signs, symbols, language, or other unique identifiers of distinction understood by the in-group and, to a lesser extent, by out-groups (Densley 2013).

Locus of custodial influence indicates that the group is a force within the custodial context. Influence is often recognized in the intergang social field (Lauger 2012; Harding 2014) or by official classification from prison authorities. But this property is about the capacity to exercise power, not reactions to it (Ball and Curry 1995, pp. 237–38; Campana and Varese 2018). This is why Maxson and colleagues (2012) differentiated between atomized street gang members and institutional gangs.

Collective behavior is based on intragang interaction. The reality of life inside prisons dictates that interaction cannot be limited to Thrasher's (1927) criteria of meeting, milling, and movement, but it also includes broader interpersonal gang-related custodial communication patterns including phone calls, text messages, legal letters, hand signs, meetings, chants, roll calls, and secretive correspondences that bring about purposive action.

Illegal activity refers to a pattern of serious misconduct occurring or originating in prison that serves the interest of the gang. Such behaviors can be opportunistic or premeditated, be conducted by a single individual or by co-offenders associated with the gang, or entail instrumental or symbolic motivations; patterns cannot be established on the basis of unrelated one-off events, such as a race riot or an instance of drug smuggling, or on self-interested actions unrelated to the gang, such as personal vendetta or drug theft for consumption. This is comparable to Maxson and Klein's (1996) distinction between homicides motivated by gangs and homicides that merely involve gang members.[4]

Many prisoner collectives satisfy one or more of these criteria, but unless they meet all five, they are not a gang. One could imagine a collective of prisoners with shared faith in a supreme power that recurrently engages in the formal practice of worship, including the performance of rituals in common spaces, and even proselytizes to the greater prisoner community. Perhaps such a collective seeks to support the mental and physical well-being of their members in prison, to the extent that, on occasion, it creates tensions with other prisoner associations. This religious collective would satisfy the first four, but not the fifth, criterion.

The aim of this definition is not to induce homogeneity in gangs, reducing prisoner collectives to gangs or nongangs. To the contrary, gangs can take on many forms and functions in prison, which is why it is critical yet again to emphasize the differences between definers and descriptors. Questions of type, such as corporate features, indigenous origins, boundaries and fluidity of affiliation, and criminal specialization, among others, are central topics worthy of empirical investigation.

Even this definition and its attendant properties awaits empirical validation. Save for Maxson's (2012) use of expert surveys to assess the Eurogang

---

[4] Still, it is important to emphasize that even though a pattern of illegal activity is a defining property of institutional gangs, the vast majority of their activities and functions serve noncriminal purposes that are indistinguishable from the wants and needs of other prisoner collectives.

definition in California juvenile facilities, none of the definitions of prison gangs has been subject to independent testing. Maitra's (2020) grounded definition stands out because it was based on his field research in English prisons. Combined, Maxson and Maitra provide a nice road map to assess what is (and is not) a gang in prison.

B. History and Theory

"I'm convinced that if you put three people on an island somewhere, two would clique up and become predatory against the other at some point" (Trulson, Marquart, and Kawucha 2006, p. 26). So said a gang investigator in the Florida Department of Corrections, referring to groups that developed to control the contraband market in Andersonville, the notorious Confederate prisoner-of-war camp during the Civil War.

Much has been made of the "first" gang to emerge in US prisons. Using interviews with prison officials, Camp and Camp (1985, p. 20) reported this to be the Gypsy Jokers, founded in 1950 in the Walla Walla Penitentiary in Washington state. This claim was repeated for decades by researchers until it was disputed by Smith (2016). Since no evidence could be unearthed to support the claim, Smith instead proposed that the Mexican Mafia, founded at the Deuel Vocational Institute in California in 1957, was the "first US prison gang" (p. 51). It is ironic that no similar effort has been made to identify the first American street gang, much less the first in various regions, states, or even cities (Howell 2015).

As the Andersonville quip suggests, prisoner groups such as gangs are not unique to the second half of the twentieth century; they seem to emerge from punishments that isolate people within custodial settings. Scott Decker, reviewing records in the Lloyd Sealy Library at the John Jay College of Criminal Justice, looked at the papers of Lewis E. Lawes, Warden of Sing Sing Prison for 21 years. The *New York Times* (1931, p. 17) quoted Lawes: "[Lewis] has had 132 different gangs in his prison and has had to watch them within the walls of the institution as carefully as the police watch the activity of their associates outside." This discovery is one basis for Roth's (2020, pp. 7–8) argument that, despite the "avalanche of American manuscripts on prison gangs," there is a pressing need for historical research. His global history of prison gangs documented the origins and evolution of *vory-v-zakone* in Russia, the Numbers gangs in South Africa, the Camorra in Italy, and various prison gangs in the Americas, Asia, Australia, and Europe.

Understanding the origins of gangs is important because it sheds light on their proliferation across prison systems and the emergent group processes that are critical to theory development and testing. Figure 2 shows the years gangs emerged in the 51 prison systems in the United States, using data collected from surveys of prison officials (Camp and Camp 1985;

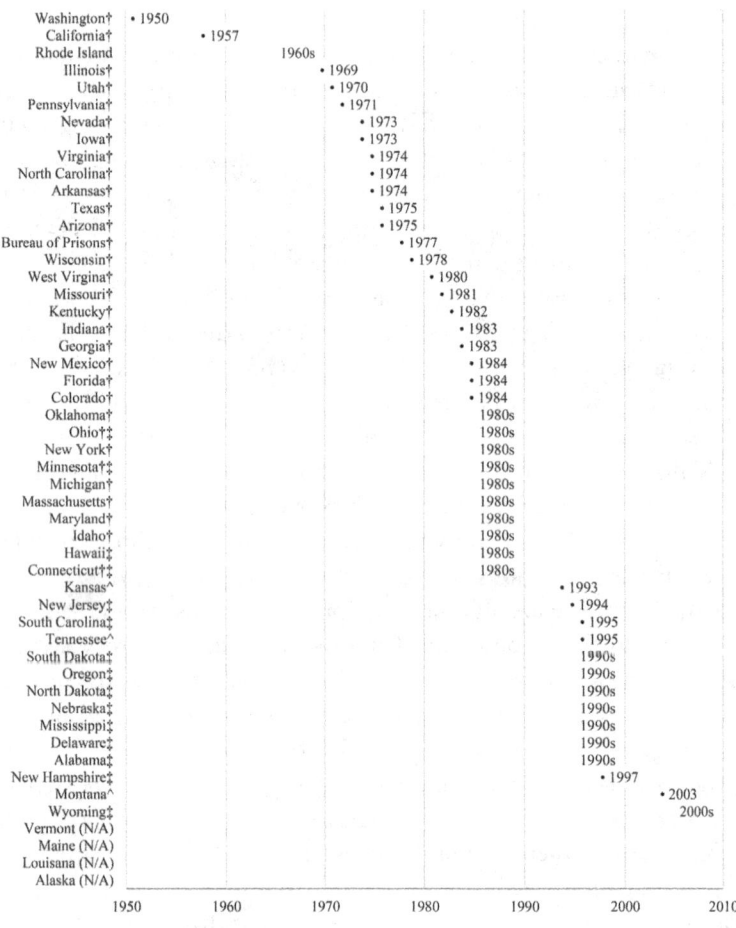

FIG. 2.—Proliferation of gangs in federal and state prison systems. † Reported in Camp and Camp (1985). ‡ Derived from data collected by Pyrooz and Mitchell (2020). †‡ Camp and Camp's (1985) findings verified in Pyrooz and Mitchell (2020). ^ Kansas: Bonner (1999); Montana: personal communication with Kuchinsky (August 14, 2017); Tennessee: public documents on security threat group unit.

Pyrooz and Mitchell 2020). Of the 49 prison systems in Camp and Camp's study, 33 reported active gangs in 1983. Sixteen stated that no gangs existed. Camp and Camp were able to provide precise years gangs emerged in 19 systems; the other 14 were estimates. Pyrooz and Mitchell obtained responses from 39 prison systems in a 2016 survey that asked about the decade when gangs emerged; the responses are used to validate the 14 estimates and supplement 16 no-gang responses from Camp and Camp. In three instances, credible alternative sources of information were used.

Figure 2 reveals several things. Just about every prison system in the United States reports the existence of gangs. This applies to systems with small and large custodial populations alike. No data were available for Alaska, Louisiana, or Maine; Vermont was the only prison system to report the absence of gangs. Differences in degree may exist but not of kind, as prison gangs are a reality throughout the United States.

There is temporal variation. Five decades separate the emergence of gangs in California and Washington from those in Montana and Wyoming. Some of this variation may be explained by the size of the custodial population. Using 2019 data from the Bureau of Justice Statistics, the correlation between custodial population and year of gang emergence is -0.37—gangs formed earlier in prison systems with larger populations. Still, it is important to emphasize that gang emergence appears tightly clustered in the latter half of the twentieth century.

The proliferation coincided with the emergence of mass incarceration. The bulk of onset has occurred since the 1980s when 36 of 47 prison systems (70 percent) reported the emergence of gangs, including 18 in the 1980s alone. That decade was notable because the prison population exploded. According to the Bureau of Justice Statistics there were 301,500 sentenced prisoners in federal and state custody in 1979; by 1989 there were 680,900. The development of gangs in prison cannot be divorced from the rise in mass incarceration.

What explains the existence of gangs in prison? Social scientists generally use three theories to answer this question; they are represented in figure 3. Any theory must account for the patterning of gang emergence across place and time.

The *deprivation* pathway assigns theoretical weight to the conditions of confinement. Beginning with Fishman (1934), and extending through Clemmer (1940), Sykes (1958), and Goffman (1961), the deprivation perspective emerged as an explanation for the social organization of prisons. These classic works emphasized the monolithic structuring of routines in

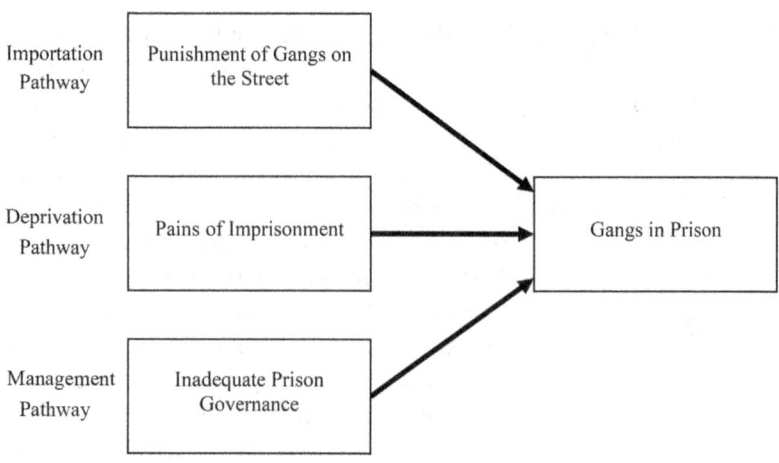

Importation Pathway	Punishment of Gangs on the Street	
Deprivation Pathway	Pains of Imprisonment	Gangs in Prison
Management Pathway	Inadequate Prison Governance	

FIG. 3.—Theoretical models on gangs in prison

prisons and the far-reaching pains of imprisonment manifesting as a prisoner culture—the convict code—distinct from that of the "free world." The convict code assists in compensating for the indignities of imprisonment, such as degradation ceremonies, insecurity, identity and status collapse, loss of citizenship and relationships, and, perhaps most importantly, loss of autonomy, by offering roles and rules that regulate behaviors, interactions, and status. The tenets of the convict code, to which people become acculturated through a process of prisonization, relies primarily on reputation-based norms shared among prisoners.

Gangs are thought to function as one (mal)adaptation to the deprivations of imprisonment. Deprivation theory was, however, based on observations of US prisons well before contemporary prison gangs appeared. Can the theory accommodate the reality of gang emergence reported in figure 2? Irwin (1980) observed that the norms of the convict code were eroding in California by the 1970s. Skarbek (2014) attributed this to the inability of the convict code to scale up when confronted with compositional changes occurring in prisons—the ballooning prison population was composed of younger, more violent, and more racially and ethnically diverse prisoners. Prisoners with common affinities band together to blunt the indignities of the institution, and gangs accomplish this through provision of selective incentives, such as companionship, resources, safety, and status. The viability of the deprivation perspective as an explanation of gang emergence is moored to temporal changes in the degree rather than the type of deprivations. In other words, the types of deprivations may have remained unchanged, but their intensity increased. This could be due to state or prison policies permitting severe overcrowding, intergroup conflicts, or other factors (see, e.g., Hunt et al. 1993). The existence of gangs in prisons thus covaries with the deprivations experienced in prisons.

The *importation* pathway assigns theoretical weight to influences found outside the prison and posits, paradoxically, that the prison itself is largely irrelevant to the social organization of prisoners. Irwin and Cressey (1962, p. 142) countered the predominant "blank slate" view of the deprivation perspective, contending that "much of the inmate behavior classified as part of the prison culture is not peculiar to the prison at all." Instead, the social organization of prisons reflects the features of people who are ultimately imprisoned, what Schwartz (1971) termed "cultural drift." These features can include biographical elements, such as geography and race; propensities, such as cognitive ability and self-control; criminal histories, such as age of onset, frequency, and violence; and cultural orientations and group involvement, such as the code of the street and gang affiliation (e.g., DeLisi et al. 2011; Mears et al. 2013; Mitchell, Pyrooz, and Decker 2021). The prison experience is not so all consuming that biography, culture, and relationships are rendered obsolete upon admission. As the composition of the prison population changes, so too will the culture of prisons.

The importation perspective must account for several factors if it is to explain the existence of gangs in prison. There must be a large enough volume of street gang activity to permit drift into prisons. Before the 1980s gangs concentrated primarily in the urban core. Klein (1995) and others (Miller 1975, 1982; National Gang Center, n.d.) documented the explosion of street gangs throughout the United States. There must be a pathway linking the street to the prison. Enough gang members must be arrested, prosecuted, and incarcerated to constitute such groups in custody. Suppression-oriented responses to gangs ensured this happened, as gangs were the subject of police crackdowns and enhanced prosecution (Klein 1995; Aspholm 2020). The prison experience must not overwhelm members of street gangs so much that it squashes gang identity. Moore (1978) recognized the continuities between the barrio and the prison in California, and Jacobs (1974) recognized the links between street and prison gang activity in Illinois. Moore (1978) observed that *carnales* from

East Los Angeles arrived in prison as "celebrities" (p. 99) and that the gangs were "alive and well inside of the prison" (p. 106). The existence of gangs in prison thus covaries with gangs outside of prison, although, once activated, prison gang culture should take on a life of its own.

The *management* pathway assigns theoretical weight to the operations of prisons. It focuses not on the people who are incarcerated or on prisoner culture but, departing from traditional criminological and sociological theorizing, on how (well) prisons are managed. This perspective is most closely associated with DiIulio (1987), who contrasted the managerial models of California (i.e., consensual), Michigan (i.e., responsibility), and Texas (i.e., control). Quality of life in prisons was characterized by order, amenity, and service, which was more likely to be found in well-managed prisons. The management perspective has broadened to include prisoner-staff interactions and relationships as well as official governance mechanisms (Wooldredge 2020). While there is an emerging literature on prisoner-staff dynamics (Sparks, Bottoms, and Hay 1996; Crewe, Liebling, and Hulley 2015; Steiner and Wooldredge 2018; Alward, Baker, and Gordon 2021; Tostlebe and Pyrooz 2022), which emphasizes procedurally fair treatment of prisoners by officers and the legitimacy of prison authority (i.e., the process-based model of regulation), it has not been linked to gang formation in prison. In contrast, the governance perspective—most closely associated with Skarbek (2011, 2014)—has yielded a productive line of inquiry that can situate prison gang emergence in time and across space.

Skarbek (2014, p. 8) argued that gangs form in prison when there is a demand for extralegal governance and official governance mechanisms are ineffective or unavailable. Self-governance in prison worked before mass incarceration, but structural changes eroded the capacity of norms- and reputation-based order in prison social systems. Gangs operate at the core of a community responsibility system created to resolve trust dilemmas—primarily around culture, history, and race—that undermine cooperation in the absence of official governance. While both governance and deprivation perspectives emphasize indigenous influences, Skarbek's theory holds that gangs fill a void in institutional governance that should be provided by the prison system. Gangs facilitate the trade of goods and services, provide protection, enforce rules, and resolve disputes. Others have pointed to the consequences for gang formation of unsafe institutions, the consolidation of power, and racialized and racist practices of correctional authorities (Lessing 2017; Maitra 2020; Weide 2020). That centralized gangs exist in prison is an indictment of the managerial regimes of prison facilities specifically and prison systems generally. Reducing the demand for extralegal governance should reduce the need for gangs in prison.

What is perhaps most conspicuous from this review of theories about prison gang emergence and persistence is the absence of empirical testing. Put simply, the jury is still out on deprivation, importation, and management theories. And while these perspectives offer theoretical scaffolding to account for the existence of gangs in prison, they are by no means exhaustive. Single-gang and single-system accounts offer rich descriptions of gang emergence. Research has heavily concentrated on California, Illinois, and Texas, and it is possible that the theoretical inventory is greater than I have described. Much work remains to be done. Any test of an existing theory, or development of a new theory, must also reckon with assumptions, propositions, and specificity. So far, only Skarbek's governance theory passes this threshold, which makes it ripe for testing.

II. Forms and Functions of Gangs in Prison

Understanding the activities, goals, organization, and structure of social groups is central to the social sciences. Religious congregations, athletic and recreational groups, service organizations, and other affinity groups bring meaning and purpose to people's lives. The many social groups found in prison are no exception. It is likely that these groups occupy an even greater position in the lives of prisoners owing to their considerable isolation from the free world.

In this section, I discuss forms and functions of gangs as groups. Forms refer to the composition, organization, and structure of gangs—what do they look like? Functions refer to the meaning, purpose, and utility of gangs—what do they do? The classic view is that prison gangs are conspiratorial, hierarchical, monolithic, predatory, and rule bound. Camp and Camp (1985, p. x) emphatically observed that "one of the distinguishing characteristics of the prison gang is the *virtual absence* of any non-criminal, non-deviant activities" (emphasis added). These views are no longer tenable; contemporary research uncovers far greater heterogeneity in gangs' forms and functions.

A. Composition, Organizational Structure, and Variation

Demographics—age, gender, and race or ethnicity—are a distinctive feature of prison gangs. Because there is a separate criminal legal system for juveniles, gangs in US prisons are composed exclusively of adults. Gang members tend to be younger than nongang prisoners. For example, using official classifications of gang affiliation, Ralph and colleagues (1996) found that the average age at prison admission in Texas between 1980 and 1991 was 26 years for 1,744 gang members and 28 years for 13,218 nongang members. Among newly admitted prisoners in Nebraska, Krienert and Fleisher (2001) reported that 85 percent of self-reported gang members, but only 26 percent of nongang members, were under age 25. But there is also significant variation in the age profiles of members across gangs. This reflects selection and retention processes commonly found in gangs with corporatized organizational structure (Skarbek 2014; Gundur 2018; Pyrooz and Decker 2019), such as requiring members to undergo prolonged periods of prospecting before joining, recruiting exclusively from a screened pool of clique-based gang members, and discouraging members from leaving gangs. I discuss these points in Section IV.

Just as prisons are occupied overwhelmingly by men (93 percent: Carson 2020), the gang phenomenon is almost exclusive to men's prisons. The gang affiliations that women maintain tend to be street based and linked to romantic partners or family members; conflicts in women's prisons are rarely motivated by gang dynamics (Belknap and Bowers 2016; Owen, Wells, and Pollock 2017). Gang identity exists among women in prison but tends to be secondary to social arrangements unrelated to gangs. This diverges sharply from research on street gangs, in which girls and women are more proportionately and actively involved (Miller and Decker 2001; Pyrooz 2014; Peterson, Carson, and Fowler 2018). Male gang members in prison acknowledge that there are female counterparts affiliated with their gangs, such as the Featherwoods linked to the Aryan Nation (Belknap and Bowers 2016), but this is more common among gangs with a broader street presence than among gangs in prison with more corporatized organizational structures (Pyrooz and Decker 2019). Far more research needs to be aimed at gang behavior and identity in women's prisons.

Prisons are highly racialized places in which categorizations based on social constructions of race and ethnicity are central to everyday life. In California, for example, prisoners become acculturated to a "carceral social order" (Lopez-Aguado 2018) and "negotiated settlement" (Goodman 2008) that is shared by prisoners and correctional officers and officials alike, enabling and enforcing institutional divisions by race and ethnicity. Race and ethnicity are also central to gangs. Neighborhood tends to be the first basis for sorting people into gangs on the street; race and ethnicity serve that function in prison. Bloch and Olivares-Pelayo (2021) described the decisions newly incarcerated unaffiliated people in California had to make with respect to who they would "run with"—Peckerwood (i.e., White), Sureno (i.e., southern Latino), Norteno (i.e., northern Latino), or Black. There is no in between, as people need to choose sides or run the risk of being deemed a "hood hopper" (Lopez-Aguado 2018, p. 105). There are mixed reports about the significance of race outside the United States, particularly in Canadian (Tetrault, Bucerius, and Haggerty 2019) and British (Phillips 2012; Maitra 2020) prisons.

Racial and ethnic diversity in gangs in prison is rare but not impossible. For example, in Illinois, Hagedorn (2015, p. 62) noted that gangs of all races and ethnicities fall under People or Folks coalitions. Still, it is common for racial or ethnic adjectives to be used when gangs in prison are described—a "White" or "Black" or "Latino" gang. In their study of the demographic composition of 38 gangs in the Texas prison system, Pyrooz and Decker (2019, pp. 113–14) observed the following self-identified single-race or ethnic breakdowns among the seven largest gangs in their sample: Tangos (125 members: 87 percent Latino, 4 percent White, and 0 percent Black), Crips (113 members: 78 percent Black, 4 percent Latino, and 1 percent White), Bloods (92 members: 68 percent Black, 6 percent White, and 5 percent Latino), Aryan Brotherhood (48 members: 92 percent White and 0 percent Black or Latino), Mexican Mafia (38 members: 84 percent Latino and 0 percent Black or White), Texas Syndicate (25 members: 92 percent Latino and 0 percent Black or White), and Aryan Circle (25 members: 96 percent White and 0 percent Black or Latino). Each of these tallies would add up to 100 percent if other, mixed-race, and ethnic heritages were included; in nearly all instances the outstanding proportions were people mixed with the dominant racial or ethnic group. And if the focus were to shift to the 12 gangs classified as STGs in Texas, none of the Latino or White gangs contained members with different (single) races or ethnicities, although both Black STGs did. Bloch and Olivares-Pelayo (2021) referred to racial incongruities in prison gangs as having as much to do with gang identity (e.g., White Crip gang member) as with phenotypic characteristics (e.g., Black-passing Sureno gang member; see also Bolden 2020). Just as gangs dictate the social order of prisons, they also complicate it.

How are gangs in prison organized and structured? It is useful to draw on two "ideal types," in the Weberian sense, since they represent the extremes of a continuum on the organizational structure of gangs. The first type, *instrumental rational*, refers to the corporatized, hierarchical, and organized groups commonly depicted in the literature on prison gangs (e.g., Skarbek 2014). The second type, *informal diffuse*, refers to weakly regulated, nonhierarchical, and disorganized groups commonly depicted in the literature on youth gangs (e.g., Decker, Bynum, and Weisel 1998). These perspectives emerged in the early 1990s out of interest in the extent to which street gangs operated as organized distributors of drugs or their members operated as "freelance" dealers (Decker and Van Winkle 1994; Hagedorn 1994), and they seem to capture the spectrum of organizational structures of gangs in prison nicely.

Whereas instrumental-rational gangs are structured vertically, informal-diffuse gangs are structured horizontally. Skarbek (2014), for example, outlined the power structure of the La Nuestra Familia, a Latino STG in California, which included a hierarchical chain of command consisting of four levels, including the general and captains, the latter of whom control a regiment of lieutenants and soldiers at their respective prison units. Crouch and Marquart (1989) outlined the structure of the Texas Syndicate, an STG in Texas, which included a system-wide president and vice president, unit-level vice chairman, captain, lieutenant, and sergeant at arms, followed by soldiers and nonmember associates and sympathizers. Like many other classic prison gangs, La Nuestra Familia and the Texas Syndicate are structured vertically with well-defined leadership that regulates the conduct of the gang. In contrast, the structure of informal-diffuse gangs is flatter. The Tangos, the largest gang in the Texas prison system, is at the informal-diffuse end of the continuum. They have at best two tiers of membership, with leadership that is more contextual to the prison unit, diffuse among members, and functional on the basis of needs and skills (Tapia 2013; Gundur 2018; Pyrooz and Decker 2019; Bolden 2020). The absence of a hierarchy led the Texas prison system to classify the Tangos as a clique rather than an STG.

Differences between the organizational structures of instrumental-rational and informal-diffuse gangs are also reflected in the rules governing the behavior of gang members. It is common to observe constitutions and manifestos in instrumental-rational gangs that dictate everything from regulating the use of violence to sharing information to determining qualifications of prospective members to stating entrepreneurial aims to establishing norms and values. Fong (1990) detailed the constitutions of the Texas Syndicate and Mexican Mafia in Texas. The Texas Syndicate's consisted of eight rules, such as requiring lifetime membership and that members wear the gang's tattoo, the gang "comes before anyone and anything," and "all members will respect each other" (p. 40). The Mexican Mafia's contained 12 rules, including uniting to "destroy the person or the other group" that disrespected the gang, requiring every member to be "prepared to sacrifice his life or take a life at any time when necessary," and as a criminal organization requiring members to "participate in all aspects of criminal interest for monetary benefits" (p. 40). Informal-diffuse gangs lack constitutions, although they do not lack purpose. Instead, the purpose of gangs like the Tangos is protection, primarily from the predatory activities of STGs like the Mexican Mafia and the Texas Syndicate but also around race or ethnicity, rather than functioning along the lines of a criminal enterprise. Unwritten rules and membership rosters are understood and shared informally, rather than documented and formally studied by members.

While the ideal types may represent extremes, it is important to emphasize that there is variation in the organizational structure of gangs in prison. Pyrooz and Decker (2019) divided gangs in prison into four categories based on classifications of groups as STGs or cliques by Texas prison officials. The categories are STGs placed in segregation (e.g., Aryan Brotherhood, Mexican Mafia, Texas Syndicate), STGs not placed in segregation (e.g., Bloods, Crips, and Texas Chicano Brotherhood), and cliques with self-reported street (e.g., Gangster Disciples, Surenos) or prison (e.g., Peckerwoods, Tangos) orientations. They compared gangs on the basis of their instrumental, expressive, communication, and profit-generation characteristics, finding that variation observed across the 38 gangs represented in the study could be explained by this four-part classification. In general, the STGs in segregation stood apart, fitting the characterization of classic prison gangs. The STGs not placed in segregation were similar to street-oriented gangs in prison, while the prison-oriented gangs lacked strong instrumental characteristics and profit generation was not a core activity.

The organization and structure of gangs in prison is not static. Although not a lot of research has been conducted on the evolution of gangs in prison, much less on the street (for exceptions, see Ayling 2011; Densley 2014; Ouellet, Bouchard, and Charette 2019), three decades ago Buentello, Fong, and Vogel (1991) proposed a four-stage model of development. They contended that prison gangs, as represented by the instrumental-rational ideal type, initially start as loose collections of prisoners who resemble cliques that gel due to homophily and social sorting, particularly around hometowns, race, or ethnicity. The next stage of development is the protection group, for which the purposes are protective, and group-based criminal activity is limited to defensive or retaliatory actions, yet there is a clear group consciousness. The predator group has the trappings of a full-fledged prison gang, with well-defined membership, purposes that extend to power and profit, and formalized codes of conduct. The prison gang, as Buentello and colleagues defined it, maintains a centralized structure with governance functions and monopolies on protection and control. This is the type of group typically represented in key statements (and definitions) on gangs in prison (Jacobs 1977; Pyrooz, Decker, and Fleisher 2011; Skarbek 2014; Ortiz 2019; Gundur 2020; Roth 2020).

The end goal for prison collectives is not necessarily a "prison gang" or organized crime group. Buentello, Fong, and Vogel (1991) did not state explicitly why some groups advanced to the next stage of prison development and others did not, although recently Gundur (2018) and Pyrooz and Decker (2019) have elaborated on the emergent group processes that bring about these transitions. Pyrooz and Decker proposed that transitions from cliques to protection groups reflected reactions to external hostility and strength in numbers, while the transition to predator group was a function of organic internal processes and member-initiated actions. Natural selection based on power and violence accounts for full-blown transitions to prison gangs. Gundur observed that gangs may make strategic decisions not to advance to the next stage because of administrative interventions and for functional purposes. Horizontal structure impedes prison officials from the blanket placement of gang members in solitary confinement, and prisoners do not want the lasting baggage that comes with the STG label. Pyrooz and Decker found that the ratio of STG to clique gang members in Texas fell from 6:1 in 2005 to nearly 1:1 in 2016—a striking shift over such a short period during which the gang population was largely stable.

In sum, the traditional view of gangs in prison as corporatized, hierarchical, and organized is outdated. There is considerable variation between and within gangs, which is observed not only in their organizational structure but also in their demographic characteristics. That these observations were made in the very prison systems from which classic representations of gangs originated is telling. Should the study of prison gangs extend beyond the usual jurisdictions it is likely to reveal even greater heterogeneity in gang composition, organization, and structure. Still, the relevance of race and ethnicity to prison gangs is the thread of continuity uniting prison systems. Gangs both contribute to and complicate prisons as racialized spaces. Interracial collaboration will occur, typically for instrumental reasons.

B. Meaning, Purpose, and Utility

Wooldredge (2020) divided research on prisons, management, and culture into three eras: 1930s to mid-1960s, mid-1960s to mid-1970s, and late 1970s to late 2010s. The most recent era, Wooldredge contended, was characterized by growth in recognition of prisoners' rights and shifts in management philosophies, resulting in prisons becoming more open systems and, consequently, "prison cultures became nearly synonymous with gang cultures in higher security facilities" (p. 170), subsuming and supplanting the long-standing "convict code" that had long defined prison social organization. This represented a marked shift from earlier eras when gangs were either nonexistent or insignificant (Camp and Camp 1985; DiIulio 1987; Crouch and Marquart 1989). If gangs now occupy a central place in the social organization of prisons, what is their meaning and purpose, and what value do they provide?

Skarbek (2014) argued that the gangs bring order to prison. In the simplest terms, order refers to safety, or as DiIulio (1987, p. 11) put it, "no assaults, rapes, or riots." Prima facie evidence of the gangs-order link is found in Bureau of Justice Statistics data on homicide in prison. Homicide rates in state prisons dropped by over 90 percent during the period when gangs proliferated, falling from 54 per 100,000 prisoners in 1980 to 4 per 100,000 in 2002 (Mumola 2005). In prior eras, the source of order in prison was the convict code. But Skarbek contended that decentralized norms no longer worked with large, diverse, and overcrowded prison systems—trustworthiness breaks down with too much anonymity and complexity. Rather than rely on individual reputations, it is more efficient to discern the trustworthiness of a group. This is the role that gangs fill.[5]

Gangs provide extralegal governance, according to Skarbek (2014). They are needed because the prison system—legal governance—is either incapable of or ineffectual in meeting the legitimate needs of prisoners.

---

[5] Weide (2022) offered a variant of this argument that focused on the structural hegemony of a single gang in California, the Mexican Mafia, contending that social controls imposed with their rise to power reduced aggregate weapon assaults.

Ultimately, gangs serve three purposes. First, they facilitate trade, particularly around contraband. Prison authorities will officially never support drug markets, much less other contraband transactions (e.g., cell phones, cash); gangs oversee acquisition and distribution, while membership affords access for use and sales. Second, and contrary to the contention that gangs only create disputes, they also resolve them. This is especially the case for interracial or interethnic conflicts. Gangs are not only responsible for their members but also accountable for their own racial or ethnic group. Conflicts over debts, trade, commissary, recreation, work assignments, and other meaningful aspects of everyday life in prison are mediated by gangs; permission often must be obtained from gang leaders before avenging disputes (Ortiz 2019). Many scholars have alluded to seemingly unlikely alliances between correctional officials and gangs (especially leaders) to govern pods, wings, and facilities, ensuring they remain clean and orderly. Finally, gangs provide protection, which can be contracted (e.g., John Gotti paid the Aryan Brotherhood while serving federal time in Marion, Illinois) or assumed (e.g., for gang members). The perpetrators of gang violence are often members of a victim's own gang, who dole out punishment for violating rules or disobeying orders. Gangs are capable of doing this because of their social power (Crewe 2012), with compliance achieved through "hard" (i.e., coercive) and "soft" (i.e., norm-setting) exercises of power, projected inside and outside prisons (Lessing 2017; Pyrooz and Decker 2019).

Prisoners, however, dispute the contention that gangs bring order. Gangs are viewed by many prisoners as a source of disorder. Pyrooz and Decker (2019) asked prisoners in Texas—gang and nongang members—about various indicators of control and order. Just one-quarter agreed that prisons would be more violent without gangs and that they would trust gangs rather than correctional staff to fix their problems. Less than 10 percent reported that gangs made them feel safer. Still, a large minority believed that gangs helped maintain order (48 percent) and fixed problems better than correctional staff (42 percent). Most prisoners disagreed that gang approval was needed for the sale of contraband or that gangs got a cut of illicit profits. About half of the sample self-reported a gang affiliation, which skewed these proportions upward. Focusing only on nongang prisoners, just 19 percent thought gangs brought about safety, 15 percent trusted gangs to solve problems, and 6 percent said that gangs make them feel safer. Nongang prisoners did not think gangs brought order to prison (34 percent) or that gangs fixed problems

(28 percent). There was one indicator gang and nongang members agreed on: slightly over 80 percent said that everyone suffers when gangs have problems. Of course, it is possible that prisoners do not discern the extralegal governance that gangs provide, but these numbers do not support conceptions of gangs as governance mechanisms. Prisoners, including people affiliated with gangs, want something different from the extralegal governance of gangs.

Still, this does not mean that gangs do not offer general or specific benefits, particularly to their members. As Roth (2020, p. 342) stated, "although the image of the prison gang remains a sinister one, summoning up the worst that prisons have to offer, such groups can also be constructive." The reform to solitary confinement in California that I described in the introduction is a good example. Todd Ashker, labeled as a member of the Aryan Brotherhood, helped orchestrate hunger strikes and litigation. Although the head of the prison system called these actions a "gang power play" (Beard 2013), they eliminated the prolonged, status-based placement of gang affiliates in solitary confinement. The perceived benefits are also evident in the motivations gang members give for joining prison gangs (see Sec. IV). Lopez-Aguado (2018), for example, highlighted the significance of "cars," which are not gangs per se but more like the cliques in Buentello, Fong, and Vogel's (1991) typology—loose collectives united by geography or neighborhood, race or ethnicity, or street gang affiliation to compensate for the pains of imprisonment, offering material (e.g., food, clothes, hygiene products) and emotional support and protection. Perhaps most obvious are the companionship and friendships gangs provide to counter the monotony of prison life. Members have an immediate social network upon being incarcerated or transferring to a new prison unit. There is also a funneling among street gangs, which Lopez-Aguado (2018, p. 66) termed a "reframing of gang identities"; trust dilemmas and street antagonisms are set aside for the broader purpose of group or racial unity while incarcerated. For example, different Latino gang sets from east Fresno came together under the Bulldog banner, while rival Laotian and Cambodian gangs came together under the Asian banner. Hagedorn's (2015, pp. 19–20) key respondent tells the story of the rise of the multiracial Folks coalition in Illinois prisons. In this sense, gangs can bring unity, whether out of necessity or strategy.

It is common to describe prisons as total institutions, as closed worlds with monolithic structuring and extensive surveillance (Goffman 1961). But prisons are not impenetrable fortresses (Ellis 2021). This is perhaps most evident in relation to gangs, particularly those with instrumental-rational organizational structure. Nearly all the members of STGs in Pyrooz and Decker's (2019) study stated that their gang was simultaneously active on the street and in the prison. There are inflows and outflows of goods, information, and people. Crouch and Marquart (1989, p. 211) described how a member of the Mexican Mafia would strategically manipulate a correctional officer to smuggle drugs into prison. Lessing (2017) and others (Jacobs 1974; Skarbek 2014) showed how prison gangs influence street gangs by projecting power through the threat of victimization upon incarceration. In the early 1990s, the Mexican Mafia in California issued an edict calling for the end of drive-by shootings (Lopez and Katz 1993). Gangs and gang members who defied the order were "green lit," treated like "a child molester, a rat, [or] a rapist" behind bars (Lopez and Katz 1993; see also Gundur 2022). Even gangs that were traditionally prison based, such as the Aryan Warriors in Nevada, set up "street programs" for their members. Gundur (2018) described how Barrio Azteca established legitimate businesses in El Paso that sold narcotics and charged a tax on drug dealers who operated in their territory. The total institution certainly exists, but between legal communications, visits, contraband cell phones, and churning of people, the walls that keep people incarcerated do not restrict them from maintaining connections and conducting business on the street.

Cullen (2013) argued that prison systems must rehabilitate, not merely warehouse, their residents. Various programmatic efforts are undertaken to this end, often in tension with the purposes of gangs. Gangs do engage in a form of programming, socializing their members to the norms and values of the group. It is common for cultural, racial, and religious ideology to constitute a component of this socialization (Pyrooz and Decker 2019; Bolden 2020). Bloch and Olivares-Pelayo (2021) showed that places of worship were often racialized and gang oriented, offering such examples as Black Muslim prayer, Native American Warrior Society, Roman Catholic Sureno, and Nordic ceremonials. For decades Black Muslim groups have in the view of prison authorities straddled the line between STG and religious group, while racial supremacy is characteristic of White gangs with ties to Asatru, Odinism, or Christian identity. More generally, longitudinal studies regularly identify changes in attitudes, beliefs, and experiences when people enter gangs. For example, Melde and Esbensen (2014) and others (e.g., Weerman, Lovegrove, and Thornberry 2015; Wu and Pyrooz 2016) found that the contours of gang membership had adverse changes on prosocial peers, school commitment, guilt, violence neutralization, parental monitoring, negative peer commitment, and unstructured socializing.

However, gang members are often excluded from participation in rehabilitative programming such as education or therapy (Winterdyk and Ruddell 2010). It is also common for restrictions to be placed on visitation, commissary access, and good time credits and for parole eligibility to be delayed (Huff and Meyer 1997; Fleisher and Decker 2001). And even if gang members had access to them, as Jacobs (2001, p. vi) pointed out, "classes and programs may become sites for conducting gang business," and "teachers and other professionals may be intimidated or demoralized by [gang] presence."

Even if prisoners and authorities see things differently, gangs do bring a semblance of order to the prison, particularly in the mass incarceration era. They also offer clear benefits, whether instrumental or symbolic. What remains unclear is whether they provide a net positive value to the prison or to their members that overcomes the negative effects of their presence.

III. Misconduct, Violence, and Gangs

Klein (1971) famously described life in the gang as boring, second only to being a researcher observing the gang's activities. Many excellent accounts of street gang life exist (e.g., Decker and Van Winkle 1996; Fleisher 1998; Rios 2011; Lauger 2012; Durán 2013; Panfil 2017; McLean and Densley 2020), but ethnographies offering rich descriptions of gang life in prisons are rare (Lopez-Aguado 2018; Bolden 2020). Yet it is the misconduct, violence, and unrest associated with gangs, not the monotony of day-to-day life in prison (which is undoubtedly even more pronounced than on the streets), that have simultaneously attracted and commanded the attention of policy makers, practitioners, and researchers. Even though prison gangs as groups are defined in part by their recurrent illegal activity, violence is not constant among prisoners involved in gangs.

In the first national survey of prison gangs in the United States, Camp and Camp (1985) offered a sobering assessment: gangs posed serious challenges to institutional order and safety, controlled drug markets in prison, recruited and intimidated nongang prisoners, and in 1983 were responsible for the deaths of four correctional staff in two jurisdictions and 20 homicides in nine jurisdictions. In 1972, 30 of 36 homicides in

California prisons were committed by a single gang, the Mexican Mafia; over a 5-year period in the late 1970s, there were 124 gang-related homicides (Porter 1982; Crouch and Marquart 1989; Fong, Vogel, and Buentello 1992). Gang violence exploded in Texas in 1984 and 1985. In a 21-month period, which became known as the "war years," there were 52 homicides, of which 43 were gang related (Fong 1990; Ralph and Marquart 1991). These alarming reports point to gangs as drivers of prison violence. Prisons in the United States have become much safer since 1980, when the homicide rate was 54 per 100,000 prisoners (Mumola 2005). The Bureau of Justice Statistics reported that there were 1,440 homicides in federal and state prisons in the United States between 2001 and 2018; that is, about six homicides per 100,000 prisoners annually (Carson and Cowhig 2021). However, killings steadily rose after the turn of the century, tripling from three per 100,000 prisoners in 2001 to 10 in 2018.

There is a wide gulf between perspectives that view gangs as bringing order and safety to prisons and those emerging from the street gang literature that attribute wide-ranging misconduct and violence to them. Nearly all the microlevel theory and research points to gang affiliation as a driver of misconduct, but there are countervailing claims at the macrolevel that produce what could be thought of as a micro-macro paradox.

A. Theoretical Perspectives on the Gang/Misconduct Link

Researchers typically draw on deprivation, importation, and managerial theories to explain misconduct and violence in prison (Steiner and Wooldredge 2020)—the theories presented above to understand the existence of gangs in prison. These theories generally focus on maladaptations to the conditions and experiences of confinement (deprivation), the sturdy characteristics and baggage that prisoners bring with them (importation), or the behavior and functioning of prison authorities (managerial). A fairly large body of research tests deprivation (Listwan et al. 2013), importation (DeLisi et al. 2011), and managerial (Steiner and Wooldredge 2018) theories; systematic reviews of the evidence are available (e.g., Steiner, Butler, and Ellison 2014).

The empirical study of gang affiliation and misconduct has largely been divorced from theory. Camp and Camp (1985, p. x), for example, claimed that "one of the distinguishing characteristics of the prison gang is the virtual absence of any non-criminal, non-deviant activities." On that account, the only purposes of gangs are to commit crimes and be violent, and gang members are simply people who commit crimes. Less extreme, but still lacking a theoretical foundation, researchers have typecast gang affiliation as a "risk factor" since it is predictive of problem behaviors (Shelden 1991; Gaes et al. 2002; Austin 2003; DeLisi, Berg, and Hochstetler 2004; Griffin and Hepburn 2006). While prediction is valuable, too little regard is afforded to why gang affiliation matters and the theoretical mechanisms that bring about rule violations and violence.

There is good reason to anticipate that the leading theories of misconduct are applicable to gangs. One could hypothesize that institutional deprivations are enhanced among gang populations, that riskier propensities are found among gang populations, and that heavy-handed managerial responses to gangs attenuate feelings of obligation to follow institutional rules. But Pyrooz and Decker (2019) argued that even these explanations miss the mark because they ignore midlevel dynamics in prisons. Short (1985, 1998), in his essays on the level of explanation problem in criminology, contended that macro- and microlevel perspectives on crime and deviance are tantamount to "ships passing in the night" when interactional and situational context is ignored. This led Pyrooz and Decker to apply Thornberry and colleagues's (1993) tripartite theoretical model—selection, facilitation, and enhancement—to the context of prison, gangs, and misconduct. The broader question inspiring this model is whether gangs attract or create offenders. Of course, prisons contain people who have been convicted of crimes, but the theoretical foundation remains relevant to explaining gang members' disproportionate involvement in misconduct.

The selection model posits that gangs consist of people with individual problems, such as poor self-control, neuropsychological deficits, or behavioral disorders (Gottfredson and Hirschi 1990; Moffitt 1993; DeLisi, Drury, and Elbert 2019). The selection model differs from arguments offered by Krienert and Fleisher (2001) and Davis and Flannery (2001), who contended that dynamic psychological or social deficits concentrate in gang populations, rather than rank-order stable individual differences; people end up in gangs because these deficits lead to associating with like-minded others, prevent them from associating with people without such deficits, or both. This is a spuriousness hypothesis, which implies that there is nothing special about the gang. High levels of misconduct are observed among gang populations because of selection; accounting for these deficits—whatever they may be—would eliminate the empirical relationship. There are clear parallels between the selection model and the importation thesis.

The facilitation model proposes that group processes are responsible for elevated levels of misconduct among gang affiliates (Short and Strodtbeck 1965; Klein and Crawford 1967; Vigil 1988; Decker and Van Winkle 1996). Interactional and situational dynamics nested within the intra- and intergang context are what give rise to misconduct and violence; they include normative influences, social status, collective behavior, and opportunities and routine activities (McGloin and Collins 2015). These midlevel dynamics depart from traditional explanations of misconduct. Given the merit of the group process perspective in explaining offending and victimization among gang members in noninstitutional settings, Pyrooz and Decker (2019) contended that it is the theoretical candidate best equipped for translation to institutional settings.

The final model, enhancement, is a blend of selection and facilitation, acknowledging that prospective gang members may be different from people who do not end up in gangs but still maintaining that the gang is a powerful influence on their behavior (and attitudes, beliefs, and experiences). Those explanations focus on individuals and groups. Probabilistically, not deterministically, gang affiliates are disproportionately involved in misconduct. The unit of analysis is the person while, at least with facilitation and enhancement models, the unit of inference is the group.

There are also higher-order units deserving of consideration in the link between gangs and misconduct, including the pod or wing, facility, and even system. Far less theoretical attention has been aimed at these units of analysis. Inmate balance, administrative control, structural disorganization, and governance constitute the theoretical inventory, but only governance theory has been fully developed and applied to the interrelations between gangs and institutional disturbances and misconduct. Whereas gangs can be understood as a source of backlash in inmate-balance theory and a source of mobilization in administrative control theory (Useem and Reisig 1999), structural disorganization and governance theory views gangs as bringing order and safety to prisons (Skarbek 2014; Weide 2022).

And despite their opposite predictions about the behavior of gangs and gang members, governance and group process can paradoxically operate simultaneously since the former concerns facilities and the latter concerns people and groups. Gangs can suppress aggregate violence in prisons while their members simultaneously engage in more violence; such nuances seem to get lost in debates, not just among practitioners and policy makers but also among academics.

B. Empirical Evidence on the Gang/Misconduct Link

Table 2 lists 33 studies that quantify the relationship between gang affiliation and misconduct in prison. They were conducted primarily in the United States; Canada and South Africa are the only other locations. Nineteen independent data sources were used to examine this relationship, with clusters based on Arizona data used by DeLisi and colleagues (five studies), Kentucky and Ohio data used by Steiner and Wooldredge (four studies), and LoneStar Project data used by Decker and Pyrooz (three studies). Six state prison systems were identified, accounting for 21 of the studies, along with four deidentified state prison systems in the Midwest. Two studies used data from the Federal Bureau of Prisons; one was based on survey data representative of US prisoners (Huebner 2003). Other sample characteristics warrant highlighting. Researchers examined this relationship among women (e.g., Berg and DeLisi 2006; Steiner and Wooldredge 2014*b*), prisoners placed in restrictive housing (e.g., Motz, Labrecque, and Smith 2020), capital offenders (e.g., Morris et al. 2010), admission/early years of imprisonment (e.g., Griffin and Hepburn 2006), and release/later years of imprisonment (e.g., Pyrooz and Decker 2019). A diversity of research sites and sample characteristics is represented. Perhaps the most important stratification is reflected in the cross-tab in table 2, which shows that most of the research measuring gang affiliation and misconduct relies on official records.

The main story that emerges is that gang affiliation is a sturdy correlate of misconduct in prison, albeit with some important qualifications. This is consistent with prior reviews of the literature. Wooldredge (2020, p. 172) found that researchers "can no longer examine individual-level violence in prison without recognizing the role of membership in security threat groups." Steiner, Butler, and Ellison (2014) identified 23 studies on the relationship between gang affiliation (or antisocial peers) and misconduct, finding that 47 percent of the 209 associations were statistically significant in the anticipated direction. That placed gang affiliation in the upper tier of misconduct correlates but nonetheless is a downward departure from the research findings on the gang-offending link in noninstitutional settings. Some of this is undoubtedly a result of Steiner and colleagues pooling together "gang" and "peer" associations, but there is more to the story. A meta-analysis of 179 empirical studies revealed weaker effect sizes in studies that were conducted in correctional settings, used official records, did not control for confounders, and analyzed nonviolent outcomes (Pyrooz et al. 2016). This seems like a fitting way to characterize

TABLE 2

Empirical Studies Examining the Relationship between Gang Affiliation and Misconduct by Official and Survey Data Sources

Measures of Gang Affiliation	Measures of Misconduct	
	Survey	Official
Survey	4. Huebner (2003) United States	14. Varano, Huebner, and Bynum (2011) Midwest
	20. Wulf-Ludden (2013) Midwest	29. Pyrooz and Decker (2019) Texas
	21. Ireland and Power (2013) Canada	30. Pyrooz, Clark, et al. (2021) Texas
	29. Pyrooz and Decker (2019) Texas	32. Fitz (2020) South Africa
	30. Pyrooz, Clark, et al. (2021) Texas	
	31. Fahmy et al. (2020) Texas	
Official	23. Steiner and Wooldredge (2014*a*) Ohio and Kentucky	1. Shelden (1991) Nevada
	30. Pyrooz, Clark, et al. (2021) Texas	2. Fischer (2002) Arizona
		3. Gaes et al. (2002) Bureau of Prisons
		5. DeLisi (2003) Arizona
		6. DeLisi and Munoz (2003) Arizona
		7. DeLisi, Berg, and Hochstetler (2004) Arizona
		8. Berg and DeLisi (2006) Arizona
		9. Cunningham and Sorensen (2006) Florida
		10. Griffin and Hepburn (2006) Arizona
		11. Cunningham and Sorensen (2007) Florida
		12. Kuanliang, Sorensen, and Cunningham (2008) Florida
		13. Morris et al. (2010) Texas
		15. Drury and DeLisi (2011) Arizona
		16. Scott and Ruddell (2011) Canada
		17. Ruddell and Gottschall (2011) Canada
		18. Worrall and Morris (2012) Texas
		19. Diamond, Morris, and Barnes (2012) Texas
		22. Walters and Crawford (2013) Bureau of Prisons

TABLE 2 (*Continued*)

Measures of Gang Affiliation	Measures of Misconduct	
	Survey	Official
		23. Steiner and Wooldredge (2014*a*) Ohio and Kentucky
		24. Steiner and Wooldredge (2014*b*) Ohio and Kentucky
		25. Morris and Worrall (2014) Texas
		26. Tewksbury, Connor, and Denney (2014) Midwest
		27. Steiner and Wooldredge (2015) Ohio and Kentucky
		28. Steiner and Wooldredge (2018) Ohio
		30. Pyrooz, Clark, et al. (2021) Texas
		33. Motz, Labrecque, and Smith (2020) Midwest

the literature on the relationship between gang affiliation and misconduct in prison. The consistency and strength of the associations fit on a continuum. On one end, researchers report large, statistically significant findings derived from bivariable relationships relying on self-reports of violent misconduct. On the other end, researchers report weak, statistically null multivariate relationships relying on official records of nonviolent misconduct. A few examples are in order.

Griffin and Hepburn (2006) found that gang affiliates in Arizona were about twice as likely to be written up for a violent disciplinary infraction in their first 3 years in prison as nongang members, yet that difference fell to 57 percent when demographics, criminal history, and custody level were accounted for in a multivariate model. Steiner and Wooldredge (2014*a*) related an official measure of gang affiliation among 5,630 prisoners in Kentucky and Ohio to official and survey measures of assault, drug, and property misconduct in the previous 6 months. They found that gang affiliation was positively and equally associated with both measures of assault, unrelated to both measures of drug misconduct, negatively related to self-reports, and unrelated to official records of property misconduct. Pyrooz and Decker (2019), by contrast, relied on a self-report measure of gang affiliation among 802 prisoners in Texas. They found no differences in official misconduct—including disorder, violent, instrumental, and substance—in the previous 6 months between current, former, and nongang members. However, there were substantively large differences in self-reports of misconduct, particularly violence. Still, former gang members committed misconduct at a rate that was indistinguishable from nongang members, which further illustrates the importance of gang status for understanding misconduct in prison.

The role gangs play in aggregate levels and trends in prison violence is unclear. Despite the reports from Camp and Camp, California, and Texas, we lack systematic knowledge about the contribution of gangs to aggregate violence in prison. There are four exceptions. Weide (2022, p. 122) interprets California's system-wide reduction of weapon assaults, but not the simultaneous rise of nonweapon assaults from 1975 to 2006, to the Mexican Mafia "enjoying dominance and control of almost every general population" facility. The remaining studies offer evidence leading to a different conclusion. In a survey of wardens from 317 medium- and maximum-security prisons conducted in 1986, Useem and Reisig (1999) found that the proportion of prisoners in "prohibited groups" was positively associated with inmate disturbances and unlawful protests but not riots. In a study of 50 prison units in Arizona, Fischer (2002) reported a strong, positive association between the concentration of gang members and violent misconduct ($r = 0.60$) and a moderate association with nonviolent misconduct ($r = 0.31$). Worrall and Morris (2012), studying 47 prisons in Texas, found that prisons containing a greater proportion and diversity of gang affiliates were associated with inmate-on-inmate assaults. This comports with qualitative observations from Bolden (2020), who described gang warfare as erratic but orchestrated, often triggered by fluctuations in the movement of gang members into and out of pods and units. Such a contextual focus is rarely the object of study in qualitative and quantitative research, at least in the United States (Kreager et al. 2016).

The growing literature on gang affiliation and misconduct has recently shown signs of theoretical and empirical maturity. However, much remains unknown, especially when contrasting the precision, sophistication, and volume of research on this relationship in noninstitutional settings with that in institutional settings. Indeed, the understanding of the gang affiliation-misconduct link is dominated by official accounts, which is important to remember; what the literature says about this relationship is filtered by administrative practices and priorities. There is an urgent need to integrate items on gang status into surveys of prisoners, to conduct longitudinal analyses that capture changes in behaviors with join-ing, persisting in, and leaving gangs, which would help address the "causal question" that long animated research on street gangs (e.g., Katz and Jackson-Jacobs 2004). Should precepts from the street gang literature prove accurate, extending social network analysis to prisons and gangs would better capture group processes, particularly cohesion (Papachristos 2011; Kreager 2019). These advances should aid in identifying the mech-anisms responsible for misconduct, while also demonstrating that the consequences of gang affiliation extend to other important behavioral, health, and social outcomes.

IV. The Contours of Gang Affiliation and Involvement

Adoption of the developmental and life-course perspective has yielded tremendous benefits for gang research (Thornberry et al. 2003; Melde and Esbensen 2011; Pyrooz and Decker 2011). It offers conceptual and methodological tools for understanding the extent to which gang mem-bership is dynamic rather than static in the life course. In contrast to cross-sectional studies, which offer a one-time snapshot of gang mem-bers, longitudinal studies, which interview people at multiple times, show that gang membership is age graded with variability in onset, continuity, and change in the life course. Unfortunately, prison research on gang af-filiation and involvement relies almost exclusively on cross-sectional data sources. But this is a problem that cuts across all prison research, which rarely tracks people over time and, when it does, usually relies on official records rather than on survey data (for exceptions, see O'Keefe et al. 2013; Wright, Hepburn, and Griffin 2020). In this section, informed by pre-cepts established in noninstitutional settings, I examine the literature on the contours of gang affiliation and involvement in prison.

A. Gang Affiliation and Embeddedness

How common is gang affiliation in prison? Some accounts indicate that "going it alone" is practically impossible, suggesting that outside of reli-gious groups, prisoners must associate with a gang (Skarbek 2014; O'Neill 2015; Bolden 2020; Roth 2020; Gundur 2022). Other accounts claim that gang affiliation is vastly overstated, since prisoners are nested within loose networks of informal associations, or "cars," defined more in terms of race, hometown, or geography than gang membership (Lopez-Aguado 2018; Bloch and Olivares-Pelayo 2021). Neither account offers an accurate representation of the proportion of prisoners affiliated with gangs, whether based on official records or self-reports; they both over-state and understate.

Table 3 shows official estimates of the proportion of prisoners affiliated with gangs from six studies. The earliest is from Camp and Camp (1985), based on data collected in 1984, and the most recent is from Pyrooz and Mitchell (2020), based on data collected in 2016. These estimates are based on official records. All demonstrate that gang affiliates constitute a minority of prisoners in the United States—about 15 percent. Hill (2009) surveyed prison systems on the indicators used to classify prisoners as gang affiliated, which were classified into five core domains (Pyrooz, Decker, and Owens 2020): personal possessions (e.g., clothing, shoes, property), physical embodiments (e.g., tattoos, branding), self-admission, associations (e.g., photos, communication, graffiti), and observations (e.g., court records, informants, staff reports). While there is a lot of variation across prison systems in the indicators used, typically prisoners have to meet three of the indicators before being classified as "confirmed" and at least one but fewer than three to be classified as "suspected." Legitimate criticisms have been offered about how these indicators are used in practice (e.g., Toch 2007; Lopez-Aguado 2018), particularly around informants, the conflation of culture and gangs, and the circular logics of association- and observation-based indicators.

There are no survey-based alternatives to official records of gang af-filiation in prison. The leading representative survey of prisoners, the Bureau of Justice Statistics' Survey of Prison Inmates, has not asked ques-tions about gang membership since 1991 (e.g., Huebner 2003; Gaston and

TABLE 3

Six Estimates of the Proportion of Prisoners Affiliated with Gangs

Study	Number of Prison Systems	Year of Data Collection	Gang Affiliated Percentage	Count
Camp and Camp (1985)	23	1984	3	12,634
Wells et al. (2002)	39	2002	10	112,148
Hill (2009)	38	2008	12	132,251
Winterdyk and Ruddell (2010)	37	2009	19	226,100
NGIC (2011)	NA	2011	15	230,000
Pyrooz and Mitchell (2020)	36	2016	15	142,023

Huebner 2015).[6] This is part of the reason Trulson, Marquart, and Kawucha (2006, p. 26) called data on gang-affiliated prisoners among the "most elusive figures in corrections." However, a comparison of official records and self-reports of gang affiliation in Texas identified a correspondence rate of 80 percent (Pyrooz, Decker, and Owens 2020), which suggests that survey data may not skew the proportions reported in table 3 too greatly upward or downward. Still, it is important to point out that official records performed worse when seeking to identify current, former, and nongang status (Pyrooz, Clark, et al. 2021), as official records were more likely to identify prisoners as active rather than as former gang members.

Even though a minority of prisoners are gang affiliated, a much larger proportion is associated with gangs. Table 4 contains data from the LoneStar Project, also known as the Texas Study of Trajectories, Associations, and Reentry (Mitchell et al. 2018), on gang embeddedness by self-reported current, former, and nongang status. Gang embeddedness captures individual immersion in gangs along dimensions of position, association, behavior, and power (Pyrooz, Sweeten, and Piquero 2013; Decker et al. 2014), drawing on relational rather than bounded perspectives on gangs—involvement rather than affiliation. A gang embeddedness scale was constructed using a mixed graded response model based on the eight items reported in table 4. The least surprising finding is that people who self-identify as active gang members are most deeply embedded in gangs, while those who have never affiliated with a gang are the least embedded; former gang members were about one-third of a standard deviation more embedded than never gang members but 1.6 standard deviations less embedded than current gang members.

Table 4 also demonstrates that prisoners who have never been in a gang or who have left the gang are nonetheless sometimes embedded in gangs. For example, at the 75th percentile of the distribution of gang embeddedness scale for subgroups, never gang members scored slightly above the sample mean while former gang members score well above. The individual items unpack this story. While never gang members almost universally hold no position in gangs or participate in gang activity, a nontrivial minority maintains associations with gangs, either through hanging out with gangs (29 percent) or having friends in gangs (34 percent). That is even

---

[6] The 2016 Survey of Prison Inmates asks about participation in drug-trafficking groups: "When you committed the [controlling offense] were you a part of any group or organization that manufactured, imported, distributed, or sold drugs?" Not all drug-trafficking groups, however, are gangs, and not all gangs are drug-trafficking groups.

TABLE 4

Embeddedness in Gangs by Self-Reported Current, Former, and Nongang Status in the LoneStar Project

Item	Full Sample	Never Gang	Former Gang	Current Gang
Gang embeddedness scale, M (SD)	.00 (1.00)	−.45 (.61)[†,‡]	−.15 (.89)*,‡	1.46 (.60)*,†
25th, 75th percentiles	−.95, .72	−.95, .04	−.95, .48	1.19, 1.82
Position in gang (0–2), M (SD)	.30 (.60)	.02 (.13)[†,‡]	.23 (.54)*,‡	1.15 (.65)*,†
% no position (=0)	77.7	98.3	82.7	14.3
Centrality in gang (0–2), M (SD)	.35 (.64)	.06 (.23)[†,‡]	.24 (.51)*,‡	1.21 (.73)*,†
% outside of bull's-eye (=0)	74.0	94.4	79.7	17.9
Contact with gang (0–2), M (SD)	.72 (.94)	.52 (.86)[‡]	.49 (.82)[‡]	1.75 (.60)*,†
% no contact (=0)	61.1	71.9	72.7	8.6
Friends in gang (0–3), M (SD)	.80 (.99)	.43 (.68)[†,‡]	.73 (.96)*,‡	1.91 (.95)*,†
% no gang friends (=0)	52.3	65.8	55.6	10.7
Gang signs, colors (0–1), M (SD)	.09 (. . .)	.00 (. . .)[†,‡]	.05 (. . .)*,‡	.41 (. . .)*,†
% never flash/wear (=0)	90.9	99.7	95.3	58.6
Intimidation, attacks (0–2), M (SD)	.10 (.37)	.00 (.05)[†,‡]	.05 (.27)*,‡	.44 (.70)*,†
% never take part (=0)	93.1	99.7	96.7	68.6
Importance of gang (0–2), M (SD)	.27 (.60)	.02 (.18)[†,‡]	.14 (.43)*,‡	1.17 (.76)*,†
% not important (=0)	81.2	98.3	88.7	21.4
Influence on gang (0–3), M (SD)	.31 (.67)	.03 (.17)[†,‡]	.24 (.58)*,‡	1.21 (.86)*,†
% gang influence (=0)	79.1	97.8	83.0	22.3
N	800	359	301	140

NOTE.—Gang embeddedness scores are standardized and generated from a graded response model. Independent sample t-tests were used to determine statistical differences. Values in parentheses in the item column refer to the range of the response categories, where higher scores equate to greater embeddedness. M = mean; SD = standard deviation.

  * Statistically different from never gang members at the .05 α level (two-tailed).
  † Statistically different from former gang members at the .05 α level (two-tailed).
  ‡ Statistically different from current gang members at the .05 α level (two-tailed).

more evident among former gang members. While a low proportion participate in gang activity, many remain embedded in the gang through their positions, associations, or influence. This illustrates that the reach of gangs in prison extends beyond bona fide members and even beyond those who were previously affiliated. It could possibly explain offending and victimization among former and nongang members (Papachristos et al. 2015), who by virtue of their embeddedness are susceptible to gang influences and liabilities. It could possibly also explain misconceptions about the prevalence of gang affiliation in prison that I described at the beginning of this section.

B. Joining the Gang

Does gang affiliation originate outside prison or inside? This is a question of great importance because it helps adjudicate the validity of deprivation and importation theories discussed in Section I. The answer offered by prison officials surveyed by Winterdyk and Ruddell (2010) was an even split; they claimed that half of gang members joined in prison and the other half brought their affiliation with them. Researchers have validated this using data based on cross-sectional interviews with prisoners (Pyrooz and Decker 2019; Paat et al. 2020), although a longitudinal study of juveniles adjudicated guilty of serious offenses—albeit including juvenile and jail incarceration in addition to prison—showed more evidence of importation (about 85 percent) than origination (Pyrooz, Gartner, and Smith 2017). It is premature to reach any firm conclusions, as research is likely to reveal variation across cities, states, and regions.

Gangs must recruit new members to maintain their numbers. Accounts of recruitment suggest that it is a ubiquitous feature of prison life. Bolden (2020, p. 97) described constant recruitment; the Hispanic gangs particularly "would never stop trying, knowing that danger and manipulation had a way of making people do things that they didn't want to do." Pyrooz and Decker (2019, p. 208) confirmed this with a representative sample of prisoners. Among 448 prisoners who were never affiliated with gangs, 51 percent stated that they were recruited by a prison gang but did not see the benefits of affiliation or viewed themselves as independent. They ultimately had to decline the invitation or "keep their heads down" (Narag and Lee 2018; Carson and Esbensen 2019), occupying lower positions in the prison status hierarchy (Kreager et al. 2021; Pyrooz, Mitchell, et al. 2021). Group organization and prison policy seemed to matter, too. Gundur (2018), for example, reported that horizontally structured gangs were able to recruit constantly since gang intelligence officers had difficulty thwarting these efforts owing to the absence of identifiable leadership. Bucerius, Jones, and Haggerty (2021) reported that the decision to disperse Indigenous gangs across prisons in the Canadian Prairie Region led to recruitment of nonaffiliated prisoners and thus the proliferation of gangs.

What motivates affiliation in prison? There are many similarities in why people join gangs in prison and on the street; they can be divided into push and pull factors (Decker and Van Winkle 1996). However, environmental and group influences in the prison contour motivations for joining. Lopez-Aguado (2018), for example, outlined the generality in seeking comfort in homophilous groups to manage the pains of institutional life (see also Narag and Lee 2018; Paat et al. 2020). Pyrooz and Decker (2019) compared motivations for joining gangs in prison and on the street for 441 self-reported lifetime gang members in their study in Texas. Normative influence relating to family, friends, and hometown provided the modal reason, but much more commonly for joining street (50 percent) than prison (30 percent) gangs. Other factors were more common in prison, such as protection (21 percent vs. 4 percent on the street) and ideology concerning race and empowerment (25 percent vs. 8 percent on the street). Other leading motivations, such as material influences, belonging, and status, were equally common in prison and on the street.

How do people join gangs in prison? As with street gangs, both active and passive entrances are characteristic. Roth (2020), for example, detailed extreme methods for joining the Numbers gangs (26s, 27s, and 28s) in South African prisons. Prospects for the 28s were instructed to commit a fatal or nonfatal stabbing. Afterward, the 28s initiated a ritual that determined whether the prospect entered on the desirable gold line (i.e., soldier) or the less desirable silver line (i.e., sexual object) based on the declaration of an influential member. Pyrooz and Decker (2019) found that STGs in Texas, particularly the instrumental-rational groups, required recruits to undergo prolonged periods of prospecting. This entailed studying gang constitutions and operations, directives to "do dirt" on the gang's behalf, and outward violence targeting snitches or rivals. Other gangs required prospects to undergo inward violence, what the Tangos called a *corrache*, or "heart check," which entailed getting beaten (i.e., jumped on) for several minutes in a secluded area of the prison. Other gang members did not have do anything to join—passive entrances—owing to gang ties, which is more consistent with gang joining practices on the street (Densley 2015; Descormiers and Corrado 2016).

C. Leaving the Gang

The constitutions of gangs like the Aryan Brotherhood, Mexican Mafia, Nuestra Familia, and Texas Syndicate explicitly forbid members ever to leave. Rule 1 in Mexikanemi's constitution is "blood in, blood out" (Fong 1990, p. 40), while the Nuestra Familia constitution states that "a Familiano will not be released from his obligations towards the organization because he is released from prison" (Skarbek 2014, p. 113). Popular rhetoric abounds when it comes to prison gangs, such as early 1990s cult classic films, *Bound by Honor*, starring Benjamin Bratt, and *American Me*, starring Edward James Olmos, portraying gang membership as a lifelong commitment. This was also once believed about street gangs—once a gang member, always a gang member—until researchers found not only that it was untrue but that people typically remained in gangs for short periods (Decker and Lauritsen 2002; Krohn and Thornberry 2008). Longitudinal research in Philadelphia and Phoenix shows that incarceration prolongs gang careers (Pyrooz, Gartner, and Smith 2017), but there is enough other evidence to conclude that claims of permanence in prison gang membership are false. People regularly leave gangs during and after prison.

The earliest evidence was reported by Fong and Vogel (1995), who administered an anonymous questionnaire to 48 former gang members in Texas who were in protective custody, owing to their dropout status. These men were previously affiliated with the Aryan Brotherhood, Mexican Mafia, Texas Mafia, or Texas Syndicate. Fong and Vogel used the terminology of "defecting" to characterize the exit, which is language more common to soldiers and spies than to street or prison gangs. Johnson and Densley (2018), using ethnographic research in two Brazilian prisons dominated by the Comando Vermelho, found that prisoners transitioned out of gangs under the auspices of the countervailing influence and structure of the prisoner-led Pentecostal church. Pyrooz and Decker (2019, p. 230) found widespread gang leaving occurred in Texas prisons, concluding that "it is more common to leave a gang than join one in prison." To be sure, this is a small body of research, but it was conducted in two very different prison systems with highly organized and structured gangs.

The reasons for leaving are asymmetrical to those for joining, a common finding in developmental and life-course criminology (Uggen and Piliavin 1998). The "defectors" queried by Fong and Vogel (1995) claimed to have lost interest, disagreed with the gang's direction, violated rules, or matured, which fits into the push (i.e., factors internal to the gang) and pull (i.e., factors external to the gang) framework introduced by Pyrooz and Decker (2011). The motivations for leaving facilitate transitions across the stages of the role exit model—"first doubts" to "anticipatory socialization" to "turning points" to "post-exit validation" (Decker, Pyrooz, and Moule 2014). Disillusionment with the gang, a push factor, was the foremost motivation (79 percent) offered by the 213 people who left a gang in prison in the LoneStar Project (Pyrooz and Decker 2019). Many realized they had been sold a bill of goods, as the gang rarely fulfilled its promises of protection, companionship, or material rewards. Family, a pull factor, was the second most common motivation (36 percent), as prison represented a time-out to consider the missed birthdays and graduations of children and value romantic partners and parents who provided emotional and social support. The personal motivations for leaving in prison were mostly similar to those on the street, although criminal justice pressures—delayed parole, placement in administrative segregation, and restricted programming—appeared to be qualitatively and quantitatively different.

There should be no mistake: leaving a gang is more complicated in prison than on the street. Much of the research on disengagement from gangs portrays a largely straightforward exit path, complicated by age, tenure, and organization (Carson, Peterson, and Esbensen 2013; Densley 2013; Decker, Pyrooz, and Moule 2014). These complications are characteristic of prison gangs, composed of adults with longer tenures in gangs that tend to exhibit stronger organizational structures than street gangs. Yet there is an added layer of complication: residing in total institutions, which shape and surveil activities, makes it harder to shake an affiliation. Pyrooz and Decker (2019) reported that gang leaving in prison was much more likely to involve an active rather than a passive exit. Fong and Vogel's (1995) respondents were placed in protective custody because of leaving. Johnson and Densley (2018) reported that the Pentecostal church was the only viable option for gang leaving in Brazilian prisons. This was also reported for gang members—many in prison—in Central America (Rosen and Cruz 2019). This worked because it sent a costly, honest, and sincere signal that the gang respected (Densley and Pyrooz 2019). Decker and Pyrooz (2020) found that religion was not the most common pathway out of gangs in Texas prisons, but religious transformations facilitated around 20 percent of exits. Unlike on the street, where the modal response from former gang members is to "walk away" or "do nothing," in prison the modal response is to "give notice" as part of seeking the gang's acknowledgment of the status transition. One-quarter of the former members of STGs placed in segregation underwent the prison system's gang renouncement program, a 2-year process yoked to leaving solitary confinement. A minority of prisoners were jumped out of the gang; in this instance the *corrache* symbolized breaking rather than making gang bonds.

V. Responding to Gangs in Prison

Peter Carlson, former assistant director and warden in the Federal Bureau of Prisons, two decades ago opened an article in a special issue of

Corrections Management Quarterly on prison gangs with these words: "Ask any veteran corrections official what the most difficult challenge associated with inmate management is today and you consistently will hear of their problems in controlling inmate gangs. Nearly all of the negative issues involved with inmate management revolve around race, drugs, power, and protection; the common factor that makes these always worrisome issues into major concerns is often gang affiliation" (2001, p. 21). What works in responding to gangs in prison? Readers would be forgiven for assuming the existence of a well-established body of evidence on the effectiveness of various policies, practices, and programs, especially because prisons are controlled environments. Ironically, several of the seven corrections agencies whose gang control strategies Carlson discussed described their approaches as "excellent." Two decades later there is still no confirmatory (public) evidence. This is reminiscent of Klein and Maxson's (2006) conclusion to a review of street gang control policies and programs—they appear promising because they have not been evaluated.

In this section, I discuss policies and practices introduced to address the behaviors and influence of gangs in prison. I draw on McGrath's (2020) systematic review of gang interventions and management strategies. Gang management strategies are specialized practices and policies involving monitoring, sanctioning, and housing of gangs and gang members. Gang intervention strategies are rehabilitative efforts that entail specialized programming designed primarily to address psychological and social deficits. The seven studies identified by McGrath are outlined in table 5.

A. Gang Management: Monitoring, Sanctioning, and Housing

Correctional agencies face a common challenge when seeking to implement policies and practices to manage gangs: intelligence and documentation. This issue permeates just about every aspect of corrections. Personnel in reception and classification must make decisions about security levels and housing assignments. Security staff need to be aware of potential conflicts between individuals or groups of prisoners on their pods or in the recreation yard. Counseling and rehabilitative staff need to understand the liabilities and obligations of prisoners in one-on-one or classroom settings. Those who oversee work details inside or outside of facilities must consider risks posed by those assigned to their teams. And if state or federal prosecutors seek to build criminal conspiracy charges (e.g., RICO) or correctional authorities seek to sanction gang affiliates by limiting visitations, phone calls, commissary access, or

TABLE 5

Prison-Based Gang Management and Intervention Strategies Identified by McGrath (2020)

Study	Title	Description	Type/Unit	Outcome
Cook et al. (2015)	Milwaukee Safe Streets, Prisoner Release Initiative	Reentry program with "reach in" prerelease services involving casework, skills training, and reentry planning	Intervention/Individuals	Postrelease employment, earnings, rearrest, and reimprisonment
Di Placido et al. (2006)	Correctional Services Canada, Cognitive Behavioral Programs	High-intensity aggression, sex, and psychiatric programs following risk-need-responsivity principles	Intervention/Individuals	In-prison misconduct; postrelease reconviction
Burrowes and McIntyre (2004)	Aboriginal Gang Initiative	Aboriginal-specific, programmatic response involving personal developmental, employment, education, and training	Intervention/Individuals	In-prison misconduct; postrelease "returns"
Fischer (2002)	Arizona STG Program	Monitoring, investigation, and sanctioning of gang affiliates; placing gang affiliates in solitary confinement	Management/System and individuals	In-prison misconduct, gang affiliate validation
Gransky et al. (1999)	Illinois Gang-Free Prison	Prisoner exchange to create a gang-free environment, exchange gang and nongang affiliated prisoners	Management/Facilities	In-prison gang membership and misconduct
Ong (2014, 2015)	New Zealand Prisoner Services	A range of behavioral, cognitive, cultural, employment, substance use, and therapeutic programs	Intervention/Individuals	Postrelease reconviction and reimprisonment
Pyrooz and Decker (2019)	Texas Gang Renouncement and Disassociation Program	Solitary confinement step-down program with programming nested within normalization, socialization, and reintegrative phases	Intervention/Individuals	In-prison gang status, gang embeddedness, misconduct, and victimization

programming, they must know whom to target. Many employees are able to discern the affiliations of prisoners intuitively, but these skills accrue with experience and do not scale very well. In Texas, for example, the outbreak of violence—and rise of prison gangs—during the "war years" of the 1980s is believed to be due, in part, to dismantling the intelligence network by removing building tenders (Crouch and Marquart 1989). Prison systems throughout the United States now have systems in place to document gangs and gang affiliates in order to manage them.

Arizona's experiences in the 1990s, documented by Fischer (2002), capture the emergence of an intelligence apparatus. Figure 4 contains a graphical representation of documentation procedures. In 1991, a general order was issued prohibiting inmates from engaging in gang activity. Orders in 1994 and 1995 better defined gangs, added sanctions for gang affiliation, and instituted systems of gang certification and officer training. Efforts intensified in 1997. The intelligence apparatus was elaborated by outlining evidentiary standards for validation, establishing practices to gather gang intelligence, and, most controversially, requiring that validated gang affiliates be placed in restrictive housing. Eight groups were identified as gangs, and 649 prisoners, as gang affiliates. The 1997 order offered a semblance of due process, as it established validation hearings and an appeal process, along with procedures for renouncement of gang membership to permit reclassification. Yet nearly all (96 percent) prisoners whose gang packets were submitted to the initial committee were validated as gang affiliated, and nearly all (again, 96 percent) appeals of gang validation were rejected. At this point, prisoners were "put between a rock and hard place" (Hunt et al. 1993, p. 402), since their options were either to live in restrictive housing or renounce gang membership. Twenty-two percent of gang affiliates renounced, which entailed an interview about their activities as a gang member and about the gang (i.e., debriefing). While most were successful (66 percent), the outcome was stigmatizing and perhaps equally stifling since they were placed in protective custody. The remaining gang affiliates faced a fate that far exceeded the United Nations's threshold for torture (Haney 2018): indeterminate placement in restrictive housing, with visitations, phone calls, commissary access, programming, and social interaction severely curtailed or eliminated altogether.

Perhaps the most challenging issue facing correctional authorities is to develop an effective (and legal) strategy to house gang populations. The built environment of correctional settings requires authorities to decide

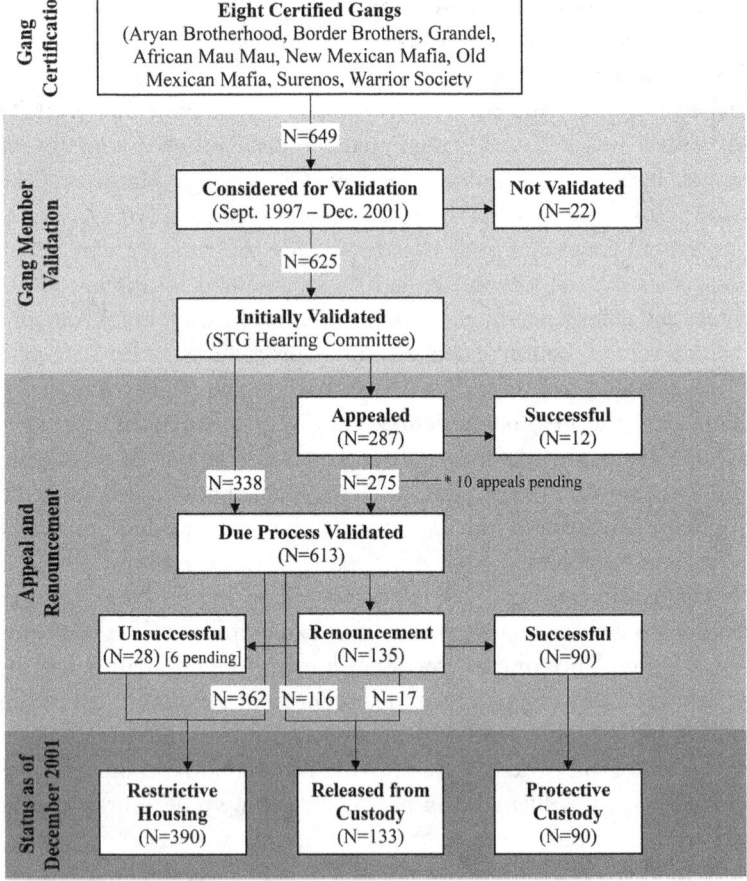

FIG. 4.—Diagram of gang certification and gang affiliate validation, appeal, and renouncement in Arizona. Data are based on the Fischer (2002, pp. 4–5) report evaluating the Arizona Department of Corrections's STG Program.

how to distribute the affiliates of various gangs across the cells, pods, and dormitories of facilities while obeying legal mandates concerning amenities, race or ethnicity, and safety (Trulson and Marquart 2010). Three housing strategies are available—dispersion, concentration, or isolation. All involve trade-offs.

Dispersion distributes the members of gangs across different settings to avoid concentrated power. Gangs are powerful because their numbers and their propensity for violence allow them to exercise control over contraband markets and other aspects of the prison experience. Dispersing gang members avoids power in numbers. This is what the Texas Department of Criminal Justice did with members of the Black Muslims, and other radicalized groups, to prevent them from gaining a foothold in areas of prisons (Crouch and Marquart 1989, p. 205; Useem and Clayton 2009). This seemed to work well with some groups that posed security threats, as prison culture may organize against political extremism. The flip side is that dispersion can lead gangs to evangelize and recruit in areas previously beyond reach (Bucerius, Jones, and Haggerty 2021), while also risking chance encounters that trigger immediate and broader conflicts (Bolden 2020).

Concentration places the members of gangs together. It is not uncommon to encounter pods dominated by a single gang. Crouch and Marquart (1989) reported that the Black Muslims in Texas were eventually concentrated together to prevent evangelizing, as they constantly sought to recruit new members (e.g., Bolden 2020). In Latin American countries, entire prison facilities are devoted to specific gangs. Dudley and Bargent (2017) called this a Faustian bargain, as it soothes prison conflicts yet empowers prison gangs. Gransky and colleagues (Gransky and Patterson 1999; Gransky et al. 1999) reported that Illinois sought to create a "gang-free" prison in Taylorville; 552 gang-affiliated prisoners were transferred out and 657 nongang prisoners from three minimum security facilities were transferred in. The culture changed in a year as prisoners became older (mean age from 32 to 37 years) and Whiter (from 21 to 46 percent). Disciplinary reports fell by over 50 percent. While anecdotes on dispersion and concentration abound, there is no systematic empirical evidence indicating that one or the other is more successful.

Isolation, in contrast, is the most extreme approach. More commonly known as solitary confinement, this typically involves isolating individual prisoners in restrictive housing for 22 or more hours daily over prolonged periods. Prisoners are typically placed in restrictive housing for protective, disciplinary, or administrative reasons. Gang affiliates are overrepresented in restrictive housing under all three approaches (Pyrooz and Mitchell 2020), but the last reason is the most controversial. Prison systems placed gang affiliates in administrative segregation, not because they "needed it" (i.e., protection) or "deserved it" (i.e., disciplinary) but because of their status as gang affiliates; this was Arizona's strategy for housing the eight certified gangs. Texas adopted this approach in September

1985 when placing gang leaders in administrative segregation failed to quell the violence (Ralph and Marquart 1991); the practice continues for affiliates of seven of the 12 STGs (Pyrooz and Decker 2019). And in California, until the hunger strikes and settlement of *Ashker v. Governor of the State of California*, gang affiliates were placed in restrictive housing indeterminately (Reiter 2016). Fewer prison systems are using administrative segregation as a gang housing strategy than in the past (Butler, Griffin, and Johnson 2013; Pyrooz and Mitchell 2019).

The isolation strategy reduces misconduct and violence among gang members. Fischer (2002) observed both deterrence and incapacitation effects of Arizona's STG program. Placement of members of eight STGs in their special management unit resulted in an 11 percent system-wide reduction in violations, including a 44 percent drop in the assault rate, and a 30 percent system-wide drop in the assault rate among gang members. Among the gang members placed in solitary confinement, the assault rate fell by 53 percent. These findings must be placed in context; segregation is expensive since the ratio of prisoners to officers is low. It is also controversial, owing to the known adverse psychological effects of solitary confinement (Morgan et al. 2016). In the long run, restrictive housing is not the "silver bullet" some have proclaimed (Vigil 2006), as the gangs have outlasted it. Gundur (2018, p. 16) observed with respect to the Tangos, the largest prison gang in Texas, "it is nearly impossible, short of subjecting the entire prison population to solitary confinement, to break a horizontal [structured] group." Restrictive housing is ultimately a management solution that ignores the individual, group, and structural factors that give rise to gangs in the first place.

B. Gang Intervention: Rehabilitating Liabilities and Obligations

Gang interventions aim to target the sources of misbehavior through rehabilitative training or therapy. One line of intervention seeks to reduce *liabilities* by addressing the economic, psychological, and social deficits that concentrate in gang populations. Another tries to eliminate *obligations* by blunting the influence of gang-related group processes. The two lines are not mutually exclusive, but the theories of change are distinct and reflect a broader debate about application of general or specific programing to gang populations (Klein and Maxson 2006; Thornberry et al. 2018; Decker, Pyrooz, and Densley 2022).

Liabilities-based interventions use training and therapy to respond to deficits that researchers have identified among gang populations (e.g.,

Davis and Flannery 2001; Krienert and Fleisher 2001). Gang affiliates in prison typically have poorer educational and employment histories, more neuropsychological deficits, more criminogenic attitudes and beliefs, and more adverse childhood background experiences than nongang prisoners. Interventions seek to address these problems by use of programming designed for general populations. Cook and colleagues (2012, 2015) detailed how the Prisoner Release Initiative in Racine, Wisconsin, delivered wraparound "reach-in" services to prisoners with gang and violent histories combined with postrelease continuity. The in-prison services included a coordinated care team that delivered cognitive-behavioral therapy, vocational training, and reentry preparedness. These services were not specially created for the group assigned at random to treatment, but they were guaranteed access; the control group had to follow standard procedures to sign up and get in line for services. Cook and colleagues found that the initiative was associated with more consistent employment, greater earnings, and lower recidivism (arrest, but not imprisonment) 1 year after release from prison. It is unclear whether the intervention worked equally well for gang and nongang prisoners,[7] but these findings are a positive sign given what is known about gang affiliation and reentry (Scott 2004; Bender, Cobbina, and McGarrell 2016; Pyrooz, Clark, et al. 2021).

Di Placido and colleagues (2006) of Correctional Services Canada described another liabilities-based intervention. They reported the results of use of risk-need-responsivity principles with gang and nongang prisoners in a maximum-security forensic mental health hospital in Saskatchewan. Three high-intensity cognitive-behavioral programs, each lasting between 6 and 8 months, were included: chronic aggression and impulsivity (79 percent), major mental illness (14 percent), and sex offender (8 percent). One hundred sixty prisoners, split evenly into four groups of 40 by gang and treatment status, were matched on age, sentence length, convictions, and recidivism risk. In terms of posttreatment in-prison misconduct, the untreated gang members fared the worst, with a monthly rate

---

[7] This was a joint initiative of the US Attorney's Office and the Wisconsin Department of Corrections, funded by the US Department of Justice's Comprehensive Anti-gang Initiative. The focus was to target "high-impact gang members," but Cook and colleagues (2012, p. 279) reported that too few prisoners met the eligibility criteria and thus the "gang-affiliation requirement was expanded to include all violent criminals." While 66 percent of the control group and 59 percent of the treatment group were designated as having prior gang affiliation, Cook and colleagues unfortunately did not distinguish treatment effects by gang and nongang affiliation.

of major misconduct about three times as great as for treated gang members and six times as great as for treated and untreated nongang members. There were no differences between treated and untreated gang members in minor incident of misconduct. In terms of postrelease recidivism, the rate of reconviction over a 2-year period was about 15 percentage points lower for treated (50 percent) than untreated (65 percent) gang members. Like the Prisoner Release Initiative (Cook et al. 2015), the quasi-experimental findings from Di Placido and colleagues showed long-term benefits from a liabilities-based intervention.

Obligations-based interventions aim to block the on-ramps into gangs or open the off-ramps. The underlying theory is that it is necessary to thwart the group processes of gangs, not just members' personal deficits, to stem problem behaviors. This means preventing gang affiliation in the first place or promoting disengagement. Gang prevention is nonexistent in US prison systems. Winterdyk and colleagues (2009, p. 29) concluded that there was "no one clear prevention strategy being used and/or being used successfully," and they did not tabulate the findings from the prevention component of their survey. There are, however, interventions that seek to promote disengagement.

It is important to distinguish between renouncement exit strategies and programmatic-based exit strategies. The end result of renouncement is reclassification that results in a (seemingly) better housing assignment. Prisoners renounce their gang affiliation by signing a proclamation, which is often accompanied by an interview or investigation to validate their claims. If the validation requires that prisoners disclose the inner workings of the gang, such as naming members, identifying leadership, or reporting on gang rules, that is usually referred to as debriefing. This is controversial, especially when tied to exiting solitary confinement, since would-be renouncers are often no longer privy to the dynamics of the evolving gang landscape and thus the honesty and sincerity of their intentions are questioned (Toch 2007). Debriefing is a one-way street: once entered, there is no returning, which is why renouncing prisoners often end up in protective custody. Pyrooz and Mitchell (2019) reported that most prison systems that claim to support disengagement operate only renouncement practices, which are closer to "management" strategies than to "intervention" strategies.

Programmatic-based efforts to disrupt gang obligations are less common but exist in prison systems in Connecticut, North Carolina, and Texas. Pyrooz and Mitchell (2019) noted that many prison managers view their solitary confinement step-down programs as close proxies for disengagement programs since gang affiliates are substantially overrepresented in them. For example, about three-quarters of participants in Oregon's step-down program were gang affiliated (Labrecque et al. 2021). Texas has maintained the Gang Renouncement and Disassociation (GRAD) program since the turn of the century. Burman (2012) reported that GRAD was modeled on Connecticut's renouncement program but tailored to the nature and scope of Texas prison gang dynamics. It is effectively solitary confinement, but only gang affiliates are eligible. Gang affiliates must sign a form indicating their intention to participate, followed by an investigation that can last up to 12 months. There are three phases of GRAD: normalization, socialization, and reintegration. Transitions lead to more expansive contacts (from single- to double-cell to general population), privileges (from fewer to more visits, phone calls, commissary), and programming (from in-cell videotaped lessons to classroom-based programs to vocational opportunities). There has been no formal impact evaluation, although Burman (2012) detailed its processes and Pyrooz and Decker (2019) used data from the LoneStar Project to compare 53 GRAD participants with a matched sample of 64 nonparticipants. GRAD participants maintained lower gang embeddedness and were more likely to identify as a former gang member, but there were no statistical differences in misconduct or victimization. These results are promising but not definitive.

VI. Conclusion

The last paragraph of Camp and Camp's (1985, p. 208) report called for a "follow-up to this study" to be conducted within 3 years to "ascertain the changes in prison gang nature and extent, as well as further impacts on prison operations and strategies that are being used to deal with the problems." Never happened. Federal funding has never been earmarked for research and evaluation concerning prison gangs. Items on prison gang dynamics elude the instruments used when surveying correctional populations. Prison systems have not paired their gang management and intervention strategies with evaluations. The gangs never went away; an absence of evidence is not evidence of their absence. Prison gangs have not been completely ignored by researchers, but that this survey of the literature fits into a single essay reflects a knowledge base not very different from those at earlier stages of research on street gangs when

Crime and Justice last published essays on gangs (Spergel 1990; Hagedorn 1998).

In this section I outline five main conclusions from research on prison gangs and identify areas especially worthy of sustained attention. First, questions concerning gang definitions and emergence are intimately related and foundational, but the absence of empirical validation is a clear takeaway from this essay. None of the mainstream definitions of prison gangs have been formally and independently tested. I offered a definition that avoids misconceptions of prison gangs—*a durable group that shares a collective identity, maintains a locus of custodial influence, exhibits collective behavior, and engages in a pattern of illegal activity*—but that too awaits confirmation. It can be said with confidence that widespread emergence of prison gangs coincided with the rise of mass incarceration. Deprivation, importation, or management theories offer theoretical scaffolding to account for the existence of gangs in prisons, but far too little research has been done to be confident about their validity. Skarbek's (2014) governance theory demonstrated logical consistency, propositions, and specificity that warrant formal testing.

Second, there is far greater variation in the forms and functions of gangs in prison than is commonly acknowledged. The traditional view of them as corporatized groups lacks support. There is considerable variation between and within gangs in their organizational structures and their demographic characteristics. Nonetheless, two robust conclusions emerge. The first is the significance of race and ethnicity; gangs contribute to and complicate the prison as a racialized space. The second is that gangs bring a semblance of order, particularly in the mass incarceration era. It remains unclear whether they provide a net positive value to the prison or their members that might counterbalance formal and informal negative consequences.

Third, a micro-macro paradox about links between prison gangs and disorder is emerging. A sizable literature points to concentration of misconduct among gang populations. This literature, including more than 30 studies, shows signs of theoretical and empirical maturity, but it relies far too heavily on official data, and far too much remains unknown about causal inferences and underlying mechanisms. Moreover, countervailing hypotheses propose that gangs, especially centralized ones, bring order to prisons. Skarbek's (2014) governance theory stands out, as it has been subject to critiques and comparative analysis (Butler, Slade, and Dias 2018; Peirce and Fondevila 2020; Skarbek 2020). To be sure, it is logically and empirically possible that both macro-order and microdisorder hypotheses may be confirmed. This will depend primarily on the extent to which gang activities ameliorate grievances and tensions among nongang (and majority) prisoners related to disorder.

Fourth, the contours of gang membership appear to concentrate in prison. Estimates are imprecise, but it seems that most gang members bring affiliations into prison from the street. Still, gangs of all kinds regularly recruit new members. Most prisoners elude these attempts, but those who join offer normative influences and various incentives as their reasons. Contrary to popular belief, prison gang membership is not a lifelong commitment. Gang leaving occurs frequently in prison, typically because of disillusionment or familial influences. Leaving, however, is more complicated than on the street. This reflects gang composition and organization and also the environment and management of the total institution. An important caveat to these observations is that these patterns have been documented in cross-sectional studies involving retrospective accounts of status transitions rather than in panel studies involving prospective evidence (Krohn and Thornberry 2008). Measures of gang affiliation and involvement should be regularly included in survey research in prisons; the evidence of the relevance of gangs is far too significant to ignore.

Finally, prison systems mostly try to manage gangs rather than to offer meaningful interventions that might address members' liabilities or obligations. Management of gang populations is facilitated by an intelligence apparatus designed to document, classify, monitor, and respond to gang affiliates. Interventions, in contrast, entail general programming that is indifferent to the particular needs and challenges faced by gang populations or associated with solitary confinement. McGrath (2020) demonstrated that the inventory of gang management and intervention strategies in prisons is scant, especially when compared to responses to gangs in noninstitutional settings. Two decades ago, surveying the National Institute of Justice's portfolio on gang research, Decker (2002, p. 19) remarked: "The lack of even basic knowledge about the impact of interventions on gangs should be a clarion call to researchers, practitioners, and policymakers." The evidence base on responses to street gangs has increased in rigor and volume since Decker wrote, but that is not true of prison gang interventions. The evidence is far too sparse for any conclusions to be offered about managing or intervening with gangs in prison.

The conclusions offered in the five main sections of this essay are based on piecemeal rather than systematic efforts to generate knowledge. Each of the core issues deserves sustained empirical inquiry, but a coordinated agenda would likely yield the greatest advances in understanding.

It is fitting in thinking about an agenda for future research to recall Katz and Jackson-Jacobs's trenchant appraisal of street gang research in "The Criminologists' Gang" (2004). They identified three core "perversions" in "gang criminology" that are as salient to gangs in prison as to gangs on the street.

Loss of a Naturalistic and Comparative Perspective.   Katz and Jackson-Jacobs described Thrasher (1927) as the standard to which street gang scholarship should aspire, and for good reason. There is, however, no work on prison gangs equivalent to Thrasher's. Naturalistic description of life in the gang and its environs ignores prison gangs, especially in the era of mass incarceration. Bolden's (2020) biographical account of his incarceration experiences in Texas is an exemplary exception. There is also little comparative emphasis on the diversity of gangs in prison. Camp and Camp's (1985) description of the development and nature of several dozen gangs in nine prison systems probably comes closest, but it was filtered through the perspectives of corrections officials.

The Gang as a Window.   Katz and Jackson-Jacobs (2004, p. 103) lamented criminologists' "seeing through gangs in the desire to explain them." The gang as a window is transparent; the worry is what is hidden by the framing. The popular image of gangs is highly contoured by criminal activities, especially violence, made public by officials and media that portray gangs as nonsensical, incorrigible enterprises. Even researchers pay disproportionate attention to the gang-misconduct link. However, some academics have "outfitted" their theories with their preferred economic and social conditions to explain the gang. In both instances, the "gangs themselves never provide the origin of the theory" (p. 102). Katz and Jackson-Jacobs were commenting on street gangs, but the meager theoretical literature on the emergence and existence of gangs in prison is equally vulnerable to their critique.

These two perversions are unlikely to be resolved by use of quantitative methodologies. They have advantages of generalizability, inference, and, potentially, comparison but lack feeling and meaning; attitudes, behaviors, and experiences are encapsulated in numbers. In-depth qualitative research—interviews and ethnographies—is probably the only approach capable of painting rich pictures of gang life behind bars. But gaining access is a huge problem. Few researchers have enjoyed the access Jacobs had when he published the first scholarly work on gangs in prison (1974) and his book on Stateville (1977). The best and, perhaps, only viable strategy involves accounts by people with lived experience of incarceration: current or former correctional officers (e.g., Crouch and Marquart 1989) and prisoners (e.g., Bolden 2020). Given the emergence of convict criminology (Tietjen 2019) and the scale of mass incarceration, a legion of writers could inject the naturalistic and comparative perspective into the study of prison gangs. Their perspectives are not immune to the framing follies Katz and Jackson-Jacobs spotlighted but could undoubtedly enrich understanding of gang life in prison.

Gangs, Crime, and Causal Analysis. Katz and Jackson-Jacob's third perversion concerned causal inferences. They did not mince words (Katz and Jackson-Jacobs 2004, p. 107): "If gangs were no more criminal than a random sample of the youth populations from which they emerge, why base theory and policy on images of gangs as opposed to the social dimensions of that larger population?" Indeed, with that broader focus, the study of gangs would (and should) move away from etiological criminology and even, perhaps, criminal justice policy and practice. Anthropologists, economists, linguists, psychologists, and sociologists are interested in gangs for many reasons, but crime and legal responses to it are what command the attention of criminologists. No doubt misconduct concentrates among gang populations, but the limitations of current knowledge extend beyond theoretical mechanisms, reliance on official data, and causal identification. There is too little description of misconduct and violence by gang members in prison. There is no equivalent to Maxson, Gordon, and Klein's (1985) comparison of the characteristics of gang and nongang homicides in Los Angeles. There is no equivalent to Decker's (1996) cycle of gang violence model. There is no equivalent to Fagan's (1989) description of the social organization of gangs' drug use and sales. There is no equivalent to Thornberry and colleagues's (1993) demonstration that criminal activity rises and falls with gang joining and leaving. Katz and Jackson-Jacobs's critique must be taken seriously, without dismissing or dramatizing the violence associated with gangs but recognizing that many causes and consequences of prisons gangs apart from crime are equally if not more important.

Knowledge about gangs in prison has advanced in important ways since Jacobs's (1974) earliest observations and even since his turn-of-the-century lament (2001). But lawsuits, riots, uprisings, or violence should not be necessary to attract the interest of social scientists or command the attention of prison officials or policy makers. Short's (2006) call should be enough: gangs are a rich subject of interest that reveals a great deal about human behavior and social organization, and prisons are no exception.

REFERENCES

Alward, Lucas M., Thomas Baker, and Jill A. Gordon. 2021. "Procedural Justice and Incarcerated People's Obligation to Obey Institutional Rules: An Examination of Current, Former, and Never-Gang Members." *Journal of Criminal Justice* 73(March–April):1–12.

Aspholm, Roberto. 2020. *Views from the Streets: The Transformation of Gangs and Violence in Chicago.* New York: Columbia University Press.

Austin, James. 2003. "Findings in Prison Classification and Risk Assessment." Washington, DC: US Bureau of Prisons, National Institute of Corrections.

Ayling, Julie. 2011. "Gang Change and Evolutionary Theory." *Crime, Law and Social Change* 56(1):1–26.

Ball, Richard A., and G. David Curry. 1995. "The Logic of Definition in Criminology: Purposes and Methods for Defining 'Gangs.'" *Criminology* 33(2):225–45.

Barrows, Julie, and C. Ronald Huff. 2009. "Gangs and Public Policy: Constructing and Deconstructing Gang Databases." *Criminology and Public Policy* 8(4):675–703.

Beard, Jeffrey. 2013. "Hunger Strike in California Prisons Is a Gang Power Play." *Los Angeles Times*, August 6. https://www.latimes.com/opinion/la-xpm-2013-aug -06-la-oe-beard-prison-hunger-strike-20130806-story.html.

Belknap, Joanne, and Molly Bowers. 2016. "Girls and Women in Gangs." In *The Wiley Handbook on the Psychology of Violence*, edited by Carlos Cuevas and Calliee Rennison. New York: Wiley-Blackwell.

Bender, Kimberly A., Jennifer E. Cobbina, and Edmund F. McGarrell. 2016. "Reentry Programming for High-Risk Offenders: Insights from Participants." *International Journal of Offender Therapy and Comparative Criminology* 60(13):1479–508.

Berg, Mark T., and Matt DeLisi. 2006. "The Correctional Melting Pot: Race, Ethnicity, Citizenship, and Prison Violence." *Journal of Criminal Justice* 34(6):631–42.

Bjerregaard, Beth. 2002. "Self-Definitions of Gang Membership and Involvement in Delinquent Activities." *Youth and Society* 34(1):31–54.

Bloch, Stefano, and Enrique Alan Olivares-Pelayo. 2021. "Carceral Geographies from Inside Prison Gates: The Micro-Politics of Everyday Racialisation." *Antipode* 5(1):1319–38.

Bolden, Christian L. 2020. *Out of the Red: My Life of Gangs, Prison, and Redemption.* New Brunswick, NJ: Rutgers University Press.

Bonner, Roger H. 1999. "The Brotherwoods: The Rise and Fall of a White-Supremacist Gang Inside a Kansas Prison." *Journal of Gang Research* 6(3):61–76.

Brotherton, David C., and Luis Barrios. 2004. *The Almighty Latin King and Queen Nation: Street Politics and the Transformation of a New York City Gang*. New York: Columbia University Press.

Bucerius, Sandra M., Daniel J. Jones, and Kevin D. Haggerty. 2021. "Indigenous Gangs in Western Canada." In *International Handbook of Critical Gang Studies*, edited by David C. Brotherton and Rafael Gude. New York: Routledge.

Buentello, Salvador, Robert S. Fong, and Ronald E. Vogel. 1991. "Prison Gang Development: A Theoretical Model." *Prison Journal* 71(2):3–14.

Burman, Michelle Lynn. 2012. "Resocializing and Repairing Homies within the Texas Prison System: A Case Study on Security Threat Group Management, Administrative Segregation, Prison Gang Renunciation and Safety for All." Austin: University of Texas at Austin. https://repositories.lib.utexas.edu/handle/2152/23352.

Burrowes, Michel J., and Peter McIntyre. 2004. "Effective Corrections Initiative: Aboriginal Reintegration." Final report. Ottawa: Correctional Service Canada.

Butler, H. Daniel, O. Hayden Griffin, and W. Wesley Johnson. 2013. "What Makes You the 'Worst of the Worst?' An Examination of State Policies Defining Supermaximum Confinement." *Criminal Justice Policy Review* 24(6):676–94.

Butler, Michelle, Gavin Slade, and Camila Nunes Dias. 2018. "Self-Governing Prisons: Prison Gangs in an International Perspective." *Trends in Organized Crime*. https://doi.org/10.1007/s12117-018-9338-7.

Camp, George M., and Camille Graham Camp. 1985. *Prison Gangs: Their Extent, Nature, and Impact on Prisons*. Washington, DC: US Government Printing Office.

Campana, Paolo, and Federico Varese. 2018. "Organized Crime in the United Kingdom: Illegal Governance of Markets and Communities." *British Journal of Criminology* 58(6):1381–400.

Carlson, Peter M. 2001. "Prison Interventions: Evolving Strategies to Control Security Threat Groups." *Corrections Management Quarterly* 5(1):10–22.

Carson, Dena C., and Finn-Aage Esbensen. 2019. "Gangs in School: Exploring the Experiences of Gang-Involved Youth." *Youth Violence and Juvenile Justice* 17(1):3–23.

Carson, Dena C., Dana Peterson, and Finn-Aage Esbensen. 2013. "Youth Gang Desistance: An Examination of the Effect of Different Operational Definitions of Desistance on the Motivations, Methods, and Consequences Associated with Leaving the Gang." *Criminal Justice Review* 38(4):510–34.

Carson, E. Ann. 2020. "Prisoners in 2018." NCJ 253516. Washington, DC: US Department of Justice, Bureau of Statistics. https://www.bjs.gov/content/pub/pdf/p18.pdf.

Carson, E. Ann, and Mary P. Cowhig. 2021. "Mortality in State Prisons, 2001–2018—Statistical Tables." Washington, DC: US Department of Justice, Bureau of Justice Statistics. https://bjs.ojp.gov/content/pub/pdf/msfp0118st.pdf.

Clemmer, Donald. 1940. *The Prison Community*. New York: Rhinehart.

Cook, Philip J., Songman Kang, Anthony A. Braga, Jens Ludwig, and Mallory E. O'Brien. 2015. "An Experimental Evaluation of a Comprehensive Employment-Oriented Prisoner Re-entry Program." *Journal of Quantitative Criminology* 31(3):355–82.

Cook, Philip J., Mallory O'Brien, Anthony Braga, and Jens Ludwig. 2012. "Lessons from a Partially Controlled Field Trial." *Journal of Experimental Criminology* 8(3):271–87.

Crewe, Ben. 2012. *The Prisoner Society: Power, Adaptation, and Social Life in an English Prison.* Oxford: Oxford University Press.

Crewe, Ben, Susie Hulley, and Serena Wright. 2020. *Life Imprisonment from Young Adulthood.* New York: Springer.

Crewe, Ben, Alison Liebling, and Susie Hulley. 2015. "Staff-Prisoner Relationships, Staff Professionalism, and the Use of Authority in Public- and Private-Sector Prisons." *Law and Social Inquiry* 40(2):309–44.

Crouch, Ben M., and James W. Marquart. 1989. *An Appeal to Justice: Litigated Reform of Texas Prisons.* Austin: University of Texas Press.

Cullen, Francis T. 2013. "Rehabilitation: Beyond Nothing Works." In *Crime and Justice in America, 1975–2025,* edited by Michael Tonry and Daniel S. Nagin. Volume 42 of *Crime and Justice: A Review of Research,* edited by Michael Tonry. Chicago: University of Chicago Press.

Cunningham, Mark D., and Jon R. Sorensen. 2006. "Nothing to Lose? A Comparative Examination of Prison Misconduct Rates among Life-without-Parole and Other Long-Term High-Security Inmates." *Criminal Justice and Behavior* 33(6):683–705.

Cunningham, Mark D., and Jon R. Sorensen. 2007. "Predictive Factors for Violent Misconduct in Close Custody." *Prison Journal* 87(2):241–53.

Davis, Mark S., and Daniel J. Flannery. 2001. "The Institutional Treatment of Gang Members." *Corrections Management Quarterly* 5(1):37–46.

Decker, Scott H. 1996. "Collective and Normative Features of Gang Violence." *Justice Quarterly* 13(2):243–64.

Decker, Scott H. 2002. "A Decade of Gang Research: Findings of the National Institute of Justice Gang Portfolio." In *Responding to Gangs: Evaluation and Research,* edited by Winifred Reed and Scott H. Decker. Washington, DC: US Department of Justice, National Institute of Justice.

Decker, Scott H., Tim Bynum, and Deborah Weisel. 1998. "A Tale of Two Cities: Gangs as Organized Crime Groups." *Justice Quarterly* 15(3):395–425.

Decker, Scott H., and Janet L. Lauritsen. 2002. "Leaving the Gang." In *Gangs in America,* edited by C. Ronald Huff. Newbury Park, CA: Sage.

Decker, Scott H., and David C. Pyrooz. 2020. "The Role of Religion and Spirituality in Disengagement from Gangs." In *Gangs in the Era of Internet and Social Media,* edited by Chris Melde and Frank M. Weerman. New York: Springer.

Decker, Scott H., David C. Pyrooz, and James A. Densley. 2022. *On Gangs.* Philadelphia: Temple University Press.

Decker, Scott H., David C. Pyrooz, and Richard K. Moule Jr. 2014. "Disengagement from Gangs as Role Transitions." *Journal of Research on Adolescence* 24(2):268–83.

Decker, Scott H., David C. Pyrooz, Gary Sweeten, and Richard K. Moule Jr. 2014. "Validating Self-Nomination in Gang Research: Assessing Differences in Gang Embeddedness across Non-, Current, and Former Gang Members." *Journal of Quantitative Criminology* 30(4):77–98.

Decker, Scott H., and Barrik Van Winkle. 1994. "'Slinging Dope': The Role of Gangs and Gang Members in Drug Sales." *Justice Quarterly* 11(4):583–604.

Decker, Scott H., and Barrik Van Winkle. 1996. *Life in the Gang: Family, Friends, and Violence.* Cambridge: Cambridge University Press.

DeLisi, Matt. 2003. "Criminal Careers behind Bars." *Behavioral Sciences and the Law* 21(5):653–69.

DeLisi, Matt, Mark T. Berg, and Andy Hochstetler. 2004. "Gang Members, Career Criminals and Prison Violence: Further Specification of the Importation Model of Inmate Behavior." *Criminal Justice Studies* 17(4):369–83.

DeLisi, Matt, Alan J. Drury, and Michael J. Elbert. 2019. "Do Behavioral Disorders Render Gang Status Spurious? New Insights." *International Journal of Law and Psychiatry* 62(January):117–24.

DeLisi, Matt, and Ed A. Munoz. 2003. "Future Dangerousness Revisited." *Criminal Justice Policy Review* 14(3):287–305.

DeLisi, Matt, Chad R. Trulson, James W. Marquart, Alan J. Drury, and Anna E. Kosloski. 2011. "Inside the Prison Black Box: Toward a Life Course Importation Model of Inmate Behavior." *International Journal of Offender Therapy and Comparative Criminology* 55(8):1186–207.

Densley, James A. 2013. *How Gangs Work: An Ethnography of Youth Violence.* New York: Palgrave Macmillan.

Densley, James A. 2014. "It's Gang Life, but Not as We Know It: The Evolution of Gang Business." *Crime and Delinquency* 60(4):517–46.

Densley, James A. 2015. "Joining the Gang: A Process of Supply and Demand." In *The Handbook of Gangs*, edited by Scott H. Decker and David C. Pyrooz. Chichester: Wiley-Blackwell.

Densley, James A., and David C. Pyrooz. 2019. "A Signaling Perspective on Disengagement from Gangs." *Justice Quarterly* 36(1):31–58.

Descormiers, Karine, and Raymond R. Corrado. 2016. "The Right to Belong: Individual Motives and Youth Gang Initiation Rites." *Deviant Behavior* 37(11):1341–59.

Diamond, Brie, Robert G. Morris, and James C. Barnes. 2012. "Individual and Group IQ Predict Inmate Violence." *Intelligence* 40(2):115–22.

DiIulio, John J., Jr. 1987. *Governing Prisons: A Comparative Study of Correctional Management.* New York: Free Press.

Di Placido, Chantal, Terri L. Simon, Treena D. Witte, Deqiang Gu, and Stephen C. P. Wong. 2006. "Treatment of Gang Members Can Reduce Recidivism and Institutional Misconduct." *Law and Human Behavior* 30(1):93–114.

Drury, Alan J., and Matt DeLisi. 2011. "Gangkill: An Exploratory Empirical Assessment of Gang Membership, Homicide Offending, and Prison Misconduct." *Crime and Delinquency* 57(1):130–46.

Dudley, Steven, and James Bargent. 2017. "The Prison Dilemma: Latin America's Incubators of Organized Crime." InSight Crime, January 19. https://insightcrime.org/investigations/prison-dilemma-latin-america-incubators-organized-crime/.

Durán, Robert. 2013. *Gang Life in Two Cities: An Insider's Journey.* New York: Columbia University Press.

Ellis, Rachel. 2021. "Prisons as Porous Institutions." *Theory and Society* 50(2):175–99.

Fagan, Jeffrey. 1989. "The Social Organization of Drug Use and Drug Dealing among Urban Gangs." *Criminology* 27(4):633–70.

Fahmy, Chantal, Dylan B. Jackson, David C. Pyrooz, and Scott H. Decker. 2020. "Head Injury in Prison: Gang Membership and the Role of Prison Violence." *Journal of Criminal Justice* 67(March–April):1–11.

Fischer, Daryl R. 2002. "Arizona Department of Corrections: Security Threat Group (STG) Program Evaluation." Final report. Washington, DC: US Department of Justice, National Institute of Justice.

Fishman, Joseph Fulling. 1934. *Sex in Prison: Revealing Sex Conditions in American Prisons*. New York: National Library.

Fitz, Lincoln. 2020. "The Impact That Inmates' Personal Characteristics Have on Prison Gang Membership and Misconduct: An Application of Akers' Social Learning Theory." *Acta Criminologica: African Journal of Criminology and Victimology* 33(1):1–19.

Fleisher, Mark S. 1998. *Dead End Kids: Gang Girls and the Boys They Know*. Madison: University of Wisconsin Press.

Fleisher, Mark S., and Scott H. Decker. 2001. "An Overview of the Challenge of Prison Gangs." *Corrections Management Quarterly* 5(1):1–11.

Fong, Robert S. 1990. "The Organizational Structure of Prison Gangs: A Texas Case Study." *Federal Probation* 54(1):36–43.

Fong, Robert S., and Ronald E. Vogel. 1995. "Blood-In, Blood-Out: The Rationale Behind Defecting from Prison Gangs." *Journal of Gang Research* 2(4):45–51.

Fong, Robert S., Ronald E. Vogel, and Salvador Buentello. 1992. "Prison Gang Dynamics: A Look Inside the Texas Department of Corrections." In *Corrections: Dilemmas and Directions*. Cincinnati: Anderson.

Gaes, Gerald G., Susan Wallace, Evan Gilman, Jody Klein-Saffran, and Sharon Suppa. 2002. "The Influence of Prison Gang Affiliation on Violence and Other Prison Misconduct." *Prison Journal* 82:359–85.

Gaston, Shytierra, and Beth M. Huebner. 2015. "Gangs in Correctional Institutions." In *The Handbook of Gangs*, edited by Scott H. Decker and David C. Pyrooz. Chichester: Wiley.

Goffman, Erving. 1961. *Asylums: Essays on the Social Situation of Mental Patients and Other Inmates*. Chicago: Aldine.

Goodman, Philip. 2008. "It's Just Black, White or Hispanic: An Observational Study of Racializing Moves in California's Segregated Prison Reception Centers." *Law and Society Review* 42(4):735–70.

Gottfredson, Michael R., and Travis Hirschi. 1990. *A General Theory of Crime*. Stanford, CA: Stanford University Press.

Gransky, Laura A., Ernest L. Cowles, Marisa Patterson, Barry Bass, and Beverly D. Rivera. 1999. "Evaluation of the Illinois Department of Corrections' Gang-Free Environment Program." Springfield: University of Illinois at Springfield, Center for Legal Studies. https://www.ojp.gov/ncjrs/virtual-library/abstracts/evaluation-illinois-department-corrections-gang-free-environment.

Gransky, Laura A., and Marisa E. Patterson. 1999. "A Discussion of Illinois' 'Gang Free' Prison: Evaluation Results." *Corrections Management Quarterly* 3(4):30–42.

Gravel, Jason. Forthcoming. "The History and Future of Collaboration in Gang Scholarship." In *The Handbook of Gangs and Society*, edited by David C. Pyrooz, James A. Densley, and John Leverso. New York: Oxford University Press.

Griffin, Marie L., and John R. Hepburn. 2006. "The Effect of Gang Affiliation on Violent Misconduct among Inmates during the Early Years of Confinement." *Criminal Justice and Behavior* 33(4):419–66.

Gundur, R. V. 2018. "The Changing Social Organization of Prison Protection Markets: When Prisoners Choose to Organize Horizontally Rather than Vertically." *Trends in Organized Crime*. https://doi.org/10.1007/s12117-018-9332-0.

Gundur, R. V. 2020. "Prison Gangs." In *Oxford Research Encyclopedia of Criminology and Criminal Justice*. https://doi.org/10.1093/acrefore/9780190264079.013 .397.

Gundur, R. V. 2022. *Trying to Make It: The People, Gangs, and Enterprises of the American Drug Trade*. Ithaca, NY: Cornell University Press.

Hagedorn, John M. 1994. "Homeboys, Dope Fiends, Legits, and New Jacks." *Criminology* 32(2):197–219.

Hagedorn, John M. 1998. "Gang Violence in the Postindustrial Era." In *Youth Violence*, edited by Michael Tonry and Mark H. Moore. Volume 24 of *Crime and Justice: A Review of Research*, edited by Michael Tonry. Chicago: University of Chicago Press.

Hagedorn, John M. 2015. *The In$ane Chicago Way: The Daring Plan by Chicago Gangs to Create a Spanish Mafia*. Chicago: University of Chicago Press.

Haney, Craig. 2018. "Restricting the Use of Solitary Confinement." *Annual Review of Criminology* 1(1):285–310.

Harding, S. 2014. *The Street Casino: Survival in the Violent Street Gang*. Bristol: Policy.

Hill, Cece. 2009. "Gangs/Security Threat Groups." *Corrections Compendium* 34(1):23–37.

Howell, James C. 2015. *The History of Street Gangs in the United States: Their Origins and Transformations*. Lanham, MD: Lexington.

Huebner, Beth M. 2003. "Administrative Determinants of Inmate Violence: A Multilevel Analysis." *Journal of Criminal Justice* 31(2):107–17.

Huff, C. Ronald, and Matthew Meyer. 1997. "Managing Prison Gangs and Other Security Threat Groups." *Corrections Management Quarterly* 1(4):10–18.

Hunt, Geoffrey, Stephanie Riegel, Tomas Morales, and Dan Waldorf. 1993. "Changes in Prison Culture: Prison Gangs and the Case of the 'Pepsi Generation.'" *Social Problems* 40(3):398–409.

Ireland, Jane L., and Christina L. Power. 2013. "Propensity to Support Prison Gangs: Its Relationship to Gang Membership, Victimisation, Aggression and Other Disruptive Behaviours." *Psychology, Crime and Law* 19(9):801–16.

Irwin, John. 1980. *Prisons in Turmoil*. Boston: Little, Brown.

Irwin, John, and Donald R. Cressey. 1962. "Thieves, Convicts and the Inmate Culture." *Social Problems* 10:142–55.

Jacobs, James B. 1974. "Street Gangs behind Bars." *Social Problems* 21(3):395–409.

Jacobs, James B. 1977. *Stateville: The Penitentiary in Mass Society*. Chicago: University of Chicago Press.

Jacobs, James B. 2001. "Focusing on Prison Gangs." *Corrections Management Quarterly* 5:vi–vii.

Johnson, Andrew, and James Densley. 2018. "Rio's New Social Order: How Religion Signals Disengagement from Prison Gangs." *Qualitative Sociology* 41(2):243–62.

Katz, Jack, and Curtis Jackson-Jacobs. 2004. "The Criminologists' Gang." In *The Blackwell Companion to Criminology*, edited by Colin Sumner. Malden, MA: Blackwell.

Klein, Malcolm W. 1971. *Street Gangs and Street Workers*. Englewood Cliffs, NJ: Prentice-Hall.

Klein, Malcolm W. 1995. *The American Street Gang: Its Nature, Prevalence and Control*. New York: Oxford University Press.

Klein, Malcolm W. 2012. "The Next Decade of Eurogang Program Research." In *Youth Gangs in International Perspective: Results from the Eurogang Program of Research*, edited by Finn-Aage Esbensen and Cheryl L. Maxson. New York: Springer.

Klein, Malcolm W., and Lois Y. Crawford. 1967. "Groups, Gangs, and Cohesiveness." *Journal of Research in Crime and Delinquency* 4(1):63–75.

Klein, Malcolm W., and Cheryl L. Maxson. 2006. *Street Gang Patterns and Policies*. New York: Oxford University Press.

Knox, George W. 2005. "The Problem of Gangs and Security Threat Groups (STGs) in American Prisons Today: Recent Research Findings from the 2004 Prison Gang Survey." National Gang Crime Research Center. http://faculty.uml.edu/jbyrne/44.327/The%20Problem%20of%20Gangs%20and%20Security%20Threat%20Groups.doc.

Kreager, Derek A. 2019. "A Social Network Approach to Prison Gangs." Paper presented at the American Society of Criminology, San Francisco, November.

Kreager, Derek A., David R. Schaefer, Martin Bouchard, Dana L. Haynie, Sara Wakefield, Jacob Young, and Gary Zajac. 2016. "Toward a Criminology of Inmate Networks." *Justice Quarterly* 33(6):1000–1028.

Kreager, Derek A., Jacob T. N. Young, Dana L. Haynie, David R. Schaefer, Martin Bouchard, and Kimberly M. Davidson. 2021. "In the Eye of the Beholder: Meaning and Structure of Informal Status in Women's and Men's Prisons." *Criminology* 59(1):42–72.

Krienert, Jessie L., and Mark S. Fleisher. 2001. "Gang Membership as a Proxy for Social Deficiencies: A Study of Nebraska Inmates." *Corrections Management Quarterly* 5(1):47–58.

Krohn, Marvin D., and Terence P. Thornberry. 2008. "Longitudinal Perspectives on Adolescent Street Gangs." In *The Long View of Crime: A Synthesis of Longitudinal Research*, edited by Akiva M. Liberman. New York: Springer.

Kuanliang, Attapol, Jon R. Sorensen, and Mark D. Cunningham. 2008. "Juvenile Inmates in an Adult Prison System: Rates of Disciplinary Misconduct and Violence." *Criminal Justice and Behavior* 35(9):1186–201.

Labrecque, Ryan M., Jennifer J. Tostlebe, Bert Useem, and David C. Pyrooz. 2021. "Reforming Solitary Confinement: The Development, Implementation, and Processes of a Restrictive Housing Step Down Reentry Program in Oregon." *Health and Justice* 9(1):1–15.

Lauger, Timothy R. 2012. *Real Gangstas: Legitimacy, Reputation, and Violence in the Intergang Environment.* New Brunswick, NJ: Rutgers University Press.

Lessing, Benjamin. 2010. "The Danger of Dungeons: Prison Gangs and Incarcerated Militant Groups." *Small Arms Survey* 6:157–83.

Lessing, Benjamin. 2017. "Counterproductive Punishment: How Prison Gangs Undermine State Authority." *Rationality and Society* 29(3):257–97.

Listwan, Shelley Johnson, Christopher J. Sullivan, Robert Agnew, Francis T. Cullen, and Mark Colvin. 2013. "The Pains of Imprisonment Revisited: The Impact of Strain on Inmate Recidivism." *Justice Quarterly* 30(1):144–68.

Lopez, Robert J., and Jesse Katz. 1993. "Mexican Mafia Tells Gangs to Halt Drive-Bys." *Los Angeles Times*, September 26. https://www.latimes.com/archives/la-xpm-1993-09-26-mn-39383-story.html.

Lopez-Aguado, Patrick. 2018. *Stick Together and Come Back Home: Racial Sorting and the Spillover of Carceral Identity.* Oakland: University of California Press.

Lyman, Michael D. 1989. *Gangland.* Springfield, IL: Thomas.

Maitra, Dev Rup. 2020. "'If You're Down with a Gang Inside, You Can Lead a Nice Life': Prison Gangs in the Age of Austerity." *Youth Justice* 20(1–2):128–45.

Maxson, Cheryl L. 2012. "Betwixt and between Street and Prison Gangs: Defining Gangs and Structures in Youth Correctional Facilities." In *Youth Gangs in International Perspective*, edited by Finn-Aage Esbensen and Cheryl L. Maxson. New York: Springer.

Maxson, Cheryl L., Charlotte E. Bradstreet, Danny Gascón, Julie Gerlinger, Jessica Grebenkemper, Darin Haerle, Jacob Kang-Brown, et al. 2012. *Gangs and Violence in California's Youth Correctional Facilities: A Research Foundation for Developing Effective Gang Policies.* Irvine: Department of Criminology, Law and Society, University of California, Irvine.

Maxson, Cheryl L., Margaret A. Gordon, and Malcolm W. Klein. 1985. "Differences between Gang and Nongang Homicides." *Criminology* 23(2):209–22.

Maxson, Cheryl L., and Malcolm W. Klein. 1996. "Defining Gang Homicide: An Updated Look at Member and Motive Approaches." In *Gangs in America*, edited by C. Ronald Huff, 2nd ed. Thousand Oaks, CA: Sage.

McGloin, Jean M., and Megan E. Collins. 2015. "Micro-Level Processes of the Gang." In *The Handbook of Gangs*, edited by Scott H. Decker and David C. Pyrooz. Chichester: Wiley-Blackwell.

McGrath, Karl. 2020. "A Systematic Review of the Effectiveness of Gang Interventions and Management Strategies (GIMS) in Penal Institutions." Master's thesis, Technological University Dublin, School of Languages, Law and Social Sciences.

McLean, Robert, and James A. Densley. 2020. *Scotland's Gang Members: Life and Crime in Glasgow.* Cham: Palgrave Macmillan.

Mears, Daniel P., Eric A. Stewart, Sonja E. Siennick, and Ronald L. Simons. 2013. "The Code of the Street and Inmate Violence: Investigating the Salience of Imported Belief Systems." *Criminology* 51(3):695–728.

Melde, Chris, and Finn-Aage Esbensen. 2011. "Gang Membership as a Turning Point in the Life Course." *Criminology* 49(2):513–52.

Melde, Chris, and Finn-Aage Esbensen. 2014. "The Relative Impact of Gang Status Transitions: Identifying the Mechanisms of Change in Delinquency." *Journal of Research in Crime and Delinquency* 51(3):349–76.

Miller, Jody, and Scott H. Decker. 2001. "Young Women and Gang Violence: Gender, Street Offending, and Violent Victimization in Gangs." *Justice Quarterly* 18(1):115–40.

Miller, Walter B. 1975. *Violence by Youth Gangs and Youth Groups as a Crime Problem in Major American Cities*. Washington, DC: US Department of Justice, Office of Juvenile Justice and Delinquency Prevention.

Miller, Walter B. 1982. "Crime by Youth Gangs and Groups in the United States." Washington, DC: US Department of Justice, Office of Juvenile Justice and Delinquency Prevention.

Mitchell, Meghan M., Kallee McCullough, Jun Wu, David C. Pyrooz, and Scott H. Decker. 2018. "Survey Research with Gang and Non-gang Members in Prison: Operational Lessons from the LoneStar Project." *Trends in Organized Crime*. https://doi.org/10.1007/s12117-018-9331-1.

Mitchell, Meghan M., David C. Pyrooz, and Scott H. Decker. 2021. "Culture in Prison, Culture on the Street: The Convergence between the Convict Code and Code of the Street." *Journal of Crime and Justice* 44(2):145–64.

Moffitt, Terrie E. 1993. "Adolescence-Limited and Life-Course-Persistent Antisocial Behavior: A Developmental Taxonomy." *Psychological Review* 100(4):674–701.

Moore, Joan W. 1978. *Homeboys: Gangs, Drugs, and Prison in the Barrios of Los Angeles*. Philadelphia: Temple University Press.

Morgan, Robert D, Paul Gendreau, Paula Smith, Andrew L. Gray, Ryan M. Labrecque, Nina MacLean, Stephanie A. Van Horn, Angelea D. Bolanos, Ashley B. Batastini, and Jeremy F. Mill. 2016. "Quantitative Syntheses of the Effects of Administrative Segregation on Inmates' Well-Being." *Psychology, Public Policy, and Law* 22(August):439–61.

Morris, Robert G., Dennis R. Longmire, Jacqueline Buffington-Vollum, and Scott Vollum. 2010. "Institutional Misconduct and Differential Parole Eligibility among Capital Inmates." *Criminal Justice and Behavior* 37(4):417–38.

Morris, Robert G., and John L. Worrall. 2014. "Prison Architecture and Inmate Misconduct: A Multilevel Assessment." *Crime and Delinquency* 60(7):1083–109.

Motz, Ryan T., Ryan M. Labrecque, and Paula Smith. 2020. "Gang Affiliation, Restrictive Housing, and Institutional Misconduct: Does Disciplinary Segregation Suppress or Intensify Gang Member Rule Violations?" *Journal of Crime and Justice* 44(1):49–65.

Mumola, Christopher J. 2005. "Suicide and Homicide in State Prisons and Local Jails." Washington, DC: US Department of Justice, Bureau of Justice Statistics. http://www.prisonpolicy.org/scans/bjs/shsplj.pdf.

Narag, Raymund E., and Sou Lee. 2018. "Putting out Fires: Understanding the Developmental Nature and Roles of Inmate Gangs in the Philippine

Overcrowded Jails." *International Journal of Offender Therapy and Comparative Criminology* 62(11):3509–35.

National Gang Center. n.d. "National Youth Gang Survey Analysis." Accessed December 15, 2015. http://www.nationalgangcenter.gov/Survey-Analysis/Measuring-the-Extent-of-Gang-Problems.

New York Times. 1931. "Penologists Back Wickersham Data." *New York Times*, October 23.

NGIC (National Gang Intelligence Center). 2011. "2011 National Gang Threat Assessment—Emerging Trends." Washington, DC: Federal Bureau of Investigation, NGIC. https://www.fbi.gov/stats-services/publications/2011-national-gang-threat-assessment/2011-national-gang-threat-assessment-emerging-trends.

O'Keefe, Maureen L., Kelli J. Klebe, Jeffrey Metzner, Joel Dvoskin, Jamie Fellner, and Alysha Stucker. 2013. "A Longitudinal Study of Administrative Segregation." *Journal of the American Academy of Psychiatry and the Law* 41(1):49–60.

O'Neill, Kevin Lewis. 2015. *Secure the Soul: Christian Piety and Gang Prevention in Guatemala*. Oakland: University of California Press.

Ong, S.-W. 2014. "Research to Improve Effectiveness of Rehabilitative Programmes: Phase 1 Results." Memorandum.

Ong, S.-W. 2015. "Improving Effectiveness of Rehabilitative Programmes with Gang Members: Research Phase 2 Findings." Memorandum.

Ortiz, Jennifer M. 2019. "Gangs and Environment: A Comparative Analysis of Prison and Street Gangs." *American Journal of Qualitative Research* 2(1):97–117.

Ouellet, Marie, Martin Bouchard, and Yanick Charette. 2019. "One Gang Dies, Another Gains? The Network Dynamics of Criminal Group Persistence." *Criminology* 57(1):5–33.

Owen, Barbara, James Wells, and Joycelyn Pollock. 2017. *In Search of Safety: Confronting Inequality in Women's Imprisonment*. Oakland: University of California Press.

Paat, Yok-Fong, Eddie Hernandez, Trina L. Hope, Jennifer Muñoz, Hector Zamora Jr., Michael H. Sanchez, and Sonny Contreras. 2020. "'Going Solo' or Joining Gangs While Doing Time: Perceptions of Prison Gangs among the Formerly Incarcerated." *Justice System Journal* 41(3):259–76.

Panfil, Vanessa R. 2017. *The Gang's All Queer: The Lives of Gay Gang Members*. New York: New York University Press.

Papachristos, Andrew V. 2011. "The Coming of a Networked Criminology?" In *Measuring Crime and Criminality*, edited by John MacDonald. Advances in Criminological Theory, vol. 17. New Brunswick, NJ: Transaction.

Papachristos, Andrew V., Anthony A. Braga, Eric Piza, and Leigh S. Grossman. 2015. "The Company You Keep? The Spillover Effects of Gang Membership on Individual Gunshot Victimization in a Co-offending Network." *Criminology* 53(4):624–49.

Peirce, Jennifer, and Gustavo Fondevila. 2020. "Concentrated Violence: The Influence of Criminal Activity and Governance on Prison Violence in Latin America." *International Criminal Justice Review* 30(1):99–130.

Peterson, Dana, Dena C. Carson, and Eric Fowler. 2018. "What's Sex (Composition) Got to Do with It? The Importance of Sex Composition of Gangs for Female and Male Members' Offending and Victimization." *Justice Quarterly* 35(6):941–76.

Phillips, Coretta. 2012. "'It Ain't Nothing like America with the Bloods and the Crips': Gang Narratives Inside Two English Prisons." *Punishment and Society* 14(1):51–68.

Porter, Bruce. 1982. "California Prison Gangs: The Price of Control." *Corrections Magazine* 8(6):6–19.

Puffer, Joseph Adams. 1912. *The Boy and His Gang.* Boston: Houghton.

Pyrooz, David C. 2014. "'From Your First Cigarette to Your Last Dyin' Day': The Patterning of Gang Membership in the Life-Course." *Journal of Quantitative Criminology* 30(2):349–72.

Pyrooz, David C., Kendra J. Clark, Jennifer J. Tostlebe, Scott H. Decker, and Erin Orrick. 2021. "Gang Affiliation and Prisoner Reentry: Discrete-Time Variation in Recidivism by Current, Former, and Non-gang Status." *Journal of Research in Crime and Delinquency* 58(2):192–234.

Pyrooz, David C., and Scott H. Decker. 2011. "Motives and Methods for Leaving the Gang: Understanding the Process of Gang Desistance." *Journal of Criminal Justice* 39(5):417–25.

Pyrooz, David C., and Scott H. Decker. 2019. *Competing for Control: Gangs and the Social Order of Prisons.* Cambridge: Cambridge University Press.

Pyrooz, David C., Scott H. Decker, and Mark S. Fleisher. 2011. "From the Street to the Prison, from the Prison to the Street: Understanding and Responding to Prison Gangs." *Journal of Aggression, Conflict and Peace Research* 3(1):12–24.

Pyrooz, David C., Scott H. Decker, and Emily Owens. 2020. "Do Prison Administrative and Survey Data Sources Tell the Same Story? A Multi-Trait, Multi-Method Examination with Application to Gangs." *Crime and Delinquency* 66(5):627–62.

Pyrooz, David C., Nancy Gartner, and Molly Smith. 2017. "Consequences of Incarceration for Gang Membership: A Longitudinal Study of Serious Offenders in Philadelphia and Phoenix." *Criminology* 55(2):273–306.

Pyrooz, David C., Chris Melde, Donna L. Coffman, and Ryan C. Meldrum. 2021. "Selection, Stability, and Spuriousness: Testing Gottfredson and Hirschi's Propositions to Reinterpret Street Gangs in Self-Control Perspective." *Criminology* 59(2):224–53.

Pyrooz, David C., and Meghan M. Mitchell. 2015. "Little Gang Research, Big Gang Research." In *The Handbook of Gangs,* edited by Scott H. Decker and David C. Pyrooz. Chichester: Wiley-Blackwell.

Pyrooz, David C., and Meghan M. Mitchell. 2019. "The Hardest Time: Gang Members in Total Institutions." In *Handbook on the Consequences of Sentencing and Punishment Decisions,* edited by Beth M. Huebner and Natasha A. Frost. New York: Routledge.

Pyrooz, David C., and Meghan M. Mitchell. 2020. "The Use of Restrictive Housing on Gang and Non-gang Affiliated Inmates in U.S. Prisons: Findings from a National Survey of Correctional Agencies." *Justice Quarterly* 37(4):590–615.

Pyrooz, David C., Meghan M. Mitchell, Richard K. Moule Jr., and Scott H. Decker. 2021. "Look Who's Talking: The Snitching Paradox in a Representative Sample of Prisoners." *British Journal of Criminology* 61(4):1145–67.

Pyrooz, David C., Gary Sweeten, and Alex R. Piquero. 2013. "Continuity and Change in Gang Membership and Gang Embeddedness." *Journal of Research in Crime and Delinquency* 50(2):239–71.

Pyrooz, David C., Jillian J. Turanovic, Scott H. Decker, and Jun Wu. 2016. "Taking Stock of the Relationship between Gang Membership and Offending: A Meta-analysis." *Criminal Justice and Behavior* 43(3):365–97.

Ralph, Paige H., Robert J. Hunter, James W. Marquart, Steven J. Cuvelier, and Dorothy Merianos. 1996. "Exploring the Differences between Gang and Non-gang Prisoners." In *Gangs in America*, edited by C. Ronald Huff, 2nd ed. Thousand Oaks, CA: Sage.

Ralph, Paige H., and James W. Marquart. 1991. "Gang Violence in Texas Prisons." *Prison Journal* 71(2):38–49.

Reiter, Keramet. 2016. *23/7: Pelican Bay Prison and the Rise of Long-Term Solitary Confinement*. New Haven, CT: Yale University Press.

Rios, Victor M. 2011. *Punished: Policing the Lives of Black and Latino Boys*. New York: New York University Press.

Rosen, Jonathan D., and José Miguel Cruz. 2019. "Rethinking the Mechanisms of Gang Desistance in a Developing Country." *Deviant Behavior* 40(12):1493–507.

Roth, Mitchell. 2020. *Power on the Inside: A Global History of Prison Gangs*. London: Reaktion.

Ruddell, Rick, and Shannon Gottschall. 2011. "Are All Gangs Equal Security Risks? An Investigation of Gang Types and Prison Misconduct." *American Journal of Criminal Justice* 36(3):265–79.

Schwartz, Barry. 1971. "Pre-institutional vs. Situational Influence in a Correctional Community." *Journal of Criminal Law, Criminology and Police Science* 62:532–42.

Scott, Greg. 2004. "'It's a Sucker's Outfit': How Urban Gangs Enable and Impede the Reintegration of Ex-convicts." *Ethnography* 5(1):107–40.

Scott, Terri-Lynne, and Rick Ruddell. 2011. "Canadian Female Gang Inmates: Risk, Needs, and the Potential for Prison Rehabilitation." *Journal of Offender Rehabilitation* 50(6):305–26.

Shelden, Randall G. 1991. "A Comparison of Gang Members and Non-gang Members in a Prison Setting." *Prison Journal* 71(2):50–60.

Short, James F. 1985. "The Level of Explanation Problem in Criminology." In *Theoretical Methods in Criminology*, edited by Robert F. Meier. Beverly Hills, CA: Sage.

Short, James F. 1998. "The Level of Explanation Problem Revisited: The American Society of Criminology 1997 Presidential Address." *Criminology* 36(1):3–36.

Short, James F. 2006. "Why Study Gangs: An Intellectual Journey." In *Studying Youth Gangs*, edited by James F. Short Jr. and Lorine A. Hughes. Lanham, MD: Rowman Altamira.

Short, James F., and Fred L. Strodtbeck. 1965. *Group Process and Gang Delinquency*. Chicago: University of Chicago Press.

Skarbek, David. 2011. "Governance and Prison Gangs." *American Political Science Review* 105(4):702–16.

Skarbek, David. 2014. *The Social Order of the Underworld: How Prison Gangs Govern the American Penal System*. New York: Oxford University Press.

Skarbek, David. 2020. *The Puzzle of Prison Order: Why Life Behind Bars Varies around the World*. New York: Oxford University Press.

Smith, Carter F. 2016. "When Is a Prison Gang Not a Prison Gang: A Focused Review of Prison Gang Literature." *Journal of Gang Research* 23(2):41–52.

Sparks, Richard, Anthony E. Bottoms, and Will Hay. 1996. *Prisons and the Problem of Order*. Oxford: Clarendon.

Spergel, Irving A. 1990. "Youth Gangs: Continuity and Change." In *Crime and Justice: A Review of Research*, vol. 2, edited by Michael Tonry and Norval Morris. Chicago: University of Chicago Press.

Steiner, Benjamin, H. Daniel Butler, and Jared M. Ellison. 2014. "Causes and Correlates of Prison Inmate Misconduct: A Systematic Review of the Evidence." *Journal of Criminal Justice* 42(6):462–70.

Steiner, Benjamin, and John Wooldredge. 2014*a*. "Comparing Self-Report to Official Measures of Inmate Misconduct." *Justice Quarterly* 31(6):1074–101.

Steiner, Benjamin, and John Wooldredge. 2014*b*. "Sex Differences in the Predictors of Prisoner Misconduct." *Criminal Justice and Behavior* 41(4):433–52.

Steiner, Benjamin, and John Wooldredge. 2015. "Racial (in)Variance in Prison Rule Breaking." *Journal of Criminal Justice* 43(3):175–85.

Steiner, Benjamin, and John Wooldredge. 2018. "Prison Officer Legitimacy, Their Exercise of Power, and Inmate Rule Breaking." *Criminology* 56(4):750–79.

Steiner, Benjamin, and John Wooldredge. 2020. *Understanding and Reducing Prison Violence: An Integrated Social Control-Opportunity Perspective*. Abingdon: Routledge.

Sykes, Gresham M. 1958. *The Society of Captives*. Princeton, NJ: Princeton University Press.

Tapia, Mike. 2013. "Texas Latino Gangs and Large Urban Jails: Intergenerational Conflicts and Issues in Management." *Journal of Crime and Justice* 37 (2):256–74.

Tetrault, Justin, Sandra M. Bucerius, and Kevin D. Haggerty. 2019. "Multiculturalism under Confinement: Prisoner Race Relations Inside Western Canadian Prisons." *Sociology* 54(3):534–55.

Tewksbury, Richard, David Patrick Connor, and Andrew S. Denney. 2014. "Disciplinary Infractions Behind Bars: An Exploration of Importation and Deprivation Theories." *Criminal Justice Review* 39(2):201–18.

Thornberry, Terence P., Brook Kearley, Denise C. Gottfredson, Molly P. Slothower, Deanna N. Devlin, and Jamie J. Fader. 2018. "Reducing Crime among Youth at Risk for Gang Involvement." *Criminology and Public Policy* 17(4):953–89.

Thornberry, Terence P., Marvin D. Krohn, Alan J. Lizotte, and Deborah Chard-Wierschem. 1993. "The Role of Juvenile Gangs in Facilitating Delinquent Behavior." *Journal of Research in Crime and Delinquency* 30(1):55–87.

Thornberry, Terence P., Marvin D. Krohn, Alan J. Lizotte, Carolyn A. Smith, and Kimberly Tobin. 2003. *Gangs and Delinquency in Developmental Perspective.* New York: Cambridge University Press.

Thrasher, Frederic M. 1927. *The Gang: A Study of 1,313 Gangs in Chicago.* Chicago: University of Chicago Press.

Tietjen, Grant. 2019. "Convict Criminology: Learning from the Past, Confronting the Present, Expanding for the Future." *Critical Criminology* 27(1):101–14.

Toch, Hans. 2007. "Sequestering Gang Members, Burning Witches, and Subverting Due Process." *Criminal Justice and Behavior* 34:274–88.

Tostlebe, Jennifer J., and David C. Pyrooz. 2022. "Procedural Justice, Legal Orientations, and Gang Membership: Testing an Alternative Explanation to Understand the Gang-Misconduct Link." *Criminology* 59(4):1–40.

Trulson, Chad R., and James W. Marquart. 2010. *First Available Cell: Desegregation of the Texas Prison System.* Austin: University of Texas Press.

Trulson, Chad R., James W. Marquart, and Soraya K. Kawucha. 2006. "Gang Suppression and Institutional Control." *Corrections Today* 68(May):26–31.

Uggen, Christopher, and Irving Piliavin. 1998. "Asymmetrical Causation and Criminal Desistance." *Journal of Criminal Law and Criminology* 88(4):1399–422.

Useem, Bert, and Obie Clayton. 2009. "Radicalization of U.S. Prisoners." *Criminology and Public Policy* 8(3):561–92.

Useem, Bert, and Michael D. Reisig. 1999. "Collective Action in Prisons: Protests, Disturbances, and Riots." *Criminology* 37(4):735–60.

Varano, Sean P., Beth M. Huebner, and Timothy S. Bynum. 2011. "Correlates and Consequences of Pre-incarceration Gang Involvement among Incarcerated Youthful Felons." *Journal of Criminal Justice* 39(1):30–38.

Vigil, Daryl A. 2006. "Classification and Security Threat Group Management." *Corrections Today* 68(2): 32–34.

Vigil, J. Diego. 1988. *Barrio Gangs: Street Life and Identity in Southern California.* Austin: University of Texas Press.

Walters, Glenn D., and Gregory Crawford. 2013. "In and out of Prison: Do Importation Factors Predict All Forms of Misconduct or Just the More Serious Ones?" *Journal of Criminal Justice* 41(6):407–13.

Weerman, Frank M., and Scott H. Decker. Forthcoming. "The Eurogang Definition: Past, Present, and Future." In *The Handbook of Gangs and Society,* edited by David C. Pyrooz, James A. Densley, and John Leverso. New York: Oxford University Press.

Weerman, Frank M., Peter J. Lovegrove, and Terence Thornberry. 2015. "Gang Membership Transitions and Its Consequences: Exploring Changes Related to Joining and Leaving Gangs in Two Countries." *European Journal of Criminology* 12(1):70–91.

Weerman, Frank M., Cheryl L. Maxson, F. Esbensen, Judith Aldridge, Juanjo Medina, and Frank van Gemert. 2009. "Eurogang Program Manual: Background, Development, and Use of the Eurogang Instruments in Multi-Site, Multi-Method Comparative Research." https://eurogangproject.files.wordpress.com/2018/06/eurogang-manual.pdf.

Weide, Robert D. 2020. "The Invisible Hand of the State: A Critical Historical Analysis of Prison Gangs in California." *Prison Journal* 100(3):312–31.

Weide, Robert D. 2022. "Structural Disorganization: Can Prison Gangs Mitigate Serious Violence in Carceral Institutions?" *Critical Criminology* 30:113–32.

Wells, James B., Kevin I. Minor, Earl Angel, and Lisa Carter. 2002. *A Study of Gangs and Security Threat Groups in America's Adult Prisons and Jails.* Indianapolis: National Major Gang Task Force.

Winterdyk, John, Nikki Fillipuzzi, Jessice Mescier, and Crystal Hencks. 2009. "Prison Gangs: A Review and Survey of Strategies." Ottawa: Correctional Service of Canada. https://www.ojp.gov/ncjrs/virtual-library/abstracts/prison-gangs -review-and-survey-strategies.

Winterdyk, John, and Rick Ruddell. 2010. "Managing Prison Gangs: Results from a Survey of US Prison Systems." *Journal of Criminal Justice* 38(4):730–36.

Wood, Jane. 2006. "Gang Activity in English Prisons: The Prisoners' Perspective." *Psychology, Crime and Law* 12 (6): 605–17.

Wooldredge, John. 2020. "Prison Culture, Management, and In-Prison Violence." *Annual Review of Criminology* 3(1):165–88.

Worrall, John L., and Robert G Morris. 2012. "Prison Gang Integration and Inmate Violence." *Journal of Criminal Justice* 40(5):425–32.

Wright, Kevin A., John R. Hepburn, and Marie L. Griffin. 2020. "Altering Administrative Segregation for Prisoners and Staff: A Mixed Methods Analysis of the Effects of Living and Working in Restrictive Housing." Washington, DC: US Department of Justice, National Institute of Justice. https://www.ojp.gov /pdffiles1/nij/grants/255929.pdf.

Wu, Jun, and David C. Pyrooz. 2016. "Uncovering the Pathways between Gang Membership and Violent Victimization." *Journal of Quantitative Criminology* 32:531–59.

Wulf-Ludden, Timbre. 2013. "Interpersonal Relationships among Inmates and Prison Violence." *Journal of Crime and Justice* 36(1):116–36.

Ojmarrh Mitchell

Drug Use Disorders before, during, and after Imprisonment

ABSTRACT

Drug-involved offenders have been long overrepresented in prisons. Intensified drug law enforcement in many countries increased both incarceration rates, especially for drug offenses, and numbers of drug-involved prisoners. This is attributable to four features of drugs and drug markets. Drug use disorders typically are not the only problems facing drug-involved prisoners. A high proportion exhibit severe mental health problems such as major depression, personality disorders, and psychotic disorders. Before incarceration, many drug-involved prisoners have unstable housing and are at high risk of homelessness; incarceration increases that risk. The high concentration of drug-involved offenders in prisons presents numerous challenges. After release, the most obvious are high rates of drug relapse and recidivism. Former prisoners have extraordinarily high risks of drug overdoses shortly after release; in the long term, diseases acquired during imprisonment are transmitted in the community. Effective prison-based drug treatment holds promise to break this cycle and mitigate physical and mental health problems of drug-involved prisoners. Unfortunately, access to treatment modalities proven to be effective in reducing drug use and recidivism is limited. A paradigm shift in drug enforcement and treatment is needed to meet the challenges presented by individuals with drug use disorders more effectively.

Drug-involved offenders have been long overrepresented in prisons. Intensified drug law enforcement in many countries, however, strengthened

Ojmarrh Mitchell is an associate professor in the School of Criminology and Criminal Justice at Arizona State University. I thank Eric L. Sevigny and Harold Pollack for helpful comments and constructive criticisms on an earlier draft.

Electronically published September 29, 2022

Crime and Justice, volume 51, 2022.

the relationship between drug use and imprisonment. The United States, and to a lesser extent other Western nations, adopted more aggressive drug law enforcement approaches beginning in the mid-1980s that targeted street-level users and sellers. This tactical shift represented a sharp departure from earlier efforts that primarily targeted drugs in their source countries (e.g., crop eradication/replacement), drug transportation routes, and drug smuggling on the border and at ports of entry and provided drug treatment for drug-involved offenders (see, e.g., Musto 1999; Tonry 2004; Boyum and Reuter 2005; Mitchell 2009). The expanded and reinvigorated drug war was a harbinger of a broader "tough-on-crime" movement that dramatically escalated the punitiveness of American criminal justice for all offenses, but especially for drug offenses.

This more punitive approach produced rising incarceration rates, again especially for drug offenses, and rising numbers of drug-involved prisoners. The increased numbers are attributable to at least four features of drugs and drug markets. First, drug possession and distribution are criminal offenses in themselves. Second, the illegal nature of drug markets means that marketplace disputes are resolved using extralegal means such as violence. Third, enhanced drug enforcement may cause drug prices to climb, which in turn increases the likelihood that problem users will commit crimes of various sorts including drug distribution, theft, fraud, and sex work, even though the empirical work on the relationship between drug enforcement and drug prices is equivocal at best (see, e.g., Pollack and Reuter 2014). Fourth, use of some drugs is associated with heightened aggression or agitation—states of mind conducive to violence. These mechanisms often lead to drug-involved individuals being arrested for a wide range of offenses. Further, a high proportion of drug-involved arrestees have diagnosable drug use disorders, which increase the likelihood of offending after release, returning to prison, and prolonged criminal careers. These factors result in drug-involved individuals, especially those with more severe drug abuse problems, being overrepresented in prisons throughout the world.

Drug enforcement appears to be shifting toward greater tolerance in many parts of the world, especially the European Union. Approaches have been adopted that emphasis rehabilitation and focus on minimizing the harms of uncontrolled use. Yet, many other nations, particularly the United States, have been slow to make that shift and maintain elements of tough-on-crime drug enforcement.

In this essay, I discuss the overrepresentation of individuals with drug problems in prisons around the world and problems and prospects associated with the heavy concentration of such individuals in prisons. Section I lays the groundwork for understanding the problems facing drug-involved prisoners. It begins by noting that drug addiction, but not drug use per se, is a strong risk factor for imprisonment. By some estimates, people serving prison terms are eight to 15 times more likely than the general public to have a drug use disorder. Imprisoned people are also much more likely to use hard drugs (e.g., heroin, prescription opioids, cocaine, amphetamines) and to use them intravenously than is the population at large. Drug use disorders typically are not the only problems facing drug-involved prisoners. A large percentage of drug-involved prisoners suffer from severe mental health problems such as major depression, personality disorders, and psychotic disorders. Before incarceration, many drug-involved individuals have histories of homelessness and unstable housing, and the risk of homelessness is further increased after a term of incarceration—creating feedback loops among drug abuse, incarceration, and homelessness.

All of the co-occurring conditions associated with drug use disorders are more pronounced among females. A higher proportion of female prisoners suffer from drug use disorders. And, in comparison to males, female prisoners with drug use disorders have higher probabilities of co-occurring mental health problems, histories of abuse and trauma, and homelessness. These findings strongly suggest that effective drug interventions need to address the multiple behavioral health challenges confronting drug-involved prisoners, and successful treatment programs may need to be gender specific or include gender-specific components.

Section II discusses drugs and drug users in prison. The concentration of drug-dependent individuals confined in prisons and jails presents numerous challenges. Public discourse surrounding these issues typically focuses on high rates of offending and recidivism. Much less attention is paid to the plethora of challenges drug-involved individuals present while in prison. Most centrally, the large number of drug users behind bars generates drug markets to meet their demands, yet the inconsistent availability of specific drugs and their high cost leads to reduced drug tolerance, which in turn increases the likelihood of fatal drug overdoses. Further, the limited availability of needles and syringes necessitates sharing them, which is a major source of transmission of blood-borne diseases. Upon release, parolees with drug problems face all of the stigma and social exclusions other parolees face but also contend with drug cravings and sudden, pervasive availability of potent low-cost drugs. Drug relapse is common immediately after release and extraordinarily often fatal; the risk of fatal overdoses spikes in the first 2 weeks. In the longer term, parolees infected with blood-borne diseases, often acquired in prison, transmit those diseases to the community via needle sharing, tattooing, sexual relations, and childbirth.

The clustering of individuals in prison presents an opportunity to intervene in the cycle of uncontrolled drug use, crime, and incarceration. Effective prison-based drug treatment holds the promise of breaking this cycle and mitigating the physical and mental health problems common among drug-involved prisoners.

Section III describes common treatment modalities available in incarcerative settings and obstacles to obtaining access to them. Prisons, and to a lesser extent jails, provide a variety of drug treatment options ranging from short-term, low-intensity drug education programs to long-term, demanding therapeutic communities (TCs); group-based counseling programs fall in between these extremes. An increasing number of secure facilities offer medications for opioid use disorder (MOUD). Often, these modalities are combined with one another and other treatment interventions. Many drug-involved prisoners receive drug treatment of some sort; the vast majority, however, do not receive intensive, long-term programming commensurate with the scale of their behavioral health challenges. The dearth of intensive drug interventions is fundamentally important. Evaluations only of TC programs consistently find evidence of recidivism reduction for both female and male participants—even in the most rigorous program evaluations. The effectiveness of TC programs is enhanced by continuing treatment in the community after release. By contrast, the most common treatments offered by prisons lie on the low-intensity side of the spectrum and have been found to be ineffective in suppressing recidivism and substance use after release. This should not be surprising given the limited nature and duration of most incarceration-based drug treatment interventions relative to the many interlinked problems confronting incarcerated individuals with drug use disorders. In the end, primarily because of limited access, most drug-involved prisoners go untreated or only partially treated.

Section IV offers evidence-based policy recommendations aimed at reducing the harms drug-involved incarcerated individuals do to themselves and to their communities. Most centrally, research findings convincingly demonstrate that the goal of achieving a "drug-free" society, as American "wars" on drugs sought to do, is unrealistic. No modern society has ever achieved this impossible goal, and drug problems appear to be worse in countries, like the United States, that attempt to attain it by criminalizing and punishing people with drug problems. Given the overrepresentation of drug-involved individuals in prisons in most countries and the long history of this relationship, a more realistic approach is to treat drug problems as public health imperatives that can be managed but never solved. This approach is commonly referred to as "harm reduction." Harm reduction in correctional institutions will require treatment to become a central mission of prisons and parole, equal in importance to public safety and security. Corrections-based harm reduction requires significant expansion of access to high-quality treatments for the many challenges facing drug-involved individuals (e.g., mental problems, physical and sexual abuse, trauma, housing, and employment instability). The shift of focus from abstinence to harm reduction will require research that more precisely measures not only recidivism and drug relapse but, equally seriously, health and social functioning.

I. Drug Use Disorders and Drug-Related Problems among Imprisoned Populations

In the general population, drug use is not a strong predictor of imprisonment; most users consume illicit substances in a controlled way (Anthony, Warner, and Kessler 1994; Grant 1996; Lopez-Quintero et al. 2011). A large share of the population at some point in their lives, typically in adolescence or early adulthood, consume one or more illicit psychoactive substances (Kandel and Yamaguchi 1993; Chen and Kandel 1995; Makkai and Payne 2003). The most common pattern begins with alcohol or tobacco, which are generally legal for adults, then progresses to soft illicit drugs such as marijuana, hallucinogens, and low potency prescription pills. Some users progress to harder drugs like cocaine, methamphetamine, heroin, and synthetic opioids. For the vast majority of individuals, drug use is infrequent and short-lived and has minimal consequences.

A minority of users develop problematic patterns of drug use indicative of uncontrolled, compulsive use. Their developmental patterns are characterized by early onset of drug use, harder drugs including those taken intravenously, multiple drugs, frequent use, and use that continues beyond early adulthood (see, e.g., Chaiken and Chaiken 1990; Farabee, Joshi, and Anglin 2001). A considerable number of individuals with such patterns become problem drug users (Labouvie and White 2002). Throughout the world, problem drug use greatly elevates individuals' risks of contact with the criminal justice system and imprisonment. Consequently, drug problems are a common feature of incarcerated populations the world over (see, e.g., Taylor 2002).

Drug problems are typically one of several problems confronting drug-involved prisoners. They typically suffer from high rates of one or more mental health problems, blood-borne diseases such as HIV and hepatitis C, and homelessness and housing instability. These co-occurring problems are particularly common among female drug-involved prisoners, as are histories of physical and sexual abuse and trauma. A full understanding of drug-involved prisoners must acknowledge these co-occurring issues and incorporate this knowledge into crafting effective interventions both in prison and afterward.

A. Drug Use Disorders among Prisoners

Individuals detained in jails and prisons throughout the world are substantially more likely than their corresponding general populations to use illicit psychoactive drugs, consume "hard drugs," use drugs compulsively, and exhibit drug-related problems. At the time of detention, recent drug use among those incarcerated is three to six times and drug dependence eight to 15 times greater than in the general population. In contrast to casual drug use that only modestly increases the risk of incarceration, drug dependence is a prime risk factor for incarceration. And, while the association between drug dependence and incarceration is long-standing, the proportion of prisoners with drug use disorders is increasing, especially among female detainees—the majority of whom have a drug use disorder.

Comparing rates of drug use and drug dependence between prisoners and general populations is complicated by many measurement issues. A simple and parsimonious way to demonstrate overrepresentation among detainees is to compare the rates of drug use and drug dependence among incarcerated populations in various nations to these rates in the United States. Such comparisons are imperfect but offer conservative estimates of the overrepresentation of drug-involved individuals in the world's prisons.

The nation with the highest estimated rate of past year drug dependence is the United States (Ritchie and Roser 2019).[1] Globally, in 2019, the past year dependence rate was 0.9 percent on average, and the vast majority of countries had rates below 1.2 percent. The rate in the United States was 3.4 percent, nearly four times the global average (Ritchie and Roser 2019). In terms of "current" drug use, defined as drug use in the past 30 days, 13 percent of US residents age 12 and over self-report use of an illicit psychoactive substance (SAMHSA 2021). The most commonly consumed illicit drug in the United States, by far, is marijuana (11.5 percent); approximately 75 percent of current drug users in the United States use marijuana exclusively.[2] Current use of "hard drugs" such as prescription pain medicines (~1 percent), cocaine (<1 percent), and heroin (<0.5 percent) are used by much smaller proportions of US residents; 3.4 percent of US residents age 12 and over used an illicit drug other than marijuana (SAMHSA 2021).

By contrast, research conducted throughout the world finds that individuals held in prisons and jails use psychoactive drugs, particularly hard drugs, at rates many times higher than the overall US rates. Nearly half (48.6 percent) of recent arrestees in a South African sample tested positive for at least one illicit substance (van Niekerk et al. 2002, p. 131). Marijuana was the most commonly consumed drug. Approximately 40 percent of inmates tested positive (p. 135), which is the general pattern in all but a few countries. Roughly 35 percent of the South African sample was found to have used harder drugs such as methaqualone (quaaludes), cocaine, or opiates (van Niekerk et al. 2002, p. 136). A study in Thailand found that 39 percent of male prison inmates self-reported using heroin before imprisonment (Thaisri et al. 2003). In Australia, 73 percent of arrestees tested positive for one or more psychoactive substances, and approximately half (47 percent) tested positive for hard drug use, including cocaine, heroin, or amphetamines (Coghlan et al. 2015). Studies in European nations including England and Wales, the Netherlands, and Scotland find that 61–71 percent of arrestees test positive for any illicit drug use, and roughly half had used a hard drug shortly before their arrest (Bennett

---

[1] Rates of drug dependence and hard drug use are notoriously difficult to measure (see, e.g., Reuter, Caulkins, and Midgette 2021); some caution is warranted in asserting that the United States has the highest rate of drug dependence.

[2] Of all US residents age 12 and over, 9.6 percent used marijuana exclusively; that is 74 percent of all drug users.

2002; Klerks, Plaisier, and Garnier 2002; McKeganey et al. 2002; Bennett and Holloway 2009). In North America, a drug monitoring program in five US cities in various regions of the country found that 63–83 percent of arrestees tested positive for any of 10 drugs; marijuana use was common in all five sites, but the use of hard drugs varied dramatically, ranging from 20 to 60 percent (ONDCP 2014). And in South America, a study in Chile found that 47.8 percent of arrestees had used any of 10 drugs, primarily marijuana (31 percent) or cocaine (26.7 percent; Caris and Taylor 2002). Cumulatively, this body of research indicates that the prevalence of illicit drug use among incarcerated populations worldwide is roughly three to six times higher than in the US general population, the nation with the most severe illicit drug problem. The rate of hard drug use among the world's prisoners is eight to 15 times greater than the US general population rate.

A striking proportion of people held in prisons and jails have drug problems. Researchers define drug problems in various ways and use numerous terms such as "drug dependence," "drug use disorders," and drug "addiction" to refer to inmates with drug problems. In this essay, I use these terms as the original authors do. I use the phrase "drug problems" as a catchall to refer to individuals who use psychoactive drugs compulsively and whose compulsive use negatively affects their lives in a host of domains (e.g., family, school, employment, physical and mental health).

Individuals held in prisons worldwide have much higher rates of drug problems than the general public in their country. For example, the US population rate of drug dependence is 3.4 percent; incarcerated individuals have rates of past year drug use disorders many times higher. For instance, a 2016 national survey of people imprisoned in the United States estimated that 40 percent satisfied the clinical criteria establishing the presence of a drug use disorder in the 12 months before prison admission (Maruschak, Bronson, and Alper 2021)—a rate more than 11 times higher than in the general population. When alcohol use disorders are included, nearly half (47 percent) of US state prisoners had a substance use disorder during the year before incarceration. While no other nation appears regularly to conduct large-sample surveys assessing drug problems of prisoners, numerous studies in Europe, Australia, and South America also find high rates of drug use disorders among prisoners, ranging from 14 percent in a prison in Christchurch, New Zealand (Bushnell and Bakker 1997), to 61 percent in a prison in Iceland (Einarsson et al. 2009). Fazel, Yoon, and Hayes (2017) conducted a systematic review of studies assessing drug use disorders among prisoners. They found 24 such studies from 10 countries on four continents but primarily from the United States and Western Europe. Using meta-analytic techniques, they estimated the proportion of prisoners with drug use disorders and found a pooled prevalence for males of 30 percent and for females of 51 percent.

There is also evidence that drug disorders among prisoners have become increasingly common. Fazel, Yoon, and Hayes's (2017) synthesis of the literature found that drug use disorders were significantly more prevalent in studies published after 2000 than before. Likewise, surveys of drug disorder rates among state prisoners in 2004 (Mumola and Karberg 2006) and 2007–9 (Bronson et al. 2017), using identical measures, indicate that drug dependence or abuse grew from 53.4 to 58.5 percent. An influential report of the National Center on Addiction and Substance Abuse that employed a broader definition of drug problems estimated that the percentage of "substance-involved" state prisoners rose from 81 percent in 1996 to 85 percent in 2006 (NCASACU 2010, p. 10).

High rates of intravenous drug use among prisoners are another manifestation of drug problems. Intravenous drug use is especially troubling for several reasons. It is inherently an indication that a user has become drug tolerant and wants a more efficient and effective means of drug administration; this signals compulsive, uncontrolled drug use. Another problem is that tight regulation of needle distribution in many prisons causes scarcity and results in increased needle sharing. This leads to transmission and contraction of blood-borne diseases such as HIV/AIDS, tuberculosis, and hepatitis B and C (Palmateer et al. 2013; Stone et al. 2018; Leung et al. 2019).

Precise estimates of injection rates in prisons compared to general populations are difficult to gauge, given low intravenous drug use rates in general populations. It is clear, however, that drug injectors are vastly overrepresented in prisons. Consider, for example, that estimates of the lifetime prevalence of injecting drug use among the general population are 0.2 percent in Australia (Dolan et al. 2016), 0.3 percent in Europe (EMCDDA 2012, p. 11), and 1.7 percent among US residents over age 12 (SAMHSA 2021). By contrast, the proportion of prisoners who have injected drugs is 11 percent in the United States (Marotta 2017), 2–38 percent in Europe (EMCDDA 2012, p. 11), 51 percent in a sample of male prisoners in Thailand (Thaisri et al. 2003), and 55 percent in Australia (EMCDDA 2012, p. 11).[3]

---

[3] An early review of research published in the 1980s and 1990s, conducted primarily in the United States and Australia, estimated that 30–42 percent of prisoners had used drugs intravenously (Fortuin 1991).

A large proportion of imprisoned injecting drug users report sharing drug paraphernalia. More than two-thirds of the male prisoners in Thailand reported that they had shared injection paraphernalia (Thaisri et al. 2003). A similar proportion of intravenous drug users in a US national prisoner survey acknowledged needle sharing (Marotta 2017). In New South Wales, 62 percent of imprisoned drug injectors shared injection equipment (Cunningham et al. 2018). Several Canadian studies found that approximately 30 percent of prisoners had injected drugs (Calzavara et al. 2003, 2007; Poulin et al. 2007).

Given the number of injection drug users in prisons, a majority of whom have shared needles, it is not surprising that blood-borne diseases are relatively common. In Canada, for instance, general population estimates are that less than 1 percent are infected with HIV (0.8 percent) or hepatitis C (0.18 percent). The corresponding rates among prisoners were 2.0 and 17.6 percent, and among prisoners who injected drugs these rates were 5.7 and 54.7 percent (Calzavara et al. 2007). An international research survey reports similar findings in a variety of nations. Dolan and colleagues' (2016) systematic review of 299 publications on the prevalence of HIV, hepatitis B and C, and tuberculosis among prisoners in 196 countries found overall a 2.8 percent prevalence for active tuberculosis, 3.8 percent for HIV, 4.8 percent for chronic hepatitis B, and 15.1 percent for hepatitis C. Moreover, when the data were available to allow comparisons, the rates were consistently and considerably higher among prisoners with histories of drug injection.

B. Conditions and Characteristics Associated with Problem Drug Use

Individuals with mental health problems are vastly overrepresented in prisons everywhere. In the United States, less than 11 percent of general population adults satisfy DSM-IV (*Diagnostic and Statistical Manual of Mental Disorders*, 4th ed.) criteria for a mental health disorder; the most suffer major depression (8 percent) with much smaller proportions experiencing psychotic disorders (3 percent) or mania (1.8 percent; James and Glaze 2006). Yet a representative sample of state prisoners found that 56 percent had a mental health disorder, with large proportions having major depression (23 percent), psychotic disorders (15 percent), or mania (43 percent; James and Glaze 2006). Similarly, Butler and colleagues (2011) estimated that 43 percent of Australian prisoners exhibited a mental health condition. These findings are representative of the high prevalence of mental health disorders among prisoners in all surveyed countries. More comprehensively, Fazel and Danesh (2002) synthesized 62 studies in 12 countries that estimated the prevalence among prisoners of mental health problems. Approximately two-thirds of prisoners had mental health disorders, most commonly personality disorders, major depression, or psychotic disorders. They estimated that prisoners are two to three times more likely to suffer from major depression or psychosis than the general population and roughly 10 times more likely to have an antisocial personality.

Drug use disorders are particularly high among prisoners with mental health problems ("co-occurring disorders"). For instance, 62 percent of US state prisoners with mental health problems exhibited drug dependence (44 percent) or abuse (18 percent). When alcohol is included 74 percent had a substance abuse or dependence (James and Glaze 2006). Forty-two percent exhibited both mental health and substance use disorders, 24 percent had substance use problems but no diagnosable mental health problems, 14.5 percent experienced mental health problems but no substance abuse disorders, and only one in five state prisoners (19.5 percent) had neither disorder (James and Glaze 2006). Similar findings are common elsewhere. Surveys of research throughout the world, including Australia, France, Spain, and the United Kingdom among many other nations, found that co-occurring mental health and drug problems are common characteristics of prisoners (Butler et al. 2011; EMCDDA 2012; Rebbapragada, Furtado, and Hawker-Bond 2021; Baranyi et al. 2022).

Homelessness is less frequently discussed in relation to drug use disorders. Although the vast majority of US state prisoners were not homeless before their incarceration, incoming prisoners, especially those with mental health or drug problems, have much higher rates of homelessness than does the general population. For instance, approximately 6 percent of American adults were estimated to be homeless, but data from a national prisoner study generate estimates that inmates with drug dependence or abuse were twice as likely to be homeless in the year before arrest (12.8 percent) and those with symptoms of mental health disorders were twice as likely (12.4 percent; James and Glaze 2006; Greenberg and Rosenheck 2008b).

Other research illustrates tight relationships between homelessness and substance abuse. One study before the current term of incarceration found that 78 percent of homeless inmates had both a severe mental health disorder and a substance use disorder (McNiel, Binder, and Robinson 2005).

Moreover, a comprehensive review of 116 studies evaluating individual-level predictors of homelessness demonstrated that psychiatric disorders, substance abuse problems, and incarceration were strong predictors of homelessness. The relationship between homelessness and incarceration runs in both directions; a host of studies have found that a history of incarceration increases the likelihood of homelessness (see, e.g., Metraux, Roman, and Cho 2007; Greenberg and Rosenheck 2008*a*; Mogk et al. 2019; Moschion and Johnson 2019; Adler 2021). Many individuals experience homelessness and incarceration cyclically. Mogk and colleagues (2019), for example, interviewed 101 homeless individuals in Seattle and found that 78 percent had experienced incarceration and that on average they had served 7.3 terms of incarceration.

Gender is strongly associated with drug use disorders and imprisonment. Female prisoners are substantially more likely than male prisoners to have drug use disorders. Fazel, Yoon, and Hayes (2017), in their international survey, found a pooled prevalence of drug use disorders of 30 percent for males and 51 percent for females. Female inmates' high rate of drug problems is confirmed by research in many countries. Surveys of US prison inmates consistently find that female prisoners have higher rates of drug problems. In the 2004 national survey, female state prisoners' drug dependence or abuse rate was substantially (7.2 percentage points) higher than males' (60.2 vs. 53.0 percent; Mumola and Karberg 2006). In the 2007–9 survey, the difference increased to 12.3 percentage points (69.2 vs. 56.9 percent; Bronson et al. 2017). Measurement of drug problems changed in the 2016 survey from DSM-IV's measure of "drug dependence or abuse" to DSM-V's "drug use disorders." Despite the change, the gender difference remained stable at 12.3 percentage points (Maruschak, Bronson, and Alper 2021). Similar gender differences in drug use and problems have been found in Australia (Coghlan et al. 2015), Canada (Weekes, Thomas, and Graves 2004), England (Borrill et al. 2003), and New Zealand (Morris 2001).

Female prisoners also have higher rates of mental health problems, co-occurring disorders, and homelessness. In the United States, female state prisoners had higher rates of mental health problems than males (73 vs. 55 percent), two-thirds of female prisoners with mental health problems met criteria for drug dependence or abuse (66 vs. 62 percent for all prisoners with mental disorders), and 17 percent were homeless in the year before arrest (compared to 13 percent all for prisoners with mental disorders and 6 percent of prisoners without mental problems; James and Glaze

2006).[4] Further, 68 percent of female inmates with mental health problems had histories of physical or sexual abuse, compared with 27 percent of all prisoners with mental health problems. Thus, the relationships between imprisonment, drug use disorders, mental health problems, histories of abuse, and homelessness are all stronger for female prisoners.

That most drug-involved prisoners have multiple co-occurring behavioral health problems has important implications. Effective interventions may need to address each problem facing individual prisoners or the shared underlying conditions driving them. Specialized treatment programs for dually diagnosed inmates may, for example, be most effective. Prison-based drug treatment programs that do not link participants' reentry into society with housing assistance are likely to fail, as people who are homeless are unlikely to be focused on maintaining their sobriety. Another implication is that effective interventions may also need to be gender specific or contain gender-specific components. Pathways into criminal behavior and drug use disorder are gendered, which suggests that pathways to desistance are likely also to be (see, e.g., Lynch et al. 2013; Broidy, Payne, and Piquero 2018). A final implication is that treatment programs aimed at female prisoners may be ineffective if they do not attend to trauma caused by histories of sexual and physical abuse.

II. Challenges Posed by Drug-Involved Offenders in Prison and at Reentry

People with drug problems have high incarceration risks. Many, if not most, individuals with drug use disorders will sooner or later go to prison. According to a survey conducted in nine European countries, more than half of self-reported heroin or cocaine users had been to prison (March, Oviedo-Joekes, and Romero 2006). An Australian study of a community-based sample of intravenous drug users indicated that the majority had been incarcerated (Kinner et al. 2009). Nearly 80 percent of intravenous drug users in the United States have been to prison at least once (Dolan 1999). Many problem drug users cycle in and out (NCASACU 2010).

The high recidivism rate among prisoners with drug use disorders is well known. They also present a host of challenges for prison administrators. And once released, they face numerous challenges.

---

[4] "Overall" refers to percentages based on both male and female prisoners, as gender specific rates were not consistently reported.

A. Problems Associated with Drug-Involved Offenders in Prison

The heavy concentration of prisoners with drug problems presents significant problems for prison managers. Their presence creates a demand for drugs to salve their disorders, prevent withdrawal symptoms, and break the monotony of prison life (Keene 1997). In-prison drug markets are a product of this demand. They, in turn, stimulate violence between groups fighting to control the markets and contribute to inmate-on-staff violence (O'Hagan and Hardwick 2017; Wooldredge 2020). Drug markets also corrupt prison staff, as the profits of in-prison drug markets are typically substantially greater than those in the community (Rosen 2019). Most prison staff earn modest salaries, particularly in comparison with the income potential of drug distribution. This is why prison staff are probably the single largest source of illicit drugs behind bars (Penfold, Turnbull, and Webster 2005; Trestman and Wall 2018).

Drug markets and availability undermine inmates' efforts to overcome their addictions. Most fundamentally, the security threats fueled by drug markets create unsafe environments. Assuring inmate safety is essential to maintaining an environment conducive to rehabilitation (Wooldredge 2020). The availability of drugs can reduce inmates' motivation to enter treatment and undermine efforts to achieve sobriety by inmates in treatment (Nguyen et al. 2021).

Prisons try to suppress drug availability and use (see, e.g., Trestman and Wall 2018). They attempt to keep drugs out of secure facilities in a number of ways, including searching inmates' clothes, belongings, and bodies whenever entering or returning, using drug-sniffing dogs and ion spectrometry to detect drugs on inmates and visitors, and monitoring inmates' phone and mail communications. Within facilities, administrators employ drug-sniffing dogs, random cell searches, on-demand inmate searches, and informants in drug distribution networks. Drug testing, both random and targeted, aimed at individuals suspected of drug involvement is ubiquitous. All of these efforts are backed up by the threat of sanctions imposed on anyone involved in drug trafficking.

These tactics reduce drug availability and the problems associated with in-prison drug markets (Feucht and Keyser 1999; Holsinger 2002; Trestman and Wall 2018; Bell and Leese 2021; Nguyen et al. 2021). An evaluation of Maryland's enhanced drug security measures found large reductions in contraband discovery and drug use during a period of enhanced enforcement compared with an earlier period (Holsinger 2002). Pennsylvania prisons had similar success. Heightened drug control activities included scans of correctional officers, increased phone monitoring, and drug testing of hair in addition to standard drug control activities. Compared with a prior period, positive drug tests declined sharply (35 percent for urine testing and nearly 80 percent for hair tests), discovery of drug contraband fell by 40 percent, assaults between inmates fell by 70 percent, and assaults on staff decreased nearly 60 percent (Feucht and Keyser 1999).

Reduced drug availability reduces drug use. Many inmates entirely cease using drugs while in prison (Carpentier et al. 2012; Montanari et al. 2020). And nearly all drug-involved offenders reduce their frequency of drug use from preincarceration levels because of difficulty obtaining drugs and their high cost (Dolan, Kite, et al. 2007; Carpentier et al. 2012; Montanari et al. 2020). Carpentier and colleagues (2012) reviewed 53 studies conducted in European Union countries and found that prisoners consistently reported reduced drug use in the past 30 days in prison compared to their use before imprisonment. Paksi (2009; cited in Carpentier et al. 2012), for example, found that 26 percent of those surveyed reported using illicit drug in the month before imprisonment, but only 3 percent used in prison in the past month.

While drug use is reduced by imprisonment, it remains commonplace. The literature on in-prison drug use is vast and comes from many countries, but much of it comes from the European Union where the European Monitoring Centre for Drugs and Drug Addiction regularly collects pertinent data. Carpentier and associates (2018), after conducting a global search for studies, estimated that 20–45 percent of inmates had ever used an illicit drug in prison. They found tremendous variation in prevalence estimates. Several studies reported drug use rates while in prison of 15 percent or less, and others reported 50 percent or more (Carpentier et al. 2018). Prisoners who inject drugs, most commonly heroin, are particularly likely to continue. One study estimated that 16–60 percent of such prisoners continued to use drugs intravenously in European prisons (Stöver and von Ossietzky 2001). A German study found that 75 percent of injecting drug users continued intravenous use in prison (Stark et al. 2006).

Carpentier and associates' (2018) review also found that rates of recent or regular use in prison were substantially lower than before prison entry. This confirms that frequency of use is curtailed by imprisonment. Marijuana is the most frequently used drug behind bars, as it is in free society, but use of hard drugs such as cocaine, amphetamines, and heroin is also prevalent. Montanari and colleagues (2020) estimate that the lifetime prevalence of drug use in European prisons is 70 percent for marijuana, 30 percent for heroin, 20 percent for cocaine, and 18 percent for amphetamines.

Ironically, efforts to suppress prison drug markets create incentives to prefer stronger drugs. Interdiction efforts are likelier to impede marijuana entry, as it is bulky and pungent; this encourages smuggling of more compact and potent drugs. Prison drug testing also encourages use of stronger drugs. Marijuana can be detected in urine for weeks, which makes users vulnerable to discovery for an extended period. Heroin and cocaine are metabolized quickly and detectable only for a few days. Some inmates switch to these substances in order to reduce detection risk (Singleton, Farrell, and Meltzer 2003).

Heroin has calming, sleep-inducing effects that can mitigate stress and restlessness common among prisoners, and the presence of experienced users may facilitate use (Stöver and von Ossietzky 2001). There is evidence that a substantial proportion of heroin-using inmates began its use while imprisoned; Boys and colleagues' (2002) inmate survey found that more than a quarter of users first injected heroin while in prison. It is not surprising that the prevalence of heroin use is high in prisons.

As in the community, heroin use in prison is associated with a significant risk of fatal overdose. Reduced frequency of use resulting from security measures diminishes dependent prisoners' drug tolerance; this increases the risk of overdose if users return to prior dosage levels. In addition, illicit opioids are by definition unregulated, and their potency is unknowable, including whether a substance genuinely is heroin. Much of what is sold as heroin is instead a synthetic opioid such as fentanyl or is tainted by synthetic opioids, which are much more potent than heroin.

Those features of opioid use in prison make overdoses likely. US mortality statistics illustrate the dangers. Between 2001 and 2019, the mortality rate of state prisoners attributed to drug or alcohol intoxication rose from three to 22 per 100,000 prisoners—a 633 percent increase. The recent overdose mortality rate is the highest on record (Carson 2021). Much of the increase occurred after 2015 when fentanyl was increasingly sold as or mixed with heroin. These figures are only for fatal overdoses; the many nonfatal overdoses are not counted.

Heroin use poses serious problems apart from overdoses. Intravenous drug use transmits blood-borne illnesses. Heroin use is overwhelmingly via injection. Access to clean needles and syringes is tightly constrained by prison security measures. Scarcity of needles increases how often a needle is used, and with that the risk of blood-borne disease increases (Montanari et al. 2020). Intravenous drug use as a result is the primary mode of in-prison transmission of HIV and hepatitis in most parts of the world and also increases the risk of other infections such as tuberculosis (Dolan, Khoei, et al. 2007).

Because of other common prison activities such as tattooing, body piercing, and sexual intercourse, non-drug-injecting prisoners are also at elevated risk of contracting these infections. Chronic illnesses associated with these viruses cause a substantial number of in-prison deaths. For example, as recently as 2001, 20 percent of US state prisoner deaths were attributed to liver disease (10.7 percent) or AIDS-related conditions (9.6 percent); these causes of death have steadily declined but still constitute 4 percent of in-prison deaths (Carson 2021).

Suicide is the most frequent unnatural cause of death among US prisoners (Carson 2021); mental health problems and drug use disorders are potent risk factors. Suicide mortality rates have recently nearly doubled, rising from four per 100,000 prisoners in 2001 to 27 in 2019. Research in many countries has consistently found that drug and mental health problems are key predictors of prisoner suicide. For instance, 72 percent of inmates who died by suicide in England and Wales over a 2-year period were drug dependent or exhibited another mental disorder (Shaw et al. 2004). Similarly, 73 percent of inmates who died by suicide in California prisons had previously received treatment for substance abuse or mental health disorders (Patterson and Hughes 2008). A worldwide synthesis of studies on risk factors for inmate suicide found that a current psychiatric diagnosis increased the odds of suicide by 490 percent (Fazel et al. 2008).

B. Drug-Involved Offenders and the Challenges of Reentry

Drug-involved individuals released from correctional institutions face numerous challenges. They, like all ex-prisoners, encounter stigma and social exclusions associated with felony convictions and imprisonment that make it difficult to find a place to live and meaningful employment. The combination of stigma and prolonged absence complicate reconnecting to friends, family, and community.

Ex-prisoners with drug problems face the additional challenges of addiction, particularly relapse. Relapse is most acute and deadly immediately after release. The availability of relatively inexpensive and potent illicit drugs combined often with weakened drug tolerance make the first few weeks of freedom exceptionally risky. One study of former inmates released from Washington state prisons found that the risk of death from all causes in the first 2 weeks was 12.7 times higher than for other Washington state residents (Binswanger et al. 2007). The leading cause of death was drug overdose; the rate was an astonishing 129 times that for other state residents. The risk of death quickly fell markedly but remained many times higher than for other state residents. Similar findings emerged from a Norwegian study of individuals released from prison (Bukten et al. 2017). A meta-analysis of six studies investigating mortality among former inmates in Australia, the United Kingdom, and the United States found that mortality from drug overdoses was especially high in the first 2 weeks (Merrall et al. 2010). High rates of fatal drug overdoses in the first 2 weeks of reentry makes it clear that many former prisoners return to drug use almost immediately.

Relapse in the longer term is strongly associated with rearrest and return to prison. Bruce Western's (2018) immersive investigation of reentry in the greater Boston area found that substance use was the strongest predictor of recidivism. Half of former prisoners with histories of substance abuse problems reported substance use in the year after release. Their rate of reincarceration was twice that of the full sample and thrice that of individuals with substance abuse histories who did not relapse. Some sample members were returned to prison simply for failure to stay drug free—not for new crimes. This practice illustrates that the criminal justice system heaps additional punishment on drug-involved offenders, rather than recognizing that relapse is part and parcel of drug addiction (Chandler, Fletcher, and Volkow 2009).

A large body of research confirms the relationship between drug use and recidivism (e.g., Gendreau, Little, and Goggin 1996; Bonta, Law, and Hanson 1998), but this relationship is nuanced. First, not all drug use is strongly associated with recidivism. For instance, use of marijuana, hallucinogens, sedatives, and alcohol by themselves did not predict recidivism in a cohort of former prisoners in Sweden, but polysubstance, amphetamine, and heroin use were predictive (Håkansson and Berglund 2012). Second, while recidivism rates are higher among males, the relationship between drug relapse and recidivism is stronger among females (Dowden and Brown 2002). Third, research from Australia, Sweden, and the United States finds that conditions associated with drug use disorders, namely, housing instability, mental health problems, and intravenous drug use, are independently positively associated with recidivism. Håkansson and Berglund's (2012) study of inmates released from prisons in Sweden found higher recidivism among individuals using drugs intravenously, recently experiencing housing instability, and with a history of in-patient psychiatric treatment (also see Baldry et al. 2004; Genberg et al. 2015; Winter et al. 2019).

At the community level, the return of drug-involved individuals leads to increased transmission of blood-borne diseases. This is not surprising. The prevalence of blood-borne diseases including HIV, viral hepatitis, and tuberculosis is everywhere substantially higher among drug-involved individuals than in the general population. Effective treatments exist for these conditions, and the two conditions can be cured, but many ex-prisoners have not received treatments in prison and do not have access to treatment in the community. As a result, ex-prisoners transmit blood-borne diseases in the community through sexual activity, tattooing, needle sharing, and in utero (Dolan et al. 2016). High rates of transmissible diseases are thus a direct by-product of reinvigorated criminalization of drug offenses and punitive responses to crime.

III. Prison-Based Drug Interventions and Their Effectiveness

The promise of effective prison-based drug treatment is nearly boundless. The clustering of individuals with drug problems provides an opportunity to break cycles of uncontrolled drug use, drug-related offending, and reincarceration and to address mental and physical health problems associated with heavy drug use. Successful prison-based treatment can reduce recidivism, which is strikingly high among offenders with serious drug problems, and reduce fatal and nonfatal overdose levels.

Yet, even under ideal conditions with bountiful resources and highly motivated clientele, treating individuals with drug abuse disorders is difficult. Prisons are not ideal locations for treatment generally but are in some ways well suited for drug interventions. The inconsistent availability of drugs can motivate treatment engagement and facilitate efforts to achieve abstinence. Prisoners have a wealth of time available for drug and mental health treatment activities. Prisons can also provide incentives to motivate participants such as housing that provides increased amenities or privileges or even reductions in sentence length.

A. Drug Treatment in Prisons

A variety of programs are commonly offered. They vary in methods but share aims of reducing drug use, drug-related offending, and associated health problems. Prison-based programs include drug education, drug detoxification, cognitive behavioral therapy, peer-led self-help groups (e.g., Alcoholics Anonymous, Narcotics Anonymous), group counseling, TCs, MOUD, and various combinations.

Drug education, detoxification, and peer-led self-help programs are largely self-explanatory. Prison-based drug education programs teach inmates about drug use disorders and the harms associated with drug use and dependence. Participation is often required for individuals assessed as having drug abuse histories (Leukefeld and Tims 1993). Peer-led self-help programs, typically based on the 12 steps of Alcoholics or Narcotics Anonymous, are ubiquitous. Self-help programs are networks formed by current and recovering substance-dependent individuals. Together, they meet to discuss and try to solve common problems, provide fellowship, and provide mutual support to efforts to become drug abstinent. Detoxification refers to health care services that help manage withdrawal. Discontinuing use of drugs such as cocaine, stimulants, and hallucinogens is not typically associated with florid withdrawal symptoms; detoxification can be accomplished by use of psychological and counseling services. Halting the use of alcohol or opioids, however, involves more drastic withdrawal symptoms that often require use of medication. While drug education programs usually target individuals assessed as having low-level drug abuse histories, 12-step and detoxification programs target individuals with substance dependencies. Drug education, 12-step, and detoxification programs are widely available but typically are not used as standalones for incarcerated people with serious drug problems; they are often combined with other more intensive interventions.

Cognitive behavioral therapy is another commonplace option. It aims to reduce uncontrolled drug use by fostering long-term thinking patterns and developing effective coping strategies. Such programs teach participants to anticipate the consequences of their behaviors, to recognize the early signs of drug cravings and environments likely to induce them, and to craft techniques for managing cravings and avoiding high-risk environments. Cognitive behavioral programs are sometimes used as standalones but are often integrated into other treatment modalities.

Drug counseling programs are multifaceted. They rely on combinations of group and individual sessions, cognitive behavioral and life skills training, drug education, and self-help groups. They are typically provided on an intensive outpatient basis; participants are housed in the general prison population but meet regularly for counseling sessions. Less common are inpatient programs that set aside separate housing units for participants. They usually last 30–90 days and are led by trained substance abuse counselors.

TCs are comprehensive, long-term, and residential. Participants are housed in separate units in an effort to establish a milieu focused on holistic personal reformation. TCs view drug abuse as symptomatic of underlying personal and psychological disorders, rather than as itself being the central problem requiring treatment. TC programming thus is aimed broadly at multiple problems affecting dependent prisoners including prior abuse, trauma, personality disorders, and mental health conditions. Tending to the underlying problems takes considerable time, and as a result TC programs typically last 6–12 months. Correctional staff supervise them, but they are largely run by their residents. In successful programs, residents actively nurture the treatment environment, monitor each other's behavior for compliance with program rules, maintain order, and steer treatment sessions. Residents are expected both to support one another's efforts at personal reformation and to be highly confrontational with wayward residents.

MOUD programs offer therapies for individuals with opioid use disorders. Currently, three medications are used: methadone, buprenorphine, and naltrexone. Methadone and buprenorphine are opioid substitutes that prevent withdrawal symptoms and reduce cravings. Naltrexone, by contrast, blocks opioid receptors in the nervous system and prevents euphoric highs; some studies suggest it reduces cravings (SAMHSA 2019). MOUD treatments, by reducing cravings and preventing withdrawal, should in theory lead to reductions in drug injecting, needle sharing, drug-related crime, overdoses, and transmission of blood-borne diseases.

Outside of incarcerative settings, a robust research base demonstrates that MOUD treatments, particularly methadone and buprenorphine, enhance treatment retention (Fullerton et al. 2014; Weinstein et al. 2017) and reduce illicit opioid use (Mattick et al. 2009). In prisons, MOUD treatments have several different uses including easing withdrawal symptoms of addicted incoming prisoners, continuing treatment for prisoners involved in MOUD programs before prison admission, and beginning new therapy before release that is intended to continue in the community.

These major modalities are often combined in prison or in community-based aftercare. Given the multiple challenges confronting drug-dependent prisoners and the general difficulty in overcoming drug dependence, using multiple modalities and extending treatment after release should enhance effectiveness. A growing body of research investigates the effectiveness of combining treatments in different contexts, such as group counseling in prison and MOUD treatment after release.

B. The Effectiveness of Prison-Based Treatment Programs

A voluminous body of research evaluates the effects of the drug treatment in prisons. A sizable proportion compares the relative effectiveness of a particular treatment to one or more alternatives. Another portion assesses the effects of drug treatment by comparing the experiences of participants who complete the program to those who did not. While these studies are important and informative, the clearest way to isolate treatment effects is to compare postrelease drug use and recidivism of participants in prison-based drug treatment programs to those of nonparticipants who received no treatment or treatment as usual. Such studies are sufficiently rigorous to support conclusions about effectiveness. Thus, I focus mainly on studies comparing treatment to no treatment or treatment as usual.

Numerous high-quality reviews summarize this literature (Pearson and Lipton 1999; Mitchell, Wilson, and MacKenzie 2012; Doyle et al. 2019; Strange et al. 2022). They cover evaluations made in different periods, but their results are largely consistent. Notably, evaluations of drug education, detoxification, self-help groups, and cognitive behavior therapy as standalones are too limited to support an effectiveness conclusion; I do not discuss them. They are, however, often key components of the three modalities most commonly evaluated: group counseling, TCs, and MOUD programs.

I also discuss therapies that combine modalities or are combined with postrelease care in the community. Much of my discussion draws from meta-analyses. They typically measure effects of program participation as a *positive effect size* whenever the treatment group of interest has a *more favorable* outcome than the comparison group. For example, if the treatment group has a lower rate of drug use than the comparison group—a more favorable outcome—the coded effect size will be positive. In short, all positive effect sizes indicate a better result for the treatment group.

1. *Therapeutic Communities.* TCs have been evaluated most extensively and rigorously. Mitchell and colleagues identified 35 independent contrasts

between participation in a TC and no treatment or treatment as usual. Most of this research was methodologically weak in terms of internal validity: 37 percent of coded contrasts employed either a rigorous quasi-experimental (31 percent) or an experimental design (6 percent). The remaining 61 percent were rated as standard or weak quasi experiments. Taken as a whole, the TC evaluations found strong support for reduction in recidivism measured by rearrest, reconviction, or reincarceration. Participation reduced the odds of recidivism by 40 percent relative to the comparison group over follow-ups of varying length, typically 3 years or less. Importantly, the two most rigorous studies that used experimental designs found stronger evidence of effectiveness; the average effect was a 90 percent reduction in the odds of recidivism compared with no treatment or treatment as usual.

The effects of TC participation on recidivism are long lasting. Inciardi, Martin, and Butzin's (2004) analysis of a Delaware program estimated that treatment participation increased the odds of being arrest-free by 60 percent in the 5 years after release. More impressively, a follow-up extending the postrelease period to 18 years continued to find significant reduction in the likelihood of new arrests (Martin et al. 2011). Thus, the bulk of evaluations, even the most rigorous, find that TC programs suppress recidivism and that the effects persist for years.

The effects of TC participation on drug use are equivocal. There are considerably fewer studies of drug relapse than of recidivism, 13 versus 35 in Mitchell, Wilson, and MacKenzie's (2012) meta-analysis. The confidence interval (CI) of the average effect on drug relapse, expressed as an odds ratio, ranges from 0.92 to 1.93 with a mean of 1.33. This indicates that TC participation decreased the odds of relapse by 33 percent on average, but this finding was not statistically significant. Individual studies included in the meta-analysis produced conflicting results. Some found that TC participation substantially reduced relapse (e.g., Knight, Simpson, and Hiller 1999; Prendergast, Hall, and Wellisch 2003; Inciardi, Martin, and Butzin 2004), but the majority found smaller, non-statistically-significant effects.

In-prison TCs appear to be particularly effective in reducing recidivism when combined with aftercare in the community. Inciardi, Martin, and Butzin's (2004) 5-year postrelease evaluation found that people who completed both the in-prison and the aftercare components had the highest probability of remaining arrest free (48 percent) and drug free (26 percent). These probabilities were much lower among those who completed only the in-prison program (28 and 17 percent, respectively). Evaluations of TC programs in Pennsylvania (Welsh 2007) and Minnesota (Duwe 2010) produced similar findings. However, the Pennsylvania evaluation of in-prison TC combined with aftercare found no reduction in drug relapse, another demonstration of equivocal outcomes concerning post-release drug use.

While there is ample evidence that TC participation combined with aftercare enhances effectiveness, it is important to recall that self-selection bias may affect many of these studies (see Pelissier, Jones, and Cadigan 2007). Individuals often must agree to participate in both programs; those who successfully complete both may be atypical on difficult-to-measure traits such as motivation. As a result, it is possible that large positive effects reported in evaluations of TC plus aftercare may be upwardly biased. The Mitchell, Wilson, and MacKenzie (2012) quantitative synthesis compared in-prison-only TC programs with others that included mandatory aftercare; the comparison included all participants in both kinds of programs, not only program graduates, which minimizes the effects of some sources of self-selection. The TC programs that had mandatory aftercare produced only slightly larger effects on recidivism than those without mandatory aftercare. Therefore, caution warrants against making strong claims about the combined effects of these interventions.

One subtle but important finding was that TC programs that included only females had the largest effects on recidivism. Evaluations with all-female samples were, on average, estimated to lower the odds of recidivism by 65 percent compared with 36 percent in male-only samples and 23 percent in mixed samples. This supports a conclusion that TC programs are effective for both males and females and suggests but does not prove that programs for females are more effective.

2. Group-Based Counseling. Another sizable number of evaluations assess in-prison group-based counseling. They most often conclude that participants have statistically lower recidivism rates than nonparticipants. For example, 54 percent (14 of 26) of these evaluations in Mitchell, Wilson, and MacKenzie's (2012) meta-analysis found statistically significant differences favoring counseling; the overall mean odds ratio effect size was 1.53 with a 95 percent CI of 1.20 to 1.94. This suggests that the odds of recidivism were 53 percent smaller on average for participants in counseling programs than for nonparticipants. While this may seem impressive, most of the evaluations are methodologically weak, and positive findings came almost entirely from less rigorous evaluations. The recidivism-suppressing effects declined systematically as methodological rigor increased. The two randomized experimental evaluations found that participation did not meaningfully lower recidivism rates.

The literature does not provide compelling evidence of counseling programs' effectiveness in lowering postrelease drug relapse. The knowledge base is small; only three evaluations measure program participation's relationship with relapse. There are thus too few studies to support strong conclusions. The three studies exhibited CIs ranging from 0.35 to 1.70 with a mean of 0.77. This could suggest that counseling program participants on average had somewhat higher rates of drug relapse than nonparticipants, but this difference was not reliable.

3. *MOUD.* Methadone maintenance has been available since the 1960s in community settings (Murray 1998). There is considerable evidence outside of prison settings that MOUDs reduce illicit opioid use and increase treatment engagement (see, e.g., Moore et al. 2019). Yet, until recently, only a small number of studies assessed their effects in incarcerative settings. Since 2019, however, at least three meta-analyses of MOUD evaluations in correctional settings (Moore et al. 2019; Boksán et al. 2022; Strange et al. 2022) have appeared. There was one earlier systematic review (Hedrich et al. 2012). These analyses differ in periods covered and in eligibility criteria. For instance, Moore et al.'s synthesis of recidivism studies focused primarily on experimental studies of methadone maintenance; the others also included studies with quasi-experimental designs. Boksán et al. excluded studies that examined the effects of naltrexone (which has distinctly different pharmacodynamics compared with opioid substitution medications).

Despite their differences, these reviews—with one important exception— yield similar findings. The most consistent is that MOUD participants are much more likely to engage in treatment after release (Hedrich et al. 2012; Moore et al. 2019; Boksán et al. 2022). Those who received MOUD treatments in prison had 200 percent greater odds of treatment engagement after release than did members of comparison groups (Boksán et al. 2022). MOUD participants were less likely to use opioids, use other drugs, inject drugs, and share needles in the community (Hedrich et al. 2012; Moore et al. 2019; Boksán et al. 2022).

Moore et al. (2019) estimated that MOUD programs reduced the odds of illicit opioid use and injection drug use in the community by roughly 75 percent each. Hedrich and colleagues' (2012) also found that participants in MOUD treatments had lower drug use during imprisonment than did the comparison groups. These reviews, however, do not find that MOUD programs reduced fatal overdoses or overall mortality (Hedrich et al. 2012; Strange et al. 2022). However, nonfatal overdoses appear to be significantly reduced (Strange et al. 2022).

Notably, these reviews reach divergent conclusions about recidivism effects. Two of the meta-analyses (Moore et al. 2019; Strange et al. 2022) found that individuals involved in MOUD programs did not have lower risk of recidivism. Strange and colleagues' synthesis of 16 studies found that MOUD program participation did not significantly reduce risk of reincarceration (mean odds ratio = 0.93; 95 percent CI = 0.68–1.26) or rearrest (mean odds ratio = 1.47; 95 percent CI = 0.70–3.07). Hedrich and colleagues' qualitative systematic review concluded that the effects of MOUD on recidivism were "equivocal" (2012, p. 501). However, the most recent meta-analysis (Boksán et al. 2022) concluded that MOUD program participants were less likely to have been reincarcerated than comparison group members (mean odds ratio = 1.98; 95 percent CI = 1.28–3.05). This finding, however, is tempered by the fact that the effect of MOUD programming was statistically smaller in the more rigorous studies using experimental designs. They did not find lower recidivism among MOUD program participants.

Several conclusions can be offered about the effectiveness of the three most common standalone in-prison drug treatment programs. Only TC programs have consistent and long-lasting effects in suppressing recidivism, and these effects are found even in evaluations with the strongest research designs. Most TC evaluations also find that program participation lowers postrelease drug use, but this finding is equivocal as a sizable minority of evaluations indicate no difference in drug relapse. By contrast, there is compelling evidence that in-prison MOUD programs lessen illicit opioid use and injection drug use but do not lower risk of fatal drug overdose and probably do not lower recidivism risk. Group-based counseling programs produce the weakest effects. Evaluations, particularly strong ones, find that counseling programs have no meaningful effect on drug relapse or recidivism.

Given the many co-occurring disorders and problems associated with serious drug problems, these conclusions should not be surprising. Group-based counseling is insufficiently intensive and too short to treat drug use disorders successfully, let alone address the mental health disorders and housing instability that often contribute to drug use disorders and vice versa. At best, counseling programs may be appropriate for incarcerated individuals with minor drug use problems. MOUD programs are effective in reducing illicit opioid use but typically do not provide the intensive and long-lasting interventions needed to tackle the criminal thinking, mental health, or housing instability problems associated with criminal behavior and serious drug problems. Only TCs among widely available, prison-based interventions provide long-lasting, extensive, and intensive services to address the multiple problems driving drug use disorders. Many TC participants, either voluntarily or mandatorily, continue residential treatment in the community and in doing so obtain at least short-term housing stability. The core features of TC programs make them well suited to tackle obstacles confronting incarcerated individuals with serious drug problems.

C. Access and Barriers to Drug Treatment

The sheer number of drug-involved people in the world's prisons is clear evidence of the need for effective drug treatment. There is, however, little research detailing the proportion of those in need who receive services and the type of services received. The United States is the only country that regularly collects this information in periodic surveys of nationally representative samples of prisoners. The 2016 survey estimated that 397,500 state prisoners had substance use disorders (alcohol or drug). One-third had received any type of substance abuse treatment; many had participated in multiple programs (Maruschak, Bronson, and Alper 2021). The most common "treatments" were peer-led self-help programs (27 percent) and drug education (23.5 percent); nearly all prisoners with substance use disorders in treatment participated in one of these two program types. Twenty percent of prisoners with substance use disorders indicated that they had participated in more demanding forms of treatment; 12 percent in a residential facility or unit for drug treatment (e.g., TCs, drug-free units), 10 percent engaged in counseling with a substance abuse specialist, 1.7 percent in a detoxification program, and 0.9 percent received a maintenance drug (i.e., MOUD).

These statistics highlight the large difference between the numbers of inmates who need treatment and who receive it. This gap grows further when only the treatment programs established as effective in the evidence base are considered. Just 12 percent of inmates with substance use disorders reported participation in residential programs, such as TCs, that reduce recidivism, and less than 1 percent were administered maintenance drugs that lower illicit opioid use in the community.

This stark treatment gap results primarily from lack of access to programming. As a rule, prisons throughout the world are underresourced. With their limited resources prison officials must simultaneously attend to security issues outside the prison, safety issues inside it, and the health care needs of prisoners. The low availability of drug treatments, especially more intensive ones, demonstrates clearly that administrators prioritize security and safety issues over health care. In many parts of the world, drug treatment is a peripheral concern.

It is also important to understand that the focus on security and safety creates mind-sets that devalue efforts at treatment and rehabilitation. Cultural resistance to rehabilitative programs is a consistent theme in the literature on implementation. Corrections staff often do not highly value treatment services for prisoners, which inevitably causes or exacerbates difficulties in treatment delivery (e.g., Farabee et al. 1999). Although many European Union nations have adopted in-prison MOUD services, prisons in the United States and other parts of the world have been reluctant for ideological reasons to establish opioid replacement programs. Only two small US states (Rhode Island and Hawaii) of 46 states studied made all three opioid medications available, 16 states relied solely on naltrexone, and the remaining 28 offered no opioid medications (Lopez 2018). These findings suggest that increasing funding and access to programming may not be enough unless vigorous efforts are made to change cultural norms among prison staff.

IV. Implications

I began this essay by noting that substance abuse and imprisonment have long been associated. That association in recent decades has been strengthened by policy choices in many countries that markedly increased the proportions of people imprisoned for drug offenses and drug-related offenses. If policy choices exacerbated the drugs-crime connection, however, alternative policy decisions could ameliorate it. The literature I have summarized reveals notable gaps in knowledge. Many arise from a widely held view that societal drug abuse is a problem that can be solved rather than a long-term chronic problem that requires management. Adoption of approaches that align with harm reduction principles would have important implications for drug policy, interventions, and research.

My most fundamental and essential conclusion is that drug policies that aim to achieve abstinence through punishment have failed. The United

States provides the clearest evidence. In 1988, the federal government declared "it to be U.S. policy to create a drug-free society by 1995" (Anti–Drug Abuse Act of 1988, H.R. 5210, 100th Cong.). The United States sought to achieve this goal by arresting, prosecuting, and incarcerating ever-growing numbers of people convicted of drug offenses and of drug-involved individuals. That required huge investment in law enforcement. Investment in treatment has been meager. Despite huge investments in punitive approaches for dealing with drug abuse, the US rate of drug use disorders is the world's highest, and the rate of fatal drug overdoses is at historically unprecedented levels. The punitive American approach has only exacerbated drug problems.

The necessary first step is to reject the naive goal of drug abstinence at a societal level. No modern society has achieved this goal, even in countries with extreme punishments for minor drug crimes. Iran, for instance, permits capital punishment for simple drug possession, but illicit drugs continue to be used and abused (see, e.g., Noorbala et al. 2020). The fatal flaw is in treating societal drug problems as crime problems rather that as public health priorities. Punishment-based approaches may not solve drug problems, but they do stigmatize people. This exacerbates community drug problems because it compels people to conceal their addictions, and as a result they often go untreated.

Real-world drug policy must acknowledge that drug abuse is an intractable societal problem that can be exacerbated or ameliorated by drug policy but not solved. There will always be people with drug problems who, because of the relationships between uncontrolled drug use and crime, will be disproportionately present in the world's prisons. Because drug use disorders are closely associated with other problems such as mental health disorders and housing instability, effective policies and interventions will need to target the health and social functioning of the whole person.

Punitive approaches lead to a narrow focus on abstinence and recidivism as the key measures of policy effectiveness. This is what the effectiveness literature has overwhelmingly investigated. These outcomes are important, but so are other more direct, comprehensive, and nuanced outcomes. Future effectiveness research needs to consider overall mortality, mortality from drug use, nonfatal overdoses, emergency room visits, blood-borne disease infection, and other characteristics of drug-involved people. Social functioning as measured by family engagement, housing stability, and employment also need to taken into account. Unlike the dichotomous measures currently employed—recidivism or not, abstainer or not—the most useful measures will be more precise (e.g., number of events of interest in a given period) if they are to capture improvements and setbacks in health and social functioning.

Harm reduction approaches that aim to minimize risks and negative consequences associated with drug use best embody these principles. An array of treatment services is needed to treat the whole person, and access to treatment needs to be expanded and made available to those who are ready to quit or to reduce their drug use. For those not ready to desist, other harm reduction interventions provide tools to reduce the individual- and community-level health consequences of heavy drug use and drug-using lifestyles (e.g., distribution of clean needles, safer sex supplies, safe drug use sites) and to teach people how to mitigate negative health consequences (e.g., needle cleaning techniques). Harm reduction strategies recognize that interventions must address more than drug use. Homeless people may need to secure stable housing before their drug disorders can be effectively managed. An expanding body of research finds that harm reduction strategies enhance social functioning and mitigate health consequences (e.g., DeBeck et al. 2011; Fernandes et al. 2017; Kennedy et al. 2022). Harm reduction is the dominant guiding drug policy paradigm in the European Union and is prominent in Canada (Harm Reduction International 2020).

The principles of harm reduction are amenable to institutional and community corrections contexts, but successfully applying them will require that provision of high-quality treatment services be given at least as high a priority as security and control. Correctional staff may need to be retrained or replaced with individuals who recognize the value of both treatment and security. This shift may also require agencies to incentivize incarcerated people to engage in, and maintain participation in, treatment programming (e.g., by increasing prison good time or increasing prison amenities for treatment participants).

Full integration of harm reduction principles will require the criminal justice system to assess the risks and needs of each individual more carefully. Individuals who pose low risks to public safety but have significant treatment needs should be diverted from jails and prisons into appropriate community-based treatment. Individuals posing higher risks and with significant treatment needs will need in-prison services that match the intensity of their assessed needs. Prisons will need to expand treatment access significantly, especially to intensive services such as TCs. Last, given record numbers of fatal drug overdoses, prisons should make opioid antagonists (e.g., naloxone) readily available.

Upon reentry, there is an urgent need to link released prisoners immediately to high-quality community services. The clearest evidence of this need is the high rate of fatal drug overdoses. Despite the astonishingly high rate of fatal overdose in the first 2 weeks, most individuals with opioid disorders do not receive MOUD treatment in prison, and many who do cannot continue upon release (Green et al. 2018). The Rhode Island Department of Corrections is an exception. Starting in July 2016, all people with opioid disorders exiting prisons were referred to a community-based provider that continued to dispense opioid medications. A preliminary evaluation found that, compared with a period before program implementation, fatal drug overdoses over 12 months fell by 60 percent (Green et al. 2018). And as noted above, there is ample evidence that in-prison TC participants are less likely to recidivate if their treatment continues in the community (e.g., Inciardi, Martin, and Butzin 2004; Welsh 2007; Duwe 2010). These findings illustrate that linked in-prison and postrelease treatment programs can improve health and reduce recidivism. The US federal government recently acknowledged this by funding the Justice Community Opioid Use Innovation Network to improve access to evidence-based opioid addiction treatments throughout the justice system and to develop new treatments (Ducharme et al. 2021). Increasing numbers of comprehensive reentry programs incorporate harm reduction principles and show preliminary promise. One example, the ComALERT (Community and Law Enforcement Resources Together) program, provides drug treatment, transitional housing, employment, and referrals to mental health care and other services as needed to people returning to Brooklyn from New York prisons (Jacobs and Western 2007). The services are offered within days of release and last up to 1 year. These wraparound services are well suited to treating the whole person, while providing basic resources (housing, employment) that enable individuals to concentrate on their current wellness and future success. Unsurprisingly, an evaluation finds that, compared with nonparticipants with similar criminal histories, ComALERT participants had lower rearrest rates, unemployment, and drug use. However, participants and nonparticipants did not significantly differ on markers of family well-being such as marriage, cohabitation, or contact with their children (Jacobs and Western 2007).

The ComALERT program and evaluation exemplify key elements needed in the next generation of drug evaluation research. Interventions and policies need to be long-term and comprehensive if they are to combat multiple problems. And they need to be made available immediately upon release. The ComALERT evaluation used a multi-outcome approach to capture changes in social functioning. This is essential in evaluating interventions consistent with the harm reduction approach.

The next generation of drug policy interventions and evaluations is emerging unevenly around the world. Harm reduction strategies, such as needle distribution or exchange programs, safe injection sites, and easy access to naloxone, have been widely adopted in Australia, Canada, and the European Union. Some inroads have been made in the United States; for instance, the first supervised injection site in the nation opened in New York City in 2021 (18 years after Canada opened its first site),[5] needle exchange programs are now legal in a majority of states (but are haphazardly distributed across the country), and naloxone is widely available to first responders (but not to the general public). Aside from these limited successes, harm reduction strategies have not been fully embraced. Harm reduction interventions are similarly infrequent in Africa, Asia, and Latin America (Harm Reduction International 2020). Instead, drug policy in much of the world continues primarily to criminalize drug problems in pursuit of the impossible dream of a drug-free society.

REFERENCES

Adler, Rachel H. 2021. "The Nexus of Homelessness and Incarceration: The Case of Homeless Men in Trenton, NJ." *Journal of Men's Studies* 29:335–53.
Anthony, James C., Lynn A. Warner, and Ronald C. Kessler. 1994. "Comparative Epidemiology of Dependence on Tobacco, Alcohol, Controlled Substances, and Inhalants: Basic Findings from the National Comorbidity Survey." *Experimental and Clinical Psychopharmacology* 2:244–68.
Baldry, Eileen, Desmond McDonnell, Peter Maplestone, and Manu Peters. 2004. *The Role of Housing in Preventing Re-offending*. Melbourne: Australian Housing and Urban Research Institute.
Baranyi, Gergő, Seena Fazel, Sabine Delhey Langerfeldt, and Adrian P. Mundt. 2022. "The Prevalence of Comorbid Serious Mental Illnesses and Substance Use Disorders in Prison Populations: A Systematic Review and Meta-analysis." *Lancet Public Health* 7:e557–e568.

[5] The first supervised injection site, the Insite program, began in Vancouver, Canada, in 2003.

Bell, Victoria, and Maggie Leese. 2021. "Increased Security Measures in a Drug Re-
covery Prison: Disrupting the Drug Supply." *Prison Service Journal* 252:31–38.

Bennett, Trevor. 2002. "England and Wales." In *I-ADAM in Eight Countries:
Approaches and Challenges*, edited by Bruce Taylor. Washington, DC: US Department of Justice, National Institute of Justice.

Bennett, Trevor, and Katy Holloway. 2009. "The Causal Connection between
Drug Misuse and Crime." *British Journal of Criminology* 49:513–31.

Binswanger, Ingrid A., Marc F. Stern, Richard A. Deyo, Patrick J. Heagerty,
Allen Cheadle, Joann G. Elmore, and Thomas D. Koepsell. 2007. "Release
from Prison: A High Risk of Death for Former Inmates." *New England Journal
of Medicine* 356:157–65.

Boksán, K., M. Dechant, M. Weiss, A. Hellwig, and M. Stemmler. 2022. "A Meta-
analysis on the Effects of Incarceration-Based Opioid Substitution Treatment."
Medicine, Science and the Law. https://doi.org/10.1177/00258024221118971.

Bonta, James, Moira Law, and Karl Hanson. 1998. "The Prediction of Criminal
and Violent Recidivism among Mentally Disordered Offenders: A Meta-
analysis." *Psychological Bulletin* 123:123–42.

Borrill, J., A. Maden, A. Martin, T. Weaver, G. Stimson, M. Farrell, and T.
Barnes. 2003. *Differential Substance Misuse, Treatment Needs of Women, Ethnic
Minorities, and Young Offenders in Prison*. London: Home Office.

Boys, Annabel, Michael Farrell, P. Bebbington, T. Brugha, J. Coid, R. Jenkins,
G. Lewis, J. Marsden, H. Meltzer, N. Singleton, and C. Taylor. 2002. "Drug
Use and Initiation in Prison: Results from a National Prison Survey in
England and Wales." *Addiction* 97:1551–60.

Boyum, David, and Peter Reuter. 2005. *An Analytic Assessment of U.S. Drug Policy*.
Washington, DC: AEI.

Broidy, Lisa M., Jason Payne, and Alex R. Piquero. 2018. "Making Sense of Heterogeneity in the Influence of Childhood Abuse, Mental Health, and Drug
Use on Women's Offending Pathways." *Criminal Justice and Behavior* 45:
1565–87.

Bronson, Jennifer, Jessica Stroop, Stephanie Zimmer, and Marcus Berzofsky.
2017. *Drug Use, Dependence, and Abuse among State Prisoners and Jail Inmates,
2007–2009*. Washington, DC: US Department of Justice, Bureau of Justice
Statistics.

Bukten, Anne, Marianne Riksheim Stavseth, Svetlana Skurtveit, Aage Tverdal,
John Strang, and Thomas Clausen. 2017. "High Risk of Overdose Death Following Release from Prison: Variations in Mortality during a 15-Year Observation Period." *Addiction* 112:1432–39.

Bushnell, John A., and Leon W. Bakker. 1997. "Substance Use Disorders among
Men in Prison: A New Zealand Study." *Australian and New Zealand Journal of
Psychiatry* 31:577–81.

Butler, Tony, Devon Indig, Stephen Allnutt, and Hassan Mamoon. 2011. "Co-
occurring Mental Illness and Substance Use Disorder among Australian
Prisoners." *Drug and Alcohol Review* 30:188–94.

Calzavara, Liviana, Nancy Ramuscak, Ann N. Burchell, Carol Swantee, Ted
Myers, Peter Ford, Margaret Fearon, and Sue Raymond. 2007. "Prevalence

of HIV and Hepatitis C Virus Infections among Inmates of Ontario Remand Facilities." *Canadian Medical Association Journal* 177:257–61.

Calzavara, Liviana M., Ann N. Burchell, Julia Schlossberg, Ted Myers, Michael Escobar, Evelyn Wallace, Carol Major, Carol Strike, and Margaret Millson. 2003. "Prior Opiate Injection and Incarceration History Predict Injection Drug Use among Inmates." *Addiction* 98:1257–65.

Caris, Luis, and Bruce Taylor. 2002. "Chile." In *I-ADAM in Eight Countries: Approaches and Challenges*, edited by Bruce Taylor. Washington, DC: US Department of Justice, National Institute of Justice.

Carpentier, Chloé, Luis Royuela, Linda Montanari, and Philip Davis. 2018. "The Global Epidemiology of Drug Use in Prison." In *Drug Use in Prisoners: Epidemiology, Implications, and Policy Responses*, edited by Stuart A. Kinner and Josiah D. Rich. New York: Oxford University Press.

Carpentier, Chloé, Luis Royuela, André Noor, and Dagmar Hedrich. 2012. "Ten Years of Monitoring Illicit Drug Use in Prison Populations in Europe: Issues and Challenges." *Howard Journal of Criminal Justice* 51:37–66.

Carson, E. Ann. 2021. *Mortality in State and Federal Prisons, 2001–2019: Statistical Tables*. Washington, DC: US Department of Justice, Bureau of Justice Statistics.

Chaiken, Jan M., and Marcia R. Chaiken. 1990. "Drugs and Predatory Crime." In *Drugs and Crime*, edited by Michael Tonry and James Q. Wilson. Vol. 13 of *Crime and Justice: A Review of Research*, edited by Michael Tonry. Chicago: University of Chicago Press.

Chandler, Redonna K., Bennett W. Fletcher, and Nora D. Volkow. 2009. "Treating Drug Abuse and Addiction in the Criminal Justice System: Improving Public Health and Safety." *Journal of the American Medical Association* 301:183–90.

Chen, Kevin, and Denise B. Kandel. 1995. "The Natural History of Drug Use from Adolescence to the Mid-Thirties in a General Population Sample." *American Journal of Public Health* 85:41–47.

Coghlan, Sarah, Alexandra Gannoni, Susan Goldsmid, Eileen Patterson, and Matthew Willis. 2015. *Drug Use Monitoring in Australia: 2013–14 Report on Drug Use among Police Detainees*. Canberra: Australian Institute of Criminology.

Cunningham, Evan B., Behzad Hajarizadeh, Janaki Amin, Neil Bretana, Gregory J. Dore, Louisa Degenhardt, Sarah Larney, Fabio Luciani, Andrew R. Lloyd, and Jason Grebely. 2018. "Longitudinal Injecting Risk Behaviours among People with a History of Injecting Drug Use in an Australian Prison Setting: The HITS-P Study." *International Journal of Drug Policy* 54:18–25.

DeBeck, Kora, Thomas Kerr, Lorna Bird, Ruth Zhang, David Marsh, Mark Tyndall, Julio Montaner, and Evan Wood. 2011. "Injection Drug Use Cessation and Use of North America's First Medically Supervised Safer Injecting Facility." *Drug and Alcohol Dependence* 113:172–76.

Dolan, Kate. 1999. *The Epidemiology of Hepatitis C Infection in Prison Population*. Sydney: National Drug and Alcohol Research Centre.

Dolan, Kate, Effat Merghati Khoei, Cinzia Brentari, and Alex Stevens. 2007. *Prisons and Drugs: A Global Review of Incarceration, Drug Use and Drug Services*. Oxford: Beckley Foundation, Drug Policy Programme.

Dolan, Kate, Ben Kite, Emma Black, Carmen Aceijas, and Gerry V. Stimson. 2007. "HIV in Prison in Low-Income and Middle-Income Countries." *Lancet Infectious Diseases* 7:32–41.

Dolan, Kate, Andrea L. Wirtz, Babak Moazen, Martial Ndeffo-mbah, Alison Galvani, Stuart A. Kinner, Ryan Courtney, Martin McKee, Joseph J. Amon, Lisa Maher, Margaret Hellard, Chris Beyrer, and Fredrick L. Altice. 2016. "Global Burden of HIV, Viral Hepatitis, and Tuberculosis in Prisoners and Detainees." *Lancet* 388:1089–102.

Dowden, Craig, and Shelley L. Brown. 2002. "The Role of Substance Abuse Factors in Predicting Recidivism: A Meta-analysis." *Psychology, Crime and Law* 8:243–64.

Doyle, Michael F, Anthony Shakeshaft, Jill Guthrie, Mieke Snijder, and Tony Butler. 2019. "A Systematic Review of Evaluations of Prison-Based Alcohol and Other Drug Use Behavioural Treatment for Men." *Australian and New Zealand Journal of Public Health* 43:120–30.

Ducharme, Lori J., Tisha R. A. Wiley, Carrie F. Mulford, Zu-In Su, and Julia B. Zur. 2021. "Engaging the Justice System to Address the Opioid Crisis: The Justice Community Opioid Innovation Network (JCOIN)." *Journal of Substance Abuse Treatment* 128(108307):1–6.

Duwe, Grant. 2010. "Prison-Based Chemical Dependency Treatment in Minnesota: An Outcome Evaluation." *Journal of Experimental Criminology* 6:57–81.

Einarsson, Emil, Jon Fridrik Sigurdsson, Gisli H. Gudjonsson, Anna Kristin Newton, and Olafur Orn Bragason. 2009. "Screening for Attention-Deficit Hyperactivity Disorder and Co-morbid Mental Disorders among Prison Inmates." *Nordic Journal of Psychiatry* 63:361–67.

EMCDDA (European Monitoring Centre for Drugs and Drug Addiction). 2012. *Prisons and Drugs in Europe: The Problem and Responses*. Lisbon: EMCDDA.

Farabee, David, Vandana Joshi, and M. Douglas Anglin. 2001. "Addiction Careers and Criminal Specialization." *Crime and Delinquency* 47:196–220.

Farabee, David, Michael Prendergast, Jerome Cartier, Harry Wexler, Kevin Knight, and M. Douglas Anglin. 1999. "Barriers to Implementing Effective Correctional Drug Treatment Programs." *Prison Journal* 79:150–62.

Fazel, Seena, Julia Cartwright, Arabella Norman-Nott, and Keith Hawton. 2008. "Suicide in Prisoners: A Systematic Review of Risk Factors." *Journal of Clinical Psychiatry* 69:1721–31.

Fazel, Seena, and John Danesh. 2002. "Serious Mental Disorder in 23,000 Prisoners: A Systematic Review of 62 Surveys." *Lancet* 359:545–50.

Fazel, Seena, Isabel A. Yoon, and Adrian J. Hayes. 2017. "Substance Use Disorders in Prisoners: An Updated Systematic Review and Meta-regression Analysis in Recently Incarcerated Men and Women." *Addiction* 112:1725–39.

Fernandes, Ricardo M., Maria Cary, Gonçalo Duarte, Gonçalo Jesus, Joana Alarcão, Carla Torre, Suzete Costa, João Costa, and António Vaz Carneiro. 2017. "Effectiveness of Needle and Syringe Programmes in People Who Inject Drugs: An Overview of Systematic Reviews." *BMC Public Health* 17:1–15.

Feucht, Thomas E., and Andrew Keyser. 1999. "Reducing Drug Use in Prisons: Pennsylvania's Approach." *National Institute of Justice Journal* 241:10–15.

Fortuin, Judi. 1991. "Behind Bars: Risk Behaviours for HIV Transmission in Prisons, a Review." In *HIV/AIDS and Prisons : Proceedings of a Conference Held 19–21 November 1990*, edited by Jennifer Norberry, Matt Gaughwin, and Sally-Anne Gerull. Canberra: Australian Institute of Criminology.

Fullerton, Catherine Anne, Meelee Kim, Cindy Parks Thomas, D. Russell Lyman, Leslie B. Montejano, Richard H. Dougherty, Allen S. Daniels, Sushmita Shoma Ghose, and Miriam E. Delphin-Rittmon. 2014. "Medication-Assisted Treatment with Methadone: Assessing the Evidence." *Psychiatric Services* 65:146–57.

Genberg, Becky L., Jacquie Astemborski, David Vlahov, Gregory D. Kirk, and Shruti H Mehta. 2015. "Incarceration and Injection Drug Use in Baltimore, Maryland." *Addiction* 110:1152–59.

Gendreau, Paul, Tracy Little, and Claire Goggin. 1996. "A Meta-analysis of the Predictors of Adult Offender Recidivism: What Works!" *Criminology* 34:575–607.

Grant, Bridget F. 1996. "Prevalence and Correlates of Drug Use and DSM-IV Drug Dependence in the United States: Results of the National Longitudinal Alcohol Epidemiologic Survey." *Journal of Substance Abuse* 8:195–210.

Green, Traci C., Jennifer Clarke, Lauren Brinkley-Rubinstein, Brandon D. L. Marshall, Nicole Alexander-Scott, Rebecca Boss, and Josiah D. Rich. 2018. "Postincarceration Fatal Overdoses after Implementing Medications for Addiction Treatment in a Statewide Correctional System." *JAMA Psychiatry* 75:405–7.

Greenberg, Greg A., and Robert A. Rosenheck. 2008*a*. "Homelessness in the State and Federal Prison Population." *Criminal Behaviour and Mental Health* 18:88–103.

Greenberg, Greg A., and Robert A. Rosenheck. 2008*b*. "Jail Incarceration, Homelessness, and Mental Health: A National Study." *Psychiatric Services* 59:170–77.

Håkansson, Anders, and Mats Berglund. 2012. "Risk Factors for Criminal Recidivism: A Prospective Follow-Up Study in Prisoners with Substance Abuse." *BMC Psychiatry* 12:1–8.

Harm Reduction International. 2020. *The Global State of Harm Reduction, 2020*, 7th ed. London: Harm Reduction International.

Hedrich, Dagmar, Paula Alves, Michael Farrell, Heino Stöver, Lars Møller, and Soraya Mayet. 2012. "The Effectiveness of Opioid Maintenance Treatment in Prison Settings: A Systematic Review." *Addiction* 107:501–17.

Holsinger, Alexander. 2002. *National Institute of Corrections' Drug-Free Prison Zone Project: Evaluation Component for Each of Eight State Sites*. Washington, DC: US Bureau of Prisons, National Institute of Corrections.

Inciardi, James A., Steven S. Martin, and Clifford A. Butzin. 2004. "Five-Year Outcomes of Therapeutic Community Treatment of Drug-Involved Offenders after Release from Prison." *Crime and Delinquency* 50:88–107.

Jacobs, Erin, and Bruce Western. 2007. "Report on the Evaluation of the ComALERT Prisoner Reentry Program." Brooklyn, NY: Kings County District Attorney.

James, Doris J., and Lauren E. Glaze. 2006. *Mental Health Problems of Prison and Jail Inmates*. Washington, DC: US Department of Justice, Bureau of Justice Statistics.

Kandel, Denise, and Kazuo Yamaguchi. 1993. "From Beer to Crack: Developmental Patterns of Drug Involvement." *American Journal of Public Health* 83:851–55.

Keene, Jan. 1997. "Drug Misuse in Prison, Views from Inside: A Qualitative Study of Prison Staff and Inmates." *Howard Journal* 36:28–41.

Kennedy, Mary Clare, Kanna Hayashi, M.-J. Milloy, Miranda Compton, and Thomas Kerr. 2022. "Health Impacts of a Scale-Up of Supervised Injection Services in a Canadian Setting: An Interrupted Time Series Analysis." *Addiction* 117:986–97.

Kinner, Stuart A., Jessica George, Gabrielle Campbell, and Louisa Degenhardt. 2009. "Crime, Drugs and Distress: Patterns of Drug Use and Harm among Criminally Involved Injecting Drug Users in Australia." *Australian and New Zealand Journal of Public Health* 33:223–27.

Klerks, Peter, Janine Plaisier, and Willemijn Garnier. 2002. "The Netherlands." In *I-ADAM in Eight Countries: Approaches and Challenges*, edited by Bruce Taylor. Washington, DC: US Department of Justice, National Institute of Justice.

Knight, Kevin, D. Dwayne Simpson, and Matthew L. Hiller. 1999. "Three-Year Reincarceration Outcomes for In-Prison Therapeutic Community Treatment in Texas." *Prison Journal* 79:337–51.

Labouvie, Erich, and Helene R. White. 2002. "Drug Sequences, Age of Onset, and Use Trajectories as Predictors of Drug Abuse/Dependence in Young Adulthood." In *Stages and Pathways of Drug Involvement: Examining the Gateway Hypothesis*, edited by Denise B. Kandel. Cambridge: Cambridge University Press.

Leukefeld, Carl G., and Frank R. Tims. 1993. "Drug Abuse Treatment in Prisons and Jails." *Journal of Substance Abuse Treatment* 10:77–84.

Leung, Janni, Amy Peacock, Samantha Colledge, Jason Grebely, Evan B. Cunningham, Matthew Hickman, Peter Vickerman, Jack Stone, Adam Trickey, Kostyantyn Dumchev, Michael Lynskey, Lindsey Hines, Paul Griffiths, Richard P. Mattick, Louisa Degenhardt, and Sarah Larney. 2019. "A Global Meta-analysis of the Prevalence of HIV, Hepatitis C Virus, and Hepatitis B Virus among People Who Inject Drugs: Do Gender-Based Differences Vary by Country-Level Indicators?" *Journal of Infectious Diseases* 220:78–90.

Lopez, German. 2018. "How America's Prisons are Fueling the Opioid Epidemic." *Vox*, March 26. https://www.vox.com/policy-and-politics/2018/3/13/17020002/prison-opioid-epidemic-medications-addiction (accessed September 7, 2021).

Lopez-Quintero, Catalina, José Pérez de los Cobos, Deborah S. Hasin, Mayumi Okuda, Shuai Wang, Bridget F. Grant, and Carlos Blanco. 2011. "Probability and Predictors of Transition from First Use to Dependence on Nicotine, Alcohol, Cannabis, and Cocaine: Results of the National Epidemiologic Survey on Alcohol and Related Conditions (NESARC)." *Drug and Alcohol Dependence* 115:120–30.

Lynch, Shannon, Dana D. DeHart, Joanne Belknap, and Bonnie L. Green. 2013. *Women's Pathways to Jail: Examining Mental Health, Trauma, and Substance Abuse.* Washington, DC: US Department of Justice, Bureau of Justice Assistance.

Makkai, Toni, and Jason Payne. 2003. *Key Findings from the Drug Use Careers of Offenders (DUCO) Study.* Canberra: Australian Institute of Criminology.

March, Joan Carles, Eugenia Oviedo-Joekes, and Manuel Romero. 2006. "Drugs and Social Exclusion in Ten European Cities." *European Addiction Research* 12:33–41.

Marotta, Phillip. 2017. "Exploring Relationships between Delinquent Peer Groups, Participation in Delinquency, Substance Abuse, and Injecting Drug Use among the Incarcerated: Findings from a National Sample of State and Federal Inmates in the United States." *Journal of Drug Issues* 47:320–39.

Martin, Steven S., Daniel J. O'Connell, Raymond Paternoster, and Ronet D. Bachman. 2011. "The Long and Winding Road to Desistance from Crime for Drug-Involved Offenders: The Long-Term Influence of TC Treatment on Re-arrest." *Journal of Drug Issues* 41:179–96.

Maruschak, Laura M., Jennifer Bronson, and Mariel Alper. 2021. *Alcohol and Drug Use and Treatment Reported by Prisoners.* Washington, DC: US Department of Justice, Bureau of Justice Statistics.

Mattick, Richard P, Courtney Breen, Jo Kimber, and Marina Davoli. 2009. "Methadone Maintenance Therapy versus No Opioid Replacement Therapy for Opioid Dependence." *Cochrane Database of Systematic Reviews*, no. 3, CD002209. https://doi.org/10.1002/14651858.CD002209.pub2.

McKeganey, Neil, Clare Connelly, John Norrie, and Janusz Knepil. 2002. "Scotland." In *I-ADAM in Eight Countries: Approaches and Challenges*, edited by Bruce Taylor. Washington, DC: US Department of Justice, National Institute of Justice.

McNiel, Dale E., Renée L. Binder, and Jo C. Robinson. 2005. "Incarceration Associated with Homeless, Mental Disorder, and Co-occurring Substance Abuse." *Psychiatric Services* 56:840–46.

Merrall, Elizabeth L. C., Azar Kariminia, Ingrid A. Binswanger, Michael S. Hobbs, Michael Farrell, John Marsden, Sharon J. Hutchinson, and Sheila M. Bird. 2010. "Meta-analysis of Drug-Related Deaths Soon after Release from Prison." *Addiction* 105:1545–54.

Metraux, Stephen, Caterina G. Roman, and Richard S. Cho. 2007. "Incarceration and Homelessness." In *Toward Understanding Homelessness: The 2007 National Symposium on Homelessness Research*, edited by Deborah Dennis, Gretchen Locke, and Jill Khadduri. Washington, DC: US Department of Health and Human Services.

Mitchell, Ojmarrh. 2009. "Ineffectiveness, Financial Waste, and Unfairness: The Legacy of the War on Drugs." *Journal of Crime and Justice* 32:1–19.

Mitchell, Ojmarrh, David B. Wilson, and Doris Layton MacKenzie. 2012. *The Effectiveness of Incarceration-Based Drug Treatment on Criminal Behavior: A Systematic Review.* 2012 Update. Oslo: Campbell Collaboration, Crime and Justice Group.

Mogk, Jessica, Valerie Shmigol, Marvin Futrell, Bert Stover, and Amy Hagopian. 2019. "Court-Imposed Fines as a Feature of the Homelessness-Incarceration Nexus: A Cross-Sectional Study of the Relationship between Legal Debt and Duration of Homelessness in Seattle, Washington, USA." *Journal of Public Health Policy* 42:107–19.

Montanari, Linda, Luis Royuela, Liesbeth Vandam, Ines Hasselberg, and Dagmar Hedrich. 2020. *European Prisons and Drug Use*. Lisbon: European Monitoring Centre for Drugs and Drug Addiction.

Moore, Kelly E., Walter Roberts, Holly H. Reid, Kathryn M. Z. Smith, Lindsay M. S. Oberleitner, and Sherry A. McKee. 2019. "Effectiveness of Medication Assisted Treatment for Opioid Use in Prison and Jail Settings: A Meta-analysis and Systematic Review." *Journal of Substance Abuse Treatment* 99:32–43.

Morris, Richard. 2001. "Alcohol and Drugs: A Perspective from New Zealand." *Forum of Corrections Research* 13:18–19.

Moschion, Julie, and Guy Johnson. 2019. "Homelessness and Incarceration: A Reciprocal Relationship?" *Journal of Quantitative Criminology* 35:855–87.

Mumola, Christopher J., and Jennifer C. Karberg. 2006. *Drug Use and Dependence, State and Federal Prisoners, 2004*. Washington, DC: US Department of Justice, Bureau of Justice Statistics.

Murray, John B. 1998. "Effectiveness of Methadone Maintenance for Heroin Addiction." *Psychological Reports* 83:295–302.

Musto, David F. 1999. *The American Disease: Origins of Narcotic Control*, 3rd ed. New York: Oxford University Press.

NCASACU (National Center on Addiction and Substance Abuse at Columbia University). 2010. *Behind Bars II: Substance Abuse and America's Prison Population*. New York: NCASACU.

Nguyen, Holly, Greg Midgette, Thomas Loughran, and Yiwen Zhang. 2021. "Random Drug Testing in Prisons: Does a Little Testing Go a Long Way?" *Criminology and Public Policy* 20:329–49.

Noorbala, Ahmad Ali, Armita Saljoughian, Seyed Abbas Bagheri Yazdi, Elham Faghihzadeh, Mohammad Hadi Farahzadi, Koorosh Kamali, Soghrat Faghihzadeh, Ahmad Hajebi, Shahin Akhondzadeh, and Mir Taher Mousavi. 2020. "Evaluation of Drug and Alcohol Abuse in People Aged 15 Years and Older in Iran." *Iranian Journal of Public Health* 49:1940–46.

O'Hagan, Andrew, and Rachel Hardwick. 2017. "Behind Bars: The Truth about Drugs in Prisons." *Forensic Research and Criminology International Journal* 5:309–20.

ONDCP (Office of National Drug Control Policy). 2014. "2013 Annual Report, Arrestee Drug Abuse Monitoring Program II." Washington, DC: Executive Office of the President.

Paksi, B. 2009. *Drug Use among Convicted Detainees in Hungary in 2008*. Budapest: Institute of Behavioural Science and Communication Theory Centre of Behavioral Research, Corvinus University.

Palmateer, Norah E., Sharon J. Hutchinson, Hamish Innes, Christian Schnier, Olivia Wu, David J. Goldberg, and Matthew Hickman. 2013. "Review and Meta-analysis of the Association between Self-Reported Sharing of Needles/ Syringes and Hepatitis C Virus Prevalence and Incidence among People Who Inject Drugs in Europe." *International Journal of Drug Policy* 24:85–100.

Patterson, Raymond F., and Kerry Hughes. 2008. "Review of Completed Suicides in the California Department of Corrections and Rehabilitation, 1999 to 2004." *Psychiatric Services* 59:676–82.

Pearson, Frank S., and Douglas S. Lipton. 1999. "A Meta-analytic Review of the Effectiveness of Corrections-Based Treatment for Drug Abuse." *Prison Journal* 79:384–410.

Pelissier, Bernadette, Nicole Jones, and Timothy Cadigan. 2007. "Drug Treatment Aftercare in the Criminal Justice System: A Systematic Review." *Journal of Substance Abuse Treatment* 32:311–20.

Penfold, Clarissa, Paul J. Turnbull, and Russell Webster. 2005. *Tackling Prison Drug Markets: An Exploratory Qualitative Study.* London: Home Office.

Pollack, Harold A., and Peter Reuter. 2014. "Does Tougher Enforcement Make Drugs More Expensive?" *Addiction* 109:1959–66.

Poulin, Céline, Michel Alary, Gilles Lambert, Gaston Godin, Suzanne Landry, Hélène Gagnon, Éric Demers, Elena Morarescu, Jean Rochefort, and Christiane Claessens. 2007. "Prevalence of HIV and Hepatitis C Virus Infections among Inmates of Quebec Provincial Prisons." *Canadian Medical Association Journal* 177:252–56.

Prendergast, Michael L., Elizabeth A. Hall, and Jean Wellisch. 2003. *Outcome Evaluation of the Forever Free Residential Substance Abuse Treatment (RSAT) Program at the California Institution for Women, 1997–2000.* Ann Arbor, MI: Inter-university Consortium for Political and Social Research.

Rebbapragada, Nivedita, Vivek Furtado, and George William Hawker-Bond. 2021. "Prevalence of Mental Disorders in Prisons in the UK: A Systematic Review and Meta-analysis." *BJPsych Open* 7:S283–S284.

Reuter, Peter, Jonathan P. Caulkins, and Greg Midgette. 2021. "Heroin Use Cannot Be Measured Adequately with a General Population Survey." *Addiction* 116:2600–2609.

Ritchie, Hannah, and Max Roser. 2019. "Opioids, Cocaine, Cannabis and Illicit Drugs." *Our World in Data.* https://ourworldindata.org/illicit-drug-use ?country = (accessed November 1, 2021).

Rosen, Dan. 2019. "The Never-Ending Drug Hustle Behind Bars." Marshall Project, November 7. https://www.themarshallproject.org/2019/11/07/the -never-ending-drug-hustle-behind-bars.

SAMHSA (Substance Abuse and Mental Health Services Administration). 2019. *Use of Medication-Assisted Treatment for Opioid Use Disorder in Criminal Justice Settings.* Rockville, MD: SAMHSA, National Mental Health and Substance Use Policy Laboratory.

SAMHSA (Substance Abuse and Mental Health Services Administration). 2021. "National Survey on Drug Use and Health, 2019." https://pdas.samhsa.gov /#/survey/NSDUH-2019-DS0001/crosstab/?results_received = true (accessed October 14, 2021).

Shaw, Jenny, Denise Baker, Isabelle M. Hunt, Anne Moloney, and Louis Appleby. 2004. "Suicide by Prisoners: National Clinical Survey." *British Journal of Psychiatry* 184:263–67.

Singleton, N., M. Farrell, and H. Meltzer. 2003. "Substance Misuse among Prisoners in England and Wales." *International Review of Psychiatry* 15:150–52.

Stark, Klaus, Ute Herrmann, Stephan Ehrhardt, and Ulrich Bienzle. 2006. "A Syringe Exchange Programme in Prison as Prevention Strategy against HIV

Infection and Hepatitis B and C in Berlin, Germany." *Epidemiology and Infection* 134:814–19.

Stone, Jack, Hannah Fraser, Aaron G. Lim, Josephine G. Walker, Zoe Ward, Louis MacGregor, Adam Trickey, Sam Abbott, Steffanie A. Strathdee, and Daniela Abramovitz. 2018. "Incarceration History and Risk of HIV and Hepatitis C Virus Acquisition among People Who Inject Drugs: A Systematic Review and Meta-analysis." *Lancet Infectious Diseases* 18:1397–409.

Stöver, Heino, and Carl von Ossietzky. 2001. *Study on Assistance to Drug Users in Prisons*. Lisbon: European Monitoring Centre for Drugs and Drug Addiction.

Strange, C. Clare, Sarah M. Manchak, Jordan M. Hyatt, Damon M. Petrich, Alisha Desai, and Cory P. Haberman. 2022. "Opioid-Specific Medication-Assisted Therapy and Its Impact on Criminal Justice and Overdose Outcomes." *Campbell Systematic Reviews* 18:e1215.

Taylor, Bruce, ed. 2002. *I-ADAM in Eight Countries: Approaches and Challenges*. Washington, DC: US Department of Justice, National Institute of Justice.

Thaisri, Hansa, John Lerwitworapong, Suthon Vongsheree, Pathom Sawan-panyalert, Chanchai Chadbanchachai, Archawin Rojanawiwat, Wichuda Kongpromsook, Wiroj Paungtubtim, Pongnuwat Sri-Ngam, and Rachaneekorn Jaisue. 2003. "HIV Infection and Risk Factors among Bangkok Prisoners, Thailand: A Prospective Cohort Study." *BMC Infectious Diseases* 3:1–8.

Tonry, Michael. 2004. *Thinking about Crime: Sense and Sensibility in American Penal Culture*. New York: Oxford University Press.

Trestman, Robert L., and Ashbell T. Wall. 2018. "Supply Reduction in Prison: The Evidence." In *Drug Use in Prisoners: Epidemiology, Implications, and Policy Responses*, edited by Stuart A. Kinner and Josiah D. Rich. New York: Oxford University Press.

van Niekerk, Elna, Charles Parry, Andreas Plüddemann, Antoinette Louw, Gina Weir-Smith, and D. Locke. 2002. "South Africa." In *I-ADAM in Eight countries: Approaches and Challenges*, edited by Bruce Taylor. Washington, DC: US Department of Justice, National Institute of Justice.

Weekes, John, Gerald Thomas, and Greg Graves. 2004. *Substance Abuse in Corrections: FAQs*. Ottawa: Canadian Centre on Substance Abuse.

Weinstein, Zoe M., Hyunjoong W. Kim, Debbie M. Cheng, Emily Quinn, David Hui, Colleen T. Labelle, Mari-Lynn Drainoni, Sara S. Bachman, and Jeffrey H. Samet. 2017. "Long-Term Retention in Office Based Opioid Treatment with Buprenorphine." *Journal of Substance Abuse Treatment* 74:65–70.

Welsh, Wayne N. 2007. "A Multisite Evaluation of Prison-Based Therapeutic Community Drug Treatment." *Criminal Justice and Behavior* 34:1481–98.

Western, Bruce. 2018. *Homeward: Life in the Year after Prison*. New York: Russell Sage.

Winter, Rebecca J., Mark Stoové, Paul A. Agius, Margaret E. Hellard, and Stuart A. Kinner. 2019. "Injecting Drug Use Is an Independent Risk Factor for Reincarceration after Release from Prison: A Prospective Cohort Study." *Drug and Alcohol Review* 38:254–63.

Wooldredge, John. 2020. "Prison Culture, Management, and In-Prison Violence." *Annual Review of Criminology* 3:165–88.

Katherine Beckett and Allison Goldberg

The Effects of Imprisonment in a Time of Mass Incarceration

ABSTRACT

Imprisonment has deleterious effects on prisoners' mental, physical, social, and economic well-being. These harms are long lasting and affect prisoners' partners and children. In the United States and elsewhere, imprisonment disproportionately inflicts these harms on people of color and people living in poverty. Although imprisonment is regarded as a reasonable and effective means of protecting the public, it is not, when compared with nonconfinement alternatives, an effective way to achieve public safety. Two broad sets of policy reforms would be better: retroactive and prospective sentencing reforms that reduce reliance on confinement for all types of offenses, including violent crimes, and broad initiatives that reduce reliance on prison and jails while also investing in housing, education, treatment, health, and communities. Researchers and policy analysts need to engage in problem-solving research that examines not only incarceration's effects but alternative ongoing efforts to achieve public safety and justice.

Imprisonment imposes innumerable short- and long-term harms on imprisoned people. It is psychologically, emotionally, and physically costly and undermines people's health and well-being while also increasing

Katherine Beckett is S. Frank Miyamoto Professor of Sociology and a professor in the Law, Societies, and Justice Department at the University of Washington. Allison Goldberg is a PhD student in the Department of Sociology. Many thanks to Sandra Bucerius, Michael Tonry, and several anonymous reviewers for constructive feedback and guidance.

Electronically published September 2, 2022

Crime and Justice, volume 51, 2022.
https://doi.org/10.1086/721018

morbidity over the life course. It imposes steep financial costs. Although many imprisoned people work while behind bars, few are able to save money or support their families because of the high cost of subsistence items in prison, extremely low wages, and the widespread imposition and collection of legal financial obligations. Adverse financial effects persist over time, as imprisonment reduces employment, earnings, and opportunities for wealth accumulation after release. Imprisonment also disrupts and weakens bonds between incarcerated people, their romantic partners, and their children, destabilizing families in the process. These social and relational harms extend over time and outside prison walls.

Some of these effects are intensified by the American style of imprisonment. And some have been exacerbated by mass incarceration over the past half century (Haney 2012). The US incarceration rate began an unprecedented ascent in 1973, after which the number of people under the supervision of the criminal legal system increased more than fivefold.[1] This trend continued through 2007, when nearly one in 100 adults lived behind bars, 5 million were on probation or parole, roughly 10 million spent time in jail, and nearly one in three US residents were living with a criminal record (Pew Charitable Trusts 2008; Sabol 2014; Kaeble and Cowhig 2018, table 1). By 2020, the imprisonment rate had declined by 28 percent from its peak in 2007 (Carson 2021a). Even so, the US incarceration rate remains the highest in the world (Walmsley 2021).

The terms "mass imprisonment" and "mass incarceration," coined by David Garland (2001), underscore the unprecedented scale of the US criminal justice system and the harms it causes. The scale of confinement sharply differentiates the United States from comparable democratic countries, where incarceration rates in recent years ranged from 38 per 100,000 residents in Japan to 188 in New Zealand (Walmsley 2021). By contrast, the US incarceration rate remains remarkably high—over 600 per 100,000 residents in 2020 (Kang-Brown, Montagnet, and Heiss 2021). Mass incarceration is also characterized by highly disproportionate confinement of people of color, especially young Black men with low levels of formal education (Pettit and Western 2004; Western and Wildeman 2009). These racial disparities have decreased in recent years: from 2010 to 2020, US state and federal imprisonment rates fell by 37 percent among

---

[1] Immigrant detention has also increased dramatically: on an average day in 2020, nearly 50,000 immigrants were detained in the United States, up from a few thousand in 1980 (Kassie 2019).

Black residents, 32 percent among Hispanic/Latinx residents, and 25 percent among White residents (Carson 2021*a*). Still, substantial racial inequities in incarceration nonetheless persist. For example, the imprisonment rate among Black residents in 2010 was 6 times higher than among White residents and remained 5.1 times higher in 2020.[2]

Mass incarceration is wrong for many reasons. There is little evidence that it makes Americans safer (Petrich et al. 2021). It is exorbitantly expensive (Wagner and Rubay 2017). It imposes significant human and social costs (Travis, Western, and Redburn 2014). Because racial and ethnic disparities in imprisonment have been, and remain, staggeringly high, these costs are disproportionately borne by people and communities of color (Alexander 2010). As a result of its scale, mass incarceration has damaged enormous numbers of people. While imprisonment probably has negative effects on prisoners anywhere and at any time, Americans are much more heavily burdened by its effects than are people elsewhere. The increase in the scale of the US criminal legal system has been so profound, and so consequential, that researchers now treat penal institutions and practices as key mechanisms by which race and class inequality has been reproduced over time (see, e.g., Western 2006).

For these and other reasons, concern about overuse of incarceration has grown, and many state and local governments have taken steps to reduce their prison and jail populations (Beckett 2022). The spread of COVID-19 in US prisons and jails intensified the push for decarceration (Denney and Valdez 2021), and the number of incarcerated people fell 14 percent, from 2.1 million people to 1.8 million from March 2020 to June 2021 (Kang-Brown, Montagnet, and Heiss 2021). However, most of this decline took place during the early months of the pandemic. By summer 2021, many courts had resumed operations, and jails were returning to their prepandemic practices, gradually reversing previous population declines. The jail population increased by 13 percent from mid-2020 to the spring of 2021 (Kang-Brown, Montagnet, and Heiss 2021). Several jurisdictions announced plans for prison expansion. Thus, although the pandemic triggered a nontrivial decline in US prison and jail populations, emerging evidence suggests that those drops will prove temporary.

The devastating effects of COVID-19 in prisons and jails reveal an important truth about prisons: they are places that cage human beings and

[2] Calculations are based on data from Carson (2021*a*), table 3.

deprive them of the means to ensure their health and safety. In this essay, we provide an overview of the harms of imprisonment and offer recommendations about alternative ways to pursue safety and justice. We focus on state and federal imprisonment in the United States. To be sure, state and federal prisons, which mainly house people who have been convicted of a felony offense and sentenced to 1 year or more of confinement, are only the tip of the carceral iceberg.[3] While the term mass incarceration is commonly used, the state criminalizes, supervises, and controls millions of people in prisons and jails and outside. In 2019, for example, 1.4 million US residents were in a state or federal prison, nearly 750,000 were in a local jail, close to 900,000 were on parole, and almost 3.5 million were on probation (Minton, Beatty, and Zeng 2021, table 1). Terms such as mass criminalization (Hinton and Cook 2021), the carceral state (Beckett 2018), and punitive excess (Travis and Western 2021) highlight this broad expansion of the state's capacity to surveil, punish, and control its residents. Because of space constraints, we focus on the effects of confinement in federal and state prisons. For the same reason, we draw mainly from recent scholarship and focus on the United States, although we sometimes refer to comparative and international research.

We begin in Section I by summarizing research findings about the effects of imprisonment on imprisoned people's health and well-being; their employment, earnings, and wealth; and their relationships with loved ones, including children. Where possible, we identify the mechanisms by which imprisonment has these adverse effects. In Section II we discuss the policy implications of this body of research. We first identify normative principles that, along with data and evidence, influence our recommendations for reducing the harms that imprisonment causes. We make the case for two broad sets of policy reforms: comprehensive sentencing reforms that reduce confinement time for current and future prisoners for all types of offenses, including violent crimes, and broader policy initiatives that reduce reliance on prison and jails while also investing in housing, education, treatment, health, and communities. Both strategies are crucial to ensuring that ostensible reforms actually reduce precarity, state violence, racial inequities, and marginalization. We invite researchers to engage in

---

[3] US prisons also house people who were released from prison but returned to it after violating the conditions of their release. A small number of states have combined jail and prison systems in which people awaiting adjudication or serving confinement sentences of less than 1 year are housed.

problem-solving research that examines not only mass incarceration's effects but also ongoing efforts to promote safety and justice by alternative means (Prasad 2018).

I. The Effects of Imprisonment

Imprisonment imposes myriad health-related, financial, and relational harms on prisoners and their loved ones. The negative effects sometimes vary along demographic lines. And for some who face especially grim circumstances in the "free world," prison can offer a reprieve from even more acute deprivation. For instance, some imprisoned women report that prison offers a "temporary refuge" from abuse, extreme poverty, and marginalization (Bucerius, Haggerty, and Dunford 2021, p. 525). For these women, prison "interrupted what they understood to be lethal patterns of drug use" (p. 526) and provided a rare guarantee of a "safe place to sleep" (p. 528), three meals a day, and health care. Similarly, some imprisoned people in Leipzig, Germany, describe prison as a place of rest, predictability, privacy, and care relative to their experiences of hardship on the streets (and some were therefore opposed to decarceration efforts during the pandemic; Schneider 2021). Research in England, Wales, and Norway reveals that prison can afford opportunities for some for "reinvention" and an opportunity to "get clean" (Crewe and Ievins 2020). Although many of the studies that report such findings involve people incarcerated outside the United States, Comfort (2012) similarly finds that, for some, imprisonment in the United States can also provide an opportunity for "self-reflection" (p. 314) that some describe as akin to college, although "prison's punitive mission . . . fundamentally interferes with any other purpose young adults may attempt to extract from it" (p. 317).

Although prison may thus offer particular resources and opportunities for some especially disadvantaged people, these findings ultimately reveal the deep deprivation, marginalization, and structural violence many people living in poverty experience both inside and outside of prison. These caveats notwithstanding, the literature shows that imprisonment imposes many harms on the people who experience it and on their loved ones (Haney 2012). It is true that establishing a causal connection between imprisonment and particular adverse outcomes in individual studies is challenging because of possibly uncontrolled selection bias, limited longitudinal data, variation in the operationalization of key variables, and limited measures of important health and other metrics (Travis, Western, and

Redburn 2014; Massoglia and Pridemore 2015; Massoglia and Remster 2019). Still, the accumulated evidence of adverse effects is robust. For this reason, we offer few additional disclaimers in this essay regarding the challenges of establishing the causal effects of imprisonment.

A. The Health and Well-Being of the Imprisoned

US imprisonment generally worsens the mental and physical health of the imprisoned in both the short and the long term. For some groups (especially Black men), particularly disadvantageous conditions in the free world mean that incarceration may improve access to health care and reduce mortality in the short run but exacerbate these problems in the long run.

1. *The Psychological Harms of Imprisonment.* Many researchers in the post–World War II era analyzed the complex psychological harm caused by imprisonment (Liebling and Maruna 2005). Perhaps most famously, Gresham Sykes (1958) identified five psychic pains of imprisonment. They include deprivation of liberty, which encompasses both restricted movement and social isolation; deprivation of goods and services; diminished autonomy, including the compulsion to comply with rules that are often experienced as both arbitrary and irrational; and physical vulnerability and insecurity. The fifth and most fundamental kind of pain is symbolic: "The individual's picture of himself as a person of value—as a morally acceptable adult who can present some claim to merit—begins to waver and grow dim" (p. 79). Other contemporaneous researchers similarly underscored the psychic costs of imprisonment (Haney, Banks, and Zimbardo 1973; Toch 1992) and institutionalization more generally (Goffman 1961).

During the 1980s and 1990s, however, many researchers began to operate from a very different premise, namely, that the psychological pains of imprisonment are relatively inconsequential (for a discussion and critique of this intellectual shift, see Liebling and Maruna [2005]). Yet recent studies confirm that imprisonment has a variety of negative effects on mental health and well-being both during and after incarceration (Liebling and Maruna 2005; Schnittker, Massoglia, and Uggen 2012; Turney, Wildeman, and Schnittker 2012). As psychologist Craig Haney puts it, "prisons are fraught with danger, dehumanization, and deprivation, and are pervaded by all the negative emotions that those things engender" (2017, p. 311; see also Haney 2001, 2020). This is especially true in the United States, where prison conditions have deteriorated over time and overcrowding is commonplace. Imprisonment also requires prisoners to adapt to prisons' unique features and requirements in order to stay safe. These adaptations are often referred to as "institutionalization." Such adaptations are often functional in the prison but unhelpful in the free world: "It is important to emphasize that these are the natural and normal adaptations made by prisoners in response to the unnatural and abnormal conditions of prisoner life. The dysfunctionality of these adaptations is not 'pathological' in nature (even though, in practical terms, they may be destructive in effect). They are 'normal' reactions to a set of pathological conditions that become problematic when they are taken to extreme lengths, or become chronic and deeply internalized (so that, even though the conditions of one's life have changed, many of the once-functional but now counterproductive patterns remain)" (Haney 2001, p. 7; see also Haney 2012).

While researchers agree that imprisonment is psychologically unhelpful at best and harmful at worst, they identify different dimensions of the experience as most consequential. For example, Crewe (2011) emphasizes the harm caused by correctional policies and practices that make imprisoned peoples' futures uncertain and precarious. Irwin and Owen (2005) argue that the loss of agency and a pronounced sense of unfairness are among the most significant of imprisonments' psychic harms. Liebling (1999) highlights the social dislocation caused by imprisonment as well as heightened risks of mental illness and suicide. The prevalence of violence and victimization in prisons, which can induce or heighten symptoms associated with posttraumatic stress disorder (PTSD), are also singled out as especially harmful (Liebling 1999; Haney 2012; Travis, Western, and Redburn 2014; Schappell, Docherty, and Boxer 2016). Many of these stressors, including discrimination, stigma, and disruptions to the life course that formerly incarcerated people experience, continue long after imprisonment ends (Western 2006; Turney, Wildeman, and Schnittker 2012), although the pains of imprisonment do not always result in long-term psychological harm. As Haney summarizes,

> The adaptation to imprisonment is almost always difficult and, at times, creates habits of thinking and acting that can be dysfunctional in periods of post-prison adjustment. Yet, the psychological effects of incarceration vary from individual to individual and are often reversible. To be sure, then, not everyone who is incarcerated is disabled or psychologically harmed by it. But few people are completely

unchanged or unscathed by the experience. At the very least, prison is painful, and incarcerated persons often suffer long-term consequences from having been subjected to pain, deprivation, and extremely atypical patterns and norms of living and interacting with others. (2001, p. 2)

Solitary confinement has especially adverse effects. As Haney observes, the "adverse and sometimes life-threatening psychological and physical consequences of social isolation, social exclusion, loneliness, and the deprivation of caring human touch . . . [appear in acutely] toxic forms" within solitary confinement and in the prison environment more generally (2020, p. 517; see also Nurse, Woodcock, and Ormsby 2003; Reiter et al. 2020). For this reason, the experience of solitary confinement causes significant psychological pain, exacerbates mental illness where it exists, and may induce it where it does not (Haney 2017; Reiter et al. 2020). It also appears that the experience of solitary confinement is quite common. For example, Western (2019) reports that in Pennsylvania 39 percent of people in men's prisons, and 25 percent in women's prisons, experience solitary confinement; on average, people spend more a month in solitary confinement during each spell of incarceration.

2. *Access to Health Care.* People who experience imprisonment tend to have poor health and limited access to health care before their incarceration (Wakefield and Uggen 2010; Travis, Western, Redburn 2014). A wide range of social conditions and dynamics beyond individual behaviors and conditions explain this pattern (Wang et al. 2008; Dumont et al. 2013). For example, people who are unemployed frequently lack health insurance that would allow them to secure medical care and income and therefore have difficulty eating healthfully, obtaining medication, and otherwise addressing their health needs. As Travis, Western, and Redburn observe, the poor health of many prisoners "can be attributed to overlapping synergistic epidemics (syndemics) of substance use, infectious diseases, and mental illness in the context of poverty, violence, homelessness, and limited access to health care" (2014, p. 204).

Ironically, imprisoned people are the only group of US residents for whom health care is recognized as a legally actionable right. In *Estelle v. Gamble*, 429 U.S. 97 (1976), the Supreme Court found that deliberate indifference to the medical needs of incarcerated people violates the Eighth Amendment's prohibition against cruel and unusual punishment. This ruling and subsequent litigation (including *Brown v. Plata*, 563 U.S. 493

[2011]) expanded health care services for prisoners (Simon 2016). Thus, in a country with comparatively low rates of health care insurance coverage and other barriers to health care, "incarceration can be an opportunity of last resort" for access to medical care (Meyer et al. 2014, p. 721). As Travis, Western, and Redburn (2014, p. 215) note, "Some correctional facilities have served as important public health collaborators in screening for and diagnosing various infectious diseases" such as HIV. And because of the aging of the prison population, some prisons also increasingly serve as critical delivery sites for nursing home–level care (Smith 2013). But the availability of care in prison varies widely. For example, more than one-third of all state and federal prisoners have been diagnosed with a mental health condition, but nearly two-thirds of these prisoners report not having access to mental health care during their incarceration (Prison Policy Initiative 2021; see also Bronson and Berzofsky 2017).

Moreover, even when care is available in theory, correctional institutions are not ideal settings for care provision and often fail to meet incarcerated people's health needs (Aday and Farney 2014). This is in part because people in federal and most state prisons are required to pay co-pays to get access to (privatized) health services. While these fees may appear low to outsiders, they are prohibitive for many incarcerated people (Travis, Western, and Redburn 2014). Moreover, prisons are difficult and often hostile environments in which imprisoned people must often navigate physical barriers, correctional staff indifference or even hostility, logistical challenges, and widespread assumptions about prisoner malingering in order to access health care (Vandergrift and Christopher 2021). In the absence of systematic accreditation, the courts are the main source of oversight of health care in prisons—and their willingness and capacity to ensure that prisoners' right to adequate health care is provided varies notably (Schwartzapfel 2018). Ongoing litigation about the failure of many correctional systems to provide adequate and timely care suggests that these problems are endemic.

Many people also experience gaps in care after release from prison. This stems in large part from the "inmate exclusion" policy, which mandates Medicaid termination upon incarceration and often results "in gaps in Medicaid coverage at release" (Albertson et al. 2020, p. 317; see also Winkelman et al. 2016; Pew Charitable Trusts 2017). Even after the expansion of Medicaid triggered by the enactment of the Affordable Care Act in 2014, the incidence of uninsuredness (30 percent) is about twice as high among nonelderly adults with recent criminal legal system involvement as among otherwise comparable adults (Winkelman et al. 2016; Albertson et al. 2020). In addition, discrimination based on both race or ethnicity and criminal records is associated with decreased health care access and use (Frank et al. 2014).

3. *Morbidity and Mortality during and after Imprisonment.* Imprisoned people generally have poor health before, during, and after incarceration. For example, rates of hypertension, chronic lung disease, and heart disease are two to four times higher among incarcerated people (Massoglia 2008*a*). Older adults and women who are imprisoned suffer from especially poor health (Travis, Western, and Redburn 2014). Because imprisoned people are more likely to experience poor health before incarceration, it is sometimes difficult to determine whether incarceration worsens physical health. However, studies reveal numerous likely causal pathways between incarceration and poor health. Some of these mechanisms, including acute and chronic stress and increased risk of infectious disease transmission, are operative during incarceration. Others, such as social and economic marginalization after release and discrimination against formerly incarcerated people in employment, housing, and health care, come into play following release (Massoglia and Remster 2019).

High rates of morbidity among the currently and formerly incarcerated are linked to comparatively high mortality rates. Counterintuitively, though, the mortality rate for incarcerated Black men is notably lower than for nonincarcerated Black men (Spaulding et al. 2011; Travis, Western, and Redburn 2014; Carson 2021*b*). This is because incarceration eliminates some of the main causes of mortality for Black men, including gun violence and transportation-related accidents, and because access to health care is temporarily expanded (Patterson 2010; Massoglia and Pridemore 2015; Western 2019).[4] By contrast, White male prisoners do not experience reduced mortality during incarceration, in part because lack of insurance coverage before incarceration is less common among White men. Thus, "the more equitable mortality rates among inmates are not evidence of the beneficial effects of incarceration so much as an indictment of disparities in the community at large" (Dumont et al. 2013, p. 78).

---

[4] Western (2019) reports that men's (race- and age-adjusted) homicide victimization rate is roughly four times higher for the general population than for incarcerated men. However, rates of assault in prison are more than five times higher than in the general population. Men are thus less likely to die of homicide, but far more likely to be assaulted, in prison than outside of it.

Moreover, any reductions in mortality that do occur for Black men (and possibly for Black women and other people of color) dissipate after release, after which mortality rates increase notably (Spaulding et al. 2011; Pridemore 2014; Rosen, Kavee, and Brinkley-Rubinstein 2020). For example, one study found that justice-involved individuals had 12.7 times the risk of death within 2 weeks after release compared with residents of the same age, gender, and race and 3.5 times the risk of death during the average follow-up period of 1.9 years (Binswanger et al. 2007; see also Albertson et al. 2020). The risk of death from suicide or drug overdose is especially high in the months following release (Binswanger et al. 2007; Travis, Western, and Redburn 2014). Thus, any reductions in mortality among Black men (and possibly other marginalized groups) during incarceration appear to be offset by much larger increases in mortality following release.

4. *Effects on Public Health and Racial Inequities in Health.* Many researchers have noted that US mass incarceration has profound health effects. The pandemic made those connections, and their implications, even more clear. As sociologist Hedwig Lee and her colleagues write, "The novel coronavirus 2019 (COVID-19) pandemic has brought into sharp relief the expansive nature of community. . . . To be sure, certain populations remain disproportionately burdened by COVID-19 infection risk, complications, and death, but, as we have seen, the rise in infection in any subpopulations can easily lead to infection in other communities. This new reality requires us to reimagine in a more inclusive way what 'community' and 'safety' mean. It also requires us to act in a more deliberate and universal way to protect communities. For a community to be resilient, every member of the community must be resilient" (Lee, Weiss, and Prendergast 2021, p. 1).

Findings from Wildeman's (2016) cross-national study provide support for the idea that the scale of incarceration affects the overall health of the population (even in the absence of a global pandemic). This study examined the relationship between incarceration rates and population health in 21 developed democratic countries and found that increases in incarceration are inversely associated with gains in population health. However, it appears that this effect was driven mainly by the relationship between incarceration and poor health in the United States (see also Rich, Wakeman, and Dickman 2011). This effect likely stems from the concentration of formerly incarcerated people with limited access to health care in low-income neighborhoods (Massoglia 2008a) and limitations on health care for incarcerated people and their families (Massoglia and Schnittker 2009). In addition, incarceration can increase the spread of infectious diseases, including HIV (Johnson and Raphael 2009), and sexually trans- mitted diseases more broadly, in the communities from which the incar- cerated and formerly incarcerated are overwhelmingly drawn (Grinstead et al. 2005).

Given that US mass incarceration disproportionately affects Black people and other people of color, Massoglia argues that incarceration may act "as one of the fundamental systems of stratification that contrib- utes to racial health disparities in general health functioning" (2008*b*, p. 297; see also Massoglia 2008*a*). Consistent with this proposition, Sykes and Piquero (2009, p. 214) find significant racial, educational, and marital in- equalities in health testing and test results and conclude that "the penal in- stitution is an active agent in structuring and re-creating health inequalities within prisons, thereby exacerbating existing community health inequities when inmates are released." Similarly, Nowotny and Kuptesvych-Timmer find that "mass incarceration has deleterious health effects for those directly affected by it (the incarcerated), and mass incarceration contaminates the communities where it is geographically concentrated" (2018, p. 1).

B. Employment, Earnings, and Wealth

Having been imprisoned negatively affects nearly every aspect of for- mer prisoners' lives. Compared with otherwise similar people who have never been imprisoned, former prisoners' levels of employment, current and lifetime earnings, and accumulated wealth are lower. Negative eco- nomic effects are greater for minority than for White former prisoners. Many causes have been documented. They include discrimination by employers, occupational disabilities, residence in disadvantaged neigh- borhoods offering few employment opportunities, and lack of member- ship in social networks that provide access to opportunities.

1. *Education, Employment, and Earnings before Incarceration.* Imprisonment disproportionately affects people with lower levels of formal education, spotty employment histories, and comparatively low incomes (Pettit and Western 2004; Western and Wildeman 2009; Looney and Turner 2018). For example, Looney and Turner find that "Boys who grew up in families in the bottom 10 percent of the income distribution ... are 20 times more likely to be in prison on a given day in their early 30s than children born in top-decile families" (2018, p. 2). Imprisonment has become a common

event in the lives of men with little formal education, especially men of color (Pettit and Western 2004; Western and Pettit 2010).

Although the experience of incarceration is clearly shaped by inequality, mass incarceration also masks it. This is because incarcerated people are not represented in important data sources; this exclusion notably affects metrics used to assess inequality (Western and Beckett 1999; Western and Pettit 2005; Pettit 2012). For example, Pettit (2012) shows that the exclusion of incarcerated people from most national surveys leads to underestimates of the magnitude and persistence of the racial gap in educational attainment, employment, and earnings. Similarly, Ewert, Sykes, and Pettit (2014) find that including incarcerated men in estimates of the high school dropout rate reveals that Black men have not experienced any improvements in educational attainment since the early 1990s and that sizable racial inequality persists among men in educational attainment.

2. *Employment, Earnings, and Income during Imprisonment.* Although many people who enter prison were unemployed before their incarceration, a majority work while imprisoned (Halladay 2019). However, few prisoners earn much income and even fewer are able to save or contribute much to support their families. This is mainly because the wages paid to imprisoned people are, with a few exceptions, extraordinarily low (if they are paid at all): "On average, prisoners earn $0.20 per hour if held in a state prison and $0.31 per hour in a federal prison" (Halladay 2019, p. 938). Moreover, wages for incarcerated people have declined in recent decades (Sawyer 2016). Hatton argues that labor is a central, if overlooked, feature of mass incarceration and that, for prisoners, "work is a punitive curtailment of citizenship rights, even as it is a foundation of such rights for others" (2018, p. 174). This observation appears to be especially germane given recent evidence that most prison work programs fail to contribute to later desistance from crime or help build skills that are transferable to the workforce outside of prison (Blakinger 2021).

As low as prison wages are, the figures reported above overstate the capacity of imprisoned people to earn income, for two main reasons. First, prisons increasingly charge prisoners for everyday necessities such as soap, toilet paper, food, medical co-pays, and toothpaste, and the cost of these necessities is often quite high (Eisen 2015; Raher 2018). In addition, many departments of correction now charge imprisoned people for the cost of their incarceration. For example, in Riverside County, California's pay-to-stay program charges prisoners $142.42 per day (Eisen 2015). Although this rate appears to be comparatively high, 43 states authorize prisons to charge fees for room and board (Halladay 2019). These prison-related charges coexist with other "legal financial obligations" (LFOs)—fees, fines, and restitution orders—that are increasingly assessed by courts, jails, and other legal authorities (Harris 2016; Martin et al. 2018; Kirk, Fernandes, and Friedman 2020). As a result of their increased imposition, an estimated 10 million people owe more than $50 billion in LFOs (Brennan Center for Justice 2019). The modest wages that imprisoned people earn are often garnished to cover prison and other LFOs. In Massachusetts, for example, "any and all funds" can be used to pay court-assessed fines, court costs, victim witness assessments, and other LFOs (Sawyer 2016). Similarly, New Mexico deducts 15–50 percent of each paycheck for a Crime Victims Reparations Fund and other assessments.

In short, although roughly half of all imprisoned people work while they are living behind bars, few are able to contribute much to their families or leave prison with any savings. This is because of the very low wages paid to prisoners, because many prisoners rely on these wages to obtain everyday necessities, and because of routine garnishment of prisoners' wages.

3. *Employment and Earnings after Incarceration.* Formerly incarcerated people continue to experience diminished levels of employment and comparatively low wages following their release (Pettit and Lyons 2007, 2009; Western et al. 2015; *Economics Daily* 2019). For example, Pettit and Lyons find that "incarceration appears to have important consequences for employment and wage outcomes regardless of when individuals are admitted to prison. Even the most motivated offenders suffer sizeable and significant wage penalties and, over time, decreased likelihood of employment" (2009, p. 725). Similarly, Western and Pettit conclude that "prison was associated with a 40 percent reduction in earnings and with reduced job tenure, reduced hourly wages, and higher unemployment" (2010, p. 13). More recent studies similarly find that prior incarceration notably depresses employment and earnings. Gordon and Neelakantan (2021), for example, estimate that first-time imprisonment reduces expected lifetime earnings by 33 percent and employment by 22 percent for Black men with a high school degree and by 43 and 27 percent, respectively, for their White counterparts. Some studies show that these effects are greatest for those who spend longer behind bars: earnings and employment are lowest among people who were incarcerated for more than 6 months (Ramakers et al. 2014; *Economics Daily* 2019; but see Kling 2006).

The cumulative effect of the loss of earnings associated with incarceration is substantial. As Craigie, Grawert, and Kimble write, "The lifetime effects of this earnings loss are staggering. The roughly half-million dollars lost by the average formerly imprisoned person is more than the entire lifetime earnings of someone who spends his or her life at the poverty line ($382,000). And this loss does not account for missed opportunities for additional wealth generation, from Social Security benefits to accrued interest on retirement accounts to forgone investment opportunities" (2020, p. 19). Because incarceration is more common in communities of color, incarceration contributes to racial gaps in employment and earnings. For example, Gordon et al. (2021, p. 1) find that "differences in incarceration and nonemployment can explain a significant portion of the black-white gap in lifetime earnings—44 percent of the gap for high school graduates and 52 percent of the gap for high school dropouts" among men with low levels of formal education.

While it is clear that formerly incarcerated people generally have comparatively low levels of employment and earnings, questions about causality remain challenging. This is mainly because quantitative studies are unable to control for more subtle factors—such as prior victimization—that may differentiate some people who experience incarceration from those with similar demographic characteristics and levels of education who do not (Travis, Western, and Redburn 2014). For example, Western et al. (2015) find that among people leaving prison in Massachusetts, those with histories of addiction and mental illness were the least socially integrated and had the weakest family ties, most unstable housing, and lowest levels of employment (see also Visher, Debus-Sherrill, and Yahner 2010; Western 2019). These qualitative findings regarding the importance of behavioral health issues underscores the challenge of using national survey data, which generally do not include measures that would allow researchers to control for such factors, in order to isolate the impact of incarceration. Variability in the effects of incarceration also makes establishing causality challenging. For example, some studies suggest that the relationship between incarceration and earnings may vary by race, with former incarcerated Black people paying the steepest price (Lyons and Pettit 2011; Western and Sirois 2018; Apel and Powell 2019).[5] These caveats notwithstanding, researchers have identified a number of mechanisms by which incarceration appears to suppress employment and

[5] For a discussion of some of the limitations of the survey data on which many studies rely, see Travis, Western, and Redburn (2014, pp. 241–42).

earnings among formerly incarcerated people. Each of these mechanisms is briefly described below.

4. *Stigma and Internalized Stigma.*   Criminal conviction carries significant social stigma. Experimental studies show that this stigma reduces opportunities for employment among job applicants, especially for applicants of color (Pager 2003, 2007; Pager, Western, and Bonikowski 2009; Vuolo, Lageson, and Uggen 2017). Sociologist Devah Pager's pathbreaking work on this topic found that otherwise identical (and fictional) applicants who indicated that they had been convicted of a drug-related felony were notably less likely to receive a callback from potential employers. This form of discrimination interacts with, and compounds, the effect of race: Black applicants who reported no criminal conviction were less likely to receive a callback than White applicants who reported having a conviction record. Pager, Western, and Bonikowski's (2009, pp. 792–93) replication of this study in New York City included Latino job applicants and again found significant discrimination based on conviction status but also that "black and Latino applicants with clean backgrounds fared no better than white applicants just released from prison."

It is thus evident that criminal conviction carries a stigma that reduces the job prospects of formerly incarcerated people who seek work, particularly for applicants of color who also experience racial discrimination. Yet the extent to which this stigma explains low levels of employment and earnings among formerly incarcerated people is unclear. This is because many formerly incarcerated people do not seek work, in which case employer discrimination cannot account for high levels of unemployment and poverty among the formerly incarcerated. For example, Apel and Sweeten's (2010) analysis of National Longitudinal Study of Youth (NLSY) data shows that many of the formerly incarcerated people who were unemployed were not looking for work, often for sustained periods of time.

Schnittker and Massoglia (2015) draw on social-psychological research to make sense of widespread labor market disengagement among formerly incarcerated people. In doing so, they emphasize the importance of internalized stigma, particularly in the context of the trauma associated with imprisonment: "Some of the self-defeating behavior of former inmates, including disengagement, can be seen as reflecting the psychological dilemmas former inmates face after release. . . . Although coping with stigma is difficult for all stigmatized persons, the situation of former inmates may be especially difficult given a confluence of factors, including some atypical features of incarceration stigma, institutional pressures that amplify that stigma, and the lingering psychological pains of imprisonment, which mitigate effective coping" (p. 349). Ricciardelli and Mooney's (2018) interviews with formerly incarcerated people also support the idea that "internalized stigma," along with lingering trauma, may discourage job seeking and labor force participation among the formerly incarcerated.[6]

5. *Neighborhood Conditions.* Local socioeconomic conditions also affect the labor market experiences of the formerly incarcerated. For example, Sabol (2007) analyzed the relationship between local labor market conditions and employment among former prisoners in Ohio. Formerly incarcerated people experienced longer unemployment spells, and earned lower wages, in counties with higher unemployment rates. Noting that many former prisoners return to the most disadvantaged sections of a limited number of urban areas, other researchers have also found that residential location affects labor market outcomes for formerly incarcerated people (Morenoff and Harding 2014; Kirk 2015). Sugie and Lens (2017) find that, because local conditions are generally inhospitable, the capacity of the formerly incarcerated to travel to job-rich areas is key to transcending these limitations.

International and comparative research provides additional evidence that local economic conditions affect formerly incarcerated people's financial futures. For example, Aaltonen et al. (2017) compare former prisoners' employment trajectories in four Nordic welfare states (Denmark, Finland, Norway, and Sweden) and find that postrelease employment rates were highest in the country with the lowest level of unemployment (Norway) and lowest in the country where unemployment is more common (Finland). At a more general level, these findings indicate that local economic conditions may have some influence on the employment trajectories of the formerly imprisoned. That so many formerly incarcerated people return to neighborhoods with high levels of unemployment and limited transit options thus helps explain low levels of labor market participation and earnings upon release from prison.

6. *Hidden Sentences and Collateral Consequences as Labor Market Barriers.* Emerging evidence suggests that policies that limit occupational opportunities for formerly incarcerated people are also consequential.

---

[6] Awareness that wages will be garnished to pay for LFOs may also discourage some formerly incarcerated people from seeking work in the formal labor market (Beckett and Harris 2011; Cadigan and Kirk 2020).

As of 2015, more than 35,000 laws imposed more than 40,000 penalties or disabilities beyond visible forms of punishment such as imprisonment and probation on justice-involved people in the United States (Kaiser 2016, pp. 178–79; see also Warner, Kaiser, and Houle 2020). Many of these policies restrict those with a criminal record from accepting certain types of jobs entirely or from obtaining necessary certifications or licenses.

In one of the first attempts to quantify the effects of these policies, Warner, Kaiser, and Houle (2020) examine the effects of these "hidden sentences" on the formerly incarcerated. The results indicate that recently incarcerated young adults are less likely to find employment if they live in states that have comparatively large numbers of hidden sentences. Similarly, the earnings penalty of incarceration is larger in states with more laws and policies that restrict occupational options. While additional research in this area is needed, it appears that policies that restrict opportunities to engage in certain types of labor suppress labor force participation among the formerly incarcerated.

7. *The Challenge of Returning Home and Navigating Postrelease Surveillance.* Although imprisoned people generally look forward to their release, this process can be challenging, even overwhelming, and the difficulties associated with this transition undermine the labor market prospects of formerly incarcerated people. Halushka's (2020) study of recently imprisoned men on parole in New York City, for example, shows that navigating the bureaucratic requirements of criminal justice and welfare institutions is a dehumanizing, demoralizing, tedious, and time-consuming experience that provides minimal resources and consigns many people to a life of permanent poverty (see also Miller 2021). Similarly, on the basis of interviews with people leaving prison and returning to the Boston area, Western and his colleagues conclude that

> Prison release is a disruptive event that is often unpredictable and unfolding in a context of severe hardship. The high level of material deprivation we observed was combined with feelings of anxiety, isolation, and unease with criminally involved peers immediately after prison release. New technology, crowds, mass transit, and other aspects of everyday life were unfamiliar and only slowly became part of the respondents' daily routines. While other researchers have suggested that the exposure to prison conditions or the stigma of a criminal record may produce negative effects ... the stress of transition from prison to community is a distinct channel rooted in the fundamentally segregative character of incarceration. (2015, p. 1540)

Sociologist Sarah Brayne (2014) has identified yet another way prior criminal justice system involvement may suppress employment and earnings. Her analysis indicates that people who have been stopped by police, arrested, convicted, or incarcerated "are less likely to interact with surveilling institutions, including medical, financial, labor market, and educational institutions, than their counterparts who have not had criminal justice contact. By contrast, individuals with criminal justice contact are no less likely to participate in civic or religious institutions" (p. 367). Brayne infers that fear of surveillance and subsequent system avoidance among the justice-involved shape individuals' behavior and involvement with institutions and other formal settings, such as legal employment, in ways that reproduce poverty and inequality. In short, recent studies indicate that the challenges associated with returning home and living with a criminal record also diminish employment and earnings among the formerly incarcerated.

8. *Racial Inequality in the Price of Imprisonment: The Role of Networks.* Research indicates that people of color pay the steepest price for being formerly incarcerated. For example, Western and Sirois (2018, p. 1517) find that formerly incarcerated "blacks and Hispanics have lower total earnings than whites even after accounting for health, human capital, social background, crime and criminal justice involvement, and job readiness." Racial differences in access to networks appear to help explain this pattern (Lyons and Pettit 2011; Apel and Powell 2019). That is, formerly incarcerated White job seekers are more likely to find stable, high-paying jobs through social networks. Western and Sirois conclude that "these findings support a hypothesis of racialized re-entry that helps explain the unusual disadvantage of African Americans at the nexus of the penal system and the labor market" (2018, p. 1517).

Moreover, some policies that restrict occupational opportunities and appear, at first glance, to be race neutral may not be. For example, Warner, Kaiser, and Houle's analysis of the impact of hidden sentences on the job prospects and earnings of the formerly incarcerated finds that "hidden sentences are more strongly associated with access to employment for black formerly incarcerated respondents than for whites or Hispanics. This finding is in line with, and supports, recent research that shows evidence for a 'racialized reentry.' . . . One interpretation of these findings is that hidden sentences institutionalize discrimination and make it easier for employers to discriminate against people of color" (2020, p. 147). In short, there is strong evidence that incarceration erodes the already poor job and earning prospects of the formerly incarcerated, especially for people of color. This effect appears to be attributable to various informal social processes as well as formal policies that limit opportunities for formerly incarcerated people.

9. *The Effects of Imprisonment on Wealth and Asset Accumulation.* Recent studies also examine whether and how incarceration affects people's ability to accumulate wealth. This question is especially germane given the magnitude and persistence of the racial wealth gap, which shows no sign of abating (Oliver and Shapiro 2019). Not surprisingly, these studies show that the experience of incarceration depresses rates of home ownership and other forms of asset accumulation. Maroto's (2015, p. 207) hybrid mixed effects analysis of NLSY data indicates that formerly incarcerated people "are less likely to own their homes than never-incarcerated people by an average of 5 percentage points, and their probability of home ownership decreases by an additional 28 percentage points after incarceration." As a result, the net worth of formerly incarcerated people decreases by an average of $42,000 following incarceration. Other studies report similar findings (Sykes and Maroto 2016; Maroto and Sykes 2020). These effects also affect families and children—and they sustain racial inequality. For example, Schneider and Turney (2015) find that incarceration rates are negatively associated with home ownership rates among Black people and that they widen Black-White inequalities in rates of home ownership. Similarly, Turney and Schneider (2016) find that incarceration is negatively associated with ownership of a bank account, vehicle, and home among men and that these consequences also affect formerly incarcerated men's romantic partners.

10. *Directions for Future Research.* As economic inequality climbs and wealth accumulation among millennials falls far behind that of earlier generations (Kent and Ricketts 2021), future research might consider how these broader societal trends affect the most marginalized communities, including the formerly incarcerated. Future research might also consider how the pandemic altered the effects of incarceration on labor market opportunities and outcomes. Finally, as Travis, Western, and Redburn conclude, "The collection of longitudinal data tracking individuals before and after their contact with the criminal justice system is needed" (2014, pp. 256–57).

C. Relationships with Partners and Children

Imprisonment affects prisoners' and ex-prisoners' relationships with partners and children in fundamental ways. Although methodological and design limitations of research on these subjects are significant, several adverse affects are clear. Imprisonment weakens relationships between couples and fosters breakups, although it is unclear whether this is because of imprisonment per se or because of forced separation. Parental imprisonment adversely affects children directly through weakened relationships with parents and indirectly through reduced household earnings and stability during and after parental confinement. Negative effects of mothers' imprisonment appear to be particularly strong. All of these negative effects are disproportionately more severe for Black people and members of other minority groups and their families than for Whites.

1. *Marriage and Partnerships.* Researchers have examined the effects of imprisonment on existing romantic relationships, on the likelihood of marriage/partnership following release from prison, and on aggregate rates of marriage and singlehood. Each of these topics is highly important in light of research showing that stable romantic partnerships contribute to desistance from crime (Laub, Nagin, and Sampson 1998; Sampson, Laub, and Wimer 2006; Forrest 2014). Mass incarceration has interrupted opportunities for, and the stability of, partnerships in several ways.

First, incarceration increases the likelihood that preexisting romantic relationships will end (Western and Wildeman 2009; Apel et al. 2010; Turney 2015). Early studies focused exclusively on the effects on marriage dissolution and found that incarceration had only modest effects. However, more recent studies include nonmarital cohabitation and suggest broader effects (Travis, Western, and Redburn 2014). The inclusion of nonmarital unions is important because rates of marriage among incarcerated men are about half as high as among nonincarcerated men (Lopoo and Western 2005). The effects of imprisonment on union dissolution is greatest for cohabiting couples and couples with children (Western, Lopoo, and McLanahan 2003; Turney and Wildeman 2013; Turney 2015). While these studies mainly rely on statistical methods, the adverse effects of imprisonment on partnerships has been substantiated by quasi-experimental studies (Fallesen and Andersen 2017), which find that people who served their sentence at home under electronic monitoring had a 13.3 percentage point lower risk of relationship dissolution than those who were imprisoned.

The main mechanism by which imprisonment disrupts partnerships appears to be physical separation, although the stress and strain associated with incarceration may also play a role. For example, Massoglia, Remster, and King (2011) find that incarceration has no effect on marital dissolution after duration of incarceration is taken into account, which suggests that physical separation is the key causal mechanism. This emphasis on separation is also supported by evidence that other forms of long-term separation such as military enlistment have a similar effect on rates of marital dissolution.

There is less consensus regarding the effects of incarceration on future relationship status. Raphael (2007) finds that having served time in jail or prison reduced the odds that formerly incarcerated people would subsequently marry (see also Huebner 2005, 2007). Compared to young men who had not been imprisoned, those who had been incarcerated were about 14 percent less likely to be married. Analyzing the same data set, however, Lopoo and Western (2005) found that the adverse effect of incarceration on relationship status did not persist after release (see also Apel et al. 2010). In light of these mixed findings, Bacak and Kennedy (2015), analyzing a marginal structural model, find evidence that incarceration does reduce the likelihood of entering marriage following release. In short, studies of the effects of incarceration on future relationship status produce mixed findings, although more recent studies suggest a negative effect. Future research might usefully emulate Bacak and Kennedy (2015) by studying both nonmarital and marital partnerships (including among LGBTQ people).

Finally, researchers have examined whether mass incarceration has an aggregate effect on marriage rates in the general population. This research generally relies on state-level incarceration rates to estimate the effects of incarceration on marriage and divorce. This research design assumes that marital status does not affect incarceration and that some other factor is not causing both high rates of incarceration and high rates of union instability (Travis, Western, and Redburn 2014, pp. 266–67). Some of these studies indicate that mass incarceration may have contributed to falling marriage rates, especially for Black women (Charles and Luoh 2010; Mechoulan 2011). Others suggest small or limited aggregate effects. For example, Mechoulan (2011) finds that the incarceration of Black men suppressed marriage rates among Black women up to the mid-1980s but not thereafter. The comparatively modest effect of incarceration on aggregate marriage rates is likely a function of already-low rates of marriage among men with low levels of educational attainment (Lopoo and Western 2005).

Given the broad shift away from marriage in the general population, future research might usefully assess the effects of incarceration on aggregate rates of partnerships and singlehood. In addition, researchers might wish to explore the possibility that lowered marriage rates may provide some benefits to women in particular (see Mechoulan 2011). Future studies might also shed additional light on the possibility that effects of higher rates of singlehood vary by gender and other factors.

2. *Incarcerated Parents' Relationships with Children.* There has been a dramatic rise in the number of children who experience parental incarceration. Unsurprisingly, there are notable race and class inequities in this experience (Gotsch 2018; Miller 2018; Turney and Wildeman 2018). Sykes and Pettit find that "in 1980, roughly half a million children had a parent behind bars. By 2012, nearly 2.6 million children had at least one parent in prison or jail" (2014, p. 135). The likelihood that a child will ever have this experience is even higher: more than 5.7 million kids—1 in 12—have experienced parental incarceration during their lives. Latinx and Black children are respectively 2.5 and 7.5 times more likely than White children to have a parent in a correctional institution; American Indian, Alaskan Native, multiracial, and ethnic minority children are also overrepresented among those who experience parental incarceration (Gotsch 2018; see also Sykes and Pettit 2014; Miller 2018). Western and Wildeman conclude, "Just as imprisonment had become a normal life event for young black male dropouts, so had parental imprisonment become normal for their children" (2009, p. 236). The reason so many children have been affected by mass incarceration is clear: most incarcerated people are parents, and about half of imprisoned parents lived with their children before incarceration (Glaze and Maruschak 2008; Gotsch 2018).

Although some studies suggest that parental incarceration can be a time to rebuild bonds (Edin, Nelson, and Paranal 2004) and facilitate communication (Giordano 2010), most find that incarceration fractures relationships between parents and children "in terms of physical closeness and financial contributions" and erodes "relationships that may already have been fragile" (Travis, Western, and Redburn 2014, pp. 269–70), with harmful effects on children's well-being. For example, Turney and Wildeman (2013) find that incarceration negatively affects parent-child engagement, shared responsibility in parenting, and cooperation in parenting among fathers who were living with their children before their incarceration (see also Geller 2013). Using propensity score models, Washington, Juan, and Haskins (2018) find that paternal incarceration is associated with decreased involvement with fathers of children in middle childhood.

Recent studies also shed light on the mechanisms underlying negative effects of paternal incarceration on fathers' relationships with their children. For example, Turney and Wildeman (2013) find that lower levels of paternal involvement in children's lives stem from changes in the quality of the parental relationship, in fathers' economic conditions, and in fathers' health. The first of these is especially important: virtually the entire association between paternal incarceration and fathers' parenting is explained by changes in fathers' relationships with their children's mothers. These effects are smaller (and may be nonexistent) among fathers who are not living with their children before incarceration, probably because most nonresident fathers have less contact with their children.

Most studies of the effects of parental incarceration on children focus on paternal rather than maternal incarceration. More recently, though, researchers have examined the effects of maternal incarceration on mothers' relationships with their children and their family life more generally. Although less common than paternal incarceration, maternal incarceration appears to be especially disruptive because of higher levels of parent-child cohabitation before incarceration. Turney and Wildeman (2018) find that in addition to impairing romantic relationships, maternal incarceration leads to chronic strains in family life and is a stressor from which families are often unable to recover (see also Poehlmann 2005).

In short, the experience of imprisonment generally undermines imprisoned peoples' relationships with their loved ones. These relational effects are distributed in a highly uneven manner. Nearly half (44 percent) of Black women, and one-third (32 percent) of Black men, have a family member who is imprisoned (Lee et al. 2015). By contrast, 12 percent of White women and 6 percent of White men have an imprisoned family member. The cumulative risk of ever having had a loved one incarcerated is, of course, higher, especially for people of color. A recent study found that 63 percent of Black respondents, 48 percent of Hispanic respondents, and 42 percent of White respondents indicated that they had ever experienced the incarceration of an immediate family member (Enns et al. 2019).

This literature has some limitations (see Travis, Western, and Redburn 2014, pp. 275–77). Most or all of the quantitative studies analyze Fragile Families and Child Well-Being longitudinal data, which are limited to select urban areas.[7] Qualitative studies are generally based on convenience

---

[7] For more information about the Fragile Families and Child Well-Being data source, see https://fragilefamilies.princeton.edu.

samples in a limited number of (overwhelmingly urban) jurisdictions. Future studies might draw on alternative data sources, use experimental designs, or both to address these limitations. Researchers might also explore the effects of COVID-19 on incarcerated parents and their relationships with children.

II. Implications for Policy and Research

Imprisonment causes significant harm. When it occurs on a mass scale, and in the context of pronounced inequality and widespread precarity, those harms are multiplied. The penal system is now an important mechanism by which racial and class inequalities are reproduced over time (Western 2006). At the same time, there is compelling evidence that incarceration is not an effective or humane way to protect public safety—even if we accept a narrow definition of public safety (Travis, Western, and Redburn 2014; Tonry 2016; Petrich et al. 2021). For example, a recent meta-analysis of 116 studies found that confinement either has no effect on recidivism or slightly increases it relative to use of noncustodial sanctions such as probation. Petrich et al. conclude that "this finding is robust regardless of variations in methodological rigor, types of sanctions examined, and sociodemographic characteristics of samples. All sophisticated assessments of the research have independently reached the same conclusion. The null effect of custodial compared with noncustodial sanctions is considered a 'criminological fact.' Incarceration cannot be justified on the grounds it affords public safety by decreasing recidivism" (2021, p. 353).

The strength of this conclusion may surprise many readers, yet other types of evidence provide additional support for it. Many countries with far lower incarceration rates than the United States experience far less crime, and many have enjoyed declines in crime rates that are similar to those that have taken place in the United States without increasing their use of incarceration (Doob and Webster 2006; Zimring 2007; Tonry 2014b). Similarly, US states that reduced their imprisonment rates the most in recent years have experienced the largest drops in crime rates (Pew Charitable Trusts 2014; see also Lofstrom and Raphael 2016). Research has for decades consistently shown that short sentences deter as much as long ones and that most people—including people serving long and life sentences—mature and desist from crime (Travis, Western, and Redburn 2014). Moreover, incarceration is often criminogenic (Haney 2020). For these and other reasons, the National Research Council recently concluded that "statutes mandating lengthy prison sentences cannot be justified on the basis of their effectiveness in preventing crime" (Travis, Western, and Redburn 2014, pp. 155–56).

In short, incarceration is an ineffective and harmful means of achieving public safety. Mass incarceration is, therefore, an especially unwise and destructive institutional development, one that both reflects and perpetuates poverty and racial inequality while also largely failing to achieve its ostensible mission of keeping people safe. And when we adopt a more capacious understanding of what safety means and requires, it is clear that mass incarceration not only fails to produce public safety but is a threat to it (Beckett 2022).

Many researchers are engaged in public scholarship aimed at educating the public and policy makers about the harm imprisonment and mass incarceration cause and the need for alternative approaches to achieving public safety and justice. Doing so often means "going beyond the data" to weigh costs and benefits or identify possible alternatives. This, in turn, requires that social scientists identify the normative commitments that, along with data and evidence, guide their interpretations and recommendations. In this section, we offer a normative framework that might inform these efforts. We then draw on this framework, and social scientific evidence, to argue for two broad sets of policy changes that would reduce use of incarceration while building a safer and more just society.

A. Normative Commitments in Efforts to End Mass Incarceration

We believe it is important for researchers who engage in public scholarship regarding mass incarceration to be transparent about normative commitments. A few values seem especially germane.

1. *Racial Equity.* Mass incarceration cannot be understood without reference to the long history of racial injustice throughout US history, especially the enslavement and subjugation of Black people (Alexander 2010; Muhammad 2011; Hinton and Cook 2021). The criminal justice system continues to be rife with bias and unfairness and reproduces racial inequality in communities that are struggling with poverty and numerous forms of violence (Western 2006; Lee et al. 2015; Wakefield, Lee, and Wildeman 2016). Efforts to reduce reliance on incarceration should, we believe, treat equity, fairness, and remediation of past and current racial injustices as primary objectives.

2. *Human Rights.* The principle of universal human rights should guide analysis of what needs to be done to redress mass incarceration

and reduce reliance on imprisonment (Beckett 2022). The idea that all humans are entitled to inalienable rights, including rights to hope and to dignity, has a long history in the United States and elsewhere but has been denied in practice far too often.[8] The belief in the inherent value of all people, including those who live at the margins of society or have been convicted of terrible crimes, is sometimes expressed as the idea that "no one is disposable." This value underscores the importance of considering the rights and dignity of all, including people who have been convicted of the most serious offenses (Stevenson 2014). It is for this reason that many countries allow neither the death penalty nor life sentences without the possibility of parole (Mauer and Nellis 2019; van Zyl Smit and Appleton 2019).

3. *Social Justice.* Commitment to social justice means that corrective courses of action should seek not only to reduce incarceration and the power of the carceral state but also, wherever possible, to address related sources of harm that disproportionately affect the socially disadvantaged. The concept of social justice has been articulated and theorized in numerous ways; at its core, it involves a commitment to redressing social inequality and promoting "the capacity to flourish" among the most marginalized (Sen 1989, p. 47). This value underlies our preference for changes that reduce the harm caused both by the criminal legal system and by social ills such as extreme poverty, houselessness, unmanaged addiction, and interpersonal violence. These social problems disproportionately affect people of color, people contending with poverty, and other historically marginalized groups. And as sociologist Neil Gong (2021) notes, decarceration can lead easily to abandonment and precarity if not also accompanied by increased investment in housing, income support, health care, families, and communities. Prominent proponents of abolition of imprisonment, theorists and activists alike, emphasize that ending mass incarceration requires not only dismantling coercive state institutions and practices but also imagining, building, and instituting humane approaches to safety and justice in their place (Davis 2003; Gilmore 2017; Kaba 2021). Releasing people from prison to the streets and a life of hardship, precarity, and struggle is clearly insufficient.

---

[8] Legal scholar Jonathan Simon (2016, 2017) has written eloquently and persuasively about the importance of the right to dignity.

B. Ending Mass Incarceration

Evidence of the damage caused by incarceration on a mass scale has been amassing for decades, and policy makers appear to be increasingly aware of its harmful and counterproductive effects. Some states have taken steps to reduce their reliance on prisons (Beckett et al. 2018; Beckett 2022). However, most reforms to date target the "low-hanging fruit," or what Gottschalk (2015) calls the "nons": nonserious, nonviolent, and nonsexual crimes (see also Seeds 2017; Beckett 2022). Even in relation to drug law reform most decarcerative reforms focus only on drug possession (as opposed to drug distribution). Lawmakers in recent years have more often increased penalties for drug distribution than reduced them (Beckett and Brydolf-Horwitz 2020). As a result, most of the draconian sentencing laws that contributed to the prison buildup remain on the books and continue to ensure long prison stays for many (Gottschalk 2015; Tonry 2016).

This approach ignores the reality that widespread imposition of long and life sentences, mainly in cases involving violent crime, has contributed significantly to mass incarceration. The majority of the nation's state and federal prisoners are serving time for violent crimes, and the United States imposes far longer sentences in such cases than do other democratic countries (Tonry 2016; Ghandnoosh 2019; Beckett 2022). Moreover, while people of color are overrepresented among people convicted of all types of offenses, racial disproportionality is most pronounced among people convicted of violent crimes and, relatedly, among those serving long and life sentences (Ghandnoosh 2019; Grunwald 2021). Reform strategies that do not reduce penalties for violent crime will likely increase racial disproportionality in US prisons (Grunwald 2021). Reliance on excessive sentences is also costly and consumes significant tax dollars that might otherwise be spent on crime prevention initiatives, victim services, and restorative justice (RJ) alternatives. The clear implication of this body of research—and of the normative framework we outlined—is that comprehensive sentencing reform that includes the most serious offenses is needed if we are meaningfully to reduce reliance on incarceration and the racial inequities it embodies and aggravates.[9] Limiting maximum prison sentences to 20 years would be a significant change in the United

---

[9] Pfaff (2017) argues that sentence length has not increased and that changes in sentencing policy did not fuel mass incarceration. Instead, he attributes mass incarceration to one main dynamic—the increased propensity of prosecutors to file felony charges given arrest—and

States but would bring the country into line with human rights norms and the practices of other democratic countries (Ghandnoosh 2019; Mauer and Nellis 2019). To ensure that such a policy would also redress the inequities and excesses of the past, sentencing reforms must be made retroactive and allow for meaningful opportunities for postconviction relief for people serving long and life sentences. Decreasing prison admissions would also, eventually, reduce the size of the prison population, but that alone would take much longer to reduce the size of the prison population, would leave many (disproportionately Black and Brown) people serving long and life sentences, and would not decrease racial disproportionality in prisons (Grunwald 2021).

This does not mean, however, that penalties for comparatively minor offenses should not be reduced, for several reasons. First, the routine imposition of confinement and other penalties for low-level crimes contributes to mass incarceration and mass criminalization, occasions entirely avoidable pain and suffering, and reproduces racial and socioeconomic inequality (Stuart, Armenta, and Osborne 2015; Stuart 2016; Atkinson and Travis 2021). Second, relying on confinement sentences—or even conviction—for minor crimes does not protect public safety (Agan, Doleac, and Harvey 2021). And third, it seems unlikely that lawmakers will reduce long sentences for violent and other comparatively serious crimes if they have not reduced reliance on confinement for minor offenses. At the same time, reforms aimed at reducing or eliminating penalties for minor offenses must be carefully and thoughtfully pursued. Reforms, especially those aimed at making troubling practices more procedurally fair, can create the perception but not the reality of change, thereby pacifying critics, entrenching carceral state power, and making more transformative change more difficult (Steiker and Steiker 2014; Butler 2016; Gilmore 2017). Moreover, in some cases, political actors justify their support of very modest reforms in terms of the increased capacity those reforms will generate to punish other people more severely (Beckett et al. 2018). Both social scientific research and the normative principles set out above underscore the need to reduce reliance on incarceration, including for cases involving violence. Yet the political and cultural challenges associated with violent crime pose a significant obstacle, one more difficult to surmount than

advances a reform agenda that, he argues, would lead to more meaningful change by reducing felony filings. For a critique of this perspective, see Beckett (2018, 2022).

the opposition of vested interests (Beckett 2022). Resistance to reducing punishments for interpersonal violence reflects deeply rooted and widely shared images of violent people as monstrous and irredeemable others. This myth of monstrosity (Beckett 2022) is deeply rooted in racist tropes and stereotypes (Muhammad 2011; Haney 2020). It is also irreconcilable with a substantial body of research showing that people convicted of more and less serious crimes are not two distinct moral or social categories and that extreme poverty, trauma, instability, and violent victimization typically precipitate acts of interpersonal violence (Western 2019; Haney 2020). Evidence of extensive victimization among people who subsequently commit violent acts challenges popular understandings of criminal behavior and contradicts the widespread assumption that people who commit violent acts and people who survive them are distinct groups with opposing interests. The myth of monstrosity rests on an overly narrow conception of violence, one that disregards and discounts the racial and structural violence that pervade US history and society. Yet this structural violence—including extreme poverty, racial oppression and discrimination, housing precarity, and untreated addiction and mental illness—helps explain unacceptably high levels of interpersonal violence in some US neighborhoods (Western 2019). Acknowledging the many forms violence takes, and undermining the myth of monstrosity, will be necessary if we are to develop responses to violence that reduce rather than compound it.

C. Getting from Here to There: Challenging the Myth of Monstrosity

Comprehensive sentencing reform that reduces long and life sentences—and creates viable postconviction release mechanisms—is clearly needed. What is less clear is how, given the durability and power of the myth of monstrosity, to get such laws enacted. There are few avenues for challenging the popular assumption that criminal defendants are inherently malicious individuals. In capital cases, the Supreme Court has recognized that this may not be true and requires that sentencing decisions take account of individual circumstances in order not to violate the Eighth Amendment's prohibition of cruel and unusual punishment. As a result, defense attorneys representing capital clients can introduce evidence of "mitigating circumstances" in the sentencing phase of capital trials. Some legal scholars have proposed that opportunities to present evidence of mitigating circumstances be expanded to noncapital cases (Gohara 2013). However, evidence regarding this potential strategy is discouraging. The vast majority of cases are resolved through plea bargains rather than at trial. Even in cases that go to trial, evidence of mitigating circumstances is often dismissed. As Haney notes, "A simple and seemingly irrefutable assertion that 'not everybody' exposed to one or another set of destructive background factors engaged in violent crime is used to trivialize what, in virtually any other context, we would all recognize as critically important to the decision at hand" (Haney 1995, p. 591). While the "not everybody" argument is intuitively appealing to many, it ignores the reality that peoples' experiences of broadly similar circumstances are not identical. Evidence that some smokers do not develop lung cancer, for example, does not mean that a causal relationship between smoking and cancer does not exist but rather suggests that the risk smoking poses is mediated by other factors. Similarly, gender, poverty, the age at which a person experienced abuse, the existence or absence of alternative sources of support, and myriad other factors mediate the long-term effects of childhood abuse, neglect, and trauma. Invocations of the not-everybody argument sweep these nuances aside, wrongly dismiss all evidence that social biography matters, and bolster the myth of monstrosity (Haney 2020). The effectiveness of legal mechanisms for introduction of mitigating evidence is limited for another reason. Juries' willingness to treat evidence of abuse and trauma as grounds for mercy is shaped by race. Summarizing his observations of numerous capital cases involving Black defendants, Haney concludes that "a particular kind of racially discriminatory death sentencing comes about as a result of an 'empathic divide' that exists between many white jurors and African American defendants. White jurors may have an especially difficult time understanding the mitigation that inheres in the structure of the lives that many African-American defendants have led" (2014, p. 1558). Findings from experimental studies confirm Haney's observation. Mitigating circumstances that may be perceived as exculpatory for White defendants are often ignored, or even interpreted as incriminating, when defendants are Black (Lynch and Haney 2011). Research showing that race shapes jurors' responses to evidence of mitigating circumstances casts doubt on the likelihood that such an approach will bring about a more just and fair system.

Recent studies suggest more promising avenues for undermining the myth of monstrosity. At first glance, it may seem that politicians who stress commitment to harsh penalties for violent crimes are reading public opinion reasonably accurately: many members of the public do support harsh penalties for violent offenses, and nearly all express more support for punitive responses to violent than to property crimes (O'Hear and Wheelock 2020). Interestingly, though, people who have experienced violence, or live in areas that put them at higher risk of it, are not more punitive than others. Instead, the widespread preference for long sentences for violence is associated with traditional views about individual responsibility and accountability as well as racial resentment and authoritarianism (Cullen, Butler, and Graham 2021). That support for punitive responses to violence is rooted in values and attitudes rather than in experience means that these preferences may be fungible. In particular, advocates of alternative responses to violence could make the case that less punitive responses to violence also comport with traditional values. For example, proponents of RJ often emphasize the ways in which restorative practices respect and serve the value of accountability (e.g., Boyle 2010; Sered 2019). Emphasizing these kinds of connections may help dislodge the widely accepted idea that the only way to hold people accountable is through long prison sentences.

Many advocates are doing important cultural work by disseminating biographical narratives that challenge the myth of monstrosity. Some groups, such as the Alliance for Safety and Justice (2019), amplify the voices of the survivors of crime and violence—especially survivors of color whose voices are often omitted or silenced—who do not favor the current approach to public safety. Relatedly, some advocates disseminate and amplify the stories of people who in the past were convicted of a violent offense but now lead lives of peace and integrity, whether behind bars or in the free world. Researchers could support this effort by collecting and publicizing the stories of people whose lives refute the core assumptions of the myth of monstrosity, although this needs to be thoughtfully done to maximize the transformative potential of these stories (Desmond and Martinez Rosas 2021).

These and other cultural strategies are essential to countering the myth of monstrosity, which has impeded serious consideration of comprehensive sentencing reform. In the meantime, more minor reforms may help dislodge the image of people convicted of an act of violence as monstrous others. For example, requiring that prisons and jails adopt trauma-informed practices would constitute a minor step toward acknowledging the histories of victimization that abound among inmates in those institutions. Similarly, improving conditions of confinement (e.g., around medical care, visitation, and the use of solitary confinement) would acknowledge the humanity of the people affected. These smaller reforms may also help lay foundations for more sweeping transformation of our approach to the problem of violence.

D. Ending Mass Incarceration through Social Investment

Together with social scientific evidence of mass incarceration's harmful effects and its failure to enhance public safety meaningfully, the normative framework set out above underlines the need to simultaneously diminish carceral state power, reduce racial and other inequities in the justice system, and improve underlying social conditions. This is a tall order, but we believe it is doable. We consider below what such an approach might look like.[10]

Risks of interpersonal violence are highly uneven. In the United States, for example, people of color, people who live in poverty, and people living in high-crime neighborhoods face especially high risk of victimization (Langton and Truman 2014; Sered 2019). Violent victimization is, in turn, highly correlated with negative mental health and social outcomes such as PTSD, socioemotional distress, and reduced quality of life. Individuals exposed to trauma (including violent victimization) are at increased risk of physical and mental illness; poor physical and mental health affect survivors' ability to engage successfully in education and the labor market (Sledjeski, Speisman, and Dierker 2008; Cutler, Lleras-Muney, and Vogl 2011).

Advocates of tough sentencing practices often base their arguments on the needs and wants of crime victims, but current criminal justice and sentencing policies do not serve violence survivors well, especially those from disadvantaged communities. Many people convicted of violent crimes and serving long sentences are themselves victims of abuse and violence (Western 2019). Most victims never enjoy their "day in court," either because they do not file a police report or because arrest and prosecution do not occur (Travis 2012). As Sered (2019) points out, that roughly half of people who experience violence do not report the crime to the police

---

[10] In focusing on violence, we do not mean to imply that the scale of punishment is driven solely or primarily by rates of crime or violence. Incarceration is widely viewed as a public safety intervention. Strategies that ignore threats of interpersonal violence in some US communities are neither inclusive nor credible (Desmond and Martinez Rosas 2021). Moreover, upticks in crime or violence, such as have occurred during the pandemic, often trigger calls for harsher penalties. Proposals to alter sentencing policies radically are unlikely to be politically credible if not accompanied by alternative public safety and justice strategies.

means they prefer nothing to what the state has to offer. Even among people who do report, most do not receive the services they need (Herman 2010). People who are poor, of color, or both are especially unlikely to receive needed services (Stillman 2015; Sered 2019). Moreover, many survivors who do report their victimization are dissatisfied with the process, and too many experience revictimization that amplifies their psychological distress. Some studies find that victim participation in the conventional criminal justice process exacerbates rather than alleviates survivors' trauma (Englebrecht, Mason, and Adams 2014).

Policies that allow for the imposition of long and life sentences are often said to reflect survivors' preferences, but this is also misleading. Long prison sentences do little to mitigate the negative effects of violence, are not favored by many people who have experienced interpersonal violence, and often end up punishing people who are themselves victims of abuse, crime, and violence. A recent national survey found that 61 percent of those who have experienced interpersonal violence favor shorter prison terms and enhanced spending on prevention and rehabilitation; only 25 percent preferred sentences that keep people in prison as long as possible (Alliance for Safety and Justice 2019). Similarly, significant majorities of survivors of all political orientations favor investing public safety dollars in education rather than in prisons and jails. In California, crime victims are a leading force in the movement for criminal justice reform (Stillman 2015).

Long prison sentences consume significant public dollars that could be reallocated to improve victim services and enhance crime prevention efforts (Tonry 2014a). For example, increasing access to high-quality, early education programs improves educational outcomes and reduces subsequent criminal legal system involvement (Heckman et al. 2010). The US Department of Education has, however, acknowledged that children in countries as diverse as Mexico, France, and Singapore have a better chance of receiving preschool education than do children in the United States (Ghandnoosh 2019). Other public safety interventions that do not involve incarceration have also been found to be highly cost effective. These include employment training and job assistance in the community and outpatient drug treatment (Drake 2013). Within prison settings, substance abuse treatment, education (both K–12 and postsecondary), and vocational training are cost-effective means of reducing recidivism and improving public safety. Community-based organizations that focus on violence prevention and strengthening communities have also been found to reduce violent crime (Sharkey, Torrats-Espinosa, and Takyar 2017; see also Sharkey 2018). Sharkey, Torrats-Espinosa, and Takyar (2017, p. 1214) found that "every 10 additional organizations focusing on crime and community life in a city with 100,000 residents leads to a 9 percent reduction in the murder rate, a 6 percent reduction in the violent crime rate, and a 4 percent reduction in the property crime rate" (see also Telep and Hibdon 2018).

In short, investing in youth, families, and community-based organizations will advance the cause of public safety and is a preferred strategy for many crime survivors. Increased investment in RJ alternatives would also help meet survivors' needs, improve public safety, and dislodge the cultural centrality of the myth of monstrosity. Interventions based on RJ principles vary across a number of important dimensions but generally "involve, to the extent possible, those who have a stake in a specific offense to collectively identify and address harms, needs and obligations, in order to heal and put things as right as possible" (Zehr 2002, p. 12). RJ initiatives that involve diversion from the criminal legal system have the potential to facilitate survivor healing while also holding people who cause harm to others accountable but without relying on jails and prisons. A growing body of evidence suggests that programs informed by RJ principles hold a great deal of promise in terms of improving survivor well-being, reducing recidivism, and, in some cases, decreasing reliance on prisons and jails.

When given the option, many people who have experienced violence and other harms choose to participate in RJ alternatives (see, e.g., Sered 2019). Studies of RJ programs generally indicate that all involved parties report high levels of satisfaction (Umbreit et al. 2005; Wilson, Olaghere, and Kimbrell 2018). In fact, expression of satisfaction is consistent for both victims and responsible parties across sites, cultures, and offense seriousness. In addition, research tracing the effects of RJ conferencing on PTSD symptoms associated with robbery and burglary found that RJ practices notably reduce traumatic effects (Angel et al. 2014; see also Wilson, Olaghere, and Kimbrell 2018). High levels of victim satisfaction reflect increased feelings of safety and positive attitudes toward perceptions of greater fairness (Umbreit et al. 2005; Sered 2019).

Although RJ programs tend to focus on meeting survivors' needs and repairing harms, the efficacy of criminal justice interventions is often measured in terms of reduced recidivism. Many survivors participate in RJ processes precisely because they hope doing so will ensure that the person who harmed them will not harm others (Sered 2019). For these reasons, many studies assess whether RJ processes affect the likelihood of future harm. Although significant methodological challenges are associated with these evaluations, many find that RJ programs reduce future violations (Umbreit et al. 2005; Umbreit, Vos, and Coates 2007; Sherman et al. 2015).

Unfortunately, most RJ programs are not used for violent crimes. Yet RJ may be most effective in such situations. One Canadian study found no significant effects on future violations by people convicted of low-level offenses but a 38 percent reduction in recidivism for people who committed violent crimes (Sherman et al. 2015). Another study found a direct and positive correlation between the long-term success of the program (measured mainly in terms of recidivism) and the seriousness of the offense (McCold and Wachtel 1998). The implication is that RJ programs may have the greatest potential to improve victim healing and reduce recidivism if they include cases that involve interpersonal violence (see also Sered 2019). It seems likely that RJ initiatives improve interpersonal relationships and hence communities' capacity to address harms without reliance on the police or criminal legal system.

A number of important concerns have been raised about RJ alternatives; scalability remains especially challenging. It is as yet unclear whether and how diversion frameworks based on RJ principles can be scaled up in a way that leads to meaningful improvements in survivor well-being and public safety. Yet the answers to these difficult questions will never be learned in the abstract. Increased investment in and experimentation with RJ alternatives is needed to inform assessments of its scalability and viability.

III. Conclusion

Imprisonment causes a great deal of harm to individuals, families, and communities. It causes significant psychological harm, worsens mental and physical health, and increases morbidity over the life course. Although many imprisoned people work while they are behind bars, few can contribute to their families or save money because of the meager wages paid to imprisoned workers, the high cost of subsistence items, and widespread imposition and collection of LFOs. Incarceration reduces employment, earnings, and opportunities for wealth accumulation after release from prison. Imprisonment also disrupts and weakens bonds between incarcerated people, their romantic partners, and their children, destabilizing families in the process.

As evidence of imprisonment's harms has accumulated, some researchers have tried more effectively to disseminate their findings to policy makers and public audiences. This public scholarship has an important role to play and has likely helped raise awareness of the harm caused by incarceration. We invite researchers to consider adopting a problem-solving approach. Prasad (2018) distinguishes "problem-solving sociology" from "public scholarship" in which researchers seek to engage in dialogue with affected parties or broadly disseminate their findings. The fundamental difference is that the problem-solving approach calls for researchers to identify and assess potential solutions to problems rather than describe and analyze the problem itself. A problem-solving approach thus requires focusing on (attempted) solutions and proposing new solutions rather than only studying problems or critiquing existing solutions. Prasad emphasizes that this approach is not an alternative to scientific inquiry. It will yield new substantive and theoretical insights and substantive findings and often require development of new methods.

Such an approach to the study of imprisonment in general, and mass incarceration in particular, would yield important and useful new knowledge. Mass incarceration's many harms and failures are well documented and reasonably well understood. It is true that causality is difficult to establish definitively in certain areas, especially in a single study. Absolute certainty is unlikely to ever be obtained. Alternatively, we could call the question, as climate scientists have increasingly done, and shift our focus to identifying and analyzing solutions to the problem of mass incarceration.

The seeds of such a problem-solving approach have been planted. For example, Sharkey, Torrats-Espinosa, and Takyar's (2017) study found that the presence of community-based organizations reduces violence. This finding invites a new research and policy agenda that studies approaches to public safety and justice that do not rely on police and prisons (see also Bell 2020). Prasad (2018) notes that such studies could advance general social scientific understanding of a variety of topics related to public safety and justice. They would likely also yield important insights into improving public safety and enhancing justice in ways that build, rather than harm, the communities most affected both by violence and by mass incarceration. The destruction and harm both cause are now well understood. The time has come for researchers to use our skills to help solve the problems we have usefully described and analyzed for decades.

REFERENCES

Aaltonen, Mikko, Torbjørn Skardhamar, Anders Nilsson, Lars Højsgaard Andersen, Olof Bäckman, Felipe Estrada, and Petri Danielsson. 2017. "Comparing Employment Trajectories before and after First Imprisonment in Four Nordic Countries." *British Journal of Criminology* 57(4):828–47.

Aday, Ronald, and Lori Farney. 2014. "Malign Neglect: Assessing Older Women's Health Care Experiences in Prison." *Journal of Bioethical Inquiry* 11(3):359–72.

Agan, Amanda Y., Jennifer Doleac, and Anna Harvey. 2021. "Misdemeanor Prosecution." NBER working paper. Cambridge, MA: National Bureau of Economic Research. https://doi.org/10.3386/w28600.

Albertson, Elaine Michelle, Christopher Scannell, Neda Ashtari, and Elizabeth Barnert. 2020. "Eliminating Gaps in Medicaid Coverage during Reentry after Incarceration." *American Journal of Public Health* 110:317–21.

Alexander, Michelle. 2010. *The New Jim Crow: Mass Incarceration in the Age of Colorblindness*. New York: New Press.

Alliance for Safety and Justice. 2019. *Crime Survivors Speak: The First-Ever National Survey of Victims' Views on Safety and Justice*. Oakland, CA: Alliance for Safety and Justice.

Angel, Caroline M., Lawrence W. Sherman, Heather Strang, Barak Ariel, Sarah Bennett, Nova Inkpen, Anne Keane, and Therese S. Richmond. 2014. "Short-Term Effects of Restorative Justice Conferences on Post-traumatic Stress Symptoms among Robbery and Burglary Victims." *Journal of Experimental Criminology* 10(3):291–307.

Apel, Robert, Arjan A. J. Blokland, Paul Nieuwbeerta, and Marieke van Schellen. 2010. "The Impact of Imprisonment on Marriage and Divorce: A Risk Set Matching Approach." *Journal of Quantitative Criminology* 26(2):269–300.

Apel, Robert, and Kathleen Powell. 2019. "Level of Criminal Justice Contact and Early Adult Wage Inequality." *Russell Sage Foundation Journal of the Social Sciences* 5(1):198–222.

Apel, Robert, and Gary Sweeten. 2010. "The Impact of Incarceration on Employment during the Transition to Adulthood." *Social Problems* 57(3):448–79.

Atkinson, Daryl, and Jeremy Travis. 2021. *The Power of Parsimony*. New York: Square One Project.

Bacak, Valerio, and Edward H. Kennedy. 2015. "Marginal Structural Models: An Application to Incarceration and Marriage during Young Adulthood." *Journal of Marriage and Family* 77(1):112–25.

Beckett, Katherine. 2018. "The Politics, Peril and Promise of Criminal Justice Reform in the Context of Mass Incarceration." *Annual Review of Criminology* 1:235–59.

Beckett, Katherine. 2022. *Ending Mass Incarceration*. New York: Oxford University Press.

Beckett, Katherine, Lindsey Beach, Anna Reosti, and Emily Knaphus. 2018. "U.S. Criminal Justice Policy and Practice in the 21st Century: Toward the End of Mass Incarceration?" *Law and Policy* 40(4):321–45.

Beckett, Katherine, and Marco Brydolf-Horwitz. 2020. "A Kinder, Gentler Drug War? Race, Drugs, and Punishment in 21st Century America." *Punishment and Society* 22(4):509–33.

Beckett, Katherine, and Alexes Harris. 2011. "On Cash and Conviction: Monetary Sanctions as Misguided Policy." *Criminology and Public Policy* 10(3):509–37.

Bell, Monica. 2020. "Black Security and the Conundrum of Policing." *Just Security*, July 15. https://www.justsecurity.org/71418/black-security-and-the-conundrum -of-policing/.

Binswanger, Ingrid A., Marc F. Stern, Richard A. Deyo, Patrick J. Heagerty, Allen Cheadle, Joann G. Elmore, and Thomas D. Koepsell. 2007. "Release from Prison: A High Risk of Death for Former Inmates." *New England Journal of Medicine* 356(2):157–65.

Blakinger, Keri. 2021. "Some Prison Labor Programs Lose Money—Even When Prisoners Work for Pennies." Marshall Project, September 2.

Boyle, Gregory. 2010. *Tattoos on the Heart.* New York: Simon & Schuster.

Brayne, Sarah. 2014. "Surveillance and System Avoidance: Criminal Justice Contact and Institutional Attachment." *American Sociological Review* 79(3):367–91.

Brennan Center for Justice. 2019. *Is Charging Inmates to Stay in Prison Smart Policy?* New York: New York University Law School, Brennan Center for Justice.

Bronson, Jennifer, and Marcus Berzofsky. 2017. *Indicators of Mental Health Problems Reported by Prisoners and Jail Inmates, 2011–2012.* Washington, DC: US Department of Justice, Bureau of Justice Statistics.

Bucerius, Sandra, Kevin D. Haggerty, David T. Dunford. 2021. "Prison as Temporary Refuge: Amplifying the Voices of Women Detained in Prison." *British Journal of Criminology* 61(2):519–37.

Butler, Paul. 2016. "The System Is Working the Way It Is Supposed To: The Limits of Criminal Justice Reform." *Georgetown Law Journal* 104(6):1419–79.

Cadigan, Michelle, and Gabriela Kirk. 2020. "On Thin Ice: Bureaucratic Processes of Monetary Sanctions and Job Insecurity." *Russell Sage Foundation Journal of the Social Sciences* 6(1):113–31.

Carson, E. Ann. 2021a. *Prisoners in 2020—Statistical Tables.* Washington, DC: US Department of Justice, Bureau of Justice Statistics.

Carson, E. Ann. 2021b. *Mortality in State and Federal Prisons, 2001–2018—Statistical Tables.* Washington, DC: US Department of Justice, Bureau of Justice Statistics.

Charles, Kerwin Kofi, and Ming Ching Luoh. 2010. "Male Incarceration, the Marriage Market, and Female Outcomes." *Review of Economics and Statistics* 92(3):614–17.

Comfort, Megan. 2012. "'It Was Basically College to Us': Poverty, Prison, and Emerging Adulthood." *Journal of Poverty* 3:308–22.

Craigie, Terry-Ann, Ames Grawert, and Cameron Kimble. 2020. *Conviction, Imprisonment, and Lost Earnings: How Involvement with the Criminal Justice System Deepens Inequality.* New York: New York University Law School, Brennan Center for Justice.

Crewe, Ben. 2011. "Depth, Weight, Tightness: Revisiting the Pains of Imprisonment." *Punishment and Society* 13(5):509–29.

Crewe, Ben, and Alice Ievins. 2020. "The Prison as a Reinventive Institution." *Theoretical Criminology* 24(4):568–89.

Cullen, Francis T., Leah C. Butler, and Amanda Graham. 2021. "Racial Attitudes and Criminal Justice Policy." In *Crime and Justice: A Review of Research*, vol. 50, edited by Michael Tonry. Chicago: University of Chicago Press.

Cutler, David M., Adriana Lleras-Muney, and Tom Vogl. 2011. "Socio-Economic Status and Health: Dimensions and Mechanisms." In *The Oxford Handbook of Health Economics*, edited by Sherry Glied and Peter C. Smith. New York: Oxford University Press.

Davis, Angela Yvonne. 2003. *Are Prisons Obsolete?* New York: Seven Stories.

Denney, Matthew G. T., and Ramon Garibaldo Valdez. 2021. "Compounding Racialized Vulnerability: COVID-19 in Prisons, Jails, and Migrant Detention Centers." *Journal of Health Politics, Policy, and Law* 46(5):861–87.

Desmond, Matthew, and Greisa Martinez Rosas. 2021. "Beyond the Easiest Cases: Creating New Narratives for Criminal Justice and Immigration Reform." New York: Square One Project.

Doob, Anthony, and C. Webster. 2006. "Countering Punitiveness: Understanding Stability in Canada's Imprisonment." *Law and Society Review* 40(2):325–67.

Drake, Elizabeth. 2013. *Inventory of Evidence-Based and Research-Based Programs for Adult Corrections*. Olympia: Washington State Institute for Public Policy.

Dumont, Dora M., Scott A. Allen, Bradley W. Brockmann, Nicole E. Alexander, and Josiah D. Rich. 2013. "Incarceration, Community Health, and Racial Disparities." *Journal of Health Care for the Poor and Underserved* 24(1):78–88.

Economics Daily. 2019. "Employment of Young Men after Arrest or Incarceration." *Economics Daily*, March 20.

Edin, Katherine, Timothy Nelson, and Rechelle Paranal. 2004. "Fatherhood and Incarceration as Potential Turning Points in the Criminal Careers of Unskilled Men." In *Imprisoning America: The Social Effects of Mass Incarceration*, edited by Mary Patillo, David Weiman, and Bruce Western. New York: Russell Sage.

Eisen, Lauren-Brooke. 2015. *Charging Inmates Perpetuates Mass Incarceration*. New York: New York University Law School, Brennan Center for Justice.

Englebrecht, Christine, Derek T. Mason, and Margaret J. Adams. 2014. "The Experience of Homicide Victims' Families with the Criminal Justice System: An Exploratory Study." *Violence and Victims* 29(3):407–21.

Enns, Peter K., Youngmin Yi, Megan Comfort, Alyssa W. Goldman, Hedwig Lee, Christopher Muller, Sara Wakefield, Emily A. Wang, and Christopher Wildeman. 2019. "What Percentage of Americans Have Ever Had a Family Member Incarcerated? Evidence from the Family History of Incarceration Survey (FamHIS)." *Socius: Sociological Research for a Dynamic World* 5:1–45.

Ewert, Stephanie, Bryan L. Sykes, and Becky Pettit. 2014. "The Degree of Disadvantage: Incarceration and Inequality in Education." *Annals of the American Academy of Political and Social Science* 651:24–30.

Fallesen, Peter, and Lars H. Andersen. 2017. "Explaining the Consequences of Imprisonment for Union Formation and Dissolution in Denmark." *Journal of Policy Analysis and Management* 36(1):154–77.

Forrest, Walter. 2014. "Cohabitation, Relationship Quality, and Desistance from Crime." *Journal of Marriage and Family* 76(3):539–56.

Frank, Joseph W., Emily A. Wang, Marcella Nunez-Smith, Hedwig Lee, and Megan Comfort. 2014. "Discrimination Based on Criminal Record and Healthcare Utilization among Men Recently Released from Prison: A Descriptive Study." *Health and Justice* 2(6):1–8.

Garland, David. 2001. *Mass Imprisonment: Social Causes and Consequences.* Beverly Hills, CA: Sage.

Geller, Amanda. 2013. "Paternal Incarceration and Father-Child Contact in Fragile Families." *Journal of Marriage and Family* 75(5):1288–303.

Ghandnoosh, Nazgol. 2019. *The Next Step: Ending Excessive Punishment for Violent Crimes.* Washington, DC: Sentencing Project.

Gilmore, Ruth Wilson. 2017. "Abolition Geographies and the Problem of Innocence." In *Futures of Black Radicalism*, edited by Gaye Theresa Johnson and Alex Lubin. New York: Verso.

Giordano, Peggy C. 2010. *Legacies of Crime: A Follow-Up of the Children of Highly Delinquent Girls and Boys.* New York: Cambridge University Press.

Glaze, Lauren E., and Laura M. Maruschak. 2008. *Parents in Prison and Their Minor Children.* Washington, DC: US Department of Justice, Bureau of Justice Statistics.

Goffman, Erving. 1961. *Asylums: Essays on the Social Situation of Mental Patients and Other Inmates.* New York: Anchor.

Gohara, Miriam S. 2013. "Grace Notes: A Case for Making Mitigation the Heart of Noncapital Sentencing." *American Journal of Criminal Law* 41(41):41–88.

Gong, Neil. 2021. "California Gave People the 'Right' to be Homeless: But Little Help in Finding Homes." *Washington Post*, May 20.

Gordon, Grey, John Bailey Jones, Urvi Neelakantan, and Kartik Athrey. 2021. "Incarceration, Earnings, and Race." Working Paper WP 21-11. Richmond, VA: Federal Reserve Bank of Richmond.

Gordon, Grey, and Urvi Neelakantan. 2021. "Incarceration's Life-Long Impact on Earnings and Employment." Economic Brief no. 21-07. Richmond, VA: Federal Reserve Bank of Richmond.

Gotsch, Kara. 2018. "Families and Mass Incarceration." *Criminal Justice Involvement of Children in Child Welfare.* Minneapolis: University of Minnesota School of Social Work.

Gottschalk, Marie. 2015. *Caught: The Prison State and the Lockdown of American Politics.* Princeton, NJ: Princeton University Press.

Grinstead, Olga A., Bonnie Faigeles, Megan Comfort, David Seal, Jill Nealey-Moore, Lisa Belcher, and Kathleen Morrow. 2005. "HIV, STD, and Hepatitis Risk to Primary Female Partners of Men Being Released from Prison." *Women and Health* 41(2):63–80.

Grunwald, Ben. 2021. "Toward an Optimal Decarceration Strategy." *Stanford Law and Policy Review* 33(1):1–78.

Halladay, Josh. 2019. "The Thirteenth Amendment, Prison Labor Wages, and Interrupting the Intergenerational Cycle of Subjugation." *Seattle University Law Review* 42:937–63.

Halushka, John M. 2020. "The Run-Around: Punishment, Welfare, and Poverty Survival after Prison. *Social Problems* 67(2):233–50.

Haney, Craig. 1995. "The Social Context of Capital Murder: Social Histories and the Logic of Mitigation." *Santa Clara Law Review* 35(2):547–609.

Haney, Craig. 2001. "The Psychological Impact of Incarceration: Implications for Post-prison Adjustment." In *From Prison to Home: The Effect of Incarceration and Reentry on Children, Families and Communities*. Washington, DC: US Department of Health and Human Services, Office of the Assistant Secretary for Planning and Evaluation.

Haney, Craig. 2012. "Prison Effects in the Era of Mass Incarceration." *Prison Journal*. https://doi.org/10.1177/0032885512448604.

Haney, Craig. 2014. "Condemning the Other in Death Penalty Trials: Biographical Racism, Structural Mitigation, and the Empathic Divide." *DePaul Law Review* 53:1557–89.

Haney, Craig. 2017. "'Madness' and Penal Confinement: Some Observations on Mental Illness Prison Pain." *Punishment and Society* 19(3):310–26.

Haney, Craig. 2020. *Criminality in Context: The Psychological Foundations of Criminal Justice Reform*. Washington, DC: American Psychological Association.

Haney, Craig, Curtis Banks, and Philip Zimbardo. 1973. "A Study of Prisoners and Guards in a Simulated Prison." *Naval Research Reviews* 30:4–17.

Harris, Alexes. 2016. *A Pound of Flesh: Monetary Sanctions as a Punishment for the Poor*. New York: Russell Sage.

Hatton, Erin. 2018. "When Work Is Punishment: Penal Subjectivities in Punitive Labor Regimes." *Punishment and Society* 20(2):174–91.

Heckman, James, Lena Malofeeva, Rodrigo Pinto, and Peter Savelyev. 2010. *Understanding the Mechanisms through Which an Influential Early Childhood Program Boosted Adult Outcomes*. Chicago: University of Chicago Press.

Herman, Susan. 2010. *Parallel Justice for Victims of Crime*. New York: National Center for Victims of Crime.

Hinton, Elizabeth, and DeAnza Cook. 2021. "The Mass Criminalization of Black Americans: A Historical Overview." *Annual Review of Criminology* 4:261–86.

Huebner, Beth M. 2005. "The Effect of Incarceration on Marriage and Work over the Life Course." *Justice Quarterly* 22(3):281–303.

Huebner, Beth M. 2007. "Racial and Ethnic Differences in the Likelihood of Marriage: The Effect of Incarceration." *Justice Quarterly* 24(1):156–83.

Irwin, John, and Barbara Owen. 2005. "Harm and the Contemporary Prison." In *The Effects of Imprisonment*, edited by Alison Liebling and Shadd Maruna. New York: Routledge.

Johnson, Rucker, and Steven Raphael. 2009. "The Effect of Male Incarceration Dynamics on AIDS Infection Rates among African-American Women and Men." *Journal of Law and Economics* 52(2):251–93.

Kaba, Mariame. 2021. *We Do This 'Til We Free Us: Abolitionist Organizing and Transforming Justice*. Chicago: Haymarket.

Kaeble, Danielle, and Mary Cowhig. 2018. *Correctional Populations in the United States, 2016*. Washington, DC: US Department of Justice, Bureau of Justice Statistics.

Kaiser, Joshua. 2016. "Revealing the Hidden Sentence: How to Add Transparency, Legitimacy, and Purpose to Collateral Punishment Policy." *Harvard Law and Policy Review* 10(1):123–84.

Kang-Brown, Jacob, Chase Montagnet, and Jasmine Heiss. 2021. *People in Jail and Prison in 2020.* New York: Vera Institute of Justice.

Kassie, Emily. 2019. "Detained: How the United States Created the Largest Immigration Detention System in the World." *Guardian*, September 24.

Kent, Ana Hernández, and Lowell R. Ricketts. 2021. "Millennials Are Catching Up in Terms of Generational Wealth." *On the Economy Blog.* St. Louis, MO: Federal Reserve Bank of St. Louis.

Kirk, David S. 2015. "A Natural Experiment of the Consequences of Concentrating Former Prisoners in the Same Neighborhoods." *Proceedings of the National Academy of Sciences* 112(22):6943–48.

Kirk, Gabriela, April Fernandes, and Brittany Friedman. 2020. "Who Pays for the Welfare State? Austerity Politics and the Origin of Pay-to-Stay Fees as Revenue Generation." *Sociological Perspectives* 63(4):921–38.

Kling, Jeffrey R. 2006. "Incarceration Length, Employment, and Earnings." *American Economic Review* 96(3):863–76.

Langton, Lynn, and Jennifer Truman. 2014. *Socio-Emotional Impact of Violent Crime.* Washington, DC: US Department of Justice, Bureau of Justice Statistics.

Laub, John H., Daniel S. Nagin, and Robert J. Sampson. 1998. "Trajectories of Change in Criminal Offending: Good Marriages and the Desistance Process." *American Sociological Review* 63(2):225–38.

Lee, Hedwig, Tyler McCormick, Margaret T. Hicken, and Christopher Wildeman. 2015. "Racial Inequalities in Connectedness to Imprisoned Individuals in the United States." *Du Bois Review* 12(2):269–82.

Lee, Hedwig, Liza Weiss, and Finola Prendergast. 2021. *Health (Care) as Justice Reform: Protecting the Health and Well-Being of Incarcerated Populations, Their Families, and Their Communities.* New York: Square One Project.

Liebling, Alison. 1999. "Prison Suicide and Prisoner Coping." In *Crime and Justice: A Review of Research*, vol. 26, edited by Michael Tonry. Chicago: Chicago University Press.

Liebling, Alison, and Shadd Maruna. 2005. "Introduction: The Effects of Imprisonment Revisited." In *The Effects of Imprisonment*, edited by Alison Liebling and Shadd Maruna. New York: Routledge.

Lofstrom, Magnus, and Steven Raphael. 2016. "Prison Downsizing and Public Safety: Evidence from California." *Criminology and Public Policy* 15(2):349–65.

Looney, Adam, and Nicholas Turner. 2018. *Work and Opportunity before and after Incarceration.* Washington, DC: Brookings.

Lopoo, Leonard M., and Bruce Western. 2005. "Incarceration and the Formation and Stability of Marital Unions." *Journal of Marriage and Family* 67(3):721–34.

Lynch, Mona, and Craig Haney. 2011. "Looking across the Empathic Divide: Racialized Decision Making on the Capital Jury." *Michigan State Law Review* 2011:573–607.

Lyons, Christopher J., and Becky Pettit. 2011. "Compounded Disadvantage: Race, Incarceration, and Wage Growth." *Social Problems* 58(2):257–80.

Maroto, Michelle Lee. 2015. "The Absorbing Status of Incarceration and Its Relationship with Wealth Accumulation." *Journal of Quantitative Criminology* 31:207–36.

Maroto, Michelle Lee, and Bryan L. Sykes. 2020. "The Varying Effects of Incarceration, Conviction, and Arrest on Wealth Outcomes among Young Adults." *Social Problems* 67(4):698–718.

Martin, Karin D., Bryan L. Sykes, Sarah Shannon, Frank Edwards, and Alexes Harris. 2018. "Monetary Sanctions: Legal Financial Obligations in U.S. Systems of Justice." *Annual Review of Criminology* 1:471–95.

Massoglia, Michael. 2008a. "Incarceration as Exposure: The Prison, Infectious Disease, and Other Stress-Related Illnesses." *Journal of Health and Social Behavior* 49(1):56–71.

Massoglia, Michael. 2008b. "Incarceration, Health, and Racial Disparities in Health." *Law and Society Review* 42(2):275–306.

Massoglia, Michael, and Alex Pridemore. 2015. "Incarceration and Health." *Annual Review of Sociology* 41:291–310.

Massoglia, Michael, and Brianna Remster. 2019. "Linkages between Incarceration and Health." *Public Health Reports* 134(1):85–145.

Massoglia, Michael, Brianna Remster, and Ryan D. King. 2011. "Stigma or Separation? Understanding the Incarceration-Divorce Relationship." *Social Forces* 90(1):133–55.

Massoglia, Michael, and Jason Schnittker. 2009. "No Real Release." *Contexts* 8(1):38–42.

Mauer, Marc, and Ashley Nellis. 2019. *The Meaning of Life: The Case for Abolishing Life Sentences*. New York: New Press.

McCold, Paul, and Benjamin Wachtel. 1998. *Restorative Policing Experiment: The Bethlehem Pennsylvania Police Family Group Conferencing Project*. Bethlehem, PA: Community Service Foundation.

Mechoulan, Stéphane. 2011. "The External Effects of Black Male Incarceration on Black Females." *Journal of Labor Economics* 29(1):1–35.

Meyer, Jaimie P., Javier Cepeda, Johnny Wu, Robert L. Trestman, Frederick L. Altice, and Sandra A. Springer. 2014. "Optimization of Human Immunodeficiency Virus Treatment during Incarceration: Viral Suppression at the Prison Gate." *JAMA Internal Medicine* 174(5):721–29.

Miller, Keva M. 2018. "Exploring the Intersection of Child Welfare and Criminal Justice." In *Criminal Justice Involvement of Children in Child Welfare*. Minnesota: University of Minnesota School of Social Work.

Miller, Reuben Jonathan. 2021. *Halfway Home: Race, Punishment, and the Afterlife of Incarceration*. New York: Little, Brown.

Minton, Todd D., Lauren G. Beatty, and Zhen Zeng. 2021. *Correctional Populations in the United States, 2019—Statistical Tables*. Washington, DC: US Department of Justice, Bureau of Justice Statistics.

Morenoff, Jeffrey D., and David J. Harding. 2014. "Incarceration, Prisoner Reentry, and Communities." *Annual Review of Sociology* 40:411–29.

Muhammad, Khalil Gibran. 2011. *The Condemnation of Blackness: Race, Crime and the Making of Urban America*. Cambridge, MA: Harvard University Press.

Nowotny, Kathryn M., and Anastaslia Kuptesvych-Timmer. 2018. "Health and Justice: Framing Incarceration as a Social Determinant of Health for Black Men in the United States." *Sociology Compass* 12(3):e12566.

Nurse, Jo, Paul Woodcock, and Jim Ormsby. 2003. "Influence of Environmental Factors on Mental Health within Prison: Focus Group Study." *British Medical Journal* 327:1–5.

O'Hear, Michael, and Darren Wheelock. 2020. "Violent Crime and Punitiveness: An Empirical Study of Public Opinion." *Marquette Law Review* 103(3): 1035–71.

Oliver, Melvin, and Thomas Shapiro. 2019. "Disrupting the Racial Wealth Gap." *Contexts* 18(1):16–21.

Pager, Devah. 2003. "The Mark of a Criminal Record." *American Journal of Sociology* 108(5):937–75.

Pager, Devah. 2007. *Marked: Race, Crime and Finding Work in an Era of Mass Incarceration*. Chicago: University of Chicago Press.

Pager, Devah, Bruce Western, and Bart Bonikowski. 2009. "Discrimination in Low Wage Labor Markets." *American Sociological Review* 74:777–99.

Patterson, Evelyn J. 2010. "Incarcerating Death: Mortality in U.S. State Correctional Facilities, 1985–1998." *Demography* 47(3):587–607.

Petrich, Damon M., Travis C. Pratt, Cheryl Lero Jonson, and Francis T. Cullen. 2021. "Custodial Sanctions and Reoffending: A Meta-analytic Review." In *Crime and Justice: A Review of Research*, vol. 50, edited by Michael Tonry. Chicago: University of Chicago Press.

Pettit, Becky. 2012. *Invisible Men: Mass Incarceration and the Myth of Racial Progress*. New York: Russell Sage.

Pettit, Becky, and Christopher J. Lyons. 2007. "Status and the Stigma of Incarceration: The Labor Market Effects of Incarceration by Race, Class, and Criminal Involvement." In *Barriers to Reentry? The Labor Market for Released Prisoners in Post-industrial America*, edited by Shawn Bushway, Michael Stoll, and David Weiman. New York: Russell Sage.

Pettit, Becky, and Christopher J. Lyons. 2009. "Incarceration and the Legitimate Labor Market: Examining Age-Graded Effects on Employment and Wages." *Law and Society Review* 43(4):725–56.

Pettit, Becky, and Bruce Western. 2004. "Mass Imprisonment and the Life Course: Race and Class Inequality in U.S. Incarceration." *American Sociological Review* 69:151–69.

Pew Charitable Trusts. 2008. *One in 100: Behind Bars in America*. Washington, DC: Pew Charitable Trusts.

Pew Charitable Trusts. 2014. *Prisons and Crime: A Complex Link*. Washington, DC: Pew Charitable Trusts.

Pew Charitable Trusts. 2017. *Prison Health Care: Costs and Quality* Washington, DC: Pew Charitable Trusts.

Pfaff, John. 2017. *Locked In: The True Causes of Mass Incarceration—and How to Achieve Real Reform*. New York: Basic.

Poehlmann, Julie. 2005. "Incarcerated Mothers' Contact with Children, Perceived Family Relationships, and Depressive Symptoms." *Journal of Family Psychology* 19(3):350–57.

Prasad, Monica. 2018. "Problem-Solving Sociology." *Contemporary Sociology* 47(4):393–98.

Pridemore, William Alex. 2014. "The Mortality Penalty of Incarceration: Evidence from a Population-Based Case-Control Study of Working-Age Males." *Journal of Health and Social Behavior* 55(2):215–33.

Prison Policy Initiative. 2021. *Mental Health: Policies and Practices Surrounding Mental Health*. Northampton, MA: Prison Policy Initiative.

Raher, Stephen. 2018. *The Company Store: A Deeper Look at Prison Commissaries*. Northampton, MA: Prison Policy Initiative.

Ramakers, Anke, Robert Apel, Paul Nieuwbeerta, Anja Dirkzwager, and Johan van Wilsem. 2014. "Imprisonment Length and Post-prison Employment Prospects." *Criminology* 52(3):399–427.

Raphael, Steven. 2007. "Early Incarceration Spells and the Transition to Adulthood." In *The Price of Independence: The Economics of Early Adulthood*, edited by Sheldon H. Danziger and Cecilia Elena Rouse. New York: Russell Sage.

Reiter, Karamet, Joseph Ventura, David Lovell, Dallas Augustine, Melissa Barragan, Thomas Blair, Kelsie Chestnut, Pasha Dashtgard, Gabriella Gonzalez, Natalie Pifer, and Justin Strong. 2020. "Psychological Distress in Solitary Confinement: Symptoms, Severity, and Prevalence in the United States, 2017–18." *American Journal of Public Health* 110(supp. 1):S56–S62.

Ricciardelli, Rosemary, and Taylor Mooney. 2018. "The Decision to Disclose: Employment after Prison." *Journal of Offender Rehabilitation* 57(6):1–24.

Rich, Josiah D., Sarah E. Wakeman, and Samuel L. Dickman. 2011. "Medicine and the Epidemic of Incarceration in the United States." *New England Journal of Medicine* 364(22):2081–83.

Rosen, David L., Andrew L. Kavee, and Lauren Brinkley-Rubinstein. 2020. "Post-release Mortality among Persons Hospitalized during Their Incarceration." *Annals of Epidemiology* 45:54–60.

Sabol, William. 2007. "Local Labor-Market Conditions and Post-prison Employment Experiences of Offenders Released from Ohio State Prisons." In *Barriers to Reentry? The Labor Market for Released Prisoners in Post-industrial America*, edited by Shawn Bushway, Michael A. Stoll, and David A. Weiman. New York: Russell Sage.

Sabol, William J. 2014. *Survey of State Criminal History Information Systems, 2012*. Washington, DC: US Department of Justice, Bureau of Justice Statistics.

Sampson, Robert J., John H. Laub, and Christopher Wimer. 2006. "Does Marriage Reduce Crime? A Counterfactual Approach to Within-Individual Causal Effects." *Criminology* 44(3):465–508.

Sawyer, Wendy. 2016. "Punishing Poverty: The High Cost of Probation Fees in Massachusetts." Northampton, MA: Prison Policy Initiative.

Schappell, Ashley, Meagan Docherty, and Paul Boxer. 2016. "Violence and Victimization during Incarceration: Relations to Psychosocial Adjustment during Reentry to the Community." *Violence and Victims* 31(2):361–78.

Schneider, Daniel, and Kristin Turney. 2015. "Incarceration and Black-White Inequality in Homeownership: A State-Level Analysis." *Social Science Research* 53:403–14.

Schneider, Luisa T. 2021. "Let Me Take a Vacation in Prison before the Streets Kill Me! Rough Sleepers' Longing for Prison and the Reversal of Less Eligibility in Neoliberal Carceral Continuums." *Punishment and Society*, forthcoming.

Schnittker, Jason, and Michael Massoglia. 2015. "A Sociocognitive Approach to Studying the Effects of Incarceration." *Wisconsin Law Review* 2015:349–74.

Schnittker, Jason, Michael Massoglia, and Christopher Uggen. 2012. "Out and Down: Incarceration and Psychiatric Disorders." *Journal of Health and Social Behavior* 53(4):448–64.

Schwartzapfel, Beth. 2018. "How Bad Is Prison Health Care? Depends Who's Watching." Marshall Project, February 26.

Seeds, Christopher. 2017. "Bifurcation Nation: American Penal Policy in Late Mass Incarceration." *Punishment and Society* 19(5):590–610.

Sen, Amartya. 1989. "Development as Capability Expansion." *Journal of Development Planning* 19:41–58.

Sered, Danielle. 2019. *Until We Reckon: Mass Incarceration and the Road to Repair.* New York: New Press.

Sharkey, Patrick. 2018. "The Long Reach of Violence: A Broader Perspective on Data, Theory, and Evidence on the Prevalence and Consequences of Exposure to Violence." *Annual Review of Criminology* 1:85–102.

Sharkey, Patrick, Gerard Torrats-Espinosa, and Delaram Takyar. 2017. "Community and the Crime Decline: The Causal Effect of Local Nonprofits on Violent Crime." *American Sociological Review* 82(6):1214–40.

Sherman, Lawrence W., Heather Strang, Evan Mayo-Wilson, Daniel J. Woods, and Barak Ariel. 2015. "Are Restorative Justice Conferences Effective in Reducing Repeat Offending?" *Journal of Quantitative Criminology* 31(1):1–24.

Simon, Jonathan. 2016. *Mass Incarceration on Trial: A Remarkable Court Decision and the Future of Prisons in America.* New York: New Press.

Simon, Jonathan. 2017. "The Second Coming of Dignity." In *The New Criminal Justice Thinking*, edited by Sharon Dolovich and Alexandra Natapoff. New York: New York University Press.

Sledjeski, Eve M., Brittany Speisman, and Lisa C. Dierker. 2008. "Does Number of Lifetime Traumas Explain the Relationship between PTSD and Chronic Medical Conditions? Answers from the National Comorbidity Survey-Replication (NCS-R)." *Journal of Behavioral Medicine* 31(4):341–49.

Smith, Amy. 2013. *Health and Incarceration: A Workshop Summary.* Washington, DC: National Academies.

Spaulding, Anne C., Ryan M. Seals, Victoria A. McCallum, Sebastian D. Perez, Amanda K. Brzozowski, and N. Kyle Steenland. 2011. "Prisoner Survival Inside and Outside of the Institution: Implications for Health-Care Planning." *American Journal of Epidemiology* 173(5):479–87.

Steiker, Carol S., and Jordan M. Steiker. 2014. "Judicial Developments in Capital Punishment Law." In *America's Experiment with Capital Punishment: Reflections on the Past, Present and Future of the Ultimate Penal Sanction*, 3rd ed., edited by James R. Acker, Robert M. Bohm, and Charles S. Lanier. Durham, NC: Carolina Academic Press.

Stevenson, Bryan. 2014. *Just Mercy: A Story of Justice and Redemption*. New York: Spiegel & Grau.

Stillman, Sara. 2015. "Black Wounds Matter." *New Yorker*, October 15.

Stuart, Forrest. 2016. *Down, out and under Arrest: Policing and Everyday Life in Skid Row*. Chicago: University of Chicago Press.

Stuart, Forrest, Amada Armenta, and Melissa Osborne. 2015. "Legal Control of Marginal Groups." *Annual Review of Law and Social Science* 11:235–54.

Sugie, Naomi F., and Michael C. Lens. 2017. "Daytime Locations in Spatial Mismatch: Job Accessibility and Employment at Reentry from Prison." *Demography* 54(2):775–800.

Sykes, Bryan L., and Michelle Maroto. 2016. "A Wealth of Inequalities: Mass Incarceration, Employment, and Racial Disparities in U.S. Household Wealth, 1996 to 2011." *Russell Sage Foundation Journal of the Social Sciences* 2(6):129–52.

Sykes, Bryan L., and Becky Pettit. 2014. "Mass Incarceration, Family Complexity, and the Reproduction of Childhood Disadvantage." *Annals of the American Academy of Political and Social Sciences* 654(1):127–49.

Sykes, Bryan L., and Alex R. Piquero. 2009. "Structuring and Re-creating Inequality: Health Testing Policies, Race, and the Criminal Justice System." *Annals of the American Academy of Political and Social Science* 623(1):214–27.

Sykes, Gresham M. 1958. *The Society of Captives: A Study of a Maximum Security Prison*. Princeton, NJ: Princeton University Press.

Telep, Cody W., and Julie Hibdon. 2018. "Community Crime Prevention in High-Crime Areas: The Seattle Neighborhood Group Hot Spots Project." *City and Community* 17(4):1143–67.

Toch, Hans. 1992. *Mosaic of Despair: Human Breakdowns in Prison*. Washington, DC: American Psychological Association.

Tonry, Michael. 2014*a*. "Remodeling American Sentencing: A Ten-Step Blueprint for Moving Past Mass Incarceration." *Criminology and Public Policy* 13(4): 503–33.

Tonry, Michael. 2014*b*. "Why Crime Rates Are Falling throughout the Western World." *Crime and Justice* 43(1):1–64.

Tonry, Michael. 2016. *Sentencing Fragments: Penal Reform in America, 1975–2025*. New York: Oxford University Press.

Travis, Jeremy. 2012. "Summoning the Superheroes: Harnessing Science and Passion to Create a More Effective and Human Response to Crime." In *25th Anniversary Essays*, edited by Marc Mauer and Kate Epstein. Washington, DC: Sentencing Project.

Travis, Jeremy, and Bruce Western. 2021. *The Era of Punitive Excess*. New York: New York University Law School, Brennan Center for Justice.

Travis, Jeremy, Bruce Western, and Steven Redburn. 2014. *The Growth of Incarceration in the United States: Exploring Causes and Consequences*. Committee on

Causes and Consequences of High Rates of Incarceration, National Research Council Committee on Law and Justice. Washington, DC: National Academies.

Turney, Kristin. 2015. "Liminal Men: Incarceration and Relationship Dissolution." *Social Problems* 62(4):499–528.

Turney, Kristin, and Daniel Schneider. 2016. "Incarceration and Household Asset Ownership." *Demography* 53(6):2017–103.

Turney, Kristin, and Christopher Wildeman. 2013. "Redefining Relationships: Explaining the Countervailing Consequences of Paternal Incarceration for Parenting." *American Sociological Review* 78(6):949–79.

Turney, Kristin, and Christopher Wildeman. 2018. "Maternal Incarceration and the Transformation of Urban Family Life." *Social Forces* 96(3):1155–82.

Turney, Kristin, Christopher Wildeman, and Jason Schnittker. 2012. "As Fathers and Felons: Explaining the Effects of Current and Recent Incarceration on Major Depression." *Journal of Health and Social Behavior* 53(4):465–81.

Umbreit, Mark S., Betty Vos, and Robert B. Coates. 2007. "Restorative Justice Dialogue: Evidence-Based Practice." *Contemporary Justice Review* 10(1):23–41.

Umbreit, Mark S., Betty Vos, Robert B. Coates, and E. Lightfoot. 2005. "Restorative Justice in Action: Restorative Justice in the Twenty-First Century." *Marquette Law Review* 89(2):251–304.

Vandergrift, Lindsey, and Paul P. Christopher. 2021. "Do Prisoners Trust the Healthcare System?" *Health and Justice* 9(15):1–8.

van Zyl Smit, Dirk, and Catherine Appleton. 2019. *Life Imprisonment: A Global Human Rights Analysis*. Cambridge, MA: Harvard University Press.

Visher, Christy A., Sara A. Debus-Sherrill, and Jennifer Yahner. 2010. "Employment after Prison: A Longitudinal Study of Former Prisoners." *Justice Quarterly* 28(5):698–718.

Vuolo, Mike, Sarah Lageson, and Christopher Uggen. 2017. "Criminal Record Questions in the Era of 'Ban the Box.'" *Criminology and Public Policy* 16(1):139–65.

Wagner, Peter, and Bernadette Rubay. 2017. *Following the Money of Mass Incarceration*. Northampton, MA: Prison Policy Initiative.

Wakefield, Sara, Hedwig Lee, and Christopher Wildeman. 2016. "Tough on Crime, Tough on Families? Criminal Justice and Family Life in America." *Annals of the American Academy of Political and Social Science* 665:8–21.

Wakefield, Sara, and Christopher Uggen. 2010. "Incarceration and Stratification." *Annual Review of Sociology* 36:387–406.

Walmsley, Roy. 2021. *World Prison Population List*. London: Institute for Criminal Policy Research.

Wang, Emily A., Mary C. White, Ross Jamison, Joe Goldenson, Milton Estes, and Jacqueline P. Tulsky. 2008. "Discharge Planning and Continuity of Health Care: Findings from the San Francisco County Jail." *American Journal of Public Health* 98(12):2182–84.

Warner, Cody, Joshua Kaiser, and Jason N. Houle. 2020. "Locked out of the Labor Market? State-Level Hidden Sentences and the Labor Market Outcomes of Recently Incarcerated Young Adults." *Russell Sage Foundation Journal of the Social Sciences* 6(1):132–51.

Washington, Heather M., Shao-Chieu Juan, and Anna R. Haskins. 2018. "Incapacitated Involvement: Incarceration and Fatherhood in Fragile Families at Age 9." *Journal of Family Issues* 39(13):3463–86.

Western, Bruce. 2006. *Punishment and Inequality*. New York: Russell Sage.

Western, Bruce. 2019. *Homeward: Life in the Year after Prison*. New York: Russell Sage.

Western, Bruce, and Katherine Beckett. 1999. "How Unregulated Is the U.S. Labor Market? The Penal System as a Labor Market Institution." *American Journal of Sociology* 104(4):1030–60.

Western, Bruce, Anthony A. Braga, Jaclyn Davis, and Catherine Sirois. 2015. "Stress and Hardship after Prison." *American Journal of Sociology* 120(5):1512–47.

Western, Bruce, Leonard M. Lopoo, and Sara McLanahan. 2003. *Incarceration and the Bonds among Parents in Fragile Families*. Princeton, NJ: Center for Research on Child Wellbeing.

Western, Bruce, and Becky Pettit. 2005. "Black-White Wage Inequality, Employment Rates, and Incarceration." *American Journal of Sociology* 111(2):553–78.

Western, Bruce, and Becky Pettit. 2010. "Incarceration and Social Inequality." *Daedalus* 139(3):8–19.

Western, Bruce, and Catherine Sirois. 2018. "Racialized Re-entry: Labor Market Inequality after Incarceration." *Social Forces* 97(4):1517–42.

Western, Bruce, and Christopher Wildeman. 2009. "The Black Family and Mass Incarceration." *Annals of the American Academy of Political and Social Science* 621:221–42.

Wildeman, Christopher. 2009. "Parental Imprisonment, the Prison Boom, and the Concentration of Childhood Disadvantage." *Demography* 46(2):265–80.

Wildeman, Christopher. 2016. "Incarceration and Population Health in Wealthy Democracies." *Criminology* 54:360–82.

Wilson, David B., Ajima Olaghere, and Catherine S. Kimbrell. 2018. *Effectiveness of Restorative Justice Principles in Juvenile Justice: A Meta-analysis*. Washington, DC: US Department of Justice, Office of Juvenile and Delinquency Prevention.

Winkelman, Tyler N. A., Edith C. Kieffer, Susan D. Goold, Jeffrey D. Morenoff, Kristen Cross, and John Z. Ayanian. 2016. "Health Insurance Trends and Access to Behavioral Healthcare among Justice-Involved Individuals: United States, 2008–2014." *Journal of General Internal Medicine* 31(12):1523–29.

Zehr, Howard. 2002. *Little Book of Restorative Justice*. Philadelphia: Good Books.

Zimring, Franklin E. 2007. *The Great American Crime Decline*. Oxford: Oxford University Press.

Sara Wakefield

Incarceration, Families, and Communities: Recent Developments and Enduring Challenges

ABSTRACT

Mass incarceration has fundamental adverse effects that include weakening families and intimate relationships, altering children's life chances, and undermining communities. Serious work on those effects began in the late 1990s and laid foundations on which subsequent research has built. More recent work, especially in the past dozen years, is more complex and has produced findings that are more nuanced and mixed. It is also theoretically and conceptually richer. The newer work involves substantially greater cross-disciplinary engagement, draws on new and more diverse data sources, and pays greater attention to pathways into prison. Fundamental challenges persist. They include measurement problems, overlap between the criminal justice and other governmental systems (e.g., education, public health, social welfare), and generalizability issues. Mixed results, definitional disagreements, and measurement challenges should encourage researchers to embrace complexity in the study of the effects of incarceration on family and community life.

Mass incarceration fundamentally alters family and community life for millions of people. In the United States, the high rate of incarceration is central to efforts to understand the lives of many families and the communities

Sara Wakefield is associate professor of criminal justice, School of Criminal Justice, Rutgers University, Newark.

Electronically published September 21, 2022

Crime and Justice, volume 51, 2022.

https://doi.org/10.1086/721741

in which they live as well as entrenched racial and class inequality. The effects of incarceration on families and communities, however, were largely ignored by the public, politicians, and many scholars until well after the start of the prison boom in the early 1970s. While it is not surprising that social scientists failed to predict the historically unprecedented rise in incarceration, it is more surprising that possible harms of mass incarceration for families and communities began to receive attention only in the 1990s.

That nearly quarter century time lag is at least partly attributable to inherent difficulties associated with slow and deliberate social sciences. It takes a long time for research on any complex subject to catch up with large and unexpected social change, which the emergence of mass incarceration surely was. Incarceration in the United States, however, presents specific and significant challenges to researchers. First, while punishment processes and outcomes have long been understood to reflect existing patterns of societal and structural disadvantage (e.g., Wacquant 2000; Muhammad 2011), researchers have been slow to make connections between incarcerated people, their loved ones, and the communities from which they come and to which they usually return. Second, extreme concentration of incarceration within disadvantaged families and communities likely influenced the attention scholars paid to mass incarceration's effects. Those effects, especially for families and communities, are difficult to assess with existing data sources and are often described as invisible (Pettit 2012) or hidden (Walker 2022). Finally, mainstream theories of the family, communities, and crime and punishment offered few conceptual tools or adequately developed data sets for understanding widespread family and community harms (e.g., Wakefield and Apel 2018).

Research since the late 1990s and early 2000s clearly demonstrates the core importance of families and communities in a full accounting of mass incarceration. Theoretical innovation and improved data infrastructure produced an enormous amount of scholarship on its collateral consequences. Research findings more clearly demonstrated that mass incarceration destabilized communities (Clear 2007), upended families (Comfort 2007), and contributed to declines in children's well-being (Wakefield and Wildeman 2013). Those harms were distributed unequally, producing widespread racial and class inequalities in the lifetime risk of imprisonment (Pettit and Western 2004). Mass incarceration is associated with a variety of family and community harms, including educational handicaps of children of incarcerated parents (Hagan and Foster 2012*a*;

Haskins 2014; Lageson 2016), family dissolution (Apel 2016), racial inequality in childhood well-being (Wakefield and Wildeman 2013), population health (Wildeman and Wang 2017), civic engagement (Sugie 2015), and community cohesiveness (Braman 2004; Kirk 2019). Research findings demonstrated substantial spillover to nonincarcerated significant others and massive inequalities in the risk of such harms (Pettit 2012; Shannon et al. 2017).

Scholarship from the late 1990s to roughly 2010 thus laid the theoretical, conceptual, and empirical foundations for more recent research, justifying a great degree of confidence in the conclusion that mass incarceration has been harmful to US families and communities; the National Academy of Sciences Committee on the Causes and Consequences of High Rates of Incarceration unanimously so concluded (National Research Council 2014).

More recent results paint more complex pictures. Greater rigor and exploitation of policy shocks to isolate causal effects confirmed some earlier findings but modified or qualified others. The clear weight of the evidence supports a general conclusion that mass incarceration has caused net harms for families and communities, but the findings are neither global nor applicable to every outcome of interest. As a consequence, researchers ask and try to answer more productive questions, such as how and for whom incarceration has particular harmful effects. Similarly, focusing on the extent to which selection into incarceration drives observed harmful effects has led to more complex research designs that encompass experiences before incarceration, conditions of confinement, and reentry pathways. Such holistic models can more fully investigate interactions between incarceration and broader social systems of exclusion and disadvantage.

Contemporary research grapples with a variety of challenges. Accurate measurement of incarceration experiences, for example, remains very difficult but has improved (Finlay and Mueller-Smith 2021; Enns et al. 2022). Definitions of "family" and "community," similarly, have broadened beyond partner or parental incarceration to include broader family and community networks. Finally, at a time when some scholars use more advanced research designs to isolate causal effects, others increasingly ask whether such a thing is possible or useful. Is it advisable, for example, to isolate the effects of incarceration from broader experiences of deep poverty, entrenched racism, social marginality, and vulnerability throughout the life course? The overarching takeaway from this essay is that researchers must continue to recognize and work to disentangle conceptual and empirical complexity.

Here is how this essay is organized. Section I briefly introduces foundational works that underpin the sizable literature that has since accumulated, and Section II discusses research on the effects of incarceration on family and community life, using as examples parental incarceration, partner incarceration, and extreme concentration in particular communities of people who have been or will be incarcerated. Section III discusses important recent developments including greater cross-disciplinary collaboration, improvement of data sources, and heightened attention to selection bias and pathways into prison. Section IV explores enduring challenges, particularly measurement issues and the need to disentangle the effects of interactions between the criminal justice system and other systems of social control (Western and Harding 2022).

I. Foundations for the Study of Family, Community, and Incarceration

More than two decades after the dawn of the prison boom in the United States in the mid-1970s, several classic contemporary works focused attention on communities with high concentrations of former and current prisoners and families of incarcerated people. Earlier works foreshadowed attention on racial disparities and the enormous growth in incarceration in the United States (e.g., Zimring and Hawkins 1993; Tonry 1995; Beckett 1997).

A number of early works laid foundations for an explosion of scholarship on collateral consequences of incarceration for families and communities. David Garland (2001*b*, pp. 5–6) defined "mass incarceration," as the term is now commonly used, as a pattern of historically and comparatively high rates of confinement that produce very large disparities between groups in the likelihood of incarceration over the life course. John Hagan and Ronit Dinovitzer (1999) laid out a series of competing theories about incarceration's effects and proposed research designs for understanding how mass incarceration could be expected to affect the children and families of incarcerated people. Influential collections of articles outlined a series of potential consequences for families, their communities, and racial inequality more broadly (Garland 2001*a*; Mauer and Chesney-Lind 2002). These works largely anticipate findings from a host of studies published in the following few years.

Several books offered deep dives into the families and communities of incarcerated people, offering new conceptual tools and powerful descriptions. Megan Comfort, for example, introduced the concept of "secondary prisonization" to describe the experiences of "legal bystanders"—families and friends of incarcerated people—and showed how the pains of incarceration are transferred to them (Comfort 2003, 2007). Donald Braman's *Doing Time on the Outside* (2004) did much the same with communities, describing ways the prison system structures relationships in communities far beyond prison walls. Anne Nurse's *Fatherhood Arrested* (2002), and Todd Clear's *Imprisoning Communities* (2007), among others, respectively offered new theories and much needed descriptions of the lives of family members of the incarcerated and of the experiences of high incarceration communities. Taken together, these works upended any assumption that mass incarceration is somehow beneficial to families and communities.

Finally, an additional set of foundational works tied mass incarceration to historic and contemporary systemic racism, detailing large racial and class disparities in incarceration risk over the life course (Pettit and Western 2004). Others framed mass incarceration as a continuation of systemic racism in the United States, directly connecting it to legacies of enslavement and Jim Crow (Wacquant 2000; Muhammad 2011; Alexander 2012) and describing the effects of mass incarceration on Black family life and communities (Harris and Miller 2003; Roberts 2004; Western 2006). The result was a clear series of statements implicating the criminal justice system as a driver of deep inequalities in the United States.

II. Current Knowledge

To summarize recent scholarship on incarceration, families, and communities, a research assistant and I began with core articles and books and followed the development of research flowing from them via citation tracking. We then expanded our efforts by searching data bases using a variety of terms related to family, community, incarceration, and reentry. Finally, we looked at research on the intersection of the criminal justice system and what we termed "surveilling or stratifying institutions." By this we meant institutions and contexts that overlap with criminal justice systems or produce or sustain family and community-level inequalities; these include schools, child welfare systems, and health care systems.

Several caveats are in order. First, we surely did not locate every article and book on these topics in the last 20 years, but I am confident we found enough to identify general trends in scholarship and salient examples of approaches and findings. An exciting development is that the literature on incarceration and family and community life has recently spread across diverse disciplines and subjects. More scholars in public health, economics, and political science have joined the large number of sociologists, criminologists, social workers, and psychologists who are trying to understand and document the harms caused by mass incarceration. Interest in incarceration and family and community life has expanded into many disciplines.

Second, we identified a relatively provincial literature that focuses primarily on the United States. Presumably this is because American incarceration rates are vastly higher than those in other Western and developed countries. Nearly a quarter of the world's incarcerated people are in jails and prisons in the United States. When we learned about work from other countries, I weave it into the discussion. American mass incarceration presents many challenges to efforts to produce generalizable knowledge, establish causality, and implement policies to redress harms.

Early twenty-first-century scholarship precipitated a major turn in the framing and quantity of research on incarceration and its collateral consequences. These works collectively reversed the causal ordering of earlier models that connected incarceration to outcomes for families and communities and centered racial and class disparities in the risk of lifetime incarceration. The argument that incarceration creates disruptions apart from the conditions that lead to it is too often taken for granted, but the intellectual work involved in to connecting time spent in a prison or jail to harmful outcomes for families and communities was substantial. It required collaboration among diverse disciplines, repurposing of old data sets, creation of new ones, and development of new concepts. The next stage of this work, discussed below, was largely devoted to detailing associations between incarceration and a variety of critical social outcomes, including health and well-being, crime and delinquency, and economic hardship.

A. Parental Incarceration

Research at the dawn of the prison boom highlighted potentially harmful effects of parental incarceration for children (Sack, Seidler, and Thomas 1976; Fishman 1983), and criminologists have long studied the intergenerational transmission of crime and punishment (Hagan and Palloni 1990; Giordano et al. 2019; Wildeman 2020). Few early works, however, explicitly asked whether incarceration itself—as distinct from involvement in crime, lack of opportunity, or exposure to maltreatment and violence—produces a broader set of family and community harms. The causal effect of parental incarceration on children remains contested, and researchers continue to ask important questions about the strength of the evidence. That said, the bulk of (mostly observational) research on parental incarceration is generally consistent with the proposition that, on average and with caveats, it is harmful to children in a variety of ways.

The evidence base is larger with respect to the incarceration of fathers, in part because vastly more men than women are incarcerated. Studies conducted primarily but not only in the United States find that paternal incarceration is associated with a host of children's mental health and behavioral problems (Geller et al. 2011), including aggression (Wildeman 2010) and internalizing problems (Wakefield and Wildeman 2013). The initial evidence was stronger for aggression and externalizing behavioral problems (Murray, Farrington, and Sekol 2012), especially for boys (Wildeman 2010) and younger children (Turney 2022). Internalizing behavioral problems (e.g., depression and anxiety) appear to affect children at older ages (Wakefield and Wildeman 2013; Turney and Goodsell 2018). Paternal incarceration also increases the risk of delinquency (Murray and Farrington 2005; Porter and King 2015), drug use (Roettger et al. 2011), and early sexual onset (Turney and Goldberg 2019).

Such findings anticipate later work documenting difficulties of children of incarcerated parents in school settings. Paternal incarceration is associated with declines in school readiness and special education placement (Haskins 2014) and early grade retention (Turney and Haskins 2014). A history of parental incarceration has knock-on effects, reducing parental involvement in children's schooling (Lageson 2016; Haskins and Jacobsen 2017) and in children's overall educational attainment (Hagan and Foster 2012b; Miller and Barnes 2015). Experimental evidence suggests that important mechanisms behind these findings include stigma and teachers' lowered expectations of children because of their parent's incarceration history (Dallaire, Ciccone, and Wilson 2010; Wildeman et al. 2017).

The literature on the effects of maternal incarceration offers a useful contrast, although there are fewer plausibly causal studies and greater variation in findings. Several studies find that maternal incarceration is associated with poor outcomes for children, including entry into the foster care system (Johnson and Waldfogel 2002; Andersen and Wildeman 2014) and later justice involvement (Huebner and Gustafson 2007; Muftić, Bouffard, and Armstrong 2016).

Other studies, however, find null or heterogeneous effects of maternal incarceration. Wildeman and Turney (2014), for example, find that maternal incarceration has consistently null average effects across nearly 21 measures of well-being and suggest that much of that result can be explained by preincarceration instability in children's lives. In this conception, the incarceration of a mother is but the latest instability in a long line that affect children. In later work, Turney and Wildeman (2015) examine heterogeneity in the effects of maternal incarceration on mental health and behavioral problems and find countervailing effects; maternal incarceration is most harmful for children of mothers who have the lowest risk of being incarcerated.

Still other studies have found that maternal incarceration may be beneficial for some children. Cho, for example, finds that maternal incarceration results in a lower likelihood of grade retention (2009*b*) and has no effect on educational achievement as measured by reading and math test scores (2009*a*; see also Norris, Pecenco, and Weaver 2021). In summary, maternal incarceration effects are more often mixed, and findings contrast sharply with those concerning paternal incarceration.

It is, of course, unclear how much of this difference is driven by differences in study samples and methods, difficulty associated with smaller cell sizes that reflect mothers' relatively low rate of incarceration compared to fathers', or differences in the preincarceration experiences of children of incarcerated mothers compared with incarcerated fathers. In general, the more rigorous the study, the more likely paternal incarceration effects remain and maternal incarceration effects fade, but this may well depend on what is being studied.

Qualitative research on maternal incarceration offers a possible reconciliation for findings derived from studies using surveys and administrative data. They highlight substantial and lengthy histories of instability for children whose mothers will later be incarcerated and suggest that such experiences may blunt the effects of incarceration (Siegel 2011; Giordano et al. 2019) or make it more difficult to separate the effects of incarceration from the effects of earlier disadvantages (Giordano and Copp 2015). At the same time, instability that results from maternal incarceration may be greater relative to instability related to paternal incarceration. Mumola (2000) shows that less than half of incarcerated parents lived with their children before they were incarcerated and that children were much likelier to be living with mothers (~64 percent) than with fathers (~44 percent). Along the same lines, 90 percent of incarcerated fathers reported that their children lived with their mother while they were in prison; only 28 percent of mothers said this of fathers. The rate of foster care placement of children during incarceration was much higher for incarcerated mothers (~10 percent) than fathers (~2 percent). Taken together, these examples of family complexity have pushed researchers away from looking for average causal effects and toward answering questions concerning how and for whom incarceration has particular consequents.

Debates about the precise nature of parental incarceration's effects on children remain unresolved but highlight a major challenge. Myriad disadvantages and traumatic experiences often precede incarceration in children's lives, and incarceration often makes them worse. Detailing the mechanisms that link parental incarceration to poor outcomes for children offers some potential for reconciling contradictory research findings. Among potential mechanisms, parental incarceration may increase material insecurity (Schwartz-Soicher, Geller, and Garfinkel 2011), housing insecurity (Wildeman 2014), parenting stress (Turney 2014a; Wakefield 2014), entry into the foster care system (Johnson and Waldfogel 2002), and social exclusion (Foster and Hagan 2007; Shaw 2019). A counter view, however, is that it may be impossible to separate effects of incarceration fully from the larger constellation of disadvantages faced by incarcerated people, their families, and their communities. Instead, as Giordano and Copp (2015, p. 165) argue, researchers might better conceptualize incarceration as part of a "difficult-to-pry-apart package" of risks and disadvantages.

B. Family Dissolution and Family Burdens

Similar difficulties affect research on incarceration's effects on a broader set of family members, including romantic partners, parents, and siblings. In general, research with varying degrees of rigor suggests that the net effect of incarceration is to destabilize romantic relationships. Findings suggest that incarceration has larger effects in breaking up intact partnerships than in preventing family formation after release from prison (Massoglia, Remster, and King 2011; Apel 2016); incarcerated people, however, have relatively low marriage rates generally (Lee and Wildeman 2021). Black families face much higher rates of family dissolution following incarceration than do White and Hispanic families (Widdowson et al. 2020).

Incarceration of a romantic partner introduces a variety of stresses and abrupt changes for the partner left behind. Some of the poor outcomes observed for children of incarcerated parents probably result from burdens transferred to the remaining parent. Material insecurity, homelessness, and other forms of financial strain are common following incarceration, but a partner's incarceration also increases parenting stress (Besemer and Dennison 2018), risks of neglect and harsh parenting practices for children (Turney 2014a; Wakefield 2014), and risks of infant mortality (Wildeman 2012; Light and Marshall 2018).

Additional strains include lengthy separations (McKay et al. 2019), costly visits to distant prisons (Grinstead et al. 2001; Christian 2005), and spillover stigma and punishment because of attachments to incarcerated people (Comfort 2007). As incarceration rates increased over time and access to programs and services in correctional facilities declined, families and partners of incarcerated people have borne more of the burden of managing incarceration and reentry for family members (Mowen and Visher 2016). Partners struggle to remain connected, and the reentry period is often described as an acute stressor when families try to reunite with little access to supportive services (Grieb et al. 2014). During reentry, for example, prison systems routinely rely on family members to shore up gaps in services and, in so doing, place tremendous burdens on people who may be unwilling or unable to provided needed support (Turanovic, Rodriguez, and Pratt 2012; Mowen and Boman 2018). Incarceration need not be lengthy to introduce such burdens. Comfort's (2016) study of people cycling between jail and home for low-level offenses details enormous caretaking burdens that fall on family members (see also Miller 2021).

Finally, incarceration of a partner or family member has important implications for physical health. A large literature has focused on the public health consequences of incarceration (Massoglia and Pridemore 2015; Wildeman and Wang 2017); such problems also spill over into families and communities. Several studies, for example, document how incarceration and associated drug use places incarcerated people and their sexual partners at risk for sexually transmitted infection/HIV transmission (Khan et al. 2009). Similarly, the COVID-19 pandemic provided an especially salient example of how disease transmission spreads outside prisons via prison releases and the cycling of staff members from work to home (Charles et al. 2021; Maruna, McNaull, and O'Neill 2022; Towers et al. 2022). Alarming levels of community spread of other transmissible diseases owing to incarceration are common in many countries (e.g., Altice et al. 2016; Walter et al. 2021).

C. Community Concentration of Incarceration

The extreme concentration of incarceration in a small set of locations is well documented (Clear 2007; Simes 2018). Incarceration rates are highly stable in some places; incarceration is a core feature of neighborhoods characterized by high poverty, unemployment, family disruption, and segregation, creating a "self-reinforcing cycle that keeps some communities trapped in a negative feedback loop" and becoming more vulnerable over time (Sampson and Loeffler 2010, p. 21). Other work finds much the same pattern; incarceration is concentrated in a small number of extremely disadvantaged places (Simes 2018; Chamberlain and Boggess 2019; Kirk 2019). That increases risks of crime and recidivism for community members and the formerly incarcerated (Chamberlain and Boggess 2019), degrades neighborhood quality (Remster and Warner 2018), and limits mobility of formerly incarcerated people from poor to nonpoor neighborhoods (Warner 2016).

The concentration of incarceration is implicated in health consequences. Negative health consequences are not limited to formerly incarcerated people or their close contacts but have implications for whole communities and for inequalities in population health (Wildeman and Wang 2017). As one example, men's incarceration rates are strongly associated with HIV/AIDS infection rates in the community (Johnson and Raphael 2009) and linked to poor heart health among Black men who live in high-incarceration-rate communities (Topel et al. 2018). Thus, the individual-level implications of the health consequences of incarceration are significant, and the concentration of incarceration experiences within communities creates broader public health problems (Dumont et al. 2012; Wildeman and Wang 2017). Reliably measuring costs and benefits of mass incarceration for community outcomes is incredibly difficult, but at least one study finds that reductions in homicide are outweighed by increases in infant mortality (Light and Marshall 2018).

Neighborhoods with high incarceration rates often are targeted by police surveillance (Stuart, Armenta, and Osborne 2015; Stuart 2016). Inspired by Wacquant's (2000) framing of the overlapping nature of prison and community, Forrest Stuart and Reuben Miller (2017) describe how adaptations and knowledge of prison culture are shared within communities via "prisonized old heads." Incarceration thus shapes both the structural features of high incarceration neighborhoods (Sampson and Loeffler 2010) and cultural frames that incorporate adaptations to prison experiences (Stuart and Miller 2017).

Community connections to incarceration may be direct, as in the case of neighbors and family members cycling from prison to community, or more subtle, as in the case of prison gerrymandering that dilutes the political power of already marginalized communities (Remster and Warner 2018). More recent works focus not on the urban neighborhood origins of most incarcerated people but on the rural siting of many prisons, documenting complicated relationships between local economies and prison building (Eason 2017). The concentration of individual incarceration experiences spills over into community life, influencing the lives of people whose only connection to incarceration is living there.

III. Recent Themes

Incarceration changes the lives of the families and communities of incarcerated people and is associated with a wide variety of social harms that, taken together, implicate the criminal justice system in maintenance and exacerbation of inequality (Wakefield and Uggen 2010). In the last 10 years, however, efforts have shifted from simply cataloging the consequences of incarceration toward better explaining how and for whom it is most detrimental. Greater cross-disciplinary collaboration and debate are occurring, large improvements have been made in relevant data sets, and there is greater recognition of how experiences before incarceration influence family and community responses to incarceration.

A. Cross-Disciplinary Collaboration

One challenge is that many disciplines have a core interest in families but assumptions vary widely about how incarceration affects them. Similar issues arise when community work in sociology overlaps with epidemiology and public health. Not surprisingly, early scholarship in a field is often unfamiliar with scholarship in closely related fields. Things are improving, however, with cross-disciplinary engagement that acknowledges the complex ways incarceration affects families and communities.

Collections of articles and meetings in the 2010s have usefully brought family scholars from various disciplines together. Christopher Wildeman, Anna Haskins, and Julie Poehlmann-Tynan's *When Parents Are Incarcerated: Interdisciplinary Research and Interventions to Support Children* (2018) is an example; it includes selections on sociological (Haskins and Turney 2018), criminological (Wakefield and Apel 2018), and developmental perspectives on parental incarceration (Poehlmann-Tynan and Arditti

2018) and marries theoretical perspectives with research on interventions for children of incarcerated parents. Efforts to catalyze cross-disciplinary synergy continue (e.g., Loury and Western 2010; Sampson 2011; Wakefield, Lee, and Wildeman 2016; Laub 2018; Turney and Wakefield 2019). Disciplines do, of course, tend to emphasize different things—sociologists have long had a keen interest in inequality, criminologists in reentry, psychologists in family dynamics, and economists in isolating causal effects. The literature in the last decade is nonetheless more cohesive and better mutually informed. The value of greater cross-disciplinarity interaction is multiply evident but, perhaps most usefully, has brought greater theoretical innovation and methodological rigor to the study of incarceration and social life.

Family stress models in developmental psychology and life course models in sociology and criminology dominated much of the early literature on incarceration and families, but more recent research integrates these perspectives with others, including social learning, strain, and control theories. Arditti's (2016) family stress–proximal process model conceives of parental incarceration as upending family roles and scrambling external and internal processes that govern family life (Besemer and Dennison 2018; Charles, Muentner, and Kjellstrand 2019). Turney (2014b) applies stress proliferation and family stress models to parental incarceration and health (see also Turney and Sugie 2021). Life course and social learning theories remain important, often combined with theories focused on family dynamics, for interpreting the interplay between parental crime and punishment (Giordano et al. 2019) and social exclusion driven by incarceration (Hagan and Foster 2012b). These developments offer more conceptual tools and, importantly, solidify the increasingly multidisciplinary nature of scholarship on incarceration and the family.

B. Better Data

The data available to researchers have improved considerably. Older data sets containing measures of incarceration and other criminal justice system contacts were repurposed to new ends (Murray and Farrington 2008; Apel and Powell 2019). Measures of incarceration, although often crude, were added to large-scale surveys (Harris et al. 2009) or included in newer data sources (Reichman et al. 2001; Earls et al. 2002), allowing researchers to connect incarceration to a broad array of family and community measures. Linked administrative data sets, albeit often limited to employment, education, recidivism, or mortality in a small number of jurisdictions, improved the data infrastructure for researchers interested in mass incarceration (Binswanger et al. 2016; Harding et al. 2018; Finlay and Mueller-Smith 2021). More recent cross-sectional surveys (Enns et al. 2022), longitudinal data sets (Bir and Lindquist 2017; Giordano, Longmore, and Manning 2017; Dirkzwager et al. 2018), demographic estimates of racial disparities and spatial concentration of incarceration (Muller and Wildeman 2016; Shannon et al. 2017), and large-scale administrative data (Finlay and Mueller-Smith 2021) offer great promise for fully capturing the who, what, and how of incarceration's effects on families and communities.

Research designs have likewise improved. Researchers continue to use longitudinal surveys, administrative data sets, and interviews, but recent scholarship is more rigorous and multifaceted. Researchers have exploited policy shocks, or legal changes that abruptly change the risk of imprisonment for individual offenders. Wildeman and Andersen (2017), for example, investigated a policy change in Denmark that shifted more convicted people from prison to community service to disentangle the causal effects of paternal criminality and paternal incarceration on children's risk of being charged with a crime. They find that both a parent's criminal involvement and incarceration independently contribute to children's risk of criminal charges. Others have used variations in sentencing judges' punitiveness, or their tendencies to sentence convicted people to prison or the community, to isolate causal effects of imprisonment and pretrial detention on labor market outcomes and recidivism (Loeffler 2013; Dobbie, Goldin, and Yang 2018; Harding et al. 2018). Finally, innovative qualitative and mixed-methods designs offer greater insight into the complex family relationships that have produced mixed results in other forms of research (Bir and Lindquist 2017).

Unsurprisingly, greater rigor in causal identification yields mixed results that complicate assessment of earlier findings that outcomes were due solely to incarceration (e.g., Loeffler 2013; Norris, Pecenco, and Weaver 2021). Mixed-methods studies demonstrating substantial family complexity likely explain why (e.g., Giordano et al. 2019; McKay et al. 2019). Work in the area has recently become more rigorous, more complex, and a good bit messier.

C. Aligning Experiences before, during, and after Incarceration

One bit of messiness now being tackled more concretely concerns massive selection effect problems. Experiences that increase the risk of incarceration at individual or community levels (e.g., unemployment) tend to be things that researchers expect to be worsened by incarceration. Lacking data sets that document complex sets of experiences that precede incarceration, researchers often have little insight into the pathways that bring people to prison (Sampson 2011; Rodriguez 2016). Moreover, findings often conflate measures of criminal justice system contacts with measures of criminal offending. Separating the effects of parental criminality from effects of parental punishment, for example, requires recognition that they are not the same thing, but few data sets measure criminal involvement and criminal justice system contacts equally well (Wildeman 2020).

An early example concerns the effects of maternal incarceration on children; the nature and direction of these effects remains contested because research has produced decidedly mixed results. Whether maternal incarceration is, on average, harmful for children, dependent on the outcome being studied, or something else altogether is important. Rodriguez (2016) and others argue, however, that we should expect heterogeneity in the effects of incarceration because incarcerated people (and their families and communities) have often lived seriously unstable lives and endured exposure to violence and maltreatment (Bodkin et al. 2019), racism (Muhammad 2011; Alexander 2012), and deep poverty long before entering a prison (Giordano and Copp 2015).

Strong causal designs remain important, but the bar for achieving them has been raised considerably by greater recognition of the difficulties many people face before entering prison. This weakens the credibility of strong causal claims but has the advantage of focusing attention on the pathways that lead people to prison in the first place. The twin influences of rapidly rising standards for the demonstration of causal effects coupled with greater insight on the complex lives of incarcerated people and their families provide both enduring challenges and new opportunities for researchers.

IV. Enduring Challenges and New Opportunities

I turn now to enduring challenges to future progress. They revolve around measurement issues—what counts as incarceration and what counts as a family—and reflect growing recognition that the criminal justice system affects far more people and institutions than is usually recognized.

A. What Counts as Incarceration?

Describing the population of incarcerated people, their families, and their communities completely and accurately poses fundamental challenges. Connecting incarceration to family and community outcomes requires that incarceration be measured. Doing this is especially difficult in the United States (Kirk and Wakefield 2018). Many commonly used data sets pertinent to the study of families and communities were not primarily geared toward the criminal justice system and are often limited to crude measures of arrest, incarceration, or conviction. Incarceration is more highly concentrated in some places than in others, in some social groups than in others, and in some communities than in others. Especially in the United States, incarceration experiences are ubiquitous in some places and for some groups and largely hidden or invisible for others (Pettit 2012). Counting incarceration experiences well presents myriad difficulties.

The United States with its world-leading incarceration rate can be used as an example (Fair and Walmsley 2021). Figure 1 shows US imprisonment rates for state and federal prisoners per 100,000 population from 1978 to 2019 (Carson and Mulako-Wangota 2021). Those rates, however, are understated because, unlike imprisonment rates in other Western countries, they do not include people in pretrial confinement (Dobbie, Goldin, and Yang 2018) or most people serving sentences of a year or less

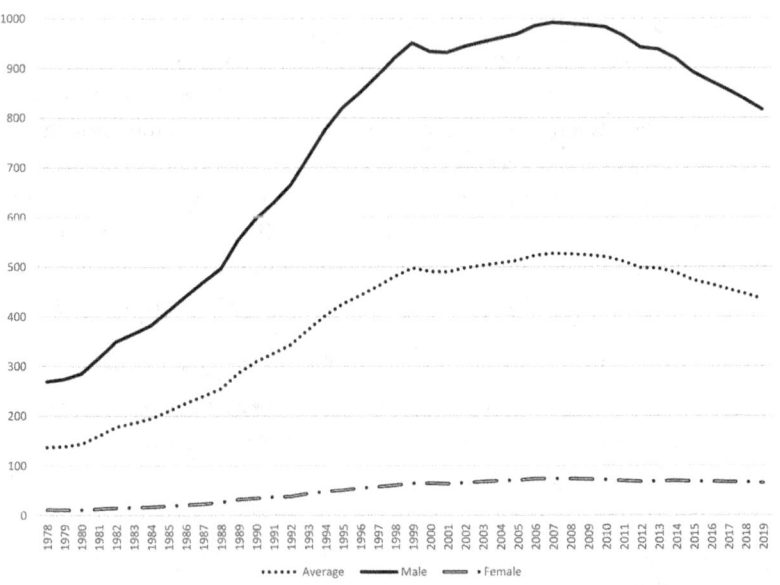

Fig. 1.—Imprisonment rates in the United States, by sex, 1978–2019. (Source: Carson and Mulako-Wangota 2021.)

(usually in county jails; Turney and Connor 2019). Mostly in this essay I refer to total rates, which I refer to as incarceration rates.

These US data, and much more, can easily be downloaded from the US Bureau of Justice Statistics using its Corrections Statistical Analysis tool (Carson and Mulako-Wangota 2021). Even though annual imprisonment and incarceration rates are readily accessible, connecting them to the complex lives of families and communities most affected by incarceration remains difficult. During the prison boom, however, even the reasonably well understood distinction between prison and jail inmates broke down in some states when increased numbers of people served lengthy sentences in local jails because of overcrowding in state prisons.

These data, whether they reflect incarceration rates or the narrower imprisonment rates, provide little insight into flows of people into and out of correctional institutions. US Bureau of Justice Statistics reports, for example, show that more than 10 million people were admitted to local jails in 2019 (Wagner and Sawyer 2020; Zeng and Minson 2021). It is unclear to what extent this huge number reflects many individuals who experienced a single admission and how many were admitted more than once or in what proportions. Clever scholars have pooled data sources to estimate the number of people who have been incarcerated (Pettit and Western 2004; Muller and Wildeman 2016), have been convicted of a felony (Shannon et al. 2017), or have had a parent who experienced incarceration (Sykes and Pettit 2015). These estimates, however, are not easily paired with other data sources to allow deeper examination into families or finely grained analyses of the concentration of incarceration in specific communities.

Data sources that allow measurement of histories of various forms of incarceration and can be connected to detailed family and community measures are thus in short supply. There is little reason to think that imprisonment for more than a year has important consequences for families and communities but that pretrial detention, short spells in jails, or time spent in a holding cell do not. Much research nonetheless relies on data sets that cannot reliably distinguish among different kinds of confinement. That fundamentally limits the kinds of questions that can usefully be asked and confidently be answered. A recent effort to match survey respondents who reported they had been incarcerated to administrative data on incarceration does not inspire confidence; the matching procedure increased the number of fathers who had been incarcerated and triggered concern that earlier research using the same data set missed a substantial number of incarceration spells (Geller, Jaeger, and Pace 2016).

All of this means that some questions are difficult, if not impossible, to answer. For example, is it more disruptive for children to experience a lengthy incarceration or a series of short jail terms of a parent over the course of childhood and adolescence? Tying sentence length to outcomes for children is difficult in most cases, although research from countries with better data available suggests it is important (e.g., Andersen 2016). Similarly, available data sources in the United States are likely to miss short jail spells or especially time spent in holding cells, but these experiences are not ignorable. As one example, Michael Walker's *Indefinite: Doing Time in Jail* (2022) begins by describing the dehumanizing and traumatic experience of a short time spent in a holding cell, and Kohler-Hausmann (2013) describes the calamities that follow even misdemeanor-level contact with the criminal justice system, undermining assumptions that short spells in jail are inconsequential for families and communities or that only felony convictions have far-reaching consequences.

These distinctions are especially important during this era of mass incarceration. Were incarceration levels much lower, inability to distinguish between short and long stays or pretrial detention might not radically change conclusions. Similarly, largely ignoring the effects of pretrial detention on families and communities when pretrial detention was much less common or jail terms were shorter might not substantially distort findings. Those differences are no longer ignorable if ever they were.

Linking data on incarceration histories to other data sources on families and communities is difficult and time consuming but worth pursuing. Several projects attempt to do so. Progress has been made, but the attempts so far either are limited in what outcomes can be investigated (e.g., only other social influences that are captured by administrative data sets; Finlay and Mueller-Smith 2021) or detail troubling levels of error in linking administrative data sets and surveys (Geller, Jaeger, and Pace 2016). Such findings challenge researchers toward more caution as they expand the variety of incarceration experiences studied.

B. *Who Counts as Family? What Makes a Community?*

Measurement problems are equally common and important concerning families and communities. Who counts as family? Blood relatives? Household members (which begs the question, before or after incarceration)? Kin-like friends and significant others? What about incarcerated people for whom criminal involvement and punishment broke family ties long ago? Questions like these reflect important scope condition decisions that must be made before attempting to connect incarceration to family outcomes. However, most research on incarceration and family life is devoted to the children and partners of incarcerated people. This is driven primarily by the measures of family incarceration that are available but is irreconcilable with extensive ethnographic work demonstrating the concentration of incarceration within families far beyond children and partners (Braman 2004; Wildeman and Wakefield 2014).

Just how extensive is the concentration of incarceration in families? Colleagues and I recently fielded a survey to improve estimates of how many people have experienced the incarceration of a family member; we sought to account for difficult-to-measure jail incarceration and expand familial scope beyond parents, partners, and children (Enns et al. 2022). Our results suggest that far more people have experienced the incarceration of a family member than previous estimates indicate (Bonczar 2003; Pettit and Western 2004; Lee et al. 2015). Using a nationally representative panel, we asked respondents a series of questions about incarceration of immediate and extended family members. All questions were anchored to incarceration experiences of more than one night to exclude short spells in holding cells but include pretrial detention, jail incarceration more broadly, and conventional imprisonment of more than 1 year. While this cross-sectional and short survey can offer no insight into histories of criminal justice system contacts, it can shed light on how taking account of pretrial detention or jail sentences affects estimates of how many US families and communities are affected by incarceration.

Figure 2 shows prevalence estimates, with confidence intervals, from the Family History of Incarceration Survey (FamHIS) of when respondents identified a specific immediate family member (parents, siblings, partners, and children, including foster, step, and adoptive relationships) who had experienced incarceration for at least one night. About 45 percent of Americans, with very large race and class disparities, have had an immediate family member incarcerated. Race and ethnicity prevalence estimates range from a high of 63 percent for Black and Native Americans to a low of 34 percent for Other Race (mostly respondents with Asian or multiracial identities) and 43 percent for Whites.[1]

---

[1] Estimates for Native Americans and Other Race have very large confidence intervals given their small sample sizes; these estimates should be interpreted with caution.

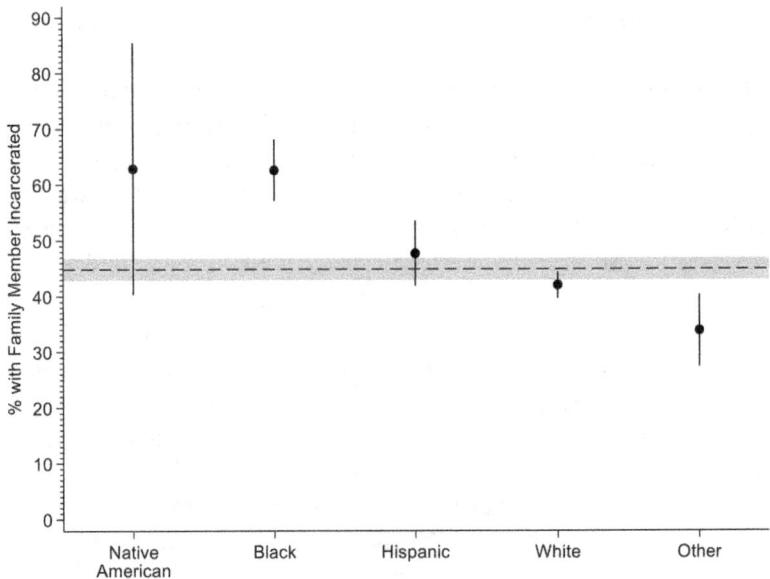

Fɪɢ. 2.—Prevalence of immediate and extended family member incarceration. $N = 4{,}030$. Weighted estimates and 95% error bars are shown. The horizontal line is the sample mean for immediate family member incarceration, with the shaded band indicating 95% error bars. (Source: Family History of Incarceration Survey; see Enns et al. 2022.)

FamHIS echoes prior estimates of the prevalence of incarceration experiences (Lee et al. 2015), but the overall estimate—including forms of incarceration not well measured in other data sets—suggests that family member incarceration is much more common than was previously understood. Figure 3 presents the distribution of family member incarceration for the full sample and by selected racial and ethnic groups. It includes both immediate family member incarceration and that of extended family (grandparents, aunts and uncles, cousins, and others not included in the immediate family definition) and presents a count of family members incarcerated offered by FamHIS respondents. There are large racial and ethnic disparities, with Black and Hispanic respondents much more likely to report 10 or more family members who have been incarcerated (see also Wildeman and Wakefield [2014] for overlap between mother and father incarceration).

Much research on family incarceration relies on relatively crude measures of incarceration, limited to a specific relationship or truncated with

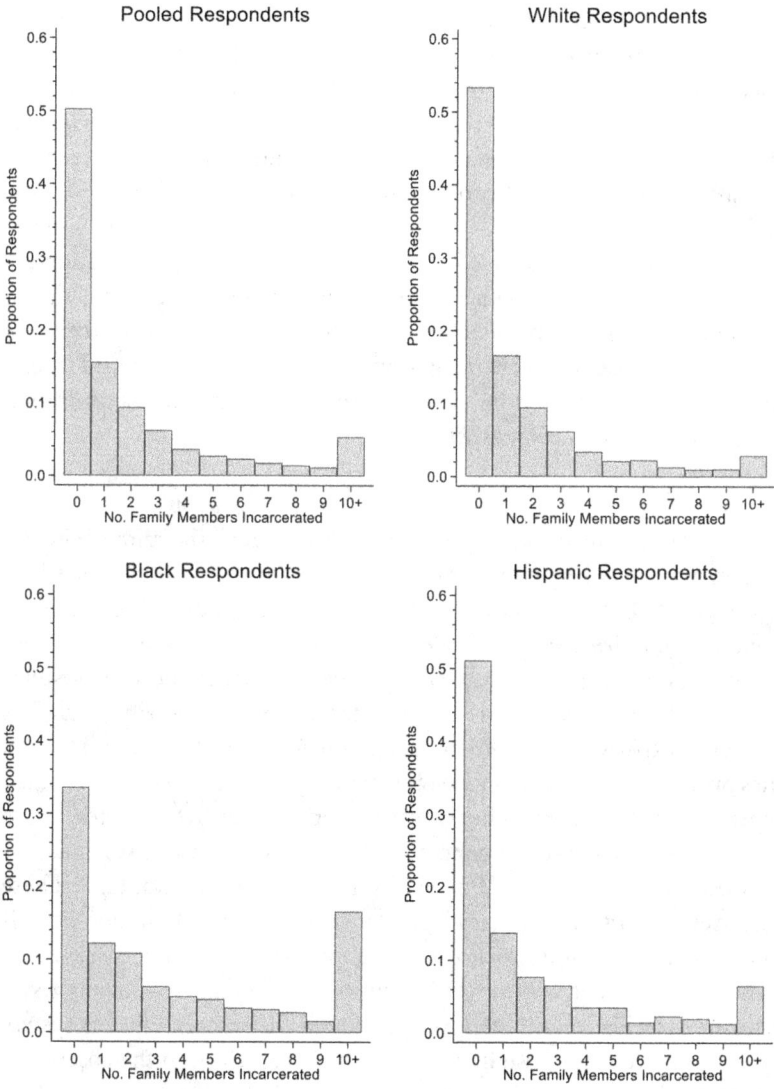

FIG. 3.—Distribution of family member incarceration, by race/ethnicity. $N = 3{,}690$. Immediate and extended family members are included. (Source: Family History of Incarceration Survey; see Enns et al. 2022.)

respect to family members beyond partners or children. Yet FamHIS found that many people have multiple family members who have experienced incarceration. Incarceration of a sibling, not a parent or partner, was the most common form reported (Enns et al. 2019). Two conclusions emerge. First, much research on incarceration and the family is potentially missing a substantial number of family incarceration experiences. Second, and more troubling, comparison groups designated as "no family incarceration" may include people with substantial vicarious incarceration experiences. It is difficult to know whether this results in over- or underestimation of incarceration effects on the family (perhaps the incarceration of a distant cousin or uncle really is inconsequential) but justifies investments in research that would better capture the range and concentration of vicarious incarceration experiences.

C. Other Systems That Work in Concert with Incarceration

A third enduring challenge concerns ways in which the criminal justice system overlaps with other institutions and systems to maintain racial inequality. Scholarship on incarceration's effects on families and communities tends to minimize the importance of traumatizing and destabilizing experiences before incarceration. Many of these experiences occur in systems that, like the criminal justice system, reflect pervasive inequality. Scholars may view experiences before incarceration as primarily posing selection bias problems to be overcome or as a pathway problem to be investigated more deeply; both approaches would be improved by greater attention to other systems that work in concert with the criminal justice system.

Most incarcerated people have histories of deep disadvantage. These histories are not merely the accumulation of adverse childhood experiences, such as exposure to violence, poverty, or racism, but involve sustained engagement with other institutions that create overlapping systems of surveillance and exclusion in which the criminal justice system is part of a broader constellation (Beckett 2018). Even in the absence of incarceration, it is difficult to imagine unraveling the effects of each of these overlapping systems. Harmful outcomes of incarceration for families and communities reflect widespread exposure to surveillance systems and system exclusion. Consider health outcomes. Incarceration precipitates a distinct set of health problems (Massoglia and Pridemore 2015) but also reflects structural racism in health care delivery (Bailey et al. 2017; Homan, Brown, and King 2021) and system avoidance of "surveilling" institutions such as hospitals (Brayne 2014).

Or consider educational systems. Systematic exclusion is readily apparent in school systems (Foster and Hagan 2007). Ewert, Sykes, and Beckett describe America's prisons and jails as "repositories for high school dropouts" (2014, p. 24), finding that the concentration of people excluded from high school in prisons obscures racial gaps in high school completion and labor market attainment (Pettit 2012; Rios 2017). Schools thus play a role in criminalizing behavior (Gerlinger et al. 2021), reflect deep poverty and institutional racism (Crawley and Hirschfield 2018), and exclude people with family incarceration experiences (Hagan and Foster 2012*a*; Lageson 2016).

A final example. Exposure to child welfare systems often precedes or follows involvement with the criminal justice system. Involvement in the child welfare system increases the risk of prison entry (Font et al. 2021). The racial and ethnic composition of children in child welfare systems looks remarkably like those in prison and jail populations. Figure 4, for example, shows cumulative prevalence rates for children, by race and ethnicity, for child welfare investigations, foster care placements, and termination of parental rights (Edwards et al. 2021; see also Roberts 2002, 2004). The foster care placement rate among incarcerated populations is much higher than in the general population (Uggen and Wakefield 2008). Moreover, children are more likely to be placed in foster care in states with more punitive punishment regimes (Edwards 2016), and increases in the maternal

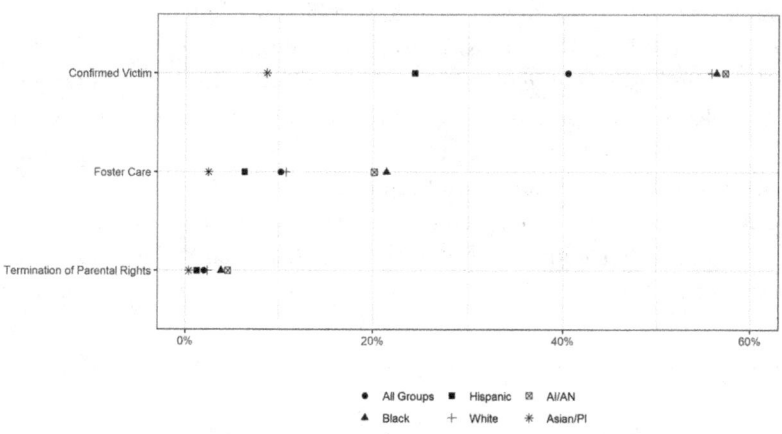

FIG. 4.—Cumulative prevalence of Child Protective Services investigation, foster care placement, and termination of parental rights. (Source: Edwards et al. 2021.)

incarceration rate correspond to increases in foster care placement (Johnson and Waldfogel 2002).

These are but three examples of how a collection of outcomes from studies of a variety of state institutions are best characterized as reflecting overlapping or joint systems of surveillance, exclusion, and disadvantage. Such systems often drive people into the criminal justice system (Font et al. 2021; Gerlinger et al. 2021) or increase the harmful consequences of criminal justice system contacts for families and communities (Hagan and Dinovitzer 1999; Kirk and Wakefield 2018). We lack a full understanding of surveillance and exclusion systems that characterize the lives of incarcerated and formerly incarcerated people, their families, and their communities.

D. What Should We Learn from the Extreme?

The United States is an unusual place in which to study incarceration, especially concerning the effects of incarceration on families and communities. That is probably why so much of the research is American but also why US data cannot validly be used as bases for generalizations about incarceration's effects (or, conversely, why findings from research elsewhere may not recur in the United States). It is equally unclear that findings from research in especially punitive US states or cities should be expected to apply to other US states or cities.

Prisons have long reflected historical legacies of social exclusion, but the forms and nature of these patterns differ substantially across times and places. It is nearly impossible to claim confidently that incarceration affects families or communities in a particular way most of the time in most places. Unfortunately, much of the literature on mass incarceration ignores generalizability problems and tends to extrapolate findings from places to other places that have little in common.

Researchers should not pretend (or assume) that the United States is comparable to Denmark (Wakefield and Andersen 2020), Colombia (Arteaga 2021), or the Netherlands (Ramakers et al. 2014) with respect to incarceration. Nor should the goal be to produce general answers to what are inherently distinctly local questions.

V. Conclusion

I have highlighted advances in the study of incarceration, family, and community over the last 20 years. Work in the early 2000s sought primarily to investigate whether high levels of incarceration are on balance harmful to families and communities. The answer is clear: research in many disciplines on many subjects has cataloged numerous direct and indirect harms. The evidence base has expanded to encompass additional effects on families and communities and has done so by means of greater cross-disciplinary collaboration and a focus on harm-producing mechanisms. A fair reading of the evidence is that incarceration has harmful effects on families and communities, much as Hagan and Dinovitzer (1999) predicted in *Crime and Justice* more than 20 years ago.

The evidence base is now very large, but fundamental challenges must be overcome before full accountings can be made. Early observational estimates of incarceration harms, for example, are likely to have been overestimated; more rigorous research tends to find smaller effects. However, it is also increasingly clear that netting out incarceration effects from the effects of other prior forms of disadvantage risks missing forests for trees. Incarceration has always been associated within a constellation of forms of deep disadvantage and often reflects long legacies of racism, class disadvantage, and weakened community supports.

Although scholarship on incarceration and social harms has increased enormously, our gaze remains partly obscured. Many forms of incarceration are difficult to measure well, which precludes deep analysis of how heterogeneity in incarceration experiences influences outcomes for families and communities. Research on families focuses mostly on children and partners, to the exclusion of broader kinship networks. Nascent research on the intersection between the criminal justice system and other systems that produce disadvantage suggests important overlaps but remains underdeveloped. Generalizability issues related to the study of incarceration in extreme carceral contexts continue to be bedeviling. Continued advances in understanding of the effects of incarceration will depend on researchers turning these challenges into opportunities.

REFERENCES

Alexander, Michelle. 2012. *The New Jim Crow: Mass Incarceration in the Age of Colorblindness*. New York: New Press.

Altice, Frederick L., et al. 2016. "The Perfect Storm: Incarceration and the High-Risk Environment Perpetuating Transmission of HIV, Hepatitis C

Virus, and Tuberculosis in Eastern Europe and Central Asia." *Lancet* 388 (10050):1228–48.

Andersen, Lars H. 2016. "How Children's Educational Outcomes and Criminality Vary by Duration and Frequency of Paternal Incarceration." *Annals of the American Academy of Political and Social Science* 665(1):49–70.

Andersen, Signe Hald, and Christopher Wildeman. 2014. "The Effect of Paternal Incarceration on Children's Risk of Foster Care Placement." *Social Forces* 93(1):269–98.

Apel, Robert. 2016. "The Effects of Jail and Prison Confinement on Cohabitation and Marriage." *Annals of the American Academy of Political and Social Science* 665(1):103–26.

Apel, Robert, and Kathleen Powell. 2019. "Level of Criminal Justice Contact and Early Adult Wage Inequality." *RSF: The Russell Sage Foundation Journal of the Social Sciences* 5(1):198–222.

Arditti, Joyce A. 2016. "A Family Stress-Proximal Process Model for Understanding the Effects of Parental Incarceration on Children and Their Families." *Couple and Family Psychology: Research and Practice* 5(2):65–88.

Arteaga, Carolina. 2021. "Parental Incarceration and Children's Educational Attainment." *Review of Economics and Statistics*. https://doi.org/10.1162/rest_a _01129.

Bailey, Zinzi D., Nancy Krieger, Madina Agénor, Jasmine Graves, Natalia Linos, and Mary T. Bassett. 2017. "Structural Racism and Health Inequities in the USA: Evidence and Interventions." *Lancet* 389(10077):1453–63.

Beckett, Katherine. 1997. *Making Crime Pay: Law and Order in Contemporary American Politics*. New York: Oxford University Press.

Beckett, Katherine. 2018. "The Politics, Prospects, and Perils of Criminal Justice Reform in an Era of Mass Incarceration." *Annual Review of Criminology* 1:235–59.

Besemer, Kirsten L., and Susan M. Dennison. 2018. "Family Imprisonment, Maternal Parenting Stress and Its Impact on Mother-Child Relationship Satisfaction." *Journal of Child and Family Studies* 27(12):3897–908.

Binswanger, Ingrid A., Patrick J. Blatchford, Simon J. Forsyth, Marc F. Stern, and Stuart A. Kinner. 2016. "Epidemiology of Infectious Disease–Related Death after Release from Prison, Washington State, United States, and Queensland, Australia: A Cohort Study." *Public Health Reports* 131(4):574–82.

Bir, Anupa, and Christine Lindquist. 2017. "Multi-Site Family Study on Incarceration, Parenting and Partnering, 2008–2014 [5 States]." Ann Arbor, MI: Inter-university Consortium for Political and Social Research.

Bodkin, Claire, Lucie Pivnick, Susan J. Bondy, Carolyn Ziegler, Ruth Elwood Martin, Carey Jernigan, and Fiona Kouyoumdjian. 2019. "History of Childhood Abuse in Populations Incarcerated in Canada: A Systematic Review and Meta-analysis." *American Journal of Public Health* 109(3):e1–e11.

Bonczar, T. P. 2003. *Prevalence of Imprisonment in the U.S. Population, 1974–2001*. Washington, DC: US Department of Justice, Bureau of Justice Statistics.

Braman, Donald. 2004. *Doing Time on the Outside*. Ann Arbor: University of Michigan Press.

Brayne, Sarah. 2014. "Surveillance and System Avoidance: Criminal Justice Contact and Institutional Attachment." *American Sociological Review* 79(3):367–91.

Carson, E. Ann, and Joseph Mulako-Wangota. 2021. "Corrections Statistical Analysis Tool (CSAT)—Prisoners." Washington, DC: US Department of Justice, Bureau of Justice Statistics. https://perma.cc/4H5T-VM7N.

Chamberlain, Alyssa W., and Lyndsay N. Boggess. 2019. "Parolee Concentration, Risk of Recidivism, and the Consequences for Neighborhood Crime." *Deviant Behavior* 40(12):1522–42.

Charles, Pajarita, Luke Muentner, Sarah Jensen, Chiara Packard, Chloe Haimson, John Eason, and Julie Poehlmann-Tynan. 2021. "Incarcerated during a Pandemic: Implications of COVID-19 for Jailed Individuals and Their Families." *Corrections*. https://doi.org/10.1080/23774657.2021.2011803.

Charles, Pajarita, Luke Muentner, and Jean Kjellstrand. 2019. "Parenting and Incarceration: Perspectives on Father-Child Involvement during Reentry from Prison." *Social Service Review* 93(2):18–61.

Cho, Rosa Minhyo. 2009*a*. "The Impact of Maternal Imprisonment on Children's Educational Achievement Results from Children in Chicago Public Schools." *Journal of Human Resources* 44(3):72–97.

Cho, Rosa Minhyo. 2009*b*. "Impact of Maternal Imprisonment on Children's Probability of Grade Retention." *Journal of Urban Economics* 65(1):11–23.

Christian, Johnna. 2005. "Riding the Bus: Barriers to Prison Visitation and Family Management Strategies." *Journal of Contemporary Criminal Justice* 21(1):31–48.

Clear, Todd R. 2007. *Imprisoning Communities: How Mass Incarceration Makes Disadvantaged Neighborhoods Worse*. New York: Oxford University Press.

Comfort, Megan. 2003. "In the Tube at San Quentin: The 'Secondary Prisonization' of Women Visiting Inmates." *Journal of Contemporary Ethnography* 32 (1):77–107.

Comfort, Megan. 2007. "Punishment beyond the Legal Offender." *Annual Review of Law and Social Science* 3(1):271–84.

Comfort, Megan. 2016. "'A Twenty-Hour-a-Day Job': The Impact of Frequent Low-Level Criminal Justice Involvement on Family Life." *Annals of the American Academy of Political and Social Science* 665(1):63–79.

Crawley, Kayla, and Paul Hirschfield. 2018. "Examining the School-to-Prison Pipeline Metaphor." In *Oxford Research Encyclopedia of Criminology and Criminal Justice*. New York: Oxford University Press.

Dallaire, Danielle H., Anne Ciccone, and Laura C. Wilson. 2010. "Teachers' Experiences with and Expectations of Children with Incarcerated Parents." *Journal of Applied Developmental Psychology* 31(4):281–90.

Dirkzwager, A. J. E., et al. 2018. "Cohort Profile: The Prison Project—a Study of Criminal Behavior and Life Circumstances before, during, and after Imprisonment in the Netherlands." *Journal of Developmental and Life-Course Criminology* 4(1):120–35.

Dobbie, Will, Jacob Goldin, and Crystal S. Yang. 2018. "The Effects of Pre-trial Detention on Conviction, Future Crime, and Employment: Evidence from Randomly Assigned Judges." *American Economic Review* 108(2):201–40.

Dumont, Dora M., Brad Brockmann, Samuel Dickman, Nicole Alexander, and Josiah D. Rich. 2012. "Public Health and the Epidemic of Incarceration." *Annual Review of Public Health* 33(1):325–39.

Earls, Felton J., Jeanne Brooks-Gunn, Steven W. Raudenbush, and Robert J. Sampson. 2002. *Project on Human Development in Chicago Neighborhoods (PHDCN)*. Ann Arbor, MI: Inter-university Consortium for Political and Social Research.

Eason, John. 2017. "Prisons as Panacea or Pariah? The Countervailing Consequences of the Prison Boom on the Political Economy of Rural Towns." *Social Sciences* 6(1):7.

Edwards, Frank. 2016. "Saving Children, Controlling Families: Punishment, Redistribution, and Child Protection." *American Sociological Review* 81(3):575–95.

Edwards, Frank, Sara Wakefield, Kieran Healy, and Christopher Wildeman. 2021. "Contact with Child Protective Services Is Pervasive but Unequally Distributed by Race and Ethnicity in Large US Counties." *Proceedings of the National Academy of Sciences* 118(30):e2106272118.

Enns, Peter K., Christopher Wildeman, Youngmin Yi, Megan Comfort, Maria D. Fitzpatrick, Alyssa W. Goldman, Hedwig Lee, Christopher Muller, Sara Wakefield, and Emily A. Wang. 2022. "Family History of Incarceration Study (FamHIS)." Release 3. Roper no. 31115615, Roper IPoll. Roper Center for Public Opinion Research.

Enns, Peter K., Youngmin Yi, Megan Comfort, Alyssa Goldman, Hedwig Lee, Christopher Muller, Sara Wakefield, Emily Wang, and Christopher Wildeman. 2019. "The Family History of Incarceration Survey (FamHIS): Motivation, Design, and Preliminary Findings." *Socius* 6:1–45.

Ewert, Stephanie, Bryan L. Sykes, and Becky Pettit. 2014. "The Degree of Disadvantage: Incarceration and Inequality in Education." *Annals of the American Academy of Political and Social Science* 651(1):24–43.

Fair, Helen, and Roy Walmsley. 2021. "World Prison Population List." 13th ed. London: Birkbeck College, International Centre for Prison Studies.

Finlay, Keith, and Michael Mueller Smith. 2021. *Criminal Justice Administrative Records System (CJARS)*. Ann Arbor: University of Michigan, Institute for Social Research.

Fishman, Susan Hoffman. 1983. "The Impact of Incarceration on Children of Offenders." *Journal of Children in Contemporary Society* 15(1):89–99.

Font, Sarah, Lawrence M. Berger, Jessie Slepicka, and Maria Cancian. 2021. "Foster Care, Permanency, and Risk of Prison Entry." *Journal of Research in Crime and Delinquency* 58(6):710–54.

Foster, Holly, and John Hagan. 2007. "Incarceration and Intergenerational Social Exclusion." *Social Problems* 54(4):399–433.

Garland, David. 2001*a*. *Mass Imprisonment: Social Causes and Consequences*. Thousand Oaks, CA: Sage.

Garland, David. 2001*b*. "The Meaning of Mass Imprisonment." *Punishment and Society* 3:5–7.

Geller, Amanda, Carey E. Cooper, Irwin Garfinkel, Ofira Schwartz-Soicher, and Ronald B. Mincy. 2011. "Beyond Absenteeism: Father Incarceration and Child Development." *Demography* 49(1):49–76.

Geller, Amanda, Kate Jaeger, and Garret T. Pace. 2016. "Surveys, Records, and the Study of Incarceration in Families." *Annals of the American Academy of Political and Social Science* 665(1):22–43.

Gerlinger, Julie, Samantha Viano, Joseph H. Gardella, Benjamin W. Fisher, F. Chris Curran, and Ethan M. Higgins. 2021. "Exclusionary School Discipline and Delinquent Outcomes: A Meta-analysis." *Journal of Youth and Adolescence* 50(8):1493–509.

Giordano, Peggy C., and Jennifer E. Copp. 2015. "'Packages' of Risk: Implications for Determining the Effect of Maternal Incarceration on Child Wellbeing." *Criminology and Public Policy* 14(1):157–68.

Giordano, Peggy C., Jennifer E. Copp, Wendy D. Manning, and Monica A. Longmore. 2019. "Linking Parental Incarceration and Family Dynamics Associated with Intergenerational Transmission: A Life-Course Perspective." *Criminology* 57(3):395–423.

Giordano, Peggy, Monica Longmore, and Wendy Manning. 2017. "Toledo Adolescent Relationships Study (TARS): Wave 5, 2011." Version 1. Ann Arbor, MI: Inter-university Consortium for Political and Social Research.

Grieb, Suzanne M. Dolwick, Amelia Crawford, Julie Fields, Horace Smith, Richard Harris, and Pamela Matson. 2014. "'The Stress Will Kill You': Prisoner Reentry as Experienced by Family Members and the Urgent Need for Support Services." *Journal of Health Care for the Poor and Underserved* 25(3):1183–200.

Grinstead, Olga, Bonnie Faigeles, Carrie Bancroft, and Barry Zack. 2001. "The Financial Costs of Maintaining Relationships with Incarcerated African American Men: A Survey of Women Prison Visitors." *Journal of African American Men* 6(1):59–69.

Hagan, John, and Ronit Dinovitzer. 1999. "Collateral Consequences of Imprisonment for Children, Communities, and Prisoners." In *Crime and Justice: A Review of Research*, vol. 26, edited by Michael Tonry. Chicago: University of Chicago Press.

Hagan, John, and Holly Foster. 2012a. "Children of the American Prison Generation: Student and School Spillover Effects of Incarcerating Mothers." *Law and Society Review* 46(1):37–69.

Hagan, John, and Holly Foster. 2012b. "Intergenerational Educational Effects of Mass Imprisonment in America." *Sociology of Education* 85(3):259–86.

Hagan, John, and Alberto Palloni. 1990. "The Social Reproduction of a Criminal Class in Working Class London, circa 1950–1980." *American Journal of Sociology* 96(2):265–99.

Harding, David J., Jeffrey D. Morenoff, Anh P. Nguyen, and Shawn D. Bushway. 2018. "Imprisonment and Labor Market Outcomes: Evidence from a National Experiment." *American Journal of Sociology* 124(1):49–110.

Harris, K. M., C. T. Halpern, E. Whitsel, J. Hussey, J. Tabor, P. Entzel, and J. R. Udry. 2009. "The National Longitudinal Study of Adolescent to Adult Health: Research Design." University of North Carolina at Chapel Hill. https://addhealth.cpc.unc.edu//documentation/study-design.

Harris, Othello, and R. Robin Miller. 2003. *Impacts of Incarceration on the African American Family*. New Brunswick, NJ: Transaction.

Haskins, Anna. 2014. "Unintended Consequences: Effects of Paternal Incarceration on Child School Readiness and Later Special Education Placement." *Sociological Science* 1:141–58.

Haskins, Anna, and Wade C. Jacobsen. 2017. "Schools as Surveilling Institutions? Paternal Incarceration, System Avoidance, and Parental Involvement in Schooling." *American Sociological Review* 82(4):657–84.

Haskins, Anna R., and Kristin Turney. 2018. "The Demographic Landscape and Sociological Perspectives on Parental Incarceration and Childhood Inequality." In *When Parents Are Incarcerated: Interdisciplinary Research and Interventions to Support Children*, edited by Christopher Wildeman, Anna R. Haskins, and Julie Poehlmann-Tynan. Washington, DC: American Psychological Association.

Homan, Patricia, Tyson H. Brown, and Brittany King. 2021. "Structural Intersectionality as a New Direction for Health Disparities Research." *Journal of Health and Social Behavior* 62(3):350–70.

Huebner, Beth M., and Regan Gustafson. 2007. "The Effect of Maternal Incarceration on Adult Offspring Involvement in the Criminal Justice System." *Journal of Criminal Justice* 35(3):283–96.

Johnson, Elizabeth I., and Jane Waldfogel. 2002. "Parental Incarceration: Recent Trends and Implications for Child Welfare." *Social Service Review* 76(3):460–79.

Johnson, Rucker C., and Steven Raphael. 2009. "The Effects of Male Incarceration Dynamics on Acquired Immune Deficiency Syndrome Infection Rates among African American Women and Men." *Journal of Law and Economics* 52(2):251–93.

Khan, Maria R., Irene A. Doherty, Victor J. Schoenbach, Eboni M. Taylor, Matthew W. Epperson, and Adaora A. Adimora. 2009. "Incarceration and High-Risk Sex Partnerships among Men in the United States." *Journal of Urban Health* 86(4):584–601.

Kirk, David S. 2019. "Where the Other 1 Percent Live: An Examination of Changes in the Spatial Concentration of the Formerly Incarcerated." *RSF: The Russell Sage Foundation Journal of the Social Sciences* 5(1):255–74.

Kirk, David S., and Sara Wakefield. 2018. "Collateral Consequences of Punishment: A Critical Review and Path Forward." *Annual Review of Criminology* 1(1):171–94.

Kohler-Hausmann, Issa. 2013. "Misdemeanor Justice: Control without Conviction." *American Journal of Sociology* 119(2):351–93.

Lageson, Sarah Esther. 2016. "Found Out and Opting Out: The Consequences of Online Criminal Records for Families." *Annals of the American Academy of Political and Social Science* 665:127–41.

Laub, John H. 2018. "Reducing Justice System Inequality: Introducing the Issue." *Future of Children* 28(1):3–10.

Lee, Hedwig, Tyler McCormick, Margaret T. Hicken, and Christopher Wildeman. 2015. "Racial Inequalities in Connectedness to Imprisoned Individuals in the United States." *Du Bois Review: Social Science Research on Race* 12(2):269–82.

Lee, Hedwig, and Christopher Wildeman. 2021. "Assessing Mass Incarceration's Effects on Families." *Science* 374:277–81.

Light, Michael T., and Joey Marshall. 2018. "On the Weak Mortality Returns of the Prison Boom: Comparing Infant Mortality and Homicide in the Incarceration Ledger." *Journal of Health and Social Behavior* 59(1):3–19.

Loeffler, Charles E. 2013. "Does Imprisonment Alter the Life Course? Evidence on Crime and Employment from a Natural Experiment." *Criminology* 51(1): 137–66.

Loury, Glenn C., and Bruce Western. 2010. "Introduction: The Challenge of Mass Incarceration in America." *Daedalus* 139(3):5–7.

Maruna, Shadd, Gillian McNaull, and Nina O'Neill. 2022. "The COVID-19 Pandemic and the Future of the Prison." In *Prisons and Prisoners*, edited by Michael Tonry and Sandra Bucerius. Vol. 51 of *Crime and Justice: A Review of Research*, edited by Michael Tonry. Chicago: University of Chicago Press.

Massoglia, Michael, and William Alex Pridemore. 2015. "Incarceration and Health." *Annual Review of Sociology* 41(1):291–310.

Massoglia, Michael, Brianna Remster, and Ryan D. King. 2011. "Stigma or Separation? Understanding the Incarceration-Divorce Relationship." *Social Forces* 90(1):133–55.

Mauer, Marc, and Meda Chesney-Lind, eds. 2002. *Invisible Punishment: The Collateral Consequences of Mass Imprisonment*. New York: New Press.

McKay, Tasseli, Megan Comfort, Christine Lindquist, and Anupa Bir. 2019. *Holding On: Family and Fatherhood during Incarceration and Reentry*. Berkeley: University of California Press.

Miller, Holly Ventura, and J. C. Barnes. 2015. "The Association between Parental Incarceration and Health, Education, and Economic Outcomes in Young Adulthood." *American Journal of Criminal Justice* 40(4):765–84.

Miller, Reuben Jonathan. 2021. *Halfway Home: Race, Punishment, and the Afterlife of Mass Incarceration*. Boston: Little, Brown.

Mowen, Thomas J., and John H. Boman. 2018. "A Developmental Perspective on Reentry: Understanding the Causes and Consequences of Family Conflict and Peer Delinquency during Adolescence and Emerging Adulthood." *Journal of Youth and Adolescence* 47(2):275–89.

Mowen, Thomas J., and Christy A. Visher. 2016. "Changing the Ties That Bind: How Incarceration Impacts Family Relationships." *Criminology and Public Policy* 15(2):503–28.

Muftić, Lisa R., Leana A. Bouffard, and Gaylene S. Armstrong. 2016. "Impact of Maternal Incarceration on the Criminal Justice Involvement of Adult Offspring: A Research Note." *Journal of Research in Crime and Delinquency* 53(1): 93–111.

Muhammad, Khalil Gibran. 2011. *The Condemnation of Blackness: Race, Crime, and the Making of Modern Urban America*. Cambridge, MA: Harvard University Press.

Muller, Christopher, and Christopher Wildeman. 2016. "Geographic Variation in the Cumulative Risk of Imprisonment and Parental Imprisonment in the United States." *Demography* 53(5):499–509.

Mumola, Christopher J. 2000. *Incarcerated Parents and Their Children*. Washington, DC: US Department of Justice, Bureau of Justice Statistics.

Murray, Joseph, and David P. Farrington. 2005. "Parental Imprisonment: Effects on Boys' Antisocial Behaviour and Delinquency through the Life-Course." *Journal of Child Psychology and Psychiatry* 46(12):1269–78.

Murray, Joseph, and David P. Farrington. 2008. "The Effects of Parental Imprisonment on Children." In *Crime and Justice: A Review of Research*, vol. 37, edited by Michael Tonry. Chicago: University of Chicago Press.

Murray, Joseph, David P. Farrington, and Ivana Sekol. 2012. "Children's Antisocial Behavior, Mental Health, Drug Use, and Educational Performance after Parental Incarceration: A Systematic Review and Meta-Analysis." *Psychological Bulletin* 138(2):175–210.

National Research Council. 2014. *The Growth of Incarceration in the United States: Exploring Causes and Consequences*. Washington, DC: National Academies.

Norris, Samuel, Matthew Pecenco, and Jeffrey Weaver. 2021. "The Effects of Parental and Sibling Incarceration: Evidence from Ohio." *American Economic Review* 111(9):2926–63.

Nurse, Anne M. 2002. *Fatherhood Arrested: Parenting from within the Juvenile Justice System*. Nashville: Vanderbilt University Press.

Pettit, Becky. 2012. *Invisible Men: Mass Incarceration and the Myth of Black Progress*. New York: Russell Sage.

Pettit, Becky, and Bruce Western. 2004. "Mass Imprisonment and the Life Course: Race and Class Inequality in U.S. Incarceration." *American Sociological Review* 69(2):151–69.

Poehlmann-Tynan, Julie, and Joyce A. Arditti. 2018. "Developmental and Family Perspectives on Family Incarceration." In *When Parents Are Incarcerated: Interdisciplinary Research and Interventions to Support Children*, edited by Christopher Wildeman, Anna R. Haskins, and Julie Poehlmann-Tynan. Washington, DC: American Psychological Association.

Porter, Lauren C., and Ryan D. King. 2015. "Absent Fathers or Absent Variables? A New Look at Parental Incarceration and Delinquency." *Journal of Research in Crime and Delinquency* 52(3):414–43.

Ramakers, Anke, Robert Apel, Paul Nieubeerta, Anja Dirkzwager, and Johan Van Wilsem. 2014. "Imprisonment Length and Post-prison Employment Prospects." *Criminology* 52(3):499–527.

Reichman, Nancy E., Julien O. Teitler, Irwin Garfinkel, and Sara S. McLanahan. 2001. "Fragile Families: Sample and Design." *Children and Youth Services Review* 23(4–5):303–26.

Remster, Brianna, and Cody Warner. 2018. "Residential Insecurities and Neighborhood Quality Following Incarceration." In *Handbook on the Consequences of Sentencing and Punishment Decisions*, edited by Beth M. Huebner and Natasha A. Frost. New York: Routledge.

Rios, Victor M. 2017. *Human Targets: Schools, Police, and the Criminalization of Latino Youth*. Chicago: University of Chicago Press.

Roberts, Dorothy. 2002. *Shattered Bonds: The Color Of Child Welfare*. London: Civitas.

Roberts, Dorothy. 2004. "The Social and Moral Cost of Mass Incarceration in African American Communities." *Stanford Law Review* 56:1271–305.

Rodriguez, Nancy. 2016. "Bridging the Gap between Research and Practice: The Role of Science in Addressing the Effects of Incarceration on Family Life." *Annals of the American Academy of Political and Social Science* 665(1):231–40.

Incarceration, Families, and Communities 431

Roettger, Michael E., Raymond R. Swisher, Danielle C. Kuhl, and Jorge Chavez. 2011. "Paternal Incarceration and Trajectories of Marijuana and Other Illegal Drug Use from Adolescence into Young Adulthood: Evidence from Longitudinal Panels of Males and Females in the United States." *Addiction* 106(1):121–32.

Sack, William H., Jack Seidler, and Susan Thomas. 1976. "The Children of Imprisoned Parents: A Psychosocial Exploration." *American Journal of Orthopsychiatry* 46(4):618–28.

Sampson, Robert J. 2011. "The Incarceration Ledger." *Criminology and Public Policy* 10(3):819–28.

Sampson, Robert J., and Charles Loeffler. 2010. "Punishment's Place: The Local Concentration of Mass Incarceration." *Daedalus* 139(3):20–31.

Schwartz-Soicher, Ofira, Amanda Geller, and Irwin Garfinkel. 2011. "The Effect of Paternal Incarceration on Material Hardship." *Social Service Review* 85(3):447–73.

Shannon, Sarah K. S., Christopher Uggen, Jason Schnittker, Melissa Thompson, Sara Wakefield, and Michael Massoglia. 2017. "The Growth, Scope, and Spatial Distribution of People with Felony Records in the United States, 1948–2010." *Demography* 54:1795–818.

Shaw, Marcus. 2019. "The Reproduction of Social Disadvantage through Educational Demobilization: A Critical Analysis of Parental Incarceration." *Critical Criminology* 27(2):275–90.

Siegel, Jane A. 2011. *Disrupted Childhoods: Children of Women in Prison.* New Brunswick, NJ: Rutgers University Press.

Simes, Jessica T. 2018. "Place and Punishment: The Spatial Context of Mass Incarceration." *Journal of Quantitative Criminology* 34(2):513–33.

Stuart, Forrest. 2016. "Becoming 'Copwise': Policing, Culture, and the Collateral Consequences of Street-Level Criminalization." *Law and Society Review* 50(2):279–313.

Stuart, Forrest, Amada Armenta, and Melissa Osborne. 2015. "Legal Control of Marginal Groups." *Annual Review of Law and Social Science* 11(1):235–54.

Stuart, Forrest, and Reuben Jonathan Miller. 2017. "The Prisonized Old Head: Intergenerational Socialization and the Fusion of Ghetto and Prison Culture." *Journal of Contemporary Ethnography* 46(6):673–98.

Sugie, Naomi. 2015. "Chilling Effects: Diminished Political Participation among Partners of Formerly Incarcerated Men." *Social Problems* 62(4):550–71.

Sykes, Bryan L., and Becky Pettit. 2015. "Severe Deprivation and System Inclusion among Children of Incarcerated Parents in the United States after the Great Recession." *RSF: The Russell Sage Foundation Journal of the Social Sciences* 1(2):108–32.

Tonry, Michael. 1995. *Malign Neglect: Race, Crime, and Punishment in the United States.* New York: Oxford University Press.

Topel, Matthew L., Heval M. Kelli, Tené T. Lewis, Sandra B. Dunbar, Viola Vaccarino, Herman A. Taylor, and Arshed A. Quyyumi. 2018. "High Neighborhood Incarceration Rate Is Associated with Cardiometabolic Disease in Nonincarcerated Black Individuals." *Annals of Epidemiology* 28(7):489–92.

Towers, Sherry, Danielle Wallace, Jason Walker, John M. Eason, Jake R. Nelson, and Tony H. Grubesic. 2022. "A Study of SARS-COV-2 Outbreaks in US Federal Prisons: The Linkage between Staff, Incarcerated Populations, and Community Transmission." *BMC Public Health* 22(1):482.

Turanovic, Jillian J., Nancy Rodriguez, and Travis C. Pratt. 2012. "The Collateral Consequences of Incarceration Revisited: A Qualitative Analysis of the Effects on Caregivers of Children of Incarcerated Parents." *Criminology* 50(4):913–59.

Turney, Kristin. 2014*a*. "The Consequences of Paternal Incarceration for Maternal Neglect and Harsh Parenting." *Social Forces* 92(4):1607–36.

Turney, Kristin. 2014*b*. "Stress Proliferation across Generations? Examining the Relationship between Parental Incarceration and Childhood Health." *Journal of Health and Social Behavior* 55(3):302–19.

Turney, Kristin. 2022. "Chains of Adversity: The Time-Varying Consequences of Paternal Incarceration for Adolescent Behavior." *Journal of Quantitative Criminology* 38(1):159–96.

Turney, Kristin, and Emma Connor. 2019. "Jail Incarceration: A Common and Consequential Form of Criminal Justice Contact." *Annual Review of Criminology* 2:1–26.

Turney, Kristin, and Rachel E. Goldberg. 2019. "Paternal Incarceration and Early Sexual Onset among Adolescents." *Population Research and Policy Review* 38(1):95–123.

Turney, Kristin, and Rebecca Goodsell. 2018. "Parental Incarceration and Children's Wellbeing." *Future of Children* 28(1):147–64.

Turney, Kristin, and Anna R. Haskins. 2014. "Falling Behind? Children's Early Grade Retention after Paternal Incarceration." *Sociology of Education* 87(4):241–58.

Turney, Kristin, and Naomi F. Sugie. 2021. "Connecting Models of Family Stress to Inequality: Parental Arrest and Family Life." *Journal of Marriage and Family* 83(1):102–18.

Turney, Kristin, and Sara Wakefield. 2019. "Criminal Justice Contact and Inequality." *RSF: The Russell Sage Foundation Journal of the Social Sciences* 5(1):1–23.

Turney, Kristin, and Christopher Wildeman. 2015. "Detrimental for Some? Heterogeneous Effects of Maternal Incarceration on Child Wellbeing." *Criminology and Public Policy* 14(1):125–56.

Uggen, Christopher, and Sara Wakefield. 2008. "Young Adults Reentering the Community from the Criminal Justice System: The Challenge of Becoming an Adult." In *On Your Own without a Net: The Transition to Adulthood for Vulnerable Populations,* edited by D. W. Osgood, E. M. Foster, C. Flanagan, and G. R. Ruth. Chicago: University of Chicago Press.

Wacquant, Loïc. 2000. "The New 'Peculiar Institution': On the Prison as Surrogate Ghetto." *Theoretical Criminology* 4(3):377–89.

Wagner, Wendy, and Peter Sawyer. 2020. "Mass Incarceration: The Whole Pie 2020." Prison Policy Initiative, March 24. https://www.prisonpolicy.org/reports/pie2020.html.

Wakefield, Sara. 2014. "Accentuating the Positive or Eliminating the Negative: Paternal Incarceration and Caregiver-Child Relationship Quality." *Journal of Criminal Law and Criminology* 104(4):905–28.

Wakefield, Sara, and Lars Højsgaard Andersen. 2020. "Pretrial Detention and the Costs of System Overreach for Employment and Family Life." *Sociological Science* 7:342–66.

Wakefield, Sara, and Robert J. Apel. 2018. "Criminological Perspectives on Parental Incarceration." In *When Parents Are Incarcerated: Interdisciplinary Research and Interventions to Support Children*, edited by Christopher Wildeman, Anna R. Haskins, and Julie Poehlmann-Tynan. Washington, DC: American Psychological Association.

Wakefield, Sara, Hedwig Lee, and Christopher Wildeman. 2016. "Tough on Crime, Tough on Families? Criminal Justice and Family Life in America." *Annals of the American Academy of Political and Social Science* 665(1):8–21.

Wakefield, Sara, and Christopher Uggen. 2010. "Incarceration and Stratification." *Annual Review of Sociology* 36(1):387–406.

Wakefield, Sara, and Christopher Wildeman. 2013. *Children of the Prison Boom: Mass Incarceration and the Future of American Inequality*. New York: Oxford University Press.

Walker, Michael L. 2022. *Indefinite: Doing Time in Jail*. New York: Oxford University Press.

Walter, Katharine S., et al. 2021. "The Escalating Tuberculosis Crisis in Central and South American Prisons." *Lancet* 397(10284):1591–96.

Warner, Cody. 2016. "The Effect of Incarceration on Residential Mobility between Poor and Nonpoor Neighborhoods." *City and Community* 15(4):423–43.

Western, Bruce. 2006. *Punishment and Inequality in America*. New York: Russell Sage.

Western, Bruce, and David F. Harding. 2022. "Careers in Criminalization: Reentry, Recidivism, and Repeated Incarceration." In *Prisons and Prisoners*, edited by Michael Tonry and Sandra Bucerius. Vol. 51 of *Crime and Justice: A Review of Research*, edited by Michael Tonry. Chicago: University of Chicago Press.

Widdowson, Alex O., Wade C. Jacobsen, Sonja E. Siennick, and Patricia Y. Warren. 2020. "Together despite the Odds: Explaining Racial and Ethnic Heterogeneity in Union Dissolution after Incarceration." *Criminology* 58(1):129–55.

Wildeman, Christopher. 2010. "Paternal Incarceration and Children's Physically Aggressive Behaviors: Evidence from the Fragile Families and Child Wellbeing Study." *Social Forces* 89(1):285–309.

Wildeman, Christopher. 2012. "Imprisonment and Infant Mortality." *Social Problems* 59(2):228–57.

Wildeman, Christopher. 2014. "Parental Incarceration, Child Homelessness, and the Invisible Consequences of Mass Imprisonment." *Annals of the American Academy of Political and Social Science* 651(1):74–96.

Wildeman, Christopher. 2020. "The Intergenerational Transmission of Criminal Justice Contact." *Annual Review of Criminology* 3(1):217–44.

Wildeman, Christopher, and Signe Hald Andersen. 2017. "Paternal Incarceration and Children's Risk of Being Charged by Early Adulthood: Evidence from a Danish Policy Shock." *Criminology* 55(1):32–58.

Wildeman, Christopher, Kris Scardamalia, Elizabeth G. Walsh, Rourke L. O'Brien, and Bridget Brew. 2017. "Paternal Incarceration and Teachers' Expectations of Students." *Socius* 3(January):1–14.

Wildeman, Christopher, and Kristin Turney. 2014. "Positive, Negative, or Null? The Effects of Maternal Incarceration on Children's Behavioral Problems." *Demography* 51(3):1041–68.

Wildeman, Christopher, and Sara Wakefield. 2014. "The Long Arm of the Law: The Concentration of Incarceration in Families in the Era of Mass Incarceration." *Journal of Gender, Race and Justice* 17:367–89.

Wildeman, Christopher, and Emily A. Wang. 2017. "Mass Incarceration, Public Health, and Widening Inequality in the USA." *Lancet* 389(10077):1464–74.

Wildeman, Christopher, Anna R. Haskins, and Julie Poehlmann-Tynan, eds. 2018. *When Parents Are Incarcerated: Interdisciplinary Research and Interventions to Support Children.* Washington, DC: American Psychological Association.

Zeng, Zhen, and Todd D. Minson. 2021. "Jail Inmates in 2019." In *Prison and Jail Inmates at Midyear.* Washington, DC: US Department of Justice, Bureau of Justice Statistics.

Zimring, Franklin E., and Gordon J. Hawkins. 1993. *The Scale of Imprisonment.* Studies in Crime and Justice. Chicago: University of Chicago Press.

Bruce Western and David J. Harding

Careers in Criminalization: Reentry, Recidivism, and Repeated Incarceration

ABSTRACT

Criminalization is the process by which people are classified by authorities as criminal and become subject to the control of criminal justice agencies—police, courts, and correctional departments. "Careers in criminalization" refers to sustained criminal justice involvement through repeated incarceration and ongoing police and court contact. Careers in criminalization are produced through a mutually reinforcing process of system-induced harms and criminal justice traps that combine to prolong surveillance and penal control. System-induced harms are physical, psychological, and reputational injuries that may be criminogenic or otherwise impede adjustment to community life. Criminal justice traps are cycles of involvement created through intensive surveillance, compliance enforcement, and system marking. The idea of careers in criminalization has special relevance for understanding prisoner reentry, in which criminal justice institutions and officials sustain surveillance and penal control, delaying social integration.

A fundamental question for students of crime concerns patterns of offending over the life course. In the language of research from the 1980s, the study of arrest and incarceration over the life course was motivated by an interest in "criminal careers." Findings of a decline in the arrest rate

Bruce Western is Pryce Professor of Sociology and Social Justice and directs the Justice Lab at Columbia University. David J. Harding is professor of sociology and faculty director of the D-Lab at the University of California, Berkeley.

Electronically published September 22, 2022

Crime and Justice, volume 51, 2022.

with age past adolescence and of heterogeneity in offending in the population established the terms of a long-standing debate (Wolfgang, Figlio, and Sellin 1972; Gottfredson and Hirschi 1986; Blumstein and Cohen 1987; Moffitt 1993). Life course scholars emphasized a steady decline in criminal justice contact with the transition to adulthood (Sampson and Laub 1993). In this approach, the informal social controls of employment and marriage brought routine to daily life, created stakes in conformity, and monitored conduct. Another line of research observed that most criminal justice contact in a cohort over a period of time can be traced to a small number of individuals (Wolfgang, Figlio, and Sellin 1972). Enduring traits like impulsiveness or aggressiveness were used to explain persistent antisocial behavior that resulted in ongoing involvement with police and repeated incarceration (Moffitt et al. 2011). Although research often examined criminal justice outcomes such as arrest, theory and hypotheses had a behavioral focus on violence and other antisocial behavior.

In this essay, we bring together several lines of research, largely from the United States, on criminal justice case processing and the effects of criminal justice contact, to develop an account of careers in criminalization. The focus on careers in criminalization on crime over the life course aims to account for how criminal justice contact progresses with age. Ongoing criminal justice contact is reflected, for example, in recidivism statistics, failures of prisoner reentry, aging of the prison population, and repeated jail incarceration. We examine how police, courts, and correctional agencies themselves create new criminal justice contact and how criminal justice contact is created from noncriminal behavior. This perspective emphasizes how social conditions such as racial segregation and poverty can lead to arrest and incarceration, how untreated mental illness and addiction elevate risks for people affected by them, how cycles of criminal justice contact can endure over the life course, and how high rates of recidivism are often observed for some people convicted of less serious crimes.

To describe careers in criminalization, we draw on a diverse literature that includes well-established lines of research on labeling and the criminalization of poverty. We also draw on more recent work on low-level criminal justice contacts, such as police stops, misdemeanor arrests, jail incarceration, and, after incarceration, prisoner reentry. The idea of careers in criminalization is consistent with many of the stylized facets of criminal careers but puts criminal justice processes at the center of analysis. Our perspective is motivated by work on prisoner reentry that studies the transition from prison to the community. However, reentry research tends to view community return as a one-time event, in which the policy challenge involves addressing the deficits of formerly incarcerated people. The careers in criminalization perspective views any single reentry as one of an age-graded sequence of criminal justice contacts, in which renewed criminal justice involvement may be rooted in the actions of line officials and the design of criminal justice institutions.

We define "careers in criminalization" as a process in which system-induced harms interact with criminal justice traps that penalize nonharmful conduct to create continuing involvement with police, courts, and correctional control. Criminalization is not just determined by law but also produced by justice system officials who label, surveil, and confine individuals, often using morally inflected categories that embody ascriptions of race and class. The concept of careers in criminalization proposes an alternative explanation for continued involvement in the criminal justice system over the life course. Instead of appealing to stable psychological traits or age-graded social roles, the concept proposes that continuing justice system involvement is a product of system-induced harms and traps.

In Section I we introduce the theory and concept of careers in criminalization. In Section II we outline its motivation and basic contours, linking our approach to recent studies that provide empirical evidence for the process. We then in Section III delve more deeply into four research areas that show how criminalization is sustained by different stages of criminal processing: through policing, in courts and jails, by prison conditions, and through parole and probation supervision. The conclusion discusses implications for future research and policy making.

I. Defining Careers in Criminalization

The term "criminalization" is used in different ways across a variety of disciplinary perspectives. Some criminal lawyers and philosophers, for example, develop ethical, moral, and policy arguments concerning whether, why, and when behavior should or may be legally defined as criminal (e.g., Husak 2008; Simester and von Hirsch 2011). Sociologists, criminologists, political scientists, and historians have empirically examined political, social, economic, and other influences on policy decisions to define behavior as criminal or to enforce criminal laws in particular ways (Chambliss 1964; Dubber 2001; Jenness 2004; Hirschfield 2008; Thompson 2015). Our usage encompasses the term as applied in empirical research but is broader. By criminalization, we refer to the processes by which acts or people are classified by authorities as criminal and become subject to the control of criminal justice agencies—police, courts, and correctional departments. This idea of criminalization indicates that the criminal law, arrests, convictions, and prison sentences are not only or even chiefly indicators of harmful conduct but result from active processes of classification and control by state agents. Criminalization is an institutional process.

Like the related sociological ideas of labeling and stigma, criminalization describes a moral action in which individuals are judged to have violated laws or rules in ways that render them candidates for punishment (Durkheim 1973; Garland 1990). The criminal justice system is a blaming institution, and the assessment of violation extends well beyond the courtroom to include police suspicion, prison management and operation, and the surveillance functions of probation and parole. The moral dimensions of criminalization can be seen in a variety of ways. Throughout criminal processing, from pretrial detention to sentencing and parole hearings, judges and parole boards make judgments about "character" that describe the moral status of those subject to their judgment (Redmayne 2015; Sampson and Smith 2021). The expressive character of punishment, which conveys authorities' disapproval and condemnation, also reflects a moral judgment. Public conversations about crime have an emotional resonance in which criminal offenders are ascribed a status outside the moral community that the rest of us occupy. "Thugs," "career criminals," and "super predators" are moral descriptions not of conduct but of people.

Authoritative judgments of violation happen not in a social vacuum but in contexts of social power that reflect steep social and economic inequalities. In the United States, institutional processes of criminalization have been entwined with historic projects of racial classification and exclusion. Khalil Gibran Muhammad (2011) describes how assumptions about Black criminality formed part of academic understanding of crime in the late nineteenth century and the measurement of crime since the inception of the Uniform Crime Reports in the 1920s. Elizabeth Hinton and DeAnza Cook (2021) trace the use of police and prisons as a leading mode of social control in Black communities since the emergence of Jim Crow in the American South at the end of the nineteenth century.

A broader literature describes the criminalization of poverty in the United States and in Europe as a central element in the development of modern criminal law. For a long line of sociological and historical research, the state's response to crime aimed to regulate and preserve social order in general, and particularly the prerogatives of private property, instead of specially taking action against those individuals who have harmed others (Garland 1990, chaps. 4–5; Bridges and Myers 1994). Medieval laws against vagrancy, theft, and poaching have been understood to treat the survival strategies of landless peasants as criminal acts subject to harsh punishment (Chambliss 1964; Thompson 2015). The idea that modern criminal law is class blind yet still outlaws the poor is captured by Anatole France (1930, p. 91), who remarks on "the majestic equality of the laws, which forbid rich and poor alike to sleep under bridges, to beg in the streets." Contemporary laws against the possession of drugs and other contraband (Dubber 2001), criminal trespass (Beckett and Herbert 2010), and loitering (Collins 2007) and ordinances against panhandling (Duneier 2000) are similarly class blind yet regularly bring poor people to the attention of police.

The social conditions of poverty also provide the context for a long continuum of antisocial behavior. At one end lie the small public norm violations and disruptive behavior that can accompany untreated mental illness or drug addiction, which John Irwin (1985) associated with "the rabble" among whom jail incarceration was concentrated. At the other end lie the high rates of homicide in low-income communities of color in US cities that fall on one side of Peterson and Krivo's (2010) "racial-spatial divide." In our perspective, even killings must be processed by police and the courts to be transformed into "crimes." Because criminal law is not self-executing, individuals become criminals when the label of criminality is attached to them by officials with the authority to do so. Individual behavior and interpersonal harm are central to projects of criminalization, but state responses are not automatic. Conduct becomes crime only through the terms of the criminal law, police arrests, and criminal court sentencing.

Over the last two decades, a large body of empirical research was developed to examine how police and prisons surveil and exert control in poor communities under contemporary conditions of racial and economic inequality (e.g., Western 2006; Wacquant 2009; Alexander 2010; Fassin 2018; Garland 2020). Recent contributions from US research show how proactive policing tactics expanded the reach of the criminal justice system (Stuart 2016; Bell 2017) and how punitive sentencing policies increased US imprisonment rates to historically high levels (Tonry 1995; Raphael and Stoll 2013; Travis, Western, and Redburn 2014). These processes of social control are age graded and sequential. Criminalization is age graded in the sense that an individual's history of criminal justice contact is frequently incorporated into decisions about further criminal justice control. Sanctions of increasing severity are often imposed because of a history of prior criminal justice contact. The noncustodial sentence of probation is often given to people for first-time felony convictions (Petersilia and Turner 1986; Petersilia 1997). A prior conviction, however, then increases the risk of jail detention before sentencing, and jail detention increases the risk of conviction, which for a second felony offense carries the increased risk of imprisonment (Dobbie, Goldin, and Yang 2018). Sentence enhancements are often added for prior convictions, so older criminal defendants are at risk of more severe treatment because of their criminal records. Careers in criminalization emerge through the sequence of criminal justice contacts that, for some, sustains control and surveillance over the life course.

II. System Harm and Institutional Traps

Whereas research on crime and the life course indicates peak criminal involvement between age 15 and 18 (Hirschi and Gottfredson 1983; Farrington 1986; Neil and Sampson 2021), the median age of state prisoners was 37 years old in the 2016 US Survey of Prison Inmates (US Bureau of Justice Statistics 2020). In a cohort of released prisoners, 10–20 percent will return to prison at least two more times (Rhodes et al. 2016). For people in the prison system, criminalization is often sustained well beyond the average age of harmful behavior. Trends in US criminal justice policy have developed to create long periods of criminalization that extend across the life course. Long sentences, criminogenic punishment, collateral consequences of imprisonment, and effects of labeling all operate to generate careers in criminalization. This idea shares something with Goffman's (1959) writing on the "moral career of the mental patient" in which hospital processes of classification and treatment can involve degradations and the stripping of selfhood that accompanies institutionalization.

Careers in criminalization extend beyond institutionalization and include life after release from incarceration, what Reuben Miller (2021) has called the "afterlife of mass incarceration." Our review of research points to two main ways in which careers in criminalization are produced. A mutually reinforcing combination of system-induced harms and criminal justice traps create cycles of system involvement. System harm refers to the injuries to individual physical and mental health and stymied development of life skills and work experience that result from criminal justice contact. System harm leaves those who come into contact with the criminal justice system worse off in many domains, including the labor market; mental, physical, and behavioral health; social support; and material security. Criminal justice traps induce repeated contacts with police, courts, and incarceration that result partly from the operation of the criminal justice system itself. Numerous popular and academic terms are used to evoke the concept of cycles of involvement, from "frequent flyers" in the context of misdemeanor policing, court appearances, and short jail stays (Ford 2005) to the "revolving door" of prison (Harding et al. 2017). Improving the social and economic integration of formerly incarcerated people and cutting short careers in criminalization requires an understanding of how criminal justice systems create system harm and drive cycles of involvement.

System harm has been a dominating concern for research on the socio-economic effects of incarceration and a new parallel literature on policing. Researchers have studied the economic, health, and social harms of imprisonment (Western 2006; Wakefield and Uggen 2010; Travis, Western, and Redburn 2014; Massoglia and Pridemore 2015). These harms affect not only the people imprisoned (Beckett and Goldberg 2022) but also their families and communities (Clear 2007; Western and Wildeman 2009; Wakefield and Wildeman 2013; Wakefield 2022; cf. Norris, Pecenco, and Weaver 2021). Recent police research shows that police contact adversely affects mental health and confidence in social institutions and that the quantity and form of policing in disadvantaged communities have community-wide effects (Lerman and Weaver 2014; Zimring 2017; McCarthy, Hagan, and Herda 2020; Kazemian 2021). Less well understood is the specific role of policing in prisoner reentry and reintegration (a subject we discuss below). A burgeoning literature has begun to investigate the harms created by other components of the criminal justice system, including the courts (Van Cleve 2016; Kohler-Hausmann 2018; Clair 2020), community supervision (Phelps and Ruhland 2022), jails (Dobbie, Goldin, and Yang 2018), and nonstate actors that are closely intertwined with the criminal justice system, such as purveyors of criminal records databases (Lageson 2020), for-profit companies that expand the social control functions of the state (Latessa and Lovins 2019), and nonprofit organizations that perform the dual role of providing social services and monitoring those under justice supervision (Haney 2010; Miller 2014).

A key challenge for research on the harms of incarceration and police contact is the steeply selective character of criminal justice intervention. Arrests and incarceration are concentrated in communities and among people who are poor, in poor health, and highly exposed to violence and other crime. Assessing system harm involves a causal analysis that can isolate the effects of system contact from preexisting disadvantages. Empirical studies are sometimes able to control for observed disadvantages. Although observational designs are relatively weak, researchers can examine the robustness of results by studying the sensitivity of results to possible confounders and subsamples in the data. Other studies go further by fitting fixed effects to panel data, examining policy changes that induce changes in criminal justice contact, or exploiting natural experiments such as the random assignment of judges to cases. Qualitative research—interview studies and ethnography—is also able to trace the social process leading from, say, incarceration to adverse outcomes after release.

The empirical phenomenon of cycles of involvement is well documented and particularly important to reentry, as rates of return to prison for new crimes and technical violations are high. Consistent with the idea of careers in criminalization, risks of returning to imprisonment are highest for those with prior prison records (Tonry 2004; Rhodes et al. 2016). Among people on parole in the United States in 2020, about 20 percent of all exits from parole are the result of reincarceration, and technical violations of probation or parole account for 29 percent of prison admissions nationwide (Carson 2020). Research on reentry and recidivism indicates several paths to rearrest and reincarceration for those who have been released from prison and jail. The criminal justice system itself maintains surveillance through probation and parole supervision. Common conditions such as sobriety, maintaining employment, paying supervision fees, and avoiding others with criminal convictions may be violated in daily living, even in the absence of any harmful behavior. Violating conditions elevates the risk of revocation and may result in returning to incarceration. When incarceration is related to chronic health conditions such as mental illness or addiction, criminal justice contact may happen repeatedly. Jail incarceration, in particular, has been subject to this kind of analysis (Western et al. 2021).

The social process of cycles of involvement is often attributed to characteristics of those under criminal justice control and the operations of the system itself. One long-standing explanation focuses on individual deficits like low human capital, mental health problems, and social isolation. By this explanation, the same individual-level barriers that led to involvement in crime and system contact in the first place also drive the behavior that prompts repeated incarceration. Accordingly, community supervision and corrections have simply inherited the social problems created by a highly unequal American society with a thin and porous social welfare state. The individual deficits explanation misses two key aspects of cycles of involvement: individual deficits are in part produced by the harms of the wider criminal justice system, and the criminal justice system creates "traps" that lead to continued and sometimes continuing involvement through features of the system itself rather than individual behavior.

The concept of criminal justice traps is particularly important to reentry given the often intense surveillance and control faced by those who leave prison into community supervision. However, we also emphasize that the process of prisoner reentry and reintegration is affected by other criminal justice elements as well, including police, courts, jails, and allied nonsystem actors. Existing research provides evidence of three features of criminal justice systems that serve to trap people in cycles of involvement: monitoring and surveillance, dilemmas of compliance, and system marking.

First, monitoring and surveillance by police and community corrections officers increase the risk of sanctions for low-level offenses. For example, as we discuss below, the intensive policing of high-poverty, minority neighborhoods to which many formerly incarcerated people return increases risks of arrest, and technical violations of parole or probation drive myriad punishments, including not only returns to prison but also noncustodial sanctions, brief jail stays, mandatory treatment programs, or more intensive supervision.

Second, the requirements of criminal justice control often create dilemmas in which compliance with one condition results in violation of another. A common example across stages of criminal processing involves conflicts between the demands of supervision and maintaining regular employment. Court appearances, short periods of jail detention, and meetings with parole and probation officers have all been found to disrupt employment, while employment is often a condition of community release or taken as a marker of rehabilitation (e.g., Western 2018, p. 131; Harding, Morenoff, and Wyse 2019, pp. 192–93).

Third, the system marks people sometimes to indicate successful compliance but also to signal danger, incorrigibility, or greater culpability requiring greater control. Devah Pager (2007, p. 33) likened the mark of a criminal record to a credential: "With a criminal record comes state certification of an individual's criminal transgressions; a wide range of social, economic, and political privileges become off-limits." For those who are actively being processed through the system, official marking may not indicate guilt but instead records compliance with authority. "Marks document a range of behaviors and accomplishments, including the fact and frequency of prior encounters, whether defendants have properly complied with prosecution's demands, [or] court mandates" (Kohler-Hausmann 2018, p. 145). Marks are a penal technique that indicate to officials what level of social control is warranted. In some cases additional control is formally prescribed, as with sentencing guidelines (Kurlychek and Johnson 2019) or risk assessments (Harcourt 2015) that assign greater punishment or control to those with greater prior involvement in the system. Criminal justice marks are also used informally when, for example, people sentenced for felonies who were on parole at the time of the offense are more likely to be sentenced to prison, even beyond what is specified in applicable sentencing guidelines (Hickert et al. 2022). Menefee et al. (2021) show that otherwise identical people sentenced to probation are more likely to be placed on more intensive supervision when they were also sentenced to a short jail term.

The labeling process that is central to criminal justice operations is by no means impervious to the agency of those under penal control. While labeling theory in the sociology of deviance also includes the pernicious process of self-labeling, scholars have written powerfully about the importance of shifting self-understandings of life trajectories. Thus, Shadd Maruna (2000) describes how the development of narratives of redemption contributes to desistance among people with long criminal justice involvement. John Braithwaite (1989) also describes how stigma can be overcome in his account of reintegrative shaming, in which punishment is followed by rituals of forgiveness and normalization. While labelling is a powerful mechanism for criminalization, research also indicates directions for its reversal.

III. Criminal Justice Institutions and Careers in Criminalization

System-induced harms and criminal justice traps create cycles of involvement that accumulate into careers in criminalization. Our focus is on the ways these various criminal justice institutions structure prisoner reentry and reintegration, but we also note that these institutions contribute to careers in criminalization for many others who come into contact with the criminal justice system through police arrest and court involvement.

A. Police

Policing is the most common form of criminal justice contact and a typical entry point for criminal justice system involvement. About one-quarter of all survey respondents in a US national sample report contact with the police in a year, and about half of those contacts are police initiated (Langton et al. 2013). Such police stops are disproportionately experienced in communities of color (Pierson et al. 2020). Despite the intensive policing of poor communities of color (Lerman and Weaver 2014) to which formerly incarcerated people often return after prison (Simes 2021), policing has largely been neglected in the reentry literature (Travis, Davis, and Lawrence 2012).

As reentry became an important domain of criminal justice policy making in the 1990s, police began to play a role in newly forming collaborations with community corrections agents and other state and nonstate actors intended to reduce recidivism (Matz and Kim 2013). Police could participate in reentry partnerships in many ways, including by improving access to social services (LaVigne 2006; Herbert, Beckett, and Stuart 2018). But in practice, the documented roles of police agencies in reentry partnerships have been concentrated on enhancing the capacities of community corrections to surveil, monitor, and apprehend those under their charge (Parent and Snyder 1999; Byrne and Hummer 2004). This role in community corrections suggests that police may contribute to cycles of involvement among the reentry population through surveillance and monitoring. Intensive policing of poor communities of color is a function of not simply the level of police presence but also the police tactics that are employed in such neighborhoods (Oberman and Johnson 2015). Broken windows policing, zero-tolerance, stop-and-frisk, and other high-intensity and proactive policing strategies can place those on community supervision at increased risk of arrest and technical violations, as police contact is a potential violation. The economic insecurity of formerly incarcerated people may place them at particular risk for police contact in jurisdictions that employ such tactics (Beckett and Herbert 2010). This type of policing may also instill feelings of marginalization that extend to entire communities (Bell 2017). As police have been thrust into the role of responding to mental health crises, homelessness, and other social problems, they are likely to come into contact with formerly incarcerated people even more frequently (Seim 2020). Because contact with police is recorded by police themselves or by community corrections officers, police contact can enhance system marking.

Policing also contributes to system-induced harms. Contact with the police, even when not resulting in arrest, is associated with a wide range of outcomes, including employment, education, and mental health effects such as stress, anxiety, and depression, although much of this research focuses on youth and young adults (for a recent review, see Kazemian 2021). Aggressive forms of policing may lead to legal cynicism, lack of confidence in social institutions, and other social harms (Geller and Fagan 2019; McCarthy, Hagan, and Herda 2020). An additional potential harm is the risk of exposure to injury and death at the hands of police (Howell 2015; Edwards, Lee, and Esposito 2020). Furthermore, avoidance of public spaces for fear of police contact has the potential to restrict access to employment opportunities, social support and housing opportunities, and medical care (Brayne 2014; Lara-Millán 2014).

B. Courts and Jails

The closely linked institutions of courts and jails also play a role in careers in criminalization. Jails account for about one-third of all incarceration in the United States, and jail incarceration rates tripled between 1982 and 2008, when they were at their peak. The jail incarceration rate on any given day is 229 per 100,000 in the United States (Kaeble and Cowhig 2018). More than 10 million people are admitted to jail annually in the United States (Sawyer and Wagner 2020). Jail incarceration forms an important part of the process of prisoner reentry, as almost half of parolees have been found to spend some time in jail in the 2 years following release from prison (Harding, Morenoff, and Herbert 2013). Jail incarceration can result from parole violations, misdemeanor convictions, or new arrests.

Less studied than imprisonment, an emerging literature documents the harms created by jail incarceration (Turney and Conner 2019). Jail incarceration is associated with reduced employment, reduced access to welfare benefits, and an increased risk of poverty. There is also suggestive evidence that jail incarceration negatively affects physical and mental health as well as sobriety, particularly for those who cycle between courts, jails, and the community. The effects of jail incarceration may radiate outward to family members, increasing stress, material hardship, and stigma (Turney and Conner 2019).

Jails are commonly linked to cycles of involvement through observed patterns of repeated incarceration. For example, nearly 5 percent of all Black men in New York City have been incarcerated in the city's jail system 10 or more times by age 38 (Western et al. 2021). To the extent that jail incarceration represents a police response to largely nonharmful offenses to public order among poor people, repeated jail incarceration reflects the enduring poverty of a "permanent underclass," to quote Irwin's (1985, p. 103) language of another era. Lara-Millán (2021) documents how procedures designed to manage the jail population that classify inmates on the basis of gang affiliations, perceived propensity for violence, and medical needs dictate both the services received in jail and the severity of punishment experienced while in the jail.

Courts have also been found to be sources of harm and repeated criminal justice involvement. Courts are a primary mechanism for system marking, as warrants, open court cases, and prior convictions mark people for greater police scrutiny and prior convictions result in harsher future sentences (Kurlychek and Johnson 2019). Pretrial detention increases the probability of conviction through plea bargaining (Dobbie, Goldin, and Yang 2018), and even misdemeanor prosecution can lead to greater likelihood of future criminal complaints, particularly but not exclusively for first-time defendants (Agan, Doleac, and Harvey 2021). The criminal mark of a felony record has also been found to be linked to later community corrections supervision; people who have been sentenced to short sentences in jail tend to receive more intensive community supervision on probation (Menefee et al. 2021).

Courts create dilemmas of compliance for those whose cases are moving through the judicial process. Feeley (1979) documents the delay and inconvenience involved in being a defendant in a misdemeanor court: wasted time, missed work, attorney and court fees, and bail and pretrial detention. Issa Kohler-Hausmann (2018) shows how New York City's misdemeanor courts developed a "managerial model" in response to broken windows policing that sought to control defendants through compliance with court requirements. Compliance with these requirements can influence eventual punishments and imposes significant time and financial costs. These studies also demonstrate the ways in which court actors monitor and surveil those with open cases. Clair (2020) shows how compliance with court expectations is structured by race and class and affects conviction and sentencing outcomes. Van Cleve (2016) shows the ways in which race and ethnicity influence the treatment of defendants in Cook County criminal court.

C. Prisons

The process of criminalization culminates in punishment. In the period of mass incarceration in the United States this has often meant incarceration in state or federal prisons, typically for a year or longer. Often research on the effects of incarceration focuses not on the experience of penal confinement but on the stigma of a criminal record (Pager 2007; Pager, Western, and Bonikowski 2009; Sugie, Zatz, and Augustine 2020). The experience of incarceration itself, however, may contribute to reincarceration or renewed contact with police and courts. Incarceration is often not an end point; many people in prison are incarcerated repeatedly (although see Rhodes et al. 2016).

Four pathways—each describing system-induced harms—are indicated by research on US prisons that may impair the adjustment to community life after incarceration. First, US conditions of incarceration are severe and increase the distance between prison conditions and conditions of life in free society. Second, prison violence can be associated with trauma and mental illness. Third, levels of custody in US prisons have increased, reflected most notably in evidence of the increased use of solitary confinement. Finally, prison imposes severe health risks, particularly elevated risks of infectious disease. The harms suffered through each of these channels impair adjustment back to community life after prison.

Although rehabilitation has been conceived of as an important function of the modern American penitentiaries of the early twentieth century, support for rehabilitative programming in prison has ebbed and flowed among correctional administrators and policy makers. Policy makers of the 1980s and 1990s largely rejected rehabilitation and adopted incapacitation and deterrence as the main goals of penal policy. The rejection of rehabilitation is captured in figures on prison program participation. The Survey of Inmates of State Correctional Facilities (renamed the Survey of Prison Inmates in 2016) indicates reductions in program participation in US prisons across the country and across program areas. Participation in drug treatment programs in the northeast and the Midwest fell from highs of 30–50 percent in the 1980s to below 20 percent by 2016. Educational programming was also reduced in all regions except the west. Job training became less common. Participation in work assignments also fell across the country. Trends toward declining participation were strong in the northeast and Midwest where program participation rates are highest (Western 2021).

The retreat from rehabilitation was accompanied by other changes in the internal operation of prisons. As incapacitation and deterrence became the main purposes of penal policy, prison populations grew rapidly and lengths of stay increased. Increases in length of stay have clearly contributed in a direct way to sustained criminal justice involvement. Sentencing policy changes, mostly in the 1980s and 1990s, increased the duration of imprisonment, particularly for those convicted of violence. Length of stay in prison is difficult to measure because the duration of imprisonment is not observed for those who have not been released, so those serving longer sentences are undercounted in estimates of length of stay among releasees. Neal and Rick (2014) counted the number of people in prison who had served at least 5 years and found that the rates of 5-year imprisonment had increased 2 to 5 times from 1985 to 2000 for those incarcerated for violent offenses. They trace the increase in time served to truth-in-sentencing laws that mandated that 85 percent of a nominal sentence be served and to three strikes, mandatory minimum sentence, and other sentence enhancement laws applicable to violent crimes. Increased length of stay has contributed to the aging of the prison population. Many jurisdictions have also reduced the use of parole and other forms of conditional release. These policy changes contribute to an aging out of criminalization, although at a relatively advanced age. Long sentences have created an aging cohort of releasees who are returning to communities at the expiration of their sentences, without any subsequent criminal justice supervision.

The escalating US prisons population since 1973, particularly in the 1980s and 1990s, contributed to severe overcrowding. Overcrowded prisons faced many court challenges in this period (Levitt 1996; Simon 2014; Guetzkow and Schoon 2015). A series of California cases demonstrated links between overcrowding, health care, and prison safety. In 2007, 13 percent of all state prisoners in the United States were incarcerated in California, and the system had regularly exceeded its designed capacity by 150 percent or more since at least the 1980s. By the early 2000s, prison gymnasiums in California were being used as housing units and triple bunking was used in some facilities. Jonathan Simon (2014, p. 117) described the conditions of incarceration by quoting from a federal court opinion following Governor Arnold Schwarzenegger's State of Emergency proclamation on prison overcrowding in 2006: "The risks enumerated by the Governor in his Proclamation include 'increased, substantial risk for transmission of infectious illness'; security risks caused by line-of-sight problems for correctional officers, particularly in areas where inmates are triple-bunked and in 'tight quarters'; and 'thousands of gallons of sewage spills and environmental contamination' from overloading the prisons' sewage and wastewater systems.... Governor Schwarzenegger also declared that the suicide rate in the 29 severely over-crowded prisons '[was] approaching an average of one per week.'" Overcrowding severely undermined the delivery of health care, which led a panel of federal judges to declare the entire California state prison system of more than 150,000 incarcerated people unconstitutional, in violation of the Eighth Amendment prohibition against cruel and unusual punishment. The US Supreme Court in *Brown v. Plata*, 563 U.S. 493 (2011), affirmed. In the period of rapid growth in incarceration when extreme overcrowding became persistent in many states, researchers described prisons as warehouses, operating chiefly as storage units for prime-age men from poor communities (Lynch [2009] and Phelps [2011] discuss the warehouse prison).

Violence has been a long-standing focus of prison research, but prison conditions of the 1980s and 1990s that combined overcrowding, the decline of rehabilitative programs, and the influx of new and younger prisoners exacerbated conditions that undermine prison safety. For prison researchers, the fear of violence casts a broad shadow over prison life. Bowker's (1980) catalog of the forms of prison violence includes threats, assaults, rapes and other sexual assaults, and homicide. The classic prison field study, *The Society of Captives* by Gresham Sykes (1958), described the loss of security as one of five "pains of imprisonment." Psychologist Hans Toch (1977), in a detailed survey of male prisoners in New York state in the 1970s, found that safety—protection against "being attacked"— was among the most important concerns about the prison environment. Focusing on violence of a different kind, Alison Liebling (1999, p. 341) writes that "fear, anxiety, loneliness, trauma, depression, injustice, powerlessness, violence, rejection, and uncertainty are part of the experience of prison" in which "suicide is perhaps its most dramatic outcome." Violent victimization and a fear of violence have been found to be associated with social withdrawal, hypervigilance, a tough exterior, and flat affect as incarcerated people try to avoid conflict (Haney 2006, pp. 172–73). These adaptations to the threats and hardships of incarceration have classically been called "prisonization," foreshadowing their enduring effects beyond incarceration (Clemmer 1940). The long-lasting effects of violent victimization in prison are indicated by research finding evidence of later drug use, emotional distress, depression, and criminal offending (Wooldredge 1999; Hochstetler, Murphy, and Simons 2004; Zweig et al. 2015).

Levels of violence in prison, indicated by European and US data, have consistently been shown to exceed rates of violence in the general population (Bottoms 1999). One indication of the scale of violence in US prisons is provided by statistics on homicide victimization. Like homicide in the community, the US prison homicide rate declined significantly from the early 1980s to the late 2010s. In 1980, the homicide rate in state prisons was five times higher than in the general population—54 per 100,000 compared to 10.2. By 2001, the prison homicide rate had fallen to 3 per 100,000, although it then doubled to 8 per 100,000 in 2016, the latest year for which statistics have been published (Mumola 2005; Carson and Cowhig 2020). Homicide rates in prison can be expected to be higher than in the general population; prisons are occupied by people—younger, mostly male, and disproportionately non-White—who face high risks of homicide even without imprisonment. Age-, race-, and gender-adjusted homicide rates show that men under 35 face significantly lower rates of homicide victimization in prison than in the general population. Unusually when compared to community patterns, the prison victimization risk increases with age over age 45 (about a third of the prison population). For prisoners over age 55, the homicide victimization rate is equal to the rate in free society. The relatively low rate of homicide in prison, on an age-, race-, and gender-adjusted basis, is related to the absence of firearms in prisons and high rates of firearms deaths in the community. When prison homicides are compared to nonfirearm community rates, homicide victimization in prison is about twice as high as in the community, indicating the high level of manual violence in prison (Western 2021).

Prison also clearly impairs health through the transmission of infectious disease. COVID-19 is only the most recent example (Maruna, McNaull, and O'Neill 2022). Research on infectious disease in US prisons reports particularly high rates of HIV and Hepatitis B and C. HIV prevalence in prison has been found to exceed community rates by a factor of 3 to 5, and HBV and HCV prevalence exceeds community rates by 5 to 10 times (Bick 2007; Gough et al. 2010). Although precise numbers are difficult to estimate, screening at prison intake suggests around 80–90 percent of cases were present before incarceration, with the remainder transmitted in prison, mostly through sexual activity and needle use. A related line of research studies outbreaks of infectious disease, focusing on the spread of tuberculosis, influenza, and varicella (Beaudry et al. 2020). These infections are airborne and spread through aerosol transmission (droplets) and contact with surfaces. The congregate living areas, dining halls, and recreation areas that make up the physical plants of prisons facilitate the spread of airborne pathogens, particularly in overcrowded conditions (Wang et al. 2020). Population turnover associated with staff movements and prison admissions and discharges multiply the risk of importing infectious disease from the community and transmitting disease from prison to community.

The significance of correctional facilities for the transmission of infectious disease was strikingly illustrated by the coronavirus pandemic (Maruna, McNaull, and O'Neill 2022). Prisons and jails were consistently among the leading hot spots for COVID-19 outbreaks throughout 2020 (Wang et al. 2020). Facilities such as Rikers Island Jail in New York City, Cook County Jail in Chicago, and Marion Correctional Institution in Ohio suffered ferocious outbreaks that resulted in dozens of fatalities among staff and incarcerated people.

The harms of incarceration are reflected in long sentences in overcrowded facilities with few educational or training programs, an elevated risk of violent victimization, and exposure to infectious disease. These harms create significant obstacles to reintegration after incarceration. Here, evidence for the effects of prison conditions is less direct, but resulting unemployment and health problems after prison release are both associated with ongoing criminal justice involvement. Unemployment can trigger noncompliance with parole conditions, and a large research literature finds a consistent relationship between education and employment and reductions in crime and recidivism (e.g., Wilson 1987; Bound and Freeman 1992; Uggen 2000; Raphael and Winter-Ebmer 2001; Lochner and Moretti 2004). Poor health and disability have also been widely found to be associated with parole violations and rearrest after incarceration (Lamberti 2007; Link, Ward, and Stansfield 2019; Semenza and Link 2019; Wallace and Wang 2020). In some cases the line from harm to criminalization is quite direct, when, for example, unemployment represents a violation of parole. But in other cases, harms are criminogenic and contribute to criminal involvement after incarceration.

D. Community Supervision

Along with the rise in mass incarceration came a less noticed but equally important rise in community supervision, now termed "mass probation" (Phelps 2017; McNeill 2018). One in 46 Americans is on community supervision; about 4.4 million people are on probation or parole (Oudekerk and Kaeble 2021). Although only a small minority of the community supervision population is on postprison parole, many of those experiencing reentry have been or will be on probation at some point, and probation and parole are similar in their structures and administration in many jurisdictions, with parolees typically experiencing more intensive supervision

(Petersilia 2003). Probation is also central to criminal justice policy because it is the putative alternative to imprisonment as a widespread form of punishment. As the institution charged with both surveilling and reintegrating those who leave prison, community supervision plays a central role in the careers of criminalization of formerly incarcerated people; researchers are increasingly documenting its role in producing system-induced harms and cycles of system involvement.

Research studying community supervision from an institutional perspective has generally taken two approaches, micro and macro. The micro literature explores the dual roles of community supervision officers, typically probation officers, which include both control/law enforcement and rehabilitation. Historically, community supervision, like other criminal justice institutions, has swung between these two orientations (Goodman, Page, and Phelps 2017; Rengifo, Stemen, and Amidon 2017). Klockars (1972) first argued that most probation officers adopt a "synthetic" role that attempts to balance the two. More recent research confirms that most officers and supervisors understand their work as a hybrid between law enforcement and social work (Miller 2015). Successfully balancing the two orientations may be central to reducing recidivism (Skeem and Manchak 2008). However, more recent research has documented the dominance of the control and punishment functions in the day-to-day work of community supervision (Hoover 2018; Viglione, Blasko, and Taxman 2018), consistent with the argument that the rehabilitation functions of criminal justice institutions have largely devolved into rhetoric (Lynch 2000). A related literature shows that officers approach supervision differently according to the gender of the supervised person, using their discretion to impose different restrictions and recommend different programs (Wyse 2013; Welsh 2019).

A second, more macro, literature views supervision as a form of "poverty governance" (Soss, Fording, and Schram 2011), an extension of the punitive state that rose alongside historical declines in supportive social welfare policies in the United States (Wacquant 2009; Alexander 2010). These changes occurred at the same time as the advent of what Feeley and Simon (1992) call the "new penology," which emphasized more efficient management of growing caseloads, actuarial methods of risk assessment, and a focus on preventing offending rather than on rehabilitating or reintegrating offenders. This era brought corresponding changes in the role of parole officers, whose primary responsibilities were reframed as managing risks to public safety (Simon 1993; Lynch 2000). The benchmarks by which parole officers' work is evaluated shifted toward parole violations and subsequent revocations (Feeley and Simon 1992; Simon 1993). Violations and use of sanctions expanded (Burke and Tonry 2006). The poverty governance framework views the criminal justice system as a tool for managing the poor, particularly poor people of color, although scholars disagree on whether the emphasis is on forcing employment in the low-wage labor market (Soss, Fording, and Schram 2011; Seim and Harding 2020) or managing those excluded from the labor market entirely (Simon 1993). Simon argues that parole has shifted toward "managerial parole" since the 1970s, with an emphasis on control and surveillance. Comparisons with community supervision in Europe buttress arguments about the relative punitiveness of US parole systems (Rhine and Taxman 2017).

Thus, both the micro and macro literatures on community supervision are consistent with the argument that parole and probation contribute to system-induced harms and cycles of justice system involvement. Prior research has documented four different types of harms generated by community supervision. First, fines and fees impose significant financial burdens on individuals and their families, absorbing resources needed for immediate material security and investment in long-term mobility (Harris 2016; Harris, Pattillo, and Sykes 2022).

Second, complying with supervision requirements such as curfews, meetings with parole officers, attending treatment programs, and avoiding contact with others with criminal records can hinder finding and maintaining employment, stable housing, and supportive social ties (Capece 2022; Ortiz and Wrigley 2022; Phelps and Ruhland 2022). For many, complying with parole can itself feel like a full-time job, especially in the weeks and months after release (Harding, Morenoff, and Wyse 2019; Halushka 2020). People on community supervision must learn to become good subjects of the state or risk returning to prison or receiving other sanctions (Miller and Stuart 2017).

Third, people on supervision report considerable stress and mental strain not only from supervision requirements but also from suspicion and distrust in the ways in which officers interact with them, projecting an assumption of criminality and feelings of disrespect (Phelps and Ruhland 2022). Patterns of interaction in police stops, courtrooms, and penal facilities and the ritual character of their organization are important parts of the process of criminalization (Irwin 1985, chap. 5; Van Cleve 2016).

Fourth, supervision exposes people to the risk of sanctions that stop short of reimprisonment, including short-term custodial sanctions that can interfere with housing stability and employment (Herbert, Morenoff, and Harding 2015; Harding, Siegel, and Morenoff 2017). Community supervision generates cycles of escalating criminal justice involvement through such harms but also through its emphasis on surveillance and punishment and the ways it marks individuals for further and increasing punishment. Almost 30 percent of US state and federal prison admissions nationwide are for technical violations of probation or parole (Carson 2020). The more intensive supervision of parole, compared with probation, produces more prison admissions for violations despite having no effects on criminal convictions for serious crimes (Harding et al. 2017) or violent crimes (Harding et al. 2019). Such effects are more common among those with earlier ages of first arrest or more severe substance use problems, who may be most susceptible to ongoing surveillance (Franco Buitrago et al. 2022). Regarding marking, prior parole "failure" is typically scored by risk instruments as necessitating more intensive supervision in the future. Furthermore, individuals on parole face harsher future punishment if they are convicted of a new crime, including a greater likelihood of being sentenced to prison, an effect that is attributable to both formal sentencing guidelines and the discretionary decisions of judges and prosecutors (Hickert et al. 2022). Intensive probation serves as a cautionary tale; heightened surveillance and punishment can make seemingly alternative forms of punishment causes of escalating involvement (Palumbo, Clifford, and Snyder-Joy 1992; Petersilia 1999). Intensive probation, originally promoted as a community-based alternative to incarceration, was commonly used by prosecutors and judges for defendants who would otherwise have been sentenced to traditional probation, a phenomenon known as net widening (Austin and Krisberg 1981; McMahon 1990; Tonry and Lynch 1996; Phelps 2013). More intensive supervision led to increased technical violations and incarceration (Caplow and Simon 1999; Lin, Grattet, and Petersilia 2010). Instead of an off-ramp for high-risk offenders, intensive probation became an on-ramp for medium-risk offenders.

IV. Conclusion

Research on prisoner reentry and recidivism frequently focuses on the characteristics of individuals involved in long-term contact with the criminal justice system. Antisocial personality, low self-control, high school dropout, joblessness, drug addiction, and many other factors are associated with continuing contact with police and the penal system long after the population-level peak of criminal involvement in late adolescence.

The concept of careers in criminalization shifts the focus from the characteristics of individuals to the role of the criminal justice system in sustaining police contact and incarceration over the life course. A key conceptual implication is that researchers and policy makers must shift their focus from ameliorating the deficits of individuals to systematic study and reform of institutions and organizations. From this perspective, a significant component of what is labeled "recidivism" is system produced. Shifting perspective in this way will help fill in gaps between macro level arguments about punitive cultural logics rooted in history, public opinion, and political expediency (e.g., Garland 2001; Wacquant 2009; Enns 2016) and the lived experiences of people in conflict with the law who contend in daily life with police stops, imprisonment, and community supervision. We came to this approach through our ongoing interactions with policy makers, criminal justice practitioners, and advocates and with those who are currently or were formerly incarcerated.

The concept of careers in criminalization suggests that reentry into community life from prison is just one stage in a larger life process of criminalization. This has several implications for future research. First, reentry is often studied as a discrete event with its own characteristic dynamics. Formerly incarcerated people are, however, often entangled in cycles of correctional supervision that involve repeated incarceration, periods of probation and parole, periods of jail detention, arrests, and police stops. These cycles in their cumulative effect may in turn affect social and economic well-being differently from any discrete episode of reentry (Sampson and Laub 1997).

Second, the operations of police, courts, prisons, jails, and community supervision have often fallen outside the literature on reentry. Careers in criminalization point toward further probing these institutions and their interrelationships. Echoing an approach in prison field studies (Sykes 1958; Liebling 2004), recent ethnographies by Stuart (2016) and Miller (2021) exemplify research that encompasses the experience of those under penal control and the officials that staff the system.

Third, studies of reintegration consistently demonstrate that a significant number of formerly incarcerated individuals are excluded from conventional or mainstream social roles that structure daily lives in contemporary society, despite managing to avoid continued involvement with the criminal justice system (Petersilia 2003; Crutchfield 2014; Western 2018; Harding, Morenoff, and Wyse 2019). Careers in criminalization may help us understand why an important subset of this group "ages out" of crime without "aging into" full participation in the economy, community, and polity.

Fourth, the notion of cycles of involvement points toward the moments of transition between components of the criminal justice system as critical. For example, contemporary parole decisions (Greene and Dalke 2021) are understudied but may carry important implications for the organization of both prison services and postrelease supervision.

Finally, although we have focused on state actors who are part of the criminal justice system, the role of nonstate actors in careers of criminalization is an important area for further research. Core state functions extend to nonprofit social service providers and private for-profit businesses, greatly expanding contemporary systems of social control and raising important questions about democratic accountability when private actors take on state functions. For example, nonprofit service providers, often operating under contract with the state and serving as "hybrid state institutions" (Haney 2010) or as a "shadow carceral state" (Balfour, Hannah-Moffat, and Turnbull 2018), play monitoring roles even as they attempt to support people on community supervision. This contradiction often limits their ability to provide real prosocial opportunities to their clients (Kaufman 2015). The criminal records industry provides another example. As these businesses meet the "needs" of employers to learn about potential and current workers' contact with the criminal justice system, they heighten the effect of stigma and propagate system marking (Lageson 2020). Private corrections companies are a third example. As the prison-industrial complex has extended into community supervision through the for-profit provision of electronic monitoring, the state's capacity to monitor, punish, and generate compliance-induced harms has also expanded (Kilgore 2013; Latessa and Lovins 2019).

The concept of careers in criminalization encourages shifting policy discussions away from "fixing individuals" toward fixing systems and institutions by reducing system-induced harms and dismantling system traps. Improving reentry and reintegration outcomes can be reimagined as disrupting careers in criminalization. More broadly, institutionalized "off-ramps" are needed to help people exit the control and surveillance of the criminal justice system, become free of compliance-induced dilemmas, and shed the labels and stigma of prior system marking.

Shortening careers in criminalization may depend less on changes in criminal justice policy than on changes in other policy domains, particularly social policy. The criminal justice system is organized to assess risk and impute blame; criminalization is central to how criminal justice institutions are organized and how they operate. Agencies for health care, education, housing, and employment have service delivery as a central function. Although racism, criminal suspicion, and punitive withholding are well documented among social service agencies (Soss, Fording, and Schram 2011; Kohler-Hausmann 2017), assignment of blame is not central to their functions, and social policy has been shown to have positive effects. Expanding education, employment services, health care, and income support have all been shown to reduce criminal justice contact across the life course (e.g., Uggen 2000; Carneiro and Heckman 2004; Wang et al. 2017; Deshpande and Mueller-Smith 2022; Simes and Jahn 2022). Eligibility for programs might be viewed as part of the process of erasing criminal stigma. Program recipients are people in need, not objects of blame. Social programs can be understood as a tool for reversing system-induced harms and long-standing processes of blaming and exclusion that are at the heart of criminalization.

REFERENCES

Agan, Amanda Y., Jennifer L. Doleac, and Anna Harvey. 2021. "Misdemeanor Prosecution." NBER Working Paper no. 28600. Cambridge, MA: National Bureau of Economic Research. https://doi.org/10.3386/w28600.

Alexander, Michelle. 2010. *The New Jim Crow: Mass Incarceration in the Age of Colorblindness.* New York: New Press.

Austin, James, and Barry Krisberg. 1981. "NCCD Research Review: Wider, Stronger, and Different Nets; The Dialectics of Criminal Justice Reform." *Journal of Research in Crime and Delinquency* 18(1):165–96.

Balfour, Gillian, Kelly Hannah-Moffat, and Sarah Turnbull. 2018. "Planning for Precarity? Experiencing the Carceral Continuum of Imprisonment and Reentry." In *After Imprisonment*, edited by Austin Sarat. Bingley: Emerald.

Beaudry, Gabrielle, Shaoling Zhong, Daniel Whiting, Babak Javid, John Frater, and Seena Fazel. 2020. "Managing Outbreaks of Highly Contagious Diseases in Prisons: A Systematic Review." *BMJ Global Health* 5(11). https://doi.org/10.1136/bmjgh-2020-003201.

Beckett, Katherine, and Allison Goldberg. 2022. "The Effects of Imprisonment in a Time of Mass Incarceration." In *Prisons and Prisoners*, edited by Michael Tonry and Sandra Bucerius. Vol. 51 of *Crime and Justice: A Review of Research*, edited by Michael Tonry. Chicago: University of Chicago Press.

Beckett, Katherine, and Steven Herbert. 2010. *Banished: The New Social Control in Urban America*. New York: Oxford University Press.

Bell, Monica C. 2017. "Police Reform and the Dismantling of Legal Estrangement." *Yale Law Journal* 126(7):2054–150.

Bick, Joseph A. 2007. "Infection Control in Jails and Prisons." *Clinical Infectious Diseases* 45(8):1047–55.

Blumstein, Alfred, and Jacqueline Cohen. 1987. "Characterizing Criminal Careers." *Science* 237(4818):985–91.

Bottoms, Anthony E. 1999. "Interpersonal Violence and Social Order in Prisons." In *Prisons*, edited by Michael Tonry and Joan Petersilias. Vol. 26 of *Crime and Justice: A Review of Research*, edited by Michael Tonry. Chicago: University of Chicago Press.

Bound, John, and Richard B. Freeman. 1992. "What Went Wrong? The Erosion of Relative Earnings and Employment among Young Black Men in the 1980s." *Quarterly Journal of Economics* 107(1):201–32.

Bowker, Lee H. 1980. *Prison Victimization*. New York: Elsevier.

Braithwaite, John. 1989. *Crime, Shame and Reintegration*. Cambridge: Cambridge University Press.

Brayne, Sarah. 2014. "Surveillance and System Avoidance: Criminal Justice Contact and Institutional Attachment." *American Sociological Review* 79:367–91.

Bridges, George S., and Martha A. Myers, eds. 1994. *Inequality, Crime, and Social Control*. Boulder, CO: Westview.

Burke, Peggy B., and Michael Tonry. 2006. *Successful Transition and Reentry for Safer Communities: A Call to Action for Parole*. Bethesda, MD: Center for Effective Public Policy.

Byrne, James M., and Don Hummer. 2004. "Examining the Role of the Police in Reentry Partnership Initiatives." *Federal Probation* 68:62–69.

Capece, Jesse. 2022. "Community Supervision and Employment." *Annals of the American Academy of Political and Social Science*, forthcoming.

Caplow, Theodore, and Jonathan Simon. 1999. "Understanding Prison Policy and Population Trends." In *Prisons*, edited by Michael Tonry and Joan Petersilia. Vol. 26 of *Crime and Justice: A Review of Research*, edited by Michael Tonry. Chicago: University of Chicago Press.

Carneiro, Pedro, and James J. Heckman. 2004. "Human Capital Policy." In *Inequality in America: What Role for Human Capital Policies?* edited by Benjamin M. Friedman. Cambridge, MA: MIT Press.

Carson, E. Ann. 2020. "Prisoners in 2017." Washington, DC: US Department of Justice, Bureau of Justice Statistics.

Carson, E. Ann, and Mary P. Cowhig. 2020. "Mortality in State and Federal Prisons, 2001–2016: Statistical Tables." Washington, DC: US Department of Justice, Bureau of Justice Statistics.

Chambliss, William J. 1964. "A Sociological Analysis of the Law of Vagrancy." *Social Problems* 12:67–77.

Clair, Matthew. 2020. *Privilege and Punishment*. Princeton, NJ: Princeton University Press.

Clear, Todd R. 2007. *Imprisoning Communities: How Mass Incarceration Makes Disadvantaged Neighborhoods Worse*. New York: Oxford University Press.

Clemmer, Donald. 1940. *The Prison Community*. New York: Henry Holt & Co.

Collins, Reed. 2007. "Strolling While Poor: How Broken-Windows Policing Created a New Crime in Baltimore Note." *Georgetown Journal on Poverty Law and Policy* 14(3):419–40.

Crutchfield, Robert D. 2014. *Get a Job: Labor Markets, Economic Opportunity, and Crime*. New York: New York University Press.

Deshpande, Manasi, and Michael G. Mueller-Smith. 2022. "Does Welfare Prevent Crime? The Criminal Justice Outcomes of Youth Removed from SSI." NBER Working Paper no. 29800. Cambridge, MA: National Bureau of Economic Research. https://doi.org/10.3386/w29800.

Dobbie, Will, Jacob Goldin, and Crystal Yang. 2018. "The Effects of Pre-trial Detention on Conviction, Future Crime, and Employment: Evidence from Randomly Assigned Judges." *American Economic Review* 108(2):201–40.

Dubber, Markus Dirk. 2001. "Policing Possession: The War on Crime and the End of Criminal Law." *Journal of Criminal Law and Criminology* 91(4):829–996.

Duneier, Mitchell. 2000. *Sidewalk*. New York: Farrar, Straus & Giroux.

Durkheim, Émile. 1973. *Moral Education: A Study in the Theory and Application of the Sociology of Education*. Mineola, NY: Free Press.

Edwards, Frank, Hedwig Lee, and Michael Esposito. 2020. "Risk of Being Killed by Police Use-of-Force in the US by Age, Race/Ethnicity, and Sex." *Proceedings of the National Academy of Sciences* 116(34):16793–98.

Enns, Peter K. 2016. *Incarceration Nation: How the United States Became the Most Punitive Democracy in the World*. New York: Cambridge University Press.

Farrington, David P. 1986. "Age and Crime." In *Crime and Justice: A Review of Research*, vol. 7, edited by Michael Tonry and Norval Morris. Chicago: University of Chicago Press.

Fassin, Didier. 2018. *The Will to Punish*. New York: Oxford University Press.

Feeley, Malcolm M. 1979. *The Process Is the Punishment: Handling Cases in a Lower Criminal Court*. New York: Russell Sage.

Feeley, Malcolm M., and Jonathan Simon. 1992. "The New Penology: Notes on the Emerging Strategy of Corrections and Its Implications." *Criminology* 30(4):449–74.

Ford, Marilyn Chandler. 2005. "Frequent Fliers: The High Demand User in Local Corrections." *Californian Journal of Health Promotion* 3:61–71.

France, Anatole. 1930. *The Red Lily*. New York: Dodd-Mead.

Franco Buitrago, Catalina, David James Harding, Shawn D. Bushway, and Jeffrey D. Morenoff. 2022. "Failing to Follow the Rules: Can Imprisonment Lead to More Imprisonment without More Actual Crime?" NHH Department of Economics Discussion Paper. SSRN. https://ssrn.com/abstract=4054666.

Garland, David. 1990. *Punishment and Modern Society*. Chicago: University of Chicago Press.

Garland, David. 2001. "Introduction." In *Mass Imprisonment*, edited by David Garland. London: Sage.

Garland, David. 2020. "Penal Controls and Social Controls: Toward a Theory of American Penal Exceptionalism." *Punishment and Society* 22(3):321–52.

Geller, Amanda, and Jeffrey Fagan. 2019. "Police Contact and the Legal Socialization of Urban Teens." *RSF: The Russell Sage Foundation Journal of the Social Sciences* 5(1):26–49.

Goffman, Erving. 1959. "The Moral Career of the Mental Patient." *Psychiatry* 22(2):123–42.

Goodman, Philip, Joshua Page, and Michelle Phelps. 2017. *Breaking the Pendulum: The Long Struggle over Criminal Justice*. New York: Oxford University Press.

Gottfredson, Michael, and Travis Hirschi. 1986. "The True Value of Lambda Would Appear to Be Zero: An Essay on Career Criminals, Criminal Careers, Selective Incapacitation, Cohort Studies, and Related Topics." *Criminology* 24(2):213–34.

Gough, Ethan, Mirjam C. Kempf, Laura Graham, Marvin Manzanero, Edward W. Hook, Al Bartolucci, and Eric Chamot. 2010. "HIV and Hepatitis B and C Incidence Rates in US Correctional Populations and High Risk Groups: A Systematic Review and Meta-analysis." *BMC Public Health* 10(1):1–14.

Greene, Joss, and Isaac Dalke. 2021. "'You're Still an Angry Man': Parole Boards and Logics of Criminalized Masculinity." *Theoretical Criminology* 25(4):639–62.

Guetzkow, Joshua, and Eric Schoon. 2015. "If You Build It, They Will Fill It: The Consequences of Prison Overcrowding Litigation." *Law and Society Review* 49(2):401–32.

Halushka, John M. 2020. "The Runaround: Punishment, Welfare, and Poverty Survival after Prison." *Social Problems* 67(2):233–50.

Haney, Craig. 2006. *Reforming Punishment: Psychological Limits to the Pains of Imprisonment*. Washington, DC: American Psychological Association.

Haney, Lynne. 2010. *Offending Women*. Berkeley: University of California Press.

Harcourt, Bernard E. 2015. "Risk as a Proxy for Race: The Dangers of Risk Assessment." *Federal Sentencing Reporter* 27(4):237–43.

Harding, David J., Jeffrey D. Morenoff, and Claire W. Herbert. 2013. "Home Is Hard to Find: Neighborhoods, Institutions, and the Residential Trajectories of Returning Prisoners." *Annals of the American Academy of Political and Social Science* 647:214–36.

Harding, David J., Jeffrey D. Morenoff, Anh P. Nguyen, and Shawn D. Bushway. 2017. "Short- and Long-Term Effects of Imprisonment on Future Felony Convictions and Prison Admissions." *Proceedings of the National Academy of Sciences* 114(42):11103–8.

Harding, David J., Jeffrey D. Morenoff, Anh P. Nguyen, Shawn D. Bushway, and Ingrid A. Binswanger. 2019. "A Natural Experiment Study of the Effects of Imprisonment on Violence in the Community." *Nature Human Behaviour* 3(7):671–77.

Harding, David J., Jeffrey D. Morenoff, and Jessica J. B. Wyse. 2019. *On the Outside*. Chicago: University of Chicago Press.

Harding, David J., Jonah A. Siegel, and Jeffrey D. Morenoff. 2017. "Custodial Parole Sanctions and Earnings after Release from Prison." *Social Forces* 96(2):909–34.

Harris, Alexes. 2016. *A Pound of Flesh: Monetary Sanctions as Punishment for the Poor*. New York: Russell Sage.

Harris, Alexes, Mary Pattillo, and Bryan L. Sykes. 2022. "Studying the System of Monetary Sanctions." *RSF: The Russell Sage Foundation Journal of the Social Sciences* 8(2):1–33.

Herbert, Claire W., Jeffrey D. Morenoff, and David J. Harding. 2015. "Homelessness and Housing Insecurity among Former Prisoners." *RSF: The Russell Sage Foundation Journal of the Social Sciences* 1(2):44–79.

Herbert, Steve, Katherine Beckett, and Forrest Stuart. 2018. "Policing Social Marginality: Contrasting Approaches." *Law and Social Inquiry* 43:1491–513.

Hickert, Audrey, Shawn D. Bushway, David J. Harding, and Jeffrey D. Morenoff. 2022. "Prior Punishments and Cumulative Disadvantage: How Supervision Status Impacts Prison Sentences." *Criminology* 60(1):27–59.

Hinton, Elizabeth, and DeAnza Cook. 2021. "The Mass Criminalization of Black Americans: A Historical Overview." *Annual Review of Criminology* 4:261–86.

Hirschfield, Paul J. 2008. "Preparing for Prison? The Criminalization of School Discipline in the USA." *Theoretical Criminology* 12(1):79–101.

Hirschi, Travis, and Michael Gottfredson. 1983. "Age and the Explanation of Crime." *American Journal of Sociology* 89(3):552–84.

Hochstetler, Andy, Daniel S. Murphy, and Ronald L. Simons. 2004. "Damaged Goods: Exploring Predictors of Distress in Prison Inmates." *Crime and Delinquency* 50(3):436–57.

Hoover, Larry T. 2018. "Effect of Contracted Treatment Referrals on Probation Officer Role." *Journal of Offender Rehabilitation* 57(7):506–24.

Howell, K. Babe. 2015. "The Costs of Broken Windows Policing: Twenty Years and Counting." *Cardozo Law Review* 37:1059–73.

Husak, Douglas. 2008. *Overcriminalization: The Limits of the Criminal Law*. New York: Oxford University Press.

Irwin, John. 1985. *The Jail: Managing the Underclass in American Society*. Berkeley: University of California Press.

Jenness, Valerie. 2004. "Explaining Criminalization: From Demography and Status Politics to Globalization and Modernization." *Annual Review of Sociology* 30:147–71.

Kaeble, Danielle, and Mary Cowhig. 2018. "Correctional Populations in the United States, 2016." Washington, DC: US Department of Justice, Bureau of Justice Statistics.

Kaufman, Nicole. 2015. "Prisoner Incorporation: The Work of the State and Non-governmental Organizations." *Theoretical Criminology* 19(4):534–53.

Kazemian, Lila. 2021. "Pathways to Desistance from Crime among Juveniles and Adults: Applications to Criminal Justice Policy and Practice." In *Desistance from Crime*, edited by Marie Garcia, Benjamin Adams, and D. Michael Applegarth. Washington, DC: US Department of Justice, National Institute of Justice.

Kilgore, James. 2013. "Progress or More of the Same? Electronic Monitoring and Parole in the Age of Mass Incarceration." *Critical Criminology* 21(1):123–39.

Klockars, Carl B. 1972. "A Theory of Probation Supervision." *Journal of Criminal Law, Criminology, and Police Science* 63(4):550–57.

Kohler-Hausmann, Issa. 2018. *Misdemeanorland: Criminal Courts and Social Control in an Age of Broken Windows Policing*. Princeton, NJ: Princeton University Press.

Kohler-Hausmann, Julilly. 2017. *Getting Tough: Welfare and Imprisonment in 1970s America*. Princeton, NJ: Princeton University Press.

Kurlychek, Megan C., and Brian D. Johnson. 2019. "Cumulative Disadvantage in the American Criminal Justice System." *Annual Review of Criminology* 2:291–319.

Lageson, Sarah Esther. 2020. *Digital Punishment: Privacy, Stigma, and the Harms of Data-Driven Criminal Justice*. New York: Oxford University Press.

Lamberti, J. Steven. 2007. "Understanding and Preventing Criminal Recidivism among Adults with Psychotic Disorders." *Psychiatric Services* 58(6):73–81.

Langton, Lynn, et al. 2013. *Police Behavior during Traffic and Street Stops, 2011*. Washington, DC: US Department of Justice: Bureau of Justice Statistics.

Lara-Millán, Armando. 2014. "Public Emergency Room Overcrowding in the Era of Mass Imprisonment." *American Sociological Review* 79(5):866–87.

Lara-Millán, Armando. 2021. *Redistributing the Poor: Jails, Hospitals, and the Crisis of Law and Fiscal Austerity*. New York: Oxford University Press.

Latessa, Edward J., and Lori Brusman Lovins. 2019. "Privatization of Community Corrections." *Criminology and Public Policy* 18(2):323–41.

LaVigne, Nancy G. 2006. *Prisoner Reentry and Community Policing: Strategies for Enhancing Public Safety*. Washington, DC: Urban Institute.

Lerman, Amy E., and Vesla M. Weaver. 2014. *Arresting Citizenship*. Chicago: University of Chicago Press.

Levitt, Steven D. 1996. "The Effect of Prison Population Size on Crime Rates: Evidence from Prison Overcrowding Litigation." *Quarterly Journal of Economics* 111(2):319–51.

Liebling, Alison. 1999. "Prison Suicide and Prisoner Coping." In *Prisons*, edited by Michael Tonry and Joan Petersilia. Vol. 26 of *Crime and Justice: A Review of Research*, edited by Michael Tonry. Chicago: University of Chicago Press.

Liebling, Alison. 2004. *Prisons and Their Moral Performance: A Study of Values, Quality, and Prison Life*. Oxford: Oxford University Press.

Lin, Jeffrey, Ryken Grattet, and Joan Petersilia. 2010. "'Back-End Sentencing' and Reimprisonment: Individual, Organizational, and Community Predictors of Parole Sanctioning Decisions." *Criminology* 48(3):759–95.

Link, Nathan W., Jeffrey T. Ward, and Richard Stansfield. 2019. "Consequences of Mental and Physical Health for Reentry and Recidivism: Toward a Health-Based Model of Desistance." *Criminology* 57(3):544–73.

Lochner, Lance, and Enrico Moretti. 2004. "The Effect of Education on Crime: Evidence from Prison Inmates, Arrests, and Self-Reports." *American Economic Review* 94(1):155–89.

Lynch, Mona. 2000. "Rehabilitation as Rhetoric: The Ideal of Reformation in Contemporary Parole Discourse and Practices." *Punishment and Society* 2(1):40–65.

Lynch, Mona. 2009. *Sunbelt Justice: Arizona and the Transformation of American Punishment*. Stanford, CA: Stanford University Press.

Maruna, Shadd. 2000. *Making Good: How Ex-Convicts Reform and Rebuild Their Lives*. Washington, DC: American Psychological Association.

Maruna, Shadd, Gillian McNaull, and Nina O'Neill. 2022. "The COVID-19 Pandemic and the Future of the Prison." In *Prisons and Prisoners*, edited by Michael Tonry and Sandra Bucerius. Vol. 51 of *Crime and Justice: A Review of Research*, edited by Michael Tonry. Chicago: University of Chicago Press.

Massoglia, Michael, and William Alex Pridemore. 2015. "Incarceration and Health." *Annual Review of Sociology* 41:291–310.

Matz, Adam K., and Bitna Kim. 2013. "Policy Implications of Police-Probation/ Parole Partnerships: A Review of the Empirical Literature." *Federal Probation* 77(1):9–16.

McCarthy, Bill, John Hagan, and Daniel Herda. 2020. "Neighborhood Climates of Legal Cynicism and Complaints about Abuse of Police Power." *Criminology* 58(3):510–36.

McMahon, Maeve. 1990. "'Net-Widening': Vagaries in the Use of a Concept." *British Journal of Criminology* 30(2):121–49.

McNeill, Fergus. 2018. *Pervasive Punishment: Making Sense of Mass Supervision*. Bingley: Emerald.

Menefee, Michael R., David J. Harding, Anh P. Nguyen, Jeffrey D. Morenoff, and Shawn D. Bushway. 2021. "The Effect of Split Sentences on Employment and Future Criminal Justice Involvement: Evidence from a Natural Experiment." *Social Forces*. https://doi.org/10.1093/sf/soab132.

Miller, Joel. 2015. "Contemporary Modes of Probation Officer Supervision: The Triumph of the 'Synthetic' Officer?" *Justice Quarterly* 32(2):314–36.

Miller, Reuben Jonathan. 2014. "Devolving the Carceral State: Race, Prisoner Reentry, and the Micro-Politics of Urban Poverty Management." *Punishment and Society* 16:305–35.

Miller, Reuben Jonathan. 2021. *Halfway Home: Race, Punishment, and the Afterlife of Mass Incarceration*. New York: Little, Brown.

Miller, Reuben Jonathan, and Forrest Stuart. 2017. "Carceral Citizenship: Race, Rights and Responsibility in the Age of Mass Supervision." *Theoretical Criminology* 21(4):532–48.

Moffitt, Terrie E. 1993. "Adolescence-Limited and Life-Course-Persistent Antisocial Behavior: A Developmental Taxonomy." *Psychological Review* 100 (4):674–701.

Moffitt, Terrie E., et al. 2011. "A Gradient of Childhood Self-Control Predicts Health, Wealth, and Public Safety." *Proceedings of the National Academy of Sciences* 108(7):2693–98.

Muhammad, Khalil Gibran. 2011. *The Condemnation of Blackness: Race, Crime, and the Making of Modern Urban America*. Cambridge, MA: Harvard University Press.

Mumola, Christopher J. 2005. "Suicide and Homicide in State Prisons and Local Jails." Washington, DC: US Department of Justice, Bureau of Justice Statistics.

Neal, Derek, and Armin Rick. 2014. "The Prison Boom and the Lack of Black Progress after Smith and Welch." NBER Working Paper no. 20283. Cambridge, MA: National Bureau of Economic Research.

Neil, Roland, and Robert J. Sampson. 2021. "The Birth Lottery of History: Arrest over the Life Course of Multiple Cohorts Coming of Age, 1995–2018." *American Journal of Sociology* 126(5):1127–78.

Norris, Samuel, Matthew Pecenco, and Jeffrey Weaver. 2021. "The Effects of Parental and Sibling Incarceration: Evidence from Ohio." *American Economic Review* 111(9):2926–63.

Oberman, Jonathan, and Kendea Johnson. 2015. "Broken Windows: Restoring Social Order or Damaging and Depleting New York's Poor Communities of Color." *Cardozo Law Review* 37:931–54.

Ortiz, Jennifer Marie, and Kimberly Wrigley. 2022. "The Invisible Enclosure: How Community Supervision Inhibits Successful Reentry." *Corrections: Policy, Practice and Research* 7(3):230–45.

Oudekerk, Barbara, and Danielle Kaeble. 2021. *Probation and Parole in the United States, 2019*. Washington, DC: US Department of Justice, Bureau of Justice Statistics.

Pager, Devah. 2007. *Marked: Race, Crime, and Finding Work in an Era of Mass Incarceration*. Chicago: University of Chicago Press.

Pager, Devah, Bruce Western, and Bart Bonikowski. 2009. "Discrimination in a Low Wage Labor Market: A Field Experiment." *American Sociological Review* 74:777–99.

Palumbo, Dennis J., Mary Clifford, and Zoann K. Snyder-Joy. 1992. "From Net-Widening to Intermediate Sanctions: The Transformation of Alternatives to Incarceration from Benevolence to Malevolence." In *Smart Sentencing: The Emergence of Intermediate Sanctions*, edited by James M. Byrne, Arthur J. Lurigio, and Joan Petersilia. Newbury Park, CA: Sage.

Parent, Dale, and Brad Snyder. 1999. *Police-Corrections Partnerships*. Washington, DC: US Department of Justice, National Institute of Justice.

Petersilia, Joan. 1997. "Probation in the United States." In *Crime and Justice: A Review of Research*, vol. 22, edited by Michael Tonry. Chicago: University of Chicago Press.

Petersilia, Joan. 1999. "A Decade of Experimenting with Intermediate Sanctions: What Have We Learned?" *Justice Research and Policy* 1(1):9–23.

Petersilia, Joan. 2003. *When Prisoners Come Home: Parole and Prisoner Reentry*. New York: Oxford University Press.

Petersilia, Joan, and Susan Turner. 1986. "Prison versus Probation in California: Implications and Offender Recidivism." Santa Monica, CA: Rand.

Peterson, Ruth D., and Lauren J. Krivo. 2010. *Divergent Social Worlds: Neighborhood Crime and the Racial-Spatial Divide*. New York: Russell Sage.

Phelps, Michelle S. 2011. "Rehabilitation in the Punitive Era: The Gap between Rhetoric and Reality in U.S. Prison Programs." *Law and Society Review* 45:33–68.

Phelps, Michelle S. 2013. "The Paradox of Probation: Community Supervision in the Age of Mass Incarceration." *Law and Policy* 35:51–80.

Phelps, Michelle S. 2017. "Mass Probation: Toward a More Robust Theory of State Variation in Punishment." *Punishment and Society* 19:53–73.

Phelps, Michelle S., and Ebony L. Ruhland. 2022. "Governing Marginality: Coercion and Care in Probation." *Social Problems* 69(3):799–816.

Pierson, Emma, et al. 2020. "A Large-Scale Analysis of Racial Disparities in Police Stops across the United States." *Nature Human Behaviour* 4(7):736–45.

Raphael, Steven, and Michael A. Stoll. 2013. *Why Are So Many Americans in Prison?* New York: Russell Sage.

Raphael, Steven, and Rudolf Winter-Ebmer. 2001. "Identifying the Effect of Unemployment on Crime." *Journal of Law and Economics* 44(1):259–83.

Redmayne, Mike. 2015. *Character in the Criminal Trial.* New York: Oxford University Press.

Rengifo, Andres F., Don Stemen, and Ethan Amidon. 2017. "When Policy Comes to Town: Discourses and Dilemmas of Implementation of a Statewide Reentry Policy in Kansas." *Criminology* 55(3):603–30.

Rhine, Edward E., and Faye S. Taxman. 2017. "American Exceptionalism in Community Supervision." In *American Exceptionalism in Crime and Punishment*, edited by Kevin R. Reitz. New York: Oxford University Press.

Rhodes, William, Gerald Gaes, Jeremy Luallen, Ryan Kling, Tom Rich, and Michael Shively. 2016. "Following Incarceration, Most Released Offenders Never Return to Prison." *Crime and Delinquency* 62(8):1003–25.

Sampson, Robert J., and John H. Laub. 1993. *Crime in the Making: Pathways and Turning Points through Life.* Cambridge, MA: Harvard University Press.

Sampson, Robert J., and John H. Laub. 1997. "A Life-Course Theory of Cumulative Disadvantage and the Stability of Delinquency." In *Developmental Theories of Crime and Delinquency*, edited by Terence P. Thornberry. New York: Routledge.

Sampson, Robert J., and L. Ash Smith. 2021. "Rethinking Criminal Propensity and Character: Cohort Inequalities and the Power of Social Change." In *Crime and Justice: A Review of Research*, vol. 50, edited by Michael Tonry. Chicago: University of Chicago Press.

Sawyer, Wendy, and Peter Wagner. 2020. "Mass Incarceration: The Whole Pie, 2020." *Prison Policy Initiative* 243(December):112618–27.

Seim, Josh. 2020. *Bandage, Sort, and Hustle: Ambulance Crews on the Front Lines of Urban Suffering.* Berkeley: University of California Press.

Seim, Josh, and David J. Harding. 2020. "Parolefare: Post-prison Supervision and Low-Wage Work." *RSF: The Russell Sage Foundation Journal of the Social Sciences* 6(1):173–95.

Semenza, Daniel C., and Nathan W. Link. 2019. "How Does Reentry Get under the Skin? Cumulative Reintegration Barriers and Health in a Sample of Recently Incarcerated Men." *Social Science and Medicine* 243(December):112618–27.

Simes, Jessica T. 2021. *Punishing Places: The Geography of Mass Imprisonment.* Berkeley: University of California Press.

Simes, Jessica T., and Jaquelyn L. Jahn. 2022. "The Consequences of Medicaid Expansion under the Affordable Care Act for Police Arrests." *Plos One* 17(1): e0261512.

Simester, A. P., and Andreas von Hirsch. 2011. *Crimes, Harms, and Wrongs: On the Principles of Criminalisation*. London: Bloomsbury.

Simon, Jonathan. 1993. *Poor Discipline*. Chicago: University of Chicago Press.

Simon, Jonathan. 2014. *Mass Incarceration on Trial: A Remarkable Court Decision and the Future of Prisons in America*. New York: New Press.

Skeem, Jennifer L., and Sarah Manchak. 2008. "Back to the Future: From Klockars' Model of Effective Supervision to Evidence-Based Practice in Probation." *Journal of Offender Rehabilitation* 47(3):220–47.

Soss, Joe, Richard C. Fording, and Sanford F. Schram. 2011. *Disciplining the Poor: Neoliberal Paternalism and the Persistent Power of Race*. Chicago: University of Chicago Press.

Stuart, Forrest. 2016. *Down and out and under Arrest: Policing and Everyday Life in Skid Row*. Chicago: University of Chicago Press.

Sugie, Naomi F., Noah D. Zatz, and Dallas Augustine. 2020. "Employer Aversion to Criminal Records: An Experimental Study of Mechanisms." *Criminology* 58(1):5–34.

Sykes, Gresham M. 1958. *The Society of Captives: A Study of a Maximum Security Prison*. Princeton, NJ: Princeton University Press.

Thompson, Edward P. 2015. *Whigs and Hunters: The Origin of the Black Act*. New York: Pantheon.

Toch, Hans. 1977. *Living in Prison: The Ecology of Survival*. New York: Free Press.

Tonry, Michael. 1995. *Malign Neglect*. New York: Oxford University Press.

Tonry, Michael. 2004. *Thinking about Crime: Sense and Sensibility in American Penal Culture*. New York: Oxford University Press.

Tonry, Michael, and Mary Lynch. 1996. "Intermediate Sanctions." In *Crime and Justice: A Review of Research*, vol. 20, edited by Michael Tonry. Chicago: University of Chicago Press.

Travis, Jeremy, Ronald Davis, and Sarah Lawrence. 2012. "Exploring the Role of the Police in Prisoner Reentry." NCJ 238337. Washington, DC: US Department of Justice, National Institute of Justice.

Travis, Jeremy, Bruce Western, and Stevens Redburn, eds. 2014. *The Growth of Incarceration in the United States: Exploring Causes and Consequences*. Washington, DC: National Academies.

Turney, Kristin, and Emma Conner. 2019. "Jail Incarceration: A Common and Consequential Form of Criminal Justice Contact." *Annual Review of Criminology* 2:265–90.

Uggen, Christopher. 2000. "Work as a Turning Point in the Life Course of Criminals: A Duration Model of Age, Employment, and Recidivism." *American Sociological Review* 65(4):529–46.

US Bureau of Justice Statistics. 2020. "Survey of Prison Inmates, United States, 2016." Version 4. Ann Arbor, MI: Inter-university Consortium for Political and Social Research. https://doi.org/10.3886/ICPSR37692.V4.

Van Cleve, Nicole Gonzalez. 2016. *Crook County: Racism and Injustice in America's Largest Criminal Court*. Stanford, CA: Stanford University Press.

Viglione, Jill, Brandy L. Blasko, and Faye S. Taxman. 2018. "Organizational Factors and Probation Officer Use of Evidence-Based Practices: A Multilevel Examination." *International Journal of Offender Therapy and Comparative Criminology* 62(6):1648–67.

Wacquant, Loïc. 2009. *Punishing the Poor: The Neoliberal Government of Social Insecurity.* Durham, NC: Duke University Press.

Wakefield, Sara. 2022. "Incarceration, Families, and Communities: Recent Developments and Enduring Challenges." In *Prisons and Prisoners*, edited by Michael Tonry and Sandra Bucerius. Vol. 51 of *Crime and Justice: A Review of Research*, edited by Michael Tonry. Chicago: University of Chicago Press.

Wakefield, Sara, and Christopher Uggen. 2010. "Incarceration and Stratification." *Annual Review of Sociology* 36:387–406.

Wakefield, Sara, and Christopher Wildeman. 2013. *Children of the Prison Boom: Mass Incarceration and the Future of American Inequality.* New York: Oxford University Press.

Wallace, Danielle, and Xia Wang. 2020. "Does In-Prison Physical and Mental Health Impact Recidivism?" *SSM—Population Health* 11(August):100569–86.

Wang, Emily A., Clemens S. Hong, Shira Shavit, Roland Sanders, Eric Kessell, and Margot B. Kushel. 2017. "Engaging Individuals Recently Released from Prison into Primary Care: A Randomized Trial." *American Journal of Public Health* 102(9):e22–e29.

Wang, Emily A., Bruce Western, Emily P. Backes, and Julie Schuck, eds. 2020. *Decarcerating Correctional Facilities during COVID-19.* Washington, DC: National Academies.

Welsh, Megan. 2019. "Conceptualizing the Personal Touch: Experiential Knowledge and Gendered Strategies in Community Supervision Work." *Journal of Contemporary Ethnography* 48(3):311–38.

Western, Bruce. 2006. *Punishment and Inequality in America.* New York: Russell Sage.

Western, Bruce. 2018. *Homeward: Life in the Year after Prison.* New York: Russell Sage.

Western, Bruce. 2021. "Inside the Box: Safety, Health, and Isolation in Prison." *Journal of Economic Perspectives* 35(4):97–122.

Western, Bruce, Jaclyn Davis, Flavien Ganter, and Natalie Smith. 2021. "The Cumulative Risk of Jail Incarceration." *Proceedings of the National Academy of Sciences* 118(16):e20234291.

Western, Bruce, and Christopher Wildeman. 2009. "The Black Family and Mass Incarceration." *Annals of the American Academy of Social and Political Science* 621:221–42.

Wilson, William Julius. 1987. *The Truly Disadvantaged: The Inner City, the Underclass, and Public Policy.* Chicago: University of Chicago Press.

Wolfgang, Marvin E., Robert M. Figlio, and Thorsten Sellin. 1972. *Delinquency in a Birth Cohort.* Chicago: University of Chicago Press.

Wooldredge, John D. 1999. "Inmate Experiences and Psychological Well-Being." *Criminal Justice and Behavior* 26(2):235–50.

Wyse, Jessica J. B. 2013. "Rehabilitating Criminal Selves: Gendered Strategies in Community Corrections." *Gender and Society* 27(2):231–55.

Zimring, Franklin E. 2017. *When Police Kill*. Cambridge, MA: Harvard University Press.

Zweig, Janine M., Jennifer Yahner, Christy A. Visher, and Pamela K. Lattimore. 2015. "Using General Strain Theory to Explore the Effects of Prison Victimization Experiences on Later Offending and Substance Use." *Prison Journal* 95 (1):84–113.

Index